Contemporary Authors®
Autobiography Series

ISSN 0748-0636

Contemporary

Authors

Autobiography Series

Joyce Nakamura
Editor

Shelly Andrews
Associate Editor

volume **21**

 **Gale Research Inc.**

An International Thomson Publishing Company

I(T)P

NEW YORK • LONDON • BONN • BOSTON • DETROIT • MADRID
MELBOURNE • MEXICO CITY • PARIS • SINGAPORE • TOKYO
TORONTO • WASHINGTON • ALBANY NY • BELMONT CA • CINCINNATI OH

EDITORIAL STAFF

Joyce Nakamura, *Editor*

Linda R. Andres, Shelly Andrews, Motoko Fujishiro Huthwaite, Thomas F. McMahon,
Sharon R. Gunton, and Diane Telgen, *Associate Editors*
Marilyn O'Connell Allen and Paul Zyskowski, *Assistant Editors*
Laurie C. Hillstrom and Lori J. Sawicki, *Contributing Copyeditors*

Victoria B. Cariappa, *Research Manager*
Andrew Guy Malonis and Maureen Richards, *Research Specialists*
Frank Vincent Castronova and Norma Sawaya, *Research Associates*
Julia C. Daniel, Shirley Gates, Michele P. Pica, and Amy Terese Steel, *Research Assistants*

Hal May, *Publisher*

Mary Beth Trimper, *Production Director*
Shanna Philpott Heilveil, *Production Assistant*

Cynthia Baldwin, *Art Director*
C. J. Jonik, *Keyliner*
Willie Mathis, *Camera Operator*

Theresa Rocklin, *Manager, Technical Support Services*

Gale Research Inc.
835 Penobscot Building
Detroit, MI 48226-4094

Library of Congress Catalog Card Number 86-641293
ISBN 0-8103-4518-8
ISSN 0748-0636

Printed in the United States of America

I(T)P™ Gale Research International Ltd., an International Thomson Publishing Company.
ITP logo is a trademark under license.

10   9   8   7   6   5   4   3   2   1

Contents

Preface

A Unique Collection of Essays

Each volume in the *Contemporary Authors Autobiography Series (CAAS)* presents an original collection of autobiographical essays written especially for the series by noted writers.

CA Autobiography Series is designed to be a meeting place for writers and readers—a place where writers can present themselves, on their own terms, to their audience; and a place where general readers, students of contemporary literature, teachers and librarians, even aspiring writers can become better acquainted with familiar authors and meet others for the first time.

This is an opportunity for writers who may never write a full-length autobiography to let their readers know how they see themselves and their work, what brought them to this time and place.

Even for those authors who have already published full-length autobiographies, there is the opportunity in *CAAS* to bring their readers "up to date" or perhaps to take a different approach in the essay format. In some instances, previously published material may be reprinted or expanded upon; this fact is always noted at the end of such an essay. Individually, the essays in this series can enhance the reader's understanding of a writer's work; collectively, they are lessons in the creative process and in the discovery of its roots.

CAAS makes no attempt to give a comprehensive overview of authors and their works. That outlook is already well represented in biographies, reviews, and critiques published in a wide variety of sources. Instead, *CAAS* complements that perspective and presents what no other ongoing reference source does: the view of contemporary writers that is shaped by their own choice of materials and their own manner of storytelling.

Who Is Covered?

Like its parent series, *Contemporary Authors,* the *CA Autobiography Series* sets out to meet the needs and interests of a wide range of readers. Each volume includes essays by writers in all genres whose work is being read today. We consider it extraordinary that so many busy authors from throughout the world are able to interrupt their existing writing, teaching, speaking, traveling, and other schedules to converge on a given deadline for any one volume. So it is not always possible that all genres can be equally and uniformly represented from volume to volume, although we strive to include writers working in a variety of categories, including fiction, nonfiction, and poetry. As only a few writers specialize in a single area, the breadth of writings by authors in this volume also encompasses drama, translation, and criticism as well as work for movies, television, radio, newspapers, and journals.

What Each Essay Includes

Authors who contribute to *CAAS* are invited to write a "mini-autobiography" of approximately 10,000 words. In order to give the writer's imagination free rein, we suggest no guidelines or pattern for the essay.

We only ask that each writer tell his or her story in the manner and to the extent that feels most natural and appropriate. In addition, writers are asked to supply a selection of personal photographs showing themselves at various ages, as well as important people and special moments in their lives. Our contributors have responded generously, sharing with us some of their most treasured mementoes. The result is a special blend of text and photographs that will attract even the casual browser. Other features include:

Bibliography at the end of each essay, listing book-length works in chronological order of publication. Each bibliography in this volume was compiled by members of the *CAAS* editorial staff and submitted to the author for review.

Cumulative index in each volume, which cites all the essayists in the series as well as the subjects presented in the essays: personal names, titles of works, geographical names, schools of writing, etc. To ensure ease of use for these cumulating references, the name of the essayist is given before the volume and page number(s) for every reference that appears in more than one essay. In the following example, the entry in the index allows the user to identify the essay writers by name:

> Auden, W.H.
>   Allen **6:**18, 24
>   Ashby **6:**36, 39
>   Bowles **1:**86
>   etc.

For references that appear in only one essay, the volume and page number(s) are given but the name of the essayist is omitted. For example:

> Stieglitz, Alfred **1:**104, 109, 110

CAAS is something more than the sum of its individual essays. At many points the essays touch common ground, and from these intersections emerge new patterns of information and impressions. The index is an important guide to these interconnections.

For Additional Information

For detailed information on awards won, adaptations of works, critical reviews of works, and more, readers are encouraged to consult Gale's *Contemporary Authors* cumulative index for authors' listings in other Gale sources. These include, among others, *Contemporary Authors, Contemporary Authors New Revision Series, Dictionary of Literary Biography,* and *Contemporary Literary Criticism.*

Special Thanks

We wish to acknowledge our special gratitude to each of the authors in this volume. They all have been most kind and cooperative in contributing not only their talents but their enthusiasm and encouragement to this project.

A Brief Sampler

Each essay in the series has a special character and point of view that sets it apart from its companions. A small sampler of anecdotes and musings from the essays in this volume hint at the unique perspective of these life stories.

Andrea Dworkin, explaining the mysterious process of writing: "Writing is alchemy. Dross becomes gold. Experience is transformed. Pain is changed. Suffering may become song. The ordinary or horrible is pushed by the will of the writer into grace or redemption, a prophetic wail, a screed for justice, an elegy of sadness or sorrow. It is the lone and lonesome human voice, naked, raw, crying out, but hidden too, muted, twisted and turned, knotted or fractured, by the writer's love of form, or formal beauty: the aesthetic dimension, which is not necessarily familiar or friendly. Nor does form necessarily tame or simplify experience. There is always a tension between experience and the thing that finally carries it forward, bears its weight, holds it in. Without that tension, one might as well write a shopping list."

Harry M. Geduld, upon exiting the bomb shelter from his street in London after it was hit by the Luftwaffe, September 7, 1940: ". . . I noticed a bizarre sight that was to become very familiar during the hundreds of other air raids I lived through. It was due to the weird effects of Blast. A bomb that had struck a nearby house had shorn away everything except one of the four walls, which remained absolutely intact. It was like looking at a stage set. On the upper floor you could see the bathtub and toilet seemingly hanging in mid-air: they were attached to the wall by plumbing pipes. Downstairs was a dresser, displaying totally unbroken crockery: all the cups and saucers were still hanging from hooks. There was also a fireplace, pictures on the wall, and someone's coat on a hanger behind a door. That side of the house was exactly as its occupants had left it a couple of hours earlier. The rest had disintegrated to become part of the debris in the street."

Larry Heinemann, remembering benefits of military service and the diversity of its enlisted ranks: "Still and all, being in the service was a cheap way to get off the street and travel; many working-class kids (especially from the South) saw it as an obligation, a step toward manhood, a way to learn a trade, and simply a way to get out on their own. And it is undoubtedly true that an enlisted barracks is one of the few democratic institutions left in the republic, and that you meet people you would not encounter in any other circumstance. Every barracks I ever lived in was a virtual parody of itself and seemed to have one of everything: black guys angry about losing their trumpet lips and Irish Republican Army trainees; dumb-fuck Texans with all their brains in their necks, college 'fags' like me, Arlington Park jockeys, historians, barracks lawyers, and dipstick 'operators' always working the angles; guys who loved it (lifers-in-training), self-discovered killers, and dumbshit California goody-two-shoes who still believed what the army recruiters had told them; Georgia dirt farmers and Northwest loggers for whom the work was a piece of cake, Ivy League ROTC dropouts, New Yorkers who talked in that parody of World War II war movies, rural Southerners for whom the army was a godsend, and guys on their way to Airborne Rangers (good luck to you, pal); Montana ranchers, San Francisco tailors, undiscovered geniuses, superb athletes, short-order cooks, future officer candidates (God help us), foreigners (Poles and Canadians), and non-English speaking Puerto Rican amateur gang-bangers. A rich, democratic mishmash. That's the genius of a conscription army."

Colleen J. McElroy, recalling her early love of the movies: ". . . By mid-summer, I was sitting through another run of the cartoons and serial. 'Don't tell me you can't read that clock,' Aunt Jennie said. 'Been taking you a long time to get out of that movie,' my grandmother said. My mother sent Mildred, one of the older neighbor girls, to fetch me home. I didn't falter. The next weekend, I added a second screening of the feature film. I learned the trick of hiding behind the seats when the usher shined his flashlight down the row, hunting for me in response to my mother's urgent phone call to the theater. 'I guess I fell asleep,' I told her. After that, I eased up for a week, but the temptation was too great. The next week, my name was flashed on the screen on a little piece of paper inserted between the projector and the light. 'I didn't see my name up there. Honest,' I said. Then, on the Saturday Aunt Claudia sent her oldest son, James Jr., the policeman, to track me down, I ran out of excuses. By the time James caught me, I had learned to hide among the seats long enough to watch four sets of the cartoons. My cousin James simply had the manager turn up the houselights and waited until I showed myself, then he snatched me down the aisle . . . That was the last time I've ever sat through more than one showing of any movie. To this day, I expect the house lights to go up, to see my name flash on the screen, to turn and face my mother and her sisters waiting for me in back of the theater . . ."

Kalamu ya Salaam, declaring the relationship between art, audience, and ancestors: "Every expression requires a transmitter, a message and a receiver—and, of course, whatever it takes to make all three work. In the West the artist is severed from the audience (or the 'auditors' as Julio Finn says). My art is incomplete without an audience because our culture is a culture of affirmation. The old folks used to say, when you enter a room, speak to the people who are already there. When we enter the room of Black culture we should speak to the ancestors and we should expect to get a reply—after all, *the ancients are culture(d)* and will surely respond when spoken to. Affirmation leads us to appreciate the continuum of life. Louis Armstrong would never have been whole, not to mention noble and bold, without the ancestors (King Oliver and Buddy Bolden) in his horn even when he blew notes that had never been blown before. By creating something new from something old, Louis, and Langston Hughes too, became ancestors of the future. These are the people we go back to know who we are in the present. To be mature is to make yourself worthy of being an ancestor."

These brief examples only suggest what lies ahead in this volume. The essays will speak differently to different readers; but they are certain to speak best, and most eloquently, for themselves.

Acknowledgments

Grateful acknowledgment is made to those publishers, photographers, and artists whose works appear with these authors' essays.

Photographs/Art

Andrea Dworkin: p. 1, © Ephrat Beloosesky; p. 13, Ellen Stark; p. 20, Eva Dworkin.

Jesse Hill Ford: p. 23, James H. Bateman; p. 42, Charles Lindgren.

Larry Heinemann: p. 75, Larry Rottmann; p. 93, © Jerry Bauer; p. 95, © 1988 Chicago Tribune Company; p. 97, © Kevin Bowen.

Colleen J. McElroy: p. 136, Bry Photography.

Molly Peacock: p. 145, © Star Black.

Sterling D. Plumpp: p. 165, Sanders Hicks; p. 167, The Reverend Father Thorne; p. 171, Eugene B. Redmond; pp. 172, 173, Nancy Ortenberg.

Kalamu ya Salaam: p. 197, Phil Cutts Photography; p. 228, Eugene B. Redmond; p. 231, © Terri A. Mimms; p. 248, Andrew Rawson/Daily Cardinal.

Ed Sanders: p. 262, Tove Neville; p. 271, Lou Barranti.

Text

Kalamu ya Salaam: Poem "The Meaning of Life" in *What Is Life?*, by Kalamu ya Salaam. Published by Third World Press, 1994. All other poetry published by permission of the author.

Contemporary Authors®
Autobiography Series

Andrea Dworkin

1946-

Andrea Dworkin at the International Jewish Feminist Conference, Jerusalem, 1988

I come from Camden, New Jersey, a cold, hard, corrupt city, and—now having been plundered by politicians, some of whom are in jail—also destitute. I remember being happy there.

First my parents and I lived on Princess Avenue, which I don't remember; then, with my younger brother, Mark, at my true home, 1527 Greenwood Avenue. I made a child's vow that I would always remember the exact address so I could go back, and I have kept that vow through decades of dislocation, poverty, and hard struggle. I was ten when we moved to the suburbs, which I experienced as being kidnapped by aliens and taken to a penal colony.

I never forgave my parents or God, and my heart stayed with the brick row houses on Greenwood Avenue. I loved the stoops, the games in the street, my friends, and I hated leaving.

I took the story of the three little pigs to heart and was glad that I lived in a brick house. My big, bad wolf was the nuclear bomb that Russia was going to drop on us. I learned this at Parkside School from the first grade on, along with reading and writing. A bell would ring or a siren would sound and we had to hide under our desks. We were taught to cower and wait quietly, without moving, for a gruesome death, while the teacher, of course, stood at the head of the class or policed the aisles for

1

elbows or legs that extended past the protection of the tiny desks. And what would happen to her when the bomb came? Never, I believe, has a generation of children been so relentlessly terrorized by adults who were so obviously and stupidly lying. Eventually, the dullest of us picked up on it; and I was far from the dullest.

I remember trying to understand what the bomb was and how it would come and why. I'd see blinding light and heat and fire; and when my brain got tired of seeing burning humans, empty cities, burning cement, I would console myself with the story of the three little pigs. I was safe because my house was brick.

It is that feeling of my brain meeting the world around me that I remember most about being a child. The feeling was almost physical, as if I could feel my brain being stretched inside my head. I could feel my brain reaching for the world. I knew my brain did more than think. It could see and imagine and maybe even create something new or beautiful, if I was lucky and brave. I always wanted engagement, not abstract knowledge.

I loved the world and living and I loved being immersed in sensation. I did not like boundaries or want distance from what was around me. I saw adults as gatekeepers who stood between me and the world. I hated their evasions, rules, lies, petty tyrannies. I wanted to be honest and feel everything and take everything on. I didn't want to be careful and narrow the way they were. I thought a person could survive anything, except maybe famine and war, or drought and war. When I learned about Auschwitz my idea of the unbearable became more specific, more informed, sober and personal.

I began to think about survival very early, because we were Jewish on the heels of the Holocaust; because of the ubiquitous presence of those Russian bombs; and also because my mother was ill with heart disease. She had scarlet fever when she was a child, and in her family, big and poor, both parents immigrants, one did not call the doctor for a girl. The scarlet fever turned into rheumatic fever, which injured her heart long before there was open-heart surgery. She had many heart failures, maybe heart attacks, and at least one stroke before I became officially adolescent. She would be short of breath, maybe fall down; then she'd be gone, to a hospital, but Mark and I never really had

any way of knowing if she had died yet. We would be farmed out to relatives, separated most of the time. This could happen day or night, while doing homework or sleeping. We'd be told to get dressed fast because Mother was very sick and we couldn't stay here now; and Dad was at work or at the hospital and he would explain later: be quiet, don't ask questions, cooperate. We never knew anything we could count on. I usually didn't even know where Mark was. Or she might be sick, at home but in bed and off-limits, maybe dying. Sometimes I would be allowed to sit on her bed for a little while and hold her hand.

She was Sylvia, and I loved her madly when I was a child, which she never believed, not even by the time she did die, in 1991 at the age of seventy-six. I did stop loving her when I was older and exhausted by her repudiations of me; but it would not be wrong to say that

"My mother, Sylvia, with her mother, Sadie,"
Camden, New Jersey, November 1943

as a child I was in love with her, infatuated. I remember loving her long, dark hair, and the smell of coffee, which she drank perpetually when she was able to walk around, and the smoke from her cigarettes. Maybe it was my child's fear of death, or her sudden, brutal absences, that made me adore her without ever flinching when she pushed me away. I wanted to be around her, and I would have been her slave had she been generous enough to accept me. She was my first great romance.

But I was the wrong child for my mother to have had. She preferred dull obedience to my blazing adoration. She valued conformity and never even recognized the brazen emotional ploys of a child to hold on to her. My emotions were too extravagant for her own more literal sensibility. One could follow her around like a lovesick puppy, but if the puppy peed on the floor, she thought its intention was to spite her. She saw malice in almost anything I said or did. When I would be stretching my brain in curiosity—and dancing my brain in front of her to dazzle her—she thought it was defiance. When I asked her questions, which was a way for me to be engaged with her, she considered the questions proof of rebellion, a wayward delinquency, maybe even treason to her authority. I could never excite her or make myself understood or even comfort her. I do remember her reading to me sometimes at night when I couldn't sleep, and I remember feeling very happy.

She often told me that she loved me but did not like me. I came to believe that whatever she meant by love was too remote, too cold, too abstract or formulaic, to have anything to do with me as an individual, as I was. She said that a mother always loved her child; and since this was an important rule in her world, she probably followed it. I never understood what she meant even when I was fully grown up—which feelings this generic and involuntary love might include. But to the extent that she knew me, there was no doubt that she did not like me, and also that I could not be the child that she would find likable. I wasn't, I couldn't be, and I didn't want to be. She understood only that I didn't want to be.

I had to be independent, of course. I had to learn to live without her or without anyone special. I had to learn to live from minute to minute. I had to learn to be on my own, emotionally alone, physically alone. I had to learn

to take care of myself and sometimes my brother and sometimes even her. I never knew what would happen next, or if she'd be sick or dying, or where I'd be sleeping at night. I had to get strong and grow up. I'd try to understand and I'd ask God how He could make her so sick. Somehow, in stretching my brain to beat back the terror, I'd assert my own desire to live, to be, to know, to become. I had many a Socratic dialogue in my head before I ever read one. I had a huge inner life, not so strange, I think, for a child, or for a child who would become a writer. But the inner lives of children were not an acknowledged reality in those days, in the fifties, before I was ten and we moved to the suburbs, a place of sterility and desolation where no one had an inner life ever.

I have idyllic memories of childhood in Camden: my brother, my father, and me having tickling fights, wrestling, on the living room floor; me in my cowgirl suit practicing my fast draw so I could be an American hero; a tiny sandbox on our front lawn where all the children played, boys and girls together, our Eden until a certain year when the girls had to wear tops—I may have been five but I remember screaming and crying in an inarticulate outrage. We girls played with dolls on the stoops, washed their hair, set it, combed it out, dressed the dolls, tried to make stories of glamour in which they stood for us. I remember being humiliated by some girl I didn't like for not washing my doll's hair right—I think the doll was probably drowning. Later, my grandfather married her mother across the street, and I had to be nice to her. I was happier when we moved from dolls to canasta, gin rummy, poker, and strip poker. The children on the street developed a collective secret life, a half dozen games of sex and dominance that we played, half in front of our mothers' eyes, half in a conspiracy of hiding. And we played Red Rover and Giant Steps, appropriating the whole block from traffic. And there was always ball, in formal games, or alone to pass the time, against brick walls, against the cement stoops. I liked the sex-and-dominance games, which could be overtly sadomasochistic, because I liked the risk and the intensity; and I liked ordinary games like hide-and-seek. I loved the cement, the alleys, the wires and telephone poles, the parked cars that provided sanctuary from the adults, a kind of metallic barrier against their eyes and

"My father, Harry, with me at five weeks and six days old"

ears; and I loved the communal life of us, the children, half *Lord of the Flies,* half a prelude to *Marjorie Morningstar.* To this day, my idea of a good time is to sit on a city stoop amid a profusion of people and noise as dark is coming on.

I would say that it was Sylvia who started fighting with me when I was an exuberant little pup and still in love with her. But eventually I started fighting back. She experienced my inner life as a reproach. She thought I was arrogant and especially hated that I valued my own thoughts. When I kept what I was thinking to myself, she thought I was plotting against her. When I told her what I thought, she said I was defiant and some species of bad: evil, nasty, rotten. She often accused me of thinking I was smarter than she. I probably was, though I didn't know it; but it wasn't my fault. I was the child, she the adult, but neither of us understood that.

Our fights were awful and I don't doubt that, then as now, I fought to win. I may have been around eight when I dug in; and we were antagonists. I may have been a little older. Of course, I still wanted her to take me back and love me, but each crisis made that harder. Because of the wrenching separations, the pressing necessity of taking care of myself or Mark or her, the loneliness of living with relatives who didn't particularly want me, I had to learn to need my mother less. When we fought she

said I was killing her. At some point, I don't know exactly when, I decided not to care if she did die. I pulled myself away from her fate and tried to become indifferent to it. With a kind of emotional jujitsu, I pushed my mother away in my mind and in how I lived. I did this as a child. I knew that she might really die, and maybe I would be the cause, as they all kept saying. I also knew I was being manipulated. I had to make a choice: follow by rote her ten thousand rules of behavior for how a girl must act, think, look, sit, stand—in other words, cut out my own heart; or withstand the threat of her imminent death—give up the hope of her love or her friendship or her understanding. I disciplined myself to walk away from her in every sense and over time I learned how. She told me I had a hard heart.

I made good grades, though I had trouble conforming in class as I got older because of the intellectual vacuity of most of my teachers. I followed enough of the social rules to keep adults at bay. There weren't therapists in schools yet so no adult got to force-fuck my mind. I was smart enough to be able to strategize. I wasn't supposed to take long, solitary walks, but I took them. I wasn't supposed to go to other parts of our neighborhood, but I went. I had friends who were not Jewish or white at a time when race and religion lines were not crossed. I knew boys who were too old for me. I read books children weren't allowed to read. I regarded all of this as my private life and my right. My mother simply continued to regard me as a liar and a cheat with incomprehensible but clearly sinister tendencies and ideas.

When I was ten we moved to Delaware Township in New Jersey, a place *New York Times* writer Russell Baker described in a column as "nowhere along the highway," after which the outraged citizens changed the name to Cherry Hill. It was an empty place with sporadic outbreaks of ranch-type and split-level housing projects. There were still wild cherry trees and some deer. With the deer came hunters who stalked them across flat fields of ragweed and poison ivy. It was virtually all-white, unlike Camden in which the schools were racially and ethnically mixed even as residential blocks were segregated according to precise calibrations: Polish Catholics on one block, Irish Catholics on another. It was intellectually arid, except for a few teachers, one of whom liked to play sex-and-seduction games with smart little girls. It was wealthy while we were quite poor. We moved there because my mother could not climb steps and the good Lord had never made a flatter place than Delaware Township/Cherry Hill. I lived for the day that I would leave to go to New York City, where there were poets and writers and jazz and people like me.

Harry, my daddy, was not a rolling stone. He wasn't at home because he worked two jobs most of the time and three jobs some of the time. He was a schoolteacher during the day and at night he unloaded packages at the post office. Later he became a guidance counselor at a boys' academic high school in Philadelphia and also in a private school for dropouts trying to get their high school diplomas. I don't know what the third job was, or when he had it. My brother and I would go stretches of many days without seeing him at home; and when we were in other people's houses, it could be weeks. There were times when he would go to college classes on Saturdays in an effort to get his Ph.D. degree, but he never had the time to write a dissertation so he never got the degree. My dream was that when I grew up I would be able to give him the money to write his dissertation; but I never did make enough money and he says he is too old now anyway (though he still goes to the library every week). He was different from other men in how he acted and how he thought. He was gentle and soft-spoken. He listened with careful attention to children and women. He wanted teachers to unionize and the races to integrate. He was devoted to my mother and determined that she would get the very best medical care, a goal entirely out of reach for a low-paid schoolteacher, except that he did it. He borrowed money to pay medical bills. He borrowed money to take my mother to heart specialists. He borrowed money for professional nurses and to get housecleaning help and some child care and sometimes to hire a cook. He kept us warm and fed and sheltered, even though not always at home or together. He was outspoken and demonstrative in expressing affection, not self-conscious or withdrawn as most men were. He was nurturant and emotionally empathetic. He crossed a gender line and was stigmatized for it; called a sissy and a fairy by my buddies on the street who no doubt heard it from their parents. He loved my mother and he loved Mark and me; but especially me. I will never know why. He

said I was the apple of his eye from the time I was born and I believe him. I did nothing to earn it and it was the one great gift of my life. On Sundays he slept late but he and I would watch the Sunday news shows together and analyze foreign crises or political personalities or social conflicts. We would debate and argue, not the vicious arguments I had with my mother but heightened dialogue always touching on policy, ideas, rights, the powerful and the oppressed, discrimination and prejudice. I don't know how he had the patience; but patience was a defining characteristic. He enjoyed my intelligence and treated me with respect. I think that to be loved so unconditionally by a father and treated with respect by him was not common for a girl then. I think he kept my mother alive and I think he kept Mark and me from being raised in foster care or as orphans.

He was appalled by the conflict between me and my mother, and certainly by the time

"Me at two years old on Princess Avenue (before my brother was born) with my sandbox," October 1948

I was a teenager he held me responsible for it. He knew I was adult inside. He let me know that my mother's well-being would always come first with him. And I remember that he hated it when I would cry. He must have thought it cowardly and pitiful and self-indulgent. I made many eloquent but to him unpersuasive declarations about my right to cry.

I trusted and honored him. I guess that I trusted him to love me more even than to take care of us. In an honors history seminar in high school, the class was asked to name great men in history. I named my father and was roundly ridiculed by advocates for Thomas Jefferson and Napoleon. But I meant it—that he had the qualities of true greatness, which I defined as strength, generosity, fairness, and a willingness to sacrifice self for principle. His principle was us: my mother, Mark, and me. When I was an adult we had serious ruptures and the relationship broke apart several times—all occasions of dire emergency for me. I think that he did abandon me when I was in circumstances of great suffering and danger. He was, I learned the hard way, only human. But what he gave me as a child, neither he nor anyone else could take away from me later. I learned perseverance from his example, and that endurance was a virtue. Even some of his patience rubbed off on me for some few years. I saw courage in action in ordinary life, without romance; and I learned the meaning of commitment. I could never have become a writer without him.

I wrote my first novel during science class in seventh grade in the suburbs. My best friend, a wild, beautiful girl who wanted to be a painter, sat next to me and also wrote a novel. In the eighth grade, my friend gone from school to be with a male painter in his late twenties or thirties, I wrote a short story for English class so disturbing to my teacher that she put her feelings of apprehension into my permanent record. The ethos was to conform, not to stand out. She knew the writing was good, and that troubled her. There was too much vibrancy in the language, too much imagination in the physical evocations of place and mood. Highly influenced by the television series "The Twilight Zone" and grief-stricken at the loss of my soulmate girlfriend, I wrote a story about a wild woman, strong and beautiful, with long hair and torn clothes, on another planet, sit-

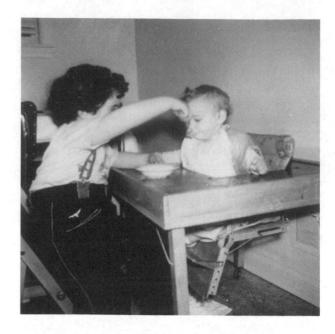

Andrea feeding her brother, Mark, April 11, 1950

ting on a rock. My story had no plot really, only longing and language. I remember getting lost in descriptions of the woman, the sky, the rock, maybe wind and dirt. In formal terms, I believe I kept circling back to the woman on the rock through repeating images and phrases that worked almost like music to my ear—a way of creating movement yet insisting on the permanence of some elements of the scenario. I had a picture in my mind, which was involuntary. I don't know why it was there or how it got there. The picture was stubborn: it didn't move or change. I could see it as if it were real with my eyes open, though it was conceptual and in my head. It wasn't in front of my eyes; it was behind them. I had huge emotions of pain and loss. I had the need to keep moving through life, not be held back or stopped by anything I felt. I remember finding words that resonated with the emotions I felt: not words that expressed those emotions or described them, but words that embodied them without ever showing them. It was the unrevealed emotion—attached to the words but invisible in them, then used to paint the picture in my head in language that was concrete and physical—that gave the prose an intensity so troubling to my teacher. Was she troubled by the homoeroticism of the story? I don't believe she recognized it.

In the eighth grade, of course, I did not have any consistent internal standards for how prose must be or what prose must do. But I did know much more about what I wanted from language when, thirty years later, I brought that same picture, the same wild woman on the same rock, into my novel *Mercy,* first published in 1990 in England.

The rock was Massada: a steep, barren mountain surrounded by desert, a refuge in ancient Palestine for a community of Jews known as zealots who committed, as the traditional story goes, mass suicide rather than surrender to the occupying Roman army. Ten men used their swords to slit the throats of everyone else; then one man killed the nine men and himself.

Mercy's narrator is a contemporary figure who in one of the novel's endings (it has two) sees herself as the wild woman on Massada at the time of the so-called suicides: "A child can't commit suicide. You have to murder a child. I couldn't watch the children killed; I couldn't watch the women taken one last time; throats

bared; heads thrown back, or pushed back, or pulled back; a man gets on top, who knows what happens next, any time can be the last time, slow murder or fast, slow rape or fast, eventual death, a surprise or you are waiting with a welcome, an open invitation; rape leading, inexorably, to death; on a bare rock, invasion, blood, and death. Massada; hear my heart beat; hear me; the women and children were murdered."

I wasn't missing my old girlfriend. I didn't have the same picture in my head because I was feeling what I had felt in the eighth grade. In my experience nothing in writing is that simple. Both memory and consciousness are deeper and wider than the thinking mind, which might find meaning in such a facile association.

I felt, certainly, a much larger abandonment, a more terrifying desolation, essentially impersonal: how the lives of women and children were worthless to men and God. In the despair of that recognition, the barren landscape of the rock became a place to stare men and God in the face, and my wild woman the one to do it. When the picture first came into my head, I dismissed it but it would not go. When I started to work with it in words, I saw Massada, I saw her, and I saw the murders. I, the writer, became a witness. Real history out in the world and a picture etched in my brain but forgotten for three decades converged in words I felt compelled to keep bringing together. Each word brought with it more detail, more clarity. My narrator, who is a character in my book, knows less than I do. She is inside the story. Deciding what she will see, what she can know, I am detached from her and cold in how I use her. I do not ever think she is me. She is not my mouthpiece. She does not directly speak my views or enumerate my ideas or serve as a mannequin in words displaying my wounds of body or soul. I am more than the sum of all her parts; and she can live in the reader's mind but the reader's mind cannot know me through knowing her. I have never been to Massada. However dull it may seem, I am the person who sits at the typewriter writing words, rewriting them, over and over, night in and night out (since I work at night), over months or years. *Mercy* took three years to write.

In using the picture in my head from my eighth-grade story, I broke the picture open

Four years old, April 1950

"Me, my mother, and my brother," December 1957,
Cherry Hill (or Delaware Township), New Jersey

into a universe of complex and concrete detail dreadful with meaning, in particular about incest and the power of the father—the patriarchal right of invasion into the bodies of women and children. At the end of writing *Mercy*'s Massada chapter, I felt as if I had finally seen that earlier picture whole. When I was younger I could only see a fragment, or a line drawing, but now I had seen everything that had been implicit in the picture from the beginning, from its first appearance in my mind, as if I had uncovered something pre-existing. It was always real and whole; what I had done as a writer was to find it and describe it, not invent it. In the eighth grade, I had not known how to use my mind or language to explicate the picture in my head, which was a gift or a visitation; I couldn't see the human destiny that had been acted out on that barren rock. But the time between my childhood and now had collapsed. The time between Massada and now had collapsed.

This strange but not unusual aftermath of creating helps to explain why so many writers disclaim responsibility for their characters and ideas. The character made me do it, most writers say. But the truth is that one starts out with a blank page, and each and every page is blank until the writer fills it. In the process, the mind

uses itself up, each cognitive capacity—intellect, imagination, memory, intuition, emotion, even cunning—used to the absolute utmost, a kind of strip-mining of one's mental faculties. At the same time, with the mind as scavenger and plunderer, one cannibalizes one's own life. But one's own life for the writer includes everything she can know, not just what happened to her in the ordinary sense. If I know about you—a gesture, an emotion, an event—I will use you if I need your gesture, your emotion, your event. What I take will seem to me to be mine, as if I know it from the inside, because my imagination will turn it over and tear it apart. Writers use themselves and they use other people. Empathy can be invasive. Friendship is sometimes a robbery-in-progress. This omniscient indifference takes a certain coldness, and a certain distance, which writers have and use.

Facts and details are the surface. The writer needs the facts and everything underneath them. One wanders, bodiless, or goes on search-and-destroy missions using one's mind. One needs a big earth, rich soil, deep roots: one digs and pulls and takes.

But after, when the writing is finished, one looks at the finished thing and has a feeling or conviction of inevitability: I found it, not I made it. It—the story, the novel—had its own laws; I simply followed them—found them and followed them; was smart enough and shrewd enough to find them and follow them; wasn't sidetracked or diverted, which would mean failure, a lesser book. Even with nonfiction, which in the universe of my writing has the same cognitive complexity as fiction, in the aftermath one feels that one has chiseled a pre-existing form (which necessarily has substance attached to it) out of a big, shapeless stone: it was there, I found it. This is an affirmation of skill but not of invention. At best, one feels like a sculptor who knows how to liberate the shape hidden in the marble or clay—or knew the last time but may not know the next, may be careless, may ruin the stone through distraction or stupidity. Once finished, the process of writing becomes opaque, even to the writer. I did it but how did I do it? Can I ever do it again? The brain becomes normal. One can still think, of course, but not with the luminosity that makes intelligence so powerful a tool while writing, nor can one think outside of literal and linear time anymore.

Writing is alchemy. Dross becomes gold. Experience is transformed. Pain is changed. Suffering may become song. The ordinary or horrible is pushed by the will of the writer into grace or redemption, a prophetic wail, a screed for justice, an elegy of sadness or sorrow. It is the lone and lonesome human voice, naked, raw, crying out, but hidden too, muted, twisted and turned, knotted or fractured, by the writer's love of form, or formal beauty: the aesthetic dimension, which is not necessarily familiar or friendly. Nor does form necessarily tame or simplify experience. There is always a tension between experience and the thing that finally carries it forward, bears its weight, holds it in. Without that tension, one might as well write a shopping list.

My fiction is not autobiography. I am not an exhibitionist. I don't show myself. I am not asking forgiveness. I don't want to confess. But I have used everything I know—my life—to show what I believe must be shown so that it can be faced. The imperative at the heart of my writing—what must be done—comes directly from my life. But I do not show my life directly, in full view; nor even look at it while others watch.

Autobiography is the unseen foundation of my nonfiction work, especially *Intercourse* and *Pornography: Men Possessing Women.* These two

Thirteen years old, in Cherry Hill, 1960

nonfiction books are not "about" me. There is no first-person writing in them. Conceptually, each involved the assimilation of research in many intellectually distinct areas using analytical skills culled from different disciplines. The research materials had nothing to do with me personally. They were freestanding, objectively independent (for instance, not interviews conducted by me). Yet when I wrote *Intercourse* and *Pornography: Men Possessing Women,* I used my life in every decision I made. It was my compass. Only by using it could I find north and stay on course. If a reader could lift up the words on the page, she would see—far, far under the surface—my life. If the print on the page turned into blood, it would be my blood from many different places and times. But I did not want the reader to see my life or my blood. I wanted her to see intercourse or pornography. I wanted her to know them the way I know them: which is deeply.

I'd like to take what I know and just hand it over. But there is always a problem, for a woman: being believed. How can I think I know something? How can I think that what I know might matter? Why would I think that anything I think might make a difference, to anyone, anywhere? My only chance to be believed is to find a way of writing bolder and stronger than woman hating itself—smarter, deeper, colder. This might mean that I would have to write a prose more terrifying than rape, more abject than torture, more insistent and destabilizing than battery, more desolate than prostitution, more invasive than incest, more filled with threat and aggression than pornography. How would the innocent bystander be able to distinguish it, tell it apart from the tales of the rapists themselves if it were so nightmarish and impolite? There are no innocent bystanders. It would have to stand up for women—stand against the rapist and the pimp—by changing women's silence to speech. It would have to say all the unsaid words during rape and after; while prostituting and after; all the words not said. It would have to change women's apparent submission—the consent read into the silence by the wicked and the complacent—into articulate resistance. I myself would have to give up my own cloying sentimentality toward men. I'd have to be militant; sober and austere. I would have to commit treason: against the men who rule. I would have to betray the noble, apparently humanistic premises of civilization and civilized writing by conceptualizing each book as if it were a formidable weapon in a war. I would have to think strategically, with a militarist heart: as if my books were complex explosives, minefields set down in the culture to blow open the status quo. I'd have to give up Baudelaire for Clausewitz.

Yes, okay, I will. Yes, okay: I did. In retrospect, that is just what I did: in *Mercy* and *Intercourse* and *Pornography: Men Possessing Women* and *Ice and Fire*.

It was in Amsterdam in 1972 that I made the vow, which I have kept, that I would use everything I know in behalf of women's liberation. I owed the women's movement a big debt: it was a feminist who helped me escape the brutality of my marriage. Escape is not a one-time run for your life: you keep running and hiding; he shows up out of nowhere and beats you, menaces you, threatens, intimidates, screams a foul invective at you in broad daylight on crowded streets, breaks into wherever you find to live, hits you with his dirty fists, dirtied by your pain, your blood.

I left the marital home toward the end of 1971, some two months after I turned twenty-five. I fled the country in which I had been living for five years in November 1972. I have no continuous memory of the events of that year. Even with the events I can remember, I have no sense of their sequence. I was attacked, persecuted, followed, harassed, by the husband I had left; I often lived the life of a fugitive, except that it was the more desperate life of a battered woman who had run away for the last time, whatever the outcome.

I have written about the experience of being a battered wife in three nonfiction essays: "A Battered Wife Survives" (1978) and "What Battery Really Is" (1989), both of which are included in the U.S. edition of *Letters from a War Zone;* and "Trapped in a Pattern of Pain," published in the *Los Angeles Times,* June 26, 1994. I wrote "A Battered Wife Survives" to celebrate my thirty-first birthday. I still shook and trembled uncontrollably, but not all the time; had nightmares and flashbacks, but less. I had published two books: *Woman Hating* (1974) and *Our Blood* (1976). I had survived and was not alone in a universe of pain and fear. The other two essays were written in behalf of other battered women: Hedda Nussbaum and Nicole Brown Simpson. I felt the need to try to make

people understand how destructive and cruel battery is—and how accepted, how normal, how supported by society. With enormous reluctance, I revisited the site of this devastation in my own life. I had to say what battery was from the point of view of the woman being hurt, since I knew.

Everything I have written in these nonfiction essays about myself is true. It would be wrong, however, to read my fiction as if it were a factual narrative, a documentary in words. Literature is always simpler and easier than life, especially in conveying atrocity. As the infrequency of my nonfiction essays about battery suggests, I am extremely reluctant to write about it: partly because I can't bear to think about it; partly because I feel physically ill when I literally trip over absent memory, great and awful blank areas of my life that I cannot recover— I am shaky with dread and vertigo; and partly because I still hide.

But the year of running, hiding, to stay alive is essential to the story of how I became a writer, or the writer I am, for better or worse. He kept our home; I was pushed out. This was fine, since I just wanted not to be hit. I had no money. I was isolated as battered women usually are but also I was a foreigner with no real rights except through my husband. My parents refused to have me back. His family was his—I was too afraid of him ever to tell them anything, though I believe they knew. I slept first on the floor of a friend's room—his friend, too—with her two dogs. Later, I slept where I could. I lived this way before I was married but not with an assassin after me, nor having sustained such brutality that my mind didn't quite work—it failed me in everyday situations, which it no longer recognized; it failed me with ordinary people who couldn't grasp my fear.

A feminist named Ricki Abrams helped me: gave me asylum, a dangerous kindness in the face of a battering man; helped me find shelter repeatedly; and together she and I started to plan the book that became *Woman Hating*.

I lived on houseboats on the canals—a majestic one near the Magere Brug, a stunningly beautiful bridge, a plainer one infested with mice. I slept in someone's kitchen. I lived for a while in the same house as Ricki, a narrow, teetering building on a cobblestone street that ringed a canal in Amsterdam's historically preserved old city. I hid on a farm far outside

Amsterdam with a commune of hippies who made their own cloth with a spinning wheel and a loom. I slept in a cold and deserted mansion near the German border. In one emergency, when my husband had broken into where I was living, had beaten me and threatened to kill me, I spent three weeks sleeping in a movie theater that was empty most of the time. Experimental movies were shown in a big room where I hid. The whole building was empty otherwise. On some nights small audiences of artistes would sit and watch formless flashes of light. When the avant-garde cleared out, I was allowed to open a cot. I lived in a state of terror. Every trip outside might mean death if he found me.

No one knew about battery then, including me. It had no public name. There were no shelters or refuges. Police were indifferent. There was no feminist advocacy or literature or social science. No one knew about the continuing consequences, now called post-traumatic stress syndrome, which has a nice dignity to it. How many times, after all, can one say terror, fear, anguish, dread, flashbacks, shaking, uncontrollable trembling, nightmares, he's going to kill me?

At the time, so far as I knew, I was the only person this had ever happened to; and the degradation had numbed me, disoriented me; changed me; lowered me; shamed me; broken me.

It was Ricki who first gave me feminist books to read. I remember especially *Sexual Politics* by Kate Millett (whose class at Barnard Ricki had taken), *The Dialectic of Sex* by Shulamith Firestone, and the anthology *Sisterhood Is Powerful* edited by Robin Morgan. I had left the United States in 1968 a second time (the first being in 1965, after a rapelike trauma in Manhattan's Women's House of Detention, where I was taken after an arrest for protesting the Vietnam War). I had not read or heard about these books. I argued with them in Amsterdam. I argued with Ricki. Oppression meant the U.S. in Vietnam, or apartheid in South Africa, or legal segregation in the U.S. Even though I had been tortured and was fighting for my life, I could not see women, or myself as a woman, as having political significance. I did know that the battery was not my fault. I had been told by everyone I asked for help the many times I tried to escape—strangers and friends—that he would not be hitting me if I didn't like it or

want it. I rejected this outright. Even back then, the experience of being battered was recognizably impersonal to me. Maybe I was the only person in the world this had ever happened to, but I knew it had nothing to do with me as an individual. It just never occurred to me that I was being hit because I was a woman.

Woman Hating was not a book written out of an ideology. It came out of an emergency, written half underground and in hiding. I wanted to find out what had happened to me and why. I knew *only* that it was impersonal. I made a list of what I thought might bear on what had happened to me, and that list became the table of contents in the published book. I looked at fairy tales—what did they teach about being female; at pornography—I was part of a generation that used it—what did it say about being female; at Chinese footbinding and the persecution of the witches—why was there culturally normalized violence against females; at androgyny—the myths and contemporary ideas of a community not organized on the principle of gender, the falseness of gender itself. I wanted to examine the culture: sex roles; sex; history; mythology; community.

Somehow, I had been given a key and access to a space in the basement of Paradiso, one of the clubs the Dutch government sponsored for counterculture, hashish-smoking, rock-and-roll–addicted hippies. The basement under the huge church building was dark and dank with a colony of misfits and homeless, mentally disoriented strangers, most of whom were hiding from someone, often the police. I was allowed to work there on the book—I had a desk and chair—but I was not supposed to sleep there, and I tried not to. My cohabitants did not inspire confidence and my husband, who worked upstairs at night when Paradiso was open, was dangerous for sure. Like other escaping battered women (I have since learned), I lived in a shared or overlapping social and economic world with the batterer; I tried to believe it would be all right.

The book Ricki and I were going to write together became, of course, very important to me. I don't know if the attempt was interrupted by the violence or the violence was interrupted by the attempt. I know that I devoted myself to the book, even though it was hard for me to concentrate because I lived in constant fear. I held on to the book as if it were a life raft, even though I was drowning in poverty and fear. There were times of hope, near normalcy. At one point my husband got a new apartment and offered me our old one. I took it, for all the obvious reasons. He left a mattress; someone gave me a small radio; and I lived on potatoes. Then he started breaking in; and it was there that he bloodied me and said he would kill me, run me down when he saw me, and I knew it was true finally, and I had to hide in the movie theater after that for three weeks, the time it took to get a restraining order. My lawyer, assigned by the court, at first didn't believe me or didn't care when I told him about the beatings or how dangerous my husband was; but later my husband apparently roughed up the lawyer's secretary. This time, when driven from the apartment by my husband's threats to a phone in a store around the block, the lawyer told me to go somewhere else for a while, though he didn't know where or how and didn't care. I had had to go to the store to use the phone because the apartment phone was in my husband's name, and he had it disconnected and it was a two-year wait for a new line. As I came out of the back room of the store where the phone was, the woman who owned the store opened her cash register, grabbed a handful of bills, pushed them at me, and said: "Run for your life. Now." I did.

Through all this, I held on to this idea of a book; and I kept working on it. Ricki and I did research together and some writing together. But then she pulled away from it. The book itself, in taking on counterculture pornography, brought us into conflict with friends and acquaintances in the exilic, counterculture community in Amsterdam. Some of these folks produced a pornography tabloid called *Suck*. Ricki and I drafted a chapter on *Suck* and gave it to them to read. I, at least, believed that they would see the insult to women in what they were publishing, and that there was danger in some of their photographs—I remember in particular a photo of an Asian woman inserting a huge, glass, bowl-shaped jar into her rectum. I had begun to identify with other women. Our friends, the makers of the pornography, reacted with outrage to our effrontery in challenging them. They said they had always been for civil rights (against segregation based on race) and this was sex—what kind of chicks were we anyway? We thought we were perfectly fine chicks at the time, even though the word "chick" itself was beginning to have an ugly sound to

it. Ricki decided that she couldn't take the social ostracism these folks threatened. We agreed that I would finish the book and get it published. I had to get out of there anyway or I'd be killed. I knew I had to disappear and that there could be no mistakes. I planned a secret escape and in November 1972 I disappeared suddenly.

The vow that I made—out loud, to myself but with Ricki as witness—was that I would become a real writer and I would use everything I knew to help women. I didn't know how much I knew, how valuable it would be; nor did she. But we both did understand that in 1972 what I knew was not part of feminism: what I knew about male dominance in sex or rape in marriage, for instance. The knowledge about male dominance in sex came not only from this one marriage but from several years of prostituting before I got married. I called it "being on the streets," and it consisted of equal parts whoring, poverty and homelessness, and just being a tough girl. I had never kept it a secret, not from my husband, not from any friend. Ricki and I both understood that I had experience that could be knowledge. I made a vow to use it for women.

Writers need to be damned hard to kill. So do women, of course. I have never believed in suicide, the female poet's alternative to standing her ground and facing down the power of men. I don't like it that Plath and Sexton wrote strong and beautiful poems capturing the horror and meanness of male dominance but would not risk losing socially conventional femininity by sticking around to fight it out in the realm of politics, including the politics of culture. I always wanted to live. I fought hard to live. This means I did something new. I have been bearing the unbearable, and facing men down, for a long time now.

I began messing with men when I was in high school, though, sadly, they began messing with me earlier than that—I was raped at nine, though not legally, since fingers and a hand were used for penetration, not the officially requisite penis. That ended up in my hand as he twisted and contorted with a physical omnipresence that pinned me and manipulated me at the same time. This breach of a child's body does count. It does register. The boundary of the body itself is broken by force and intimidation, a chaotic but choreographed violence. The child is used intentionally and reduced to less than human by the predator's intelligence as well as his behavior. The commitment of the child molester is absolute, and both his insistence and his victory communicate to the child his experience of her—a breachable, breakable thing any stranger can wipe his dick on. When it is family, of course, the invasion is more terrible, more intimate, escape more unlikely. I was lucky—it was a stranger. I was lucky by the standards of today: neither kidnapped nor killed. The man became part of the dark—not "the dark" in its usual symbolic sense, bad, with a racist tinge, but part of the literal dark: his body, almost distinct, got folded into every dark room like the one in which he hurt me and he got folded into the dark of every night I had to get through, with eyes open, waiting. I didn't like to sleep, because then I couldn't guard my mother against death. So I kept my eyes open. I could feel that the night was occupied with tangible creatures, and the man, hiding, was one of them.

As a child with an immense ambition to live, to know, to feel, I moved toward everything that frightened me: men, night, the giving up of my own body. I wanted to be an artist, by which I meant a writer. I despised commercial writing. My heroes were Rimbaud and Baudelaire. I had a paperback of Baudelaire's poems with me, in French with an English prose translation, when the man molested me. A few years later I had a high school teacher who said that most girls of my social class who worked (the ideal was not to work) became hairdressers, but I was so smart that I could become a prostitute, which at least was interesting. He was my tutor in sex; a guide; a charlatan and an exploiter. But he made the sameness of art and opening my legs palpable, urgent: there wasn't one without the other. I thought he was a philosopher and someday we would found a school of philosophy; I would be his acolyte. He introduced me to Camus and Sartre. I was a motherless child with spirit and intelligence in a world that abhorred both in girls. I wanted knowledge but distrusted formal education because the adults were enforcers and transparently wanted to break my spirit; except for the seducer. He wanted to appropriate it for his own purposes but I didn't begin to imagine that. I would find ways to go to New York City to find poems and on the bus I would

At Bennington College, 1967

find a way to get money from old guys who liked teenage girls to touch them. I'd use the money to go to Greenwich Village and buy mimeographed collections of poems. I loved Allen Ginsberg especially. More than anyone he expressed the sense of pain I felt, the anger and rebellion, but also the undifferentiated infatuation I felt for the world of possibility around me. I had no sense of evil and I didn't believe that harm could defeat me—I'd make poems out of it. High school was hell, to be endured, the teachers behavior-police who took books away and tried to shut the mind down. For instance, a tenth-grade teacher in a study hall confiscated my copy of *Hamlet,* which I had been reading. She said we weren't allowed to read it until the twelfth grade. I told her that I had already read it several times so why take it from me? She did take it and countered with her certainty that one day she would read about me in the newspapers. In those days only politicians and criminals made news. Girls didn't become politicians. I was bad for reading *Hamlet.* Each day the enforcers pushed me into a sustained rage laced with contempt; and each day the seducer manipulated my anger and loneliness, pushed me further into experiencing intelligence as a sexualized mark of Cain and artistic ambition as a sexualized delinquency.

Meanwhile, my father worked hard so that I could have a formal education that would be excellent, not mediocre, on the college level. The high school guidance counselors wanted me to go to a state college for girls to get a teaching degree "to fall back on when your husband dies." My intelligence had no significance to them; my desire to write, which I confessed, was beneath consideration. My father knew I would not stay in any college that was high school redux. In September 1964 I went to Bennington College on scholarships and loans, loans he took out, not me. I did have jobs there for money but not enough to carry any of the real economic burden. I stayed there one year, left, returned for two years, left, mailed in my thesis from Amsterdam. In 1969 my father, fittingly, attended my graduation and picked up my diploma. I am considered a graduate of the class of 1968, however, because that is how Bennington keeps track of students. In those years, so many students left—some of the richer ones to Austin Riggs, a mental institution not too far away, some taking other detours—that the college always reckoned you a member of the class in which you entered and optimistically added four years to signify graduation; it would be hard for an already overtaxed administration to know who returned when, for how long, and to what end.

Bennington had a reputation for academic excellence and a bohemian environment. In fact, Bennington trained mistresses, not wives, for artists, not businessmen. To illustrate the ambience: the year before my first year, seniors in literature had, as a group project, recreated the brothel scene in Joyce's *Ulysses,* themselves the whores. A lot of the faculty preyed on the nearly all-female student body; and the deep conviction of most of the faculty that these girls would never become artists themselves was openly articulated when, in my third year of attendance, coeducation was discussed and eventually adopted. Students, including me, got to hear how useless the mostly male faculty felt teaching girls. We never became anything, they said, each a dozen times in a dozen ways. We seemed to be fine for fucking and serial marriage, some faculty actually going through as many as four marriages with successive students

and countless adulteries. But we could never become what in our hearts we thought we were: creative, ambitious, risk-taking doers and thinkers and makers. I had three brilliant teachers at Bennington, each of whom was ethically scrupulous with respect to me; and I owe them a lot. They taught me with an astonishing intellectual generosity; they supported my aspirations; they even protected me, from other faculty and sometimes from myself. They extended friendship without the sexualization. The rest of it was intellectually boring. After my first few weeks there, my philosophy professor telephoned me at the student house where I lived and asked me please not to leave: she knew I was bored. I distracted myself with drugs, sex, and politics.

Bennington had a nine-week work period in the winter—a long two months—and long Thanksgiving, Christmas, and spring breaks, a big problem for a girl with no real home and no money. For my first work period in December 1964 I took marginal political jobs in New York City and fucked for food and shelter and whatever cash I needed. I worked with the Student Peace Union and the War Resisters League opposing the war in Vietnam. I had other jobs, too, for instance as a receptionist at a New York University institute for remedial reading. In February 1965 I was arrested outside the United States Mission to the United Nations for protesting America's involvement in Vietnam. I had a book of poems by Charles Olson with me when I was arrested. I spent four days in the Women's House of Detention before I was released on my own recognizance. While in jail, in addition to the many strip-searches by hand that police and nurses made into my vagina and anus, I was brutalized by two male doctors who gave me an internal examination, the first one I ever had. They pretty much tore me up inside with a steel speculum and had themselves a fine old time verbally tormenting me as well. I saw them enjoy it. I witnessed their pleasure in doing it. I couldn't understand why they would like to hurt me. I began to bleed right after. When I came out of jail I was mute from the trauma. I wandered around the city, homeless and resourceless, silent and confused, for several days, until I showed up at the apartment of a stranger who had taken a bag I had packed for jail from me when, toward the end of the day, it seemed as if we would not be arrested. I sort of vaguely remembered her name and looked it up in the phone book when I needed underwear badly enough. She was the writer Grace Paley and this was before she herself had gone to jail to protest Vietnam. She made me come in and sit; I stared silently. Grace got me to talk but instead of normal talk I said what had happened to me. I didn't even know the words for speculum or internal examination, so I was exceptionally blunt and used my hands. She thought that what had been done to me was horrible and she immediately called a woman reporter to say that this monstrous thing had been done to this girl. The reporter said: so what? But that night I went to the Student Peace Union office and typed letters to newspapers to tell what had happened to me in the jail: blunt letters. The antiwar boys, whose letters I typed during the day, whose leaflets I mimeographed, laughed at me; but I mounted a protest against the prison. The *New York Times,* the *Daily News,* and the *New York Post* carried the story. The city was forced to conduct a grand jury investigation. An assistant to the governor also investigated. A liberal Republican, John V. Lindsay, challenged entrenched Democratic incumbent Robert Wagner for mayor partly by holding Wagner responsible for the corruption in the jail and promising to shut it down. Lindsay won. Television news shows did documentaries on the prison, which had a long history of brutalizing women, some of whom had died. Eventually, the grand jury vindicated the prison, and the governor's assistant was defunded by the legislature. My parents were ashamed of my arrest and of the way in which I had been hurt. They were enraged with me and pretty much abandoned me. I left school, my parents, the country. I went to Greece with less than a hundred dollars in my pocket. I gave most of it to an old woman, Mildred, whom I met on a train. She said she had lost hers but had money waiting in Athens. I showed up at the appointed place, at the appointed time, but she never came. That night, my nineteenth birthday, I picked up a Greek army officer: I needed food and money. Since the hill overlooking Athens was beautiful and the night sublime, it was easy to pretend this was romance. I remember saying to him after, "You really hate women, don't you?" I hadn't anticipated woman hating but I recognized it in his abrupt post-coital tristesse. I learned not to voice the observation however many times I made it,

whatever the post-coital mood. Men don't like to be seen or remarked on by what my friend Judith Malina, director of the Living Theatre, calls "talking women." I wrote poems and a novel called *Notes on Burning Boyfriend,* a surrealistic screed against the Vietnam War built on the self-immolation of protester Norman Morrison. I published a small collection of poems and Genet-like prose called *Child* (Heraklion, Crete, 1966). It wasn't until I published *Woman Hating* in 1974 that I became a talking woman who could say with some authority: you really hate women, don't you?

The authority was never my own plain experience. I always thought other people's lives worth more than mine. As a matter of temperament I had an interest in the collective or communal, not the personal. I thought psychology was a phony science, and I still do. I didn't think something was important simply because it happened to me, and certainly the world concurred. I had learned that I would not be believed. I knew that from the world's point of view, though never my own, I was trash, the bottom. The prison authorities said I lied and the grand jury claimed to believe them, not me. No one really believed me about my husband. I had a deep experience of the double standard but no systematic understanding of it. The writers I had loved and wanted to emulate—Baudelaire or Artaud or Dostoevsky or Henry Miller or Jean Genet—were apparently ennobled by degradation. The lower they sunk the more credibility they had. I was lowered and disgraced, first by what was being called sexual liberation, then by the violence of domestic sexual servitude, without any concomitant increase in expertness: I paid my dues, baby, I know the price of the ticket but so what? When I emerged as a writer with *Woman Hating,* it was not to wallow in pain, or in depravity, or in the male romance with prostitution; it was to demand change. I wanted to change the power structure in the social world that had made degradation a destiny for many of us, or lots of us, or maybe even all of us— for women. I didn't want to write the female suicide's poem nor did I want to write another male-inspired lyric celebrating the sewer. I wanted to resist male dominance for myself and to change the outcome for other women. I did not want to open my legs again, this time in prose. I did not believe that to do so would persuade or bring change. I found, then and over the next twenty years, a stubborn refusal to credit a woman with any deep knowledge of the world itself, the world outside the domain of her own introspection about romantic love, housekeeping, a man. This refusal was so basic and so widespread that it could stay an unspoken assumption. Women who wanted to write about social issues did it through anecdote. Books that could only have been written out of an extensive and significant knowledge of what it meant to be pornographized or sexually colonized—my books—were dismissed by patriarchy's intellectual ruling class as Victorian or puritanical—empirical synonyms for ignorant.

Instead of using my own experience as the immediate subject of discourse, I used a more complex method of exposing bone and blood: I found the social phenomena that could be pulled apart to show what I knew to be the essential heart of the experience—rape, prostitution, battery, for instance; woman hating, sexualized insult, bias, discrimination—and I found the language to carry it: to carry it far, way past where critics could reach or, frankly, most men could imagine. I had the luck of having my books last over enough time to reach women—not élite women but grassroots women and marginalized women. Slowly women began to come to me to say, yes, that's right; and I learned more from them, went deeper. I used writing to take language where women's pain was—and women's fear—and I kept excavating for the words that could bear the burden of speaking the unspeakable: all that hadn't been said during the rape or after, while prostituting or after; truths that had not been said ever or truths that had not been said looking the rapist, the batterer, the pimp, the citizen-john, in the eye. This has been my contribution to literature and to the women's movement.

I saw my mother's strength. Illness seems a visitation, a particular affliction to test the courage of the stricken person, a personal challenge from God. It is hard to know what one can learn from the example even of someone as heroic as my mother surely was. In my mother, I saw Herculean strength in the face of pain, sickness, incapacitation, and the unknown. I have never thought that much of it rubbed off, because I am a coward in that realm: any minor illness makes me feel as if life has stopped. The heroic person, as I saw from my mother,

never accepts even the suggestion that life might stop. She keeps pulling the burden, illness as a stone weight; she never stops pulling. Nothing in my mother's life suggested that women were wimps.

In school—grade school and college—my female friends were rebels with deep souls: bad children in adulthood; smart adults in childhood; precocious; willful; stubborn; not one age or one sex or with one goal easily advanced by a conforming marriage and inevitable motherhood. Despite the best efforts of parents, teachers, to bind our feet Chinese-style, we kept kicking. Ain't none of us got out with unbroken feet; we all got some bones bent in half; we got clipped and pushed and stepped on hard to make us conform; and in our different ways we kept walking, even on the broken bones. It was a time when girls were supposed to be virgins when we married. The middle-class ideal was that women were not supposed to work; such labor would reflect badly on our husbands. Anyone pregnant outside of marriage was an outcast: a delinquent or an exile; had a criminal abortion or birthed a child that would most likely be taken away from her for adoption, which meant forever then. In disgrace, she would be sent away to some home for pregnant girls, entirely stigmatized; her parents ashamed, shocked; she herself a kind of poison that had ruined the family's notion of its own goodness and respectability. She would be socially reprehensible and repulsive—and the social ostracism would be absolute. I had close friends who resisted, who never quite gave in, despite appearances to the contrary. The cost was high sometimes; but it is my impression that my friends, like most women, paid the highest price when they did give in, not when they resisted. The cost needs to be spread out over time: the many marriages and the midlife depression. On the streets there were women who were both strong and fragile at the same time: immensely strong to bear the continuing sexual invasion, consistent brutality, and just plain bad weather (no joke); immensely strong to accept responsibility as the prostituting persona—I want this, I do this, I am this, ain't nothin' hurts me; and much too fragile to face either the cost of prostituting or its etiology. The cost was physical disintegration and mental splitting apart. The cost was getting dirtier and lonelier and anesthetizing pain with more and meaner drugs. The cost was accepting the physical violence of the johns, moving through it as if it didn't matter or hadn't happened, never facing that one had been hurt, then hurt again, nor asking why. Some girls were straight-out battered and forced. But even without a violent man in sight, the etiology always had to do with sexual abuse, in the present or in the past; also with homelessness and poverty; with the willingness of men to use any girl for small change; with abandonment—the personal abandonment of family, the social abandonment choreographed by the users. It may be harder to face abandonment than to endure exploitation; and there were no models for articulating the realities and consequences of sexual abuse. The point of dealing with political oppression has never been that the oppressed are by nature weak, therefore pitiful: the more injustice on one's back, the stronger one must be. Strong girls become strong women and use that strength to endure; but fighting injustice requires a dynamic strength disciplined to resistance, focused on subverting illegitimate power, eventually to level it. In a system valuing men over women, girls with piss and vinegar carried a heavier burden than girls brimming over with sugar and spice; the stronger were punished more, and still are. In this world, female friendships, deep and sustained loves, romances and infatuations, also love affairs, helped keep one's heart alive, one's sense of self, however unratified by the larger universe, animated and sensate. The political use of female strength to change society for the benefit of women is a different choice: a harder, better choice than endurance, however noble (or stylish) the endurance.

In my early adult life as a writer, there were three women especially who helped me and taught me and believed in me: Grace Paley, Barbara Deming, and Muriel Rukeyser. Each one sort of took me in and took me to her heart for some significant period of my life. Each one was mother and sister and friend. Each one was a distinguished and powerful writer, a social rebel, an original moral thinker. Each lived a life that combined writing and political action. Each put herself on the line for the oppressed, the powerless; was repelled by exploitation and injustice; and was devoted to women—had deep and intimate friendships with women and fought for women's rights. I met Grace in 1965, shortly after I got out of the Women's House of Detention. She fed me and

gave me a bed to sleep in; I went to her when I was distressed, exhausted, in trouble—or more trouble than usual. She helped me when I came back from Greece; then again later when I came back from Amsterdam. I met Barbara in 1965 a few months later than Grace, on a television program about the Women's House of Detention, where she too had spent some time as a political protester (see "Letter to M.," *Lavender Culture,* edited by Jay and Young); and then we met again and became close after *Woman Hating* was published. In 1976, my friend John Stoltenberg (about whom more later) and I went down to Sugarloaf Key in Florida to live on shared land with Barbara and her lover, Jane Verlaine. I couldn't tolerate the subtropical climate so after five months John and I moved north to the Berkshires. I met Muriel in 1972 after I had returned to New York City from Amsterdam at an antiwar meeting. She tried very hard to help me survive as a writer, including by hiring me as her assistant (see "Introduction," *Letters from a War Zone*). My apprenticeship to her had a slightly formal quality, because she paid me for the duration. She opened her home to me and her heart; she advised me and counseled me; and she made sure I had a bare minimum of money. She was attuned to the concrete necessities. A woman who has been poor and entirely on her own, as Muriel had been, knows that one's life can slip through a crack; good intentions can't match the value of a dime.

These friendships were of enormous importance to me; I doubt I would have survived without them. But the friendships went far beyond any utility for survival. Each of these women had faith in me—and I never quite knew why; and each of these women loved me— and I never knew why. It was a lucky orphan who found each of these women and it was a lucky striving writer who found each of these writers. They are all taken more seriously now than they were then; but I had the good sense to know that each was an American original, wise with common sense and plain talk, gritty with life; they were great craftswomen, each a citizen and a visionary. I know what I took; I hope I gave enough back.

It is hard to say what keeps a writer writing in the face of discouragement. It helps to have had a difficult childhood; to have a love of writing itself, without regard to the outcome;

and eventually to have an audience, however small, that wants you, wants those troublesome books, is like a lover to you, very intimate with enormous expectations—embraces you through the language you find and the truth you are willing to tell. I have had that audience, which I meet when I travel to lecture or to give readings, a U.S. underground unrecognized by the media in small towns, on college campuses, at political rallies, tender, luminous, brave women of all ages, and mostly but not exclusively young men who want fairness for women. They have shown me respect and love.

One can be derailed by savage reviews, certainly poverty, a ubiquitous cultural contempt, violent words or violent gestures or violent acts, invisibility as a writer or, in the American tradition, too much fame or notoriety. My own view is that survival is a matter of random luck: the right blow, the one that will finish you, does not hit you at the right time in the right place. I have not made money nor had an easy time publishing my work, which has been anathematized. I had a hard childhood, which is good; and I have the audience that wants my work, which is essential; and I love to write regardless of the outcome in publishing, which is damned lucky or I'd have died of a broken heart. But especially I have had the love of John Stoltenberg, with whom I have lived now for twenty years, and the love and friendship of Elaine Markson, who has been my agent for the past twenty-two years. They are fierce and brilliant friends. Neither has been intimidated by the anger against my work or against me. Each has stayed with me when I thought they would leave or should leave. I love John with my heart and soul; but what is more extraordinary is the way in which he has loved me (see his "Living with Andrea Dworkin," *Lambda Book Review*, May/June 1994). I never promised him anything; but he promised me right from the beginning that he would stay with me for the rest of his life. I am just entertaining the idea that he might. He undertook to live the life I needed. He has taken on my hardships as his own; indeed, they have become his own. We share the circumstances created by the antagonism to my work on Grub Street. We share the politics of radical feminism and a commitment to destroying male dominance and gender itself. We share a love of writing and of equality; and we share each and every day. He is a deeply kind person,

"My friend John Stoltenberg on July 6, 1986, in Atlanta, Georgia, addressing an antisexist men's conference"

and it is through the actual dailiness of living with him that I understand the spiritual poverty and the sensual stupidity of eroticizing brutality over kindness. Elaine has been a loyal friend and colleague in circumstances both complex and difficult. She has stayed loyal to me and to my work through years when she didn't make enough in commissions to cover the postage she spent sending out my manuscripts. Pornographers and their flunkies have tried to bully and intimidate her; so have publishers, as if silencing me would further freedom of speech. She has kept sending out manuscripts of mine for years as publishers stubbornly refused them. It was she who finally made it possible for me to publish my work in England when U.S. publishers were a dead end. *Ice and Fire*, published by Secker & Warburg in the United Kingdom in 1986, was the first of several books to have widespread British distribution while remaining unsold in the U.S. I had written a good first draft in 1983, which Elaine tried to sell in the U.S., then a final version in 1984. *Ice and Fire* was finally published here in 1987—by an English company; but was never brought out in a paperback edition. The paperback is still in print in England. These are trying difficulties that no slick, money-driven agent would tolerate. Elaine will tell you that she doesn't always agree with me; but why should she—and why should anyone assume that she does? The assumption comes from the lazy but popular stigmatizing ploy of guilt by association, a form of hysteria that pervades any discussion of me or my work in publishing circles. She refuses to give in to this discrediting ruse. Her faith in me has sometimes had to stand in for my faith in myself: I have become shaky but she stands firm. Many times, in the quiet of the room where I work, I have had to face the fact that I would not still be writing—given how hard the hard times have been—were it not for Elaine's passionate commitment and integrity. We've walked many miles together.

So the right blow may still strike in the right place at exactly the right time: to break my writer's heart and stop me in my tracks. I do believe that survival is random, not a result of virtue or talent. But so far, especially in knowing John and Elaine, I have been blessed with monumental grace and staggering good luck.

On April 30, 1992, at the age of forty-two, my brother Mark died of cancer. This was exactly eighteen years after the publication date of *Woman Hating,* an anniversary that will never make me happy again.

He was living in Vienna when he died, a molecular biologist, married to his wife of ten years, Eva Rastl, also a molecular biologist, forty at the time of his death.

He was chair of the department of molecular biology at the Ernst Boehringer Institute of Vienna. He and Eva worked together there and also earlier at Columbia University in New York City. He had done post-doctoral work in biochemistry at the Carnegie Institution in Baltimore, the National Cancer Institute in Bethesda, and the University of California at Davis. At the time Mark got ill, he and Eva were doing research on the metabolism of cancer cells. They were wonderful together, sharing love, friendship, and work. She, a Catholic from Austria, he, Jewish, born in Camden in 1949, reconciled cultural differences and historical sorrow through personal love, the

recognition of each other as individuals, and the exercise of reason, which they both, as scientists, valued. A belief in reason was key to a world view that they had in common.

When my brother died, part of me died. This is not hyperbole or cliché. I could feel some of the light that is life going dead inside me and when he died, it went out. He was a gentle boy, the one life I knew from infancy. I had a utopian memory of loving him, a kind of ecstatic love for him that was non-verbal, inexplicable, untouched by growing older. Although we were separated from the time I left home to go to college—there was a period of eleven years when I didn't see him at all, although we wrote each other—the closeness of early childhood never changed, his emotional importance to me, mine to him. But he didn't remember his early childhood or his later childhood; he didn't remember anything from childhood. This terrified me. Because we had usually been sent to stay at separate places when my mother was ill, I had no idea what might have happened to him. As an adult, he had recurrent nightmares that he couldn't understand. I was able to explain or identify the elements of one of them for him. He saw a big man dressed in black carrying a black bag and coming into the house at night—then he woke up in fear. This was my mother's doctor, a cold, frightening figure. I always thought of him as death but I did know who he was. My brother didn't. The childhood years were still blank when he died.

He was the kind child, the nurturer of my parents. As they grew older, he took care of them, with his company, his true concern. My mother died a year before Mark and I don't believe he recovered from her death before his own. Like my father, like John, he was a good and giving man.

I saw him about three weeks before he died. He had asked me to come to Vienna in October 1990 to visit. I didn't want to go to Austria ever, but put these feelings aside to see him. Told he had cancer in November 1991, he submitted to a major operation in which a large part of his esophagus near his stomach was removed. He recovered from the surgery but lost the use of his larynx. There were signs that the malignant cells had spread. I found myself the bearer of this knowledge, a confidant for Eva, the one who had to keep my father hoping and eventually the one who had to tell him that Mark would die soon, probably within a few days. In our childhood, Mark and I had learned to be alone with our troubles whatever they were. Mark undertook to die the same way. Eva was with him and they were close, tender, inseparable; but he didn't want family or friends to make the journey to see him. I told him that I was coming to Vienna and he didn't have to see me but I would be there; I had made the arrangements. I believe he was glad, but he got sicker much faster than he or Eva or I anticipated. When I went he was unbearably ill. He had asked me to bring him Skippy peanut butter, which was our staple as children. He was starving to death, a not unusual effect of cancer, and so Eva and I hoped he would eat it. But he couldn't. I also took him marbles, especially cats' eyes, which we had played with when we were children. Marbles and bottlecaps were currency among the kids in our neighborhood. Once he had stolen all mine and my mother had let him keep them because he was a boy—they were boys' wealth, not girls'. He smiled when I told him but I don't think he remembered. He kept the marbles near him.

I sat with him during the day for as long as he would let me. Sometimes he could whisper—it was air, not sound, shaped by his mouth. But sometimes he was too weak for that, and I sat at a table in the same room—a modern living room with a large picture window that looked out on trees and bushes, a room filled with daylight—and read, or tried to read. I think it was only after he died and Eva sent me some photographs of him from those days of my visit that I realized how frail he had been, how much I hadn't seen—how hard it had been for him to appear clean and groomed and calm and smiling. The cancer had spread to his liver. Tumors were growing on his neck, which he kept covered, and on other parts of his body.

Then I'd go back to my hotel and I would wail; I'd scream and cry and wail. I would call John—it would still be late afternoon in Vienna, too expensive to call—and I'd howl and keen and cry wildly, again and again, until I was worn out. Then I'd take a walk in the park across from my hotel. The cold air would be bracing, and my head would stop hurting. Then I would return to my room and sit down to write. I had brought a legal pad with me and also an article that John Irving had recently

published in the *New York Times Book Review* castigating feminists for opposing pornography, charging that we were purveyors of a new puritanism (see John Irving, "Pornography and the New Puritans," March 29, 1992). I knew that to survive the pain I felt on seeing my brother dying I would have to find a way to use the pain. I truly thought that otherwise it would kill me. I decided, coldly and purposefully, to confront the most painful theme in my own life—repeated sexual abuse. The logic of my answer to Mr. Irving was that no one with the kind of experience I had could be called a puritan; and maybe I and other women actually knew more about sexual violence than he did; and it was the pornographers, not feminists, who punished women in the public square, as puritans had, for being sexual. The narrative was a first-person detailed telling of rapes and assaults (see the *New York Times Book Review,* May 3, 1992). The day my piece was published as a nearly full-page letter edited from the article I had intended, my father and I

"My brother, Mark, taken on his last walk,"
early 1992

were on a plane to Vienna to bury Mark at the Central Cemetery. The chief rabbi of Vienna conducted the service. My father simply refused to sit with the men, as is orthodox practice, and sat with Eva and me. My brother wasn't religious but he loved walking in that great European graveyard. He was someone who walked miles for pleasure; and the Central Cemetery, miles from where he lived, had been one of his favorite places to walk to, then wander in. What does a man with no memory of childhood think of on long, solitary walks to the civilized, well-tended graves of the Austrians, the abandoned, overgrown graves of the Jews? My brother had taken me there on my first trip to Vienna—he had wanted me to see this place that was special to him. I had reacted with horror to the sight of the neglected Jewish graves, the latest stone I saw dated 1938. On my 1992 trip back to Vienna when Mark was sick, I saw on television that the mayor of Vienna had just made a speech acknowledging the importance of Jews, always, to life in Vienna, to its greatness as a city, and that a committee of non-Jewish Austrians was trying to make some restitution by cleaning up the abandoned graves and trying to find out what had happened to the families. Because of this change, we felt able to bury Mark in the Central Cemetery, in the contemporary Jewish burial ground, where he could rest near Eva, though she cannot be buried with him. I have gone back to visit his grave. Eva says it has helped her to have Mark buried there.

I am less alive because I lost my brother. Yet I used what I felt while I watched him dying to write something I considered necessary. I think this is a deep and perhaps terrible truth about writing. Surely, it is a deep and terrible truth about me. As long as I can, I will take what I feel, use it to face what I am able to know, find language, and write what I think must be written for the freedom and dignity of women.

Brooklyn, New York
July/August 1994

Copyright © 1994 by Andrea Dworkin.

BIBLIOGRAPHY

Nonfiction:

Woman Hating, Dutton, 1974.

Our Blood: Prophecies and Discourses on Sexual Politics (collected lectures), Harper, 1976.

Pornography: Men Possessing Women, Putnam, 1981.

Right-wing Women, Coward McCann, 1983.

Intercourse, Free Press, 1987.

(With Catharine A. MacKinnon) *Pornography and Civil Rights: A New Day for Women's Equality,* Organizing Against Pornography, 1988.

Letters from a War Zone (essays), Secker & Warburg (London), 1988, Dutton, 1989.

Fiction:

the new womans broken heart (short stories), Frog in the Well, 1980.

Ice and Fire, Secker & Warburg, 1986, Weidenfeld & Nicolson, 1987.

Mercy, Secker & Warburg, 1990, Four Walls Eight Windows, 1991.

Other:

Child (poems published on Crete), n.p., 1966.

Morning Hair (poems and fiction), designed, printed, and published by the author, hand-set type, hardbound, 1968.

Author of novels *Notes on Burning Boyfriend* and *Ruins,* and a book of poems titled *(Vietnam) Variations.*

Contributor to periodicals, including *America Report, Christopher Street, Feminist Studies, Gay Community News, Los Angeles Times, Mother Jones, Ms., New York Times Book Review, Newsday, San Francisco Review of Books,* and *Village Voice.* Also contributor to numerous anthologies, including *Take Back the Night, Transforming a Rape Culture, Violence Against Women: The Bloody Footprints,* and *Wild Women.*

Jesse Hill Ford

1928-

I envy authors whose lives have gone smoothly, those who published early and kept at it with never a pause or so much as a ripple, and who made the transition to old age, blessed with cakes and ale.

Such was never the case with me. My first novel did not appear in print until I was almost thirty. I had meanwhile been variously employed in a series of jobs beginning at ten years old when I delivered the *Saturday Evening Post* to six subscribers scattered about the neighborhood.

The mailed editions reached subscribers on Wednesday. My edge was to put the magazine in their hands on Tuesday, a day early. In those days serialized fiction had great appeal and was a mainstay of the magazines.

My next job of any consequence was for Walgreen's drugstore in downtown Nashville, Tennessee. I was hired on as stockboy. My duties were to keep the store shelves filled with merchandise. The stockroom was a couple of flights up a steep stairway above the store. I was expected to paste price labels on each item, hand letter the prices, and hustle the full boxes down the stairs where I put the merchandise on the store shelves in the proper places.

One stockboy had easily managed this until I got the job. But when the job became mine, war had broken out, and soldiers from Fort Campbell, Kentucky, and other nearby army camps, flooded the store in throngs. They needed all manner of remedies but mostly bought lotions for chiggerbite, poison ivy rashes, and sunburns.

As World War II progressed, the demands on the stockboy became overwhelming, but hiring more help was something the management never thought of, and at age fourteen, the after-school-hours job was a necessity, for I was paying my tuition to Montgomery Bell Academy with my earnings.

In my rush to open cartons of Lydia Pinkham's Vegetable Compound, something in great demand for women back in those days, I

Jesse Hill Ford, Humboldt, Tennessee, 1960

drew the blade knife down a carton edge. It slipped, blades dulled often and had to be changed frequently.

When the blade slipped, I gashed my inner forearm a sickening slice some three inches long. I saw tendons and muscles in the instant before the wound filled with blood.

Luckily the janitor heard me cry out just as he was passing the stockroom door and he helped me down the steep steps which came out on the main floor next to the pharmacy.

The dear middle-aged Jewish lady, who filled prescriptions, was just then dusting the pharmacy shelves with a filthy rag. When she saw my wound she slapped the filthy rag into it to stanch the bleeding.

I was hurried to a tiny nearby clinic inhabited by the lone physician who tended such calamities. As he sewed me up I could smell the bourbon on his breath. I was given nothing to quell the pain of that operation. I still vividly recall the untidy clinic room and the drunken doctor's stitching method. Before each stitch he *licked* the needle, something one might suppose he'd learned from his grandmother.

But, for a reward, once I was bandaged, I got the rest of the afternoon off. I quickly phoned another fourteen-year-old, a Montgomery Bell Academy classmate, and we arranged to meet that afternoon at a dove field behind some houses out on West Meade, an old farm soon to be subdivided.

Bobby Akers' dad was away in the U.S. Navy and had left behind an entire case of .12 gauge shotgun shells, especially loaded for shooting ducks. With a war on, such ammunition was not to be had and Bobby's father, away serving his country, probably dreamed of the day when he'd be home again and out hunting with those rare shells.

Bobby and I shot up the entire case of shells in two glorious days of dove shooting. My left forearm, where I was stitched up, still bears the scar. In the stress of handling our shotguns and shooting those heavy loads (they bruised your shoulder black and blue) my wound opened a bit, as it had every right to do. This made a very *nice* scar. Miraculously neither the filthy pharmacy dustrag nor the drunken old doctor's saliva caused an infection. But then, as the saying goes, germs won't live on some people.

Although I grew up in Nashville, I was born in Troy, Alabama, where my mother taught school and my father worked in the local pharmacy. Soon after my birth they moved to Jasper, Alabama. There we lived with my grandparents in their comfortable two-storey house on Florida Avenue. And there we remained, for three years in that wonderful household.

Bessie, the black cook, gave me baths in the kitchen; Mrs. Mooney, the white washerwoman, told tales of her son, Little Frank, who was, as she put it, "plumb pretty." Little Frank

Lucille Elizabeth Musgrove,
the author's mother at sixteen years

was away doing time in prison, but why that was Mrs. Mooney never said.

Foxy, my teenaged Uncle Rossie's fox terrier, never bit me even though I chewed his ears; Sophie Jo, my grandmother's Persian cat, kept her kittens in a box behind the wood-burning cook stove.

The milk from Bossie, the family cow, was churned. My two young uncles took turns milking her. They would direct a stream from Bossie's teat directly into my open mouth while I crouched, devoutly watching while Bossie was milked. The taste of milk, warmed by Bossie's generous body, was delectable.

In the kennel behind the house my father's bird dog bitch nursed her liver-patterned puppies. Near the kennel in an oblong wooden box, buried to keep its content cool, my grandfather's bait minnows swam, serenely unaware of the fate awaiting them.

Every afternoon Grandmother Musgrove rocked me to sleep while she sang lullabyes.

After three idyllic years we left Jasper for Nashville. My father had taken a job with a pharmaceutical company. His duties as a travelling salesman took him out of town days at a stretch.

Visits back to Jasper somehow only made things worse when we'd return to Nashville. Had the Depression of the thirties not intervened to displace my father from his work as a pharmacist in Alabama, we'd have never moved to Tennessee.

When I was five years old, my parents bought a house a short distance from Parmer Elementary School on what had been, before it was subdivided, the great Southern plantation, Belle Meade.

Early on, my mother had striven to bring me up to be a conscientious objector. It was not clear to me, as a youngster, exactly what the term meant.

Later she gave up and resigned herself to having in me a staunchly patriotic son. All my schoolmates were staunch patriots. We served on the school safety patrol. Our job was to direct traffic before and after school hours. Another duty was raising and lowering the American flag which flew in front of Parmer School. We respected the flag.

Middle Tennessee is at the center of what was the battleground of the Confederacy. Our elementary schoolteachers led us in the singing of both "The Star-Spangled Banner" and in "Dixie," the rollicking battle song of the defeated Confederacy. We had drilled into us every day we spent in school that, while we were Americans who might someday be privileged to serve our country in time of war, we were also Southerners.

Being a Southerner meant being a good citizen, determined to live a godly, righteous, and sober life; to work hard, and to excel, not only in studies, but in athletics and public speaking as well.

We were not expected to be concerned with sex. As a subject, sex was studiously ignored, both at home and at school.

But information, much of it misinformation, got through to us anyway, via the yard men and household domestics.

One myth had it that women were possessed of two inner routes up the nether orifice referred to as the pussy. Sperm sent up the hole to the right got a girl baby. To the left got a boy.

When I was twelve my father showed me a medical book containing horrifying depictions of venereal disease. He warned that masturbation would imperil my health and added that nothing was sadder than the sight of a pregnant, unmarried girl.

And our "talk" was over, period. The "subject" was never brought up again.

School lectures on health concentrated on nutrition, pictures of big glasses of milk and generous servings of orange juice and leafy vegetables, with a special emphasis on spinach.

There was a Victorian purity about it that would be considered quaint today, even comical.

For a brief time I attended meetings of the Boy Scout Troop headquartered at Parmer, but when confronted with the requirement to memorize Scout regulations, I ducked out and never went back. The physical aspect of scouting had appealed to me. I had passed the endurance tests with flying colors. But when it came to memorizing rules which I could look up and read, I drew the line. This was too much like school. And I never really liked school, never really took to homework, never really felt otherwise about it than it was something to be endured.

My coaches were my idols, football was my game. I was captain of my eighth grade team. But the job at Walgreen's to earn tuition ended my football career.

Reading, however, had become such a large part of my life, from the third grade onward, that the notion of authorship for my life's work was never far from my thoughts. Who wrote the many books I was reading?

It would be years before I would lay eyes on a real author, and for too many years in school, the only works we would study would be written by people long since dead. Was all the really good stuff already written: And were the people who wrote the good things all dead? One got that impression. . . .

Montgomery Bell Academy, where I spent four happy years before going on to Vanderbilt University, had that no-nonsense approach to schooling that is especially appealing to boys.

Our teachers were tough-minded gentlemen. They expected the best from us as a matter of course. Even slight misbehavior brought demerits which had to be worked off in Saturday school study hall.

Our all-male student body teemed with pride. School spirit at such a high level affected every aspect of our lives.

Besides school activities there was a social life centered about fraternities and sororities. Formal dances at the Belle Meade Country Club were evenings we would remember always.

After the dances, which lasted from ten in the evening until two in the morning, there were elaborate breakfasts.

To be sure there was some drinking and a great deal of cigarette smoking, but illegal drugs were never a problem. In our world they didn't exist.

World War II ended. This signalled establishment of the GI Bill for education. Vets, who had been away to war, some for nearly five years, thronged college campuses across America.

I entered Vanderbilt University just as this onslaught began. Many vets were most interesting. Owen Duckworth had been felled by a Japanese sniper's bullet on Saipan. Owen walked with a brace on his leg. During the battle for Saipan, Owen had lost a lot of sleep and had finally lost his temper in an argument over a flash hider, something used in night combat operations to obscure the muzzle flash of a rifle. Crazed with anger, he had stood up, whereupon a Japanese sniper had shot him in the neck. While he lay thus wounded, fragments from a mortar round struck his chin, producing the only pain he felt, since he had lost feeling in his body from the neck down.

Owen had the combat ex-marine wry sense of humor and the always happy outlook of a man glad to have survived the hell of war.

Another Vanderbilt student hailed from the Philippines. He told hair-raising stories of guerilla war behind the Japanese lines.

The veterans in our midst enriched our collegiate experience, but their excellent scholarship created intense competition for grades. This worked hardship on the young freshmen who had come to Vanderbilt in hopes of finding college a fun place. The joys of college which we had anticipated simply failed to materialize.

And I must add that while I made top grades in English and was elected president of both my junior and senior college literary clubs, I did poorly in most of my studies. The scut work required for top grades had no allure

Friends from Parmer School: (from left) Jesse Hill Ford, Bob Sneed, and Warner McNeily, 1940

for me. Not until I became a Korean War veteran did I make a straight–A average, in graduate school at the University of Florida.

While an undergraduate student at Vanderbilt, there was always the risk of being drafted into the military. Those of us who had not joined the campus Navy ROTC unit soon felt the heat. In order to remain in school I enlisted in the U.S. Navy reserve and attended drill sessions every Wednesday night. My rank was the Navy's lowest—Seaman Recruit, and I signed on for a destroyer cruise to Bermuda.

Shore leave in Bermuda was rollicking fun, laced with black rum, riding a bicycle through that island paradise, raising innocent hell as only a young sailor can. But slave-master conditions aboard ship, under the thumb of a sadistic chief petty officer, more than convinced me that the life of an enlisted man was not for me, if there were *any* way to avoid it.

When word came down that officer training would be available to those of us attending college, if we'd sign on for two summers of training at Newport, Rhode Island, I was the first in line.

At our training base in Newport cram courses in naval science were alternated with sailing, boxing, volleyball, and close order drill.

Five battalions into which we were divided each strove for the honor of first place each week in scholarship and athletics.

Our battalion, consisting mostly of Southerners, took first-place honors week after week. We had the advantage of military school graduates in our ranks. In sailing competition we were fortunate to have for our boat skipper a Chattanooga boy, Pendle Meyers, who had crewed on his father's ocean yawl.

In our second summer's competitions our battalion managed a clean sweep of all events for first place. To signify victory we hoisted a broom to the roof of our barracks.

This proved too much for the runner-up battalion. They attacked our barracks en masse and engaged us in what would have been a harmless series of pillow fights. This wouldn't have been so bad, but they also broke out the barracks fire hoses and doused our bedding.

Order was finally restored, but to our chagrin no punishments were forthcoming. Our officers in charge wrote the incident off to friendly competition.

When we saw that nothing would be done about the unwarranted attack, we vowed revenge.

We formed a commando of our strongest and fastest men. Well after midnight, when the members of the offending battalion were soundly asleep, we slipped down to the bay and filled five-gallon buckets with sea water.

Avoiding the dozing barracks duty sentinels, we entered each dormitory and proceeded to douse our enemies while they lay sleeping. For further effect we threw down the empty buckets, raising an enormous ruckus. By the time the drowned-out victims had roused and sounded the alarm, we were back in our barracks, snugly in our bunks, every man, pretending to be sound asleep.

Seawater is a dreadful destroyer of mattresses. The tiny living organisms in the water die when soaked into the mattress and the stench that results is downright horrible. Our revenge was total.

Our victims had an awful time with their bedding during the final days before graduation. We enjoyed their discomfort mightily.

But we were paid back. The night before graduation the lights flashed on at 2 A.M. A loading detail had been assigned our battalion. For the rest of the night we transferred heavy boxes into trucks.

During those two training summers at Newport we put out a newspaper. I wrote a column entitled "Dear Gertrude." In epistolary form it related the problems of a dim-witted officer written to his girlfriend Gertrude.

"Dear Gertrude" was very popular because it poked fun, in a good-natured way, at all phases of our life as officer trainees.

During chow hall, in the evenings, we sang for our adopted fight song "Goodnight, Irene." We vowed, in a jocular fashion, that we'd all have a beer in Korea.

As it turned out a good many of us were sent to Korea, and one classmate of mine from MBA and Vanderbilt, John Donelley, was severely wounded when a North Korean shore battery shelled his mine sweeper.

I graduated fourteenth in my class of two thousand and put in for flight training. But when I graduated from Vanderbilt, it happened that the Navy had too many fighter pilots left from World War II. Because these men were being recalled for Korean War combat, I was told I'd have to serve a year's sea duty before I could attend flight school.

My final two years in Vanderbilt I held down a full-time job as a reporter for the *Nashville Tennessean*.

The author (right) with Merchant Marine friend Peter Perry at Hettie Ray's Nightclub, 1944

Soon after graduation from Vanderbilt, Sally Davis and I were married. Two months later I got orders to report for sea duty with the Seventh Fleet aboard the seaplane tender *Salisbury Sound*.

My departure was a sad moment for my new bride and my parents. None of us knew where I was headed. All we knew was that I was off to the Far East.

Assignment to the Sixth Fleet, which many of my classmates got, meant they would serve in the Atlantic, out of danger, far from the fighting in Korea.

The Korean War, sandwiched between World War II and Vietnam, remains largely ignored. It is termed, by those of us who served in it, as "the forgotten war." Yet 54,246 Americans died in Korea, 103,284 were wounded there, and 8,177 were missing in action.

Our soldiers had the war won when the Chinese armies poured in upon them from the north and drove them back, creating a stalemate. But thanks to that war, South Korea remains free.

My ship, the *Salisbury Sound,* remained at sea for ten months at a stretch, all of it in the Far East. Once on board and settled into my duties as assistant operations officer in charge of the training program, I settled into that life of enforced idleness which Tolstoi describes so vividly in *War and Peace*.

Every third day I stood two watches of four hours each as officer of the deck. Every third day I was free to go ashore.

My fellow shipmate, Charles Pearson Lindgren, had an engineering degree from the Illinois Institute of Technology.

A superb scientist, he taught me what I did not know about sea duty. When we both bought 35mm Canon cameras from the Army PX on Okinawa, he taught me photography, including how to process and develop film and make enlargements.

Four years as an NROTC midshipman at IIT had prepared him for the Navy in ways my two summer sessions at Newport could not approximate.

I was transferred after one idle year at sea into a job that would prove extremely confining and most secret.

My writing ability was something the Navy was looking for when our Navy joined the Armed Forces Special Weapons Program in 1952. When my transfer came I was taken by surprise.

My new duty assignment sent me to an isolated base located in a remote area of a large Army reservation. Its ten square miles were ringed by four tall, electrified fences. Its borders were patrolled on two paved roads within the fences. U.S. Marine guards patrolled this electrified perimeter constantly in trucks mounted with fifty-caliber heavy machine guns.

Elaborate investigations of my background were carried out by the FBI prior to my first duty assignment inside the base. I was granted the highest available security clearance, namely, Top Secret/Restricted Data.

My U.S. Air Force Counterpart, Lt. Bert Gibbs, had been a five striper in the Air Force ROTC, as a Texas Aggie. I replaced him as Assistant Base Adjutant, and was, then and there, the *only* Assistant Adjutant in the U.S. Navy, since the Navy *had* no such term.

But the Navy was replacing the Air Force man for man on this Special Weapons Base and was even adopting Air Force terminology.

The job facing me, first to last, was translating into Navy Operations Orders a workable set of special weapon's regulations taken from Army and Air Force models.

On top of this task, I was made Top Secret Control Officer, personally responsible for thousands of extremely secret technical data manuals. Losing or misplacing even one page spelled court martial and years in prison. The men under me in Top Secret Control carried the same heavy responsibility.

My biggest problem as Top Secret Control consisted in destroying obsolete literature. Every last page of it had to be burned while two commissioned officers stood present.

This pre-dated the invention of the shredder. Indeed, this problem led to the invention of the shredder, that machine about which so many scandals would arise when U.S. presidents and others dared use the machine to destroy embarrassing materials.

I recall painfully boring hours spent with the base Adjutant, LCDR. D. J. McMillan, beside our incinerator, consigning national secrets to the flames, page by page.

But duty assignment all told, it proved an invaluable period of growth for me. I discovered how hard I could work, and how much I could accomplish, and I was sent to a series of special schools in New Mexico and Colorado to be indoctrinated in the intricate mys-

Ensign Jesse Hill Ford, October 8, 1951

teries of mass destruction weaponry and its strategic and tactical applications.

With the A-bomb already perfected, the H-bomb was soon to be added to our doomsday arsenals. Only the best and the brightest, drawn from Navy and Marine Corps ranks, were privileged to be a part of this awesome program. It would soon put aboard Navy ships and submarines firepower so destructive as to defy mankind's capacity to imagine it. For a twenty-three-year-old Navy Lieutenant–Junior Grade the experience was an intellectual baptism so intense that the lure of staying with the program, and making a career of it, was hard to resist. My superior officers urged me to sign over and stay on for what all of us realized would be the fountainhead of our nation's future security. With deep reluctance, I left the Navy when my two years were up.

I was relieved as Assistant Base Adjutant by Ensign Irenee DuPont May, a grandson of the "Better Things for Better Living" Duponts, who, with his wife Ursula, would find, as had

Sally and I, just how demanding and confining—but yes, fascinating—Special Weapons Service could be.

I next sought the advice of my Vanderbilt University creative writing master, Donald Davidson. I had in hand acceptance to the doctoral program at Princeton. With a Ph.D. in English, I could teach on a college faculty and write fiction on the side.

"What do you *really* want to do?" Davidson asked. A World War I veteran, Donald Davidson was a graduate of the British School of Musketry and had been an expert with the bayonet, something few people knew of him. He excelled as a poet, essayist, teacher, textbook author, and musician. His only failure had been in the arena of fiction writing. He had attempted to write novels, but simply could not. His exalted scholarly and academic reputation tended to obscure his practical side.

"Write fiction—" I replied.

"Then avoid Princeton. A Ph.D. would smother your talent. You're too gifted for life as a mere professor writing on the side. Think about it, Jesse!"

"What do you advise, then?"

"The University of Florida."

"Florida?"

"The man there is Andrew Lytle. His program is what you're looking for—an M.A."

I took Davidson's advice and entered Lytle's program at Gainesville, Florida, where I remained two years. I soaked up everything I could about the art of fiction.

A Tennessean, born in Murfreesboro, Lytle had studied under George Pierce Baker at the Yale Drama School. He had been Baker's pet, as Ed Barry Roberts put it. Lytle was deemed "student most likely to succeed" by the renowned Baker.

But life after Yale had not opened up for Lytle as he had hoped. His playwriting efforts flopped. He got bit parts on the Broadway stage, but never the starring role, and his disappointment over this failed ambition would haunt and rankle him ever thereafter.

At a New York cocktail party he held forth on his favorite topic, Confederate General N. B. Forrest, the famous cavalry raider. A publisher who happened to be present suggested he do a book on Forrest.

The result was a delightful, and in many ways comical, biography, *Bedford Forrest and His Critter Company*. Following its publication, Lytle had his moment of well-earned fame. But rather than follow up that success with more amusing tales of the Confederacy, he switched to writing novels. The lure of fiction writing was too strong. But write novels though he did, he could not live by and for fiction. His fiction didn't sell. He'd switched into teaching fiction while grinding out ever more obscure and obtuse novels. He was at work on the last of these when I knew him at Florida, a brilliant but bitter man, acerbic in the extreme, ruling his flock of fiction aspirants with an iron hand.

What he had going for him was Baker's Yale Drama School teaching method. He applied this to teaching fiction writing, and it worked very, very well. He was a captivating reader, holding listeners spellbound as he read stories by Flaubert, Katherine Anne Porter, and other masters.

On graduation from the University of Florida with my M.A., I had three small children and a wife to support. Life as a freelance was simply too daunting.

I looked about and landed a job which paid me far more than any of my professors at Florida were earning. My news writing as a *Tennessean* reporter, and, in graduate school, for the news wire services, qualified me for a post as public relations director of the Tennessee Medical Association. Because they were looking for someone just at that time, I applied.

I was the youngest of seventeen applicants for the job to be interviewed. A panel, all physicians serving on the public relations committee, conducted the interviews. While I sat waiting I watched as, one after the other, the sixteen other candidates were called in, grilled, and dismissed. My chances, I knew, were extremely slim.

What I did not realize was that each of the previous sixteen had been asked, for openers, if they knew anything about television. One and all they had confessed, TV being in that day very, very new, that they did not know anything about television, but could learn.

When my turn came and the question was put to me I paused to reflect that, while a graduate student at the university, I had watched about as much television as the next fellow. Not a great deal to be sure, but some, after all, and in an effort to be perfectly honest I answered the question, "Do you know *anything* about television?" with a confident *"Yes!"*

A pleased expression flooded the faces of the nine members of the public relations committee. With *that* question out of the way they proceeded with the remainder of the interview reflecting on my Navy campaign ribbons—United Nations, Korean Service, China Service, Japanese Occupation (my Special Weapons program experiences were still top secret, and nothing in that regard, therefore, came up).

I left wondering who would get the job, sure I could not possibly expect to snag it ahead of those older, much experienced other guys.

The next day, to my astonishment, I got the phone call. I was hired!

Not until much later would I discover that my answer to the query about television had set me apart from all the others. On the strength of that answer and that alone, the coveted job was mine.

It followed that I was under the gun right away to show the doctors of Tennessee what a whiz I was in television. The first test came in Jackson, Tennessee, where a TV station, that as yet did not have the coaxial cable hook-up from a network, was famished for program material.

I went 120 miles down to Jackson and we drew names out of the hat each week for the names of four physicians who would then appear on camera to answer questions which they themselves formulated. A beautiful brunette speech therapist asked the medical questions. She was the best thing about the show, which, otherwise, was deadly dull. But the doctors' wives and their children were thrilled to see Papa right up there on the TV screen, in glowing black and white. And the complex questions which each one in turn answered, hardly moving anything but his mouth, and that as *little* as possible—a mumble, in other words—wowed all the doctor's relatives, but hardly anyone else.

The next call on my TV expertise came from Knoxville, 200 miles east of my Nashville headquarters.

By now I'd learned a few things about doctors on television. Thanks to the Jackson show I knew that the sure way to get TV time on any station was to find out the name of the station owner's *personal* physician. Then let that doctor call the owner and ask for a thirty-minute public service time slot once a week, in prime time. The victim was not likely to refuse, given the fact that, like all patients, the station owner might wake in the night with pains in his left arm and chest, short of breath, and in dire need of prompt medical attention. Refusing his doctor ran a risk no station owner was willing to take. We got our Knoxville time slot. I decided that the show should be called "Sun Doctor," for it was now summertime down South.

I had not counted on the problems that came up when I met the station manager. He gave me the Big Time treatment, pointing out that his studio had *two* cameras and would therefore require true two-set scripts. He went on:

"And we require drama, not just four doctors sitting in a row, still as stumps and muttering complicated answers to complicated medical questions they've made up themselves."

Right away I knew he'd heard about our TV show in Jackson. Bad news travels fast.

"This show will take advantage of *both* cameras," I told him. "And it will be *very* dramatic, I promise!"

"Good," he said, then he threatened: "It *better* be."

When I told my Knoxville doctors that we might have a problem if we didn't use the two cameras, their faces fell. They wanted a show exactly like our success in Jackson, for that was how they pictured the show in Jackson.

I had some tel-ops made up. I found some dramatic music for the lead-in. I asked if any of the doctors could suggest a pretty girl to act as on-camera hostess. They came up with a doctor's daughter, a beautiful young aspiring actress. Carol Jenkins was a blonde, seventeen-year-old bombshell. She not only had stage poise but she could memorize her lines.

My doctors' TV committee meanwhile decided they'd better *not* make up any questions. They left the decision on what questions would be asked, and just how they'd be answered to me, the hired gun, after all. I was the man who had the *experience*.

The studio at the tiny hilltop station was like a long narrow hall. Camera One would face a living room set where Carol would sit with three or four Knoxville doctors.

Camera Two, this camera operator back-to-back with the operator of Camera One, would face the opposite direction. Here my tel-ops would come into play.

Since it was summertime, I decided the show would discuss summer ailments. The tel-op for the sunburn show would be a picture of some blistered human skin. For the show on chiggerbite, the tel-op was a chigger, magnified 500

times, in the act of biting a human victim. Thus magnified, the chigger resembled an aardvark burrowing at the foot of a California redwood. The tree was a human hair, magnified 500 times. We had what I felt was a swell show on poison ivy, the doctors for their part discussing the three-leaf plant that caused the rash, and my tel-op showing our audience a picture of poison ivy, very up close.

But after the chiggerbite show the station manager flagged me. He had bad news. Our show was to be cancelled. A news program would be put in its place.

Because doctors had drawn by lot their names from a fishbowl, the lucky winners were nervously awaiting their turns on the tube. So were their wives and children and in some cases their mothers.

When the station manager told me the bad news, I was shocked. By now I was making up topics week to week, researching in the encyclopedia, writing the script in less than an hour.

"Too bad. Our *next* show was really great. dramatic as all get out—" I shrugged.

"What's this great show?" the station manager sneered.

"Snakebite," I said.

"Oh, sure, tel-ops again, *pictures* of snakes, right?"

"Wrong," I said. "Real snakes. Deadly poisonous—too bad we're cancelled."

"You better not be shitting me. Real snakes? You promise?"

I nodded. "Live," I said.

"I gotta see this," he said.

"We're not cancelled?"

"No, no! Real snakes, eh?" He was thrilled.

Up to now "Sun Doctor" had required little in the way of effort on my part. The day before the show I'd think up a summertime ailment, research it, and type up the script. Then I'd order the tel-ops, 35mm slides, and my job was done. I'd drive to Knoxville the evening before the show and give the tel-ops to the production crew with a copy of the script. Then I'd take a script to Carol Jenkins. And we were set.

This time, after driving back to Nashville, I set about looking for someone, *anyone,* to handle live poisonous snakes on television. My first call was to Nashville's Children's Museum.

Yes, they said. They had poisonous snakes, but no, they did not touch them. Nobody they knew ever touched them. Sorry.

The days before the show passed swiftly while I searched frantically to no avail.

Now when one is desperate, and I was desperate, one will begin to reach out in all directions. Your thoughts will go back to that guy you met when the two of you were students, a fellow who now just happens, at this point, to be working in the Governor's office.

I reached for the phone and called Douglas Fisher and explained my problem. In every Governor's office in the fifty United States, when there comes a call nobody knows how to deal with, the highway patrol is notified. And when any state highway patrol in the fifty states is confronted with a problem they have no idea how to deal with, they resort to the patrol two-way radio system. They broadcast a bulletin. This one went something like this:

"Attention all cars, all units, all counties—" (Tennessee, by the way has 96 counties) "—emergency from the Governor's office! Someone, anyone is required who can and will handle poisonous snakes! If you locate such a person contact the Governor's office immediately! Attention! Attention!"

And so it went. No one could be found for the job within the boundaries of Tennessee, but a ham radio operator in North Carolina heard the message on his radio while driving along a remote winding highway in neighboring North Carolina. Just then he happened to be approaching what the roadside signs announced as: "DEN OF DEATH! DEADLY POISONOUS REPTILES! DEATH DEFYING SHOW! STOP!"

So the ham operator motorist stopped and, sure enough, there by the roadside, in a deep pit full of rattlesnakes, he spied a man in the midst of the deadly reptiles and he called down to him:

"Hey!"

"Yeah?"

"Somebody is wanting a man to handle snakes over in Tennessee. It's a real emergency."

"Uh-huh," said the snake man.

"What's your phone number?" the ham operator asked. He wrote it down, radioed Tennessee Highway Patrol from his car set, gave them the snake man's number, and drove on.

Doug Fisher called from the Governor's office and gave me the phone number. I immediately called it. I explained my problem to the snake man.

Meanwhile I had been doing extensive research. I had *World Almanac* open on the desk in front of me as I spoke.

"No, I couldn't, no. I just couldn't," said the snake man.

"But think of *all* the people who are snakebitten *every* summer," I insisted.

"Hadn't thought about that," he said. "It's a big problem, I know."

I found the statistics for that year. Less than twenty-nine bites reported, two fatal . . .

"You gotta know what kind of snake it was bit you or you can get the wrong antivenin shot in your veins, and all," he went on. "It's a big problem—"

"Enormous," I assured him. "A terrible problem affecting great numbers of people in America—"

"Yeah," he said. "I been bit myself enough to know."

"What about it?" I said. "Will you be on the show?"

He asked me if I could meet him at the Fort Ware Game Park, a roadside animal show near Knoxville. I said I would meet him there. "Okay," he said, "I'll do it. But I want you to know that me and my brothers had a pygmy elephant one time and we went on TV with it and it got sick and died. TV is dangerous, you know."

I didn't argue the point, and on the appointed day I drove up to the Fort Ware Game Park a few miles above Knoxville, in my blue four-door Pontiac. My man, sure enough, was there.

The snakes were kept in glass cabinets like candy cases. He proceeded to remove enormous rattlesnakes, using his hands and a snake hook, and he slipped them one after the other into a flimsy chicken crate. Each snake had the look of death coming at you, from those cruel eyes with the pit between them to the flickering tongue. They writhed restlessly in the crate. When he had filled it to his satisfaction, he tapped the screen wire covering closed with the snake hook. Then he hoisted the crate under his arm and we headed out to my car. I opened the trunk, but no, never mind that, he said. Snakes could ride in the backseat just fine. He opened the rear door and installed the death crate behind the driver's seat.

He got in the front passenger seat and we began the drive down to Knoxville, around the winding mountain curves. Behind me I could hear the restless den of death reptiles rattling their dismay. Summer though it was, those sounds chilled my blood.

"That crate," I said. "Isn't it sort of flimsy?"

"How's that?" he said in a puzzled tone of voice.

We entered yet another long curve.

"What if they got out?" I said.

"Oh, yeah. You know, one time I lost a nearly six-foot diamond-back rattler? Sure did. Looked everywhere. Guess where I found him?"

"Where?" I said.

"Coiled up under the driver's seat of my old pickup!" He laughed at the recollection. And so, if they got out, he would know right where to look for them.

We arrived at the TV station on top of the high hill. We got out. He removed the crate from the backseat and we went in the tiny studio.

At the far end in front of Camera One, beauteous Carol Jenkins was already seated in the living-room set. With her were four Knoxville physicians, none of whom, ever in their lives, had treated a single case of snakebite. But they were ready to tell us all about it. Their cameraman stood with his back to us as my friend and I stepped into place before Camera Two. This cameraman had heretofore only taken shots of tel-ops during our shows.

The snake man put the crate on the floor against the wall. Above us, looking down on the set from the control room through a glass window, sat the station manager. He ran the camera switchboard. I was determined not to disappoint him. I waved.

On came the opening "Sun Doctor" music, weird music with lots of scary timpani. Carol opened the show. The four happy doctors were introduced. She announced our topic.

The snake man opened the flimsy crate and removed a writhing six-foot rattler. He held it up to the camera. The light on top of the camera flashed on, *red.*

I've wondered since if he thought there was some sort of radiation being emitted from the TV cameras, and that this maybe had caused his pygmy elephant's illness. In any event he began his spiel, talking a mile a minute, and trembling violently.

On all previous shows I'd witnessed, a running incessant chatter had been ongoing between the two cameramen, standing back-to-back, and the bored station manager upstairs in the control room, content talking back and forth. The Camera Two guy, a slender hillbilly with slicked-back hair, was a gum chewer.

The first thing I noticed, from where I stood just off camera watching, was that the Camera Two man had quit chewing his gum. Moreover he'd gone pale about the mouth. He was staring at something behind me against the wall.

I turned to see the huge pit vipers slithering out of the chicken crate onto the studio floor.

In that primitive era TV lights were strong and put out a lot of heat. Our snakes, maybe reminded of back home in the Mexican desert where they came from, had warmed up and were crawling out. I turned to my man.

He was still talking to beat sixty. I said, as quietly as I could:

"The snakes are getting away!"

He gave no indication he'd heard me. None.

Meanwhile the station manager above it all was screaming on the intercom. Camera Two was also sounding the alarm, and backing, dollying away from the death dealers.

But Camera One operator, facing the opposite direction, had as his bounden duty to keep his camera focused on lovely Carol Jenkins and the medical snakebite authorities hall where they sat peacefully chatting away, totally unaware impending doom was just a few steps away.

So what the luckless Camera One guy heard on the intercom, from the station manager and the terrified operator on Camera Two, were things like:

"God, look at that one! Hey, there comes *another* one out of the box! Watch it—whoa! God almighty! Somebody *do* something!" On and on, while the hapless Camera One fellow (there is always a victim in these situations) could only ask:

"Where are they? Where?"

And he began lifting his feet and dollying his rig forward into the living-room set.

"The snakes are getting away!" I said again.

The snake man glanced at me with a look of outraged irritation. "Well, get your snake hook and put 'em back in the box!" he whispered.

"I don't *have* a snake hook!" I reminded him.

Until now, I would guess, he'd never been without an assistant who had no snake hook. "Well, then," he said, "better get a broom."

"Broom! Broom! Broom!" Camera One yelled into the intercom.

There was a furious clatter from above. The station manager came stumbling down from the control room stairway waving a push broom which he threw at me before staggering backwards and darting back up the stairs, meanwhile muttering: *"God! God! God!"*

I spent the rest of the show sweeping the big snakes back into the corner while they did their damnedest, lunging and striking at me, thoroughly infuriated, hell-bent on revenge.

At long, long last the closing "Sun Doctor" music signalled the show's end. My friend deftly rounded up his little pets and thrust them back into the box for the car ride back to the game park in my backseat.

Until now the studio had been quiet when a show of ours ended, quiet as a chiggerbite. Not so this time. The phones were ringing off the hook.

"We've scared Knoxville, Tennessee, outta their goddamned pants!" the station manager screamed. "This will cost me my job! FCC could take away our license! *Ohhhhh!"*

The two of us began answering the phones, expecting the worst. What we got was quite the opposite.

The calls, mostly from women, kept coming. One and all, they said how much they and their *children* had enjoyed the show. "It was so educational!" On and on, praise upon praise.

For, as it happened, no hint of our terror had gotten on camera. All had been smooth as sand, our watching audience as unaware as were Carol and her snakebite specialists at the other end of the studio.

Before heading back to Fort Ware with my guest and his cargo, the station manager said tel-ops henceforth were fine with him and the crew, and if I wanted to do a show on talcum powder, fine with him. He hoped the next show was not on hydrophobia and that I'd planned to bring in some rabid dogs.

On our way back to Fort Ware I asked my friend if he'd ever had any interesting experiences. He began telling stories, one of which as it turned out a few years later became the gist of my first story published in the *Atlantic Monthly,* "The Surest Thing in Show Business," about a man who borrows some snakes to put on a show. It won the Atlantic First Award in 1959 for the best story by a new writer. The snake experience gave me a valuable source of material for the lecture platform, when, years later, I went on the national lecture circuit.

My work for the Tennessee physicians proved such a success that I was offered a post with the American Medical Association, with a very considerable boost in salary.

My unhappiness with the business manager of the Tennessee association and his endless imaginary illnesses (mostly having to do with chronic constipation, nervous stomach, and a conviction that he was dying with cancer, if only someone of our many doctors could correctly diagnose him) made me jump at the AMA offer.

I had written and produced a movie that had been shown on every TV station in Tennessee with the result that a program for hospitalization of the indigent in Tennessee had been funded by the State legislature.

My presentation at the Association of American Medical Schools annual convention, at White Sulphur Springs, Virginia, that year, had saved American Medical Education Week from cancellation.

And my medical public relations newsletter, mailed to our membership, had been a solid hit because it proved I was *doing* something and not just sitting on my butt.

Having settled my wife and our three young children in a comfortable apartment near the lakeside, I went to work at AMA Chicago headquarters. I discovered once again, as I had with my Navy experience in Special Weapons, that there is room at the top.

By this I mean that, in the best jobs, your associates are not only efficient and intelligent, they are also happy, positive personalities. After my hard scrabble experience in Tennessee, the AMA was a piece of cake,

A number of factors right away began to converge. These would finally lead to my resigning from AMA to strike out on my own as a fiction writer.

A friend from Vanderbilt student days, Peter Farb, walked into my AMA office. He needed help with a book he was writing. Pete was publishing articles in *Reader's Digest* and was successful enough to have an apartment on Riverside Drive in New York. He would not let me buy his lunch on my expense account. We had to go Dutch treat.

Over lunch he demanded that I tell him what I was doing working for the AMA.

When I gave what to me were the obvious reasons, he sneered. With my talent I could be a freelance such as he was! It set me thinking. His words hit home.

Not long thereafter another New Yorker walked into my office, a beautiful redhead, with tons of energy and scads of enthusiasm. She had just published a book which would be responsible for the new math.

She gave me an autographed copy of the *Tractenberg System of Speed Mathematics,* which I still treasure.

Ann Cutler let me take her to lunch on the AMA, at a very good French restaurant. Over cocktails, seafood, and coffee, she related the story of her life as a foreign correspondent. She was now researching for a book on hypnosis and needed AMA guidance.

Finally she asked if I wrote. I said I had tried fiction. The *Atlantic Monthly* had sent back letters, but never an acceptance.

"Letters? Not printed rejection slips? *Letters?*"

When I said yes, she said she wanted to see these letters. Back at the office I handed over my letters from Edward Weeks, editor of the *Atlantic Monthly,* and Peter Davison of Atlantic Monthly Press.

"My God, Jesse, what are *you* doing *here?* These men want to publish you! They believe in your talent! Otherwise they'd *never* have written these *letters.* Don't you realize that?"

I said that I didn't realize it and had figured their letters were like the letters one writes when one is in public relations, a courtesy, so to speak, nothing more.

This beautiful woman was flabbergasted. "I know someone at *Harper's* and I'm going to get you an advance so you can write your novel."

I wanted to believe her.

The third event, and the clincher, happened a few months later. An AMA executive, who'd been telling me about a novel he planned to write someday, dropped dead from a heart attack.

All I could think was that now he'd never write that novel.

And about then Ann Cutler's efforts with *Harper's* paid off. I got a letter offering me a Saxton Fellowship. Just send an outline of the proposed novel and the grant was mine.

I sent off an outline of what would be my first novel, including in it an element of incest, a bad mistake. The plot didn't need incest to make it work. I guess now that my reason for including it was my way of assuming a needless handicap. Then if I were turned down, I could console myself and say the publisher was a gutless wonder.

But Ann was so certain the grant was a sure thing that I went in for a talk with my AMA boss, Leo Brown.

He was shocked. Leave the AMA? When my future was here? He couldn't believe me. He was sure I was unhappy with my apartment.

No, I *had* to write my novel, I insisted.

We settled on a leave of absence, after which I could come back to the AMA. Of course I'd have to finish up the projects I was currently working on; I would, I said, and we settled it that I would leave around October 8, the same day I'd reported for active duty in the Navy.

I moved with my family to Humboldt, Tennessee, my wife's hometown. There she got a job teaching school. Her father, Dr. Davis, a Humboldt physician, encouraged our move. He and my father would help us make ends meet until I began to earn from my fiction writing.

At the last minute *Harper's* had regretfully informed me that the Saxton Fellowship would not be forthcoming after all. I left the AMA in spite of this, determined.

My father-in-law had a very large medical practice. He had a spare back room at his clinic that he let me have for my writing place.

There, with my books and my typewriter and a sofa to stretch out on when I got tired, I went to work on my novel.

My back-room office was a noisy place. I could hear patients reciting their complaints in the nearby treatment rooms. Now and then the doctor would knock on my door to introduce me to one of his patients. Many were curious to meet someone actually writing a book.

I did not have a publishing contract nor a literary agent. But the correspondence I had struck up with Edward Weeks and Peter Davison continued. A year went by. The newspapers announced that Edward Weeks was scheduled to lecture in Memphis. I made plans to attend and was seated in the front row when Mr. Weeks was introduced.

His lecture was eloquent, his audience spellbound. I was to learn long afterwards that Ted memorized his lectures word for word, thanks to his fabulous photographic memory.

After the speech, I was first in line to introduce myself.

The handsome editor broke into a broad smile. "Jesse!" he said, pleased and surprised. "I'm just headed out to dinner with Ike Meyers. But perhaps you would meet me for breakfast tomorrow. I'm staying at the Peabody Hotel." When I asked what time I should meet him, he named 7 A.M.

I drove the eighty miles back to Humboldt, slept the night in uneasy anticipation of breakfast with the most distinguished editor in America, the great Edward Weeks. I sprang up at four, hurriedly bathed, and dressed, and set out to drive the eighty miles back to Memphis.

Promptly at seven I knocked on the door to Weeks's hotel room. He was nearly dressed. He invited me to sit down while he donned his beautifully tailored gray suit. He wore suspenders. His shoes, I saw, were very expensive, very conservative British oxfords.

Over a long and leisurely breakfast in the hotel dining room, Edward Weeks told stories about authors he had known. I asked about Somerset Maugham, one of my favorites, and he told me an interesting story.

Maugham had agreed to appear on a network radio show Ted hosted many years back, before television. During rehearsals Ted was distressed. Maugham had a *terrible* stutter. Ted left the rehearsal worried about the upcoming live broadcast and the mess of it that Mr. Maugham's stutter would surely make.

For his part, Maugham, unbeknownst to Ted, returned to his hotel, drew a hot bath, and while soaking in the tub, went over every word of the script, taking out the trouble spots that caused the stutter. He replaced those words with language he found comfortable.

During the live broadcast Maugham never stuttered once.

When time came for Ted's departure for the airport, we were still engaged in that most fascinating conversation. I offered to drive him to his plane. He accepted, and we talked all the way, riding in my little Volkswagen.

As I saw him off at the departure gate, he turned to wave. "Keep those manuscripts coming!" he called.

By now I must have sent him revised versions of my story "A Strange Sky" at least thirteen times. I was not aware that when an editor turns a story down the first time he is, by and large, through with it.

Buoyed and inspired, encouraged and walking on air, I rushed back to Humboldt. By what

sure instinct only God knows, I dug out of my trunk of story manuscripts a rough version of my story about a roadside snake show.

Here again, I was ignorant. I did not know that magazines, for the most part, never publish snake stories. I did a quick revision and mailed the story to Edward Weeks in Boston.

Back came his letter, accepting the story I had titled "Doug." He wanted to change the title to "The Surest Thing in Show Business." Enclosed with his acceptance was a check for $700.

I sprinted the four blocks back home from the Humboldt post office where I had picked up my mail. Fifteen long, anxious months had passed while I had tried time and again to sell a story. Success at last!

My long apprenticeship had made me a careful writer. Two years with Lytle had taught me, among many other things, how to revise a story to make it better. At Florida a great deal of our work was concerned with revisions, so much so that I learned patience and persistence.

Genius, infinite willingness to take pains, is a direct outgrowth of a terrible persistence.

As more stories poured forth and were published, things began to break for me in other avenues of endeavor. By mid-1959 I had won an Atlantic Grant. This helped with living expenses while I finished my first novel, *Mountains of Gilead*.

And by late 1959 my persistence had again paid off. The CBS television network accepted my one-hour play, *The Conversion of Buster Drumwright*.

It paid me handsomely and got excellent reviews.

By the time my TV play was aired, my first novel was accepted and scheduled for publication. It was the spring of 1961. I was tired.

Almost forgotten by the spring of 1961 was the fact that many months before, I had applied for a Fulbright Fellowship to the University of Oslo, Norway. When my U.S. Congressman friend, Robert A. Everett, called to inform me that I had been accepted and would be leaving for Oslo to attend language school in early June, I was pleasantly surprised. Edward Weeks had written a strong letter to the Fulbright people. He now said he knew the year in Scandinavia would add cubits to my stature.

For a send-off he commissioned me to write a "Report on Norway" for the *Atlantic Monthly*. The owner of the *Courier-Chronicle*, Humboldt's weekly newspaper, awarded me a paid assignment for a weekly column from Norway. My father told me he would pay first-class airfare for my wife and four children to Oslo.

A paperback sale of *Mountains of Gilead* to Modern American Library added to royalties from the hardback. I was confident I could support my wife and four children for our months in Oslo. And finally, we rented our house in Humboldt and I sold my VW.

Rental housing in Oslo was scarce. Five years of German occupation during World War II had depressed Norway's economy drastically. House building had come to a standstill.

I applied to NATO headquarters near Oslo to see what might be found and was rewarded with the discovery of a Norwegian university professor and family on the verge of departure for Germany where he would spend his sabbatical year of leave.

Svere Aalen's flat consisted of the ground floor of a two-storey house. The upper floor was owned by a notorious Quisling named Mirk, a Quisling being one who had sympathized with and worked for the Nazi army of occupation during the five-year occupation. Then Norwegians had lived on the verge of starvation, all except the German soldiers and the Quislings.

When I moved into the house I had not been told about Mirk upstairs and I didn't learn the truth about him until he complained that my seven-year-old son had stolen the apples from his tree, this being the year the apples were his. In alternate years the Aalen family got the fruit.

During an angry verbal barrage, Mirk expressed his bile over having Americans living below him, and thieving Americans besides. I said that my son, Jay, had not known the apples were not his to pluck. Nothing helped. Norwegian friends explained that Mirk was a known traitor. Then I understood why he hated Americans. After all, Americans helped defeat his idol, Adolf Hitler.

While in Norway I wrote a short story, "Fishes, Birds, and Sons of Men," which, upon my return to the United States in late 1962, I sent to Andrew Lytle, who by then was editor of the *Sewanee Review,* a small quarterly published by the University of the South in Sewanee, Tennessee.

Back my typescript came with a note from Lytle. Some of the people around the office liked my story, he wrote. He ordered me to remove the mechanical breaks and send it back. Then he would think about buying it.

Andrew Lytle had written to say he would like to publish a story of mine in his quarterly. Otherwise I would *never* have submitted a story to him, and it was not the return of my manuscript blemished with Lytle's bourbon spills and coffee stains that riled me. It was, rather, the high-handed tone of his letter, demanding a revision with no promise that, even if I revised it as requested, he would publish it.

By now my reputation for short stories was firmly established. I revised the story, replacing the mechanical breaks with graceful transitions. Lytle had been right about what was needed.

In my next letter to Edward Weeks I mentioned that I had revised the story as ordered and was about to send it back to Lytle.

Edward Weeks wrote back by return mail.

"Don't send that story back to the *Partisan Review*. Let me see it," he wrote. Did he get the name Lytle's little magazine wrong on purpose?

When the *Atlantic Monthly* bought "Fishes, Birds, and Sons of Men," which became the title story of my successful collection a few years later, I was happy. And never again would I submit a story to the *Sewanee Review*.

In this regard, my Vanderbilt mentor, Donald Davidson, said I should not worry about *belles lettres,* as he termed the petty literary jealousy that almost all good writers encounter.

Edward Weeks had been on target when he predicted that my year in Norway would be a good thing. On returning to Humboldt I set about building a soundproof study with private entry where a screened porch had been. Svere Aalen's study, where I had worked at writing while in Norway, had been soundproof. I could not face a return to my father-in-law's noisy clinic. Included in my new soundproof study was a lavatory and a toilet.

The only disadvantage was the heating. An unvented gas chill chaser, intended for very large, airy rooms, was my heat source. In cold weather it gave me pounding headaches. The wonder is I was not asphyxiated.

My year abroad had awakened me to a new awareness of the racial divisions brewing in the South. Outsiders, I now realized, and Europeans especially, were puzzled that the U.S. of the modern sixties could *have* such a divisive problem.

Conversations with our black housekeeper, Mrs. Tee Wallace, led to my second novel. She told details of a never-solved murder covered up by local and district authorities due to its having involved an incident dealing with sex between a black woman and a white man.

In working out my plot, with that incident as my gist, I realized that my novel would answer many of the questions about the racial problem then being asked by populations abroad.

My working title was *Death, Wheat, and Thorns.* Peter Davison and Edward Weeks were thrilled with the completed manuscript. During the writing the *Atlantic Monthly* had published several segments of the novel as short stories.

The one thing that didn't please them was my title. Anyone reading *The Liberation of Lord Byron Jones* has only to look for poetic images about death, wheat, and thorns to understand the beauty of my working title. But I was quite willing to abandon it in favor of *The Liberation of Lord Byron Jones.*

A secretary at Little, Brown and Company, which at that time co-published novels with Atlantic Monthly Press, had suggested, upon reading the manuscript, that it should be called *The "something" of Lord Byron Jones.* She had no idea what the "something" might be, however.

On hearing of her suggestion, Ted Weeks liked it so much he phoned to ask if I had any idea what the "something" might be.

Intuition came to my rescue. On my office shelf was Ted's delightful autobiography, *In Friendly Candor.* I opened it to his dedication to me, penned on the title page:

"To my dear Jesse, whose success and liberation will always have a special meaning for me. With love, Ted."

"Is the word *liberation?*" I asked.

"That's it! That's it!"

I then told him where I'd found the word.

As publication day drew near, black rioters were savaged by police dogs in Birmingham, Alabama. Farther South in Selma, Alabama, black and white marchers protesting Jim Crow were blocked, beaten, and turned back by state troopers. Alabama Governor George Wallace had stood in the doorway of the University of Alabama to block entry of a lone Negro already enrolled in the university. Incident after incident of senseless hatred took place as when black

children in a Birmingham Sunday school were killed by a racist bomb blast during worship services.

I was lecturing at Lincoln College in Lincoln, Illinois, when a long distance call from Peter Davison in Boston brought stunning news. *The Liberation of Lord Byron Jones* would be the midsummer selection of the Book-of-the-Month Club.

The reviews were raves.

"Magnificent," wrote Catherine Drinker Bowen. "It is powerful, compassionate and above all original, unlike any novel I've ever read about the South and the Problem." John Fowles described it as "The best American novel that I've read for many a long day. Quite apart from its literary skill it presented the great color-problem dilemma more vividly and freshly than I thought possible." And Paul Horgan called it both "terrible and beautiful . . . a work of passion, courage and eloquence."

Dewey Pruit, curator of the Mississippi Valley Collection at Memphis State University, visited me following publication of *Mountains of Gilead.* He wanted the manuscript for his collection. Should I ever have a research project, this prestigious collection would be open to me, he promised.

Had not Hollywood intervened, I might have begun work on my saga novel sooner. I kept writing Edward Weeks about my plans for the book. Ted kept sending encouragement. He continued to publish my best stories in the *Atlantic Monthly.*

Soon after publication, *The Liberation of Lord Byron Jones* was optioned for a movie.

Stirling Silliphant, famous in television circles for writing *"Route 66,"* agreed to script my movie. He did so. But many months went by. I co-wrote subsequent script versions with Silliphant, to no avail. Time dragged. Then one afternoon, I got a call from a Hollywood director friend, George Cukor. George was in the top rank of Hollywood directors. He was close to Katharine Hepburn and Spencer Tracy. He had directed many of their best movies.

"Jesse," he said, "I believe your movie is going to be made! I've just seen a picture of Spencer's. It's called *Guess Who's Coming to Dinner?* I believe it's going to break open the way for your movie."

Sure enough, not very long afterwards, good news reached me from the West Coast. William Wyler, who was just finishing the movie version of *Funny Girl,* had decided to direct *The Liberation of Lord Byron Jones.*

I had paid many visits to Hollywood. There I had been shown about by my generous cousin Stanley Musgrove. Now I had a contract with Columbia Pictures. I would share screen credit with Silliphant. Stan was very proud and pleased.

I had a beachview apartment near the foot of Sunset Boulevard and was well along into scripting the movie with Silliphant. We labored under the benign tutelage of William Wyler.

Willie and I became fast friends. I was making more money every week than I had ever imagined I would.

Down the beach from me at Malibu, Laurence Harvey had built a house with Joan Cohn. The gossip was that Larry had promised to marry Joan if she lost, in some impossibly short time, some improbable amount of weight.

Lose it she did, and as Larry had promised, they were married. Larry, meanwhile, invited me to his lavish parties. He hoped Willie would cast him in the role of Willie Joe Worth in the movie. It was a rich part. Larry could have played it beautifully. He did a Southern accent to absolute perfection. And his movie successes, beginning with *Room at the Top,* set him apart, I felt, as one of the very top actors of his generation.

But Willie cast a lesser-known actor. Budget was a problem, as was Willie's cousin, Paul Kohner, whose talent agency he favored. Sammy Davis pled with Willie for the role of Lord Byron Jones. Willie turned him down in favor of Roscoe Lee Brown. So it went. Lee J. Cobb won the lead role as the bigoted lawyer.

Willie was suffering from emphysema but could not break himself of a compulsive cigarette habit. Cigarettes were such a part of his creative routine that a lack of cigarettes rendered him impatient and short-tempered. So he would relent, light up, and suffer awful consequences.

He had just completed *Funny Girl* when we began work on *Liberation.* He threw a large party at his house and invited all the actors he was considering for the role of the bigoted Oman Hedgepath. These included Charlton Heston and Burt Lancaster, either of whom I wished to God he *had* cast, but budget interfered. Barbra Streisand came to the party. She struck me as a neurasthenic oddball. She had given Willie many problems on the *Funny Girl* set. He had,

finally, one day, announced that he was going home and his assistant, Bob Swink, would take over. Leave he did. Take over Bob Swink did. Two days later a tearful Streisand begged Willie to come back. Back he went and had less trouble with her afterwards. And the *Funny Girl* movie was a resounding success.

But that experience had taken its toll. Willie's failing health was going against him.

Nevertheless my picture got made. Its release was to bring grim consequences which I never could have foreseen, consequences that would almost break my own health.

Columbia Pictures had a studio executive dining room where Stirling and I often had lunch. The food was good and the camaraderie was refreshing. Stirling and my association with Willie made us big stuff indeed. Peter Fonda and his friends, at work then on *Easy Rider,* were sometimes turned away. Fonda's picture would make big money, but nobody knew it at the time. Thus he got short shrift.

That was and is Hollywood. Stirling had enrolled in a Chinese martial arts class taught by a then unknown, Bruce Lee. Bruce would strut into our office while we were working and implore me to slug him—beg me! I knew better, of course, but to indulge him I'd throw a half-hearted punch. He'd grab my fist and put me into a headlock, all in fun. High on our office door Bruce had hung a little round target. It was Stirling's assignment, from Bruce, to kick the tiny medallion. Stirling split out his trousers in the crotch attempting the stunt.

Silliphant and I wrote our script for Willie. The months whispered by, version after version, scene after scene. It was good experience and paid me several thousands a week in salary. I made weekend runs to Las Vegas when Eddie Fisher, whom I'd met at a friend's house, was on stage at Caesar's Palace.

Our shooting schedule called for exteriors to be shot in West Tennessee. The first day of principal photography took place on the majestic lawn of the bigot lawyer character's mansion. William Wyler ordered a director's chair for me placed beside his own, behind the camera.

I would remain at his side throughout the production.

Interiors were filmed back at the studio in Hollywood. Here Willie connived to put me in a scene. I answered the phone in the mayor's office.

Wardrobe suited me up, makeup dusted my face, and I delivered my one line of dialogue on the set with Dubb Taylor. Dubb's comic scenes with Chill Wills made for bright interludes in an otherwise hard-hitting movie about bigotry and murder in a small, corrupt Southern town.

With the movie completed, I took up Dewey Pruitt's offer of access to the research resources of the Mississippi Valley Collection.

Memphis State University let me teach one creative writing class per week in return for a salary covering my expenses, including a townhouse just off campus for a writing studio and living quarters.

I was well along with my research in Pruitt's Collection when construction workers, tearing down an old warehouse on the Mississippi riverfront, came upon a log kept by one of the area's first traders. It detailed hides, pelts, and furs.

He listed his Indian customers by name, and carefully logged what he paid for their deer hides and other peltry. He just as carefully noted what they bought in return—combs, lace shawls, and finery for their womenfolk; gun powder, lead gunstocks, flints, and horse tack for themselves.

This priceless trove gave me insights I needed to portray, with vivid accuracy, my Indian characters in my novel *The Raider.*

Having found much of what I needed, I set to work writing, dividing my time between my Memphis quarters and my writing studio at my Humboldt country house. I named the place Canterfield.

It was a beautiful setting, a twenty-eight-acre estate with nearly a half mile of paved private driveway. . . .

It was in November on a very dark night. Our son Charles was studying for a next-day test at his girlfriend's house. My daughter Sarah was at school in Norway. Our youngest, Elizabeth, was in her bed asleep. My son Jay was away in college at Vanderbilt.

I lay asleep. When my wife shook me awake to say a car without headlights had entered our drive and was heading for the house, I leaped up. In our drive, directly below, with its headlights off, a mysterious car went by and passed to the rear of the house. Moments later it came back and went out into the long driveway and backed into a copse of trees just where

the driveway made an elbow. The strange car sat facing a several-hundred-yard stretch down which my returning son would have to come head-on—a perfect ambush position.

I took my loaded deer rifle from the corner of the bedroom. I ran downstairs and out the back door, after first asking my wife to call the police. I went out by the door to the carport to see if anyone had been let off behind the house by the strange vehicle. Finding no one, I went around to the front of the house and proceeded across eight acres of front yard towards the mysterious parked car. It sat concealed by the thicket of sapling sassafras trees. Halfway across the lawn I fired my .30-06 into the air. From the bedroom window my wife saw the blue muzzleflash. She had called the police for the second time and was pleading with me to come back.

My heart was in my throat. Examples of what can happen to people in isolated locations such as ours flooded my consciousness. There was the Sharon Tate massacre in Hollywood. There were the Clutters, the *In Cold Blood* murder victims on their isolated farm; and there was the Illinois Senator Percy's daughter, slaughtered in bed while the Senator and the rest of his family slumbered. But finally, there had been the shooting death of Stirling Silliphant's son, Loren. Stirling and I had been at work on the screenplay for *Liberation* when that never-solved murder took place. Seventeen-year-old Loren had answered the door to his apartment. A black assassin shot him dead. Loren's uncle was there, visiting at the time.

During the weeks following the release of the movie version of my novel, threatening phone calls had put me on edge.

A female voice would ask for my son Charles. Told he was at school the caller would reply:

"Well, he won't be there long!"

Hence my loaded gun in the bedroom corner. The phone company's efforts to trace the threatening calls had failed. Was the mysterious car parked in the sassafras thicket somehow connected with the anonymous caller?

Firing a shot in the air should have had the effect of prompting whoever it was in the strange car to come out and explain why it was they were parked on my property in the dead of the night.

I had posted, at regular intervals beside our long, long driveway that dog-legged into my property, signs from Abercrombie and Fitch.

These best quality reflector signs forbade trespassing in no uncertain terms, yet another reason to wonder why anyone would ignore such plain notice, unless they were up to no good.

Using my rifle butt, I knocked on the rear fender of the car. Standing opposite the driver's door, I shouted: "The police have been called! Come out with your hands up! You are under arrest!"

The car lights came on. The car's engine started. Would I have been justified to pull the trigger then and there? After all, if the intruder got away, wasn't it reasonable to assume that, on another dark night, he might return? I did not shoot. Instead I watched in angry frustration. The mysterious car proceeded down the drive in the very direction from which my seventeen-year-old son must soon come. I fired a shot from the hip, fully expecting it would pass harmlessly above the offending vehicle.

To my surprise, the instant the trigger was pulled, the car skidded to an abrupt stop and remained stopped, engine idling. Suddenly the passenger door was flung open, out came a screaming female. She fled up the drive towing a small child by the hand. She rounded the elbow and disappeared.

Had I accidentally killed the head of a family? A flood of remorse whelmed over me. Holding the rifle in readiness I was approaching the car when a police cruiser rounded the elbow and drove up. It paused beside the intruder's car and then came to where I stood.

"It's a dead black under the wheel, Mr. Ford," the cop announced.

I told him about the female and the child. "I'll go look," he said.

I said I was awaiting the return of my son.

He spun the cruiser about and roared off, back around the elbow, out of sight. Moments later he was back. With him in the front seat he had the teenaged black girl and the infant I had seen.

"I'm taking her in," said the cop. "More help is coming."

I thanked him. He drove off. To my relief my son Charles drove in safely. I told him what had happened.

This night capped a string of menacing incidents for him. Blacks had stoned his new Mustang car at the high school. The threatening anonymous calls, while he was away at school, had worried him. His high school, only recently integrated, had an excellent football team, in this, his senior year. He was the star running back. His sub in that position was a black runner almost as talented. Tensions ran high.

Through that long night lawmen swarmed to the scene. The district attorney himself oversaw things. Hundreds of photographs were taken, many measurements were made and noted.

Very late that night the D.A. entered my house flanked by dozens of cops and detectives. I gave my statement. Turning to my mother-in-law, who was recently widowed, the D.A. piously reminded her that her late husband, the beloved doctor, had saved his son's life. Then he told us to consider the case closed, not to worry, to get a good night's sleep. It was all bullshit contrived to put us off guard. It did. We took him at his word. We trusted the scumbag.

Naturally, we should have known better. Here I was, responsible for a movie that showed up local cops, they felt. My novel highlighted just how local murders down South could go overlooked, and remain unsolved, thanks to the likes of the scumbag who was now on my case.

The teenaged female passenger in the mystery car was none other than a niece of the widow of the murdered undertaker, whose never-solved murder had inspired my novel.

The accident victim, shot from eighty paces away while driving a moving vehicle, was an AWOL soldier from Fort Leonard Wood, Missouri. The little tot in the car was a child the teenaged female was supposed to be babysitting. Her soldier buddy had picked her up at home and driven her out to my place with the infant. Packed in his soldier's bag was his bus ticket back to Fort Leonard Wood that night.

Also in the mystery car was a loaded World War I German Luger pistol. But this evidence the second cop on the scene had decided wasn't needed, so he had appropriated the pistol then and there, to sell later, when things died down. He also appropriated a bag of marijuana. He went through the dead soldier's pockets. The dead no longer need money, after all. Standard practice?

The next day the D.A. called a press conference. He announced to the world that I was about to be arrested for malicious, premeditated murder in the first degree.

But after my ride to city hall in a squad car, I posted a $20,000 property bond and went free. And all hell broke loose.

Jesse Hill Ford and his second wife, Lillian, vacationing in the Virgin Islands shortly after they were married in 1975

The media went into a feeding frenzy. Correspondents from as far away as the *London Times* showed up in Humboldt, Tennessee, to track my progress on the road to the electric chair.

The D.A. was loudly calling for my execution, the death sentence, every time he opened his mouth.

Months later, on July 3, a jury of twelve men, including one black man, found me innocent. I was acquitted thanks to a former circuit judge, my friend John Kizer, and a lawyer friend James Senter, III. They had teamed up to mount a very successful defense.

The anonymous phone calls turned out to be from the female in the front seat. The calls had been made by her from home during the day. Though she was registered at the high school, she did not attend. Her doctor gave the excuse that she had a spine ailment and had to be taught at home. As it came out at the trial under cross examination, the real reason

she didn't attend school was that she had been elected homecoming queen of her black high school, just before the black and white schools were amalgamated. Thereupon she was no longer a homecoming queen. She had it in for my son because he ran first string in the position her boyfriend had run before the teams were joined, and her pal became our son's second-string sub. Hence the stoning of his car by black students. Hence the threatening calls. And hence, maybe, the loaded pistol in the AWOL soldier's possession that dark night, when accidental death so suddenly took him. And hence, too, his unwillingness to surrender, given that I had told him the police were on the way. Caught with marijuana, caught with a loaded pistol, caught with a girl below the legal age of consent, caught with the tot she was thought to be babysitting . . . well, he chanced it.

Did the undertaker's widow complain to her niece about my movie? Did these two, in their outrage over a movie and a lost opportunity to be homecoming queen, dream up a plan for revenge? In that cornered, isolated setting, that late at night, anything was possible.

Life never again would be the same. Our beautiful twenty-eight acres, our house, pony barn, horses, mastiffs and whippets, our pond where my beloved Boston editor, Edward Weeks, my daughter, Elizabeth, and I had fished when my friend paid us visits—all were lost to debt and foreclosure. And when, finally, my first marriage ended in divorce, I left Humboldt, Tennessee, never to return, having known there the country life at its ideal best, while it lasted.

But my saga novel of frontier settlement and Civil War was well begun. My research in the Mississippi Valley Collection was completed. Upon my return to Nashville in October 1973, friends I had known from childhood gave me a warm welcome. One in particular, Neil Cargile, introduced me to polo. Under Neil's tutelage I gained a sense, at first hand, of what cavalry fights must have been like during Civil War engagements. This helped enormously when I wrote the horse action scenes for *The Raider*.

Late in 1973, while in Spain at Fuenjirola, playing tennis at the Australian champion Lew Hoad's tennis complex, I met a beautiful Nashville girl, Lillian Chandler. Her marriage, to a Beverly Hills psychiatrist, had ended in divorce. On returning to Nashville again I called on her and we became friends.

The following summer Lillian and I found a seaside cottage in Curacao. The Dutch couple who had the place asked us if we would take care of their dog, Klippy, their cat, Lumpstral, and their four huge Diffenbachia plants while they took home leave in Holland. A car and a sailboat came with the deal. There I toiled every night to complete the saga novel, working until daybreak. My signal that it was time to quit came in the form of the pre-dawn rain cloud from Venezuela that pounded the roof for twenty seconds, like clockwork.

In 1975, when *The Raider* was finally published, Lillian and I decided to tie the knot. For our wedding trip we went to Water Island, which lies a mere cannon shot across Gregory Channel from St. Thomas in the U.S. Virgin Islands.

I had a script assignment from Warner Brothers to keep me busy.

The American colony on Water Island, in 1975, was a tightly knit society of very old, exceptionally bright, highly independent retirees. They kept their little island spotless. There was no crime. There were no property taxes. Residents drove jeeps and old cars at a snail's pace over the rough, one-lane roads. They staged cocktail parties, one after the other, in a constant round of delightfully bibulous entertaining.

Since my first glimpse of the Caribbean in 1951, it had been a compelling ambition of mine to make a major ocean crossing under sail. Mel Stone, who owned the fifty-foot schooner *Tempe Wick,* afforded me that opportunity while Lillian and I were living on Water Island.

It was June, hurricane season. With one additional man as crew, the three of us set sail heading west for the coast of Venezuela, more than five hundred miles from Water Island and St. Thomas.

Our first night we began hitting storm cells, *Tempe Wick* began leaking so furiously we had to man the pumps every half hour. This we kept up around the clock for days on end until, at last, 450 nautical miles out of St. Thomas, at Margarita Island, we put in and made repairs.

Hurricane season seas knocked us about so furiously that we passed blood in our urine. After cruising to several of the Margarita Islands, we set sail again for home. The home crossing proved even rougher. But there were quiet nights, with the moon as our compan-

ion, our sails full, *Tempe Wick* leaning like an eager greyhound through glorious open seas. Sunrises and sunsets were magnificent. If invited to make the voyage again, I would, but only during the smooth winter months. Never again would I risk it in hurricane season.

In the mid-eighties I wrote editorial columns for *USA Today* and enjoyed hearing from fans who read my columns in faraway London and Japan. I did turn-arounds, columns that had to be written on the spur of the moment, when breaking news made my editors decide to change a page they had already planned in favor of another. Those bylines afforded great satisfaction. But all good things must come to an end, and after perhaps too many years of it I stopped crafting columns in favor of a return to fiction.

Of my professional memberships, none has given more satisfaction than the Overseas Press Club of America. I earned the right to belong while corresponding from Norway during my Fulbright year. I was put up for membership by Ann Cutler, the bright lady who encouraged me to abandon my solid job with the American Medical Association and take the risk.

Thank goodness I took her advice!

BIBLIOGRAPHY

Fiction:

Mountains of Gilead, Atlantic-Little, Brown, 1961.

The Conversion of Buster Drumwright, Vanderbilt University Press, 1964.

The Liberation of Lord Byron Jones (also see below) Atlantic-Little, Brown, 1965.

Fishes, Birds, and Sons of Men (stories), Atlantic-Little, Brown, 1968.

The Feast of St. Barnabas, Atlantic-Little, Brown, 1969.

The Raider, Atlantic-Little, Brown, 1975.

Co-author (with Stirling Silliphant) of screenplay *The Liberation of L. B. Jones,* Columbia, 1970.

Harry M. Geduld

1931-

YES, VIRGINIA, I REALLY DID SEE THE BATTLE OF BRITAIN: A KID'S-EYE VIEW OF WORLD WAR II
(for Marcus and Daniel)

Harry M. Geduld, advisory editor for the New York Times Encyclopedia of Film *and author of various other works about Charlie Chaplin*

Like most London children I was evacuated a few days before World War II in Europe actually began on September 3, 1939. I was eight years old.

In the immediate post-Munich period, the British government assumed that the Germans would begin their offensive with massive air raids on the British capitol: hence the evacuation. Instead, the next few months became that relatively quiescent period now known to historians as "The Phoney War" or "The Sitzkreig." London remained unscathed throughout 1939 and well into 1940—a period when Hitler fondly imagined that the British would come to their senses and sue for peace.

On the morning I was to be evacuated, my mother packed my suitcase and a brown bag of sandwiches, fruit, and chocolate. She took me to the assembly-point (the schoolyard), where the various classes were lined up. Each child was wearing an identification label and carrying a gas mask: poison gas attacks were expected well into 1942. In due course we were marched off to a bus which took us to a main line station. There we saw thousands of children (many as young as five) from other schools as well as mothers with toddlers and babes-in-arms—all assembled for the same purpose. Teachers acting as stewards assigned the different school groups to various trains.

Where were we headed? Our teachers would say nothing. For reasons best known to the organizers, the evacuation destinations were to be kept secret until we arrived and could send postcards to our parents. Many of the evacuees had never been away from home before, and the station platforms were witness to countless pathetic scenes of children saying tearful good-byes to parents who, at the same time, were trying to achieve that famous British stiff upper lip and failing miserably.

An invasion was expected. If that happened, would we ever see our parents again? My train shunted slowly out of the station then speeded up. London, grimy, glorious London, sped by and vanished in a blur of suburbs and clouds of train smoke. Some children wept uncontrollably for most of the journey; others were travel-sick; the very young ones refused to eat and became listless. Many soiled their pants and were reeking by the time we reached our destination.

As journeys go it was nothing, of course, to compare with the experiences of the million Jewish children whom the Germans transported across Europe in sealed cattle cars to be gassed in extermination camps. If the Germans *had* actually invaded England, doubtless I too would have found myself in one of those sealed cattle cars, closeted for days without food, water, or toilet facilities only to arrive on the selection ramp at Auschwitz. But the Royal Air Force and twenty-two miles of the English Channel stood between me and the gas chamber—a stroke of fortune for which I am eternally thankful.

At last our train came to halt at Taunton in Somerset, a picturesque county in the southwest of England, located about two hundred miles or so from London. During the next several hours we children were distributed among various "hosts" in the locality. I call them "hosts" euphemistically, for by government decree they were actually obliged to take in a certain number of evacuees whether they liked it or not. A sizeable number did not: and as a result many children found themselves in homes where they were subjected to abuse or mistreatment. I was to wind up in one such home briefly in 1941 when I was evacuated for the second time. But on this first occasion I was lucky. My "host" was a farmer who lived four or five miles from Carhampton, a tiny village near the Bristol Channel. He had a young son, Peter, about a year older than me, and we quickly became good friends. I had never been on a farm before, and Peter lost no time showing me all kinds of fun things to do, such as feeding calves or trailing hens when they wandered off to lay their eggs. The farmhouse was an old thatched Tudor cottage: I remember that adults had to bend down to enter the front door, while the ceiling inside was supported by low, gnarled beams from which sides of bacon and hams were suspended. I missed my parents but soon settled into a routine of school and life on the farm.

Geduld at age five, before World War II devastated London

As you can imagine I was quite an oddity, a Cockney urchin set down amidst a secluded West-of-England village. The locals made fun of my London accent, but on the whole I was treated with kindness and good humor, and they attempted to "civilize" me in their own way. I was introduced to cider (the best kind: "Somerset Rough"), and at the village school I was taught some old songs that I still love: "Widdecombe Fair" and "The Helston Floral Dance." I also learned morris dancing. A few months passed. Now we were into 1940, and suddenly in late spring or early summer of that year the time of tranquility came to an end—at least in the Bristol Channel area. The Battle of Britain had begun—but for the time being the Luftwaffe had been ordered to avoid hitting London. Their main objectives were to destroy British radar installations and to sweep the RAF from the skies. Aerial dogfights began to take place, and Peter and I had a grand-stand view of the action. German fighters would often swoop low in order to machine-gun indiscriminately houses and anything or anyone moving. Believing we were safer out-of-doors than in, we would cover ourselves with sacks for camouflage and stretch out on our backs in a field, remaining as motionless as possible while we watched the combat raging overhead. At times the planes came so low that we could discern not only their markings but the heads of the pilots. Aircraft-recognition was a popular hobby among British kids at this period, and Peter and I would argue as to whether we had just seen a Messerschmitt or a Heinkel. We easily recognized "our own" Spitfires and Hurricanes, and as they skimmed low over our heads we'd stand up, wave at them, and cheer. Sometimes the pilots waved back at us, and once or twice an airplane did a "Victory Roll" just for us—or so we thought. We often saw dogfights, and

I'm glad to say it was usually the German airplanes that were on the losing end—either fleeing from RAF fighters or actually on fire and spiralling downwards to crash somewhere over the horizon. Several times we saw pilots bail out, but they never landed near us.

Meanwhile, back in London—which had not yet experienced an air raid—my parents heard about the dogfights that were going on over the Bristol Channel area and decided to bring me back home—to safety (so they thought!).

Dad's journey to Carhampton was a nightmare. It should have taken about three hours but it took him ten. His train was shot up and derailed. He boarded another. That was shot up too. I knew nothing about all that at the time—or even that he was coming to take me home—until he appeared suddenly at the door of the farmhouse, looking very tired and worried. By now it was dusk. Peter's mother packed my things. I said farewell and shouldered the then-obligatory gas mask. Dad took my hand and we headed for the station. I remember Peter running after us, weeping and yelling, "Come back! Come back!" I never did. The last I saw of him he was on the platform waving at me and wiping away his tears.

Our trip back to London, in a train darkened for the Blackout, was uneventful. It was night and the train was probably invisible to any marauding German airplanes. We arrived eventually at Victoria Station (I think it was), which was swarming with people in uniform. Outside, on the slow bus journey home, London seemed very different from the city I had left a few months earlier. Then it had looked like a city at peace. Since then it had assumed the appearance of city prepared for war. I looked out at it through bus windows crisscrossed with tape—supposedly protection against shattering by bomb-blasts. Inside the bus there were ads warning passengers that "Careless Talk Costs Lives." Outside, the streets were darker than I could ever remember, but searchlight-beams were cutting across the sky. The Blackout was in full force, and the buildings we passed were mere silhouettes except, here and there, for glimmers of light where some careless householder's blackout curtains were less than adequate. Passersby shouted, "Put that bloody light out!" and in some streets air raid wardens were already rapping at the doors of the worst offenders. There were no streetlights and vehicles drove slowly, with dimmed headlights. I saw little traffic

With his father at Westcliff-on-Sea, 1936

other than buses and military transports. (Strict gas rationing had been enforced.) In the gloom I caught glimpses of pedestrians holding flashlights and carrying tin hats and gas mask cases over their shoulders. When we got off the bus at last I saw that many shops and houses had their entrances flanked by sandbags. On walls and billboards were huge posters appealing to the public for war savings ("Lend to Defend the Right to Be Free") or proclaiming propaganda slogans ("We Work or Want" . . . "Three Words to the Whole Nation: Go To It!"). Prominent here and there were brightly painted "detectors" that were supposed to change color in the presence of poison-gas. And everywhere were signs pointing directions to the nearest air raid shelters. It was far too dark, however, to see the most remarkable sight of all. Not until the following morning, when I looked out of my bedroom window, did I observe the dozens of barrage balloons hovering overhead like a scattered herd of bloated elephants.

It was September 1940. Although the majority of evacuees had drifted back to London, no schools were open. I didn't realize it at the time, but I would not see the inside of a school for many months.

Came Saturday, September 7, 1940. Incensed by an RAF raid on Berlin, Hitler ordered Goering to destroy London. That afternoon, three hundred German bombers, escorted by six hundred fighters, crossed the English Channel and followed the meandering Thames Estuary to their undefended target. There was to be little or no resistance to this ruthless armada. The RAF was acutely short of airplanes and could not afford to divert aircraft from the defenses of its vital airfields and radar stations. And so, on that day, the Luftwaffe was to bomb and bomb at will. Their primary targets were the London and Surrey Docks and the houses and factories in the adjacent East End, the heart of "Cockneydom."

Like my mother before me I am a Cockney. I was born in the London Hospital, Whitechapel Road. In my childhood, the area was a bustling, working-class Jewish neighborhood like the Lower East of New York at the turn of the century. It is a locale with many historic associations. For example: Chaucer and Harold Pinter were born in the vicinity, the latter only a hundred yards or so from Senrab Street, my first elementary school. In 1381, at Mile End, the eastern extension of Whitechapel Road, Richard II was forced to put an end to serfdom. It was in this district that Jews first settled when Cromwell readmitted them into England in 1657, where Captain Cook's home was located, and where William Booth established the Salvation Army in 1868. In the late Victorian period, the London Hospital, my birthplace, housed the Elephant Man. Opposite the hospital, in Buck's Row, Jack the Ripper committed one of his grisly murders in the fall of 1888. And close by, some twenty-three years later, occurred the Sidney Street Siege, in which soldiers and police battled a group of Jewish anarchists. Quite a neighborhood!

To be a Cockney one must be born within the sound of the bells of Stratford-atte-Bow Church. In a literal sense, I suppose I am one of the last of the breed since no one has heard those bells since the church was destroyed in 1942.

In the autumn of 1940, we were living in a small row-house, 36 Thomas Road, in Limehouse, a side-street of Burdett Road which led into the East India Dock Road. At around 4:30 in the afternoon, I was sprawled on the sofa reading a comic book. Mom was in the kitchen, preparing dinner. Dad was at work. Suddenly the ominous wail of an air raid siren began, and in a moment Mom and I were out at the front door.

The street was already full of neighbors, heading for the nearest shelter, located in the cellar of the Melox Marvel Dog Biscuit factory, a block from our house.

Everyone had gas masks ready. Even the babies had gas masks, but they were different from those for children and adults, which were worn over the face. A gas mask for a baby was a cylindrical container about two feet long with a window on the upper surface. On one side was an air pump for filtering out poison gas. In the event of gas attack the baby had to be placed in the container, which was then sealed. The mother then had to pump in clean air. If she stopped pumping the baby would die of asphyxiation.

We made ourselves as comfortable as possible on wooden benches scattered among boxes full of packaged dog biscuits. (Inside each of those packages, I knew, was a red rubber ball for a dog: a fact that will have some significance later in this account.) People in the shelter were very friendly. They passed chocolate and

Geduld, age eight, 1939

cigarettes around. Someone started a sing-song: "There'll Always Be an England," "Roll Out the Barrel," and "Bless 'Em All." By this time the siren had stopped and between the songs I noticed it was very quiet outside. Suddenly, there was an ear-piercing whistle and screech—the sound of a falling bomb—and we heard a tremendous explosion. The factory shook violently and showers of dust and plaster descended on us. Everyone either ducked or hit the floor. We were OK: the ceiling had held. Then followed more whistles, more screeches. The shelter shook again and again. Then the lights went out. There were a few muffled screams and some pretty raw language: I really increased my vocabulary that day. Then someone, I think it was the air raid warden, shone a flashlight. Everyone looked deathly pale. Soon there was more light. Someone had lit a candle. People began laughing and talking. The sing-song started up again. We could still hear explosions but

they seemed to get more distant. We stayed in that shelter for an hour, maybe, until, at last, the "All Clear" sounded and we headed for the shelter entrance.

Outside it was still daylight. But that was the only familiar sight. Thomas Road was a scene of utter chaos. Several houses had collapsed into the street, which was now buried under mounds of debris: bricks, roof-slates, broken glass, bits of metal, shattered wood, fragments of furniture—you name it. Wardens and ambulance men were combing the debris to find people who had not bothered to take shelter. During the next hour or two they brought out several bodies and left them stretched on a patch of sidewalk that had been cleared of wreckage. (Vehicles couldn't get into the area to take them away.) In the meantime, to add to the chaos, the water mains had burst and cascades of water were pouring into the street. Amidst this unbelievable mess and confusion was one of the most extraordinary—and quite ludicrous—sights I have ever seen. One side of the Melox Marvel factory must have taken a direct hit, and thousands of red rubber balls were floating in the huge puddles that were forming among the mounds of debris.

Number 36 Thomas Road hadn't collapsed, but the roof was gone and the upper floor was twisted askew and lurching crazily over the lower floor as if it were ready to slide over and join the wreckage in the street. Mom and I wanted to enter the house to rescue our most precious possessions, but an air raid warden stopped us. It was too dangerous. All we could do for the time being was wait in the street. Mom was afraid to leave the area in case Dad turned up and was unable to locate us.

Now, looking around some more, I noticed a bizarre sight that was to become very familiar during the hundreds of other air raids I lived through. It was due to the weird effects of Blast. A bomb that had struck a nearby house had shorn away everything except one of the four walls, which remained absolutely intact. It was like looking at a stage set. On the upper floor you could see the bathtub and toilet seemingly hanging in mid-air: they were attached to the wall by plumbing pipes. Downstairs was a dresser, displaying totally unbroken crockery: all the cups and saucers were still hanging from hooks. There was also a fireplace, pictures on the wall, and someone's coat on a hanger behind a door. That side of the house was ex-

"The last class photo before World War II," Senrab Street Elementary School, London, 1937.
Geduld is in the second row, far left. His friend Muriel Barbanel, who was killed during
the war, is in the same row, fourth from left.

actly as its occupants had left it a couple of hours earlier. The rest had disintegrated to become part of the debris in the street.

I later discovered that I had lost a number of friends that day. I'll mention by name only the one whose loss was the most painful to me. I remember going to Muriel Barbanel's birthday party when she was six. There wasn't very much of anything in the way of food and drink because the Barbanels didn't have very much. The Depression was in full swing, and like my family they had been hit very badly. Like Mom and Dad, Mr. and Mrs. Barbanel were both unemployed. Nevertheless, it was a wonderful party mainly because of Muriel's father, who regaled us with an inexhaustible supply of stories and games.

The Barbanels lived in a flat on the second floor. Mr. Barbanel was handicapped. Apparently, when the air raid siren sounded, he couldn't get down to a shelter in his wheelchair. The family (I think there were two other daughters besides Muriel) stayed up there with him. One bomb did for them all. Now, as far as I know, all that remains of Muriel—not to mention the rest of her family—is my childhood memory of her and her face in a school photo.

I thought of her recently when I saw a documentary about the Blitz. The film incorporated captured footage showing that same air raid on London. It was unspeakably eerie watching the view from a German bomber as it crossed the Channel and headed up the Thames, a silver thread glimmering in the afternoon sunlight. I saw the Docks and the East End come into view. I had been down there, somewhere. And Muriel too. Then came a close-up of the face of the pilot as he pressed a button that released his stick of bombs. They fell like dark crayons to explode below a few seconds later. The pilot, one of Hitler's blond Supermen, had snuffed out the lives of people he had never known, people who had never intended him or his country any harm. His face was lit up with joy. Afterwards, according to the film, he flew back to his base and toasted his achievement in champagne.

In Thomas Road it was still light when Dad showed up. At that period of the war he was an air raid warden. A few months later he would be appointed one of London's eight Incident Officers, responsible for coordinating the various civil defense services during air raid emergencies. Dad had been on duty near the Surrey Docks—the area that received the worst pounding. He hadn't been able to take shelter, but had seen the sky black with German airplanes heading up the river towards him, and had witnessed God-knows-how-many ghastly sights as their tons of bombs began to tear the Docks apart. He was white-faced as he told Mom about a colleague who had been standing next to him one moment and was riddled with shrapnel (bomb splinters) the next. I wasn't allowed to hear the rest.

Despite Mom's fears, he crept into Number 36 and retrieved the family photos and a few other precious items, among them two books: my earliest English textbook and *Old Rhymes for All Times,* a relic of my infancy (I still have both). He also brought out a small, single-ring kerosene stove and a can of kerosene, and in a few minutes had the stove working. This was to prove a boon for everyone in the neighborhood. For not only the water mains but all the other utilities had been put out of action, and for the rest of the day that little kerosene stove became, locally, the only means of heating water. The word quickly spread and people came from blocks away to heat water for cups of tea.

Where would we spend the night? Where would we find food? Dad had heard that shelter and food were available at the People's Palace in Mile End Road. Turning our backs on Thomas Road for the last time, we picked our way through street after street of rubble until we reached our destination. Inside the People's Palace was a huge hall swarming with families like us, made homeless by the bombing. All that most of us had were the clothes we were wearing. Women's Voluntary Service workers were on hand, providing clothes and shoes and offering sandwiches and cups of tea or milk for the babies. There were no beds. The WVS handed out blankets and we made ourselves as comfortable as we could on the floor.

It was a strange night. Impossible really to sleep with the lights on and the hubbub: more and more homeless kept arriving, children and babies were crying (some had lost their parents), and eventually came another air raid . . . and another.

As Churchill promised, that day we'd had blood, sweat, and tears. But in spite of that and in spite of the hundreds of raids that were to follow, I don't recollect ever hearing defeatist talk from anyone. Londoners were stunned at first and upset at losing their homes. But I never saw anyone demoralized. The raids intensified their patriotism, galvanized their determination to survive at all costs, and made them united in common hatred of the enemy. Wherever one went there were signs proclaiming British defiance: shops with their windows shattered were placarded with signs like, "Better luck next time, Adolf" and "Business as usual: try our back entrance." Ruined houses displayed posters reading: "They can break our bones but not our hearts" and "God Bless the RAF" After that first raid I saw an old Cockney, who'd lost everything he owned, shake his fist at the sky and proclaim: "You're a dirty bastard 'itler, but our boys'll get you in the end."

We couldn't stay for long at the People's Palace. Others also needed food, drink, and a night's rest. So we moved on—at first to stay with relatives in Romford, Essex, a few miles east of London. But after a couple of nights they let us know we were no longer welcome.

Since I have just mentioned food, I should say a few words about rationing. Like the U.S., Britain had just emerged from the Depression, during which many Britons—my family among them—had not known where their next meal was coming from. Curiously, despite the fact that the war brought acute food shortages, rationing meant that the average person ate more wholesome food and more regularly than during the years of unemployment, the Dole, and the Means Test. Food wasn't plentiful, but everyone got a fair share, and as there were no longer any unemployed, everyone could now afford to eat. Those in the armed forces were, of course, fed at government expense. Aside from that, each civilian had his or her ration book containing coupons that limited but at the same time guaranteed the quantities of available food (and also clothes and soap) he

"With my mother, outside the house in Willesden, where the ceiling caved in on me," 1944

or she could obtain. And people made sure they got whatever they were entitled to. I should mention that you had to give up ration coupons not only in food stores but also if you ate in restaurants. Tea was rationed—a major hardship for the tea-swilling British—but Mom and I always had sufficient because Dad drank only coffee (which was not rationed), and so we helped ourselves to his tea coupons and were able sometimes to swap them for food coupons. Sugar and candies were drastically rationed (kids got two ounces of "sweets" a week). We were also allowed two ounces of butter and one egg a week, and the meat ration was half a pound per person per week—whenever meat was available.

This last reminds me of a story that seems amusing now but seemed disastrous at the time. One afternoon when my mother's back was turned, our cat sneaked up on the kitchen table and stole the week's meat. A catastrophe! It meant that we had to live on bread and vegetables only for the next seven days! Bread and vegetables were not rationed, and many people also grew their own vegetables and fruit (mainly berries) to liven up their humdrum diet. There was little fruit available in the stores. I didn't see an orange or a banana for five years: overseas fruit was not imported during the war. But babies received rations of orange juice and extra milk.

I don't remember ever going hungry during the war years: but food was often deadly dull despite the efforts of the BBC and the Food Ministry to come up with all sorts of creative ways to cook carrots and cabbage.

The next few weeks after we left Romford is a blurred memory of Mom and me staying in many different places—sometimes with relatives or friends, more often than not in any air raid shelter we could find. Meanwhile the air raids continued for about two months. Often they would last all night. I've read somewhere that in this period about fifty bombs per hundred acres were falling on the area where we were sheltering: it was the heaviest bombardment of any place in England during World War II.

Dad, for his part, was bunking down at the local wardens' post when he wasn't on duty—which was much of the time, since after that first afternoon the raids intensified by day and night. For several weeks which seemed like an eternity, Mom and I seldom saw him, and after each brief visit we never knew if we would ever see him again.

Years later I read other eloquent words of Winston Churchill, spoken in the House of Commons that autumn of 1940: "Death and sorrow will be the companions of our journey, hardship our garment; constancy and valor our only shield." Beyond measure his words were true of what Londoners—and especially the East-Enders—suffered and endured at that time. However, tragic nobility is not the whole story. We also encountered some pretty ugly anti-Semitism while we were drifting around London that autumn. I remember, for example, a sign reading "No Jews Wanted" at the entrance to an air raid shelter. I recall a hefty red-faced woman telling Mom (who was a quarter of her size), "You Jews are living on the fat of the land while the rest of us are starving." And one night I heard a couple of men in the London Underground (subway) discussing in loud voices how "The Jews got us into this war" and how "Our Boys are doing all the fighting while the Jews are raking in the money." Their comments impressed me no end since I had three uncles in the army (one was a professional soldier, a master-sergeant) and a cousin in the RAF, while my father—who is handicapped and was thus ineligible for the draft—saw more action in the war than many who were conscripted.

London in 1940–45 was Front Line for Jews as well as non-Jews, but anti-Semitism then as now, whether the purveyor is Hitler, Mosley, or Farrakhan, is blind to truth. Let me stress that these were far from isolated instances, and they were by no means my first experiences of anti-Semitism. Indeed, among my earliest memories are Oswald Mosley's Blackshirts parading with their arms outstretched in fascist salutes, standing on soapboxes spouting their anti-Semitic venom, and handing out leaflets proclaiming "Mosley for Peace" and "The Jews Want War." They used to shove their pamphlets, adorned with pictures of Hitler and Mosley and thunder-flash logos, into our mailbox. We generally used them as toilet paper.

In the mid-thirties, by the way, the only Londoners who battled the Blackshirts—in violent street confrontations—were East End Jews and Communists: they were sometimes one and the same. I think it is worth noting that much later, soon after I had moved to the U.S. in the early sixties, I happened to catch Oswald Mosley being interviewed on television. He was insistent that he and his followers had never, absolutely never, been anti-Semitic! And he assured his American interviewer that "some of his best friends were Jews." He never mentioned their names.

To return to 1940. While the air raids were becoming almost routine experiences, like other kids I was "doing my bit"—which meant making sandbags, collecting scrap paper and scrap metal, and learning how to use a stirrup pump

Carolyn and Harry Geduld with their first child, Marcus, 1968

in case we had to deal with incendiary bombs. I was also a devotee of the latest "hobby": collecting shrapnel after air raids. Previously, I had collected marbles, cigarette cards, and "conkers." But shrapnel was more exciting. You never knew what you'd find after an air raid. Like most other kids in London I soon had a box full of interesting souvenirs: the tail-fin of an incendiary bomb, dozens of jagged shell or bomb splinters, and some curious strips of metal foil which the Germans dropped by the cartload, and which, I later gathered, were intended to disrupt British radar. Later on in the war the Germans put a stop to this collecting mania when they began dropping anti-personnel bombs. These were devices designed to look like toys. They exploded if kids picked them up. After a few children were maimed or killed in this way, there were strict taboos against souvenir-hunting after air raids.

By this time I had seen quite a few night raids. I would creep out of a shelter with other kids to watch the action as the ack-ack guns blasted away and searchlights crisscrossed the sky. Once in a while I saw a German bomber caught in a searchlight. When that happened it didn't take long for other searchlights to converge on the same spot; then the ack-ack guns would give the plane all hell, and we'd duck back into the shelter in case the plane crashed down on top of us. The precaution was ridiculous—it would have spiralled down and crashed miles away—but we didn't know any better. Actually, we were in much more danger from shell-shrapnel from the ack-acks which, during a heavy raid, would shower down like white-hot rain.

I think it was early or mid-December 1940 when my parents decided to send me out of London again. It must have been before December 29 because I wasn't in London for the massive incendiary (fire bomb) raid that destroyed much of the city, London's banking district, that night. The Germans deliberately hit London when they knew the Thames was at low tide and it would be impossible for firemen to get water from the river to cope with the firestorm.

Evacuated for the second time, I wound up in Camberley, Surrey, near Sandhurst, England's West Point, about an hour's journey from central London. Although I wasn't actually present at the Great Fire of December 29, I did, in fact, see it. Even thirty miles away, as

I was then, night was turned into day by the thousands of fires that were consuming the city.

In Camberley I stayed first with the Millers. Mr. and Mrs. Miller had three children: a retarded son who was my age, a daughter two years older, and another daughter a year or two younger. This was my worst "billet." Mr. Miller was built like a bull and had huge hands. I never found out why he wasn't in the army. He was very scary, always threatening dire punishments. He never actually beat me—or any of his own kids as far as I knew—but we lived all in fear of him. He once threatened to make me eat a rat because I'd left some food on my plate. And I believed him at the time. He would talk about "knocking sense" into us with his "strap" and enjoyed watching us tremble as he made the gesture of unbuckling his belt.

I wrote Dad and he soon turned up and persuaded the local billeting officer to move me to a new place. This was the home of Mr. and Mrs. Goddard, an elderly couple. They were not abusive but deadly dull for a nine-year-old boy. The Goddards believed children should be seen and not heard, and their idea of entertainment was what they called "a quiet read." It consisted, as far as I could tell, of a diet of religious tracts and sermons. My only worthwhile experience with the Goddards was discovering in their bookshelf the nearest thing they had to sensational fiction: *The Pilgrim's Progress.*

The Goddards eventually decided that looking after a well-behaved nine-year-old was too much of a handful. And so I moved again. If I hadn't, I would probably have died of boredom. My last home in Camberley turned out to be the best. Mrs. Marsden was about thirty, and her husband was in the army. I think she wanted children of her own but couldn't have any. She was a very kind and generous person, and I have very happy memories of the few weeks I stayed with her. I remember that she was very upset when I left, in June 1942, to return to London.

While in Camberley I had resumed elementary school at France Hill House, which provided tuition for evacuees. I'd missed a lot of school before that, but my parents had agreed to let me return to London if I managed to win a Junior County Scholarship, the equivalent of the Eleven Plus Examination, which would provide fees and admission to high school. (I should explain here that high school in En-

gland was only for the affluent or for working-class children who won scholarships.) I took the Junior County exam at France Hill and was one of the two or three successful children. Thus it was that I returned to London in the summer of 1942 and in September began the first of my eight years at Latymer Upper School, Hammersmith (West London).

My life at Latymer is another, long story which I'll recount in detail elsewhere. I shall mention briefly only two or three disturbing recollections.

The only time I have ever been mortally afraid was when I happened to be at Latymer during an air raid. The school shelter was located in the boiler-room, and when we had go down there all I could think of was that I'd be boiled alive if a bomb hit the school and burst the boilers. Fortunately, it never did and I never was.

Disturbing in a different way was the sight of teachers who were scarred by the war. When I began at Latymer in 1942, most teachers were elderly men, way beyond the age of military service. But as the war dragged on, a few younger teachers turned up. They had been discharged from the forces because of various injuries. One English teacher was shell-shocked. He would tremble and shake, sometimes quite violently, for minutes at a time. Another teacher had been burned severely in a tank or airplane. The burns and plastic surgery had left his face a ghastly mask.

Then there was morning assembly. The headmaster (principal) would often read aloud to us the names of Old Boys (alumni) who had recently been killed. Some of them had left school only a year before I arrived. I remember thinking: There but for the grace of God . . .

Meanwhile, during the raids of 1941, my parents had lost another home. By the time I began attending Latymer, we were living in a first-floor flat in Westbourne Park, North Kensington. It was fairly close to my school. But sometime before the end of the year the flat was demolished too. We moved again, this time to a row-house in Willesden, North-West London, about forty-five minutes by trolley-bus from Latymer. This home survived the war. But about five years later, around 1949 or 1950, I was sitting in an armchair, reading a book, when the ceiling collapsed on top of me. I was dazed

That mad surge down the staircase was scary and potentially very dangerous. At one station in East London someone slipped and more than a hundred people fell down the steps on top of one another. It took the rescue services many hours to extricate the heap of bodies.

If you got downstairs safely, places to avoid were near the toilets (which stank to high heaven) and the ends of the platform, where terrific draughts blew through the tunnel. It was usually kids who got down first, and they would stake out places for the rest of the family by stretching out blankets on the platform. Families would often quarrel about who'd got there first. In staking out a place, you had to leave about two feet clear of the edge of the platform so that passengers could get on and off the trains. For some months we simply stretched out on the platform: the blankets didn't provide much padding, but it was better than nothing. But in 1943, the government installed bunks. These were much more comfortable and could be reserved. Mom and I had bunks on one of the platforms at Oxford Circus Station. We would arrive there at around 9 p.m. and leave at 5 a.m., when the first morning trains came through. The only relatively peaceful time was between around 11 p.m. and five in the morning. Between 9 p.m. and "bedtime" (around 11 p.m., when the trains stopped running) there were always people milling around, talking and singing, playing radios, stepping over your blankets to get the toilets, etc., etc. St. John's Ambulance men were on duty to take care of anyone who got sick. For adults the WVS dispensed tea and coffee, and for kids they provided an intensely sweet cocoa which I've never encountered since, but whose taste I'll never forget.

By morning, after hundreds had spent the night down there, even though blasts of air blew through the subway tunnels, the platforms were foul and litter was everywhere. One side effect of life in the Underground was that most people wound up with head lice and fleas, and kids particularly (myself included) got scabies. Fortunately there were no serious epidemics.

Occasionally we would hear the sounds of a raid overhead, and as we went home in the morning we would see the latest bomb damage, but, as I said, the Underground was generally safe. The only exception was what happened at Bank Station. Freakishly, a bomb hit the elevator shaft and exploded on those shel-

"Three generations: with my mother and Marcus," 1969

but unhurt. Like many London houses, this one had been structurally weakened by the bombing, but it took a few years for the damage to take effect.

To return to 1942. By day I went to school. At night, Mom and I sheltered in the London Tube or Underground (subway). All told, we slept in the Underground every night for about two years. It was the only place in London where you could get some undisturbed sleep and be guaranteed safety from the bombing. While we were living in Westbourne Park, we sheltered every night in Queensway Tube Station.

The routine was to take blankets and pillows, buy a ticket at the station, and line up outside the station stairway entrance at around 6 p.m. At around 9 p.m., or earlier if there was a raid, the stairway entrance would be opened and everyone would rush down to get a good place on the platform.

tering directly below. Among those who were killed there was my father's best friend, Julius Akop, who had fled from Stalin's Russia and Hitler's Germany. His wife, who adored him, later committed suicide.

Our life in the Underground came to an end in early 1944 when my father installed a Morrison Shelter in the living-room of our house in Willesden. The Morrison was one of the two kinds of domestic air raid shelter. A rectangular box of reinforced steel, it was about the height of a table and the length and width of a queen-size bed. We sheltered and sometimes slept in it during raids: and there would be as many as six at a time in there when our next-door neighbors, a couple with two children, joined us. The Morrison was strong enough to support the weight of our house if it collapsed, but it could not have withstood the impact of a direct hit.

The other kind of domestic shelter was the Anderson, made of corrugated steel. This would be erected in a square-shaped trench dug in one's back garden. We opted for a Morrison because it was cold and damp inside the typical Anderson, a very unappealing place to bunk down during a rain-soaked British summer—not to mention a winter's night.

In addition to Andersons and Morrisons in private houses, there were small, brick shelters, equipped with bunks, situated adjacent to the sidewalk on many streets. They looked like outhouses and often smelled like them. (You can see them to this day in the film *Odd Man Out*.) I had to dodge into street shelters many times during the raids that took place while I was on my way to school.

In those years London was alive with Allied troops, seemingly from every part of the world. Most memorable to me were the Canadians and Americans (the latter, of course, began arriving in 1942, soon after Pearl Harbor). They were all part of the buildup to what, on June 6, 1944, would become D-Day. They attracted hordes of kids, starved for candies. The Americans dispensed apparently inexhaustible quantities of chewing-gum. I would follow their familiar uniforms and utter the magic words, "Got any gum, chum?" It never failed. They would dig into their uniforms and produce strange flat packets so unlike the chiclet-shaped chewing-gum I was used to that I was utterly perplexed when a GI first put one into my hand. The Americans were generous, good-humored,

The author with his parents, Bloomington, Indiana, 1990

and above all glamorous: they had accents like characters in Hollywood movies. The word quickly spread that there wasn't anything you couldn't get from them if you happened to have a good-looking young sister. I was not so fortunately endowed—but all in all didn't do too badly not only for gum but also for comics. The Canadians, in particular, would dole out reams of them—marvelous, thick, colored comics full of great cartoons I'd never seen before: *Superman, Tarzan, Dick Tracy, L'il Abner, Gasoline Alley, Little Orphan Annie, Mandrake the Magician.* Wonderful, wonderful comics! It was a whole new world.

In 1944 the raids seemed to have tailed off and people were predicting that the war would be over before the end of the year. It wasn't. Hitler still had a couple of tricks up his sleeve.

One evening a relative dropped in to see Dad. He was puzzled. He had been clearing a building site where an enemy plane had crashed. At least he thought it was a plane—although from the fragments that remained the aircraft appeared too small to have contained a pilot. It was, of course, a V-1 (a pilotless, flying bomb), one of the first to hit London, and soon everyone knew exactly what it was. The Germans lost no time in sending them over in force, each tipped with a warhead containing a ton of high explosive. Londoners quickly nicknamed them "Doodlebugs" or "Buzz Bombs." Those nicknames were the only funny things about them. They approached London so rapidly there was seldom time for an air raid siren. But you could usually hear their monotonous, droning motors before they became visible. By day and night they zipped across the sky at about six hundred miles an hour. When they did appear they looked like dark pencils shooting out flames and exhaust from a jet engine in their upper-rear ends.

Often, travelling to and from school, when there was no shelter nearby, I would leap off the bus and take cover in a doorway or behind a wall as a Doodlebug came over. Sometimes the damn thing would pass by overhead, taking its packet of destruction to some other poor devil. At other times its engine would cut out quite suddenly and everyone in the vicinity would hit the sidewalk and cover their heads. After a moment or two of silence there would be a huge explosion somewhere nearby. If you were lucky—i.e., still in one piece—you picked yourself up and went on your way. There was nothing you or anyone else could do about it.

I once saw an RAF plane try to bring a V-1 down over a park where there were no houses. He got close to it and tilted its wing. But at that moment the damn thing blew up. I didn't see anyone bail out of the plane.

I mentioned earlier that the V-1s emitted a distinctive buzzing or droning sound. When one of them approached you knew you were OK as long you could still hear the sound of its engine. But in due course, the Germans began sending over V-1s with engines that would cut out, then start up again, then cut out. This might continue half a dozen times. It was terrifying.

I've read that the South of England was hit by over 2,000 V-1s. Most were aimed at London, and I must have seen at least fifty coming over—on one occasion three at the same time.

The V-1s were bad enough. But then came the V-2s, which injured and killed hundreds more Londoners and wrecked thousands more houses. These were Wernher von Braun's stratospheric rocket bombs, the ancestors of the rockets used to develop the American space program. The V-2s were even more invulnerable than the V-1s. They sped to their targets at thousands of miles per hour and carried far greater explosive payloads. You had no warning that they were coming.

I was walking home from the bus stop one day when a V-2 struck a row of houses a few hundred yards ahead of me. One moment I could see the houses in the distance—then a second later they blew up. Only *after* the explosion(!) did I hear the swoosh of the bomb's arrival: it had travelled faster than sound.

Years later I saw a Hollywood movie about Wernher von Braun. By then he had become a great American hero, the head of the U.S. space program. The movie was called *I Aim at the Stars.* Its makers, I assume, had not been in London in 1944–45, or they might have given it a subtitle: *Sometimes I Miss and Hit London.*

By the spring of 1945 the Allies had overrun the launching pads for the V-1s and V-2s. The raids came to an end and early in May the Germans surrendered. World War II in Europe had come to an end.

On May 8, my parents and I joined the celebrating crowd outside Buckingham Palace. King George VI, Queen Elizabeth, and their two young daughters (the elder is now Queen Elizabeth II) came out on a balcony to wave to the crowd. They were joined by Winston Churchill. The applause was deafening. Then everyone, in unison, sang the national anthem and "Rule Britannia." I have never been patriotic but one couldn't be there and not be profoundly moved.

Noel Coward has summed up what I (and probably millions of other Britons) felt at that moment: "I loved British courage, British humor and British understatement . . . I loved the people—the ordinary, the extraordinary, the good, the bad, the indifferent—and what is more I belonged to that exasperating, weather-sodden little island with its uninspired cooking, its muddled thinking and its unregenerate pride, and it belonged to me whether I liked it or not."

Mom, Dad, and I left the crowds around the Palace, walked back through the Mall, under the Admiralty Arch where Churchill had conducted the war, into Trafalgar Square where Nelson and Landseer's lions stood guard, as always, and on up St. Martin's Lane and Monmouth Street into New Oxford Street. Everyone was waving flags, dancing, singing. There were bonfires and firecrackers . . . and no more Blackout. For the first time in five years

Harry Geduld (center) with sons Daniel (left) and Marcus, 1993

lights blazed everywhere: street lamps, neon signs, and the illuminations of thousands of uncurtained windows. So it was really true. It was all over at last: the evacuations, the sirens, the gas masks, the air raids. The Germans had thrown everything they could at us—and we had survived.

At Oxford Circus we caught a number 8 bus home. That night we all slept well.

A few months later I was staying with relatives in Brighton. It was my first visit to the seaside since before the war, and I was about to leave for the beach when someone rushed into the house and turned on the radio. There was a special bulletin. An American airplane had dropped an atomic bomb on a Japanese city called Hiroshima. What did it mean? No one I knew had heard of the place or knew what an atomic bomb could possibly be. To me it sounded like something out of H. G. Wells, whose novels I was reading avidly by this time. Within a few days came the atomic bombing of Nagasaki and then the Japanese surrender. World War II was over.

At the time, the war in the Far East had seemed very remote and unconnected with "my" war. But as the months went by I began to encounter not only wounded, blinded, and crippled soldiers from the European theater, but the victims of Japanese prison camps who looked like walking skeletons, and others too, survivors of German concentration camps, like the four orphaned boys my parents took in and tended for several years. And I began to realize then that it was all the same war, waged by the forces of hatred, prejudice, and inhumanity. I know now that it's a war that has never ended.

Sometimes, at night, as I lay awake, vague memories of the war drift through my mind like dreams. Did those things really happen? Did I live through those events when I was eight . . . nine . . . ten . . . eleven . . . twelve . . . thirteen . . . fourteen . . . ? Then the vague images become clearer and I seem to be back there again in 1940, 1941, 1942 . . . and the sirens are ringing in my ears. And I know for certain that it wasn't a dream, that it really happened, that I was there in England at the hour Winston said was Britain's finest.

Yes, I saw the Battle of Britain and the Few to whom so Many owed so Much. I saw London burning. I saw the death, destruction, and misery, but I also saw the Londoners, my Londoners, unbeaten, enduring, and ultimately triumphant. Yes, I was there.

And I have promised myself that one day I shall go back, back to that place I have carefully avoided on every visit to London. One day I shall find the courage to return to Thomas Road and see where my childhood ended on that unforgettable afternoon in the autumn of 1940.

BIBLIOGRAPHY

Editor:

George Bernard Shaw, *The Rationalization of Russia,* Indiana University Press, 1964.

Film Makers on Film Making: Statements on Their Art by Thirty Directors, Indiana University Press, 1967.

(And contributor with Ronald Gottesman) *Sergei Eisenstein and Upton Sinclair: The Making and Unmaking of 'Que Viva Mexico!',* Indiana University Press, 1970, published in England as *The Making and Unmaking of 'Que Viva Mexico!' by Sergei Eisenstein and Upton Sinclair,* Thames & Hudson, 1970.

Focus on D. W. Griffith, Prentice-Hall, 1971.

(With Ronald Gottesman) *Guidebook to Film: An Eleven-in-One Reference,* Holt, 1972.

Authors on Film, Indiana University Press, 1972.

(With Ronald Gottesman) *An Illustrated Glossary of Film Terms,* Holt, 1973.

(With Ronald Gottesman) *The Girl in the Hairy Paw,* Avon, 1976.

Robots, Robots, Robots, New York Graphic Society, 1978.

The New York Times Film Encyclopedia, thirteen volumes, Times Books, 1984.

Charlie Chaplin's Own Story, Indiana University Press, 1985.

Chapliniana, Volume 1, Indiana University Press, 1985.

The Definitive Time Machine, Indiana University Press, 1986.

(With David Y. Hughes) *Critical Edition of H. G. Wells's War of the Worlds,* Indiana University Press, 1993.

(With Ronald Gottesman) *Critical Essays on Film,* Macmillan, 1993.

Other:

Prince of Publishers: A Study of the Life and Work of Jacob Tonson, Indiana University Press, 1969.

James Barrie: A Study, Twayne, 1971.

Filmguide to Henry V, Indiana University Press, 1973.

The Birth of the Talkies, Indiana University Press, 1975.

The Definitive Jekyll and Hyde Companion, Garland Publishing, 1983.

German Requiem (play), produced at Fine Arts Auditorium, 1990.

Warsaw: Year Zero (docudrama), produced at Center for Jewish Culture and Creativity, 1991.

Also author of liner notes for Pelican record albums *My Man Godfrey, Tales for a Winter's Night, Flash Gordon's Trip to Mars, Sounds from the Silent Screen, The Rogue Song, The New Moon,* and *Garbo Soundtracks.* General editor, "Filmguides" and "Visions" series, Indiana University Press, 1987—; "Film Focus" series, Prentice-Hall; and "The Literature of Mystery and Detection" series, Arno.

Contributor of articles and book reviews to numerous journals, including *Denver Quarterly, Journal of Popular Culture, Modern Drama, Quarterly Journal of Film Studies, Quarterly Journal of Speech, Radio Times, Shaw Review, Studies in Short Fiction,* and *Victorian Studies.* Film reviewer for *Humanist,* 1967–90.

John Heath-Stubbs

1918-

John Heath-Stubbs

The Stubbses, originally a Staffordshire family (with Welsh connections), were linked by marriage to the Heaths, another legal family. In my grandfather's day, the last of the Heaths made us Stubbses her heirs, so long as we changed our name to Heath-Stubbs. My paternal grandmother's family were the Yorkshire Emmets. Some went to Ireland, and the Irish Nationalist Robert Emmet was one of their descendants.

My mother was one of the Aberdeenshire Marrs, a sept of the Gordons. A brilliant concert pianist, she studied with Tobias Matthay, who taught (among others) Myra Hess, Harriet Cohen, Irene Scharrer and York Bowen. My father was a qualified solicitor, who did not need to practise. His eyesight was very poor, due to the glaucoma that I was to inherit. My parents' wartime wedding was by special licence. I was born on July 9th, 1918, in Room 9 of a nursing home in Streatham.

My parents lived in Hampstead then; but my own first memories are of Cherrydale, a house they owned at Shoreham, Kent, and also of a garden tea-party at Lord Dunsany's. I was about three. I vaguely recall a bearded man— unusual then. Most men of his age had been in the army, so were beardless. Dunsany was a well-known dramatist of the day and specialized in fantastic subjects. He wrote *A Night at an Inn,* about sailors stealing a god's eye, which gave me nightmares.

I was still only three when my eyesight first gave cause for concern. A Unitarian oculist called Bishop Harman diagnosed glaucoma, a condition seldom found in children. He said I should give up reading, which I loved, and take up sport, which I loathed.

My parents did not stay long at Shoreham. They moved around the southern counties, and also lived for a while in Brittany. I spent my fourth birthday in the village of Saint-Jean-du-Doigt. I became vaguely aware of the Celtic tradition in Brittany, and specifically recall my father quoting:

> When great King Arthur ruled this land
> he was a goodly King.
> He stole three pecks of barley meal
> to make a bag pudding . . .

My father said Brittany had been one site of Arthur's battles. That comment has been with me ever since, prompting my largest-scale work, *Artorius.*

After returning (via Paris) to England, we lived for a time in London but mostly in the country, finally settling in New Milton, Hampshire, where we lost all our possessions in a fire. My father was found to be afflicted with multiple sclerosis. He died in 1938.

We moved into Seaward Cottage, Barton on Sea, about 1925 and stayed there till the war. I attended a private village school where a Miss Barnes taught history from *Our Island Story.* This book starts quite rightly with England's mythic history: the Giant Albion and Brutus the Trojan. It was here I first became conscious of poetry: "The Lady of Shalott," "Daffodils" and "Hiawatha." More recently I heard the story of Hiawatha's initiation on the radio and realized that (facile as Longfellow's verse may be) its symbolism had prepared me for *The Golden Bough* and for *The Waste Land.*

I progressed to another private school, Speedwell School in New Milton, and developed an interest in natural history. On our daily walks through the Hampshire countryside, my father would identify birdsongs. I especially recall, when I was eight, seeing a male stonechat close up: red breast, black head, a call-note like the chink of stones. My grandfather had also been interested in ornithology. Years later, reviewing James

Fisher's book about sea-birds, I learned that a "Mr. Stubbs" had recorded seeing a Wandering Albatross displayed in a poulterer's shop in Leadenhall Street, with its amazing eleven-foot wing span. That "Mr. Stubbs" must have been my grandfather.

New Milton society was like E. F. Benson's Rye: bridge, tennis, amateur dramatics. Later on, my mother founded an orchestra there. Operatic and choral societies existed. In the "silent" 1920s there was one cinema; later another was built to screen "talkies." I missed out on the cinema in early childhood. My parents' concern for my eyes (and their low esteem for the film as a medium) saw to that.

On December 1st, 1925, my brother George was born. I awoke in a strange room: mine had been requisitioned by the midwife. My grandmother, who lived with us, explained this, and then took me in to see George. I resented him. During our childhood together we were, consequently, not on the best of terms. When World War II broke out, George was sent to my uncle Fred in Rhodesia, where, after having served in the South African army, he subsequently settled. Our relations as adults were cordial until 1983, when he died.

Both our parents were devout Christians, but my father took me to Old Milton Church, while my mother helped Dora, our cook, prepare the Sunday lunch. There had been a Chapel of Ease at Old Milton since King John's time.

The New Forest was approximately a mile away. By no means all woodland, much of it is moor and bog. In my time, conifers were planted to replace deciduous woodlands for commercial purposes—and not much flourishes beneath conifers. Nor was there as much wildlife as one might expect: only wild ponies and deer. There was a gap between what books said had been there, and what actually remained of New Forest flora and fauna.

Indeed, I have always been slightly in fear of the place. One would of course "do" the Rufus Stone, the monument to William II's strange death there. In *The God of the Witches* Margaret Murray says Rufus was a "closet" pagan and suggests he died as a sacrifice.

At the age of about nine I was sent to Dorset House, a prep school in Littlehampton, Sussex. The teaching there was antiquated even then. Latin predominated in the shape of Ovidian myths, retold in the original language in a book called *Fabulae Faciles.* Nathaniel Hawthorne and

Charles Kingsley had already introduced me to these stories. Our history stopped at the Tudors. Poetry was Lord Macaulay's *Lays of Ancient Rome,* which I now respect for attempting to reproduce Livy's oral sources in terms of the English ballad tradition.

Each Sunday we went to church, wearing straw boaters. Afterwards we had to write home and learn the collect for that day. We were meant also to read one prescribed Bible chapter every evening before bed; but as this was never monitored I was at liberty to make my own discoveries: the Song of Songs, Ezekiel, Daniel and Revelations. These fed the poet in me; Leviticus's list of clean and unclean beasts and Job's Leviathan and Behemoth fed the scientist also.

At the age of twelve I was sent to Bembridge, a public (i.e. independent) school on the Isle of Wight, run on Ruskinian principles. This well-intentioned choice was a disaster. Judge Peter McNair wrote to me recently: "You, I and Robin Day went to the worst school in England." This school's warden, J. Howard Whitehouse, disbelieved in classical education; so I added nothing to my Latin and could not continue Greek. None of the English teachers had a degree in English. The emphasis was on arts and crafts.

I have never quite got over the tensions I experienced at Bembridge. Liberal ideas put across by hateful people clashed with my family background of loyalty to Church and Throne. Life was a constant battle with teachers, other boys and my own physical limitations.

The one blessing in this benighted place was its library, containing the 1888 *Encyclopaedia Britannica,* Brewer's *Dictionary of Phrase and Fable* and Lemprière's *Classical Dictionary.* The first was my main source of education—containing articles by Thomas Huxley, Ray Lancaster and Andrew Lang.

In addition to works of reference, I read poetry and fiction. My own first poem, "Winter," was written when I was twelve. I learned that I had a mysterious source of strength denied to my enemies—and I have never looked back since. In the library I had also discovered the modern novel, finding science- and detective-fiction (Wells and Chesterton) more to my taste than realism.

Despite Bembridge I am fond of the Isle of Wight. Its first invaders were Jutes—Stuf and Witgar. "Stuf" may be an early form of "Stubbs." When I was fifteen I went by bus to another side of the Isle to be confirmed. Whitehouse, who saw no purpose in the sacraments, had done his best to obstruct my parents' wishes; and the great day was devalued for me by poor preparation by the local vicar and by the school's indifference.

Politically and personally, life was getting grimmer. World War II and my father's incapacitation loured on the horizon. My mother was obliged to resume her musical career, this time as a teacher.

I read Frazer's *Golden Bough* and parts of Gibbon's *Decline and Fall.* The "Thinker's Library" series, which had prepared me for Gibbon and Frazer, included *The City of Dreadful Night* by James Thomson (BV[1]), an expression of total despair which foreshadows *The Waste Land.* When, much later, I knew T. S. Eliot, I asked his opinion of the Victorian poem. His reply was typically cryptic; "It was my favourite poem at the age of sixteen."

When I was seven or eight I had seen Elgar conduct his cello concerto at the Bournemouth Pavilion: a white-haired elderly gentleman with "presence." At twelve I saw Pavlova dance there. *Lohengrin* was the first, *Boris Godunov* one of the finest operas I heard. I came to these great works via our Gilbert and Sullivan operettas.

I also saw *The Magic Flute* on tour at Bournemouth. But Mozart made his greatest impact on me when, at nineteen, I heard *Don Giovanni* from Glyndebourne on the radio. An entire erotic universe unfolded before me. At the same time, I heard Bach's Mass in B Minor. Could such wonderful music be inspired by a lie? Was not Christianity true after all?

I had quit Bembridge at fifteen—it was obviously frustrating my development—and prepared to matriculate under two first-rate private tutors: Miss Ludwig and Miss Edwards of Christchurch. Miss Ludwig (who was Herbert Read's sister-in-law) introduced me to Thomas Hardy and Jane Austen, as well as Wordsworth; rekindled my love of Latin; and pointed me (via *Aeneid VI*) to Dante. My debt to this lady is very great. After matriculating, I studied with a Miss Hunkin. She had known Harold Monro's

---

[1]BV were initials by which the poet signed himself. It served to distinguish him from the eighteenth-century poet James Thomson ("The Seasons"). BV stands for "Bysshe Vanolis"—a tribute to Percy Bysshe Shelley and the German poet Novalis.

Poetry Bookshop, where Georgians and Modernists met, and where poets first read their work to live audiences.

At eighteen my eyes required surgery. My operation over, I was sent to Worcester College for the Blind. Worcester College was intended for "the blind sons of gentlemen," but many of the boys came from working-class homes. It was a strange place. Most of us, at whatever stage whole- or part-blindness had occurred, were damaged emotionally. I read to my blind companions books borrowed from Salmon and Glückstein's, an equivalent of Boots. From the section marked "for the sophisticated" I borrowed Robert Graves' *I Claudius* and *Claudius the God;* also *Descent into Hell* by Charles Williams, who was to be so important to me later.

The Barker Exhibition at Queen's College, Oxford, was for a blind or nearly-blind student wishing to read English. I was accepted for this.

Because of my eyesight I was exempt from military service. Most of my contemporaries were on short courses, which they hoped to complete after the war.

It was at the beginning of the Michaelmas term that I went up to Queen's to read English. I studied English Literature from Chaucer onwards with Herbert Brett-Smith of Corpus Christi College. With his daughter Hilary, I studied parts of the Anglo-Saxon Chronicle and Aelfric's lives of St. Edmund and St. Oswald. My Latin tutor, the Rev. Craddock Ratcliffe, had just been responsible for King George VI's coronation service.

I passed Pass Moderations and went on to read for Finals under the imperturbably genial Brett-Smith (for literature) with John Bryson of Balliol (for language). At first I resented Anglo-Saxon; but I learned to appreciate *Beowulf*'s heroic stoicism as World War II progressed. In 1936 J. R. R. Tolkien had published his famous lecture, arguing that *Beowulf* was no philologist's relic but a noble and tragic epic. I have recently learned that the first draft of *The Lord of the Rings* was written on the back of some of my examination papers.

C. S. Lewis ruled that a book should survive a century before being thought worth studying. This was bad in that we did not read Dickens, George Eliot, Tennyson or Browning at Oxford; good in that we learned about contemporary verse from each other.

In wartime Oxford, with younger male dons away, we had fine women lecturers such as Helen Gardner (later Dame Helen). Of the men, Nevill Coghill, David Nichol Smith and C. S. Lewis stood out. Coghill had been Auden's tutor and was to become my friend. Nichol Smith had edited the *Oxford Book of Eighteenth-Century Verse*— a welcome antidote to Bembridge's stress on Romanticism and Pre-Raphaelitism.

The reader may suppose that Oxford is all dreaming, mediaeval Gothic spires; but my college, Queen's, though founded in the fourteenth century, was burned down in the mid-seventeenth century and entirely rebuilt by Wren and Hawksmoor in an English baroque style. I think this influenced my sensibility. I developed a passion for the poetry of Dryden—not just his satires, but his great odes, his occasional poems and his heroic tragedies.

The star of Oxford English was C. S. Lewis. I heard the lectures which became *The Discarded Image*—and my world expanded. Lewis preferred the mediaeval to the modern world. The only modern writer he seemed to like was the allegorical Kafka.

Nevill Coghill lectured brilliantly on Langland; but I treasure his *Timon, Twelfth Night* and *Measure for Measure*—all outdoor productions.

Merton's Edmund Blunden was the first published poet I met. One saw in his eyes something of what he had gone through in World War I.

Charles Williams gave lectures, having been evacuated (along with his OUP colleagues) from London, where he had taught at the City Literary Institute. Lewis and Tolkien snapped him up for their Inklings set, and arranged an honorary M.A., enabling Williams to lecture at Oxford.

In my second year I began to be sociable— even then steering clear of communist contemporaries like Edmund Dell (now a merchant banker) or George Lehmann (now at the privately-funded University of Buckingham).

Drummond Allison, however, was unavoidable. Wittily talkaholic, he had no social inhibitions at all. I knew very little about current writing; Drummond already knew a good deal, modelling his verse on Auden, his prose on Hemingway. He was strong on Malory and in his own poems often explored Arthurian themes in modern contexts. T. H. White had been a family friend.

Drummond accosted anyone he suspected of poetry, requiring proof. In Queen's cloisters he introduced me to a poet who was handsome in an unusual, almost Levantine way—Sidney Keyes. We three became firm friends, setting up what is now called a "poetry workshop" at Queen's.

Sidney and Drummond were very different. As soon as I met him, Sidney denied that Auden was a poet. This was probably part of a then widespread anti-Auden movement. Sidney professed a deep belief in the philosophical roles of Wordsworth, Yeats and Rilke—but he read no philosophy.

Allusions in Sidney's copious verses were often from other people's reading. Reviewing for *Cherwell* a ballet he had not seen, he mistook which Browning poem it was based on.

He moved from Queen's to Number 37 "The High," where David Wright lodged; and where I and also William Bell later lodged. This house thus became an Oxford poets' haven.

There were two sides to Sidney's poetry (which maybe he found it too easy to write): pastoral and mythological. He also wrote two plays. I did theatre reviews for *Cherwell* when Sidney Keyes was its literary editor. There were of course also poetry magazines (for instance *Platitude,* edited by Ian Bancroft, now Lord Bancroft and formerly head of the Civil Service). Other Oxford poets included the then unpublished Alan Ross; and ebullient John Waller, whom I got to know better in London, and whose own magazine, *Kingdom Come,* was one of those that survived the war.

Blackwells had published annually a selection of verse from Oxford. Paper shortages meant they could not do this in wartime. So Sidney Keyes and Michael Meyer asked T. S. Eliot. He referred them to Herbert Read. Thus it came about that Read's firm, Routledge, published *Eight Oxford Poets.*

This book included verse by Keith Douglas, whom I never met; but who was World War II's finest poet. Others in this anthology were: Gordon Swaine; Alan Shaw, subsequently a canon of Wakefield Cathedral; Roy Porter, who became a professor at Exeter; Drummond Allison; Sidney Keyes; Michael Meyer; and myself.

There existed another set of poets at St. John's, about which we knew little. Kingsley Amis and Philip Larkin were this group's leaders—and I now know that they resented Sidney's influence.

Amis and I never met at Oxford. Larkin I knew: we seemed to get on well. Sidney had published him in *Cherwell.* But Sidney and Michael

Meyer, after careful thought, excluded Larkin's verse from *Eight Oxford Poets*—for which Larkin bore a grudge against Sidney, vilifying him whenever he could. In the 1950s, at Leeds, I was shaken by Larkin's hostile review in a student periodical, *Poetry & Audience,* of one of my own books. I had actually recommended him for the job, which he should have had the tact to refuse.

Sidney Keyes was killed in North Africa in 1943, Drummond Allison in Italy the same year. On a last visit, Sidney went back to Oxford, Tonbridge (his school) and London. He showed me his long poem "The Wilderness." In this semi-allegory, the poet traverses a desert of red rock. Sidney knew he'd be posted to North Africa; but that does not make this a war poem. Sidney was a symbolist, influenced at this time by Maud Bodkin's Jungian *Archetypal Patterns in Poetry.* The "wilderness" was Sidney Keyes's "waste land."

I obtained first-class honours in English in 1942—and for a while went off English, turning instead to European literature. In an anthology of Italian verse I found Leopardi's "The Chorus of the Dead." This made me want to read more of Leopardi's work. I also read Mallarmé in Roger Fry's edition and studied the French symbolists who had mattered so much to Sidney Keyes.

I made new friends in Merton College: Ronald Bright, later Father Laurence Bright O.P., and William Bell. These mainly Anglo-Catholic friends encouraged me to resume church-going—at St. Paul's, Walton Street: now a wine-bar—and so I slowly journeyed back to faith.

I also began in my fourth year to catch up with how I should have behaved in my first year. My thesis on the eighteenth-century poet James Thomson's philosophical background increasingly couldn't compete with my new Bohemian foreground.

It was, however, in my fourth year that I heard Charles Williams lecture on *The Prelude.* I will not forget his account of Wordsworth's dream of the Arab with the stone and the shell (which represent mathematics and poetry) and of "the romantic experience."

I also heard Williams chant parts of *Taliessin through Logres* and what would later be published as *The Region of the Summer Stars.* His southeastern accent was somewhat harsh. He recited these Arthurian poems quasi-liturgically and memorably.

Ian Davie, another friend of mine, arranged for him to read jointly with me. I seized my chance to sound Williams out on Milton. By putting Leavis's case that Milton is too sonorous, I elicited this splendid defence: "Sat'st dove-like brooding on the vast abyss," he quoted, "And mad'st it pregnant." It was simply not possible to shout these lines. Precisely the clotted consonants enforced our sense of awestruck mystery.

More even than Milton, Wordsworth or Shakespeare, Charles Williams revered Dante. Drummond had presented me with Williams's *Religion and Love in Dante;* but my true discovery of that poet came courtesy of Sidney's Roman Catholic aunt, Phyllis Keyes. She gave me *The Figure of Beatrice,* revealing new landscapes of art and of faith.

Routledge published my first volume, *Wounded Thammuz,* during my fourth year. Long and tripartite, the poem envisions death and resurrection as an archetypal pattern repeated in Thammuz-Adonis and Christ. My postgraduate work, however, did not prosper. At the end of my fourth year, I left Oxford.

Wounded Thammuz was produced on radio by Edward Sackville-West; and Routledge followed it up a year later with my second book of verse, *Beauty and the Beast.* I posted a copy to Charles Williams. He replied appreciatively, asking me to contact him when I next visited Oxford.

I did so with pleasure; and we had a long, in-depth conversation. He cast doubt on Herbert Read's psychoanalytical study of Wordsworth and Shelley. We agreed in holding Coventry Patmore and Lascelles Abercrombie in high esteem. I then expressed a preference for Christina Rossetti over Mrs. Browning; his was the opposite choice. We parted on excellent terms. When I next came to Oxford, it was to the news that he'd died the day before.

I worked on verse- and prose-elegies for Sidney: "The Divided Ways" and my critical book *The Darkling Plain.*

The second task I set myself in 1945 was a Leopardi translation, published by John Lehmann in 1946 and by the OUP twenty years later. To study Leopardi was to study a man in pain. Having discarded Christianity as a teenager, I was now starting a slow return journey. But this pilgrimage required me to identify with Leopardi's despair. I came finally to believe that

God accommodates despair; but my despair in New Milton could not accommodate God. Now as then my dog, Scepticism, guards my house of Faith against the squatter, Escapism.

Escape from New Milton came in the form of a job as an English teacher at a private school in Hampstead. Percival Coke, whom I was replacing, found a room for me in his West Hampstead lodgings. My time as a teacher was short. It is difficult to discipline children if you have not yet overcome your own problems. Once I read to a class this stanza from "The Ancient Mariner":

> O Wedding-Guest! this soul hath been
> Alone on a wide, wide sea:
> So lonely 'twas, that God himself
> Scarce seemed there to be.

—it was all I could do not to break down, sobbing, in front of them.

Shortly after France was freed in 1944, I was invited to William Empson's house to participate in a poetry reading. This was in honour of Pierre Emmanuel, and the company was very distinguished. I shall never forget hearing, for the first time, T. S. Eliot reading:

> . . . As we grow older
> The world becomes stranger, the pattern
>   more complicated
> Of dead and living . . .

The chief location for London verse-recitals in the '40s and '50s was the Ethical Church in Queensway (now the Catholic church of Our Lady, Queen of Angels). I read there often, as did George Barker, Dylan Thomas and Maurice Carpenter. Later the church was sold, and the circle moved to Prince of Wales Terrace on the other side of the park, continuing there until the '60s, when its original organizer, Alec Craig, died.

The most popular of many poetry magazines, from the war years on, were Tambimuttu's *Poetry London* and Charles Wrey Gardiner's *Poetry Quarterly.* "Tambi" published volumes of verse by David Gascoyne, W. S. Graham, Charles Williams and David Wright. In 1948 he brought out a festschrift for T. S. Eliot, to which I contributed. Charles Wrey Gardiner was a poet who also published a series of pocket selections for which I compiled selections of Swift, Shelley and Tennyson.

My next job was with Hutchinson, the publishers, in their encyclopaedia department. My interest in biology meant I at first specialized in foods, flora, fauna and ornithology. I went on to cover English verse and prose, divinity and music. We were researching "G" when I left—my last entry was about Glück.

I began to achieve a literary reputation, and hoped I could earn my living as a critic. John Lehmann's *New Writing*, Lady Rhondda's *Time & Tide* and the *New English Weekly* published reviews by me. The *New English Weekly* was A. R. Orage's creation, but the editor was now Philip Mairet. Its philosophy was Anglo-Catholic. Eliot's second, third and fourth *Quartets* were first published there. I also reviewed for the *New English Review,* thanks to Hugh Kingsmill, who was the literary editor. His friends included Denis Saurat, who believed creation began when Jesus was born. Time, he thought, had flowed both backwards and forwards ever since.

While I was still at Oxford, a youth called Tony Brown was despatched by John Lehmann, then in Cambridge, to negotiate the setting-up of a journal which should reflect the new poetic talent of both universities. "Z" was the result; but it was uninfluential and only published once.

It was Tony Brown, then living in Percy Street, who introduced me to the pub and club society of Soho and Fitzrovia. By the time the war was over, David Wright, then on the *Sunday Times,* and I regularly frequented the area where three boroughs met.

From a literary perspective, the most significant pub in the area was the Wheatsheaf in Rathbone Place. Julian Maclaren-Ross loomed large there, playing a game called "Spoof." Nearer Charing Cross Road, the Pillars of Hercules had been one of the haunts of Francis Thompson. He slept in the crypt of St. Martin-in-the-Fields until rescued from this sad way of life by the editors of *Merry England.*

The creative people who met in Soho organized themselves into a sort of community, with unwritten rules and a pecking-order. When the pubs were shut, we would go to a club—the Gargoyle or the cheaper Mandrake—and drink on till midnight. The Mandrake's owner was Boris Watson, a Russian whose real name was Protopopoff, and whose father had been Interior Minister under the last Tsar. Being Russian, Watson played chess. Many strong players (e.g. the cartoonist Vicky) haunted the club's

back room. But it was really just a late-night bar.

Nina Hamnett was royalty in Soho. You bought her a gin. You were amply rewarded with story and song. For instance:

> Every Saturday afternoon we tries to
>   drown our sorrers.
> We always goes to the waxwork shows to
>   see the Chamber of Horrors.
> There's a beautiful statue of mother
>   there, what gives us pleasure, rather,
> With the same old smile on her dear
>   old dial
> As the night she strangled father.

Nina introduced me to Liam O'Flaherty, who asked me who and what I was?—"A poet."—In his day, he said, young men said they wrote "verse." I took his point.

Some Soho denizens could not afford alcohol. Their scene was a Greek restaurant: Café Alix. Bernard Kops the playwright was one of these.

But of those at home in Soho, the most remarkable were poets. In Dylan Thomas, Welsh eloquence was more apparent than a Welsh accent, which speech-training had all but erased. He showed off a bit, surrounding himself with inferiors for that purpose. I recall an evening in the Wheatsheaf: Dylan read from work then in progress, later entitled *Under Milk Wood.*

I first heard Dylan read at the Ethical Church; here I first also heard George Barker. But George and I truly became friends in the Wheatsheaf on V-J night. Japan's entry into the war had left George and his wife Jessica stranded in America, where Elizabeth Smart helped them.

George Barker was in my view the best poet of his generation. His first book, *Thirty Preliminary Poems* (1933) preceded *Eighteen Poems* (1934)—Dylan Thomas's first book, both published by David Archer. Both their styles are distinctive and ornate. Melchiori's critique *The Tightrope Walkers* labels Thomas a "Mannerist." Dylan became the cult figure, but Yeats and Eliot held George Barker's verse in higher esteem—George was the youngest poet in Yeats's *Oxford Book of Modern Verse,* and Eliot preferred the Catholic Barker to the Nonconformist Thomas.

Barker always retained a certain loyalty to the faith of his fathers; and it is his strong sense of sin, allied to a modern view of sex, which makes his verse unique.

In Cornwall and elsewhere, George was my mentor. I showed him my work, which he was always willing to read. Some would not be—I'm happy to do so face-to-face, but I can't bear receiving poems in the post.

People sometimes view George Barker as lazy and narcissistic. This is far from true. His standards were high: his criticism could devastate.

The True Confession of George Barker is probably his masterpiece. Faber editors were so appalled by the poem's sexual content that they declined to include it in all but his last *Collected Poems*. Jack Lindsay first published it in 1950; then David Archer in 1955. George had completed his *Confession* in 1948; he said, on his thirty-fifth birthday. In this he was following Dante—beginning his major work "nel mezzo del cammin," in the middle of the way. I vividly recall George 'phoning me and inviting me round. I was the first to hear George Barker's *Confession*.

Among my contemporaries, W. S. Graham regularly frequented Soho. Our relations were fairly strained, despite goodwill on both sides. He could be very charming; he was confused and aggressive when drunk. But I liked Sydney, and I admire his beautiful poetry.

Paul Potts was in Soho. He lived in Hampstead, so we often went home together. I learned much from our conversations. Paul stood for English and American populist traditions.

I was not on such close terms with Soho's painters. Most famous amongst these were Robert Colquhoun and Robert MacBryde. They drank during the '40s also in the Old Swan, formerly at the top of Kensington Church Street. Inside were two mirrors, featuring white swans with black and yellow beaks, which you can see in Lambert and Marks's *English Popular and Traditional Art*. Colquhoun was the more talented, MacBryde the more charming of the two.

Soho was a Bohemia for the 1940s on a par with Montmartre in the 1840s—and it endured for just one generation. The sole relic now is the Coach and Horses, made artificially famous by Jeffrey Bernàrd.

By the end of the forties I had left West Hampstead for unfurnished rooms in John Waller's Kensington house. Here I first learned to cook. Now that I am completely blind and rely on the help of friends, it is a joy to be able to offer such friends a meal.

Kensington had literary pubs. Muriel Spark and Roy Campbell drank in them, Roy's local was the Catherine Wheel in Church Street. The "fascist bully" image bears no relation to the companionable Roy I knew. It is true that his wife, Mary, and he were pro-Franco (and "Flowering Rifle" is a silly pro-Franco poem) but it's equally true that he never fought in Spain, loath as he may have been to deny rumours that he had.

In the early 1950s, Roy Campbell cast himself as Saint George versus Geoffrey Grigson, the "dragon" who had breathed critical "fire" all over Edith Sitwell. Roy met Geoffrey in Regent Street and challenged him. Grigson fled into an arcade, becoming incontinent as he did so.

Roy Campbell sometimes behaved disgracefully; but there was no real vindictiveness about him. When, in 1957, he died in a car crash in Portugal, I wrote to Mary. She replied that she had received condolences from many countries—". . . but you are one of the very few English poets who wrote."

It was in my time at Kensington that Muriel Spark edited *The Poetry Review* for the Poetry Society. She has related in her own memoirs the saga of her conflict with the ancient regime of that institution—in particular, the confused and elderly Marie Stopes and the lugubrious and elderly Lord Alfred Douglas.

I still frequented the Soho pubs. In the Wheatsheaf I met Peter Avery, with whom I translated first Hafiz and later the *Rubaiyat of Omar Khayyam*, using the same (essentially Poundian) combination of free verse and a focus upon images.

It was George Every, then a lay brother of the Anglican Society of the Sacred Mission but now a Roman Catholic, who introduced me to Patrick McLaughlin, the vicar of St. Anne's, Soho. I started to attend services regularly. Consequently I met Dorothy Sayers while she was translating Dante. Every also introduced me to Eliot. We were invited to dinner at the great poet's club.

Faber was about to publish *The White Goddess*. Eliot called it Graves's *Golden Bough* and said I should review it—I soon did. Some years later, Eliot asked me to edit *The Faber Book of Twentieth-Century Verse*. I collaborated with David Wright on this. The book has gone into many editions.

Patrick McLaughlin, his sister Oonagh and I toured Provence in the early 1950s. The intensely colourful landscape amazed me. It was like being in a painting by Van Gogh. Once we traversed the Camargue wasteland in order to visit the shrine of Les Saintes-Maries-de-la-Mer. I was seeing the Mediterranean for the first time—and sensing, at the gypsy shrine in the crypt, an occult power.

My attempts to earn a living by criticism and reviewing were proving vain. I was to be rescued from a desperate financial situation by being offered the Gregory Fellowship of Poetry at Leeds University. Eliot and Herbert Read were my patrons in this—as was Bonamy Dobrée, then the Professor of English at Leeds. My duties were to write, and to encourage students to read and write verse. Apart from Professor Dobrée, my best friends at Leeds were Arthur Creedy, also a lecturer in the English department, and Kenneth Severs, the head of the Leeds BBC.

I had already met John Betjeman when he was literary editor at *Time & Tide.* After a broadcast for the BBC Northern Service, he and I spent an evening at the Leeds City Varieties. "What a nice girl," Betjeman enthused over an exotic puppeteer, "A canon's daughter, wouldn't you say?" But on the whole I was unhappy at Leeds. The university was unpopular with the locals: it was wise not to be seen carrying books.

Within the English department, my contacts proved more auspicious. I saw G. Wilson Knight's production of *Othello;* years later, he commented at helpful length on my play *Helen in Egypt* from a producer's point of view. While I was still at Leeds, a vacancy for a lecturer arose. I warmly recommended Geoffrey Hill, who got the job and became a close friend. In my second year at Leeds, I shared a house at Armley with the painter Tom Watt. His portrait of me hangs in the English department to this day.

Bonamy Dobrée's chance meeting in the Athenaeum with a mediaeval historian, who had just returned from a visiting professorship in Alexandria, led to my next job as a visiting professor of English at the same university. The boat had no sooner docked than two colleagues came aboard to welcome me: Mustapha Badawi, a Shakespearean scholar, and Mahmoud Manzalaoui, who specialized in Late Mediaeval and Renaissance literature (as befitted a former pupil of C. S. Lewis). I would be free to specialize in the Augustans, with whom I felt most at home.

My students were a lively lot and did well, considering I taught in English. Hardy's novels strongly appealed to them. Like Wessex, Egypt was moving from ancient rural to modern urban values. To Samuel Johnson's *Rasselas,* which is set in Egypt, they equally responded.

They evinced a natural talent for acting, and I directed Thomas Heywood's play *A Woman Killed with Kindness.* This play challenges the aristocratic and Renaissance code of honour and revenge. Mr. Frankford, an English gentleman, detects his wife Nan in the act of adultery. He refrains from killing her and exiles her to a country mansion which he owns, forgiving her on her deathbed. The girl-student playing Nan would not be named in the programme.

I taught postgraduate students too, one of whom had appeared as an interned student in D. J. Enright's novel *Academic Year.* Also among my graduates were Fuad and Shafik Megally. Shafik went on, at my prompting, to do a Ph.D. on Landor. These two brothers now live in Belgium and England respectively and later on I was invited to the consecration of the Coptic Church in Kensington, on which occasion I was presented to the Patriarch.

My companion Jim and I had hardly arrived in Alexandria, when a youth called Abdul Latif Qassar ("Cut-throat") appointed himself our Mr. Fixit. He was very useful, though he was also a police spy. His English was learned from newspaper headlines and film subtitles. "No cinemascope this" meant "Don't make what you're doing too obvious." He was a night creature, and so "You're looking very cheerful today" got translated into "You very Charlie Chaplin tonight."

I saw something of the Egyptian countryside and I saw the Buff-Backed Heron, or Cattle Egret—a lovely bird like a lily with wings. Linnaeus gave it the name of Ardea Ibis, supposing it to be the sacred ibis of the ancient Egyptians. The ibis is no longer found in Egypt and its true identity was only established when Napoleon's archaeologists discovered mummified bodies of this sacred bird.

On another occasion I heard a gobbling noise in a field. My Egyptian friends said this was a "field-chicken." Years later I identified it from a radio recording as a Little Bustard.

In October 1956, Israel, Britain and France attacked Egypt. I had just read my class the line from *Lycidas*—"Look homeward, Angel, now, and melt with ruth . . ."—when someone came in and said we were at war. My students thought I would be shot.

But in fact Jim and I were summoned to the town hall along with other British and French residents and told to leave Egypt within ten days or else be interned. But when the officials learned that the university still required my services, and that I needed Jim as my assistant, this order was rescinded.

The university remained closed until March 1957, but I then resumed my duties there and continued into the following year. Officially we were under house arrest, but were largely free to come and go as we liked—after all Abdul was telling the police everything he found out about us.

I received great loyalty and support from my academic colleagues and also from my students and indeed from the ordinary Egyptian shopkeepers and working people we had dealings with. But it was a worrying time; one never knew when the authorities' attitude might change or when there might be an outbreak of murderous mob violence as there had been some years previously at the time of Nasser's revolution.

At this time I wrote *Helen in Egypt,* a verse-drama, which was performed by Manzalaoui's friends in a flat. I played the Pharoah. It has only been performed once since: in 1988 at Westminster by the Roman Court Theatre Company.

In 1955 I had visited America as a delegate to Henry Kissinger's Harvard Summer School. A year or so later I was offered another visiting professorship this time at the University of Michigan, Ann Arbor. I was to initiate freshmen; go on to tutor them in Wordsworth; and I would lecture to the fourth year on Eliot, Joyce and Graves.

The poet X. J. Kennedy was my valued assistant. My colleagues and friends included Donald Hall, Geoffrey Hill, Dorothy Donnelly and Prince Ostrovsky. (As a young guardsman, Ostrovsky had witnessed the Russian Revolution.)

My first semester successfully concluded, I was offered a second. In between the two, I visited Mexico with Kenneth Leisenring, a mathematician and another Ann Arbor friend. We examined ancient sites together. Teotihuacán impressed us most. This was the shrine of the Toltecs, precursors of the Aztecs, and was made up of two pyramids (for sun and moon) and a vast temple devoted to Quetzalcoatl.

This consisted of an enclosed "temenos." At the back was a concealed inner sanctum.

Here were two enormous carved serpents' heads: gifts were placed in their jaws. Quetzalcoatl is an oddity in the Mexican pantheon: no human sacrifices for him. He is masked. Unlike his worshippers, he is bearded: was he from the Old World?

I returned to Ann Arbor to teach Dryden, Swift and Pope, and to expound the old tradition of eighteenth-century Toryism. Courtesy of John Van Domelen, I gave a reading at Calvin College, Grand Rapids. I also spent a couple of days in New York with John Guenther, the biographer of Sidney Keyes. He lived on Long Island Sound in Great Gatsby country.

Exposure to ultraviolet light in Mexico may have been the reason that, when I returned to London in 1961, I experienced alarming problems with my one good eye.

John Wain set up, in 1962, a week-long poetry festival at the Mermaid Theatre. The climax was a gala night on the Saturday: Sir Ralph Richardson, Dame Flora Robson, William Empson and Nevill Coghill all took part. I read my own poems, Tennyson's "Edward Grey" and Pope's "A Hymn Written in Windsor Forest." Sir Ralph very kindly complimented me on my reading.

At this time I lived in a basement flat at Lancaster Gate. I still drank in Soho, but the place was becoming less interesting and exciting. However, I did meet Patrick Kavanagh, Brendan Behan and Malcolm Williamson (now Sir Malcolm) then. Another friend was Frank Norman, famous for his prison memoirs, *Bang to Rights.*

At the Highlander in Dean Street I first met Eddie Linden. In his and Sebastian Barker's account of his life, *Who Is Eddie Linden?,* Eddie recounts how he came from a Lanarkshire mining family, which rejected him, bequeathing him a piecemeal education and reading problems. In spite of this, he set up a poetry magazine. That's how *Aquarius* began. I had proposed *Python* for the title. Stevie Smith disagreed with me; and another friend of Eddie's suggested *Aquarius,* one of the sixties' buzz-words.

Brian Higgins, also, drank in Soho at this time. Of Irish descent, he came from Hull. David Wright and Patrick Swift published him in *X* magazine. Higgins's long poem "The North" includes a satirical dig at Larkin. When I knew Higgins, he just lingered hopefully at the bar, reduced to finishing up heel taps if no one had bought him a drink when time was called.

By good fortune I bumped into my old friend Charles Wrey Gardiner, who said I could rent two rooms in his house at Sutherland Place, off Westbourne Grove. Of other tenants, the most amusing was John Gawsworth, whose real name was Terence Fytton Armstrong, and who claimed the title The King of Ridonda.

Early on in the 1960s I was still desperate for secure employment. For a short while I worked in Battersea, where I taught speech-training. I told my students they should not be ashamed of the way they already spoke. After this, chance landed me a job as English lecturer at the College of St. Mark and St. John, a teachers' training college in Chelsea. Initially I was taken on for just one term; but I stayed there till 1972, when the college moved to Plymouth.

Before beginning at Chelsea I went to Northern Nigeria as an external examiner at the university colleges of Zaria and Kano. My old Leeds friend, Arthur Creedy, was the professor at Kano. His colleagues included the poets Tony Harrison and James Simmons. My plane touched down in Nigeria just after dawn. I heard the hooting of hornbills as they flopped about overhead.

On a second visit a year later to Kano, the Muslim Hausa tribe had begun to massacre the mainly Christian Ibos. A colleague showed me the whole city from an ancient hill. Then he took me through, first, the old Muslim quarter; second, a devastated, corpse-strewn area; then finally to the flashily modern zone of the Ibo, "the Irish of Africa." No wonder they clashed. All night I heard a Tuareg watchman play repeatedly the same phrase upon his flute.

The head of English at St. Mark and St. John was the talented but tormented Thomas Blackburn. He had succeeded me as Gregory Fellow at Leeds, and was himself succeeded at Chelsea by Ronald Banks. Peter Dickinson the composer was in the Music department there. He and I were to have collaborated on an opera for children called *The Unicorns.* Alas, only two songs emerged, which later Elisabeth Söderström recorded.

My forties coincided with the "swinging" sixties, when youngsters rejected elders, Beatles music polluted the U.K., and well-intentioned idiots resurrected Marxist ideology. This was not an easy time for me.

In 1971 John Jones, who had been one of my Merton friends during my Oxford days, invited me to teach part-time at that college, where he was now Reader in English. The guest room I occupied for this purpose had once been used by Andrew Lang, an early influence on me. So, after thirty-five years, I had found my way slowly back to Oxford.

While still in Charles Wrey Gardiner's house, I visited Carol Whiteside of an evening, so that she might type out my long poem *Artorius* to my dictation. The Matter of Britain had long haunted me, and I drew upon Gibbon, Geoffrey of Monmouth and the *Mabinogion* to this end.

I wished above all to avoid writing a novel in verse. So I gave *Artorius* a cyclical structure and symbolic superstructure. The first I based on the Zodiac; the second involved the nine Muses, the twelve Olympian gods and Hercules' twelve labours. *Artorius,* which took over six months to complete, was well received. I believe it earned me the Queen's Gold Medal.

I was presented to Her Majesty by John Betjeman, then the Poet Laureate. The Queen asked me how I wrote poems, but we rapidly passed to more general topics. I said I had stayed in Egypt throughout the Suez crisis because that was the best way then to serve my country. She replied: "I am sure that was so." Some years later I received the OBE (Most Excellent Order of the British Empire). The Queen asked me if I still wrote poetry. I said, "It becomes an ingrained habit, Ma'am." She smiled, I am told.

In 1978 I finally went completely blind, just before my sixtieth birthday. My right eye had been removed in 1956. When, twenty-two years on, the left eye went, it transpired I had been blind for some while. I was not conscious of this. My imagination had been creating what it knew I should see. If, waiting on a kerb, I heard the bus coming, I would "see" it too.

Shortly before my operation, I revisited America with my close friend Guthrie MacKie. We followed up a week in New York with Robin Prising and Willy Coakly with a return trip to Ann Arbor. Here, despite great pain in my diseased eye, I lectured on "Five Poets, Five Cities"—Joyce's Dublin, Eliot's London, Hart Crane's New York, Cavafy's Alexandria and Apollinaire's Paris. These were all poets I had admired and cities I had known.

I have been lucky in having had to adjust to blindness over the longer term. It must be devastating for those who suddenly lose their sight. I do not experience, either, "total eclipse." Before my left eye there seems to me continuously to hover rectangular shapes inside a triangular frame like a shield. These change from faint yellow through orange to red, and from green to blue. Tiredness or hunger makes them brighter. They are neither dreams nor symbols. This is to do with physiology, not psychology. In front of these shapes move a mass of tiny dots, which I already experienced when sighted and a child. Fatigue or stress brought them on.

To lose one's sight is traditionally deemed a sign of divine wrath. Divine mercy, it's believed, makes the other senses more acute to compensate; but in fact one simply pays more attention to those senses. Walking down Artesian Road in the spring, I hear more than six species of birds—ignored, I suspect, by my sighted neighbours.

I am now approaching my seventy-sixth birthday. It is not uncommon these days for people to pass their hundredth birthdays. My last twenty-five years have been my happiest, because I no longer have to struggle to see. Death is not a problem for me; death-agony or senility obviously would be. And beyond death?

One is saddened by the loss of friends. Among my Oxford contemporaries the poets Sidney Keyes and Drummond Allison were killed in the war, and William Bell died in a mountaineering accident shortly afterwards. And tragic loss of friends continues to dog me.

There was Douglas MacKay, a companion of my thirties, a North American lost in the wildernesses of London and Soho; and, in my fifties, Charles Harwood, whose potentially brilliant mind could never find its full scope, due to an unfortunate family background and childhood illness. Both of these took their own lives, though in the case of Douglas the evidence was inconclusive.

Then there was Jim, who stood by me loyally in Alexandria when we were both under a certain amount of danger and threat, but who turned out later to be a twister and a thief. Then there was the brilliantly gifted young poet Adam Johnson, who died in 1993 shortly after his twenty-eighth birthday of an AIDS-related disease.

Other friends remain and I go on—I hope to see the third millennium.

BIBLIOGRAPHY

Poetry:

Wounded Thammuz, Routledge, 1942.

Beauty and the Beast, Routledge, 1943.

The Divided Ways, Routledge, 1946.

The Charity of the Stars, Sloane, 1949.

The Swarming of the Bees, Eyre & Spottiswoode, 1950.

A Charm against the Toothache, Methuen, 1954.

The Triumph of the Muse and Other Poems, Oxford University Press, 1958.

The Blue-Fly in His Head, Oxford University Press, 1962.

Selected Poems, Oxford University Press, 1965.

Satires and Epigrams, Turret (London), 1968.

Thomas Blackburn and John Heath-Stubbs, Longman, 1969.

Artorius, Book I, Burning Deck (Providence, Rhode Island), 1970, Enitharmon (London), 1973.

(With Stephen Spender and F. T. Prince) *Penguin Modern Poets 20,* Penguin, 1971.

Four Poems in Measure, Helikon (New York), 1973.

The Twelve Labours of Hercules, Arion (San Francisco), 1974.

A Parliament of Birds (for children), Chatto & Windus, 1975.

The Watchman's Flute, Carcanet New Press (Manchester), 1978.

The Mouse, the Bird, and the Sausage, Ceolfrith (Sunderland), 1978.

Birds Reconvened, Enitharmon, 1980.

Buzz Buzz: Ten Insect Poems, Gruffyground, 1981.

This Is Your Poem, Pisces (London), 1981.

Naming the Beasts, Carcanet New Press, 1982.

New Poems, Other Branch Readings (Leamington Spa), 1983.

Five Poems from the South, Yellowsands Press (Isle of Wight), 1984.

The Immolation of Aleph, Carcanet, 1985.

Cats' Parnassus, Hearing Eye (London), 1987.

Time Pieces, Hearing Eye, 1988.

Collected Poems 1943–1987, Carcanet, 1988.

A Partridge in a Pear Tree: Poems for the Twelve Days of Christmas, Hearing Eye, 1988.

A Ninefold of Charms, Hearing Eye, 1989.

The Game of Love and Death, Enitharmon, 1990.

The Parson's Cat, illustrated by Emily Johns, Hearing Eye, 1993.

Sweetapple Earth, Carcanet, 1993.

Chimeras, Hearing Eye, 1994.

Translator:

Poems from Giacomo Leopardi, Lehmann, 1946.

Aphrodite's Garland, Latin (St. Ives), 1952.

(With Peter Avery) *Thirty Poems of Hafiz of Shiraz,* Murray (London), 1952.

(With Iris Origo) Giacomo Leopardi, *Selected Poetry and Prose,* Oxford University Press, 1966, New American Library, 1967.

Alfred de Vigny, *The Horn/Le Cor,* Keepsake (Richmond, Surrey), 1969.

(With Shafik Megally) *Dust and Carnations: Traditional Funeral Chants and Wedding Songs from Egypt,* TR Press (London), 1977.

(With Carol Whiteside) *Anyte,* Greville (Warwick), 1979.

(With Peter Avery) *The Rubaiyat of Omar Khayyam,* Allen Lane (London), 1979.

Criticism:

The Darkling Plain (study of Victorian romantic poetry), Eyre & Spottiswoode, 1950, Folcroft Press, 1970.

Editor:

(With David Wright) *The Forsaken Garden: An Anthology of Poetry 1824–1909,* Lehmann, 1950.

William Bell, *Mountains beneath the Horizon,* Faber, 1950.

(With David Wright) *The Faber Book of Twentieth Century Verse: An Anthology of Verse in Britain 1900–1950,* Faber, 1953, revised, 1965, 1975.

Images of Tomorrow: An Anthology of Recent Poetry, SCM Press (London), 1953.

Selected Poems of Alexander Pope, Heinemann, 1964, Barnes & Noble, 1966.

(With Martin Green) *Homage to George Barker on His Sixtieth Birthday,* Brian & O'Keeffe (London), 1973.

Thomas Gray, *Selected Poems,* Carcanet, 1981.

(With Phillips Salman) *Poems of Science,* Penguin, 1984.

Other:

Charles Williams, Longman, 1955.

Helen in Egypt and Other Plays, Oxford University Press, 1958.

(Contributor) Bruce Alvin King, editor, *Dryden's Mind and Art,* Oliver & Boyd (Edinburgh), 1969.

The Ode, Oxford University Press, 1969.

The Pastoral, Oxford University Press, 1969.

The Verse Satire, Oxford University Press, 1969.

Hindsights: An Autobiography, Hodder (London), 1993.

Contributor to numerous journals, including *New English Review, New Republic, Poetry London, Poetry Quarterly,* and *Times Literary Supplement.* The author's manuscripts are collected at the University of Texas, Austin, and the State University of New York, Buffalo.

Larry Heinemann

1944-

Larry and Edie with Pham Van Hang and his wife in Van Hang's sculpture garden, Da Nang, 1992

I was born and raised in Chicago, the second of four sons, and have lived here all my life. As a matter of fact, my wife and I own a house about two miles from the hospital where I was born; I suppose that makes me what you might call a homeboy.

My family first lived in a two-flat on North Claremont in the Germantown neighborhood—Lincoln, Lawrence, and Western—near the Ravenswood elevated line, in Chicago, called the "el." My brothers and I were told always to be quiet in our second floor apartment, because the old German couple downstairs complained. I clearly recall at night hearing the big old lumbering St. Louis "el" cars screech-

ing as they rounded a very sharp curve into the Western Avenue station. There were still streetcars on Western Avenue; Red Rockets, they were called, and they *were* fast.

In 1949 we moved into one of the first postwar, tract house subdivisions in the small farming community of north-suburban Northbrook. The day we moved into our little house, the first thing I did was jump up and down, flat-footed, on the concrete slab floor, which of course stung my feet and legs, to prove that I would never again tiptoe. For some years after the street was still dirt with a duckboard sidewalk.

At age three years old, "mounted on a pony named Snuffy"

All the years of my childhood my brothers and I and the neighbor boys played in the houses being built around us, in the grown-over orchard and abandoned nursery beyond the subdivision, and the Techny farm pastures and dairy barns beyond that—Techny, a hamlet owned by the Catholic Church; The Divine Word missionary retreat, a school, a retirement home, and a farm (I well recall hearing cowbells in the morning when the cows were turned out to pasture after milking). There were increasingly elaborate forts and dugouts, far ranging war games, hide-and-seek, and cowboys and Indians. In the winter there was ice skating. Northbrook had two huge outdoor rinks, one several acres in size. The town was serious about speed skating and in the 1950s and 1960s sent kids named Rudolph, Blatchford, and Henning to the Olympics. It was common to take your skates to school, and hang out at the rink until your mother phoned the knocked-together warming house for the caretaker to call over the public address system (which broadcast music otherwise) that you were wanted home.

My mother, Dorothy (the sixth of eleven children), came from St. Cloud, Michigan, when she was seventeen to work as an *au pair* for a wealthy Winnetka doctor. Not long after, she met my father; surviving letters written by her from Miami Beach tease him about the good-looking young men on the beach as she minded the children.

My mother's father was a "retired farmer" and lived with us on and off for ten years. The Dentons were cousin to Abraham Lincoln—such was the family story—and in an odd way my grandfather resembled him; the melancholy eyes; the thin, weary face. He had stunning blue eyes and snow-white hair, but didn't have a tooth in his head and only one arm. He lost the arm in a strip-mining cave-in shortly after he was married and buried it under the farmyard apple tree. My grandparents' wedding picture show him seated and my grandmother standing beside him; the fashion of the time to show off the bride's dress. What is most odd about the picture is that my grandfather has both of his hands settled formally in his lap. I always thought it remarkable that a man could work a farm and raise eleven kids with only one arm. He had the odd habit of tucking his empty shirt or coat sleeve into his breast pocket. That stump was a source of endless fascination. It was both compelling and queer to see him naked to the waist, shaving—that bit arm with the skin folded into itself like wax paper wrapped around a sandwich. He had more than forty grandchildren and we all thought him wonderful. He was gregarious and funny—a storyteller—the embodiment of what Samuel Clemens once described as old enough to remember only those things that never happened. He would sit on the concrete stoop at our back door and tell wonderful stories to us and the neighbor kids gathered around him. The ongoing saga of the Texas cattle ranch that he and Pecos Bill owned; stories of magic horses, sailing ships, and remarkable travels; him gesturing emphatically with his cane and that stump, the empty sleeve with the cuff carefully buttoned jogging in air—stories outrageous in their plausibility, just the sort of thing kids thrive on. It never occurred to me until the year he died that this wonderful nonsense was helped along with what he called "Kentucky windage"; he was always about half lit. He was a wonderful old man, and I expect I got my love of story from him.

I have two strong memories of him.

One was his daily ritual of reading the newspapers. He read the *Chicago Tribune*, the *Detroit Free Press*, and the *St. Louis Post-Dispatch*. He would take a kitchen chair into the backyard, in the middle of the truck garden he had created and tended. Then he'd come back to the house for the papers. He'd sit with his back to the house, stick that bit of stump straight out from his shoulder, hang his cane on it, and read through the papers, discarding the sections into the squash vines around his chair. The cane would swing back and forth like a pendulum as he struggled with the pages. Sometimes he'd laugh right out loud. Sometimes he'd launch into the most wonderful, lengthy and thorough curses—oaths, he called them; he could swear like a sailor.

My other memory of him was that he was a barfly. After dinner he would dress in trousers, collarless shirt (Northbrook still half a farm town and the local haberdasher still carried such things), gray suspenders, straw fedora and cane, then walk up to the Cypress Inn saloon and be funny for drinks. In the morning we'd come downstairs and grandfather would be asleep on the couch in his clothes. It didn't click until years later that he'd arrive home drunk, and the couch was as far into the house as he could get.

My father, John, was born and raised in Evanston, the suburb just north of Chicago, the eldest son of a LaSalle Street lawyer.

My father's family came from Germany in the 1870s after a family dispute when my grandfather was two. The story goes that my great-grandfather's family were bankers, but that my great-grandfather was more interested in making beer; his brewery burned down and he tried to borrow money to rebuild, but the family refused; so he borrowed money from a family friend, brought his wife and children to the United States, and changed his name to Heinemann out of respect for his benefactor. He arrived in Chicago and bought a grocery store and small hotel across the street from what is now the Merchandise Mart (the bedrock of the Kennedy family fortune; bought for taxes in 1936—at that time the largest commercial building in the world). My grandfather went to the University of Michigan Law School (Class of '03) and practiced law for better than fifty years—outlived three sets of partners, he liked to brag. And even though his specialty

was real estate he died virtually broke—unusual for a lawyer who did his business on LaSalle Street, I'd say. My grandparents were not warm people; I cannot recall ever seeing them exchange an embrace or other displays of affection—even at Christmas when all the family would gather.

I recall my grandfather sitting in his easy chair with cigar ashes sprinkled down his shirt and vest, next to a pedestal ashtray with a large marble knob in the middle. My grandmother strongly disapproved of cigar smoking—and drinking, too, for that matter. Every time we visited I would walk up to him in his chair, he'd look at me critically, shake my hand, and say, "How's your mathematics?" I did poorly in school and math was the worst, and I sharply felt his disappointment. Every couple years he would take me to his tailors and have me fitted for a suit, always one of those three-piece flannel numbers that itched like crazy. The tailor would make a great fuss and I was both pleased and embarrassed by the attention, but wore the suits with great pride.

My father went two years to Grinnell College (I have his footlocker with the sticker), but dropped out. He said that Grandfather wanted him to study law and he didn't. It wasn't until the last year of his life and close to the publication of my first novel that my father told me he had wanted to become a writer, but that he and his father had argued about that, and my grandfather yanked him out of school.

When I was ten years old or so I was invited to spend Saturday afternoons with my great-aunt Harriette, my grandfather's older sister, and these weekly outings lasted for a number of years until she was too old to go out. She was a thin and an elegant old woman and the story went that she'd been married once when she was young, but, as you might expect, she never spoke of it. I would meet her in downtown Evanston for lunch in an elegant tea room near the Orrington Hotel where the waitresses wore tidy black uniforms with petite maid's aprons. After lunch we would sometimes shop and then go to the matinee movies at the Varsity Theater, down the street and around the corner from Northwestern University. Now that I think about it, it amazes me that she had the patience to sit through all those afternoons of westerns and war movies with a theater full of screaming kids, year after year. I was in my middle teens when she died, and hers was the first funeral I was allowed to attend. It may seem odd and something of a waste of time for a kid to spend those years of Saturdays with an old maid aunt, but I remember those times with great warmth. It's hard to say what I learned from her, but she had an elegance and dignity, a sweet nature and beautiful hand-writing, and an old-fashioned, Old World sense of taste.

I suppose we could say that my father was a lifelong, failed businessman. During the war he had a Skelgas franchise, but it went bust before I was born—this at a time when every-body was making money hand over fist. In the 1950s he owned for a time a small commuter bus company—the Deerfield Bus Company. Even-tually that failed, too; an enterprise too many decades ahead of its time. We didn't have a car in those years, so he would drive one of the prewar, stick shift GMCs (called Jimmy's) home and park it in front of the house (be-cause we didn't have a driveway or garage), which mightily irritated the neighbors—white-collar up-and-comers. (Years later, when we boys were teenagers, everyone had a car and parked in the street which positively infuriated the neigh-bors—it *always* looked like a party at our place.) In summer, on weekends, we'd pile into the bus and drive out to one of the Chain-of-Lakes for picnics. It was wonderful fun to have the whole bus to ourselves; my dad was a great one for shortcuts and we were always getting lost, which exasperated my mother to no end.

My father was one of those men who was simply not comfortable in his body; awkward and not athletic at all. Driving a bus was the only work I ever saw him do, and his clothes always smelled of grease and diesel fuel. He seemed never happy, but loved us so much that he worked like a dog at a job he didn't particularly like—he died when he was sixty-two, just as he retired.

I don't know that my mother was ever happy, either. We were four boys in a small house, and I think we were too much for her. There is a photograph of her when we were young, and she looked like those mid-nineteenth-cen-tury portraits of Great Plains pioneer women; thin and wraithlike, perpetually exhausted and practically hopeless. To make extra money she struck on the idea of an agency for baby-sit-ters, which she ran from our dining room table.

(From left) Philip, Santa Claus, Richard, Jim, and Larry: "My brothers and me," Christmas, 1957

It was all phone work, and she was always on the phone matching the baby-sitters (working class women making extra money on the side) with several hundred well-heeled client fami-lies up and down the North Shore; she had practically everything memorized, including phone numbers. Over the years my mother was quite successful and made as much money as my fa-ther.

I grew up in a house where there were no books, and "education" was not a large word. You were expected to get a job, as in many another household that came through the Great Depression. Of the four boys I am the only one to finish college; two of my brothers never did graduate high school.

I started working when I was twelve, cad-dying at a WASP country club nearby. I was skinny, rundown, and nervous (as Grandfather Denton used to say) so for the first couple years could only manage one golf bag. A round of golf paid $3.00; the typical tip was two bits; but I learned early how to suck up to rich people, how to hustle tips, and to literally keep my eye on the ball. I also learned that women (in those days referred to as "the members' wives") were lousy tippers. These women were terrible golfers, too, hacking and duffing their way through all eighteen holes, but owned huge, expensive golf bags (trunks, we called them) packed with every club obtainable and the zippered pockets stuffed with every appurtenance and accoutrement they could get their hands on; by the end of an afternoon it was all I could do to finish the round and get the bag and clubs back to the pro shop. I was one of those kids who always seemed on the caddy master's shit list and so never much got the good golfers and therefore an easy round and decent tip. Golf, the game itself, seemed pointless and dreary, if not downright stupid. But it was the only work kids like me could get; the only money I had in those years—none of us boys got an allowance. Because of the child labor laws, anyone under sixteen had to have a work permit—which none of us did. Every once in a while the woman from the Illinois Department of Labor came out to check. On those mornings, when we arrived at the caddy shack at 6:00 A.M., the caddy master would pass out the Clincher sixteen-inch softballs and a couple bats and tell us underage kids to go to the other side of the golf course and play softball until somebody came to get us. (Sixteen-inch slow-pitch softball is a style of baseball peculiar to Chicago; you don't need a glove to play; columnist Mike Royko once said that only sissies play softball with a glove—and around here it's true.) Caddying, I learned to smoke and swear, play cards, shoot pool, and horse around.

As I said, I was not an especially good student. School was simply not interesting. I'm one of those people who learned to read by moving his lips, and wouldn't be surprised to find out that I had what is nowadays regarded as a learning disability. In high school I never took the hard-core college preparatory courses expected of everyone. But I took mechanical drawing (complicated machine parts) and architectural drawing (designing a house top to bottom) along with English and history because I liked them. I didn't do very well and always wound up with middling grades. The first book I can recall anything from is *Andersonville* by MacKinlay Kantor, the first book I read at least twice. I also recall two of Ole Edvart Rölvaag's historical novels about pioneering in the Old

Northwest Territory and the Great Plains. As far as sports were concerned, in four years I never tried out for a thing—not intramural flag football, softball, nothing; it wasn't that I was unathletic, just not interested.

And becoming a writer never entered my mind.

The one thing that happened in high school that I can look back and declare a "turning point" was a summer trip to Japan. My junior year I was in the Sea Cadets, a sort of paramilitary boys' club run by the Navy League (it was never clear to me what that was). In 1961, there was a spring gathering of the different posts at the Great Lakes Naval Training Center. By some odd distribution of points I "won" a trip, along with about thirty or forty kids from all over the country—mostly California.

It would be the first time in my life that I'd be out of the house; the first time I would see how the other half lived. I was seventeen.

Myself and three other guys from around Chicago took a three-day bus ride to San Francisco—an adventure all by itself; we were definitely on the local. Then it was two weeks on a troopship, taking army replacements for a year's tour in Korea. Those guys were not happy; half the troops sick as dogs before we cast off from the pier; bunks stacked five high; the stainless steel urinal troughs soon clogged with cigarettes and such, and piss sloshing all over everything. Absolutely nothing to do but find a spot on deck and watch the water and the sky; bored to death. It was wonderful. In Japan, the navy put us up in an old wooden barracks at Yokohama Naval Base. We spent two weeks sight-seeing and hanging out; playing "sailor on shore leave." The Japanese were definitely different—elegant and stylish; they even drove on the left. Then two weeks coming back with a shipload of guys coming back from a year's tour. There was a whole different feeling to that bunch—Get to Frisco and I'm outta here!, seemed to be about it; I wouldn't know the fulsome meaning of that until I did it myself. I arrived home with what is nowadays referred to as an "attitude." Dropped out of Sea Cadets and got a job at Onwentia Stables in Lake Forest, following horses round with a coal shovel, waiting for school to end. Sunday afternoons the polo players would get up a game in the backyard of the Swift estate—the meat-packing Swifts, mind you. Each player owned a set of matched horses (chestnut or sleekly black or palomino—beautiful animals). Undersized thoroughbreds seemed best suited for this work, and I made good tips "walking hots" between chukkers, the sweat lathered to foam around the complicated leather tack and horses plenty fagged, smelling of hot sweat and saddle soap; it was like leading sleepwalkers around.

Graduation night my parents didn't attend which I didn't mind. The senior class rented a Milwaukee Road train for a trip to some Wisconsin resort, but I didn't go—why spend the money to be with people you've hung out with all your life? That night there was a mysterious fire at the station and it burned to the ground while the train waited up the track; a prank that was never solved that I know. At our twenty-fifth class reunion no one remembered it.

I had the discouragingly vague ambition to become an architect and got a job downtown—in the mail room at Perkins and Will, Architects. I had the old-fashioned idea of becoming an architect by apprenticeship; that lasted six months. My family and I scrapped together the money for college. Kendall College, a two-year liberal arts college across the street from Northwestern University (in later years it became a four-year liberal arts college; it's now a cooking school). I began doing plays, which I liked to think I had a knack for, but my studies still weren't that hot and I flunked out.

I got a job in the mail room for Sara Lee Bakery, working for a jerk who talked about Elvis movies and cleaned his nails all day. The most fun on that job was riding a little golf cart to "Production" out back, through the warehouse where they kept the truckloads of ingredients, huge cubic-foot chunks of chocolate and such—that sweet, overpowering smell of chocolate and sugar—skidding the cart across the flour-slick floors, past the long industrial ovens. I saw how they made pastry; watched the guys working the line scoop up carload dough spills with snow shovels; haven't had much appetite for store-bought bakery stuff since.

I got fired, but was not sad to leave; working there cured me of wanting ever again to work in a factory. I got a job in a local greasy spoon restaurant, washing dishes. The place was so small there was no machine so I did the dishes by hand. The guy who ran it was a Guadalcanal marine. After closing he would sit at the counter while I finished up the pots and pans and tell me stories of the war, in-

cluding driving from San Diego to Alabama when he mustered out to see the family of his best friend (who'd been killed), and marrying the guy's girlfriend.

The fall of 1964 I went back to school with the promise to do better, and did. I did more theater, and began "writing." The summer of 1965 I got a job in a summer stock theater company at Lock Haven, Pennsylvania—literally a converted dairy barn. Five dollars a week, room and board; had a great time, but discovered I was no actor. One of the company was Miss New Jersey, and years later another guy made a name for himself on the "L.A. Law" TV show.

I graduated from Kendall in January 1966 and ran out of money at the same time. I thought I might transfer into Northwestern, but couldn't manage the money. I planned to transfer that fall to San Francisco State University, because of its theater department, but I didn't make it half that far.

I was drafted into the army in May 1966 along with my younger brother Richard, and submitted to conscription with soul-deadening dread; I was twenty-two.

Looking back I can see that theater, both performing and writing, was timely and lucky, and deeply affected my life as a writer. I am one of those writers who thinks that "story" doesn't simply happen from the neck up, but involves the whole body, that perception, point of view, image, literary diction—the deepest understanding of craft—proceed from a visceral and sensual awareness of story, and that writers who deny or ignore this enrichment exclude what is often best and most poignant. Joseph Conrad said, "My task . . . is, before all, to make you *see.*" That is what theater taught me.

O f all the influences on my life as a writer, there is no doubt that spending two years in the army has been the largest and most enduring—definitely a mixed blessing. It was also the radicalizing experience of my life, a civics lesson without equal. All in all, I never met so many stupid people in one place in all my life; I had to "sir" and "sergeant" people I knew perfectly well were not my betters, men who in any other circumstance would be "shoveling shit in Louisiana," in the immortal words of General George S. Patton. But if the army was a waste of time, you nevertheless *did* acquire a lot of out of-the-way knowledge that,

With Edie in front of Nazareth College dorm, 1966

like Mark Twain's uncle who once carried a cat home by the tail, was never going to become dim or doubtful.

Richard and I did our basic training at Fort Polk in Louisiana, my first trip to the South. At the end of those eight weeks my take on Louisiana was that during the Civil War when it seceded from the Union, they should have declared New Orleans an international city and let the rest go. Fort Polk, what a shit hole.

I especially recall one of our drill sergeants (an uncommonly dim bulb). Back then it was not unusual for twins to be drafted together, and he somehow got it into his head that Richard and I were twins even though I was three years older and a head taller. We'd be standing in formation outside our barracks, and this drill sergeant would look first at Richard and then me, eyeballing us severely, and then say, nastylike, "I know you two squirrels are trying to pull something, and when I find out what it is, you're in *big* trouble." There was no point trying to explain—it would take all day and he still wouldn't get it.

We trained for "Europe," which meant sitting bunker guard at the Iron Curtain on the Czech border, then on our off-time fighting Communism with a beer mug. Anyone who has ever had to stand a guard mount can tell you what a monumental, irremediable bore it is. Still, being bored to death definitely beat the shit out of being killed, so I was downright eager to go to Germany.

By and large, basic training was a waste of time and I have no doubt still is. The "training" given you was worthless, irrelevant even for Europe. About the only thing you learn is to wear the same clothes day after day, that between meals the kitchen is closed, to spit-shine boots, and jog flat-footed (called the Airborne Shuffle), while singing sexist/racist rhyming songs about punching-bag whores and ugly bitches and killing gooks—not exactly skills you can take into the civilian workplace. (Nowadays the racism has changed from the "gooks" of Asia to the "rag-head sand-niggers" of the Middle East.) Nevertheless, at the end of eight weeks I had gained twenty pounds and was in the best physical shape of my life, and *that* was fine. Being a grunt means, simply and emphatically, hard physical work—the hardest I've *ever* done. And if you're not in shape, you just don't last.

My other strong memory of basic training was that our father would send Richard and me weekly letters, but one was always a carbon copy of the other. Neither Richard nor I had the heart to tell him that our bunks were right next to each other, and more often than not we got his "letters" the same day.

If there was any political understanding of the war in Vietnam in our house, or an awareness of an antiwar movement, I do not remember it. We never heard of resisting the draft, refusing conscription, or leaving for Canada. The attitude in the house was, It's your duty; it will make a man of you. All I knew was that two years in the army was going to be a pause in my life that I did not need.

Still and all, being in the service was a cheap way to get off the street and travel; many working-class kids (especially from the South) saw it as an obligation, a step toward manhood, a way to learn a trade, and simply a way to get out on their own. And it is undoubtedly true that an enlisted barracks is one of the few democratic institutions left in the republic, and that you meet people you would not encounter in any other circumstance. Every barracks I ever lived in was a virtual parody of itself and seemed to have one of everything: black guys angry about losing their trumpet lips and Irish Republican Army trainees; dumb-fuck Texans with all their brains in their necks, college "fags" like me, Arlington Park jockeys, historians, barracks lawyers, and dipstick "operators" always working the angles; guys who loved it (lifers-in-training), self-discovered killers, and dumbshit California goody-two-shoes who still believed what the army recruiters had told them; Georgia dirt farmers and Northwest loggers for whom the work was a piece of cake, Ivy League ROTC dropouts, New Yorkers who talked in that parody of World War II war movies, rural Southerners for whom the army was a godsend, and guys on their way to Airborne Rangers (good luck to you, pal); Montana ranchers, San Francisco tailors, undiscovered geniuses, superb athletes, short-order cooks, future officer candidates (God help us), foreigners (Poles and Canadians), and non-English speaking Puerto Rican amateur gang-bangers. A rich, democratic mishmash. That's the genius of a conscription army.

After basic training, Richard went to Fort Sill and Germany. He was assigned to the crew of a Pershing Missile—the rocket designed to accommodate a nuclear warhead launched from the back of a huge trailer truck. Later he came home with truly frightening stories of such routine negligence and institutional carelessness that it should give any rational private citizen the willies ("physic a woodpecker," as my grandfather Denton used to say) to think that these guys had access to nuclear weapons.

I was sent to Fort Knox and then Vietnam.

Fort Knox, in the middle of bluegrass country in Kentucky, was truly beautiful—if you ignored the rocks painted white along the roadways. It was the "Home of Armor" and the Gold Depository, which looked like a deluxe mausoleum with a broad lawn and a high, serious fence; all that gold surrounded by all those tanks. For eight weeks I trained for the armored cavalry—the scouts; reconnaissance (recon, we called it), "The eyes and ears of the combat arms." The day we graduated the colonel stood us in formation for one of his informal inspections, and I was the only man who could spell reconnaissance—two n's and two s's.

Most of our training company were National Guard (NGs, we called them) from Ohio who worked for Goodyear.

Labor Day Sunday afternoon I met Edie Smith at a student mixer at Nazareth College, near Bardstown; she was short with flaming red hair and possessed with boundless energy. The school was originally the Mother House of the Sisters of Charity of Nazareth, first established in 1812—it might well be that the good sisters beat Daniel Boone to Kentucky. At the end of the evening I took her number—the dormitory floor pay phone. We started dating, and saw each other as often as we could until I transferred overseas six months later; a month after I returned we got married; still are.

The war had a peculiar effect on campus life. Many soldiers dated women at Nazareth, but the antiwar sentiment of the women had more to do with the bodily safety of the men they dated rather than politics. When the men left for overseas there were the inevitable exchanges of letters. But every once in a while a letter would come back from overseas stamped DECEASED in large, red letters; other men simply stopped writing, and, for all intents and purposes, disappeared. Years later Sister Barbara, the Dean of Women, told me that I was one of the few GIs who "came back," which made me feel creepy.

That fall Edie invited me to the Thanksgiving Dance; I sent home for my suit. When we walked into the ballroom who should be standing in the receiving line but the lieutenant colonel who was the commander of the Armored Officer Candidate School. He was tricked out in his dress blue uniform complete with white gloves, yellow cavalry braids, and buzz-saw haircut. I had just received my orders for Vietnam; the last thing I wanted to do was stand in front of some lifer and shake his hand. (The collar insignia for a lieutenant colonel was a brass eagle, but it so resembled a spread-eagled chicken that lieutenant colonels were often called chicken colonels—also short for chickenshit colonel.) Edie naively insisted we go through the receiving line and I couldn't talk my way out of it. I thought I could somehow frump-down—dufus and gawky—and sneak by, but when I came to stand in front of him, he took one look at my regulation dress shoes, *my* buzz-saw haircut (freshened every Friday or you didn't get a weekend pass), and said, "Don't you know enough to stand at attention when you come before an *officer?* What's your unit, *troop?*" And right then and there I had to brace—heels together and feet at a 45-degree angle, arms at my sides with my fingers cupped and thumbs at the seams of my trousers, stomach in, shoulders back, head up, eyes locked front—and *then* salute.

Of all the medal-eager, career-tending, ticket-punching lifers I had to kowtow—all the endless and nitpicking, chickenshit harassment; the pointless, bullshit marching and drill; the jumping up and down, screaming mad-fit lectures; the arrogant and sadistic punishments; the chaplains' cheerleading "character" talks (which amounted to variations of New York Cardinal Spellman's famous exhortation to "Kill a Commie for Christ"); the entire fabric of the muddled and narrow, racist military mind—*this* was a humiliation I have never forgotten.

To be fair about this, I ought to mention three men I remember with honest respect.

The first was the first sergeant of D Troop of the 32nd Armor at Fort Knox. First Sergeant Alva was a full-blood Navaho Indian, a kindly man (built like a fireplug) who ran our orderly room and conducted the troop's business with a dignified efficiency that impressed everyone. He reminds me of Sergeant Warden in James Jones' *From Here to Eternity*. The day I left for Vietnam he brought me into his office, sat me down (the only time I can recall sitting in his presence), and said, "Remember, Heinemann, this is not a white man's war," in his gruff, heavily accented voice; as succinct a description of the war as anyone has ever said out loud.

Then there was Sergeant Shiflett from Pennsylvania. He was the recon platoon sergeant when I was at Cu Chi; lean and outdoorsy, with a wrinkled neck and a farmer's tan—the one truly skilled soldier I met there. We had the feeling that he genuinely liked us, we certainly liked him, and looked after our welfare. He didn't care if we drank or smoked grass or messed around with the roadside hookers; but did not permit the workaday atrocities (shooting up villages and hooches for the hell of it, beating up prisoners, or fucking with body-count corpses, etc.) that infantrymen become inured to and commit with appalling casualness. In a place where the spirit of atrocity was in the very air, where the permissions for that sort of thing were broadly given, Sergeant Shiflett firmly

insisted we act like human beings and treat the Vietnamese like human beings. All these years later I am grateful for his sincere *leader*ship, because it could easily have been worse.

And thirdly was First Lieutenant Opsahl, an ROTC officer from the University of Wisconsin at Madison with a degree in history (after his tour he went back for his Ph.D., a study of the Knights of Malta, but did not finish). By then I had transferred to Dau Tieng—the headquarters for the Michelin Rubber Plantation just south of Tay Ninh City and the Nui Ba Den (what the French called the Black Virgin Mountain). Lieutenant Opsahl came to the platoon from Bravo Company, certainly one of the premier hard-luck rifle companies in the whole of Cochin China; those guys took casualties leaving the motor pool. I was by then a buck sergeant. Lieutenant Opsahl called a meeting of the NCOs, and simply said that it was our job to make sure that everyone went home in one piece. We quickly agreed with him and complimented him on his excellent judgement; the egregious stupidity of the war was clear; and it was clear he'd had enough. It was ironic that from the time he arrived until I left in March we saw much bitter fighting, and, as hard as we tried, the platoon took many casualties. He and I got along because we were close in age and trusted each other; he never did anything stupid and didn't act like John Wayne.

But I am getting ahead of myself.

From the time I received my orders that fall until I left for overseas in March, all I could think of was all those rainy-day gym-class games of dodge ball when I was in grammar school. On those days when gym class couldn't go outside the coach would haul out this big bag of cheap, thick-rubber utility soccer balls. The class was split into two teams—one at each end of the gymnasium. He set the dodge balls in the center circle of the basketball court, and when he blew his whistle thirty or forty kids would rush in, try to grab a ball, and throw them back and forth. The rules were simple: if you threw a ball and hit someone on the fly, he was out; if you threw a ball and he caught it, you were out. What kept going through my mind in those months was that I never lasted very long at these games. In other words, my ass was grass—as we used to say.

That winter I spent most of my time hiding out in the barracks and reading Joseph Heller's *Catch-22*, a book at once falling-out-of-your-bunk screamingly funny, and not funny in the least; a story of such raucous and raw, death-row-gallows, darkly bitter humor that it is a wonder Heller survived the writing of it. During that time there were large numbers of guys coming back from Vietnam from armored cavalry outfits, and they looked *physically* terrible—exhausted and mean—and sounded worse. They sincerely didn't give a shit about anything, and drank morning, noon, and night. Some talked about the war and some did not. Those of us with orders looked at them as at a reflection.

Vietnam was going to be dreadful.

The middle of February I took my month's leave before I shipped overseas. The day I left, Richard arrived home with his discharge in his hand. He hadn't had time to let us know he was coming. Both he and the army had had enough of each other; he'd told off a bunch of officers, a couple chaplains, and army shrinks; he was mustered out. We sat for an hour in the kitchen, talking, before I absolutely had to leave for the airport; as brief and blunt a conversation as I ever had with any of my brothers. He felt terribly guilty, but I told him to cherish his discharge; that he had done something everyone I knew *wanted* to do and for him not to think another thing about it.

Nevertheless, all the time I was overseas his letters were full of apology, worry, and concern.

Even though I still had the half-baked idea in the back of my mind to "be an actor" or some unrealistic, inert ambition about "writing," I did not go to Vietnam looking for a literary or artistic experience. Hemingway, Mailer, and others had done it; James Jones, a man whose work I greatly admire, was famous for walking around Schofield Barracks in Hawaii with a notebook and even took classes at the university there.

My thought was: first things first; let's get through this in one piece, and then we'll see. Years later, an editor of a prominent literary magazine told me that he regarded *not* having gone to Vietnam as a missed literary opportunity; I sat and listened to him with astonishment and thought him a fool. I told him as kindly as I could that it was nothing of the kind, that he had not missed a thing and saved himself a good deal of grief, but that if he had wanted to go overseas that badly, he should have let me know.

Generally, I think the people who see service in war as *the* literary opportunity of a lifetime should have their heads examined—Hemingway, Mailer, and Jones included. And those people who think that war is the making of a man should be told that there is nothing ennobling or enriching or manful about the infantry. To be a soldier in the army of a modern industrial country is the destruction of manhood (the ultimate exploitation); an army doesn't want "warriors," it wants killers, capable of berserk viciousness.

The summer of 1965 I was in Lock Haven, having the time of my life at a summer stock theater; the summer of 1966 I was in the army at Fort Knox (good duty as garrison life goes); and the summer of 1967 I was in Vietnam, in the infantry. There it is, we used to say.

On the plane ride to Saigon I was as numb as a person can be.

When I arrived at Tan Son Nhut Air Base, I quickly passed from one repple depple (replacement detachment) to the next until I reached the Recon Platoon of the 4th Battalion (Mechanized) of the 23rd Infantry (nicknamed the Tomahawks) in the 25th Division at Cu Chi—the namesake of the famous hand-built VC tunnels that spread out beneath us two hundred kilometers worth; the base camp about half a morning's drive north of Saigon.

Being "mechanized" meant we rode armored personnel carriers—APCs; tracks, we called them. The "regular," straight-leg, ground-pounding infantry (as we called them) simply walked. We called ourselves troopers, never grunts. "Grunt" was slang used by the Marines, up-country, and didn't come into general use until I'd been home many years. And we never called each other "buddy," either—that irksome journalists' cliche.

The tracks were boxy, squat, and ugly with inch and a quarter aluminum alloy armor plate, diesel engines with a straight pipe muffler that came right off the exhaust manifolds, and a ninety-gallon fuel tank; the things weighed something like thirteen tons. In recon we had four men on each of the ten tracks, a .50-caliber machine gun (called "the fifty") mounted on the main hatch and two smaller M-60 machine guns (called pigs) mounted to the sides toward the back. Each track carried upwards of ten thousand rounds of ammunition, several cases of grenades, and perhaps a hundred pounds of C-4 plastic explosive (with small wooden boxes of blasting caps and hefty spools of detonation cord). For sidearms we had M-16s (assault rifles that *always* jammed), 12-gauge shotguns, M-79 grenade launchers, and .45-caliber semiautomatic pistols. You were also invited to carry personal weapons—usually belt or shoulder holster revolvers, or serious knives brought from home. And floating around were grease guns—.45-caliber machine guns with thirty-round magazines (also called burp guns because of the sound)—and captured AK-47s picked up after firefights. Along with the AK-47s, probably the best assault rifles in the world, the Viet Cong also had shoulder fired RPGs (armor-piercing rocket propelled grenades), a weapon of blunt and functional ugliness; you see them on the news every once in a while, carried with haughty and casual disregard. These were used against the tracks, and they were "very effective"—to use the arcane phrase of the time. Basically, an RPG round would go through the armor plate like spit through a screen.

Undoubtedly, every soldier can recall his first firefight—his first action. The first time I "went outside the wire" was as part of an ambush patrol, and it was a grand fiasco. There were six of us, including the platoon medic and a forward observer (the FO) for the battalion's mortar platoon. I was to hump an

"Me and my track, No. 31—my ride home," 1967

M-60 machine gun, carried by a strap over the shoulder so that I could fire it "from the hip," so to speak. Everyone else carried their sidearm M-16s, M-79 40mm grenade launchers with double-ought buckshot "canister" rounds (basically sawed-off shotguns), and plenty of grenades and claymore antipersonnel mines. After dark we left the base camp and went into the woods. We walked down a narrow footpath in thick woods for a long time, me pouring sweat, then came to a clearing. In the moonlight I could see a truck garden with crosshatched bamboo pea fences, melon vines, and such; we were on somebody's farm. Off to one side through the trees I could also see a streetlight at the top of a utility pole; did anyone else see it? What on earth are we doing anywhere *near* a village. What did I know, I was the new guy? We moved off through the clearing, one at a time, and turned right. As we did the woodline opposite us exploded with gun fire; we were ambushed. I knew I was going to be killed, but in my extreme panic finally did make the machine gun work. After a brief exchange of gun fire and grenades, loud and angry shouting and sincere cursing, we finally established that we were American GIs and the guys behind the woodline were South Vietnamese soldiers; called ARVNs, the acronym for Army of the Republic of Vietnam. We radioed in what had happened, and were told to return to the base camp. We retreated the way we came. On our way back through the woods we could hear army ambulances roar down the road to our right, heading for the base camp. We were told to assemble in the mess hall, the colonel wanted to talk with us; I was still pouring sweat. The ambush had passed in front of an ARVN compound on the outskirts of the village of Cu Chi; we had fired into the village, killed three and wounded fifteen (whether soldiers or civilians we were never told). The colonel said he was proud of the way we comported ourselves— bringing everyone back in one piece; nothing was said of the Vietnamese. We were dismissed and sent to bed.

Welcome to Vietnam; good God.

My battalion, my platoon rode roughshod over that part of Cochin China (as the French called it), road running, pulling day sweeps through the countryside trying to engage the VC, and busting jungle (pushing over trees as big around as you could reach) in the Iron Triangle, the Ho Bo and Bo Loi Woods, north of Saigon. We tracked the VC down like dogs and shot them on sight (those we could actually find, though most of the time they found us). It was our custom that after a firefight we would tie the heels of the Vietnamese body count together with a length of black communications wire and drag the corpses behind our tracks out to the road and leave them, like so many roadkills. We were not pleasant people and this was not a pleasant business, and I'm sure that we radicalized more Vietnamese to Ho Chi Minh's revolution than we "saved." What comfort we had came in small things: we slept on collapsible canvas cots in wood and screen wire hooches with tin roofs; hot meals flown out to us every night; beer and mail. There was a Red Cross center at Cu Chi, and the women—called Donut Dollies—were earnestly sincere, unbelievably naive, and strictly untouchable. The first time I went up to the Red Cross center I was met at the door and invited to sit down and write a letter home. What was the point? And what was the point of their being there?

It didn't take long to understand that the war was an evil, foul thing, purposeless and egregious. But if there was any antiwar sentiment among the people around me it only reached as far as: This is bullshit; let me out of here. We didn't need the Red Cross or the Donut Dollies, those pathetic touring USO shows, or Bob Hope's Christmas tour. We wanted out, and every guy knew to the day how much time he had left; some guys had calendars; some had obscene drawings of nude women (the bodies segmented with numbers that you inked out); and some notched off the days on the camouflage cover of their steel helmets (卌) We were bitter about the war and took our frustration and resentment out on the Vietnamese. There is an old saying, you know, "Sometimes the best way to disobey an order is to obey it to the letter"; and what Michael Herr said later in *Dispatches* was true, we wanted to give you a Vietnam you could put in your ashtray. We were treated like meat and expected to behave like meat, you understand.

I started drinking more than ever I drank in my life and smoked marijuana—a kind of post-modern Dutch courage. It is no exaggeration to say that you could buy a five-pound bag of excellent marijuana for five bucks; you couldn't smoke it fast enough. It got so I pre-ferred grass to beer because you didn't have to keep it cold (the beer was never cold anyway), and didn't have to deal with the empty can; you just ate the roach. What could be simpler than that? Later we found out that we could get ready-rolled, brand name opium-soaked marijuana cigarettes, the smokes still wrapped in their cellophane packs. If it seems crazy to be drunk or stoned in a war zone, in a firefight, let us remember that during World War I it was established practice in the British Army to give the troops "going over the top" a heaping cupful of rum, so much so that years later one man remembered that after a battle the trenches smelled of "rum and blood." We smoked some grass before we went on ambush (while making due with handfuls of No Doz instead of amphetamines; falling asleep on ambush was a no-no; *every*body stayed up), smoked some after we set up, then smoked some more the next morning to mellow down so we could get some rest.

Edie wrote every day, and her letters became cherished objects. Indeed, the first time I got mail it was a stack of eleven letters. Practically the only things that I brought back from Vietnam were her letters—well over three hundred. Edie's college was forty miles south of Louisville, surrounded by farmland, an hour's walk from town, and there was absolutely nothing going on, but her letters were simply fine (somebody knew I wasn't dead). Several years ago our daughter spent the better part of a Saturday afternoon going through our box of letters, and said that Edie was a much better writer than I was. She sent me two photographs of herself which I mounted on a bit of C-ration cardboard, covered with acetate and green cloth tape we used to mount maps, and kept it with me on the track, plastered to the inside wall where we also taped *Playboy* centerfolds.

I have those photographs of her still, hanging in my study; one of the few "war souvenirs" I brought home.

That spring I heard my mother had allowed my youngest brother Philip to drop out of high school; she signed him into the Marine Corps. And not only that, but the first day of boot camp he had "volunteered" for Vietnam.

The way *that* worked was this: the drill sergeant would stand all these scared-to-death seventeen- and eighteen-year-olds in front of their bunks and scream in their faces that they had "better" goddamned volunteer for Vietnam; a

Marine *dies* for his country. The ones who didn't volunteer would be taken outside where another NCO would beat the shit out of them until they *did.*

Anyway, it was not long after that I was told by letter that Philip was in Vietnam, so I put in for an in-country emergency leave to go see him. This would have to be verified by the Red Cross.

During the time of selective service—the draft—it often happened that brothers would spend basic training together (like Richard and I), but, because of the "Sullivan Rule," would split up. The "Sullivan Rule" goes back to World War II. Five Sullivan brothers joined the navy and served aboard the same ship. The ship was sunk and all five were killed. Thereafter, to save a family what could be regarded as generational suicide, blood kin were forbidden to serve together, and during the Vietnam War only one brother was supposed to be in a combat zone at a time.

I wanted to go see Philip and talk him into going home; and if he wouldn't go, then I would.

Well, the Red Cross took its sweet time to okay everything, and by the time I got to Danang Philip was already wounded, had convalesced aboard a hospital ship, and was sent home to heal up. He was caught in a mortar attack and the concussion of one of the rounds screwed up his right ear and eye. I didn't see him until I got off the plane at O'Hare Airport in Chicago when I came home. He looked terrible. When he was well enough to go back on active duty he was sent to Pearl Harbor, and in 1969 went back to Vietnam for a second tour. I was heartsick; I couldn't stand the thought of him going back a second time and tried to get him out of it; get his orders changed. He found out about it and was not pleased. Of my three brothers I always felt the closest to him, but I couldn't bring myself to write him the whole time he was overseas. When he came back, we did not exchange a word for ten years. Shortly after he got out of the Marine Corps he married and quickly had two daughters, but the marriage didn't last. He lost his job, fell behind in his child support and alimony, and one day simply disappeared. No one has seen hide nor hair of him since—one of those guys ruined by the war—something happened to him overseas that he simply could not overcome.

Larry in Dau Tieng, 1967

In July 1967 I was transferred to the Recon Platoon of the 2nd Battalion (Mechanized) of the 22nd Infantry at Dau Tieng. The base camp itself was squalid; we lived in pathetic canvas tents, rotten and sagging ruins shot through with bullet holes and shrapnel nicks walled in by waist-high sandbags; unlike Cu Chi we were to wear our steel pots and carry our sidearms everywhere. The battalion tracks were gas powered with a 283 cubic inch Chevy V-8 with a four barrel carburetor and a blower the size of a room fan. These were truly death traps because if an RPG round hit the gas tank the track would go up like the head of a match; a gallon of gasoline is equivalent to nineteen pounds of TNT and can lift one thousand pounds one thousand feet into the air, instantly. We operated around Trang Bang, Tay Ninh City, and the Nui Ba Den—a spiritual place that is sacred to the Cao Dai religion. The countryside around the Michelin and the Nui Ba Den was beautiful—that mountain one thousand feet high looked as if Mount McKinley had been set down in the middle of Kansas.

There was more fighting here, and as a matter of fact the famous 1968 Tet Offensive began for us around Thanksgiving when, for the first time, we got into firefights with regular North Vietnamese soldiers coming down off the Ho Chi Minh Trail; these guys as well trained and equipped as we were. By then I was a buck sergeant, had charge of a track, and stood behind the fifty; for a sidearm I carried an AK-47. We drove a lot of convoys from Dau Tieng to Tay Ninh City and back. During lunch we would often park along the road next to the Cao Dai Temple, and I'd stand on my track, look over the compound wall, and admire the famous Cao Dai church. In 1990 I had a chance to go back to Vietnam; one of the places I asked specifically to see was the Cao Dai, and the inside was spectacular, airy as a barn, decorated with dragons and armored spirits with swallows swooping and diving during the noon worship.

In December, just as I was coming to the last one hundred days of my tour (you were called a two-digit midget, but most often just short-timer), I went on R&R. I took my thousand dollar savings in cash, went to Tokyo, and stayed at a western style hotel called the Perfect Room. The minute we walked into the lobby and checked in, the desk clerk said "the women" were in the bar. I hired a woman who called herself Suzi for one hundred dollars a day. And like many another, my R&R was a culinary and sexual rampage. The last night there was some trouble with the plane taking us back to Vietnam, so I went back to town. I thought seriously about going AWOL; Suzi had kin on Hokkaido, the northern island of Japan. After much drinking and much talk, conniving and ciphering, I just couldn't bring myself to do it. I had honest-to-God responsibilities; I could not imagine myself a man without a country, and did not want to rot in a military prison. So I decided to take my chances and went back with the rest.

We spent Christmas in the field and then drove straight north to a place called Soui Cut, about three quarters of a mile from the Cambodian Border; the trip took three days. In the perimeter were two howitzer batteries and two battalions of infantry—my battalion and the 3rd Battalion of the 22nd (straight-leg grunts).

The night of January 1, 1968, we were attacked by what we were later told was the 272nd NVA Regiment (about fifteen hundred men); it was the worst night of my life.

The fighting began late in the evening, and, simply, went on all night. I worked the fifty, went through many, many boxes of hundred-round belts, and threw grenades just as hard as I could throw them; firing that fifty—the

slow and heavy, pounding shudder—the next morning my whole body tingled from it. I clearly and cleanly recall bodies and pieces of bodies flying through the air; the knees and feet and tire-tread sandals of some of the corpses; some guys simply disappeared into spray. The artillery fired salvos of point-blank canister rounds and other large-bore artillery from other base camps was called in. We heard that the NVA had broken through the perimeter and were fighting the straight-leg grunts hand to hand. I remember the grim and purposeful hysteria, the dust and muzzle flashes, the weird light, the choking smell of gunpowder, the sound of the fifty slugs (as big as your thumb) thwacking into the bodies and the artillery shrapnel whacking the back of the tracks, the screaming and yelling (in both English and Vietnamese, mind you), the overwhelming sound of the low-flying helicopter gunships and Air Force F-4 Phantom air strikes as they made pass after pass—the booming crack of the jet's bombs and napalm; large trees crashing to earth. When we saw a guy blown back with a burst of machine gun fire or simply disappear the only thought was, "One less to worry about." Years later when I read Faulkner's *As I Lay Dying*, Dash (the carpenter-son) talks about making his mother's coffin, holding up each plank for her to see through her death-bed room window; Faulkner describes the sound of the saw going, "One lick less, one lick less"—that's what it felt like.

Toward morning the fighting stopped, and when it was light enough we finally saw what we had done. The meat of five hundred corpses all over everything and the woodline looked like ruined drapes, their dust-covered equipment looking suddenly antique; always afterward we called this the Great Truce Day Body Count. We cleared away the firefight junk and looked around to see who was left. There were many casualties. The body count corpses were gathered up and thrown into a ditch dug by a bulldozer we brought with us. We buried the bodies and parts of bodies like you'd make a lasagna: a layer of corpses, then a layer of quick lime brought out on a chopper in one hundred pound bags, then another layer of corpses. It was a matter of sanitation and that work went on all day. In the middle of the morning the search party brought in the Bravo Company ambush; all eight men dead before they knew what hit them, their arms jogging loose as the litter bearers brought them through the woodline and up the road, and carried them to the chopper pad where they would be put into body bags and medevaced after the wounded (dusted-off, we called it). Recon had one man missing until I found his incinerated corpse in his burned-to-the-ground track. A chopper-load of reporters and journalists and that kind arrived to gawk at the body count, film the troops, and interview the captains and colonels; I am told we made the front page of the *New York Times*. We drank our water, cleaned our guns with gasoline, smoked our grass, catnapped, and waited for dark. In the days that followed, the sharp and pathetic, gagging stench of five hundred rotting human corpses—an aura of smell like no other in the world, you understand—was simply in the air and our clothes, our food and our mustaches; a sensory memory of pervasive ugliness and appalling carnage, distinct and permanent, which never fails to bring tears to my eyes all these years later.

Since 1968 our family celebrations of Christmas and New Year's have never been the same, and, try as we may to make them pleasant and joyful, it is a time of year saturated with unshakably unpleasant memories.

Almost twenty years later I went to see Oliver Stone's film *Platoon*. I used to read all the Vietnam novels and see the films out of professional curiosity—an impulse I no longer obey. Stone was in Vietnam the same time as I and operated in much the same area. I watched the film and was struck with the unmistakably familiar coincidences. I wrote and asked if he'd been at Soui Cut that night; he had—a straight-leg grunt. How strange—odd and ironic—that I should write about it and he should film it.

We spent the rest of the month operating around that woods and I wouldn't be surprised if we drove into Cambodia. Then suddenly one day we picked up and went back to Dau Tieng because of the beginning of the Tet Offensive in the south. We worked around Dau Tieng for another month or so, fighting almost every day.

In early March my orders came. One day your plane ticket comes; you turn in your rifle and such; say your good-byes around; and simply leave. That night in Saigon a bunch of us sat on the roof of our repple depple barracks hooch (a much grander affair than my platoon tents) smoking grass and watching firefight tracers, mortars, and rockets hitting the city

(there is nothing more beautiful than someone else's firefight)—everyone thinking, Tomorrow I'm outta here!

The next day we smoked some more grass, and by the time the plane arrived we were high out of our minds. The nineteen-hour ride back to the States (Back-in-the-World, we called it) was a strange and lonely trip; sleepless and melancholy. I was still stoned when I got off the plane at Travis Air Force Base outside Oakland. We were given haircuts and issued new uniforms, handed our discharges, paid our wages in cash, and shown the door. Waiting around the San Francisco airport for my flight back to Chicago, I felt old, physically and spiritually exhausted, mean and grateful and extraordinarily sad, radicalized and relieved, and ground down by a bottomless grief that I could not right then even begin to express—"*impacted* grief," it has been called. Good friends of mine were dead or dusted-off and would continue to die through that spring and summer, but a horrible event in my life had ended, the killing time was done; I had come out of it in one piece, touched by God's luck, a walking fucking miracle. I was not ashamed of what I had just done, but I was not proud, either. How can a body be proud of such a thing? (All we can say is that we lived; we cannot say that we did our work well, we cannot say we feel good about the work we did—combat as "work" simply cannot be as satisfying as ordinary wages-work. We produced an astonishing, pervasive ugliness, and that's all.) I possessed a bitterness that was almost unconscionable; to paraphrase Samuel Clemens, it would go around the world four times and tie. I felt as if I'd been used, wasted, and then dumped. Paul Fussell, an infantryman of World War II, a scholar and essayist probably said it best: "I will always look at the world through the eyes of a pissed-off infantryman."

A number of years ago I gave a reading at a university, and one of the teachers—a guy about my age; the faculty pill someone said later—told me that if he'd seen me at the airport he'd have spit on me (as happened to any number of returning GIs). I told him that spitting on someone and shooting at them came from the same place in the heart—a simple fact he should never forget; that I'd just come from a place where I didn't take any shit from anybody, what made him think I was going to take any shit from him, and if he'd spit on me I would have kicked his ass from here to Chinatown.

It is putting it mildly to say that I keenly felt the touchy extreme of the awkward ambivalence of most Americans, even from those people who welcomed me home unconditionally—like Edie and the women at Nazareth College. No one knew what to make of us, and the thousand-meter stare was a most uncomfortable gaze.

On top of everything else, I was hornier than a five-peckered billy goat. To say it plainly and unmistakably, I wanted to get laid; skip the date; skip the dinner; skip the movie. I wanted to find out as quickly as I could if it was possible for me to feel good in my body, to connect with those good, human feelings, and rediscover my own humanity.

I went back to Edie at Nazareth to find out if we could still love each other, and received as lavish and hospitable a welcome from her as I could have wanted. As a matter of fact, the kindness and regard shown me by all the women—students and faculty—were heartfelt and extraordinary, and I remember those first months home with warm gratitude. For weeks I did nothing but eat and sleep. I had an apartment in town, showed up every night at the college for dinner, and ate Edie and her friends out of house and home; it was not uncommon for me to eat five or six dinners.

In early April Martin Luther King, Jr. was shot dead and the cities around the country erupted into furious violence; riots, fires, and killings.

The middle of April I got a letter from one of the men still with the platoon telling me of the death of Emerson Cole, my best friend; I was devastated with inexpressible sadness and could not be consoled—Cole, in many ways my opposite, the one man who was *supposed* to come home in one piece (I had simply been "lucky"). But then he was one of the most self-destructive men I ever met, and finally managed to destroy himself; what a waste.

Edie and I got married, she graduated, and we moved back to Chicago.

I got a job driving a bus for the CTA, and right from the start I was the worst bus driver who ever lived and drove my bus like a bulldozer.

In May, Robert Kennedy was murdered in Los Angles, the night he won the California

Larry and Edie in front of their two-flat apartment, Chicago, 1976

Democratic presidential primary, one of the great political tragedies of the century.

All through the summer there was extreme tension in the city, what with the riots after Dr. King's murder, the terrible news from overseas (grunts were dropping like flies), the antiwar movement seriously mobilizing, the protests getting more and more violent—a thing not discouraged by the cops.

In August, there was a wildcat black bus drivers strike—a further reverberation of the killing of Dr. King. I recall being stopped by a picket—a young white woman apparently in town for the Democratic Convention the week after—as I pulled out of the bus barn. She asked me to honor the strike. I told her no, thinking to myself that I'd done worse things than scab (a dirty word in my union family) and for a lot less money.

During convention week I got in the habit of stopping my bus at the north end of Lincoln Park to watch under the trees for lights and commotion, and sniff for tear gas (the use of which was a war crime, you understand).

The night of the famous "police riot," I stopped my bus south of the Loop at Clark Street and Congress Parkway not far from the Hilton Hotel. Parked bumper-to-bumper along Congress were many, many buses filled with many, many cops in full riot gear packed to the doors (swinging loads, bus drivers call it). I had seen this, done this many times; in the dark of night the battalion would move to a staging area and at first light ("early dawn," some called it) would surround a "VC" village and pounce on it. I sat at the light and looked at all those darkened buses, understanding full well that somebody was going to get their ass kicked, but this time it wasn't going to be me.

By the end of the summer—the war, the killing of Martin Luther King, Jr. and Robert Kennedy, then the convention and all the rest—I was wrapped pretty tight. I thought the war had followed me home and I wanted no part of it.

I looked around during those years of extraordinary social upheaval and understood that whatever empathy I had for the antiwar movement, I strongly felt that what they were doing was irrelevant to me. My war was over. I was outside all of that, and would *always* be outside. I had the undeniable feeling that I had not come home; that because of the war I was cut off from something here; that *wherever* the world was going, it was going there without me.

I could not even bring myself to join the Vietnam Veterans Against the War, not even in 1971 when the VVAW gathered in Washington to protest the war, and, among other things, throw their medals away on the Capitol steps.

That fall I went back to school at Columbia College here in Chicago—a small private arts school. "Writing" was still a vague and unrealistic ambition. Nevertheless, I took a writing course because I knew I wouldn't have to work and it would be a snap A, but I fooled myself.

The teacher's name was John Schultz, then a contributing editor for *Evergreen* magazine (one of the leading left-liberal, radical journals of that time); he had been an army medic during the Korean War. I was to be his student for three years. After I graduated he hired me to teach, and I became a glorified graduate assistant (Columbia had no graduate program back then). I would be closely associated with

him at Columbia College until I resigned in 1986. Our relationship and friendship would end badly with much sore ill-feeling, but in the fall of 1968 we began a mentor-student relationship that I will always be grateful for.

I ought to say that when I came home I was not one of those guys who "went to his room," never said boo about the war, and has been eating his liver out ever since. Right from the beginning I told anyone who asked about the war—without the polite euphemisms, the tasteful dashes, or discreet ellipses. I simply could not shut up about what I had seen, what I had done, and what I had become; the war was a story that simply would not be denied.

The first night of class John went around the room to get a sense of what everyone wanted to write about. Most wanted to write about the convention, Chicago street life, and such. I said that I'd just got back from overseas and wanted to write about the war. There was a long moment of serious stares—You're one of *them?*, seemed suddenly to be the feeling in the room. I looked around as much to say, Well, yeah, I just got back from Vietnam; anybody want to talk about it, we can step out onto the fire escape.

John, however, was very interested in what I had to say about Vietnam. The week after he started giving me books—J. Glenn Gray's *The Warriors, The Iliad,* and *War and Peace* among them. Soon I was reading Bernal Diaz, Erich Remarque, Jaroslav Hasek, Martin Russ, Dalton Trumbo, as well as the canon of contemporary war literature—Hemingway, Mailer, and Jones. In those years I read everything I could get my hands on: Grimm's folktales and Burroughs, Langston Hughes and Virginia Woolf, Faulkner and Dostoevsky, Gogol and Shakespeare, Joyce and Whitman, Tennessee Williams and Katherine Anne Porter. I had been such a poor student that I was even reading bonehead grammar books and dictionaries—and not just for the vocabulary. But the most important thing he gave me was his firm, vocal permission and approval for the frank, working-class barracks language of ordinary soldiers and the blunt imagery intrinsic to the subject. John was intense and kindly, and upheld my soldier's point of view in the face of extreme resistance of some of the other young writers around me. To John Schultz's credit he did the same for *all* the young writers who were working with strong subject matter and unpopular, difficult points of view; his interest always was the keen veracity of "story"; the very human-ness of "story."

At the end of that first year I thought of myself as a writer—said the word writer with a straight face—and that was that.

In those years veterans were called many things, and I wanted to name myself and be honest about it, not a victim and not a hero, just a man trying to come through the war in one piece. Military life is virtually a foreign culture, and combat is most profoundly an experience strictly alien to most people. I wanted to validate my own memory and come to an understanding of my war year; this *did* happen; this is what *that* was; *this* is what you make when you make war. I took my cue from Melville's *Moby Dick*, a story first and foremost about killing whales; a rich piece of work I read many, many times. I would tell the story of the work. What is a track, an ambush, how a firefight and the immediate aftermath proceed, weapons and tools, work shortcuts, R&R, and what might be called the downward path to wisdom.

Edie got a job that fall teaching and supported us—for nine years at a number of jobs as it turned out—while I wrote and taught part-time. My father was severely chagrined about this. When she and I would visit my parents, my dad would greet us at the door and say, "Get a haircut. Get a job. What do you mean letting your wife work while you're horsing around." But Edie supported my writing wholeheartedly; it was her work that made my work possible; many a writer has such a partner to thank. She was a superb typist—as I was not—and she typed all my manuscripts until 1986 when I bought myself a computer. She became a superb editor and I came to rely on her more and more.

As I worked on the story year after year, draft after draft (always an expansion), my "personal" story receded, and I incorporated ideas from other novels and expropriated stories from other veterans, and the novel took on the form of a "fictionalized memoir." The one-year combat tour was a perfect dramatic structure. The writing became a retelling, an intimate reliving (whether "it" happened or not), as well as a reminiscence; both a telling and a personal reflection. And perhaps I should add that the writing of *Close Quarters* (and *Paco's Story* for that matter) was in no way cathartic, as some

people would like to suppose (writing as "therapy," God help us); the world doesn't operate that way. In 1974, I sold an excerpted chapter as a short story to *Penthouse*, and the next year I sold them another piece; whatever anyone may think of *Penthouse* magazine, there will always be a warm spot in my heart, somewhere, for it. Even so, the book was abandoned many times—why am I putting myself through this?—but finally I was determined to finish if it was to be the last natural act of my life. By 1976, I thought I had enough to send to New York, and the manuscript was bought by Farrar, Straus and Giroux; I was to work with an editor named Pat Strachan. She was a tall and elegant woman educated at Duke; a person I would never have met in a thousand years if she hadn't been an editor and I a writer. *Close Quarters*, she said, was the first war story manuscript she'd read. We were to work together for ten years and more.

When *Close Quarters* was published in May 1977, I told a friend of mine, "It's been a long time coming. But it'll be a long time gone."

Since the middle of 1976 my father had been sick with cancer. There was an operation and a long convalescence, but by the winter we knew—and he knew—he was dying. It was

Edie, Larry, Sarah, and Preston at a friend's cabin in Wisconsin, 1980

horrible to watch him diminish, literally curl up and shrink in his hospital bed right before my eyes. The middle of May he died, a week before the book appeared. I loved my father and he was dead; I had just completed eight years work on something that meant a good deal to me. How can a body grieve and celebrate at the same time?

That fall I was offered a full-time position at Columbia College. In November our daughter, Sarah Catherine, was born. We took her name from the *Bible.* Sarah, wife of Abraham, mother of all nations. And Catherine, after Catherine the Great—a very interesting woman. Edie's labor went on so long that the doctor thought she would have to undergo a cesarian, but at the last minute Edie dilated sufficiently for a normal birth. I stood outside the delivery room, watching through the porthole window. When Sarah appeared, she was cleaned up, and a nurse wrapped her up and brought her out—on the way to the nursery. She stopped for me to see. I unfolded the blanket and did what I expect every parent does. I immediately checked for a cleft palate and counted her fingers and toes. The nurse gave her into my arms and she was not any bigger than from the palm of my hand to the crook of my elbow. And at that moment I had a strong vision of Sarah eighteen or twenty years later, a young woman with an elegant neck and thin pianist's hands and fingers; fine and long honeyblond hair; dressed in an raspberry-colored evening gown; and standing midway down a flight of steps with the hem of the dress trailing up the stairs behind her. I don't suppose I am the first father to have such an image of his daughter.

It should be said that before 1975, the year the war ended once and for all, you could count the number of good books (by the soldiers themselves) on the fingers of one hand. Michael Casey's *Obscenities,* Robert Roth's *Sand in the Wind,* the VVAW anthologies of poetry and prose *Winning the Hearts and Minds* and *Free Fire Zone,* and David Rabe's stage play *Sticks and Bones.* Since 1975, there have been *well* over three hundred novels, and no doubt a like number of volumes of poetry, biographies and memoirs, military autobiographies, and political and historical analyses of all kinds.

Any number of people, Edie among them, told me that now that I had written my "war

Book jacket photo for Paco's Story:
*"I'm wearing the sweater Edie knitted
for me as a Christmas present in 1985"*

story" I could move on to something else. But, still, in 1977 the war was like a nail on my head, like a corpse in my house. So I turned right around and began *Paco's Story.* I had been reading *Naked Lunch* and was above all impressed by the sheer energy of the storytelling. And too, there is a curious myth among writers that whatever the first effort is, the second is bound to be diminished in quality and intensity, etc. So, I felt I could take my time, experiment perhaps, and (why not?) write a parody of Burroughs's novel; wouldn't it be something to sustain that kind of intensity and energy for three hundred pages. I took what I regarded as the best of my first novel, and began with that. I struck upon the direct address because it seemed to me that, above all, storytelling is an intimate conversation with the reader. The epistle is a literary form that goes back as far as written language. The conventions are simple, and you literally write the person's name at the top of the page. And when you do that,

At the National Book Award ceremony, November 9, 1987: (from left) Edie and Larry Heinemann,
Pat Strachan, editor of Paco's Story, *and Ellen Levine, the author's literary agent*

you imaginatively bring forth this person; everything you know about him or her (or can rhetorically imagine); and if there is a history of a relationship, all this is brought forth, too. Language, upbringing, family stories, shared intimacies of all kinds—everything—and the letter (whatever the content) is directed to that person. My very first impulse was to write Paco's story to "James," taken from the street custom of referring to a stranger you might engage in conversation as "Jim" or "Jack," etc. Since the story was "literary" I would use the more formal address. I wrote the first chapter in something of a frenzy, and sent it to Pat. She immediately commented with a question, "The 'James' wouldn't be James Jones would it?" That wasn't the case, but the coincidence was so exquisite I decided to tell Paco's story to James Jones. His World War II novels had a solid impact on my own work; I learned a great deal from his novels *From Here to Eternity* and *The Thin Red Line.* I was from Chicago; he from downstate Robinson. He had been an ordinary infantryman with the 25th Division, as I had— his battalion down the road from mine at Cu Chi. He was also a man of my father's generation, and though it was clear he understood soldiers, I felt that he had little understanding of the dynamics of the Vietnam War—very like

my own father, who simply could not understand what I was telling him. And like my father, Jones had died that same week in May. At the end of the first chapter ("The First Clean Fact") all the men in the company but Paco are killed in a holocaust massacre—one fell swoop—so the story of Paco is told by dead men to a dead man; a ghost story. In Samuel Clemens' *Autobiography* (not published until after his death), he says that he is speaking from the grave and therefore can speak frankly and freely, without embarrassment.

The ninety-three men of Paco's company would do the same.

I worked on the novel, and taught at Columbia.

Our son was born in 1980; Edie gave birth to him at home in the bed we sleep in; I played Aaron Copland's "Fanfare for the Common Man" over and over all day. We named him Preston John after our fathers and grandfathers—all named John, except for my mother's father, Preston.

By the winter of 1986 my relations with John Schultz had come to an end. I resigned, irremediably fed up (it's a story for another time), and was determined to make my way by my writing, and set to work first of all to finish the novel. By spring the story was all but complete. During the kids' spring break we spent the week at a friend's cottage on a small lake in northeastern Indiana; I would write and Edie would type. It was record cold and it took our typewriters until ten in the morning to warm up enough to work. I felt good—satisfied—about the work I had done, if a body can feel "good" about such a thing.

Early Passover morning an odd and wonderful thing happened. I stepped outside with a cup of coffee. It was very cold. The sky was clear. The grass rimy with frost. The full moon was setting at one end of the lake and the sun was rising at the other. Just then a pair of geese flew over the cottage, almost low enough to reach up and touch, landed on the still water of the lake, and sailed side by side to the other end. This may sound pretentious, but it seemed a blessing of some kind; that whole moment so impressed me that I wrote a poem I called "The Geese"; one of the few I ever wrote in my life.

We got back to Chicago, and I sent off the manuscript.

Pat Strachan and I always referred to the piece generically as Paco's story, and when it came time to find a title, there it was. The novel was by any definition a difficult piece to write; for nine years Edie gulped when she typed it; Pat edited the final manuscript with her eighteen-month-old daughter sometimes sitting in her lap, reading over Ellie's shoulder; and before the story came to print Pat and I had many blunt conversations.

I immediately began work on a nonfiction book about post-traumatic stress disorder and some Vietnam veterans—so-called "tripwire" veterans—who live on the Olympic Peninsula in Washington state. I began making trips out to Port Angeles to wander around the woods there, and talk to as many Vietnam veterans as would stand still for me.

That fall Pat called and said that *Paco's Story* was on the short list for the National

Heinemann (at center), with writers Don Bodey, Steve Bosak, and Tom Nawrocki, at a bar in Chicago, 1988

The Geese

Cold April
Bodey's Lake,
Indiana,
Passover,
Six a.m.

Takes an hour
to start the fire
and make the coffee.
Hot cup stings
my palms
and fingers.
Shoes soaking
in the grass.
Wear my cardigan sweater
Edie made
of skein-ends;
knitted as her hand
came to them.
Sweater is thick
and heavy,
but warm;
a riot
of colors.

This morning,
I have the lake
to myself.

Across the way;
across the lake,
just over the farmhouse
kitchen garden,
the full moon sets.
Fat and flat,
big as a tea cup saucer
held at arm's length;
color of a thick
slice of snowy ice.

Behind me;
back of Bodey's
handbuilt cinderblock cottage,
just over the pasture grove
of hickory and burr oak,
the sun rises.
Huge and yellow
orange,
and warm,
thank God.

Hold my coffee
with both hot hands
and sip deep,
sweet as brass.
Sun and moon,
both large lights,
opposite
and poised
on the horizon.
An amazing moment,
even *I* know that.
When such a light
touches such a heart,
what happens?

Mated pair
of geese who live
on the pasture pond
fly over the house
and yard,
honking and crying,
loud.
Low enough to hear
the air fiercely
hushing over their
wings and backs;
close enough to hear
the sharp,
hard breathing
as they work.

Cruising side by side,
they ease down;
touch and coast
into the wide
shivery wedge
of moonlight;
make straight
for the shoal reeds.

Long wakes
like arrows;
with feathers,
the patina
of old silver,
clean to the tip.

The Delegation of American Veteran Writers meet General Nguyen Vo Giap, Hanoi, 1990

Book Award; I was so dumb about these things I didn't know what that was. Toni Morrison's *Beloved* and Philip Roth's *The Counterlife* were among the nominees. Edie and I were to come to New York as Farrar, Straus and Giroux's guests and be present for the award. I, like everyone else, thought that either Morrison's or Roth's book would be named. As far as we were concerned, the trip would be a rare junket to New York; I'd get to sit down to dinner with Pat, who I almost never got to see; the next morning we could make a quick tour of New York, and be home that night. At the dinner in the Grand Ballroom of the Pierre Hotel (plush carpet, velvet drapes, gaudy chandeliers, and gold leaf) Edie sat with Pat and I sat next to Roger Straus. Mr. Straus is one of the most elegant and handsome men I have ever met, and so cultured that he doesn't speak English with an American accent. When the award was announced I expected to hear Toni Morrison's name; instead, I heard my own. I'm sure my mouth dropped wide open, and I just sat there.

Finally Mr. Straus (a man not given to demonstration) turned in his chair, grabbed me around the shoulders, pulling, and loudly said, "Get up! Get up! It's you, it's you!" I'm sure the two most surprised people in the room were Ms. Morrison and myself. I was given a check for ten thousand dollars and a Louise Nevelson sculpture—worth at least as much. After dinner a group of us went down the street and around the corner to the Plaza Hotel to celebrate. We walked back to the entrance to the dining room and the bar. We asked the *maitre d'* for a table. He looked us up and down— evening gowns and tuxedos—and said the kitchen was closed and invited us to take a table in the bar. It was Monday night, the place was packed, and everyone was watching Monday Night Football. Michael di Capua, an editor at FS&G, and also a very elegant man, looked at the guy, pointed to me, and said, "This man just won the National Book Award. Are you sure there's nothing you can do for us?" Right then and there the guy's whole body changed. He scooped up a handful of menus, ushered us into the Oak Room, and sat us in a corner booth. Over the booth was a bronze plaque that read, "George M. Cohen sat in this booth and passed many pleasant hours." Heavens to Betsy! Pat ordered two fifty-dollar-a-bottle bottles of champagne, which we drank with gusto. I went to the smoke shop and bought two of the biggest, ugliest cigars I could find—I was going to celebrate this like a *man!*—and smoked them down to the lips; one right after the other. I was suddenly at the top of my profession; next year it would be someone else. I've come to think of the book award as a great gift—they don't have to give it to anyone, mind you—and that you should celebrate every good thing that comes into your life; sometimes the good things are few and far between.

In the days and weeks that followed there appeared many denunciations of the judges' choice. The nasty, vituperative tone sincerely stung me—for about a minute. Finally, all I could think to say was, The check is cashed, pal, and I ain't giving the Nevelson back.

I continued to work on the PTSD book with frequent visits to Port Angeles. Then, in 1988, I received a Guggenheim Fellowship to work on a Chicago novel. I wanted to write a funny book that didn't have anything to do with Vietnam and nobody died. I got the title, *Cooler by the Lake,* from the quintessential Chicago summertime weather report. I picked the title because I figured that every time the news gave the weather report they'd be plugging the book. The book was great fun to work on, but didn't do very well.

In 1990, while I was working on that novel, I was invited by the William Joiner Center at the University of Massachusetts at Boston to join a group of American veteran writers for a trip back to Vietnam. Ex-GIs had been going back since 1985, and the idea had been in the back of my mind, but now the impulse came together with the opportunity. There was to be a joint American-Vietnamese veteran writers conference in Hanoi, and then we were going to tour the country. All I can quickly say about my first trip back (there have been several since) was that the Vietnamese welcome of us and their hospitality toward us was astonishing—thinking about all the things that happened during the war (especially in the north). It has quickly become a cliche among American veterans who have traveled there that we receive a more warm and hospitable welcome when we return to Vietnam than we received from our own people when we came back from the war. Perhaps veterans share more with the Vietnamese than we know. How odd. I have been back a number of times since, and would go back at the drop of a hat. These trips have not been "guilt trips," and certainly not journeys of re-discovery. The Vietnam we saw during the war was not Vietnam at all, but a culture and people hidden and denied us, forbidden even to our imaginations. I discovered that the food is excellent (a combination of Chinese and French), the countryside is beautiful, and the fishing is great. And perhaps most significantly, the Vietnamese hold the United States in high regard.

I decided to write a book about contemporary Vietnam. I was tired of writing about the war; I was not qualified to write about the history, others have done that much better than I; I'm not interested in the politics, the historical structure of Vietnamese socialism will probably never be understood in this country. But I'm a train buff, and as it turns out Vietnam has this funky little railroad, so I would write about that. As of this writing the book is nearly done.

The war and its aftermath were not pleasant, not personally and not for the American culture at large. The role I discovered, writing about an event which is central to my life, is simply to witness—I don't know what else a storyteller can do. The legacy for the culture, the bizarre and selfish political stupidities, the arrogance of military careerists (who saw the war as the career opportunity of a lifetime and gave little mind to the morality), the world record tons of bombs dropped, the massacres at My Lai (more vicious and horrific than Wounded Knee or Fort Pillow, you understand) and a thousand other nameless places—the whole egregious, nasty business—exerts a push as well as a pull on our collective memory and imagination. We Americans are famous for not picking up after ourselves, but the omission of dealing directly with the aftermath reverberations of the epoch of the Vietnam War is likely to take us to a very strange place, indeed.

See you there.

BIBLIOGRAPHY

Fiction:

Close Quarters (portions originally appeared in *Penthouse*), Farrar, Straus, 1977.

Paco's Story, Farrar, Straus, 1986.

Cooler by the Lake, Farrar, Straus, 1992.

Contributor:

Best American Stories in 1980, Penguin, 1981.

Best of TriQuarterly, Washington Square Press, 1982.

Contributor of short stories and nonfiction to magazines, including *Harper's, Playboy, Penthouse, TriQuarterly,* and *Van Nghe* (Vietnam Writers Association Journal of Arts and Letters).

Andrew Hudgins

1951-

Andrew Hudgins

At a party at Stanford University, where I was a Stegner fellow in poetry, a friend suddenly asked with abrupt and aggressive intensity, "When you were growing up were there books in the house?"

"No," I said, "not really."

That was true for him too, he said, when he was growing up in an Italian neighborhood in south Philadelphia. Like me and many of the writers I knew there, most of them from poor or middle-class families, he was, I suppose, amazed and gratified to find himself at Stanford, and a little touchy about it.

"Not really" was the most accurate answer I could come up with under the pressure of the moment, the unexpected question in front of friends, and though my answer was more true than not, there were in fact some books that moved with us from house to house as my father was transferred by the Air Force. It's not that my parents were against books or afraid of them; they weren't. They simply saw no need to pay money for something that would only be used once and that could be checked out of the library for free. If anything, they believed that reading was an unalloyed good, and Mom started teaching me early. The year before I began first grade, she called the school board in Goldsboro, North Carolina—my father was stationed at nearby Seymour Johnson Air

101

Force Base—and bullied them into letting her buy copies of all the first-grade readers. Sitting on her lap, following her index finger as it moved from word to word, I stumbled through the listless adventures of Dick, Jane, Spot, and Puff, who spent their lives looking and seeing. Occasionally they ran, but mostly they looked and they saw. By the time I began first grade, I knew the books backward and forward. I'm not sure I could read them so much as I had simply memorized them from countless hours of repeating each word as my mother's red fingernail pressed a faint crescent into the white space under it. When students in other reading groups got stuck on a word, I'd lift my head from whatever work I was doing at my desk and shout the answer, out of the sheer pleasure of knowing it and out of impatience too, that the story had stalled. For some reason, the teacher tolerated my disruptions, perhaps not wanting to blunt my enthusiasm.

When we moved into on-base housing the next year, I could ride my bike to the base library. Base libraries are usually spartan places—cramped, dark, and staffed by volunteers who loaned well-worn, donated books with floppy spines. The library at Seymour Johnson was one of the spartan ones, but I know that only in retrospect. It was the first library I'd ever seen and for me it held treasures. It contained about one-third of the books in the Hardy Boys series. Like ancient documents, the books were torn, creased, stained, annotated, mildewy, and occasionally missing pages entirely, but the library would let me take them home for two weeks at a time! And then, if necessary, I could check them out for two more weeks! I even enjoyed the dignified transactions that transpired if I kept the books past the due date and had to count out a dime or two to the librarian who would expiate my shame by counting back unsmilingly the pennies I was due as change.

At home, though, the books were mine, not the library's. I could pile them up, hoard them, save them for later, or pitch myself into the heroics of F. W. Dixon's Hardy Boys—and I noticed for the first time how, as I neared the conclusion of each book, I'd read more and more slowly, drawing out the pleasure, lingering as long as I could in the world I did not want to leave. Lying belly-down on my bed with my head hanging over the side and the book cracked open on the floor, I was so deeply engaged in the world created by F. W. Dixon

that I wouldn't hear my mother calling me to supper and she'd come back and say, good-naturedly, "Hey, Mister Anti-social! Come join the rest of the family." I can still summon, though weakly through the decades, the dismay I felt when I discovered that F. W. Dixon was not really the author of the Hardy Boys books but a pseudonym for many different writers working to a formula. I felt that some tacit agreement had been violated, some faith betrayed. I'd trusted F. W. Dixon, merged my nervous system with his sentences and stories until I was oblivious to the world outside them, and then I found out he didn't exist. O cruel and faithless F. W. Dixon! You should have made me more suspicious of reading than you did. But since I had no doubts about my love for Frank and Joe Hardy, whose lives were so much more interesting and so much more understandable than my own, I yielded quickly to pragmatism: "Oh, so that's how it's done. Well, who cares as long as I get to read the books."

I learned early that reading, which I saw as a pure pleasure, was seen by my parents as work, a virtue in and of itself, something to be encouraged, a form of self-improvement, and I shamelessly exploited that chasm between our perceptions. If Mom shouted back down the hall "Andrew, what are you doing?" and I answered "nothing," I'd end up scrubbing the baseboards, mowing the lawn, or peeling carrots. But if I shouted back "reading," the odds were better than fifty-fifty that I'd get out of work. Reading was more important than baseboards, the lawn, or carrots, even though I knew—and kept the guilty knowledge to myself—that I was only reading the Hardy Boys, sports biographies, books about noble and preternaturally intelligent collies—books that had no merit other than unadulterated escapism except that they could reveal the pleasures of reading itself.

I read purely to escape, not for knowledge or wisdom, not to strengthen my reading skills or deepen my psychological acuity. A shy child, miserable and self-conscious, I plunged myself into imagined worlds where I could be a Hardy Boy or young King Arthur. Though I couldn't know it then, I was assuming, as readers do, the hero's understanding and mastery of his simplified world. In my own life, though constantly aware of how little I grasped my parents' expectations of me, I was painfully aware too of how short I fell of those expectations.

My parents were natural athletes. Their golf and bowling trophies were jumbled on the shelves. Before going in the navy, Dad had begun college at Georgia Southern University on a football scholarship, and he went from the navy to West Point, where he played football on the same team as Doc Blanchard and Glen Davis. I believe he was a deep-kicker, but I'm not sure. He never talked about it. He was, I think, slightly embarrassed because he didn't play on the first-string. My mother was, if anything, a better athlete than he. They understood sports, enjoyed them, excelled at them, and assumed without question that I would too. Every year I played baseball, football, basketball. I bowled. One of the more courageous acts I performed as a boy was when at twelve or thirteen, after weeks of agonized planning, I told my parents I didn't want to play Little League anymore because I was tired of standing out in right field praying that no fly balls would be hit in my direction. "Okay, if that's what you want," they said. And life, to my surprise, went on. The only sport I stuck with was judo because

Andrew Hudgins, age four, Hunstanton, England

my father knew nothing about it and therefore couldn't stand on the sidelines yelling instructions that were soon followed by frustrated recriminations about my failure to follow the instructions. But unlike sports, which belonged to them, reading was mine. They didn't understand it and, therefore, in their sentimental view of it as almost always good, they didn't try to direct it. With only a few exactions, books were mine and I, no matter how unformed by taste, could read what I wanted to read. I was free to pursue my pleasures.

Only a couple of times did my parents institute prohibitions about what I could read. When I was eleven or twelve, superhero comics, my favorites, were banned. I think it was because superheroes are more powerful than Christ and are therefore anti-Christian, my father being from time to time overinfluenced briefly by sermons he's heard. All my *Batman, Superman, Green Lantern, Wonder Woman* comics, even my treasured copies of *Spiderman,* were pitched, and for awhile my brothers and I were permitted only insipid "baby" comics like *Richie Rich, Mighty Mouse, Baby Huey,* and *Archie.* And we were encouraged to read a two-volume, comic-book version of the Bible that my parents bought. In comic-book form I enjoyed the Old Testament more than the New. Floods, pillars of salt, Eve and the serpent make, for a twelve-year-old, a more intriguing story than pictures of a leper clutching at the hem of Jesus' robe, especially if the twelve-year-old doesn't know what a leper is. I was fascinated by the picture of Absalom hanging by his hair from a tree limb while his murderers taunted him, though I believe the book, to spare the sensibilities of us young readers, obscured the fact that he was killed. Soon, with nothing being said, the ban on comics was abandoned and, instead of going to our friends' houses and reading their tainted comics, we could stand in the PX and honestly wheedle Mom into "wasting good money," as she put it, on *Spiderman* or *The Fantastic Four.*

A year or two later I was forbidden to read any James Bond books because the movie version of *Goldfinger* came out in 1964 and received a tremendous amount of lubricious publicity for its sex scenes and its "Bond girls" with names like Pussy Galore. I knew it would be pointless even to ask permission to see the movie but I resented being told what I couldn't

With his mother, Roberta Rodgers Hudgins,
about 1955

read. I went to the base library, sat in a corner out of sight, and over a few months systematically worked my way through the Ian Fleming *oeuvre.* Even after I'd become thoroughly bored with the Bond books, I kept on reading till I'd read them all. These were the only times my father ever restricted my reading though he certainly would have done it again if he'd discovered the copy of *My Secret Life* that, in high school, I smuggled into the house and kept hidden behind the neatly fronted-up books on my bookshelf. My parents rarely asked what I was reading and I didn't tell them. If they did ask, I'd tell them the title and nothing else.

This strategy generally worked pretty well. But when I was fourteen, *The Green Berets,* a huge best-seller, came out in paperback and I was able to talk my parents into buying it for me because my father assumed it would glorify the Green Berets. I read the book and then passed it on to my father, who wanted to see what it said about Vietnam, where within eighteen months he'd be sent, something that he must have suspected would happen.

A week or so later, he came into my room, shut the door, sat on the side of the bed, and said softly, "I want to talk to you." He was clearly upset, struggling for words, and I was frightened, wondering what I'd done wrong. A gentle approach like that usually meant a long and wrenching heart-to-heart about why I wasn't "working up to my potential" at school or how I would have to step up and be more of a man around the house and more helpful to my mother while he was on TDY (temporary duty out of town). He told me he'd read the book and he was sorry he'd let me read such filth. "Listen," he said, "I just want you to know that people don't really live like that. These writers just make a lot of wild stuff up to sell books." He insisted on the point and insisted that I agree with him that "people don't really live like that." I had no idea what he was talking about. Was he talking about the war? About killing? But of course people killed each other in war. He was there, he said, anytime I needed to talk about these things, okay? I said okay, and he slapped me affectionately on the thigh and stood up. After I'd agreed again that people don't really live like that and after he'd left, I realized he meant sex. That people don't really have sex outside marriage. I didn't know who was right, Dad or the book; to me, they both offered views of the world I had no way of judging. But the book, though I suspected it of embellishment and sensationalism, held out a richer, more complex, more frightening and therefore more compelling world than my father did.

Educational reading, on the other hand, was encouraged even though Mom and Dad resisted the blandishments of door-to-door encyclopedia salesmen after twice sitting through the entire *Encyclopedia Britannica* spiel. And I, the object of the skirmish, hunched in a corner of the couch and listened as the earnest middle-aged man and later the even more earnest young one presented themselves as vitally interested in my education while respectfully insinuating that my parents, though they of course thought they too were concerned about my welfare, were perhaps not as totally committed to it as one might hope if they denied me my own personal set of the *Encyclopedia Britannica.* Immense and frightening, the *Britannica* looked to me like something I'd never comprehend, and I understood immediately that it would be an expenditure I'd hear about every time I brought home a *C* on my report card, and since my report card consisted mostly of *C*'s I knew I'd become uncomfortably knowledgeable about the pricing structures and financing procedures of the Britannica Corporation. The huge set of books would squat on its own bookcase in the living room like a dark unsatisfiable troll called Obligation. So before my parents turned to me and asked if I really needed such an expensive thing at home when they'd be happy to take me to the base library anytime I needed to go and anyway there was a set of *Britannica* in the school library, wasn't there, I was already praying for this cup to pass.

But the sales pitch about how they'd be cheating their kids if we didn't have free and easy access to an encyclopedia must have hit home with Mom. For the only time I remember, she didn't do the weekly shopping at the commissary on base; instead she went to a local grocery store that each week sold a different child's encyclopedia volume for ninety-nine cents with a minimum purchase of twenty-five dollars. We ended up with, I think, nine of the ten volumes. Though I no longer remember the name of that encyclopedia, I loved those cheap books. Skipping from subject to subject, I read randomly: Tea, Texas, Wisconsin, Coal. I'd take a volume into the bathroom, lock the door, sit on the commode, and read for hours. I tried to keep one volume open on the toilet tank so I could read it while I stood peeing. With two brothers then and later three, I relished privacy because it was hard to come by. Sometimes I'd lock myself in the bathroom, lie on the cold floor and read. After awhile, Mom would pound on the door and say, "Boy, did you fall in?" For some reason, I was fascinated with the maps of states and foreign countries, which were marked with little symbols showing what parts of Texas grew cotton and what parts of Germany and France were rich producers of bauxite. And because we owned Volume I, *A-Ch,* I knew bauxite was the principal ore of aluminum and that it was named after Les Baux-de-Provence, the place in southern France where it was first discovered. A year ago I found a complete set of those encyclopedias in an antique store in Sunbury, Ohio, and it took a great deal of self-control not to spend thirty dollars and, by that act of sentimental ransom, assure myself of disappointment.

Andrew (right) and his brother Roger with their father, Andrew Hudgins Sr., Hunstanton, England

I loved them truly when I was a boy, but then is then and now is for books, mature loves. To buy those encyclopedias and read them now would be like trying to fall in love with a twelve-year-old girl—acceptable when you're ten or twelve yourself, or even thirteen, but morally repugnant when you're forty-three.

I dashed from book to book without plan or method. In the twelve-foot-by-twelve-foot library at Del Rosa Elementary School in San Bernardino, California, where we lived for the three years my father was stationed at Norton AFB, a boy standing next to me as I tried to choose a book revealed his method: "I go to the last page and if the last word is a good word I'll read the book."

He tipped a book off the shelf and flipped to the end. "See, this book ends with 'eagle.' That's a really good word. I'll read this one."

It sounded like a good plan, but though I tried, I couldn't make it work. To me, *all* the words looked like good ones. "Faith," "Red," "die," "should"—I couldn't judge which word possessed the greatest inherent virtue. I simply lugged home piles of books, and if I got past page two, I finished the book. But I did get on riffs. Paul Bunyon led to Pecos Bill, who led to Barnacle Bill, who begat Railroad Bill, who begat John Henry and other tall-tale heroes I've forgotten.

At Del Vallejo's Junior High the next year I signed up for a class in library work, and I got to do such temporarily interesting chores as put book covers on the books, burn call numbers on spines, and glue card pockets on the inside back covers. But after I'd performed these crafts twenty or thirty times, I volunteered to do the shelving because I would toss the books back in place quickly and have plenty of time left to find a chair outside the librarian's line of sight and read about Kit Carson and Jim Bridger. Then, because they had a lot of grotesque details about massacres and cannibalism, I began to tear through colonial captivity narratives and books about the frontier Indian wars. At Del Vallejo I also read my first best-seller, and it would be hard for me to exaggerate how proud I was to be reading an adult book that seriously engaged adult subjects: *Seven Days in May,* an edgy and, to my mind, sophisticated story of nuclear tit-for-tat with Moscow and New York being wiped out.

With his brother Roger on Christmas, Wright Patterson Air Force Base, about 1957

The books we owned and that travelled with us from house to rented house included the Bible, which I didn't really consider a book because it was holy, the Bible comics, the children's encyclopedia, and about twenty books that appeared in a magical thud followed by several magical dribbles as a result of a short-lived membership my parents took in the Book-of-the-Month Club. They'd signed up for one of those twelve-books-for-a-dollar deals and then bought the minimum number of books required to discharge their obligation, something I did myself a couple of years ago with the Record-of-the-Month Club—just so you'll know I'm not sneering at them. And why would I sneer at a legal and ethical transaction that brought under our roof a couple of Frank Yerby novels that I always meant to read but never did, a superb book of hillbilly stories called *Tall Tales from the High Hills,* and perhaps the greatest book ever written, a book even more sophisticated than *Seven Days in May* because it included literary and historical information: *Bennett Cerf's Laugh Treasury,* which collected four of

Cerf's earlier books into a Bennett Cerf *magnum opus.*

I was enthralled. For hours at a time I flipped through the thick books and read the short sketches, nothing longer than a couple of pages and most of them only a few sentences—cultural and historical anecdotes, ghost stories, jokes, odds and ends of wit. The anecdotes were heavy on stories about twentieth-century American writers—Hemingway, Fitzgerald, Faulkner, and the Algonquin wits, not a one of whom I'd heard, but Cerf's blithe certainty that these writers required no introduction made me feel included, welcome, special, even as he bewildered me. Cerf's unpatronizing assumption of shared knowledge gave his literary snippets weight and significance, and made me feel as if I were not just glimpsing, but participating in an alien and superior world. To me, a sheltered boy, poor student, and worse athlete, it was an insider's view of a sophisticated and clever life that I, as a reader, would join on privileged terms by assuming Cerf's insider status.

Long before I'd ever read a word written by Ernest Hemingway, I knew that his contract with Scribner's stipulated that no word in his manuscripts would be altered without his consent. I know because Bennett Cerf told me that Maxwell Perkins, when reading the manuscript of *Death in the Afternoon,* came across the word "fuck" and, knowing he couldn't print it, jotted the word down on his list of "What to Do Today," so he would remember to discuss alternatives with Hemingway. When Perkins's secretary saw the note, she exclaimed, "Does a secretary have to remind her boss to do *everything?*" Pretty racy stuff. But I must have read the anecdote ten times over three years before I finally understood it because Cerf was of course working under nearly the same publishing constraints as Perkins. He identifies the troublesome word only as "a four-letter Anglo-Saxon word beginning with 'f'"—a description that completely foxed me, though at first I would have been just as much in the dark if he'd used the word outright. And if I couldn't grasp "fuck," I couldn't hope to grasp the distinction between "like" and "love" that Cerf credits to William Faulkner, who quotes a young lady from Mississippi as explaining, "If I like 'em, I lets 'em. If I loves 'em, I helps." But sex was not the only thing I was blind to. Though I've read that anecdote many times, not until today, rereading it to refresh my memory, did I register the casual and unexamined racism of the time that's implicit in the dialect.

Ignorance did not detract from my fascination with these stories. Far from it. If anything, the fact that I did not wholly understand them was intrinsic to my fascination; it's what drew me back to them as I struggled to justify Cerf's faith in our shared knowingness. And what, in Cerf's stories, I understood only in part, and that part only vaguely, outweighed the little I did understand fully in my own life, which was by its nature mundane. Cerf made me feel like I could understand the clash of the titans. From Cerf, I knew that Hemingway had confronted Max Eastman for referring to him in print as the leader of the "false-hair-on-the-chest" school of writing. Cerf is vague on what happened next but gives the impression that violence ensued. The anecdote is illustrated by a caricature of belligerent Hemingway, his massive chest and simian arms covered with a thick pelt of curly black hair, while a caricature of scrawny, cowed Max Eastman pulls one curly hair straight out from Hemingway's sternum and stares at it, bemused. Seeing these complex people reduced to this silly story and sillier drawing, I felt superior to both the macho strutting novelist and the weasely critic who had chosen the wrong person to abuse from what he took to be the safe distance of print.

I didn't know who Ernest Hemingway was, I still don't really know who Max Eastman was, and I had only a rough idea what hair-on-the-chest implied, but I loved Bennett Cerf for assuming I knew as much as he did, or that I would if I just kept reading. Reading Bennett Cerf, I reverted to being the child who sat under the kitchen table, playing with blocks and listening to his mother talk on the phone. I loved listening to her voice, listening to her half of the conversation and trying to make sense of what she said about people I barely knew and happenings I didn't know at all. I tried to absorb the world through her words and F. W. Dixon's and Bennett Cerf's because eyes merely see things; they cannot connect them, explain them, make sense of them the way words can, even if that understanding is provisional, illusory, wrong.

With time and too much reflection, I also learned from *Bennett Cerf's Laugh Treasury* that a short punchy anecdote could hold complexities beyond the simple turn at the end, and that punch lines, which usually jerk a story to a tidy halt while making the reader smile, could at times deepen the story uncomfortably—like the racism in the Faulkner anecdote—enriching and darkening the emotional shadings of characters they seemed to be flattering. I learned that stories, because they put people in action with other people and the teller in action with his story, are explosive and dangerous organisms that possess a life of their own outside the cage of meaning the teller thinks he has constructed for them. Nowhere was this more true than in church. Whenever the preacher launched into a story, I'd snap out of my stunned daydreaming. I wanted to hear the story no matter what it was, and I was doubly delighted when the story didn't make, or actually undercut, the point the preacher said it made. And from Bennett Cerf not only did I begin to learn how stories were structured because his were stripped to their anecdotal bones, I also grasped that humor was serious. And that pleasure was essential to life and therefore essential to writing—something my Southern Baptist upbringing and my father's stoic Calvinism had hidden from me.

Except for a few of my father's mildewed textbooks from West Point, those are the only books I recall my family owning. At the breakfast table my brother Roger and I squabbled over who got to read the back of the cereal box. When he got up to pour more orange juice, I turned the box of Captain Crunch so I could read it, and when I turned to see if my toast was done he'd shift it back. The squabbling moderated when I was ten or so, and Dad decided I was old enough for him to share sections of the Goldsboro newspaper with me. To his amusement, my favorite section wasn't sports or comics but the editorial page. The news articles merely told me what was happening, but the editorial page revealed ways of thinking about what happened. I was especially drawn to the letters to the editor; from them, I got a clear sense of people who cared passionately about something and had definite opinions about it. Because I knew nothing about the issues being debated, I was of course always utterly convinced by the last letter or editorial I read, a susceptibility that worried me and made me wonder if I were a weak reed in the wind.

Other than the West Point alumni magazine, *Assembly,* and a quarterly publication from the Woodman of the World, a fraternal insurance company that held my burial insurance policy, the only magazines we subscribed to during my childhood were the *Reader's Digest* and, briefly, *Argosy.* Though I always read the *Reader's Digest,* it didn't interest me very much, except for the jokes, because it lacked personality. A cheap men's magazine that must have been a gift subscription from someone who didn't know my father very well, *Argosy* was not renewed when its year was up. For the year that it came, though, I pored over its true-crime stories and its articles about hunting big game and searching for lost Nazi treasure sunk in Swiss lakes, but what riveted my attention were the corny "lifestyle" pictures—I didn't know they were corny—of bikini-clad babes leaning against the rails of enormous yachts, their hair trailing out over the ocean, their moist lips parted. Though tame even by the standards of the day, the pictures exposed more female flesh than I had ever seen, and I studied them for inspira-

tion and guiltily masturbated over them and then over my memories of them well after the subscription had run out and the old copies were thrown away.

But in the ninth grade I discovered a magazine that changed my life. That school year, 1965–66, my father was stationed briefly—nine months—at an army base outside Paris, France, and I became friends with Bill Tickle, a boy who lived upstairs from us in the military apartment complex. Bill was a large boy with a crew cut and bad acne, and he liked to wear sweater vests and ties to school. Because we were nerds—the tall boy and the skinny nervous boy who hung out with him—the cool kids enjoyed taunting us on the olive-drab buses that transported us to school or the various military complexes around Paris, where we could go to English-language movies or to the base libraries.

Greek fishermen caps were popular because the Beatles wore them, and I remember sitting with Bill on the back bench of the bus coming home from a movie one night as a gang of kids wearing those caps kept looking in our direction and laughing. Finally they turned and stared at us, and one of them said, "I'll give you a nickel for a pickle, Tickle." They burst into helpless laughter that fed off its silly audacity, and when the laughter began to die down one of them said again, "I'll give you a nickel for a pickle, Tickle," and the group whooped, laughing uncontrollably now, tears running down their cheeks.

Bill ignored them and kept talking to me, although I was so cross-eyed with rage I could barely follow what he was saying.

A couple of days later, in history class, I asked him why the taunting hadn't bothered him.

"Oh, that was nothing," he said, and laughed. "My dad's nickname was Tess."

"Yeah, so what? What's so bad about Tess?"

"Just say it."

"Tess?"

"No, say the whole name," he said.

"Tess Tickle?"

He chortled and so did a couple of the boys sitting near us.

"I still don't get it," I said.

"Say it louder," one of the boys said.

"Tess Tickle," I said doubtfully, but louder. My mind raced, trying to figure out what was so damn funny.

"Louder."

"Tess Tickle, Tess Tickle," I said, articulating each syllable so distinctly I kept obscuring the word from myself.

"Louder," they said again, and I was practically shouting when the teacher stared over in my direction with the look of weary and exasperated forbearance teachers reserve for students who are being particularly puerile. Bill shushed me and under his breath whispered "testicle."

Only now do I, a teacher myself, wonder what that good woman thought when she heard an idiot boy sitting in the back of the classroom chanting "testicle, testicle," until she had to stare him back into silence. And though I wanted then to take her aside and explain, now I wish even harder that I could speak backward across time and tell her what happened that day, which she has no doubt forgotten, and tell her too that, though my grades were mediocre and though I cannot for the life of me remember her name, she was one of the few good teachers I've ever had. She introduced me to Edith Hamilton's *Mythology, The Greek Way,* and *The Roman Way.* And greater love hath no teacher than to requisition a pair of buses and take a large group of fourteen-year-olds, on at least three occasions, through the museums of Paris. It was she who cajoled me into playing Tiresias in *Antigone,* dragging a stiff leg behind me and chanting, "This is the way the blind man comes, lockstep, lockstep," as I warned Creon, played by Bill Tickle, of the consequences of his intransigence.

It was Bill Tickle, son of Tess, who, in the Quonset hut that served as the post newsstand, introduced me to one of the great discoveries of my life: *Time* magazine. Somehow I had made it to fourteen without learning *Time* magazine existed. Here was a world even larger than Bennett Cerf's, to which it bore more than a few affinities with its short takes, celebrity anecdotes, and snappy writing. I loved those famous *Time* magazine VIVID VERBS that never reduced fighter aircraft to doing anything so mundane as "taking off"; they always "scrambled." Stunned and awed by that word choice—and many others—I was positive I would never be able to come up with anything half so colorful. Even more than the clever writing, I loved the sense of a larger world opening beyond the fictional world I loved. But this one was real and it was happening now. *Time* told me

"*A family picture: (from left) Roger, Dad, Mom holding Mike, and me*"

about people, places, and things I'd never heard of, and made them all seem comprehensible to a fourteen-year-old boy with little sense of the world outside of family, school, bad books, and the Bible. Except for my age, I must have been one of the provincial but curious readers that Henry Luce fantasized about in his happiest moments.

After my father was transferred from Paris to Montgomery, Alabama—back to the Land of the Round Doorknobs, as Mom called the States—I pestered my parents to buy me a *Time* magazine every time they went near the PX or commissary. And, no, a *Newsweek* or *U.S. News* wouldn't do. I was so insistent, so relentless that they found it easier to subscribe and they kept the subscription until I left the house to get married.

Time covered politics, movies, science, and contemporary culture with more authority, sweep, and style than the local newspapers could muster, and then it covered literary books, even poetry, with a commitment it has since abandoned in its attempt to lure readers who'd rather not read at all but watch TV. Now they'll review Stephen King, maybe, but then they'd review not just James Michener and Leon Uris, but Saul Bellow, Eudora Welty, J. D. Salinger, Norman Mailer—a seriousness unimaginable now. But why am I whining? I preferred Michener, Uris, and Mary Renault to Bellow. In each issue, *Time* printed a list of the top ten best-sellers in both fiction and nonfiction, and with an adolescent's uneducated and democratic conviction that what sells best must be the best, I clipped out the lists every week, taped them to three-by-five cards, and filed them in a recipe box my mother had discarded.

While waiting for the best-sellers to come out in paperback, I'd go to the library and read the early works of Michener and Uris. It never occurred to me to put my name on the library's waiting list, which I assumed would be two years long and restricted to adults anyway. In Montgomery then there was only one bookstore, Capitol Book and News, and it was downtown, where my mother seldom went. I'd eagerly go shopping with her so, while she shopped, I could haunt the paperback racks at Woolco, Gaylords, or Bellas Hess, scouring them to see if Michener's *Source* or some other longed-for book was there. If it was, I'd beg Mom to buy it for me, and though she'd examine it dubiously and grumble about the price or extract a promise to mow the lawn without whining about it, she'd usually pony up for the book. As soon as I began to make a little money by doing yard work for the neighbors, the quarters and much-folded and unfolded dollar bills soon disappeared into cash registers at Gaylords or Bellas Hess, and ultimately, by a process I would not imagine, a portion of it made its way into the hands of Michener, Uris, or Barbara Tuchman, a thought that pleased me.

In the room I shared with my brother Roger I had a closet to myself. And at the back of the overhead shelf I contrived, out of scrap lumber, a series of paperback-sized shelves held in place by the weight of the books. It was precarious and occasionally one end of it would tilt, usually in the middle of the night, noisily dumping the books in a rude jumble. But the house was rented, and Mom wouldn't let me hammer nails into the wall. With the closet door open, I'd lie on my bed and admire the two or three rows of books I'd acquired. I read most of Uris, Michener, and Kurt Vonnegut, and struggled through Swanberg's *Citizen Hearst*

and *Theodore Dreiser* and Tuchman's *Proud Tower* and *Guns of August*. In the books, I kept an index card that doubled as a bookmark, and on it I'd jot down words I didn't know, look them up later, and quiz myself on them to improve my vocabulary. Every month, I'd take the *Reader's Digest* vocabulary test called "It Pays to Enrich Your Word Power"; then I'd tear the page out of the magazine and save it so I could work on the words I missed. Every now and then, while looking something up or checking a fact, I'll find one of those index cards or folded *Reader's Digest* pages tucked in an old book, and it's gratifying and reassuring to see that I'm now comfortable with the words that seemed foreign and cumbersome when I was fifteen. With Barbara Tuchman, my list grew so formidable so quickly I had to suspend it until I finished the book, but from her I learned "ancillary." When I used it in an assignment I wrote for eleventh-grade English at Sidney Lanier High, Mrs. Schmidt half-accused me of plagiarism because she, I suspect, didn't know it before she looked it up in order to question me about it. I was such a mediocre student that I sympathize with her doubting my honesty. I was perversely pleased that she thought my writing was good enough to have been someone else's

Mike, Roger, and Andrew Hudgins in San Bernardino, California, about 1963

and I'm still nastily gratified when, looking back, I realize that she didn't seem perturbed, or even to notice, that I pronounced the word "an-Sill-a-ree."

Like many people, I have a much larger reading and writing vocabulary than a speaking one, and on more than one occasion I've been embarrassed to realize, only after the first syllable is out of my mouth, that I don't know how to pronounce the word I've begun. As a graduate student at the University of Alabama, I worked for over a year as a teaching assistant for Dr. Robert Halli, whom I admired tremendously as a person and as probably the best lecturer I've ever heard. After class one day, trying to make a point about pastoral poetry, I described something or the other as "halcyon," which I pronounced to rhyme with "falcon." A startled look passed over Dr. Halli's face, but instead of correcting me he did what gentle teachers do. Within the next five minutes he found a way to work the word naturally into what he was saying so he could pronounce it properly. He didn't give the word undue emphasis and he didn't glance at me to see if I got the point. Though he couldn't have been more gentle, I was still so humiliated by the necessary lesson that for years I couldn't talk about it.

After a year at the Air War College at Maxwell AFB near Montgomery, my father was sent to Cam Ranh Bay in Vietnam while my mother, three brothers, and I stayed put in the rented house on National Avenue. A year later when Dad was restationed at Maxwell, he bought, on North Colonial Avenue, the first house he owned. And it's the house I lived in my senior year of high school, the four years of college, and for the seven months after graduation before I got married. Once I could drive, I'd go to the downtown library or even to the huge Air War College Library out at Maxwell. I rummaged through *Publisher's Weekly* and bound back issues of *Time* and, paying special attention to the old best-seller lists, I couldn't help noticing how regularly *Folk Medicine* by a Dr. Jarvis was listed. One of the huge best-sellers of the late fifties and early sixties, it advocated natural down-home remedies as good for what ails you, whatever that ailment may be. His panacea was, if I'm remembering correctly, eight glasses of water a day, plus two more glasses of water with raw honey and cider vinegar stirred

into them. It tasted like weak apple cider gone funky.

My mother was amused by my sudden interest in folk medicine, especially since the eight glasses of water made me, at a hundred and twenty pounds, pee every twenty minutes, and the honey and vinegar concoction made me fart a lot. Though amused, she was also, I think, concerned that I might embrace health-food faddism, a concern I fostered when I announced, "I want to be a vegetarian."

She looked up from the sink, where she was peeling potatoes, and said, "No, you don't." She lapsed into an edgy silence that meant I was going to cause a major battle to erupt if I pushed any further.

Surprised, I thought about it for a minute and realized she was right. I didn't. I really liked meat. But I also realized I didn't want to fight her and my father over meat versus vegetables. They'd grown up poor in rural Georgia during the worst of the Great Depression, and it was important to them that, when we sat down at the supper table, a piece of meat, preferably red meat, be sitting on the table. Chicken was okay but it wasn't as good as pork and pork wasn't as good as beef. Fish, usually in the form of tuna casserole, salmon croquettes, and fish sticks, was always apologized for—a budget extender. Red meat meant you'd made it. It meant you weren't in red-clay Georgia scuffling to put something, anything, on the table. She let me drink my honey-and-vinegar water, but she wasn't going to compromise on meat just because I'd read something in some book. From time to time, puzzled about my constant reading, she'd ask—occasionally teasing, occasionally serious—"why do you spend all that time reading things that never really happened? Why do you read about things that aren't true?"

By that time, high school and college, I'd given up trying to explain why I compulsively disappeared into those huge best-sellers. When I didn't know it myself and wouldn't have believed it if someone told me, I couldn't tell my mother that with each book I read—and, by reading, merged with—I was changing who I was. Changing who I was, finding out who I could be: then they were the same thing and perhaps they always are. Almost certainly I could have found out more and changed faster if I'd read better books. On my bed, my back turned to my brother's side of the room,

I read, not the classics, which I stubbornly avoided out of a silly sense that classic meant dull and out of a perverse unwillingness to read books that my teachers would approve of, but *Hawaii, Mila 18, Tai Pan, Anthony Adverse, Scara-mouche,* and *Catch-22*—as well as *The Carpetbaggers, The Adventurers,* and *Valley of the Dolls.*

In junior high in Paris, I briefly overcame my lazy and falsely democratic aversion to the classics and began reading *War and Peace* because an older boy, another military brat home for Christmas from his sophomore year at Yale, had answered my question about what the greatest novel in the world was by saying that, well, on consideration, he thought *War and Peace* was the greatest novel though he himself would not go so far as to declare Tolstoy the greatest novelist—if I could follow the distinction he was drawing. Dutifully, I went to the school library and checked out *War and Peace.* I could evade Brontë and Dickens, except for a close reading of the Classics Comics version of *A Tale of Two Cities,* but even I could not slip the obligation to read the greatest novel ever written. Besides, I felt outrageously virtuous, mature, adventurous, and almost cool lugging around that great doorstop and foot-crusher of a novel, which in study hall I opened on my desk and read ostentatiously. Though Tolstoy moved with considerably less alacrity than Albert Payson Terhune's novels about dogs or *The Green Berets,* and though I found the welter of shifting Russian names difficult to organize in my mind, I loved the richly nuanced and complex vision of the world that Tolstoy created. I was transported.

That afternoon my mother asked her usual question, "What happened at school today?" Instead of replying "nothing," the usual answer, I told her that in *War and Peace* I'd read about an elaborate, fancy-dress ball and though I knew I'd merely read it, when I thought back over my day I couldn't shake the feeling I'd actually been at the great and opulent ball in Moscow. I felt that I'd been there, dancing, living those lives I'd read about.

Mom paused, and I knew from the time she was taking to respond that she was thinking, that she was being very careful with me because she didn't know what I was talking about. She may even have been a bit concerned that I was delusional but, no, she told herself, you don't want to overreact. Boys at this age

are impressionable, inclined to enthusiasm. I'd better keep an eye on him.

She said, "That's nice, I'm glad you're enjoying your book."

And suddenly I was embarrassed for myself and Tolstoy, for the book he'd written and for my failing to understand that the book was an intimacy between him and me and that I could not expect anyone else to share it. I felt as if I'd blabbed to my mother about one of the oblivious and disdainful schoolgirls I had a crush on, and watched secretly and hungrily and with immense self-loathing. But Tolstoy, in a way they never would or could, had shared his intimacy with me, and I'd betrayed him. To this day, I've never read another word of *War and Peace,* though I've read and admired other works by Tolstoy, and I resolved I'd never again talk to my mother about my reading except in the most vague terms.

Books became, even more than ever, a secret passion, and I surrendered to them utterly. "Surrender" is T. S. Eliot's brilliantly precise word to describe how we give up our own logic and personalities to the logic and personality of what we are reading. As a child and later as an adolescent, I was never a reader like Gene Williamson, one of my graduate school professors at the University of Alabama, who told the class that as a child he'd been troubled by the anomalous final section of *Huckleberry Finn,* in which Tom and Huck insist that the captured slave Jim act like a prisoner in a gothic romance. Though I now see how ridiculous those final chapters of the novel are and how thoroughly they undermine Jim's dignity, making the grown black man the plaything of two heedless white boys, then it would never have occurred to me to question the ending. Books were as immutable as rocks, and as little susceptible to questioning. I accepted everything that happened in everything I read. What I didn't understand was my fault; what seemed confusing was merely my inability to understand. The books themselves were—not perfect, because that requires a value judgment—beyond reproach, inviolate. With each book, I simply entered the world it created, accepting its premises without question, and lived in it. And when I had to leave, booted out by the timing of the last page, I dropped into a depression, a short period of grieving, if you will, that I still experience when I finish a book that has swept me beyond the resistance of logic and personality and now returns me to them. And I must wait a decent interval, a couple of hours or a day, before I jump into another book or I feel like a widow who remarries with unseemly haste, standing at the altar saying "I do" with the dirt of her first husband's grave still damp on her pumps.

Though I envied Gene Williamson his precocious intellectual power, thinking, though an important, even essential, part of the aesthetic experience, is for me a second and secondary response to putting on the author's nervous system, or a simulacrum of it, and feeling the world through his fingertips. We think by way of his thoughts to the extent we think at all. And by doing so, we enlarge the store of feelings, perceptions, ways of thinking, and thoughts available to us. Perhaps no finer compliment has ever been paid by one great writer to another than when T. S. Eliot said Henry James possessed a mind so fine no idea could penetrate it.

As a young reader I didn't feel stupid or clueless that I couldn't analyze literature dispassionately. I didn't know such skills existed. I simply entered the book's life and grew both larger and smaller—larger to be living someone else's life unbeknownst to my mother and father, smaller because the book's world was so much larger than mine. But even when I left that other world, my own, on my return, had grown incrementally larger too because I knew it better by comparison and contrast to the other. And that, I'm slightly embarrassed to admit now, after going off into these uncharacteristic raptures, was as true of Harold Robbins as it was of James Michener and as true of Michener as it was of the Shakespeare—*Julius Caesar* and *Macbeth*—that I was forced to read in high school. The fact that only compulsion got me to read Shakespeare has given me an enduring appreciation for the benefits of coercion as an educational tool.

When I went off to college, I didn't go far. Huntingdon College, a small Methodist school, was even closer to my parents' house than Sidney Lanier High. I lived at home, took classes in the morning, worked in the afternoon, and studied—to the extent I studied at all—in the evenings, a schedule that made Huntingdon seem more like thirteenth through sixteenth grade than college. I wish I could blame my after-school jobs for my acceptable but undistinguished record at Huntingdon, but I can't. Other than my laziness and my inability to concentrate on things that don't interest me, I'll blame my reading for some of it. I continued to give my freshest and most engaged attention to reading what I wanted, while working my class assignments into the gaps. I went off on odd reading jags, reading every major Hermann Hesse novel, well after the Hesse vogue of a few years earlier had been spent, though I didn't understand the books and could barely follow the plots. Even harder for me to comprehend is my doggedly ploughing through every single Evelyn Waugh novel. After I'd read a couple of them, it began to dawn on me that Waugh was not a woman, as I'd supposed, but a man. Though I found the novels easy enough to understand on the surface, I had no way to grasp their tone or intention. Since the copy on the back cover of the paperbacks described some of them as "satirical," I had a vague sense they were supposed to be funny and I read at them almost frantically, thinking that sooner or later the humor would become clear to me and I'd find myself laughing uproariously. It never happened. I also developed a bad habit in college of going to the library or discount store the week before final exams and buying eight, nine, ten thrillers and best-sellers, and immersing myself in them with the single-minded concentration that derives from shirking responsibility. In other words, I used books as tranquilizers, a purpose they served, and from time to time continue to serve, admirably.

Huntingdon was a very small college. In my graduating class there were slightly more than a hundred people. Because course offerings were limited, I to my great good fortune was not able to load up on courses in twentieth-century literature and avoid earlier periods the way many students do now at larger schools—and the way I might well have done if I'd had a choice. With so few courses being offered, I either had to take eighteenth-century poetry, say, or nothing; and as it turned out I avoided the twentieth century because I was uncomfortable with Mrs. Stone, who taught those classes. Mrs. Stone—widow of Phil Stone, the man to whom Faulkner dedicated the Snopes trilogy—was a seventy-year-old chainsmoker who wore black vinyl go-go boots, and her loud and irritable cynicism coexisted disconcertingly with her

Gurdjieffian-cum-Jungian-cum-Episcopalian religious beliefs. Once a year in Delchamps Student Center, Mrs. Stone would, while smoking, show an ancient black-and-white PBS documentary film on Faulkner. Between drags and coughs she'd grouchily answer questions about "Bill," though no one ever had the temerity to ask if she'd had an affair with him, as rumor, born of wishful romanticism, claimed.

I liked being forced to take classes that I'd never have chosen to take. I liked being forced to read closely works I'd never have read on my own—Pope, Dryden, Milton, Shakespeare. I'd assumed they were beyond me. Beyond my ability to comprehend. Beyond even my ability to read. I'd assumed obscurely that they were for students who went to Yale while best-sellers were for people like me. Much of my deep sense of inferiority was personal of course, but a lot of it was Southern, growing out of the cultural stereotypes of the South as peopled by in-bred violent dolts who were herded through substandard schools that mistaught us just enough chemistry that we could set up jerry-rigged stills by the chicken house and kill ourselves with lead poisoning—an image that was happily promoted on TV and movies, and in the best-sellers I read so assiduously.

Huntingdon took an avid but uneducated and unformed reader, and gave me Pope, Dryden, Whitman, Fitzgerald, and Shakespeare. I loved the Renaissance classes I took with Mrs. Bell, the folklore with Mrs. Figh, the American lit with Dr. Anderson. I even loved the grammar class with Mrs. Chippell, which was "strongly advised" for those of us, like me, who were earning teaching certificates; and, dear God, I even loved the eighteenth-century English lit course with depressed Dr. Hull, who began every class by complaining about the weather, which was always too hot, too cold, too damp, or too dry for his taste. Then he discussed how bad the economy was and how unlikely it was that any of us would ever be able to get jobs anywhere. From the economy, he would move on to whatever gothic criminal case or filthy political incident was in the local news, and only reluctantly and with great weariness would he pick up his textbook, flip through it, and say with a sigh, "Well, I know y'all don't want to but I guess we'd better talk about this Dryden." Dr. Hull was so unimpressed with my gifts for literary analysis—or so pessimistic about the economy—that when I later asked for a letter

of recommendation to graduate school, he tried, in all kindness, to talk me into applying to business school and, after agreeing to write the letter, he sent me away clutching a flyer for an MBA program for humanities students at the University of Virginia.

Even less impressed was Dr. Ellison, the department chairman. Discussing the intellectual abilities of the students with another teacher, she once said pointedly, "Andrew seems like a *nice* boy." Rather than resent her opinion, I was pleased she thought even that highly of me. In her honors freshman English class, I'd certainly done nothing to impress her. Until she taught me how, I had little sense of how to think about literature and no sense of how to organize those thoughts on the page. On more than one occasion Dr. Ellison told me quite pleasantly, as a point of information, that my being permitted to take the honors class had been a misjudgment on her part. I suspect she was trying to fire my competitive instincts. If so, she failed because her assessment of me too closely accorded with my own. All the other students earned an *A* in the class; I received—and earned—a *C*. Though patronizing to those like me who deserved it, Dr. Ellison was a brilliant, demanding teacher. She required freshmen to read books as complex as *Light in August, Crime and Punishment,* and *Steppenwolf,* and what she taught me about how to write clearly and think carefully I'd long needed to know.

While I was working on an English major on the second floor of Flowere Hall, down in the basement I was also pursuing a sort of walk-through history major. Truth be told, I was majoring in Dr. Gordon Chappell, whose classes in American history I took for every single history credit I earned except for one required class in European history and another in political science. A dapper, Vanderbilt-trained historian with a pencil-thin moustache and silver hair parted just off center in the style of the twenties, Dr. Chappell was a wonderfully acerbic lecturer in the old high style of Southern Tory historians, and I loved to sit in his classes, rapidly scribbling notes from the lectures he delivered from detailed, ancient, and yellowed notes that hadn't changed more than a jot or tittle in thirty years. Though I never read the textbooks, which were boring and would've taken time from my personal reading and my English classes, Dr. Chappell also re-

"My passport photo from 1965, taken for my family's move to Camp DeLoges in Paris, France"

quired us to read four books a semester from a list he provided, and he personally grilled us on each book to make sure we had read it. Quickly learning that the biographies were the best written and easiest reading—History Lite— I grew interested in biography as a form in its own right and, over time, biographies have become my preferred light reading, all but displacing thrillers and best-sellers. Two of the books I've written grew out of my fascination with the human life as a measure of, or a way to organize, time. *After the Lost War* is a historical novel in verse that masquerades as a biography of the Civil War veteran and poet Sidney Lanier, and *The Glass Hammer* is an autobiography in verse.

My parents were concerned about my majoring in English and history, and about my wanting to write, especially about my wanting to write poetry. They never tried to talk me out of it, but they worried about money. "How are you going to get a job?" they asked.

"How are you going to put meat on the table? What can an English major do that anybody'll pay money for?" Every time we washed the car or did yard work together, my father urged me to study computers. "That's the coming thing," he said, advice I ignored. Twice earlier he'd grappled with the problem of what kind of job would be suitable for a boy who wanted to do little but read. When I was thirteen or fourteen, he asked me if I'd be interested in working in a library. Because I didn't know what to make of this question that came out of the blue, because I'd liked working in the school library, and because to me the word "work" implied "payment for work," I said sure. That was the end of it. Or so I thought, until he came home a week later and told me I'd start the following Monday. Apparently he'd simply walked into the library on Norton AFB and told them he had a book-obsessed boy. Could they put him to work? For the rest of the summer, my father would come home for lunch, dump me at the library before one and pick me up a little after five. The librarians, unsure what to do with me at first, buzzed among themselves while glancing anxiously in my direction. Finally they hit on an idea. They gave me a complete tour of the library, including the secret, behind-the-scenes room where they catalogued and processed new books, and then they sat me down and gave me a long serious speech about how important, crucial, absolutely essential order is in a library. Why, a library would be just a useless jumble of books if you couldn't go to where a book is supposed to be and find it there! The worst thing in a library is for a book to be in the wrong place. A mis-shelved book is as good as lost. I could see that, couldn't I? Yes, I said, and they put me to work reading the shelves. For four hours a day, I was to stand, crouch, or kneel before the shelves of books, making sure the fiction books were in alphabetical order and the nonfiction books were correctly slotted, down to the last of John Dewey's decimals. For free. I was, it turns out, a volunteer. I read the shelves for about an hour and a half before I said "this is stupid." I pushed a large easy chair into the furthest and least-used corner of the stacks and, hidden from sight, I sat and read for four hours a day until school started again in the fall. The librarians never said another word to me, and whenever Dad asked me how work was going I said "fine."

Andrew Hudgins in his graduation photo from Sidney Lanier High School, Montgomery, Alabama, 1969

My senior year in high school he took another stab at opening my eyes to career opportunities in library science. Escorted by my father, I wound my way around the stacks of the Air War College Library at Maxwell AFB to the book-lined office of the senior librarian, who had, my father intimated, a very high general service rating and consequently quite a nice salary. The senior librarian pumped my hand and clapped me on the shoulder. "Interested in library work, huh?"

"Yes sir," I said. He motioned me to a chair, and I sat uncomfortably while he, equally uncomfortable, extolled the infinite varieties of library work in which one could specialize. My eyes wandered, and I saw that the books lining the book-lined walls weren't books anyone could *read;* they were technical books about library science, all of them—a revelation that dropped me into a horrified boredom so profound I could barely feign interest in what the senior librarian was saying. Once or twice I

forced myself to ask a question because my father was watching me anxiously while pretending not to, hoping something would spark his lethargic son into planning for his future. At home I'd made a little shrine out of the pressed-wood-and-veneer bookshelf my parents had recently bought me, fronting the books up neatly, keeping them in strict order by subject, covering the top shelf with a length of green felt, and lining up my favorite books on top of it—acts of reverence that my parents must have decided, not incorrectly, were the mark of a librarian. But as the senior librarian talked, I realized I was interested only in what was in the books; I had no desire to become a servant to the physical artifact. The idea of spending my life serving the public by looking up Jell-O salad recipes or researching the engine options originally available on 1953 mid-sized Chevrolet sedans made suicide or teaching school seem like attractive alternatives. And so, as a concession to my parents and to my own fears about finding work, while at Huntingdon I earned a teaching certificate.

In addition to the various day jobs I held in college, I found, in my freshman year, a night job that I held for the next five years. For five dollars a night, I spent four nights a week sleeping in the house of a retired opera singer named Frederick Gunster, whose family was worried about his being alone all night. I'd arrive before 10:00, help Mr. Gunster to bed at 10:30, then check on him before I left in the morning. Later, when he became bedridden, I emptied his hand-held urinal before he went to sleep. If the pay was low, so were the demands on my time and energy, and after I turned out Mr. Gunster's light and shut his bedroom door, I'd rifle his refrigerator, rummage through his liquor cabinet, occasionally taking nips of drinks that were exotic to a boy still living in a house where liquor was disapproved of. My father was a teetotaler but, to his grumbling unhappiness if he stayed up late enough to see it, my mother would mix a very diluted scotch and water, and drink it from a small thick glass that had originally held a frozen shrimp cocktail. But Mr. Gunster possessed something more exotic and fascinating to me than booze. He subscribed to the *New Yorker,* a magazine I'd read about but never seen, and I'd vaguely assumed it no longer existed, like the *Smart Set* and the *American Mercury.* I'd sit up late in his office, playing the *Tonight Show* with the sound turned off on his old black-and-white TV and poring through the articles, stories, cartoons, and studying the poems. Huntingdon then offered no courses in contemporary literature or creative writing, and the small college library carried few literary journals besides *Poetry,* so I was thrilled to read stories by Cheever and Updike and poems by W. S. Merwin, James Dickey, James Wright, Anne Sexton, and W. H. Auden before they appeared in books. At Mr. Gunster's large mahogany desk, I copied poems from the *New Yorker* into notebooks I filled, trying desperately if desultorily to learn how poems worked. I reasoned that copying would focus my attention on rhythm, line breaks, assonance, imagery, and the unfolding structure of the poem, but more than anything else I had a magical belief that I could learn the poems by reading them out loud to make my lips move the way the author's lips had moved and by copying them to make my fingers move the way the author's fingers had moved. Mervin, Dickey, Wright, Sexton, Auden: I tried to absorb them through my skin.

I've never been entirely sure why I wanted to be a poet. Unlike, I suppose, most poets, my first love in reading was prose—novels first, then nonfiction. But the first time that words jolted my nervous system from head to toe and left it jangling for weeks afterward was in the tenth grade when I flipped ahead in the English textbook to the part we never got to in any English or history class, the part about the twentieth century, and I read T. S. Eliot's "The Hollow Men." I was transported in a way I had never been before and have seldom been since. A certain kind of self-conscious self-pity is woven into the rhythms of both "The Hollow Men" and "The Love Song of J. Alfred Prufrock," a rhythm that adolescents can bond to on a subatomic level even without grasping the surface meaning. I did. With some embarrassment I remember announcing to Dr. Ellison during my freshman year at Huntingdon that it was perfectly possible to understand "The Wasteland" without understanding it on a conscious level. No, she said. One had to be familiar with the allusions, at the very least, before one could claim to understand the poem. Then suddenly she stopped and, to my astonishment, conceded the point. I loved Eliot's poetry before I could understand it and, though

I now have the predictable personal and scholarly reservations about the very qualities that first drew me to "The Hollow Men" and "Prufrock," my love for Eliot's poems has stood up through a quarter of a century of close study and continual reading. It's even withstood the fact that I read Evelyn Waugh because he'd taken the title of *A Handful of Dust* from Eliot and I read Hesse because the paperback of *Magister Ludi,* one of the most stupefying novels I've ever staggered to the last page of, had a glowing comment by Eliot splashed across the back cover. Though I don't plan it, at least once a year I read "The Wasteland" and "The Four Quartets" out loud, and I've never made it through "The Four Quartets" without crying at some point in the poem.

I was drawn to the intensity of poetry, how concentrated it was, how much meaning, ambiguity, and emotional force it could pack in an image. I loved the intricacies of language and complexities of tone, and most of all I loved the rhythms that carried everything else along on their flood and worked on my nervous system with an immediacy that circumvented thought, and subverted it in ways that were amazing to think of. On another level entirely, I've often wondered if poems weren't the perfect things for a nervous boy with a short but intense attention span to read and write. A boy who couldn't sit at a desk for twenty minutes without blasting from his chair as if by a sudden involuntary contraction of his muscles— a boy who, when he tried to write a short story, would forget by page twelve what color his main character's eyes had been on page three and, when he could remember, didn't particularly care.

The hours I spent scouring the *New Yorker* and *Poetry* and then copying poems into my notebooks were nothing compared to the hours I spent every day writing my own bad poems and rewriting them over and over, trying to teach myself to write. I never understood the contemporary anguish over people having or not having a good "role model." To me, one of the things that made writing poetry exciting, made it possible, made it mine was that nobody I knew, including my teachers, did it or knew a damn thing about it, and while I imagine I would've been a better poet sooner if I'd had a good teacher, I also suspect I'd have given it up and found something I could do on my own. The hours I poured into writing contributed to my undistinguished academic record at Huntingdon, of course; but I had a plan. The hours I'd spent writing would come to fruition and redeem me in the eyes of my teachers, envious friends, and uncomprehending but proud parents when I was accepted into the Writers Workshop at the University of Iowa, to me a place that couldn't have been more fabled or exotic or distant if it had been a monastery in Tibet.

After graduation, I taught elementary school in Montgomery for a year so I could afford to get married, and I applied to Iowa. It was the only school I wanted to attend and the only one I applied to. I got turned down flat. I was stunned, crushed, humiliated, and devastated. For days I staggered to work and back like a zombie, and cried uncontrollably when I was at home. I flinch to admit that only my mother's death and my divorce from my first wife have ever hit me harder.

Finally, I pulled myself together enough to apply to the University of Alabama, where I was accepted late and given a teaching assistantship. As often happens, the rejection by Iowa was one of the best things that ever happened to me, despite my resentful and obstinate refusal for a long time to acknowledge that fact. It made me a serious person. For the first time I understood that no *deus ex machina* was going to save me, solve my future, justify my life. At Alabama and later at Syracuse, after a second rejection by Iowa, I worked as hard as I physically could to be a serious student of literature, a serious reader, a hedonist of enduring pleasures, one who can think as well as feel. And when at thirty, after the breakup of my marriage, I was finally writing well enough to be accepted by the Writers Workshop, I turned down a good job, stored thirty-five boxes of books in my father's utility shed, and I went.

BIBLIOGRAPHY

Poetry:

Saints and Strangers, Houghton, 1985.

After the Lost War: A Narrative, Houghton, 1988.

The Never-Ending, Houghton, 1991.

The Glass Hammer, Houghton, 1994.

Contributor of short stories and articles to literary journals, including *American Poetry Review, Antioch Review, Atlantic, Chariton Review, Crazyhorse, Iowa Review, Midwest Quartlerly, Missouri Review, Nation, New England Review, New Republic, New Yorker, North American Review, Ploughshares, Poetry, Sequoia, Shenandoah, Southern Review,* and *Texas Review.*

Colleen J. McElroy

1935-

WHEREVER I AM

During the 1940s when I started elementary school, the world was at war and the men in my family, like most other neighborhood men, were serving in the military. I was surrounded by women. Every week my mother's sisters would gather at my grandmother's house on Kennerly Avenue and dissect the world along the lines of love and war, birth and death, loyalty and treachery, and above all, black and white. I took my place under the dining room table, or by the potbellied stove, or in the corner by the window next to my grandmother, Anna Belle Long, or Mama as all of us called her. On rare occasions, my grandmother would allow her daughters into the living room, which Mama called the parlor. I remember that room as dark and overpowered by heavy furniture—the forbidden room, the one used by the preacher and the insurance man but usually off-limits to children. On the wall was a tapestry, a 1920s rendition of a desert scene full of palm trees, arrogant camels, and impossibly stylized nomads, all done in beige and rose-colored velvet.

In my memory, the house on Kennerly is cloaked in eternal summer, perhaps because during the winter, school kept me too busy to find time to do what I liked best—eavesdropping when my mother's sisters came to visit us. Summers in St. Louis are humid, and in my grandmother's house that humidity made the urgency of their conversations even more pressing. It was a slot of a house, no wider than one room and the adjacent hallway. The rooms banked off that long dim hallway like compartments on a railroad sleeping car. We lived on the second floor and the parlor was the first door at the top of the stairs. In the summer, the heat crept up the stairs as soon as the front door opened, and the women spent most of the time fanning themselves as they drank glasses of Kool-Aid and chewed on the

Colleen J. McElroy

weight of the world. And because it was so hot, they dressed the way many Southern women dressed to keep themselves cool and free of heat rash: in loose skirts, open front blouses, cotton slips, and little or no underwear. I remember them sitting in the half-light of the parlor, my grandmother humming church songs and her daughters fanning away the heat of the day. The tapestry was on the wall behind them, a scene with camels waiting under a cluster of palm trees in front of a tent while someone, who was entering that tent, turned back for a moment as if to see what was unfolding behind him. The velvet sands of that tapestry seemed to add heat to the room.

I know that I did not understand all that was said by those women, because while the memory itself seems clear, their conversations were a muddle of phrases and warnings. I know now that my grandmother's parlor represented some measure of safety at a time when the world was in chaos. There, the women talked about the war, food rationing, men who'd fled the draft, and "fast women" who spent too much time cheering up soldiers on leave. And I waited at the edge of their shadows while the desert scene above the horsehair sofa maintained its own posture of intrigue. There, my sense of the outside world, with its pitfalls and temptations, began to take shape. And I was lured away from that brownstone on Kennerly as surely as the figure in the tapestry was tempted to look back at the vast desert stretching away from the tent.

The truth is I've spent my life travelling from somewhere to the next place, either physically or in the stories I have created and retold. I grew up as a storyteller, first in a family full of women who reveled in storytelling, women who, in fact, held their families together with stories when their husbands and sons were called into the military, or when racism pushed the men into hiding or into jobs in other cities. Later, when I changed schools, which I did once my mother began to follow my father on his tours of duty with the army, I used storytelling as a way of making friends. My romance with language began in my grandmother's house, with her full-length boudoir mirror and wind-up Victrola, her feather boas and wide-brimmed hats, and stacks and stacks of thick 78 rpm records—recordings of everything from opera and vaudeville to march tunes and early blues—and all of it essential accouterments for a lonely child to play out stories. I took on the roles of both speaker and listener, and when words failed, I mimicked adult conversations with body language and intonation. That was where I learned the 1920s and '30s songs of Ethel Waters, Valaida Snow, and Florence Mills, black women I chose as my heroes because they dared to defy someone's notion of what they were supposed to be. They were the stars in my boudoir mirror stories.

"My grandmother, Anna Belle Long"

In 1938, after my mother divorced my father, Purcia Purcell Rawls, she had moved back home to live with my grandmother. After war was declared, my mother worked long hours in a defense plant, so I was under my grandmother's care. Like everyone else in the family, I called my grandmother Mama, and called my mother Ruth. Mama had raised "a houseful of girls," as Aunt Jennie would say, so I was simply another girl growing up under Miz Anna Belle Long's roof. My grandmother once told me she had "lost more than her share of babies," and I knew that two of her daughters, Fannie and Jessie, had died only a few years before my birth, but the total number of daughters depended on who was counting. "I guess the Lord missed my house when he gave out boys," Mama used to laugh. Her mother had had three girls—Dora Emma, Ethel, and my grandmother—and three boys—Son, Roman, and Bud—and my grandfather, who had one sister, Clara, was one of three boys, although his twin had died at birth. But my grandmother had only one son, my Uncle Brother, who was named after my grandfather, Perry Lee Long.

Looking at all the girls in the family, I figured Papa had been bent on having a boy and just kept at it until Uncle Brother was born. My mother and her sisters doted on their brother. For years, I thought that was a waste, then I realized that since my mother was Mama's youngest daughter, if my grandfather hadn't been so determined to have a son, I might not have been born. By the time I came along, my grandmother had buried all of her daughters except Claudia, Jennie, and my mother. Aunt Claudia had children who were the same age as her younger sisters, but since Aunt Claudia was Mama's oldest child, she thought everyone had to obey her. More than one person in the family referred to Claudia Mae Long Davis as a "battle-ax"—"That woman wouldn't give a crippled man a crutch," my mother would say when she was angry with her sister. I was a grown woman before I figured out why Aunt Claudia had been so bitter. As the oldest, she had become a surrogate mother for her brother and sisters, leaving my grandmother's house at sixteen only to become a mother to four of her own children. By my count, Claudia never had a real childhood and carried that resentment with her throughout her life. When my grandmother died in 1960, Claudia sold all the furniture for three hundred dollars, without emptying the drawers or chifforobe. I still miss my grandmother's Victrola, and even though a former student has given me her grandmother's wind-up phonograph, which I cherish, nothing will completely replace the Victrola that first brought me the ladies of torch songs and blues.

When I was growing up, I don't remember hearing my Aunt Claudia laugh. Whenever she was in the room, everyone sobered up. The only one who could keep her in check was Papa. Claudia was light-complexioned, like my grandmother, but when she tried separating people in the family by skin color or texture of hair or eye color, Papa, who was dark-skinned like my mother and me, would remind Claudia that we were all from the same family. According to Papa, we were just "plain ol' colored folks." But you only had to take one quick look at my family to know *plain* just couldn't describe them.

In the Fifties, when I was attending college in Germany, a professor asked me: What are you? I thought it was an easy question, so I answered, "I am a Negro." After all, I had been raised in the Midwest before the decision of *Brown vs. the Board of Education of Topeka,* before Black Power, even before the army had been ordered to end segregation. My parents and grandparents said "Negro" and "colored," never "black." So I told the professor, "I am a Negro." He asked me again. "American?" I replied, more a question than an answer. He asked me a third time, and when I could not answer, ordered me out of his office. "How can you expect to study the history of others if you do not know your own?" he'd demanded. So I wrote to my mother in northern Germany, where my stepfather was stationed at the time. And I wrote to my Aunt Jennie back in the States. I asked them: Who am I? Where are we from? I didn't get the answers I needed in one letter, or in two letters, but in bits and pieces over the years. By then, I had developed a built-in radar that helped me glean out what versions of a story the family agreed on. Like a detective, I had learned how to probe their memories with overlapping questions, discarding vagrant information in favor of substantiated details.

Sometimes the women surprised themselves with what they remembered. Sometimes old-fashioned prudishness made them want to cover up bad memories. Was Aunt Clara's husband in California a horse trader or horse thief? I persisted. "You're part Creole-French, from some of your folks down in Texas," Aunt Claudia told me. "And Chinese from folks building the railroad," Aunt Jennie said. And when they argued about which Indian tribe we claimed, my grandmother told me that it had to be Seminole because her mother's mother had been one of the Indians the army had marched north from some place in Florida. I tried to check all the times and places, and even what I remembered of my grandfather's stories about the Sudan Desert, where his grandfather had come from. I learned that like most African Americans, I am of mixed blood, the great-granddaughter of a slave, my past rooted in six generations of free-born and slave, native and indentured forebears alike. I am a descendent of those who survived diaspora, riding the violence of bigotry and racism until it threw them off or slowed down enough for them to hang on a little longer.

Uncle Brother had hoped my mother would have a boy, but he got me instead. He called

*"My grandfather, Perry Lee Long, Sr.,
and his sister, Clara"*

me Joe, although I only answered to that name because my grandfather, Papa, also called me Joe. I remember Papa as a tall man with long fingers, "Long and skinny like yours," my grandmother would tell me years after Papa died. When my grandfather came home from work at the Anheuser Brewery, I'd hide under the roll-top lid of his big desk until my giggles gave me away. But my reward for being found was an extra glass of milk or the chance to walk with Papa to the store at the corner of the block while I told him what I'd done all day. My day could have been capped in three sentences or less, so I made up stories about an imaginary girl and Papa always asked the right questions. The longer the stories, the longer I had Papa to myself, because once the women gathered, Papa always seemed to find something to do outside of the house. Too old to be drafted into the military, Papa was the only man left at home while the other men in our family were serving in Europe or the Pacific. When my mother's sisters came to visit and

catch up on the neighborhood gossip and news of their husbands away at war, Papa would leave the house rather than be the lone man in the company of women.

There is one summer, when I was about eight, that I mark as the time when I began to understand how fragile friendships can be. It was the summer Pussy's uncle had his fit in the middle of Kennerly Avenue. Priscilla had been nicknamed Pussy for as long as I'd known her. She was the kid whose glasses were thicker than anyone else's, the kid who lost her baby teeth and seemed to take forever to grow new ones. I know now that most neighborhoods have some kid like Pussy, the ones with the eternal cold, the snaggle-toothed ones picked last for the team and even then, failing to make the grade. But in those days, she was just the kid who lived in the middle of the block, the one whose uncle had fits. "From all that drinking," some said, but my grandmother told me that mustard gas in World War I had caused his illness. "That's why he's on pension," she'd say. And I'd stare at Pussy's uncle, not knowing what forces could have given him the mystery of fits and the miracle of a pension, neither of which any of the other men in the neighborhood had ever had. Pussy's uncle was brown as a walnut and walked with a limp, crippled by all those fits, my friends and I guessed. Only once had we seen him take ill outside of the house, and because it had happened right after we'd teased him, all of us, Pussy included, were convinced we'd caused the seizure by daring him to cross our path as we blocked the sidewalk. He'd fallen backwards into the hedges, his mouth open and sounds that were not words or screams flooding the air. Pussy's face had dissolved into a gape-toothed howl and we'd abandoned her, running home to watch from our front windows until the ambulance finally arrived and loaded her uncle onto a stretcher to carry him to the colored hospital. Our mothers had shamed us for taunting him, and after that, we took care to make sure Pussy had an extra turn at jump rope or hopscotch or a bit longer to find a place to hide.

Union Railway Station in St. Louis is adorned with a fountain sculpture called the "Wedding of the Rivers," commissioned to celebrate that part of the country where the mighty Mississippi River meets the bold Missouri River. St.

Louis is also a place where the Confederate South converged on the Yankee North and the dust never really settled. My grandfather had believed St. Louis offered his family some freedom from night-riders and the poverty of the South, and he'd educated his girls to take advantage of what little freedom the town afforded them. So the St. Louis of my youth included schoolteachers and book readers and women who were determined that I would never have to work as day-help in some white woman's kitchen. "It's a big world out there," Aunt Jennie would say, when all I could see was a city that locked me into a half-mile radius of streets bordered by Taylor, St. Ferdinand, Cottage, and Kennerly avenues. "You best make your way," my cousin, Anna Lee, a schoolteacher and Aunt Claudia's oldest daughter, would tell me. But when I was young, before my mother married an army man, my way was restricted to the part of the city that included the whites-only playground at Cote Brilliante School, the pickle jars full of stale penny candy at Farrow's store,

rumors of white folks rising out of their graves in the segregated cemetery on Ash Hill, and the sugar-soaked ice cream at Velvet Freeze around the corner from White Castle's ten-cent hamburgers. I was born into a St. Louis of segregated schools and occasional race riots, a city divided into pockets of black folks and white folks, a world caught up in a war where my stepfather would wear the uniform of a segregated army. I grew up full of determination to "get out of Dodge," as they said in the Westerns.

It is just as well I left. The St. Louis I knew as a child has disappeared into the great maw of urban blight. I can no longer recognize neighborhood streets that were once as familiar as my schoolbooks. And to blur my map of home even further, they have torn down every house I every lived in—my grandmother's on Kennerly, Aunt Claudia's house on St. Ferdinand, Aunt Jennie's house on Cote Brilliante, Uncle Brother's house on McMillan—all gone, and none of them replaced by new residences. Those houses have simply been removed, leaving behind vacant lots full of prairie smokeweed, beer cans, and discarded needles. I remember streets full of fireflies and elm trees, the arbor of purple-sweet grapes behind Farrow's store, rows of hedges bruised from kids playing hide-and-seek in the thick cover of leaves, sidewalks chalked with hopscotch windows, and backyard ash pits waiting for the pick-up trucks to gather the winter's collection of cinders. In my first book of poems, I wrote:

> *The sidewalks were long where I grew up;*
> *They were as veined as the backs*
> *Of my Grandma's hands.*
> *We knew every inch of pavement,*
> *Jumped the cracks*
> *Chanting rhymes that broke evil spirits . . .*
> *The sidewalks wrapped around corners*
> *Like dirty ribbons lacing the old houses*
> *Together in tight knots . . .*

So much for memory. I cannot find those streets when I visit St. Louis now. Now those neighborhoods are dotted with patches of wilderness where houses once stood, scraggly lots in a fortress of inner-city houses either guarded by chain-linked fences or boarded up and destined for demolition. Of course, I really don't believe my leaving St. Louis had anything to do with the demise of a house, but it is a bit unnerving to think about those empty spaces

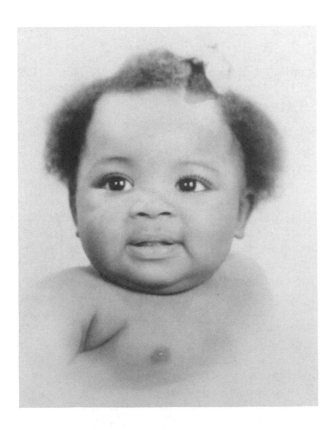

"Me at age ten months"

"At age eight with my parents, Ruth Celeste and Jesse Dalton Johnson"

replacing what was once familiar with the scars of urban deconstruction. The St. Louis I knew hasn't just changed, it has folded in upon itself like mulch.

In 1943, my mother remarried. My stepfather, Jesse Dalton Johnson, was a sergeant from Columbus, Georgia. After he was shipped overseas, my grandmother displayed two flags in the front window to show how many men in our family were away at war: one for my Uncle Brother and one for my new father. Maybe it was his uniform, or maybe it was how he looked with my mother, but I thought that next to my grandfather, my new father was the most handsome man I'd ever seen. Together, they seemed to have stepped right out of some movie like *Stormy Weather.* My mother was a beauty in those days, long-legged with hair marcelled like Joan Crawford's or in a wave over one eyebrow like Veronica Lake's. When my father teased her, her dark skin would turn even darker, deep brown undertones rising to the surface like cocoa stirred from the bottom of a cup.

While he was still stationed at Jefferson Barracks just outside of St. Louis, my father would come home some days and fix me special lunches. He listened to my stories of what had happened in school the same way Papa did in the evenings. But in the same year, soon after my father shipped out for Europe, my grandfather died.

Papa's death, like most of his life, was the subject of his daughters' speculations. Papa had gone to California to visit his sister, Clara, and her husband. On his return trip, he had been taken directly from the train to the hospital, for emergency surgery, I was told later. But at first, the family said he'd succumbed to milk poisoning, a fate that even as a child I had been unable to attach to Papa—not Papa who took me to the Anheuser stables to see the Clydesdales and walked around those big animals as if they were ponies. Not Papa who hoisted me onto his shoulders, and drop-kicked a white man's bulldog that had been commanded to "kill the niggers." Not Papa who could keep Aunt Claudia, the family whip, in check.

Over the years my mother and her sisters told me Papa had fallen victim to everything from an unknown assailant to prostate cancer. Even Uncle Brother, who had come home on furlough to attend Papa's funeral, had a different story to tell, and to this day, my mother can conjure up yet another version of how Papa died, including her insistence that he was in California to help Aunt Clara's husband, a "known horse thief." (In Los Angeles!?) Over the years, I have decided that I will never uncover the real reason Papa died, but one thing is clear: although the circumstances of his death may have been altered by time and storyteller, nothing in my life ever returned to the way it was before he died. In "More Than a Notion," a short story in my collection *Jesus and Fat Tuesday,* I have tried to capture the atmosphere of the days following Papa's death when my family tried to come to grips with our loss. I have let those versions of Papa's death swarm around me, soothing for a moment, his absence.

For a while, Mama allowed me to do my homework at Papa's desk. For a while, I'd rummage through the chifforobe, caressing whatever belonged to him—his hairbrush, tie tacks, and pipes. But the world was crowding in on me, the war was coming to an end, my father was coming home, and my mother and I would move to another house in another town. Bit by bit, I had to let my grandfather become a memory of little things: the smell of woodsmoke, witch hazel lotion and boot polish, the sound of the pull chain toilet, the lid clanging back into place and ready for all of Papa's girls. But some nights I swore I heard his footsteps echoing in long strides down that tunnel of a hallway where the whitewashed steps of the house butted right onto the sidewalk of that long sloping block down Kennerly Avenue.

I have to admit that after my grandfather died, my grandmother pampered me, allowing me into her four-poster bed where I listened to the radio and read comic books until I fell asleep, still caught up in the world of the Fat Man and the Green Hornet, Mandrake the Magician and Prince Valiant, a world where dark-haired women were fearless villains and never let men get the best of them without a fight. Since dark hair was as close as I could get to media images of people with dark skin, I cheered for them. I even favored dark-haired Claudette

Colbert paper dolls because she wore bangs like I did. Left alone, I would have spent my days dreaming of their adventures or draped in a feather boa in front of Mama's boudoir mirror, playacting the blues of Bessie Smith and the torch songs of Ruth Etting and Libby Holman. To amuse myself, I deliberately set the wrong speed on Mama's Victrola so that the records warbled out of tune. But my mother and her sisters were vigilant. Aunt Jennie dragged me from Marvel Comics to the books she had neatly lined up on the shelves in her living room, the "good" books with hardback bindings and small print. I balked at leaving my comic book "heroes-of-justice" until I discovered the magic of Aesop's fables, *The Arabian Nights,* and Boccaccio's *Tales from the Decameron.* Not even my favorite *femme fatale,* Milton Caniff's dark-haired "Dragon Lady" from "Terry and the Pirates," could quite compete with Aladdin's "Queen of the Ebony Isles" regally strolling through the gardens at midnight, her panther striding on a leash beside her. Thirty-five years later, I borrowed the images of the Dragon Lady and Aladdin's mysterious Queen as metaphors in a series of poems, and with their combined powers, they helped me win an American Book Award for poetry.

My new interest in Aunt Jennie's books suited my mother just fine. Throughout my youth she bombarded me with Shakespearean quotes. She had majored in English literature in college, and even a simple request could evoke the Bard. Her favorites were the plays with Ophelia and Lady Macbeth. Of course, I preferred the wicked Hecate, but my mother would not have me quoting witches. "Can I go out?" I'd ask, roller skates dangling from my hand. "Out, out, brief candle . . ." my mother would begin. And if I didn't show the proper patience, I was condemned to listen to the full soliloquy. My mother's quotes fed my thirst for stories, for people, who like me, seemed surrounded by men always at war. And like the books the women in my family gave me, my mother's plays offered me a glimpse of other places in the world, an escape from the scrutinizing eyes of my aunts and teachers, from neighbors who would "tell your mama" if they caught you out of line.

Another escape was the movies. On the screen, stories seemed to hold the glitter of the old music hall records in my grandmother's attic mixed with the same slick talk I heard in her parlor. But it all seemed so much more glamorous in movies like *The Bronze Buckaroo, Cabin in the Sky,* and *Stormy Weather,* featuring black folks like Lena Horne, Mantan Moreland, and Herb Jeffries, or Butterfly McQueen, Stepin Fetchit, and Bojangles Robinson, their names in tall letters on the marquee. As soon as I was old enough for a weekly allowance, I spent it on the matinee at the Antioch Theater, the "Coloreds Only" movie house a few blocks from home. Every Saturday, I met my friends—Vaughn Payne, Rosalind Townsend, and Bumpsy Pritchard. We grabbed front row seats for the double feature, the cartoons, and a serial, some "Buck Rogers" or "Tarzan" or "Bulldog Drummond" episode that never returned to the cliff-hanging scene of the previous Saturday no matter how many times the announcer said: *Last week, when we left our hero* . . . World War II unfolded for us with grainy clips on Movietone News where the military was white despite the fact that our fathers were serving overseas. Without familiar faces, that war never seemed quite real. Like the movies we saw, war was jerky movements and a projectionist who must have used his elbows to set the dials. At least three times during a show, the film would flicker, crack and die in a drawl of voices and a flash of white light. We'd hoot and whistle until it started up again but nothing stemmed our adoration for all that action on the silver screen. Unfortunately, that devotion left me with a legacy I still cannot break. Even now, even if I've entered the theater late, I cannot sit through more than one showing of the main feature. My mother and her sisters permanently cured me of that habit.

The matinee was for children, but long before my mother would have agreed, I knew I was past that stage. I plotted to be with the older kids who arrived for the later show and sat near the back of the movie house. I don't quite remember when I hatched my plan. Maybe Bumpsy Pritchard double-dog-dared me to stay— Bumpsy who was always trying to throw himself in with the bigger boys even when we were still learning to print the alphabet on thick green-lined paper—but whatever the cause, that summer when I was not yet twelve, I fancied myself old enough to hang out with the early evening crowd, the boys with letter sweaters and greasy haircuts, and the girls with lipstick and poodle skirts. I couldn't wait until eighth grade when I'd be old enough to sit with them, so that summer, I began to fudge on the time it took the matinee to end. "You best watch your step, miz-lady," my mother warned. But I watched the second showing of the newsreel edition and previews. By mid-summer, I was sitting through another run of the cartoons and serial. "Don't tell me you can't read that clock," Aunt Jennie said. "Been taking you a long time to get out of that movie," my grandmother said. My mother sent Mildred, one of the older neighbor girls, to fetch me home. I didn't falter. The next weekend, I added a second screening of the feature film. I learned the trick of hiding behind the seats when the usher shined his flashlight down the row, hunting for me in response to my mother's urgent phone call to the theater. "I guess I fell asleep," I told her. After that, I eased up for a week, but the temptation was too great. The next week, my name was flashed on the screen on a little piece of paper inserted between the projector and the light. "I didn't see my name up there. Honest," I said. Then, on the Saturday Aunt Claudia sent her oldest son, James Jr., the policeman, to track me down, I ran out of excuses. By the time James caught me, I had learned to hide among the seats long enough to watch four sets of the cartoons. My cousin James simply had the manager turn up the houselights and waited until I showed myself, then he snatched me down the aisle while Bumpsy Pritchard laughed about how I had "the FBI on my tail." That was the last time I've ever sat through more than one showing of any movie. To this day, I expect the house lights to go up, to see my name flash on the screen, to turn and face my mother and her sisters waiting for me in back of the theater— while behind me, the film flickers toward yet another crisis, fake bullets whizzing by the movie hero who stands triumphant, having once more saved the day and left me on the edge of the cliff.

In the eighth grade, I transferred from Simmons Elementary to Cote Brilliante School at the end of our block on Kennerly Avenue. Cote Brilliante had "turned over," gone from white to black as white folks fled to the outlying areas of the city, and colored folks moved in for postwar jobs. I attended that school for only one year, the eighth grade. In those days, we graduated from the eighth grade, perhaps because no one expected us to go much farther or perhaps because high school was such a giant step. At least for us it would be the latter, since we would have to criss-cross the city to reach Sumner or Vashon or the technical high school, the three options open to black kids in St. Louis. Whatever the case, we graduated eighth grade and that whole year, we practiced for graduation, everything from the processional to a choral operetta called "The Caravan," complete with Bedouins, Arabs, and slaves. The sopranos were the voices of the harem, and they sang bright and cheery lines like: *Heed not the sla-aves melancholy song / Heed not their mo-ooa-ning along*. The boys with basso voices took on the roles of slaves: *We are old with la-abor / ben-en-ded lo-oo-ow / and our steps are we-eary / weary and slow-ooh*. To add some vibrato, as the choirmaster put it, we mixed it up for the guards, traders, and Bedouins (*who a-cross the des-er-ert WANder / YONder*). Get the picture? Thirty-two black kids singing about slaves and Bedouins from September to June, and all the while not being taught that their ancestors might have been a part of such caravans. The only thing missing for this make-believe was Movietone News to break in with clips of somebody's war. By spring, everyone sang with gusto. My only problem was voice. No matter what section I chose, the choirmaster rapped his baton on the music stand and pointed my way. "Off Key!" he'd accuse, although I'd memorized the entire libretto—soprano, alto, and tenor. Even now, nearly fifty years later, I can quote whole sections of that operetta. I've even used it to test the devotion of various sweethearts. The man who can sit through my rendition of harem girls, traders, Bedouins, and caravan guards is, most certainly, worthy of my attention.

As ill-suited as "The Caravan" might have been for a class of black kids in 1947 St. Louis, it marked for me the beginning of my departure from the city. Before summer ended, I would not only leave the eighth grade, I would leave the neighborhood. The war was over and my father was stateside. That summer, my mother and I would join him on the first of many transfers to military posts, both in the States and overseas. But my exodus was not immediate. Those were the years when I'd yo-yo between St. Louis and some army post. At first, each move was punctuated by my grandmother recalling me home with the admonishment to my mother that "the army was no place to raise a child. Send that baby home." The pattern was always the same—always my grandmother would help me pack, reminding me to behave myself and be polite and act like I was in a real family with a mother *and* a father, or some such talk like that. But as soon as I'd settle into military life and the thrill of being away from St. Louis, my grandmother would have second thoughts and send for me, and the task of packing and issuing warnings fell upon my mother's shoulders.

I suppose my life as an army brat was atypical in that respect—leaving home for a few months only to return to St. Louis to finish out the school year. But those years no doubt set the pattern I continue today: the need to travel, to search out places other than where I am, and the surety of knowing that in a few months, I will return home. It is as if my grandmother is beckoning me back to Kennerly Avenue long after she, herself, had moved away.

My father moved my mother and me to Fort Francis Warren, Wyoming, soon after I said goodbye to Cote Brilliante School. Wyoming is the strongest memory I have of army life stateside. First, it was the one time the army granted my father a furlough to drive us to his new post, instead of sending for us as he had to do most of the time. We left by Route 66, the most famous highway west in those years. I'd been on that road right after the end of the war when my Uncle Brother had driven us across the country to California to see Papa's sister. Compared to today's cloverleaf, S curve, and interstate six-lane roads, Route 66 was no more than a country lane for local traffic. But in those days, that highway revealed wondrous things to a girl whose boundaries had been determined by a fifteen-block radius in St. Louis. The road was lined with cracker-barrel country stores, gas stations with pumps that looked like Pyrex blenders, and billboards advertising Philip Morris cigarettes, the Southern Pacific Railroad, and RCA radios. My favorite ads were for Burma Shave Cream, the ones with five small signs spaced out so you could read them as you rode past: four of them for a limerick and the last one holding the answer to all your troubles— *Don't lose your head / to gain a minute . . ./ You need your head / your brains are in it . . ./ Burma Shave*. I'd read the first three lines, then try to guess the rhyme of the fourth line. Half the time, I was right. (A foreshadowing of the poet I'd become?) But when we arrived in Wyoming, all guesses were put on hold.

Another reason for remembering Fort Warren is that it was my first real contact with the West. Among all those cowboys and soldiers, I suddenly felt as if I'd stepped into a matinee at the Antioch. There were uniforms everywhere, and flags and guns and tanks as big as woodsheds. Movietone News might have offered only white soldiers, but Fort Francis Warren was filled with black men fresh from the battlegrounds of World War II or in training for postwar occupation. I learned to count hash marks for the number of years in service and understand what the stars decorating combat ribbons meant. I watched my father blouse each pant leg until they were exactly the same shape along the tops of his combat boots. My mother starched and ironed everything we wore as if we were all going to line up for inspection. "Don't have your daddy swallow his spit for nothing" was her motto. But I didn't see my father's courage in the face of army-style racism. I saw his full dress uniform, combat ribbons and unit insignias. I saw him as a squadron leader and combat soldier—I saw him totally army with all the fanfare of Movietone News.

By my reasoning, my father's rank of staff sergeant gave me privilege and I used it to secure my own position among the other army brats. Besides, I was from St. Louis, and most of them were from hick towns or from the South. My only competition was a boy from New Jersey, but that wasn't any real competition because he was too busy trying to play soldier. Instead of playing army, I became a storyteller, regaling my new friends with the mystique of big-city St. Louis adventures. Some of it was true, but at times, I added a little for flavor. I learned that the story was more the art of weaving details until the telling became greater than what might have happened. In the stories I told about my neighborhood, it was true that we actually had used discarded baby buggies for makeshift races down Ash Hill—except for Vaughn Payne who had been too fat to fit into a baby's buggy. But Bumpsy had never been accidentally locked up in the cemetery overnight, and Vaughn Payne had never eaten so many pickles that his mouth had puckered shut for a week. If it was stretching the truth, I'd come by it honestly. I used what I'd learned from eavesdropping on my mother and

her sisters, and all that I'd practiced in front of my grandmother's boudoir mirror. And when I ran out of material, I listened to my father tell combat stories, stories I retold later as if I'd actually been there. The first time I heard, "And then what happened?" I was hooked. I became a weaver of tales, a purveyor of fictional truth. I didn't know that I was practicing to be a writer but from that point on, there was no turning back.

In Wyoming, I had more than the army to provide me with excitement. I had the extra added attraction of being in cowboy country—not the celluloid cowpokes of Hollywood Westerns, but real cattlemen and rodeo riders: black, white, and Indian. The first time I saw an Indian cowboy in muddy boots, worn jeans, a long ponytail, and feathers in his Stetson, I ran home to tell my mother. She looked at me and laughed. "What do you mean you never seen an Indian? Girl, you got some Indian in you," she said. "Some of your folks was Seminole." When I complained that she'd never told me about it earlier, she said, "You never asked." At the time, I used the only weapon a child could have—I sulked. Of course, years later when I was in college in Germany, I would have enough sense to ask the right questions, but when I was young, I just let this bit of information give me a new way to look at the folks I saw strolling around Cheyenne, Wyoming. I figured that with Indian blood in my family, I had to be connected to the black cowboys I saw too. After all, hadn't my mother said my uncle (in L.A.) had been in the horse business?

I remember Cheyenne as soldiers in their uniforms and cowboys decked out in their pointy-toed boots, ten-gallon hats, and ropes. I'm sure I had a crush on at least one soldier, but for the guys on post, I was just another army brat, a skinny little sergeant's daughter barely old enough to go to high school. In town, it was another matter. Boys my age or just a little older were already riding in competition and to me, seemed as reckless as any soldier. For a twelve-year-old, the connection between the men on post and in the rodeo was entirely natural. I hung around the fairgrounds to watch the cowboys try out, and over the course of the summer, I gained my first boyfriend. Sadly, I cannot remember his name. I can remember the names of my next two boyfriends—George

Darlington Love and Quentin Frederick O'Neal (every boy had three-part names in those days)—but my first boyfriend has been reduced to a silver belt buckle and isn't even held in the memory of a first kiss. (I'm not sure if this oversight is innocence or ignorance.) What I do remember is the smell of horses and leather, the noise and dust, the endless parade of pickup trucks. And I remember his nonchalant wave as he entered the arena. That, and his belt buckle, presented to me after he won the competition. I was so skinny, the first time I wore it, my father said the buckle was bigger than my waist. I still have that buckle, and although I can't remember that poor boy's name or face or whether we kissed, it is enough to know that one summer in Cheyenne, I had a boyfriend, a bronze cowpoke who called me his sweetheart. (All I needed was Movietone music.) When Uncle Brother came to fetch me, at my grandmother's request, I met him at the front door, dressed in a buckskin vest and fringed skirt, as befitting a cowboy's sweetheart.

Shortly after I returned to St. Louis from Wyoming, my mother once again came home—this time, to give birth to a son. With a little more than twelve years separating me and my brother, Keith Leslie Johnson, I still considered myself an only child in a family of adults. Uncle Brother and my mother bought a house together on McMillan Avenue, but we all referred to it as Uncle Brother's house. It was a roomy three-story house which I grew to hate once it became clear that most of the cleaning was my responsibility because my grandmother suffered from arthritis. Mama moved slower in the house on McMillan than she had in the one on Kennerly. She still did all the cooking and told stories about the old days and sang gospel hymns, but it was as if she'd left her real life behind when she moved from Kennerly. I think my grandmother felt we'd left Papa in the old house. I know I left my childhood of jump rope and hide-and-seek. Pussy's family had moved, Bumpsy had run away from home, and the city already had torn down Farrow's store. But I was looking forward to what life would bring, while my grandmother sat for hours at the window as if she could see more than the well-kept lawns on McMillan Avenue, and the overhead wires of the trolley line on the Hodiman tracks. That was the last year I ever lived with my grandmother. And

"My brother, Keith Leslie Johnson, at age eighteen"

that year, I began to call her Grandma, and my mother became Mama instead of Ruth.

When my baby brother was a year old, my mother went back to work. My grandmother offered to babysit, but most days, she slept, nodding in a chair by the window. So on those days, I had to do the babysitting too. With my grandmother less active, my father in Wyoming, and my mother at work, Uncle Brother decided to be my parent. I would have none of it. After more than a dozen years of my mother and her sisters whipping me into shape, I wasn't about to take their kid brother as a substitute. Every time I back-talked because he'd yelled at me to do something else, his cat-grey eyes burned with anger. One day, when Uncle Brother shouted at me, once again, about my cleaning methods, I aimed the mop and bucket still filled with dirty suds at his head, and walked across town to my Aunt Jennie's. And so began the year I spent under Jennie's roof.

Jennie was the family redhead, a pretty woman with a temper that could match anyone's.

I'd seen her take a swing at both Claudia and my mother. When Jennie was in her thirties, she decided to start a career in business, and her husband, Phillip, couldn't talk her out of it. Uncle Phillip also called me Joe, but I didn't mind because Uncle Phillip looked like the bandleader Cab Calloway, dapper and handsome. (At eighty, he still is.) Jennie's panache matched his style. She was stunning in her fashionable suits and high-high heels. She was the aunt with class, the aunt with clothes I wanted to borrow. She hadn't had any children of her own, but by the time I marched into her house, fourteen years old and fresh from trying to assassinate my uncle with a mop and bucket, two other cousins were in residence, both of them seeking refuge from the wrath of their mothers. So Jennie became an instant parent. Irma Jean and Cora Jean were second cousins on Uncle Phillip's side of the family. They were single children, as I had been until my brother was born. When I was older, I was positive my aunt had been a little crazy to have taken in three girls between the ages of thirteen and fifteen. But after my own children were teenagers, I decided my Aunt Jennie was a saint.

I grew up in Jennie's house, surrounded, finally, by "sisters" my own age. It was a scary step from the spotlight I had enjoyed at my grandmother's to vying for a place in line with my cousins at Aunt Jennie's. (Incidents from those days have appeared in my short stories, particularly "Ruby-Ruby," and "How I Came to Dance with Queen Esther and the Dardanelles," in *Driving under the Cardboard Pines*.) Jennie was our coach and our referee, letting us roll back the carpet and practice dancing to Little Richard, Fats Domino, and the Clovers, but paying just as much attention to what we did with homework assignments. Claudia tried to start the rumor that Jennie was running a bawdy house with all us girls as hired help. We wished. Jennie's was like a boarding school: homework and bed by ten o'clock. Only when we sneaked out of the house, shimmying down the oak tree in the front yard to go to the sock-hops at the YWCA, did we do anything the least bit risqué. And if Jennie quickly discovered our infractions of the rules, we were grounded and made to do something awful, like iron a basket full of clothes or wax all the floors. I began to sympathize with those girls in the biographies and novels about English boarding schools that I found on Jennie's book shelves in the living room. But when my cousins teased me unmercifully about my boyfriend, the one with the improbable name of George Darlington Love, Aunt Jennie defended me. "You got too much to see in this big ol' world to let folks stop you," she said. For her, the remark simply may have been a way to help me ease the pain of being teased, but I took it seriously. And on more than one occasion, as I've arrived alone in an airport in some foreign country, I have had reason to recall her words.

Twice while I was in high school, my mother joined my father when he was transferred to another stateside army base. Between assignments, he rented an apartment for my mother and me so far across town from the rest of the family, it was easy to shift my attention to high school. At Charles Sumner High, the largest black high school in St. Louis, I was thrown into a world that was color-conscious and money-struck, and family meant only one thing: where did your father work? The army didn't count. Aside from my best friend, Senesta Paige, and my on-again off-again boyfriend, Quentin Frederick O'Neal, I only remember Grace Bumbry, who is now a famous opera singer, Ronald Townsend, who would become a singer with the group The Fifth Dimension, and the science-math nerds, Harry Blackinston Jr. and Charles Sidner. And then there was Delores Green, who was rumored to date older men. My social life was restricted to the YWCA, where the boys didn't care that I was dark-skinned and skinny as long as I remembered the dance beat. A payoff for those hours of practice at Aunt Jennie's. But rumors of Delores Green's success prompted me to pretend my cousin, Warren, Claudia's youngest son, was my boyfriend, straight out of the Navy and come to pick me up after school in his Thunderbird. I don't remember how I bribed Warren to perform that little chore for a month or two. (I now know that Warren's interest in one of the girls in the senior class was greater than any make-believe I'd had.) Of my teachers, I remember nothing, except Miss Crutcher, the senior class counselor who tinted her grey hair purple. But even my mother remembered Miss Crutcher from her high school days.

Oh, I was a good student all right—National Honor Society, and a member of the Radio and Drama Clubs—but that didn't compensate for gym class, where they made us wear ugly green bloomer-leg suits and do endless jumping jacks. And then there was home economics: burnt cookies and sewing. My first garment was a dress cut from a bolt of atrociously plaid material. None of the seams matched. My triumph was starring in the senior play, *Tea and Sympathy.* I was the older woman in a May-December love affair. (Could Delores do better?) I delivered my exit line, dismissing my lover with great *savoir faire,* something terribly brittle like: "If you think of me, and you will, think of me kindly." High school. Each week I prayed for a reasonable plan of escape.

By my senior year, my mother and I were back in St. Louis awaiting orders to follow my father to Germany. At first I thought our orders would be cut so we could leave right after graduation. But the army is notorious for its hurry-up-and-wait process. My graduation, January 1953, came and went. I won a mail order course in drawing that I entered off the back of a matchbook cover. (I was bored, OK?) I took a few courses at Harris-Stowe Teachers College, but found no real challenge because after all, without any real effort I'd maintained a high school grade point average that had kept me on the rolls of the National Honor Society. Germany changed all that. My disinterest and slothful study habits put my grades in immediate jeopardy, but I was oblivious to the danger until the end of my first year.

When we arrived in Germany in the fall of '53, my mother immediately put me on a train for Munich where I would attend the university. I would not see her again for a year. For the first time, I was free of parents, aunts, and cousins. Eighteen years old and I thought I was a woman, so I blissfully enjoyed my new freedom—namely Germany's beer halls and ski slopes—all the while sliding into scholastic disaster. Since I had not bothered to cultivate a taste for beer in the States, I took to German beer with a clean palate. As potent as it was, before long I could brush my teeth and gargle with the stuff. Oh, I attended classes from time to time. That's how the professor managed to confront me with the ultimate Who-are-you? question. I'd like to say I answered by asking how his country had turned loose the devil's henchmen during World War II, but I wasn't nearly fast enough for that kind of response. I do know the question turned me around. Not enough to attend class, but enough to take a

better look at where I was. And after that look, not even the beer made me feel better. I visited Dachau, that world of ovens, windowless barracks, and stacks of prisoners' wooden shoes. Even midday with the sun hanging bright in the Bavarian sky, the place seemed grey, the ground chalky brown and dry as if nothing wanted to grow there. I thought about Billie Holiday's song, "Strange Fruit," and the race riots and lynchings back home. My German friends assumed I'd seen lynchings firsthand, yet when I asked them about Dachau, they told me they'd didn't know much about the place. I didn't believe them. That was like saying I'd grown up in St. Louis and didn't know about the Mississippi River.

I spent a lot of time in Munich's Marienplatz at the Hofbrauhaus, the beer hall Hitler had frequented in his early days. Marienplatz is cobblestoned, the buildings around it rising like a backdrop for the Grimms' fairy tales. Even the Glockenspiel, the huge clock that centers the square, holds figures cut from medieval times. In 1953, under the damage from Allied bombs, Marienplatz was more gothic than ever. The Hofbrau was like a cave, cigarette smoke clinging to the curved ceilings like stalactites. Outside, the Glockenspiel kept silent vigil, the clock cracked by bombs. But when I visited Germany again in 1982, the square was like a suburban mall, pricey shops interspersed between the Hofbrau and the Glockenspiel, except the big clock had been fixed, its life-sized figures tolling each hour.

In 1953 at the Hofbrauhaus, I learned how to argue Proust and Hegel, NATO tactics and existentialism. In those days, the Iron Curtain was just a rumor and the Berlin Wall had not yet been erected, but we were all too aware of the uneasy peace between East and West. I also learned the importance of knowing who you are. Only the Americans had an oleomargarine past, the old-fashioned kind of spread that came in large white pats with the color in a separate tube that you stirred in after you got home. Germany, 1953, made me take a close look at just what I was stirring into the mess I called home. My friends who were not Americans gave me a push. They wanted to know what my skin color meant to me and how I saw the world. I don't mean to say they were free of bigotry—not in Germany—but color was simply another way of dividing the world, along with religion, politics, and class. In the

States, it was enough to say that I was "plain ol' colored"—no other explanation necessary. I was expected to be a credit to my race, a good girl, to know my place. In Germany, I began to ask: Where was that place? Now I am certain the answer is: Wherever I am. Hadn't my grandmother once told me that there were "some of us everywhere"?

In other memoirs I've written, she is called Wilma Hessel. That name is partially right, and it doesn't matter why I promised never to reveal her real name. What matters is that Wilma freed me, finally, of the pull of St. Louis. We became friends the day I met her in front of the Deutsches Museum. She was leaning against a tree, a cigarette hanging from her mouth, her hair blowing and unhampered by pressing iron or curls. Those were the days before Afros became popular, and I'd never seen a black woman who just let her hair go natural. I stared. She spoke—in German. (Her English was even worse than my classroom German.) My second surprise. She was a "brown baby," not from a GI's encounter with a German woman, although there were plenty of young kids like that in evidence, but a German mixed blood who was only a few years older than I. I knew black GIs had been in Germany in World War I, but she wasn't that old. She told me her father had lived in Berlin where he had married her mother, a cabaret singer from New York. She told me that both of them had died in concentration camps. Another surprise. A black woman died in one of Hitler's camps! What I'd heard about the death camps involved Jews, but Wilma told me about the other prisoners: the Gypsies, the foreigners, or anyone who was different, not Aryan. She told me how her folks had managed to send her to Amsterdam, "Amsterdammit-all" she called it, and how she'd spent most of her life running away from Germany, only to return after the war. I didn't understand why anyone would return to a country that had killed their parents. She laughed and asked me if I planned to go back to America. Her hand was covering mine, one light brown, the other dark brown. One German, one American. We shared ancestry but were not the same. Like my grandmother had said, "There are some of us everywhere."

One thing is certain, whatever I learned in those two-and-a-half years in Germany was not taught in anyone's classroom. Despite my struggles with language—my ear dulled by midwestern accents—I learned how easy it was to gain friends, and boyfriends. (I prefer to pull a curtain of charity over my first brief marriage in Germany. Suffice it to say, he almost convinced me to like Proust.) Meanwhile in school, I moved from having been a National Honor Society student to dishonorable dismissal from college. My failures came as a total shock. Fail? Me? It wasn't that I couldn't answer the exam questions, I didn't remember discussing the subjects. Understandable since I couldn't remember attending the classes. I guess I wasn't yet convinced that the class had anything to do with tests. The big blow was flunking English, but the irony was that the following year, I became an *au pair* girl for a German family in Frankfurt, hired mostly because I could teach the kids English. It wasn't a bad job, and it helped me avoid moving back to the army base with my mother. That was the first in a series of odd jobs taken as a stopgap to avoid school and serious work. But it was also my first foray into the real world, a time to test my limits. I had always been teased about being skinny, but in Germany, I realized that was an asset. I took some modeling jobs, timidly at first. And I'm sure, awkwardly as well. By the time I left Germany, I'd worked part-time in a radio station and a souvenir store. "Piecemeal work," my mother called it. But it satisfied my need to be responsibly irresponsible.

Back home in the States, I ventured out even more. I went from modeling to dancing, putting to practical use those hours spent with my cousins in Aunt Jennie's living room. I wasn't spectacular, but my long legs and bad attitude lent me an assured air. I favored the Afro-Cuban and Latin beat that was popular in small Chicago clubs catering to black, Puerto Rican, and Spanish Harlem crowds. For several months, I danced the circuit along with other teams trying to cut into the big time. We did the merengue, rumba, and mambo to Perez Prado, Lord Invader, and Harry Belafonte. At one point, I had a partner whose roguishness complemented me well. That man could really dance, but he had the greasiest hair this side of the Caribbean. Once he'd brushed his hand across his hair, a cha-cha spin could send me reeling off the ends of his fingers into the tables on the other side of the spotlight. Between that partner and my aching feet, my dancing days ended

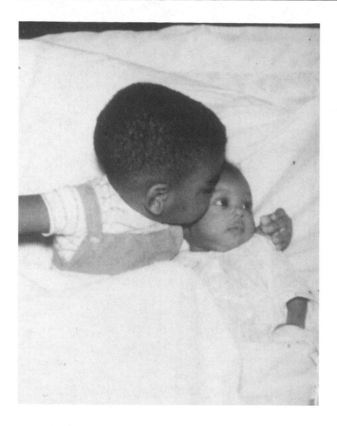

*"My children, Kevin and Vanessa, in 1962
at ages three and one"*

for a while. When I returned to the trade, I taught dance for an Arthur Murray studio near the college I was attending in Kansas. (Yes, at Arthur Murray-in-a-hurry I taught the meaning of the mambo to left-footed soldiers from Fort Reilly.) But my feet never recovered from the platform spikes of those early days when I would leave the floor with bloody shoes and a smile as wide as Chicago.

When I finally had had enough of hard luck, long hours, and low pay, I returned to college. My father was stationed at Fort Reilly, Kansas, so I moved home and attended Kansas State University. I was a little more serious about school and doubled my class load, but I didn't have a clue as to where I was going with any of those courses. I had two jobs: one cha-chaing for Arthur Murray, and the other as a work-study student at the university. It was still "piece-meal," and I suppose I would have graduated from Kansas State without a sense of direction if I had not met a professor of speech pathology who saw something in me I hadn't seen

in myself. Al Knox hired me as a receptionist for the university's speech clinic because he said I had a knack for talking to anyone and the patience to let them pace the conversation. I suppose it was a tactic I'd learned in Germany when four or five languages could invade any discussion. But under Professor Knox's tutelage, I abandoned the daily bid whist card games in the "black corner" of the Student Union cafeteria, and set out to qualify for a scholarship in speech and hearing sciences. I also acquired a boyfriend, Burl Wilkinson, who would become my second husband, and the father of my children, Kevin and Vanessa.

As I grow older, I am convinced that the pace of life simply accelerates. What seemed to take forever when I was a child, requires only a few months of my adult life, and too often, a year can be highlighted by a few days on the calendar. From 1958 to 1966, I was a student, a mother, and a speech pathologist. (I definitely count motherhood as a career.) Looking back, that period seems such a blur of children and classes and internships and patients, I can hardly separate particular events. Although a poem for my grandmother carries the title "Years That Teach What Days Don't Even Know," that title could just as well apply to those years when my life shifted and changed focus like light dancing through a crystal prism. And since the Sixties were typified by crystals, the metaphor is appropriate.

At twenty-one, I graduated from Kansas State and went east with a scholarship to the speech and hearing studies program at the University of Pittsburgh, returning to Kansas State in 1962 to complete my Master of Science degree in speech pathology. In the early Sixties, I sometimes attended fundraising rallies for equal education and voter registration for black people, but my models for living were still being pulled out of media-inspired suburban-tract middle-America, black or white. Later, I would write that in Kansas: *Entertainment was green stamps, cows with windows from the Ag-College / Carved into their sides by future farmers earning graduate degrees* . . . Both Burl and I were students, a state that finally took its toll on our marriage. We were divorced in 1964. My children were young, and the world had not yet coined the term "single parent." I did what I had to do to to keep us afloat. I was the Chief Speech Clinician at the Rehabilitation Clinic in Kansas

City, and also carried a part-time private practice, which left me with Sunday as the only full day I could spend at home. As my children learned language, I learned how to work with patients who had lost normal language function.

Graduate school provided me with a unique way to look at how words are made. I studied the neurological system and language learning patterns. My patients, at the Rehabilitation Institute in Kansas City, Missouri, ranged from children born with aphasia or other language disorders to young people and adults with traumatically induced language dysfunction. Eight to eighty, the issues were the same: how do you survive in a language-speaking world when your language system has failed? "It's like being locked in a phone booth with all the wires shorted out," a recovering patient once told me. I learned the value of unadorned language, the value of finding the most direct word upon command. I began to understand how meanings evolve, and how sounds create patterns of nuances and intonation. I suppose that's where I began to train my ear to poetic language without thinking: I-am-a-poet, but in fact, between the patients at the clinic and my own children learning how to speak, I hardly thought about my language skills at all.

Despite my elaborate lesson plans and language profiles, some of them pulled from my childhood habits of storytelling and make-believe conversations, I understood how elusive language could be. I was in a profession where words were a bonus, but I could not inject my patients with language, and most importantly, I could not equip them with the wherewithal to avoid a bureaucracy dependent on verbal skills. Without language, without a voice, anyone is at the mercy of the political/legal system. The irony is that while I taught patients to repeat words like "Ticonderoga," I also witnessed how the legal system brushed them aside because of their speechlessness. Patients could not argue for welfare assistance, educational retraining, or in the case of a young aphasic woman who was forced to hand over her baby for foster care, child custody. My patients were neurologically and legally sealed in a well of silence. At the same time, other voices were demanding to be heard. Civil rights activists across the nation could no longer be silenced. With the 1964 Civil Rights Act, the cry for FREEDOM was like a gospel song, an under-

current playing through every part of my life. In the winter of 1965–66, I took stock of my life in that city on the edge of the prairie, and something snapped.

I could say I left the Midwest because of the weather. Clearly the Kansas City area hosts some of the nation's extremes in prairie weather. My last winter there, I saw snow storms rage across the city, crippling everything in their paths. My Pacific Northwest friends give me incredulous looks when I tell them I was once trapped in the house by a snow drift that covered half of the front door, and that for the remainder of the year, I knew I could look forward to spring tornadoes and flash floods, followed by summer heat where the humidity exceeded the temperature. Or I left because of the pressure of working with patients who had been rendered mute by neurological insults, or because therapeutic techniques only carry me so far with treatment plans for a fourteen-year-old aphasic, half his head gone after his entire family perished when their car was demolished by a drunk driver. Or maybe it was the forty-two-year-old woman executive who'd been left speechless following the rupture of a cerebral aneurysm. Only her tongue was paralyzed. The rest of her bodily functions were normal, except she could not eat, or swallow, or speak, and nothing could reverse the nerve damage. She committed suicide. Or I could simply say it was the Sixties. John Kennedy had been assassinated, children were being killed in firebomb attacks on churches that supported civil rights workers, and race riots were cloaked under the rubric: civil unrest. I only needed one contact with firehoses and cattle prods to convince me that I was not heroic enough for front-line battles. And as anti-war demonstrations occurred with increasing frequency, like many other Americans, my romance with soldiers, tanks, and guns was coming to an end. Before the decade ended, two Kennedys, Medgar Evers, Martin Luther King Jr., and Malcolm X had been assassinated. The irony of trying to train patients to regain language while witnessing the swift and terrible condemnation of those who used language so persuasively was not lost on me.

Whatever the reason, I left the Midwest. I took my son's globe of the world and gave it a spin. Unless my finger landed on a body of water, I sent letters of application to those places for jobs. One such place was located in the upper left hand corner of the country—Bellingham, Washington. My brother, eighteen at the time, helped me drive to the coast. Bellingham was so far from any place my family knew, my mother swore I'd have to mush through snow to find a store. Instead of snow, I found another way to live on this planet. Perhaps because I was close to the ocean. The first time I walked along a stretch of Northwest beach studded with sculptures of driftwood and blanketed with squawking sea gulls, I cried when I realized that at that moment, the pulse of life was not dependent on skin color or political demonstrations or legal systems that recognized only one language. Or perhaps it was merely the smell of salt air, but whatever the reason, for the first time in my life, I felt I was home.

When I am in an idealistic humor, I like to think of the Sixties as a time of crystals, be-ins, and Camelot dreaming, but that sounds too prettily poetic. The hard reality is that it was a violent decade, where the phantasmagoria of the hippie culture was laced with assassinations, riots, and war. I cannot look back at those years with rose-colored nostalgia. How could I in view of the many who died, in American cities and in Vietnam, wake us up to the necessity for change? I was swept up in a mood of radical politics that I had never imagined in the presence of devil winds dancing across the prairie.

Within a year after I arrived in the Northwest, in addition to my duties as Director of Speech and Hearing Services at Western Washington University, I travelled throughout the country evaluating educational programs for the newly formed Office of Economic Opportunities. Within two years, I was hosting a television talk show with a number of noted guests: Pierre Trudeau, Dr. Benjamin Spock, and Ernest K. Gann, as well as the "variety guests": loggers who could ride the logs through white water, and one guest who had braved the Siberian Railroad only to go mute under the glare of studio cameras. On campus, black student demonstrators invaded my office after I was appointed faculty liaison to the student newspaper. I think we were all grateful to discover we were on the same side of the political fence. Such was not the case with federal politics. Toward the end of the Sixties, my children spotted two men in an unmarked car holding vigil beside our mailbox, supporting the tip I'd

been given that my name had been added to the FBI's list. (In those days, being on that list meant you were among friends.) Still, I can easily separate changes in my personal life from the great wave of political change.

To begin with, I remarried. David McElroy, who adopted my children after we were married, was a poet and a bush pilot, and with him, I began to associate more and more with those artists I'd met when I first arrived in the Pacific Northwest. The light shows, surreal theater, and experimental arts were intoxicating. My mother despaired over everything from my association with artists to my Afro hairstyle. "How'd you get mixed up with those kind of folks?" she asked. I was never quite sure whether she meant hippies or black power advocates. What saved me from her ultimate wrath was my position on the university faculty. My mother thought of teaching as a family tradition (most of my cousins had entered the profession), and she was delighted that I was going to "make something of myself," an opinion she withdrew temporarily when I told her I intended to become a writer. In my mother's eyes, writing was not a job, at least not for a young black woman out of St. Louis. Like me, the only writers my mother had studied in school were in the male-white-and-dead category of staid anthologies. But once I discovered living writers, those my age and writing about issues that also concerned me, I was irretrievably drawn into the fold.

I was in my thirties, a "late bloomer" I believe is the term, before I formally started writing. As a result of my work with language development in children, I wrote a textbook: *Speech and Language Development of the Preschool Child,* and though I wasn't aware of it at the time, that book marked the end of my work with speech pathology and language function. However, the shift from examining language to writing poetry was not a giant step, and I could not have chosen a more idyllic setting than Bellingham, Washington, to begin writing poems. (The dreary teenage verse I wrote in high school simply doesn't count.) In those days, Bellingham was the scene of grand literary soirées. Writers came and went along the "Northwest circuit" like touring companies and rock bands. And it was anything for a party, a grand bash at poet Robert Huff's castle of a house, an artist's bash at an old brick factory outside of Sultan, Washington, or some sprawl of a gathering in a communal house that might last the weekend. David and I threw our parties in a refurbished chicken coop, designated as such although no chickens had ever been inside its pine-paneled interior. And when the city re-opened the turn-of-the-century train station in Bellingham as a museum, artists and writers christened the building with a "happening." After Kansas City, I was suddenly in overdrive.

In the shadow of the rainforest, with the ocean in front of me and the mountains be-hind me, I began to write. I had found a place where my earlier attempts at art, through draw-ing, drama, and dance, seemed pale by com-parison. Those first poems appeared as if they had been waiting in the wings for the chance to be heard. I experienced a torrent of writ-ing, a virtual deluge. On good days, I wrote three or four poems. More often than not, they held the threads of stories I'd already told, except now those stories were enhanced by a more poetic vision. My artist friends applauded my efforts, and in addition to advice from my poet husband, I was encouraged to write by other poets, such as Richard Hugo, who had been David's mentor and friend, John Logan, Knute Skinner, Robert Huff, and Denise Levertov. Like the speaker in Mark Strand's poem "Eat-ing Poetry," I devoured whatever I found and wanted more, doubly delighted when I uncov-ered the works of black poets such as Langston Hughes, Joseph S. Cotter, Anne Spencer, Rob-ert Hayden, Gwendolyn Brooks, and Margaret Walker. It was then I realized that I need not be confined to Yeats and Keats as role mod-els. It was then that I began to think of the world in terms of poetry.

The mountains, the ocean, even the pres-ence of rain affects my writing, although the "triggering town" for my poems, as Richard Hugo dubbed the landscape of the imagination, has its deepest roots in my childhood. The past is important to my work because writing has been my way of setting the record straight. During those first years in Bellingham, I attended po-etry readings on campus and at coffeehouses where young white poets, in the spirit of the Sixties, attempted to explore the complexities of America's many cultures. As well-meaning as they may have been, their images of people of color were drawn from a narrow point of view. For them, race and ethnicity meant exoticism, some celluloid sense of spirituality that had been

"In California during the 1970s"

"lost" in the scientific world. (Alas, this view hasn't changed for far too many writers.) The black families and "Negro" figures drifting through their poems did not bear any resem-blance to people I'd known. And moreover, their language seemed intellectualized, stiff and unemotional. I remembered the heat of con-versations among my grandmother's daughters, my friends in Germany, even the patients at the Rehabilitation Institute. "I could do bet-ter," I complained. "So do it," my husband said. And I haven't stopped.

Richard Hugo told me that geography shapes the language of the poem, but for me, the rain shifting through the pine trees and crab apple orchard outside my study window helped me recreate the cacophony of midwestern city streets from the broadloom of Bellingham's land-scape. (I still occasionally remind myself that rain doesn't have to be shoveled.) When I first began writing, on a small farm just south of the Lummi Indian Reservation on Bellingham Bay, I realized I could vividly recall scenes from my past, none of them rural. The route from my house to campus took me past the mudflats, the Original Overhead Door Company and Buzzard Iron Works, and the docks where fishing boats nosed home, their holds filled with salmon. My son's eighth birthday party was held aboard a Lummi Island ferry. I will probably never forget how exhausted I was after chasing a dozen or so little boys from stern to port, then pulling their hands out of the aquaculture farm tanks so my family wouldn't be banned forever from the island. But in many regards, Bellingham's postcard landscape allowed me a clearer view of the stark reality of old neighborhoods without the discord of those cities.

This is not to say that the Northwest was (or is) a place of complete harmony. I arrived in Bellingham a scant two years after a sundown law against blacks and Indians was rescinded, and then only because an African diplomat's son had been arrested. I was one of three black faculty members at Western Washington, and although one was male, our names were used interchangeably because our skin color was the same. (When my daughter decided to find a new route home from school and got lost, the police took her to the other black faculty member's house. After the anonymity of Kansas City, it was hard to realize that every cop in town could find me.) It is no secret that the riots of the Sixties didn't stop at the Washington state border, and this part of the country is as culpable in its mistreatment of native peoples as any other area. But there is a multiplicity about this place that makes me rethink the more simplistic black-white color demarcation of the Midwest. When I was a speech pathologist, I had a motto on the wall above my desk that read: *Language is a steed that carries you to a far country.* Now that far country is closer to home—a world described not just in terms of black people and white people but also Asian, Pacific, Latino, Chicano, and Native American. So while this place fuels my writing, it also heightens my need to know more about the rest of the world, in short, to travel. But satisfying that need comes out of another discipline.

My grandmother used to ask me why I had to go all the way around "Coxey's barn" to do everything. I didn't know where Coxey's barn was (Coxey was an early advocate of national unemployment benefits), but I figured it must

have been big enough for somebody to get lost trying to get around it. I guess I went around Coxey's barn to become a writer, and maybe looped it a couple of times learning how to use my love of writing to pursue my passion for travel. Because if writing is my third or fourth career, then the study of linguistics and folklore must be my fifth and sixth. To be sure, I was already studying the language mechanism as a speech pathologist, but linguistics gave me a more of a world perspective. So as I began to take writing seriously, I also made the decision to go back to school again. I knew a master's degree had served me well in speech pathology, but I no longer wanted to be in a clinical field and I needed a more advanced degree to remain in academia. As a start, I selected courses on the campus where I was on faculty.

One course was an independent study with a professor emeritus in anthropology. Colin Tweddell had been a missionary in China, and his office, under the eaves of one of the old buildings on Western Washington's campus, was filled with memorabilia. I'm sure there were weekends when it didn't rain, but what I remember was the rainforest smell and raindrops streaking the windowpanes as Professor Tweddell offered me tea in English china cups. Each Saturday, in that room shadowed by stacks of books and papers and the copse of rain-soaked evergreen trees outside the windows, I began to explore the connection between language and culture. Some sessions, we'd discuss the text I'd been sent home to read the week before, and other sessions, he'd pull from the stacks of papers or piles of photographs some tidbit on cultural and linguistic patterns that he thought would entice me. He was right. I was enticed by everything. What started as a love for language that stemmed from my childhood days of storytelling and my work as a speech pathologist now included the romance of travel, of people and languages that I hadn't thought much about since I'd left Germany. Professor Tweddell told me he had seen many parts of the world and on each trip, he'd never failed to be amazed. His genuine interest in sharing his work and the intimacy of that office left me with yet another way to look at the world. Within three years, I would complete my studies at the University of Washington in ethnolinguistic patterns of dialect differences and oral traditions—none of it too far removed from tracing language systems for speech pathology, except now I could examine the art of language as well as its physiological bases.

Looking back at my final years as a graduate student, I suspect my dissertation supervisor, Professor Jack Kittell, was more intrigued with my poetry than with my research aplomb. Statistical analysis before the age of personal computers was almost my undoing, but once again, my sense of language function and storytelling techniques served me well. Kittell told me to never let go of my passion for writing, to let it be my reservoir from which I could draw strength. I've held onto those words even as my life has continued to change, sometimes drastically, from one decade to the next. Like my Aunt Jennie's encouragement to see "this big ol' world," those words have become my totem.

I received my doctorate from the University of Washington under a federal program called Teachers Training Teachers, in conjunction with the Institute for Urban Language. In 1973, I joined the faculty of the Department of English at the University of Washington, where I continue to teach. By the mid-Seventies, I was once again divorced. The pain of that last dissolution is detailed in my collection of poems *Winters without Snow*. Although I have tried to be a pragmatist, my sense of humor regarding matrimony did not surface for years. Much later, I began to suspect that divorce might be somehow connected to my status in a degree program, at least looking back at my track record the coincidence seems to be there, but I'm comforted by knowing I've run out of degrees (and marriages?).

During my early years at the university, I immersed myself in writing and teaching. I was supervisor for the English Composition Program for Minority Students and concentrated on directing my teaching staff to include such books as: *The Sound of Waves, Bless Me Ultima, The Way to Rainy Mountain, The Palm Wine Drinkard,* and *The Bluest Eye,* along with the usual diet of *Main Street* and *Huckleberry Finn.* We spent hours discussing how a book could be examined on its own merit, rather than how it could be compared to middle-class white American standards. Some of my teaching assistants have contacted me since then to express how much they appreciated the urging to "walk in some-

one else's shoes," as well as to recognize the boundaries of their own turf. I confess that I don't quite know what to say when a former student or teaching assistant tells me I was a role model. In those days, I was simply trying to maintain my footing on ground made more unsteady by my being the first or only black woman to have walked there. *First* and *only* can be scary positions—far too reminiscent of quotas for my taste—but my actions were scarcely altruistic. I was about the business of discovering my own sensibilities, my own models for creativity and success. I had survived a childhood when black people could not try on clothes in department stores, much less find realistic images of themselves in books. I remembered favoring dark-haired women in fiction in lieu of those who reminded me of my mother and her sisters. I had a Ph.D. but still searched for models that weren't ghetto-bred or welfare-bound. So while I voraciously read everything I could find by writers of color, and passed that knowledge onto those who were teaching under my guidance, I too was learning the lay of the land. At the same time, to know I was an example for others beginning their discoveries is a wonderful feeling and I am always delighted when I hear that is what has happened.

In 1973, my first collection of poems, a chapbook titled *The Mules Done Long Since Gone,* was published. In those early days, after I'd moved from Bellingham to Seattle, the company of other poets, especially black poets, sustained me as I grappled with literature and composition classes. I became a member of the Seattle-based United Black Artists Guild, and founding editor of their magazine, *Dark Waters.* Through that publication, I met a number of black writers, including Ishmael Reed, John Edgar Wideman, and Al Young. When the city of Seattle designated several buildings as public property, the Guild helped organize campaigns to have those sites declared arts centers. We just went for it with old-fashioned sit-ins and city council filibusters. It was heady stuff. The Guild maintained contact with other West Coast groups, among them Before Columbus, which included Ishmael Reed and Lawson Inada. In 1975, the two groups organized marathon readings, one of them at Seattle University that lasted well past midnight. The reading had been designated as a Third World multi-ethnic gathering, and each poet was allotted one poem of no longer than twenty minutes, ostensibly one that celebrated each reader's heritage. More than thirty poets attended, ethnicities represented by every manner of dress from full-length dashikis and breast-plated Samurai warrior outfits to Southwest Indian shamans and Samoan firewalkers in face paint. Oh yes, yours truly in dashiki and bronze earrings, a twenty-minute African-American "Genesis" poem in hand. Among all those swords, spears, feathers, and gourd rattles, I believe I was thinking: Haight-Ashbery, eat your heart out.

In the summer of 1976, I attended Bread Loaf, my only experience at being in a workshop instead of leading one. I entered not as a poet, but as a fiction writer. (During the time I was writing my dissertation—1972–73—I had cranked out a massive number of short stories to ease the tedium.) Bread Loaf gave me a chance to polish my fiction writing skills, but actually, I received the scholarship because my first full-length collection of poems, *Music from Home,* had been chosen by John Gardner, Jr., and Knute Skinner for the Southern Illinois University Press' Sagittarius Series. In one editing session, Knute Skinner drilled me on the mechanics of style. I learned how to justify every comma, capitalization, and line break according to the rhythm and meaning of the poem. At the time, it was grueling, but that lesson has been invaluable. At Bread Loaf, John Gardner, who was one of the workshop leaders, taught me to understand style in fiction in the same way Knute had done with poetry. Although I was John's protégée, and as a result, somewhat protected from the shafts of workshop criticism, that one experience as a writing student was enough. I now tell my students to remember that workshop writers are carnivorous, and if you offer them your heart on the page, they will eat it. Still, a workshop can be a risk-free environment, and its teachers should inspire such excitement that the participant's limits are constantly being challenged. This is what I have seen with teachers who hold a dedication to the craft of writing, as did the late Nelson Bentley and Richard Hugo, or those who offer standing-room-only lectures, such as Al Young and Jane Alexander. In the nearly twenty years that I have been conducting workshops, I have admired and become friends with many writers of such caliber.

I began to teach creative writing workshops around 1975 or so, first as a poet in the schools, and later, shifting from composition to creative writing on the University of Washington faculty. In 1979 and 1981, I published two collections of poems as a result of having been contacted by Ishmael Reed and Ron Trimble, editors of small presses. In 1983, I became the first black woman to be promoted to full professor at the University of Washington. In that same year, my poems found a "home" with Wesleyan University Press when *Queen of the Ebony Isles* was selected for their series. This began my association with Jeannette Hopkins, editor-in-chief at Wesleyan, and an advocate for young poets who travelled on roads seldom taken, to paraphrase Robert Frost. Jeannette was a fine, courageous editor, who was not swayed when established, usually white male writers, questioned her selections. My association with her lasted until 1988, when she retired. I was most fortunate to have made her acquaintance.

After Bread Loaf, my interest in fiction increased. I found the short story form allowed for an elaborateness that was missing in the parsimony of poetry. My mother claims it really allows me to gossip about the family. Perhaps. What I do know is that characters appear as if they have always been in my head, full-blown and assertive. The writing becomes a sort of wrestling match where I wait to see who will get the upper hand and I don't always want to win. Most of all, prose presents me with a different kind of challenge than what I find in poetry. Short fiction is, in fact, closer to storytelling and the oral tradition. In that genre, I can sustain an image and allow a fluidity of time. My most anthologized story, "Sister Detroit," was included in my first collection, *Jesus and Fat Tuesday,* published in 1987. My second collection of short fiction was published in 1990.

Once I moved into fiction, my poems moved toward more involved forms and more textured narratives. But this is also due to the influence of workshops and being around so many writers. And as a member of the creative writing faculty at the University of Washington, as well as at workshop conferences in other parts of the country, I have had the pleasure of working with a number of fine writers: Larry Levis, Al Young, Alice Fulton, David Wagoner, James Welch, Denise Levertov, Ursula LeGuin, Sonia Sanchez, to name a few. These contacts

The author's children at ages twenty-five and twenty-three

have nourished me, even those that left me anxious—as in 1978, when I inadvertently became the arbitrator on a panel with James Baldwin and Ishmael Reed: the discussion was stimulating; the sparks flew; the atmosphere was palpable. Or in 1992, when I gave a reading with Yevgeny Yevtushenko and Ron Carlson in a shopping mall in Oklahoma. I have given readings in bars and courthouses, in monasteries and ruins (new and noteworthy), and auditoriums and living rooms, but watching Yevtushenko stop traffic in a parking lot was a first.

When did I begin to think of myself as a writer? That feeling didn't come all at once, but in stages, more from a sense of belonging to a writing community than in the number of works I'd published. One such occasion was when Pulitzer Prize–winning poet Gwendolyn Brooks called me onto the stage to read from *my* work after I'd introduced her. At the time, I didn't know Gwendolyn Brooks even knew I existed. To read at the same podium with her was at once glorious and humbling. A few years

later, Maya Angelou greeted me with similar familiarity, and once again, I was surprised to know she had read my poems. Both poets urged me to keep in touch, and though I did for a while, I have let far too much time go by without contacting them. In that respect, I am like my students who tell me years later how much of an influence I have had on them. Other poets are tangibly present in my life. I have in my office several signed broadsides of poems printed for a conference at the Center for Research on Women in San Francisco. One of the broadsides is signed by Audre Lorde, who arrived at the conference before I did. The broadsides are wonderfully symbolic, with the poems and visual art complimenting the sense of women's perspectives. Audre set aside one of hers to make sure she could exchange it for one of mine when I arrived a day after the conference began. It is a gesture I will not forget.

Over the years, writing became both a necessity and a priority. I have to confess that my first poems were published when I'd written a mere ten poems—I was still counting in those days—and a friend and I selected the journals simply on the basis of the originality of their names. We also looked at earlier issues of the journals in an attempt to determine whether my poems would fit, and I suspect that test was much more valid than the name game. But before I leave the impression that writing and publishing was only a matter of choosing the journal with the catchiest name, this stuff has been hard work. Recently, a group of young black women asked me to lunch. They wanted to know what they needed to do to become writers. I said, "If you can get out now, do it." Nothing about this business is easy. Writing is sweaty and lonely, the rewards delayed until the piece is finished. When you know you've finished, nothing seems more passionate than walking—no, strutting—away from the roller coaster of creating images where there had been a blank page. On sunny days, when the work is not going smoothly, I long to be athletic. I dream about long-distance bicycle racing or competitive swimming. On rainy days, I'm tempted to become a couch potato (even inane TV sitcoms can seem interesting when the words won't fall into place). And even then, only the first part of my job has ended.

Publishing is a lot like going through customs to enter a new country—it is capricious and often depends on who was in the line before you, or what the clerk had for breakfast that morning. No matter how many papers you have to validate your passage, you are under scrutiny. I've spent more money in postage stamps sending out manuscripts than I'd like to remember. I've discovered it's easier to become personally acquainted with postal clerks than it is to get a straight answer from an editor who has had your manuscript for months. You must have faith in yourself, not in how much you've published. And when you are writing, you must put to rest those ghosts who haunt your failures as well as those who might add gloss to your success. In a recent television interview, I was asked: How do you know when what you've written is the best you could do? I answered by coining the title from Michael Ondaatje's book: *It's a trick with a knife I'm learning to do,* I said. Each piece of writing is new, something I've never done before. And therein lies the passion.

In 1985, I won an American Book Award for *Queen of the Ebony Isles,* but long before that, I had begun to write in other genres as well as poetry. I have received two National Endowment for the Arts awards—one in poetry and one in fiction. While my fiction writing officially began after John Gardner admired my short stories, I have hesitated in my attempts at a novel, snail's pace would be an appropriate description. (My novel-in-progress, *Hannibal's Children,* will be a fictionalized view of Germany, 1953.) Meanwhile, I have written television scripts and plays, enough to become a member of both the Writers Guild, for work on a public television dramatic series in 1979, and the Dramatists Guild, for stage plays in the late Eighties. In 1982, I collaborated with Ishmael Reed on a choreopoem play, *The Wild Gardens of the Loup Garou,* and in 1987, had the pleasure of using paintings by the renowned artist Jacob Lawrence in my play about Harriet Tubman, *Follow the Drinking Gourd.* I have sketched out several other scripts, but media work has been sidetracked by a particularly important change in my lifestyle.

Once my children reached high school age, I began to travel outside of the country more often. At first, it was simply a need to see those places I'd read about, and if the opportunity presented itself, to talk with poets and storytellers of the region. They were grand vis-

its, but more tourist than real. On my first trip, through five countries in South America, I saw the poet Borges strolling in a park in Buenos Aires, and on a mountainside, near the ruins of Machu Picchu, listened to a shepherd play the music of his ancestors. I have seen fortune-tellers in the boroughs of Tokyo, and visited the Caves of Ham on the Island of Majorca. In my travels, I have sailed the Sea of Finland, and stood on a bridge in Istanbul with one foot in Europe, the other in Asia. I can remember each visit by details: the way light falls on rooftops in Paris, the smell of lime and olive groves in Spain, the call for prayers on a rainy afternoon in Egypt. Like the ragman who patrolled the alley behind my grandmother's house on Kennerly Avenue, I have picked up bits and pieces of what I saw. I have woven those pieces into the tapestry of my poems, as well as into a collection of poetic memoirs, *Halfway to Nosy Be.*

But although my writing was richer in imagery, more evocative, and even more reflective, I am still learning how to use the experience of those trips to further my knowledge of oral traditions. I still was going around Coxey's barn, stumbling through most of Europe and several countries in Africa, Central and South America, Japan, the Pacific, and Southeast Asia before I could "see" what was right in front of me. Finally, between 1977, when I took that first journey through South America, and 1993, when I completed a second Fulbright Creative Writing Fellowship to Madagascar (following an earlier one to Yugoslavia), I gained a scholar's perspective. My stay in Madagascar clearly marked a turning point in my research of storytelling. (Those folktales and memoirs will be collected in a book tentatively titled "Over the Lip of the World.") I learned how to listen, how to wait for the legends and oral histories to unfold. In part, I have my dear friend Makaleia Chalk to thank for that. Maka, who died in 1982, was a master hula dancer. Through her, I began to understand the nuances of expression, how gesture and a culture's perception of time and ancestors influence what wc say and how we say it. In 1978, when I began travelling with Maka, I was only able to see the flash and flair of differences—how a hula dancer's hand turns to imply rain, or how a Fijian firedancer seems to be looking somewhere else when he steps on the burning coals.

McElroy in 1989 on a trip to Finland

With Maka, I travelled throughout the Pacific Islands. After months of watching, moving from one exhibition to another, listening to "talkstory" told through dance and song, I began to see the origins of expression—sometimes simple (the movement of the hand begins in the way the body is held) and sometimes complicated (the firedancer listens to timeless spirits of fire and air that empower the dancer and cannot be seen but must be recognized). None of this happened all at once, but gradually, I pulled away from the gloss of foreignness and came to see myself as a guest who must always remain the stranger. I was able to examine how stories are told and how they travel. This was the basis of my success in collecting folktales and oral histories in Madagascar. And this is the heart of my poetry.

I like telling my students that there was a time when poets had real jobs, a time in the days of Aesop, Beowulf, Harauec, and Merlin when poets were the griots, the soothsayers, the seers, the shamans. I say, "That was the time when Europe, Africa, Asia, and the Western worlds were composed of tribal cultures. Poets were hired to sing the praises of heroes and villains, to bring the news of other tribes, to answer the unanswerable questions of life and death: Who are we? and Where are we going? and Why? Poets are still trying to answer those questions," I tell my students.

In 1985, I held my fiftieth birthday party in one of Seattle's famous mansions. The party was a black-tie affair. (I reserved the white tie for myself, because after all, it matched my gown and the rented Rolls Royce limo.) A "World-class party," I wrote on the invitations. I watched the chair of the English department perform the limbo to a Jamaican steel-drum band. I danced out of my shoes to celebrate my half-century. That's pretty close to world-class, I'll bet. Now I'm thinking about my sixtieth. How do I go a world-class affair one better? I have my eye on the aquarium for starters. And why not? The mother ocean touches all those places I have seen and the ones I have yet to visit. My sense of travel is the one gift I hope I have bequeathed my children—it is the gift of adventure, of journeying beyond the familiar neighborhood. I suspect they've got the hang of it already. When I was in Madagascar, my son was fishing off the Aleutians and my daughter was working with a church school in St. Petersburg, Russia. But writing is another story altogether. Writing is something you do because you must do it. It is a passion, a constant discovery I make myself. Whenever I tell someone I didn't begin writing until my thirties, I always have to qualify that statement by saying my writing started before I set pen to paper. I write because I must, because part of me listens to that little girl mimicking songs on her grandmother's Victrola, and she, in turn, listens to the woman who travels to become a part of the world, not just an observer of it. To quote an image I use in a poem that will be included in my next collection, when I write, I can play back a world of what was real and what was imagined—a world where:

> *in the surprise of believing . . . / . . . logs*
>   *became*
> *chairs, dead bears, boats with roots like stars and*
> *I become a ship sailing back to the beginning*

I am working on four different manuscripts now—a novel, two sets of memoirs, and of course, poems. I am sure I will return to playwriting and short fiction again. At a glance, my writing seems as restless as I have been throughout my life, but there is rhyme and reason to all this. Each piece of writing is a new port of call, full of surprises and disappointments, pleasures and intrigue.

BIBLIOGRAPHY

Poetry:

The Mules Done Long Since Gone (chapbook), Harrison-Madrona, 1973.

Music from Home: Selected Poems, Southern Illinois University Press, 1976.

Winters without Snow, I. Reed, 1979.

Lie and Say You Love Me, Circinatum Press (Tacoma, Washington), 1981.

Looking for a Country under Its Original Name (chapbook), Blue Begonia, 1984.

Queen of the Ebony Isles, Wesleyan University Press, 1984.

Bone Flames, Wesleyan University Press, 1987.

What Madness Brought Me Here: Collected Poems, 1968–1988, University Press of New England, 1990.

Short-story collections:

Jesus and Fat Tuesday and Other Short Stories, Creative Arts Book Company, 1987.

Driving under the Cardboard Pines, Creative Arts Books, 1990.

Other:

Speech and Language Development of the Preschool Child: A Survey (textbook), C. C. Thomas, 1972.

(With Ishmael Reed) *The Wild Gardens of the Loup Garou* (choreopoem play), first produced in Stockbridge, Massachusetts, 1982, produced in New York City, 1983.

Follow the Drinking Gourd (play), first produced in Seattle, Washington, 1987.

Contributor to anthologies, including *The Encyclopedia of Short Fiction,* 1980; *The Third Woman: Minority Women Writers of the U.S.,* 1980; *Woman Poet: The West,* 1980; *Black Sister: Poetry by Black American Women 1746–1980,* 1982; *Gathering Ground: New Writing & Art by Northwest Women of Color,* 1984; *Early Ripening: American Women Poets Now,* 1987; *Breaking Ice: An Anthology of African-American Fiction,* 1990; *Northwest Originals: Washington Women and Their Art,* 1990; *The Writer's Mind,* 1990; *The Confidence Woman: 26 Women Writers at Work,* 1991; *The Graywolf Annual Eight:*

The New Family, 1991; *The Jazz Poetry Anthology,* 1991; *Writers and Their Craft: Short Stories & Essays on the Narrative,* 1991; *The Before Columbus Foundation Poetry Anthology 1980–1990,* 1992; *Poets' Perspectives: Reading, Writing, and Teaching Poetry,* 1992; *Calling the Wind: 20th-Century African-American Short Stories,* 1993; *Dreamers and Desperadoes: Contemporary Short Fiction of the American West,* 1993; *No More Masks,* 1993; *The Wesleyan Tradition: Four Decades of American Poetry,* 1993; and *Where We Stand: Women Poets on the Literary Tradition,* 1993.

Contributor of essays, poems, and short fiction to numerous literary reviews and little magazines, including *Black Warrior Review, Choice, Confrontation, Georgia Review, Kenyon Review, Manhattan Review, Massachusetts Review, Poetry Northwest, Seneca Review, Southern Poetry Review,* and *Wormwood Review.*

Molly Peacock

1947-

1

Two girls, fourteen and eleven, eat the dinner the older one has cooked as the July shadows lengthen on all the suburban lawns. School is long over and won't begin again for equally as long. They are deep into the green barbarity of a childhood summer. They listen to the swish of each car as it slows down so that the children playing baseball in the street have time to disperse, and each slowing down causes them a prick of anxiety because it might be their father's car. The later it becomes the more certain it is that he will be drunk, but what he will do is not certain. They have the dinner heating on the stove, drying out in the pans. They eat with a mix of summer doldrums and a kind of haste to finish before he comes. Then they won't have to eat with him. The day is long; it's still light out. The littler one puts her dishes in the sink and goes out to play baseball. The older one does the dishes, washing the knives first, just as her mother told her, then continuing on with the rest. "Dry those knives and put them in the drawer before your father gets home. Never leave a knife out, Molly."

Molly is obedient. Molly is good. She never leaves a knife out. Molly is not obedient or good because of her fierce moral fiber, but because she is frightened her father might kill her. Her mother has said that her father might do this. That's why she has to put the knives away. Wash them first. She slops through the suds, the scatter rug below the sink is drenched. The parakeet squawks in its cage. The sun hangs lower in the sky. This time when the sounds of the baseball players disperse, the car wheels into her own driveway. She drops the plate back into the dishwater, grabs the towel, and immediately wipes the knives. She pushes them into the drawer, shuts the drawer, and turns around. "Hi, Dad. Dinner's on the stove. Want to eat?"

Molly Peacock, 1994

She says this before she looks at his face. It is rough-red as a piece of ham. "No, I don't want nothin' to eat," the face says. The arm of her father picks up the saucepan full of creamed corn drying out on the burner from being set continually on "Low." The arm of her father flings the pan of corn at the wall. The dull creamed corn drips down the pink kitchen wall.

"You don't have to have corn, Dad. I made you some pork chops."

"Don't want no pork chops!" The workshirted arm of her father picks up the iron frying pan from the big burner on "Low."

"Dad! Don't throw it!"

He doesn't throw it.

Remember what you said just now, Molly thinks to herself, and remember how you said it. The timing. Remember how you got him not to throw the pan. Maybe you can do it again. Get him not to throw the pan when his arm grabs it like that. While she is organizing these thoughts in her mind, he has gone to the corner cabinet.

In the corner cabinet is a lazy Susan filled not with food or dishes but with files of receipts for the quarterly taxes of Peacock's Superette. Pink and yellow receipts, hundreds of them, clipped together, rubber banded, stuck in between other receipts, notebooks, little pads with columns of figures, and rolls of adding machine paper with columns of figures.

As the arm of her father opens the corner cabinet and whirls the lazy Susan faster and faster, the receipts come flying out. But they don't fly fast enough. The arm of her father, both arms of her father start grabbing the receipts and hauling them down onto the counter, then onto the floor. The kitchen is awash in receipts. Some stick to the creamed corn on the pink walls, some fall into the frying pan with the chops on the stove.

The frying pan, she thinks. I should have let him throw the pan. Next time, remember to let him throw the pan. Remember. Don't say anything. Let him throw it.

Because this is worse.

The side doorbell rings.

Molly ignores it. Her father is swearing, "Fuck the store! Don't want no dinner!" And mumbling, "Fuckin' shit, fuckin' bitch." He wades through the receipts toward the kitchen table. All this time his daughter has been moving around the kitchen, keeping at a safe distance. She makes no move to clean anything up. If she began to clean it up she'd have to turn her back. And if she turned her back, he might kill her. She watches in fascination at the destruction. Her father's legs lumber him toward her. She backs up. He turns toward the kitchen table. The doorbell rings again. Her father is still swearing. He plants his legs as two columns. His arms grab the tabletop and tip it over. Salt, pepper, napkins, and her father's place setting fly off the table. She's glad she cleaned up the other dishes. And put away the knives.

Now her father is down on his knees, bracing them against the upside down table, and using his powerful arms to wrench off the table legs one by one. It is a solid hardwood table. She has learned about adrenaline from the pediatrician who has treated her numerous allergies. Suddenly she thinks, what amount of adrenaline is coursing through him now? The doorbell rings again. He continues swearing, "Cunt, cunt," and methodically braces himself to break the last table leg. She backs into the foyer and closes the kitchen door just before her father takes a table leg and beats it like a club against the tabletop on the floor.

It is a neighbor girl at the side door. "Wanna come out and hang around, go to the drugstore?" It is the girl with cigarette burns on her legs she says are mosquito bites she scratched and made worse. Molly looks down. She still has a dishtowel in her hand. Behind the door her father grunts as he methodically beats the table. His workbooted feet make a swishing sound as he moves through the flimsy carpet of receipts. How much can she hear? What would she make of it?

"I can't. Go with you. I . . ." Molly trails off. "I . . . ," think of something normal she tells herself, think of a regular excuse, what regular parents do to normal kids. "I'm grounded," she says almost enthusiastically as she finds her normal lie. "I've got to stay in and do the dishes. He's making me." Imagine, doing something dumb and wrong and normal, and then getting punished, and then having it be over, she thinks.

Behind the kitchen door it's over temporarily. No grunts, no swearing. Then, "Molly," he growls, "get in here and clean up this goddamn mess."

"You see? Lookit, I've gotta go."

"Yeah. Well, see ya."

Inside Molly looks at her father with every ounce of censure she can muster. "Oh Dad, what's Mommy going to say?"

"Don't worry about your mother. I'll worry about your mother. Get into your room. I'll clean this up." Now he is pale and repentant. She knows he won't do anything more, like follow her into her room and start breaking things there. He is ashamed and cleans it up by himself.

After he leaves for Peacock's Superette, Molly creeps out to the kitchen. She thinks of calling the neighborhood girl, but stays in the kitchen instead, then goes into the living room to watch TV. The kitchen floor and walls are clean, the receipts somehow piled back into the corner cabinet. Of course the knives were put away earlier. She had seen to that. And he hadn't broken the chairs. Four hard maple chairs are lined up against the wall, waiting, a bit like a police lineup.

It is far too dark to play baseball now. The kids outside are playing a flashlight game. Then parents begin to call them in, so her sister comes home. The kitchen lights are ablaze, but Molly sits in the dark in the living room with only the light of the TV. "Hey, Mol, what happened to the table?" Gail asks. "I saw Dad dragging the pieces out to the garbage."

"He broke it. He broke up the table. He threw his dinner at the wall and broke the table."

"Jesus. Lookit those chairs lined up—they look like Goldilocks and the three bears," her sister says in awe.

Later their mother arrives. "What the hell happened to the kitchen table?"

"Dad broke it."

"No wonder he was such a lamb at the store," her mother says.

Even though I have told this episode countless times to friends, in therapy, and used parts of it in my poetry, I could not write it here in the first person. The only way I could tell it was to make myself and Gail and my father characters in a story.

"What happened here?" my mother asked the next morning when she opened the door to the cabinet where all the receipts were shoved in disorder.

"Dad. He did it when he broke the table."

My mother didn't ask me to tell her more about it, nor did I volunteer. She simply took in the information, groaned, and started reorganizing the receipts. "This will take me a week," she muttered. She did not say he was wrong, she did not say it was his disease, she did not say she was sorry I had to be there during it all, but neither did she wholly deny it happened. She treated it like a horrible fact of life, a hurricane you had to clean up after. I had no sense at all that change in my family was possible.

Sometimes the difference between how I see my life and how others see it is the matter of my skin. Of course, others see it as the border of my body, as anybody else's skin is

"My parents, Edward Frank (Ted) and Pauline (Polly) Peacock," 1945

the boundary between them and the world. But I have often seen my skin as permeable. And sometimes I have felt that I do not have a skin at all. At these times anybody in the world has access to me. I do not feel separate from them. This means that during those times I have found myself in a state of continuous empathy with other people. This empathic state puts me in danger of losing my self because I am attending so closely to the needs of someone else. Well into my thirties I struggled to have an identity, to have a form or shape to my life which seemed constantly to be bleeding into—or being bled by—others.

Many people, especially many women, have felt this sensation, but I felt it all the time as a teenager and as a young woman. The identity crisis that adolescents usually undergo, the questions of *Who am I?* and *What constitutes me?* were kept alive in my life. I carried far too many responsibilities to say I was in an extended state of adolescence, but there was a certain adolescent pain, the psychic growing pain, present all the time.

Years later, having to support myself as a poet, I entered a profession which requires one of the highest levels of sustained human nurturance outside of actual nursing: I became a learning disabilities specialist. The permeable skin I had allowed me to identify with the children I tried to help. These students had trouble processing language. The permeable skin also became part of my identity as a poet. It gave me an understanding of the world from the inside out.

I knew quite early I was engaged in a survival struggle, but I felt I would be alone in it, as alone as each person in my family was. It was not until I was twenty-seven, nearly twenty years ago, that I realized I could ask for help. It was my good fortune to ask for this help from Joan Stein, a psychotherapist so attuned to me that I have been able, over the years, to integrate the many aspects of me that were born and developing along, much like a healthy family of various dimensions inside me. The process of psychotherapy, what the British analyst Adam Phillips calls a "theory of censorship" (and means by this, I think, the development of ways to lift the pressure of the many internal censors our family life and growing personalities attempt to impose on us), has allowed the births and rebirths of these aspects of me, and has allowed me to see their shape, my boundaries.

For ten years (1947–1957) we lived in the duplex in Buffalo, New York, with my grandparents, then, when they retired, sold the duplex and moved to a small pink-and-white suburban house in Tonawanda, north of Buffalo. But the mortgage payments were crippling, not to mention finding the money for the cases of beer and cartons of cigarettes necessary to keep our new nuclear family afloat. My dad, Ted (Edward Frank Peacock), began to work two jobs, his regular job at the electric company, driving the truck with a huge yellow lift to repair downed wires, and a night job pumping gas in a service station a few blocks away. Anticipating my father's breaking point, my mother found a way of taking care of all of us financially, eliminating the gas station job, and getting the beer and cigarettes at cost.

What my mother, Pauline (Pauline Ruth Peacock, née Wright), found to do was to emulate her own father. My grandfather Gilbert Wright's general store and Esso station (which

"I'm in the foreground, with my mother and Gail behind me," about 1952

stood at a crossroads in the orchard country of rural upstate New York called La Grange)— with its secret peephole to spy for gypsies and the miracles of its wooden shelves of fudge bars, soda pop, clothespins, flour, oil, auto parts— fascinated all its customers, including the regulars, my grandfather's cronies, a group of pipe-smoking farmers in bib overalls. Pauline convinced Ted to borrow money from his credit union to start a business: PEACOCK'S SUPERETTE. The Superette, a low cement building next to a liquor store on a main road between Buffalo and Niagara Falls, had none of the slow conviviality of La Grange Garage. The Superette sported metal shelves, not brightly painted wooden ones, and cement floors with rows of coolers stocked with brown pint bottles and green quart bottles and flimsy aluminum cans of beer and ale.

The new arrangement Pauline constructed was that Ted would come home from his job at four, I would make him dinner, iron his shirt, and send him off to the store. There he would relieve her, so that she could come home and eat dinner. Gail and I were to come home alone from school and do our homework until the dinner I made was ready. I was to supervise my sister's homework. This was to be the clockwork, weekday routine. On weekends Pauline and Ted were to alternate shifts at the store.

Pauline would cook on Sundays. Now this is an extreme schedule for any family. The burden on my mother from her two jobs of house and store, on my father from his two jobs, on me from the two jobs of school and house, and on my sister from the job of school as a learning disabled child and home with a smarty-pants older sister who hated her mothering role all weigh so heavily in the mere description that it is exhausting for me to imagine it. Now add alcoholism.

Twelve- and thirteen-year-old humans are some of the frailest animals alive. I spent ten years of my life watching them, first as a teacher, then as a learning disabilities specialist. It is a truism among teachers that the age you teach is the age of your greatest personal crisis. Having worked with hundreds of girls and boys of the age at which I began my life as a false wife and false mother, I can say with verified sadness that no matter how adult such adolescents appear, they are not adults, but in a tunnel of travel into adult consciousness. However successful I am as a poet, or as a teacher, or even simply as an adult, there is an ever-decreasing but still apparent part of me frozen in that tunnel, for I was not allowed to traverse it in my own time or in my own skin.

"Again in the foreground, with my father and Gail, picking up marbles," about 1954

Three years of high school without change in fear, or vigilance. Sometimes the fear abates, but it never completely leaves. Sometimes I turn my attention elsewhere, but a part of me never removes my attention from the possible source of danger, which isn't only my father, but Ted and Gail and Pauline and myself in four strands of color that wind and wind. Of course the changes of growth and degeneration occur, but these aren't clear to me. My father's alcoholism degenerates. His daughters' sexuality accelerates. His wife's depression deepens. Everybody gains weight, except Gail. Either food or drink fills us up, but danger fills her up.

"I'm going out with this great guy tonight," Gail whispers over the minute steaks I've burned. "Don't tell Mom, Molly, you're always such a tattletale." I was a tattletale; she was right. "He's coming over at seven and we're going to go to the Falls." Niagara Falls was not within walking distance.

"How old is this guy? Does he drive a car?" I say incredulously.

"Sure he drives. He's nineteen. He goes to night school, isn't that cool?"

"Cool. . . ." I say nonplussed.

"He was at the JV basketball game. He likes basketball."

"Likes basketball?"

"Yeah, but Molly, don't tell Mom, what he really likes is cars. He likes to drive 'em."

"Cars?"

My sister was a JV cheerleader. I had coached her for hours before the tryouts. I hadn't been chosen as a cheerleader, but like a teenage stage mother I'd decided that my Gail should rectify my inabilities and mistakes. And so I'd hounded and nagged her until she learned a great routine and was honored with a position on the squad. She was too hip, though. She smoked; she never did her homework. I felt I was a shitty mother and worse as a sister. I just couldn't keep an eye on her. When, when, I asked myself, did she become like this?

"Look, I better call Mom," I began, but she mocked me.

"Better call Mo-om," breaking the syllable in two like a saltine.

"The guy's nineteen! He's two years older than I am!" I squawked.

"So who says you have to be the oldest thing around here? This guy is cool. Wait'll you meet him. He knows Mom, too. He hangs out at the store sometimes." The only guys who hung out at the store were dropouts. My mother collected them.

"Keep an eye on your sister," my grandparents often said.

Be vigilant. You can never tell what will happen.

She looked to me as the mother I hated to be. She told the truth to me, more or less. And whatever truth she told increasingly horrified me. She was blonde and sexual and loved danger. Personally, danger left me cold. I'd been in enough of it. I was endangered every night waiting for Ted to come home.

"That's him!" my sister squealed as she heard a muffled noise at the door.

"How could it be him? I didn't hear a car drive up."

I still listened for my father's car in the driveway every night. I listened for how he drove, whether the turn was reckless and the brake was jammed on at the last minute, or whether it was a smooth, pantherlike crawl, the turquoise Chrysler oiled with only a couple of beers. Late, later, after countless shots of whisky with beer chasers, meant either rage at full force, or maybe only a dead sleep, or maybe a few slurred questions tucked around an insult and then the blackout. A couple of beers maybe meant OK, he'd get changed and go to relieve my mother at the store, but it also meant fuller consciousness, questions, where was my sister going, what was I doing, and possible anger. This meant anything could happen.

My sister was unlocking the door and speaking to a figure in the dark she didn't ask into the light of the hallway. She left him standing outside in the cold while she ran for her coat and grabbed the keys to my mother's ancient pink Plymouth that was mysteriously harbored in the rivulet of our driveway. How had my mother gotten to work, anyway?

"You're taking Mom's car?" I was incredulous.

"I told you, Molly, he likes cars. He loves to drive. He's a really great driver, too. We'll be back before they know it's missing."

"Put those car keys on the hook!" I hissed as she swung out the door. She knew I wouldn't tackle her on the front steps. She knew I'd be slightly afraid of the nineteen-year-old boy. She knew I was confused and couldn't decide whether I was her mother or her sister, and she knew I wouldn't tell our mother because I was supposed to be her mother and I failed. And she

also knew, somehow, that my mother's car would be there for the taking. The Plymouth wheeled out of the driveway with the wild teenage daughter I couldn't control.

My father came home drunk but obedient to some unknown-to-me command from my mother that he pick her up at the store and bring her home. I said my sister was at her girlfriend's house. Just after he left, my sister came home with my mother's car, and there the two of us sat, watching "Adventures in Paradise," when my parents drove up at 10:30 P.M. I never understood how my mother had gotten to work without a car, how my sister knew this, or how my father understood the arrangement; nor did my parents—unless my mother knew some version of this from my sister— know whom my sister was with and in what vehicle. My family arrangements were often like this. I felt I had all the responsibility, and none of the control. Nothing I kept an eye on stayed still; it vaporized. Yet I had to keep my eye on·my sister, and especially on my father. If I took my eyes off him, he might kill me.

Molly and Gail at Christmas, 1955

Continually my mother reminded me to do the dishes immediately after eating and to put away the knives. "You don't want to give anybody an opportunity," my mother said. "Anybody" meant my father. It took me almost a decade of exposure to other people's lives before what a therapist said to me made sense: "She expected you to be hurt, Molly." And I expected this too.

A spring night in my senior year of high school. My sister out with her friends. I lie on my bed looking at the curtains I've designed and sewn and looking at the two orange heads of Nefertiti I've wedged as bookends for the books of poetry I've begun collecting. I have only a few friends, and they are school friends. If my mother is out when my father is home, I feel I have to stay home as well. It takes me decades to understand I am a substitute, a sacrifice. Then I only thought, if I'm not here, who knows what could happen? I have to stay home, because if I am home I will be able to . . . prevent . . . what?

Well, one thing I can prevent is his coming into my room. My bedroom has no door. It is an extension built onto the house through my sister's bedroom. Her room does have a door, but I do not want to lead him to burst through it; therefore I meet him on common ground: the kitchen and the living room. The key is to remain ever watchful. You can never tell when he will come home or what he will do when he gets there. The best tactic is to stay alert and stay away from the things of yours he could destroy.

Every evening is a defensive military maneuver, and I use the tactics of the powerless everywhere: forethought and watchfulness. I also use the good girl tactic, since it is at my disposal. I am the good girl, the obedient one. If I obey perfectly all the instructions, I can trot out obedience in my defense. I can ward off evil with my structure of goodness, of servitude. Oh yes, I am a servant. I serve my family's needs, not out of that desire for connection, not out of that love that makes us long to fulfill the needs of those whom we love, but out of self-defense, a brittle, two-faced cunning that knows the armor of the Good. And it is armor I need, for I have no skin. At best I am "thin-skinned" and sensitive, sensitive because the borders that define me are so frail.

But I have my lessons to do, and I have the phone to talk on to my occasional friends, not about socializing, but about homework and the appalling number of school activities I join. I'm in every club and on every committee. Of course there's nothing to come home for after school, so I don't. There's another reason I join everything. I want to be visible in school. I've never been rushed to a sorority. (How can I have people to my house? Who knows what will happen?) And out of a desire to reaffirm that I can be something other than a nobody, I manage to get myself elected to things, chosen for things. I do the publicity for this and this, make the posters, make the phone calls. I work on the newspaper, on the yearbook. Finally I am chosen editor of the yearbook. Everything looks normal; I am succeeding.

And I am succeeding as the substitute abused wife of my father: I am alive. A spring night here in my room admiring the overstuffed chair I acquired and the cover for the chair my grandmother helped me make and the bedspread she helped me dye to match it, and I listen. I listen for the car in the driveway. Every night for all the years between twelve and eighteen I listen for the car, and often I hope he is dead. I hope he gets into a car accident and dies. I think my father must be the luckiest man in Buffalo. He is the embodiment of the luck of the Irish. How can he be alive when he drives like that? It is about a year since my last try at getting him into Alcoholics Anonymous. I have ended a campaign which begged my mother every morning to leave him and begged him every sober early weekend morning to go to AA. I read him the ten questions from the *Buffalo Evening News* that if you answer yes to any five you are an alcoholic.

My mother surprised me. She said, "You're hurting your father." Is she crazy? I thought. He's hurting us. Me. Nothing seemed to change, except the years passing at school. I was going to go to college. I was going to get out of there, to escape a burden that was both very big and very inappropriate. The secrecy surrounding my father's alcoholism hooded every perspective. My mother had found a way of supporting us, but it was also a way of abdicating responsibility as a wife and a mother. I can still touch the anger at her strange abandonment, the lack of love and care that resulted, and that held me in a kind of perpetual pause of growth throughout my teenage

Maternal grandparents, Ruth and Gilbert Wright, about 1967

years. When I was required during literature classes or during my silly home economics classes to imagine a family, or to imagine what my own future family might be like, I could only picture my present painful one. This picture I looked away from again and again as I tried to make a life as an ordinary human being, though I was not so ordinary. I had a gift for language and a burning desire to use it to understand my life. Therefore, though I tried to turn away from it, in poem after poem I focused on that internalized picture.

2

No one who knew my mother well actually used her formal name, Pauline. Everyone called her Polly. Polly, as a child, had felt lovingly bonded to her grandmother, Molly. Her mother (my grandmother, Ruth) had named my newborn mother Ruth Isabelle, after herself. Family legend has it that my grandfather

simply started calling my mother Polly, and her name was formally changed to Pauline Ruth, dropping the wretched Isabelle. As a girl my mother lived for weeks at a time on the glorious farm with her grandparents, preferring it to the house and general store down the road where her mother was. Her brother was preferred in her parents' household, and Polly was relished by her grandparents, especially Molly, after whom I am named. When she married my father, she became Polly Peacock, a goofy name she feistily defended.

I know the history of these names is confusing—I myself was confused by it as a little girl—but I explain it here because the confusion is so emblematic of the confused identity of the child who shares too intimately a mother's thoughts. There was only one consonant's difference between my mother and me, yet I was also her obstacle. I continually felt that if I didn't exist, she somehow would have a better life. How could I, as her child, bear being her obstacle? I could become her mirror. I could reflect to her the assurances she needed to be who she was.

It was a staggering job to return this mirroring, more so because the mirroring my mother did for me was often obscured. Common wisdom says that mothers are supposed to be the mirrors of their children, for in their eyes will be reflected their children's growth and identities. But very often my mother was depressed, so depressed that the mirrors of her eyes were dull, and nearly impossible to see myself in. At these times, my mother read. I sat at her side playing—often reading myself, or writing and drawing—and admonishing myself not to interrupt her, though she tolerated what probably were a stream of interruptions from me. My mother read to escape. And I have often thought that I became a writer in order to have my mother read me. Although it is difficult to develop a positive picture of a family to internalize if the picture your mother draws for you is negative—or at least my own experience has taught me that—my mother's escape, reading, did allow me to develop other ideas of families, because as soon as I could read I loved to read about them.

Polly was an avid reader of westerns and romances. Gail and I teased her about her favorite author, Louis L'Amour, as soon as we found out what *amour* was. Before she turned to buying paperbacks to read behind the counter at the Superette, the three of us went weekly to the library. I did everything Pauline did, so I became a reader, too. My learning disabled sister, hyperactive, unable to focus, did not. My mother and I, swept into fantasy worlds at the drop of a paragraph, had one more reason to see Gail as a foreigner. This was in 1955, thirty years before schools began diagnosing learning disabilities. Pauline's escapist reading began in her own family when she herself was four and learned to read at a one-room schoolhouse, taken there every day on the back of a blind farm horse who knew the way. When her grandparents hooked up their team to their wagon and went to town for weekly supplies, Pauline stayed at the farm to ride her pony but instructed them to bring her back a book.

If I had had grandparents who hitched up a wagon and went to town, I too would have wanted to stay home and be brought a book. To wander bareback on a pony to a riverbank pretending to be this or that, and then to lie,

deliciously prone on that riverbank, and get lost in a book: I cannot think of a childhood afternoon more ideal. Very luckily I was invited to spend summers with my mother's parents at the hamlet of La Grange. A few weeks of each of my own childhood summers were as golden as those my mother described, though my mother's summers grew into apple-picking falls, and I left my grandparents' house to return to Buffalo to resume my roles as a poorly prepared substitute wife and mother. As Polly aged, she often lapsed into stories about her youth and prefaced each story with how wonderful her girlhood was. For her, childhood contained the best moments of life before adulthood went awry. For me, whose life has been so much the opposite, but who had that little taste of what she described and redescribed, those stories are clouded in my anger. I heard "Oh, I had a wonderful childhood!" with sharpening rage over the years.

It sounds hyperbolic, but the legacy of childhood reading probably saved my life. My expe-

La Grange crossroads in rural upstate New York, the site of Grandfather Gilbert Wright's general store and Esso station

rience of horror—my parents' fights, the terror I felt when the drinking was out of hand and into violence, at the least my parents' voices raised, at the worst my father pushing my mother down the cellar stairs, my sister and I running to push her back up into safety—led me to separate my experience into what happened "outside" my head and what happened "inside." Inside were fantasies of health and power and control. I was Lola the spy who controlled all (I played Lola privately well into my sophomore year of high school) or I was Mary of *The Secret Garden* or Jo of *Little Women*. I developed these fantasies from reading. The voices of authors, the comfort and wisdom and emotion expressed, allowed me to grow internally, secretly, to nurture a hidden self all on my own, the self I would save, the self I would become, unbeknownst to my family, almost unbeknownst to my conscious, practical, adult facade, the outer self I built to bear the burdens of my father's alcoholism and my mother's depression. The voices of those authors parented me. The books I read were my escape, the authors' voices mirrors of my feelings, nurturers of my imagination. All my inner world was yearnings, yearnings for solitude and freedom.

Of course I fantasized I was an orphan, that these parents were really not my own. Perhaps my real parents would come and get me. My fantasy life was composted from the emotional peelings and scraps of my parents' lives put out to rot in the backyard of literature, the weather of literature beating on them, turning them into loam. Although my parents' arguments must have had words, I do not recall them but only remember the achingly wordless nonexplanations of their behavior, the silence to my questions, the silencing of my questions, the requirement that I turn inside in order to stay sane, although many children turn inside, split off entirely, and become insane. My imagination, fueled by literature, kept alive an anchored, growing, interior life, one I could articulate to myself because of literary models, models who would save me. The books gave me this gift. But unbeknownst to me I was gifted already. I was imaginative and verbal and, best of all, I was to learn that I could write.

Polly always closed her book and put it carefully away when Ted came home. His entry into the house always threatened disruption. The threat that I felt to my life, even though my father in fact never spanked, hit,

or touched me (and in fact rarely hugged or was physically affectionate toward me) had its taproot in my father's threat to my mother's life. Ted was a hysterical nipper of a fighter, biting, darting, then sweating, bashing, and thrashing as my mother's recalcitrance fanned his hysteria into blinder rage. Polly was a growler, growling this or that comment, refusing to up her pitch, keeping a steady negative monotone that refused to react to his emotionalism, fanning it. The ways they expressed themselves completely frustrated their understanding of one another, Polly constantly protecting herself from Ted's emotional fireworks, Ted's need for an ear met instead by her protective resistance. Neither of them ever could change his or her mode.

Bright morning in the Buffalo duplex house. Gail is three and I am six. Daddy comes home after working the graveyard shift. Breakfast. French toast. Sharp rectangular delineations of sunlight on the floor. Playing, eating, unaware of the escalating voices until our mother's usual growl of stubborn annoyance hikes itself into a surprising soprano pitch, and our father's yapping descends to a deep, lung-rattling bass. The hefty Scotty dog I think he's like and the big unflappable setter I think she's like have reversed and become monstrous. They are not like dogs anymore, but like canine horrorsaurs. He is pushing her toward the open cellar door and she is screaming, "Ted, Ted don't do it!" and he is panting, "I'll kill you, you bitch," and as his broad workshirted back blocks the doorway, she is already backing down the cellar stairs. He prods her collarbone with his pointer finger. Then he pushes her again. "Ted, not in front of the kids!" is her signal to us and we run, Gail tiny enough to push between his legs to get to her, me sliding past them on the stairs. Now Gail and I are below them, pushing up against our mother's legs as he pushes down on her. It is a tangle of legs and stairs, his workpants and boots pushing down against her bare calves and slippers, while Gail and I push up against her, trying to hold her up and save her, and in saving her rescue our lives, because he is a monster now, a dragon, faced puffed and red. Her face as she twists toward us is drained an almost painted white. She looks like a geisha girl beneath her black hair. "Ted, watch out! The kids!" she screams, diverting his attention. She is the cunning girl and he is the blustering dragon, brought for a moment to his senses, outwitted because we have diverted him. He backs up the stairs, she follows, we follow her, we are saved, all of us, because of the kids, watch out for them.

The stereotypical Asian images of terrifying maleness in the shape of a red dragon and terrified femininity painted chalk white, ashen in fear, leapt into relief in my mind and seem permanently installed there. I cannot think of him in rage except to recall the dragon, or her except to recall the courtesan, highly stylized images for this Navy boy come home from World War II to work at the electric company and this farm girl come to the city. Even if he seemed like a little terrier and she like a large, long-haired lazy setter, they were a strong man and a weaker woman. He could overpower her. He could kill her. Kill us. Me. Usually the fights were verbal. Physical violence was only hinted at, but because this perennial threat wasn't quite empty, it was always powerful. Only after I escaped to college did I hear, long distance from my dorm room, the stories of increased physical violence, the police, my mother's and sister's fear escalating until they ran away. My parents divorced, and Peacock's Superette was sold, and my father briefly remarried, worked, retired early from countless alcohol-related health problems, and died; my mother finished her working life as a secretary in a hospital, never remarried, then retired and lived a life of glorious solitude until the illness of her last year, carefully budgeting her money to eat an inexpensive lunch out every day with a paperback romance or western in front of her, happy with her book, with the food which she did not have to make, brought to her by a series of solicitous waitresses with waiting coffee pots, and happy with the voice of the author speaking to her, soothing, exciting, engaging, surprising. Now I am an author.

The serious split between an internal safety I struggled to create and preserve and an external atmosphere of verbal suggestions of violence, sharpened my ideas of inner life and public life to a glittering edge. What I truly was I felt could not be revealed at the cost of its death. As a result, no one could really know me. The loneliness this causes is almost unspeakably profound. Anyone who is driven this far inward risks the "not coming back" of serious mental illness, the splitting off of internal

and external experience that can become at its worst multiple personalities. But I did not suffer a splitting off from the world so severe. When I think of the circumstances that allowed my escape from extreme illness, of the many individual adults both inside and outside my family who helped me, and of the sheer luck of my physical stamina and intelligence, the circumstance with the most profoundly rescuing shape is art. Since the first time my mother gave me a pencil and scrap paper to occupy myself, I have consistently felt the joy of processing my experiences into pictures and words. As a girl I drew and painted, and as I learned more about language I wrote, and then read. My inner life had a way out. I did not have to hold my spirit prisoner. Many times throughout my young life I imagined myself in prison, without pencil or paper. I practiced for this deprivation by imagining writing in my head and memorizing it. I was determined for my gift to save me, even if I became deprived of its instruments.

Gail next door at Grandma's, Daddy far away at work, Mommy reads her library book settled deep in a red upholstered chair with doilies on the arms to cover the cigarette burns. Mommy wears Daddy's dark green T-shirt without a bra and a pair of baggy jeans. Her shiny black hair with its exciting streak of gray to the left of her widow's peak is pushed back from her cream white forehead. The wall behind her is green, dark as the forest green of the T-shirt. It is 1952. I am five. She is thirty-three. No woman on Gunnell Avenue in Buffalo, New York, goes braless, wears jeans, buys red chairs and puts them in deep green rooms, then sits down to read a library book, popping an occasional chocolate covered cherry into her mouth after she's finished her cigarette. She's whizzed through her housework, the dinner fixings are on the counter. She is alone, alone and happy to be in her own world.

Little mouse at her side, I try to read a letter her mother, my grandmother Ruth in the country, has sent me, but I don't attend school yet and do not know how. I have my pencil and my drawing pad. I am using my inner resources. Mommy doesn't like people who can't sit and be quiet and use their inner resources. But I can't read! In exasperation I poke through the carefully constructed boundary of Mommy's world. "Read it to me, Mom."

"Read it to me, Mom, OK?"

Her hazel eyes are trained on her book.

"Read me Gram's letter, OK?"

After a few verbal tries, I place the letter on top of the open book, and Mommy turns and reads it aloud. I have never gotten a letter before, and this is an interesting thing to have, though I wonder what to do with it now.

"Well, when you get a letter, you write back," Mommy explains.

"OK," I say, picking up my pencil, making stray letterlike lines on the page. But my lines are disappointing. They don't really look like writing.

"Why don't you draw Gram a picture?" Mommy lazily says.

I *always* draw pictures. *Babies* draw pictures. "No! I want to write a letter back!"

"Oh, all right, here's the alphabet, Molly." Mommy scrawls the alphabet across the top of the paper. "Now, write DEAR GRAM." She underlines the individual letters. Of course I can't remember the order of "Dear Gram" out of ADEGMR, and I am aware that Mommy has reached her limit, so I do not ask again, but try to figure out for myself how to write them, and after a fashion, I have covered the page in something akin to a personal cuneiform. It is the hardest thing I've ever done. I couldn't be more pleased. And Mommy couldn't be more pleased. I make her smile. I draw a smile from those straight, slightly purplish lips whose carmine lipstick has disappeared to find a better home on the filter tips of cigarette butts in a square glass ashtray, an ashtray so heavy that when my father let it fly against the wall in an argument it didn't even break. Nothing can break the pleasure of this solitude of this afternoon. Like two sides of an open locket, the side that read and the side that wrote to reach the reader, my mother and I lay inside the red and green jewelbox of the afternoon.

The mutual possession of our selves, without the diverting presence of my sister or the inflaming presence of my father, gave me the sense, reinforced by my mother over and over again, that *this* was how one ought to live. "Everybody should have their own room," my mother would say. "The only way for a family to survive is for each person to have their own room." My mother had never heard of Virginia Woolf. She didn't have a room of her own as an adult until she was nearly fifty years old, divorced, and with her children grown. None of us had

rooms to ourselves, and even when my sister and I did, later in a different house, the rooms *had no doors.* Invasion was always both physically and emotionally possible. My mother's quest for a room became invested in me, and the magnitude of my need for it irrevocably shaped my life—and the lives of the people I've loved, especially the men I've lived (or tried to live) with.

Part of that driven need for a room of my own was to have room for my gift as an artist. I both drew and wrote until I reached high school. I knew I wanted to be "something special" but I didn't know what that special thing was until I got to college and decided, in a very tentative way, to try to become a poet. I know people who have denied their gifts, and I have watched their personalities wizen and shrivel, almost before my eyes, from that denial. My gift was too large, too pleasurable, too life-affirming to deny. It gave me life by ensuring my life. Without it, I would not have survived. I did not know this consciously, but since I first was able to express myself I have guarded that gift with a fierceness I have long heard described as the characteristic protective fierceness of motherhood. I take pleasure in the gift, and, animal-like, claw the mental air at any interference with the tenderness of its growing being.

3

Sex and babies. Five tiny neighborhood girls all jumping up and down on two of their children's twin beds, squealing and tickling one another in the silky, rabbit warren mess of sheets that smell of childbody sleep thick between the crumpled ridges. Burrow into Gail's bed with the shock of Gailsmell while the others use my bed as a trampoline before Grandma, alarmed at the squawk of the springs, hauls us all downstairs: I stick my finger up my underpants and find the hole, fingersized, see a color in my mind, black/red, bring my finger out and smell it. Ah! The smell of me.

"All right now, all of you girls have to go home after you finish your oatmeal cookies. Come on now, little Diane, let's get a move on." My grandmother Mildred, my father's mother who lives next door to us, has the quality of a businesslike Shetland sheepdog nosing at the heels of the three lambs she ushers out the

Paternal grandparents, Mildred and Howard Peacock, about 1950

door. She is glad to sit down. Five girls, ages four to seven, are a handful. But she leans toward me from her chair and puts her arms loosely around me. "Oh you naughty girls! I'll have to make those beds all over again."

"Hey Gram, look what I found," I say, suddenly daring. She has said "naughty" with benign acceptance. I know she thinks we weren't really naughty. I stick my finger up my underpants into my vagina and bring my finger out and thrust it under her nose. "Smell this!"

"Eeewwwhhh!" she exclaims in delight, "what a cupcake smell!" Her eyes glisten with a kind of excitement, surprise, curiosity, and wonder. I search her face for whether this is all right. I have found the secret place she also knows about, inside the place I pee from. I'm not clear at all about why this is a secret, but it is all right. "Let's go remake the beds," she says, corralling me and Gail up the stairs. I know not to startle my mother in the way that I startled Gram, just the way I know not to use the beds as trampolines, although I think it's

fine to use the beds as trampolines *quietly,* not making a disturbance.

Quietly. For all my railing at my mother's abandonment and sometimes downright neglect— one time I was forced to come home from school with a note asking my mother to please get me to brush my teeth—the policy of Quietly, and the unloosed aspect of neglect that was benign, allowed me to be uncivilized, sensuous, a barbarian. This is not the kind of thing that prepares you well for your college interviews, but it created a privacy in which my sexuality was allowed to take its own course. After I learned how to masturbate, I wasn't to be interrupted at it, disturbed in the midst, often questioned, admonished . . . my sexuality went on burgeoning without direct notice. The neglect that left me in terror, that left me holding the bag of family responsibility, left me in peace and quiet about sex. Along with writing, sex became another healthy, undisturbed part of my life.

When I worked with middle schoolers in English classes, we all enjoyed writing poems about tumbling down birth canals and the voyage from the womb to the outside. The children astonished me with their memories and images of being born: blood, and egg yolks, and pulsations galore, the imagery freshly present for them in a way it was only embedded for me. Being born is a highly contemporary subject for children's poetry. No one would have asked us to write about being born in 1955. One of my oldest friends, Katie Kinsky, a painter, swears she thought women had babies from their armpits because the deodorant commercials of the fifties showed a mysterious statue of the Venus de Milo, camera aimed at the pit of her cut-off arm and the voiceover murmuring about "that place." The language was so veiled she thought that armpits had to be the most secret part of the body.

Because my mother had a cesarean section for my sister, I thought all babies were born that way. It was only when Polly overheard me majestically explaining to Gail how babies were delivered that she corrected me. I was probably eight or nine. I simply couldn't imagine a baby coming out of my vagina, and I was horrified. It would hurt! "Oh, you expand," my mother said. Expand???

I was an angry little girl who almost never directly expressed that anger. My experience of anger was one of blowing up—not exploding, but my whole body blowing up until I was the size of an imaginary sumo wrestler. I could not name this feeling. Only as an adult did I recognize it as anger. At the time when Polly said, "Oh, you expand," I generally experienced my anger as confusion and distortion and being filled like a human balloon. This filling up felt painful and exhausting. It was a perverse pregnancy, a holding in of anger until it grew, and grew. Always having contained my anger, I never had a chance to see it being born, or expressed, and to feel a normal human cycle of being full and being empty.

Sex and babies. To have a baby "out of wedlock" was so terrible there was no worse crime. Manslaughter charges got dropped, prison sentences ended, but having a baby out of wedlock ruined your life forever. I had trouble connecting pregnancy and sex until I was in junior high. I knew you had to have a father in order to have a baby. But somehow I thought "married" conferred "future father" status on a man. However, I learned that there was a terrible danger of being "in trouble," of getting pregnant out of wedlock. I never connected my delight in myself to the sex that led to "in trouble" because I avoided knowing how children came to be and because I never asked questions. (My parents did not like to have to answer them. A child's questions shed an unwittingly bright light on their unhappiness. I grew to be a hyper-involved listener, gleaning the answers to my questions from fragments of phrases and innuendos. But sex was not a fully discussed subject, and I couldn't pick up enough information. Because, as a teenager, I was leery about bringing friends home, I didn't have the intimate conversations with them that might have led to other information.)

One day Gram drove me to see Beryl. I was eight or nine, and she was on a mission of no mercy to Beryl. I was the excuse not to stay long, just enough time to eye the mess Beryl was in and report back to other interested parties. She had had a baby out of wedlock and lived on welfare. To be on welfare was almost as bad as to be in trouble. Beryl was ironing. There probably are people alive now or in the past who don't mind ironing, or who even love it, but I have never met one. (Ironing may be distinguished from many men and women's love of washing and drying laundry, which the lovers of laundry see as a redemptive act. I know no lovers of fresh sheets

flapping on the line or shirts resurrected from their final spin who also have this deep affection for ironing.) Beryl was particularly affecting because she had a withered arm which hung at her side when she ironed.

The baby slept rather politely in a wicker laundry basket I myself wouldn't have minded curling up in. I was tired from being dragged from store to store by my tireless, domineering fireball of a grandmother. Beryl lived in welfare housing. This meant that she lived in a kind of barracks where nothing was planted to obscure the cement foundation, the grass was cut down to a yellow stubble, and the screening in the screen door sagged in convexity. This was what happened when you got in trouble. What was worse was that people like my grandmother would come and throw old baby clothes on your ripped davenport and humiliate you with a lot of judgmental questions. My grandmother *was* someone I could ask questions of and I did a substantial amount of quizzing on the fascinating, horrifying Beryl who was so skinny that her apron—obviously meant for someone who in those days would have been called more "ample"—wrapped around her one and a half times. Her eyes were red, and her hair was thin and frizzy from a home permanent that had gone wrong. "It'll grow out," my grandmother said drily. I would not be Beryl, I decided, although the image of Beryl came to me many times as I stood at the ironing board in our half-finished suburban basement, surrounded by baskets of Ted's, Polly's, Gail's and my rumpled clothes, never taken from the dryer on time. The sheer servitude of that General Electric steam iron that linked me to every housewife, housekeeper, and laundress became so fraught for me that I still can't iron more than three pieces of clothing without feeling pinned by the wings.

"I'm going to marry a collie," I announced to Gram on the way home. Some girls choose horses, some cats, some ballet shoes, and some dogs as emblems of their growing selves. Having chosen dogs for their ability to read emotions, to protect, to adore—all the qualities, alas, that Polly and Ted may have had but could not give to me—and having an encyclopedic bent, I took all the dog books out of the library and tried to memorize all the breeds. (Later, with my country grandmother Ruth in charge, I traipsed the landscape identifying flowers in the same impulse to anchor down the world.) Polly introduced me to *Lad, A Dog.* I was a goner. From sidewalk booksales to the tiny libraries at the backs of English classrooms I fetched all the Albert Payson Terhune dog novels and ate them, then ate them again. God bless him for having written so many, especially what I remember as the incomparable *Unseen,* which gives us both romance *and* dogs.

As I watched the "Lassie" family on TV, despising that horrible sap of a boy Lassie rescued week after week but loving the farmlife and the gentle goddesslike understanding of June Lockhart, the boy's mother, I reached the point of tears. (Oh, little girl who wouldn't let herself cry over the loss of what she wondered whether she deserved anyway. . . .) I did not cry at the program, knowing I would fail my mother's standard of appropriate toughness, though I would have liked to have cried, and if Gail had punched me then or if I had been injured in fake play, I would have used the opportunity to cry. The program, as the novels did, gave me a way to envision a safe life. Many people rail at the perfected, unhumanly bland vision of the fifties' television family, but it was a comfort to me. I knew it was not real. Real was home. But the kindness the "Lassie" parents showed for their son and the dog, as well as the gravely fierce kindness the dog showed toward the boy, showed *me* kindness by displaying behavior I didn't often get to see.

Animals for girls, and certainly for women poets from Emily Dickinson to Elizabeth Bishop, become a form of natural identity, identity in its unhampered state, greedy, unsocialized, an essential nature accepted simply, not transformed into the posture of continuous giving-unto-others that girls and women often must assume. I wished I could be a dog. I wished I could have a dog to recognize the essential me with its knowing eyes, just as Blake looks into the Tyger's eyes. The combination of the kindness of the family and the protection, adoration, and recognition of the dog caused such a longing for another life to well up in me that I nearly cried. I was seven years old. Would I get what I wanted? Now I had a new answer to those awful, awful questions adults always asked me, "Who are you going to marry when you grow up? And how many children will you have?"

"Lassie," I would say, "I'm going to marry Lassie." (But how would I ever meet such a

On the telephone with Michael Groden, 1964

celebrity as Lassie? Did such animals come to Buffalo? Also, Lassie would be dead by the time I needed to get married. I had heard there were *replacement* Lassies, a ghastly fact I could barely assimilate. . . .) Becoming more realistic, I would simply reply, "A collie, I am going to marry a collie." There on the windswept moor I would stand with my husband, a big, big collie with its foreleg casually, protectively, but not remotely possessively, around my shoulder. "So what kind of children are you going to have with a *dog*?" the adults asked, then answered their own question with, "*Puppies!*"

"Maybe we'll have puppies," I'd announce, then say more primly, "or we won't have anything. You can't have children with a dog." In this wish for my doghusband was a wish for cherished protection as well as a fair certainty that no progeny would come from the union. But I never got as far as imagining doing it with a dog. What was doing it, anyway? Oh, if only my parents could be dogs. Oh, to be a feral child, brought up by wolves!

"Maybe we should get a dog," I recently said to my husband who has two cats who have come to include me in their sphere of interest. "What kind of dog?" Mike says. "Oh, I don't know," I say cagily. "Do you have a favorite kind?" "A small one," Mike says. Not a collie. Oh, well, I'm years and years beyond collies. Forty years. "What kind of a small one?" "A miniature collie. I like those dogs."

Graduation day, June 1965: Molly (in cap and gown), with sister, Gail, and Mike

I did not marry this man by accident. I married him by design, although the design took thirty years and two countries, and became so vast and intricate it shaped our lives in ways only experience and greater forces could be responsible for. I am only responsible for the first move, a move I made in high school, long after I abandoned the fantasy of a collie for a husband, but not very long at all after I surrendered a fantasy about my father that I knew was entirely untrue but wanted so hard to believe I spoke it as true.

The little girl who said the cigarette burns on her legs were infected mosquito bites, the one who came to the door while my father was tearing off the hardwood maple table legs, grew up to become a creep in high school who had not been rushed to a sorority. I too had not been rushed, but I resolved to escape creephood, and did this by being yearbook editor, the keeper of the records of what everybody was, and by organizing activities, and by, as

Polly put it as she sipped her instant Maxwell House and ate a peanut donut, "not being a sheep." Really, I would have adored being a sheep if I could have just got on sheep's clothing, but I could not, and so with the Creepette I walked home. I had nothing but contempt for her, who looked up to me and believed every word I said, just like a little sister except she was my own age. But by the time I reached my sophomore year, I didn't have a single real friend. All the phone calls and checking in to see if we had gotten our periods yet that charged my group of girlfriends in junior high were gone. The years of friends squealing on the couches of our living rooms were long, long over. I was not in a sorority as my former friends were, and I had no group but those artificial clubs institutionalized by the school. I could not invite anyone home, even the Creepette. By my junior year I especially could not ask her, to whom I had lied, lied horribly and unconsciously.

"I hate my father," Creepette said as we trudged through the ice of an unshoveled sidewalk, thrown shoulder to shoulder. "He drinks too much beer. He's mean to my mother. He's not like *your* father. I know how much you like your father. I know how nice he is to you, Molly. You probably don't even understand how I could hate my father so much."

Absolutely stunned, I stammered, "Well . . . my father isn't *that* nice."

"I know he like brings you presents and stuff, like when he comes back from business trips and everything."

BUSINESS TRIPS! Oh God, how much had I lied? My lies were being presented to me as truth! When had I uttered them? When had I articulated my fantasy?

My mother dies. My sister is sent away. My father stops drinking, becomes an executive, and buys a penthouse apartment where I keep house for him, waiting in glorious solitude above downtown Buffalo, the traffic spinning below me, reading on our charcoal gray sectional couch surrounded by our shell pink walls for him to come home.

How much had I actually told her? Carefully, I question her. I refer to my mother and the store. She nods. OK, I didn't tell my mother was dead. I mention my sister. She talks about her sister. OK, sister here, not sent away. I say I'm going home. To Pilgrim Road.

"Where the hell do you live but on Pilgrim Road?" the Creepette snorts. She is tired of this ridiculous conversation. She only thinks my father is kind and doesn't drink. Well, that was the main part of the fantasy anyway. Like urine spreading through the seat of my pants, the realization, fast, warm, embarrassing and untellable, spread through my consciousness: I had fantasized, and I had *told*. I couldn't distinguish reality from fantasy. I was crazy. I had lied. My father drank. He was mean to my mother. He was just like her father. I was just like her. I was a creep, too. And I was crazy. At least the Creepette told the truth. I was lying. There was no shell pink room.

Except the one inside me. Was I crazy? Was I? Was I? OK, I hadn't lied all that much. Only to one person. *God, don't see her anymore, avoid her. At all costs don't walk home from school with her again.* She will show you to yourself in a way you will not be able to stand. *Stay longer after school,* I told myself, *work on the yearbook, hide in the stairwell, do anything.* I never walked home with her again. Now I had no friends at all, not even a creep to be contemptuous of.

The room inside me was empty. There was just that faint glow of pink in the air around the trees that in the north means eventually, after two more months of mud and cold and disbelief it will ever come, there will be spring. Oh no. I was a junior in high school, pretty old for fantasies about kind, rich fathers. And smart, too. My poor alcohol brain damaged father had become smart in my fantasy, smarter than I was. I felt really stupid now. *Don't be stupid!* With spring came a deadline. (My self-imposed deadline.) I was going to be asked to the Junior Prom. I was going to get dressed up in something those sorority girls never thought of and I was going to go. And not alone, either. I was going to get someone to ask me. This was reality. I was going to face reality. No more fantasies, Molly. Forget the penthouse. Get going. It is February 19. The Junior Prom is in June. You have three months to get a boyfriend and keep him until the Junior Prom. So go get one. Now.

Sex, attainable. Michael Groden was the smartest boy in my class. He had the kind of mind that snaps back like a brand new window shade. He had gotten perfect scores on both his math and his verbal PSATs. Not only was he the smartest boy in my class, he was smarter than many classes of kids—no one in the history of the school had gotten perfect scores. He had done the impossible. Michael

Groden was a kind boy who had friends among smart, not too nerdy boys. And he was Jewish. Polly had conveyed to me the stereotype that Jewish men were nice and always took out the garbage for their wives, bought them diamond rings, and *did not drink*. I wasn't going to go after a fraternity boy. That was a lost cause. But not just anybody was taking me to the Prom. I didn't think I was very pretty, certainly not pretty and waiflike as my sister was, off in the wilds of junior high. I was going to go after Mike Groden. I was going to go after him and I was going to get him. I was going to focus on him as I focused on my fantasy, but he was real. And I was going to get him, because he was achingly lonely. His loneliness was palpable, a force field around him. His hands jerked and shook when he answered questions in his nervously fierce intelligently shaking voice. I was going to set my hair, and put on makeup, and reach out to him. And he was going to fall.

Sex. Oh, how glad I am you are fallen. We have fallen in the backseat, we have fallen on the high school lawn. We have fallen on the plastic seats of the couch in your basement. We have fallen on my living room floor. I have reached you. And I have brought you home. Polly is always at work now. Gail is always out. Ted stays later and later at the bars. It is . . . a little bit safe . . . I am calculating. I am loved, so together we calculate . . . what we will do if my parents appear. I do not tell him all the really terrible stuff. What am I, crazy? I cannot even tell myself that terrible stuff. But in all the calculating I have not counted on falling myself. I have, but I do not admit it often. How can I let go? Not to be vigilant, not to be aware, aware, aware . . . how can I? I might get killed.

But, Mike Groden, your shirts smell so good. When we dance my nose fits under your shoulderbone and I drink in the smell of Tide soap and skin underneath. Skin. I have one. He has one. We have borders to our bodies. Oh honey, I wear a black dress to the Prom and carry a rose instead of a corsage and you cooperate. We are smart. I am not wearing pink carnations and a pink pouffy dress. I am an artiste. (An artiste of *what* it doesn't occur to me to determine. An intellectuelle.) Mike Groden works after school. He is steady. He has bought a car. A car is my equivalent of Polly's diamond ring. He delivers me to my stream of dentist appointments. This is my equivalent of taking out the garbage. He has condoms in his wallet, but don't worry, we don't take them out for another two years. We are slow. We do everything in our own rhythm.

Yes, yes, we're going to mess this up, of course, because neither of us has any model for keeping it going, and besides, we go off to college and have many neurotic adventures and mess up our lives and have our successes and thirty years later we get married, and it is a love story: happiness like this at our ages is a palpable, recognizable fact, not the wafting of a feeling. And throughout our three decades of odysseys we have much in common, so much so that when we get back together we quickly pick up the old, first threads.

Gail off with the cheerleading squad. Ted at his bar. Polly at the store. Late spring. Mike Groden at the screen door on which I have posted a note: *Come in. Lock the screen door behind you. Then go to the kitchen table and find another note.* I hear him come in from where I am ensconced: in a bubble bath with nearly three times the recommended dose of bubble juice to achieve the right effect—covered in stiff whipped foam as in a *Playboy* photograph. Mike Groden in the kitchen reading the next note to proceed to my room and take off all his clothes.

"Molly, are you here?"

"Yes, yes," I whisper, "I'm here in the bathroom, but don't come in here!" (He wouldn't have *dreamed* of coming in.)

"Where's your parents? Are we alone?"

"Yes, we're alone. They won't be home for hours. Do what the notes say!"

When you've removed all your clothes but your underpants, come to the bathroom.

And so he does. And so his eyes pop out of his sockets because there I am. We've done everything but. It is the spring of our senior year. We won't actually make love until the fall when Mike is away at Dartmouth and I take a fifteen-hour bus ride from my state university to Hanover, New Hampshire, but this spring evening in the bath is what we remember together with delight as we think of our earliest sexuality with one another, and marvel that our instincts were so right that our first choice turned out to be our best, lasting choice.

"What if your parents come home?"

"Well, I don't think they will, but we'll have to listen for them and then run to my room."

Molly Peacock and Michael Groden during their marriage ceremony, August 19, 1992, Port Angeles, Washington

"I'd better go get our clothes to have them ready just in case, Molly."

I knew he was right. What on earth had I been thinking of to trust fate so? I had been thinking of my body. I had been looking in the full-length mirror on my closet door at my almost eighteen-year-old body trying on my swimsuit for the coming summer and thinking of D. H. Lawrence and Henry Miller, whom I could never get through except to find the dirty parts, and Kenneth Rexroth's *100 Poems from the Chinese* with the first woman's sexual voice I had ever heard, the Empress Li Ching Chao who lay in her orchid boat, and then thinking of my own body: *How ripe it is,* I thought, *how ripe I am.* Ripe for what I wasn't exactly sure.

"Let's just wash each other first. All over. Then we'll get out together."

"OK," he said as I gave him the washcloth and the soap.

He was real. He was as real as my father, and as different from my father as he could be. He could have been the father to my children, as I could have been the mother to his. Our first choice was our best choice, we know that now that we are forty-seven and in our elaborately designed commuter marriage between my apartment in New York City, which we have made ours, and Mike's house in London, Ontario, Canada, which we have made ours.

When he touched my shoulders with the soapy cloth and proceeded down my breastbone and around each breast, I remembered Marie, the mother of the boys next door. Twelve or thirteen years before, Marie gave me a bath one night. How extraordinarily lightly she swiped the cloth over my arms and legs. "My boys are always covered in scrapes and bruises and scabs from the rough way they play," she said, "so I wash them very lightly, so they don't hurt and so all their bruises can heal." I was astonished. "Do they get *clean*?" I asked her. "They get clean enough." I thought you got clean only if you really scrubbed, and held Marie suspect from the point of view of Polly's cleanly values, but loved the sensuous treat of such elaborate care, and loved the safety of the big towel she wrapped around me before she led me off to pajamas, bed, and thoroughly undisturbed sleep. And here Mike was, so lightly easing the cloth down my belly and around what Lawrence called my cunt and what Gram called my cupcake and what the Empress Li Ching Chao called my orchid boat . . . and here I was, trying to slide my soapy cloth around his back and down his spine toward his buttocks and to reach underneath to his balls and then to what Lawrence called his cock, and trying to do it gently, like Marie.

What special instinct for self-preservation, what luck, led us to one another then was not only lifesaving, but enhancing. We allowed one another to grow. Our sexual companionship and literary friendship, probably the two most important, self-defining aspects of our lives then, are probably the most important now. We seemed then, and now, to free one another and to support one another simply as curious and sympathetic witnesses to the other's behavior, and ways of thinking, and needs. After we reached our freshman year in colleges many miles away from one another our fabric of support began to fray. It was not only distance, it was a creeping contempt I always felt for him that eroded my other feelings. My fear

of my father, my repulsion of him, my lonely unexpressed desire for his affection, my sadness that I did not have his love all manifested themselves in my contempt not only for him, but for Mike, especially when he did something nice for me. I simply couldn't believe a man was doing something nice for me. I thought there had to be something wrong with him; certainly there was something wrong with me. I was so deeply ashamed of my family, and so deeply ashamed of myself. Finally we broke up, and between the ages of nineteen and thirty-eight we completely lost touch with one another.

"Mike Groden!" I said to the nervously thin young woman who had joined the happy, lazy dinner trio of my former seventeenth-century literature professor, his novelist buddy, and myself, their guest of honor. My second book had come out, and I'd been invited to give a reading at State University of New York at Binghamton, where I had gone to college. The three of us had eaten nearly everything on the small menu, and here we were joined by our very late fourth for dinner, a perfectly decent woman I hated on sight because she was very very thin—we had been gobbling our chocolate cakes—and because she ordered only one thing to eat: a bowl of con-sommé. "I believe I know someone you used to know," she said, looking up from the brown watercolor in the bowl, "Mike Groden."

"Mike Groden! I remember the smell of his shirts! When we used to slow dance, my nose would rest right under his shoulderbone, and when I think of him I can't help but think of the smell of Tide, or All, or Wisk, or whatever it was then. . . ." I trailed off, having seen the discomfort on her face, and realized I had stepped in it; she must have been his girlfriend, his lover.

"He's been ill, you know," she said. "He's been very sick. He's a cancer survivor."

A cancer survivor? So, he had survived something terrible and was alive, even as I had survived something terrible to be alive. He had written a respected book, she said, and he had been the editor of the colossal many-volumed facsimile of James Joyce manuscripts. He did not have children; he had ambition, the ambition of the survivor of something terrible. This I recognized very well. I don't know what I said to her. I remember I pressed my address on her and asked if she would give it to him, but she said she was on her way to Paris and would be unlikely to see him for a long time. What could that mean? I thought. Only that she would prevent my message to him. But meanwhile she told me the name of the university where he taught, and I knew I could reach him there, if I wanted.

Unknown to me, that weekend Mike Groden would read a review of my second book, *Raw Heaven,* in the *New York Times Book Review.* He would find my address from my publisher and write to me. We would begin a long, slow, luxuriously platonic adult friendship that would last for another eight years. And one day we would finally talk about that bath.

BIBLIOGRAPHY

Poetry:

And Live Apart, University of Missouri Press, 1980.

Raw Heaven, Vintage/Random House, 1984.

Take Heart, Vintage/Random House, 1989.

Original Love, W. W. Norton, 1995.

A Complete Woman, forthcoming.

Contributor to periodicals, including *Mississippi Review, Nation, New Letters, New Yorker, New Republic, Ohio Review, Paris Review, Shenandoah,* and *Southern Review.*

Sterling Plumpp

1940-

It is never a pleasant task for one to resurrect demons he thought buried and done with. Usually I chamber a round in my revolver whenever someone requests anything about my life. I want to be helpful and reliable and I want to survive. My life, my existence, and my consciousness have truces agreed upon that forbid one from probing in order to satisfy some questionnaire's requests. I must admit that I am far more religious than I ever thought. I accept and invent and reinvent the myths which explain what I learned as the existence of God and his motley relations with humans and the attendant laws to ensure those relations. Since the religion of my grandparents was forced upon me—not really—but since it was the only avenue leading to salvation, I rejected it at the age of sixteen and accepted the paths to everlasting glory mapped out by the Pope and his various disciples. Once I found out that it was, indeed, the Catholic Church that sanctioned slavery—branding its imprimatur on the Asiento—I swore to do everything possible to render the Church impotent by proving that its God was simply manufactured, packaged, and sold. I did this by reading philosophers, social scientists, and writers in order to determine how they viewed God. I came to realize after a while that I have never had any complaint about God or religion; what I objected to and object to is the manner in which the church and its interpreters of God and his relations with humans define things. In these ecclesiastical proclamations, humans are not capable of sensing and understanding God and his laws and his plan for humans as individuals. No. It is only a select few who must erect churches and pronounce laws to govern humans who can perceive such vast mysteries.

When I say that I am religious, I mean I sense and seek connection with the completeness of existence. I long to know what is the size and shape of the universe. I long to know who are its inhabitants. I long to know who is its author. I do not seek the control over any-

Sterling Plumpp

thing except my right to explore the dimensions of existence. Therefore, death and birth are puzzles I constantly struggle to solve. I suppose it is my mortality that I am always trying to measure as I write poems. Perhaps I long to be a cartographer of the limited marriage between flesh and spirit. I am always looking for doors through which I can venture and learn. Paradoxically, I view mortality not as an end but an opportunity to invent, create, pattern—give birth within its limits. It is the margin between birth and death, which journeys throughout the entirety of existence, that must be affected and told, recorded, retrieved—invented as one's own. Therefore, the deaths which affected me greatly also fueled my desire to create. Beginning with my grandfather on January 8, 1955, and spanning my father, 1965, my mother, 1980, my uncle, 1982, my first cousin, 1989, my aunt, 1990, and concluding with my grandmother on November 16, 1993, death has forced me to write. Literally out of its ruins I construct my tales of who I am. My divorce in 1984 was also a kind of death because something within my being departed forever. My daughter's birth in 1976, her childhood, and adolescence in the 1990s serve as a counterpoint to death. Her development is a concrete work of art constantly shifting in size, shape, and composition. The dissolution of a marriage—the rupture of a shared gestalt, the termination of intimate moments and shared dreams—is a death. Two personalities merged in growth vanish. After the breakup of my marriage I had to shack up with chaos and ambivalence again. In a way, this end to one phase of my existence forced me to search for more meaning in my art. Thus I wrote more often and more experimentally.

For I am a creature who permanently resides in two worlds simultaneously. I give those who must issue, examine, cancel visas and passports a fit. I came into this world looking back. For I came to know myself, my feelings, my hopes, my fears, and my dreams within the boundaries of the utterances of my maternal grandfather and my maternal grandmother. They had been born sixty and fifty years respectively before I made my entrance on January 30, 1940, onto the crude landscape of a cotton plantation not far from Clinton, Mississippi. My grandparents had seven children born between 1914 and 1929; moreover, the grandchildren had begun coming in 1931. Of the seven children of my grandparents, three had no children or had no children to survive birth.

The boundaries of my grandparents' world had been defined by cotton fields and debts. In order to rise to see another day, my grandparents petitioned their God each night in chant-like calls to grant them space, beseeching Him to extend their time, to protect their dwelling from storms, to watch over their children, to look after their grandchildren, and to take them home if that be His wish. I learned very early that one could use words to petition for a different reality.

My grandparents lived in a place where death walked paths, taking Mr. Ike Biggs along one year, Grandpa Floyd another, Hat another, Little Black Angie another, and Miss Mahoney another. Folks older than they were crossing the River Jordan and folks their ages and younger were crossing the River Jordan. Since the arrangement at my birth was that I would live with my grandparents, I never had any hope or desire to live with either my mother or my father. And I knew that if the permanency of my grandparents crumbled that I would have to find another bonding place. I dreaded to think what I would do. I was ambivalent since I wanted to leave the cotton fields, the mud, the broken glass, the hot sun, the outhouse, the boll weevil, the cycles of droughts and storms; and yet I did not want my grandparents to depart. I did not want to have to walk into the unknown abyss of living with my mother and my stepfather or other relatives.

I wondered if my grandparents too would be the stuff of small talk about Mister Cincinnati's funeral at Mood Hood where "his chilluns put him away nice" or about Miss Mahoney who "looked just like she sleepin' and she musta gone straight to Heaven 'cause God let us know with the big storm come same day after her funeral." Within the world of my household I wondered if the death of a grandparent would destroy it. I further wondered if the outside world would catch me in a trap it done set. For I had heard repeatedly the ways and means black men and black women were ensnared by various powers, be they home brew, moonshine, somebody else's husband or wife, poisoned watermelon, or consumption or evil white folks. Somebody wanted to catch me and done already set his trap and I had no choice but to walk around in a place filled with dangers.

I found the realities of the worlds I was born into shifting when I was able to bring the strands of my existence into consciousness. The sunset of the world of slavery had not yet quite gone down and the world of freedom definitely had not shone on the horizons. I was privileged to be trapped between epochs and thus had to prepare to live in the past or get ready for the future. I inherited ambivalence and chaos; they are my birthright. Yes. I soon came to dread the possibility of my being entombed forever in the reality of slavery my grandparents had known. The world with an abbreviated circumstance in which to exist. I have always longed for space for my body and space for my spirit. Therefore, my earliest

Seventeen-year-old Plumpp (right) with a classmate, 1957

my life were a television game show its theme song or motto would be: Change for the sake of changing. The world of the sharecropper and its immediate antecedent, slavery, was dying when I was born in 1940. Like my grandparents, it, too, had little genetic reasons to expect longevity beyond my childhood. Then again, World War II itself was changing the world, reordering the foundations of power and control, and the voice of the factories in the North was calling millions to the "promised land," Chicago. Therefore, I grew into an individual never quite sure how the face of the world I inhabited would appear tomorrow. In this position of insecurity, I believe that I developed the art of telling my past in such a way that the creation or invention of my telling made it as real as any past that had been written, or any alternative. Sometimes as a child I would dream a marriage between my parents because I did not want to be a bastard nor did I want to be left alone in the world after my aged grandparents died.

I went to school for the first time at the age of eight at Sumner Hill Grammar School. I was later able to surmise that my grandparents sent me, my cousin Henry (my age), and my brother Wardell (then eleven) to school when they were sure we could fend for ourselves. I vividly remember the lunch boxes packed with liver sandwiches, cracklings, cake, or maybe a boiled egg. The indecisive soles of inexpensive shoes would willingly admit water through their soles and, in time, disappear to leave feet touching the cold earth. At school, gum, tossing spitballs, talking, or general misbehaving would bring the switch of Mrs. Latham to palms or on legs or backs. Those recalcitrant enough to fight would be taken to the principal's office for often intense encounters, with the administration of the strap that always seemed to leave blisters. I reluctantly admit that I was not only slow but—I can truly say—barely moved intellectually at all. In fact, I do not remember anything about my academic career at Sumner Hill except *A Christmas Carol*, which was taught by Mrs. Patton. Literature became a different world I could enter. I was then fourteen and in the seventh grade.

attempts to write anything were my struggles to understand exactly what was my plight as someone inheriting ambivalence and chaos. Naturally, I tried to deny my plight initially. I told myself that my reality could be what I would make of it. I could become saved and God through his son, Jesus, could dissolve the harshness of my reality. But he did not. I had to survive as someone bound to slavery and living in a time and place where my skin color relegated me to a kind of existence where if I forgot the commandments imposed on me an impromptu, "Nigger, what you doing here," or a slap side the head, or ninety days on the county farm, or a joyous "nicktie party" would surely remind me of the dangers of forgetting. I became a writer the moment I decided that I had to face the dragons of my existence and that I would fight them by becoming articulate enough to define my world and its limitations and my dreams and their infinite possibilities.

However, there are specific events, signposts, blood markers—memorable details, as it were—that delimit my world and my world alone. If

Yet I must retreat and observe that around the age of eleven I began attending Bible classes under the vigilance of Mrs. Arlene Russell, a neighbor who owned her own land. That

High school graduation, 1960

earthshaking summer in 1951 I also attended a Bible camp and made the long voyage from pews in the back of the church to moaners' bench where Sister Josie Pearl Williams told me "the Lord would make a way somehow" in her lilting voice, rising, falling, running, and dashing through the silence and into our hearts. The Reverend Younger, a liberal white evangelist from Clinton, the closest town to where I lived, conducted the camp. After the camp, I began attending Sunday school at Holy Ghost Baptist Church where I was baptized in Lake Kickapoo one Saturday afternoon. The business of being saved brought fear and guilt into my mind. For I knew I had to walk a narrow path to Salvation, always obeying the Lord and other authority figures and parents in order to succeed.

I then began having my initial curiosities about the opposite sex. But I was living in a constrained world where I heard more about the outside than I was ever able to witness. The next thing I knew I was fourteen years old, my grandfather was dead, and I would be moving away from that world. I was led from my sleep to touch Victor Emmanuel, my maternal grandfather, as he lay asleep—warm, resting forever. Two weeks later we had dug a hole and laid him safely in the ground across Highway 80 from Pleasant Green Church and I moved to Jackson with Mattie Emmanuel, Henry, and Wardell.

There had been many trials. My grandmother could not raise four teenage boys and soon I was parceled out to my mother where there was television and a telephone. My sister, Katie Mae, lived with my mother too. Wardell tried to live there but soon conflicts with Charlie Shields, my stepfather, caused him to move into the Big House, the honky-tonk that my uncle Aaron and my aunt Carrie ran; it housed space for two people to live. Wardell waited tables, helped behind the bar—was a kind of jack-of-all-trades. There he embarked on his sexual escapades and soon took the first thing smoking and headed for Chicago and the factory. He was not yet twenty years old. Henry managed to locate trouble and did everything from stealing Uncle Aaron's car to being accused of stealing from an old white women. He, too, took the first thing heading for Chicago. He was only eighteen. Neither of them had found it compelling to attend school once we moved to Jackson when both Henry and I were fourteen and Wardell was fifteen. In fact, they had gradually ceased to find the doors of Sumner Hill much after the sixth grade.

Finally, my mother lost the house we were living in when my stepfather moved out. There then began this series of apartments for her, myself, and my sister until one day I came home and found all we owned sitting on the street. I was told that my sister, who was in the bed with the flu at the time, was also set outside. Aunt Carrie took us in and I remained with her until I graduated in 1960. I did a variety of jobs: paper boy, cleaned up the Big House, and worked as a porter at a department store in downtown Jackson where I learned—as did Richard Wright and every other black boy growing up in Mississippi—the dreaded ABCs of Jim Crow. I never really developed a social life in high school because I was too busy trying to escape the boundaries of my world. I won an all-tuition-paid scholarship to St. Benedict's College in Atchison, Kansas. I entered the walls of this faraway and monastic place in the fall of 1960 and left, never to return, after my sophomore year in the spring of 1962. It was here amid these monks and farmers from Nebraska, Kansas, Missouri, and Iowa that I walked through the portals of Western literature and my life was changed forever. Greek literature did more to turn me on to the written word than anything. There was something extremely appealing to me about the Greek's hedonic way of living and their relations with their gods intrigued me. In Greek drama I faced, for the very first time, demons I carried within my bosom. By the time I finished reading "Sonny's Blues," a short story by James Baldwin, during my sophomore year, I was ready for the streets, bookstores, and life of Chicago. I was going to become a writer.

The Chicago Main Post Office was a strange and illuminating place in the fall of 1962. It was a good job; it was a "white-collar" job if one worked in first class rather than parcel post. I was strange because I was ambitious and read books. I was crazy because I wanted to write books. I was lost because I did not go out to the various parties, get drunk, or talk about my sexual encounters. I worked ten-hour days and six-day weeks as a substitute in the California Parcel Section. I learned my scheme easily. Soon I enrolled at Roosevelt University studying history, although I eventually changed to psychology. But my life was reading and talking about writing. James Cunningham, a man with a degree from Butler University, became my first mentor and introduced me to Baldwin, Wright, Ellison, Hughes, Henry Miller, Sartre, Genet, LeRoi Jones, Camus, and Tolstoy. I devoured books but did not develop distinct opinions about them at the time. During the nightmarish interlude between 1964 and 1965 when I was in the United States Army, Cunningham kept me abreast of the literary, sending me *Shadow and Act, Dutch and the Slave,* and *Lay My Burden Down.* I supplemented my reading by buying almost everything Odetta recorded and had recorded. I also bought Charlie Parker, Miles Davis, Coltrane, Monk, and Lester Young. Mostly, I read a book each day and I tried to write poems; and I tried to write narrative which never managed to be anything but disguised autobiographical attempts.

I am simply saying I did not want the limitations I saw in my grandparents' world—its midget skyline, its compressed diameter—forced on me. I am also saying that my grandparents,

like seeds planted beneath concrete, burst from the constraints limiting their possibilities but that they paid a price I felt I could not pay. If I were going to have to pay a price for my dreams then I wanted to define the parameters of those dreams and not have the ones inherited from parents or grandparents hoisted on my back as burdens of necessity. For it is never easy for one to accept the responsibility of family, clan, or community. My lifelong task as a writer has been, precisely, to locate myself and my responsibilities and possibilities within the boundaries of my history, my ancestry, my race, and my personal visions of life. I believe it is a neverending struggle; for as soon as I reach some plateau of clarity the clouds of ambivalence and chaos return to blur my vision.

I am also saying that until I was able to see how clear my grandparents were in viewing their dreams within the truncated world they were born into, I could find neither voice or vision to describe my dreams and my world. I am confessing that I stood in the windows of my grandparents' visions of themselves and their worlds—as grunted through prayers and pauses between narratives about their lives and their worlds—and that I also descended into the depths of their voices as they quavered from rumblings of blues evocations and spiritual longings. And as I descended from these heights and rose from these depths, I came to see my task as a writer as one of naming myself and recreating myself in order to exist. I was—like my history as sung in folksongs, blues, folktales, spirituals, sermons, and jazz—dependent on how successfully, how well I expressed myself for my existence.

I found myself with pen in hand in a desperate state of mind where there were no bridges between my days, where each day was an island that moved about, and there were no ferries negotiating distances between them. Then I knew what Albert King meant when he said he was "drowning on dry land." I also knew, though painfully, that the gateway to salvation opened at baptism did not bring with it a key for which to unlock one's personal experiences. I tried writing poems in order to pattern, at least, the most salient features of my life: race, oppression, spirituality, the nature of the road to be undertaken, and the search for a language. I called my initial poetic excursion *Portable Soul* (published 1969), because at the time I wanted to convey that each individual possessed the ability to express his world and his dreams. In accepting the collective call to blackness, I was reminding myself that that voice which would reply had to be personal, had to be individual. I also felt it had to be poetic. I had been, prior to writing my first volume, reading just about every and anything I could corral. Mostly I read and reread James Baldwin, Richard Wright, and Ralph Ellison, and sometimes Langston Hughes. I grappled with my family, especially my mother whom I lived with for only about a year that I could remember. *Portable Soul* is my inventing ways to express my memory, my longings, my psychic analyses, and my dreams. It is my attempt to say: I am an artist who constructs with words.

A year before my first publication I married Falvia Del Grazia Jackson whom I had known since she and I were freshmen. The year of the publication of my first volume also found me leaving the United States Post Office and entering graduate school in psychology at Roosevelt University. Since Falvia was a degreed

registered nurse, she was the main financial bearer of the family. I worked part-time as a counselor for black students at North Park College and continued to write. By 1971 I had published my second volume of poems and was hard at work on my initial nonfictional work. I was addicted to writing and did not know it. That year I began my long career as a professor at the University of Illinois at Chicago. I began as a lecturer, was promoted to instructor, then to assistant, then to assistant professor with tenure, then to associate professor, and finally to professor. My relationship with academia has freed me from a nine-to-five type job and enabled me and enables me to write. I am rich in leisure and dedication. Students inspire me with their questions and their vigor for life.

I did not come to writing "non-aligned," for I had already made treaties with the words and visions of Greek playwrights, Keats, Blake, Yeats, Baldwin, Wright, DuBois, Ellison, Dunbar, Hughes, and Dostoyevsky. Black Consciousness

Members of OBAC: (from left) Sterling Plumpp, Adelisha, Johari Amini,
Yaki Jakubu, and Walter Bradford

Celebrating the release of the magazine Literati Internationale, *edited by Lincoln T. Beauchamp, 1992*

was being shaped somewhere between the mid-1960s and the mid-1970s. It was a world filled with possibilities and equally abundant with pitfalls. On the surface of the vast ocean of possibility one could remake one's self. For one could cast off the impositions of the Oppressor and investigate ways of recasting his or her images according to specifications laid down by one's submerged culture. However, as the needs for clarity became paramount for the articulators of this newfound freedom and solidified into ideology, it became clear to me that neither the examples of blackness, as expressed in black art, or the definitions of it represented the limitless spaces of the ocean I wanted to explore. I needed to explore in order to locate my personal vision and the tools to convey it.

Portable Soul is the summation of a decade of my intense efforts at reading and a decade of attempts at trying to write poems. I further delineate elements of my style: short cryptic lines, unusual word usages to affect metaphor, use of ellipsis, concrete imagery, and allusions to events in black experience. The short poem

"Sez My Mind," captures my intentions because I am "spee/ding/to war/n my/self" as an artist. I am both in great haste and at war. "Black Ethics" extols the belief that there is something needed to propel "black men" into strength and that something is "human love." "Travelling" is my version of a blues poem which is dense with many allusions. In "You Made Them Walk," I yearn to suggest that individuals with problems can rise to a full humanity, sometimes, if they receive the proper message; that message within the poem is the call of the Honorable Elijah Muhammad of the Nation of Islam. That was written in response to seeing Muslim men selling *Muhammad Speaks*, the Nation of Islam's superb newspaper. "Sugar Woman" represents my coming to terms with my mother who, for me, did not fit the mould of a mother cast by Catholicism. She had had two sons under her maiden name by the time she reached age twenty. She lacked many of the skills that would have made her a very effective mother. She had lovers in between marriages which I knew about. I learned, through great difficulty, to

171

Chicago's Maxwell Street, 1984

accept her for herself without any hint of apology. I learned that people do what they must do in order to survive.

I was happily married by the time *Half Black, Half Blacker*, my second poetic offering, made its way from obscurity of manuscript to print in 1970. I now had reached a point where I needed to express my dissatisfaction with labels. I wanted, at least, to try to quantify labels if they had to be used to categorize. Here I returned to the world of my grandparents. I returned to a southern landscape where the blues and spirituals had their births. I sought to personally articulate my experiences with a healthy borrowing from their sounds: blues, negro spirituals, gospels, and the rural dialect associated with tenant farmers. I further paid my debts to Black Consciousness with allusions to Malcolm X, DuBois, Nat Turner, Denmark Vesey, Gabriel Prosser, John Coltrane, and black heroes and black artists in general. *Half Black, Half Blacker* situated my voice, my aesthetic battleground in the South, in the world of my

grandparents where it rightfully belongs. I became conscious of the need to find and fashion a personal language to express my individual voice and vision.

In "Daybreak" I really believed and believe that "every black man" / is an epic / sung / in the soft keys / of survival. I suppose I also believed that it was not an insult to subsume "black women" under the category of "black man." I now realize that I suffered from gender bias. Both "Black Messages" and "The Living Truth" focus on my need to tell and retell my history as a device for achieving a healthy identity. I suggest that the possibility of greatness in black culture lies in the dreams of its inhabitants where the small boys engaged in a game of basketball on the concrete are "little alcindors (Kareem Abdul-Jabbar)." "Last Ride" is my commentary on this country's treatment of black GIs who returned home after defending their country in Vietnam. "I See the Blues" and "Half Black, Half Blacker," the title poem, are examples of my vision as an African-American poet. I view identity in broad complex terms whereby there is often seemingly miles of chaos to be negotiated. In the former poem I catalogue examples of personal blues situations within my life and my history, while the latter poem finds me using irony to state the poignant fact that ideological positions which demand a litmus test for one's loyalty have pitfalls.

After my second small volume of poems, I felt somehow incomplete. Therefore, I sought to combat the broken gestalt of my vision by using my southern upbringing to fill in the blank space. I turned, naturally, back to where I was born and reared in a shack on a cotton plantation, my grandparents' home, which I knew as my place. Still, after some eighteen years, it, Clinton, was for me the lodge of my spirit. I listened to music and read and then eventually I had to unlock the ever dangerous gates to my unconsciousness and live my childhood and youth all over again amid honeysuckle blossoms, snakes, storms, Papa leaning on his hoe or plowing, and Mamma singing "Do Lord, Do Lord" while frying corn or shelling peas or butterbeans. I had to witness the sagas they told and realize that their past had been my origin. By 1972, in *Black Rituals*, a nonfictional work, I had probed my southern roots in terms of culture, autobiography, and ancestry as the sources from which I could excavate my vision and my voice. This book, more so than anything I have written, placed me firmly back in the stunted cosmos of my grandparents where I had to face monsters I had been running away from since my birth. In order to see and in order to speak, I had to see through my grandparents' voicings of their experiences. I had to somehow shed the arbitrary labels of ignorance and resignation which cast their shadows over the lives of folks born with the "shadow of the plantation" who were living out their days within the orbit it permits. I had to venture behind the masks of bowed heads, "yassuhs," "nassuhs," downcast eyes, "yes ma'ams," "no ma'ams," and bended knees. It was a world as frightening and mysterious as death itself. I sought to explore it by hoboing on its rituals.

Both *Steps to Break the Circle* (1974) and *Clinton* (1976), pamphlet-length poetic explorations, illustrate the ways I had begun to map the landscapes of my imagination and territory I was born within. In the former I catalogued the problems of logistics of making the journey from the land to the city. I envisioned the migration from the land (the South) to

the city (Chicago) as an ambiguous trek where the traveller could very well exchange Paradise for Hell. He could very well move from a place where he was articulate into one which he had not yet the wherewithal to describe. The poem was an attempt on the part of the poet to mirror what he thought happened when his family ventured from Mississippi to Chicago between 1944 and 1962 when he arrived. The poem concerns itself with the network effect of the transformation of one from a rural inhabitant of a culture that had faced problems and solutions for his people for several generations to a new urban experience in which this culture is radically changed without its nourishing institutions. *Clinton* is a blow-by-blow account of the battering my sensibility underwent from birth through childhood and adolescence in Mississippi to manhood in Chicago and the United States Army. Here the importance of self-definition and the ability to discern ideologies which might colonize are privileged. I was beginning to develop a language from viewing the ever-changing perceptions I

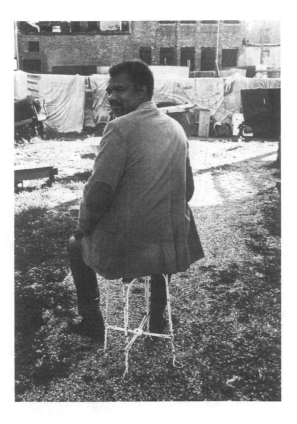

A backwards view

had of myself and the kaleidoscopic visions I had of my past.

My world was transformed almost beyond recognition in the intervening years between 1976 and 1982, when the publication of *Clinton,* the edited anthology of South African writings, *Somehow We Survive,* and the volume of poetry *The Mojo Hands Call/I Must Go* made their appearances. I had been fortunate to have a daughter born, had won tenure at the University of Illinois at Chicago, and was adjusting to the tantalizing experience of loss. My mother left this world on April 27, 1980, and my marriage to Falvia was crumbling by 1982. I had, really, a need to measure the dimensions of psychic disenchantment.

I was, like Humpty-Dumpty, split into a million pieces and had no way of putting myself back together again. "Fractured Dreams," "The Mojo Hands Call, I Must Go," and "I Hear the Shuffles of the Peoples' Feet" are poetic excursions or journeys where I sought to both reveal and heal Sterling Plumpp. I sought to invent a language with enough magic to convey my visions, memories, and realities—all of which were forever changing. My daughter, Harriet Nzinga, was the stabilizing principle in my life. I was determined to rear her so that she could find clarity in her life with choices just as I was seeking the same in my poems. I learned at this time that blackness was a discovery or a partial discovery for me and that I needed to pry through the laminated contours of my core self or the self I was making in order to breathe with assurance.

In "Fractured Dreams" I ventured into the territory of the psychic and confronted mythic bandits marauding within my mind, and I found that articulation alone could arrest them or send them off to Boot Hill after some OK Corral battle. I sought the illusive Africanity of my past and presence in "The Mojo Hands Call/I Must Go"; I personalized my history. It became a canvass onto which I invented myself through a re-creation of my past and an inventing of my present. I drew symbols from blues songs and hoodoo lexicons as I had learned them from my uncles who seemed to always have women who needed the spell of a Mojo Hand or goober dust sprinkled around the front door or an X marked up the chimney in order to keep wives or women. I sought to calibrate ways the infinite power in the songs of my ancestors could be summoned to return, as it were,

my scattered world to some degree of wholeness and harmony. "I Hear the Shuffles of the Peoples' Feet" retells the journey from slave castles to the auction blocks and the terrifying routes slaves took to their futures.

At this time I was radically shifting emphases in my writing and solidifying my poetic techniques. Exposure to the various fights or liberation in Nicaragua, Iran, Guinea-Bissau, Angola, Mozambique, Zimbabwe, Namibia, and South Africa had broadened my sense of commitment in literature and struggle. The activities of the masses of oppressed people and their perspectives became an important spring from which to draw my metaphors and references in poetry. *Somehow We Survive* represents a direct confrontation between my understanding of struggle and the concrete realities of various South African artists in exile, within the narrow confines of the apartheid state and within liberation movements. I began to understand the informing ideas of collectivity and communality better. I also understood the necessity for using the lens of class as a more useful way to view poetry than race. *The Mojo Hands Call/I Must Go* galvanized my various poetic themes, forms, devices, and languages from 1974 to 1982 into one volume so that they could be judged.

In the years between 1982 and 1989, the year in which *Blues: The Story Always Untold* appeared, I found new ways for utilizing blues as the aesthetic base from which to launch experimentations in poems that would define my personal voice. The concern for social commitment and relevancy remained a fixture in the poems, however, as evidenced by the attention given to blues song, blues lyric, blues mood, blues form, blues singers, and blues people in my poetry. For me, blues is ancestry and blues is history and *Blues: The Story Always Untold* is an opportunity for the poet to express his readings of blues. The book is tribute, self-definition, history, celebration, affirmation in the face of dangers, and voicings of my own "impulse to keep the painful details of a brutal experience alive." It is the vehicle where I launched new journeys into self and poetic language.

At the core of *Blues: The Story Always Untold* is my concern for and fascination with history, time, ancestry, and a sense of place. I trace varied and varying ways "blues people"

With friend Gerri Oliver at her Palm Tavern on Forty-seventh Street, Chicago, 1984

draw on blues as inspiration and invent and reinvent blues as language and as narrative. I try to say thanks to blues and blues creators. This is so because blues is a kind of Rosetta Stone I use to decode the complex and shifting versions of reality I long to tell. In "Under Class" and "Callings," I situate my identity deep within experiences of the collective voice of the slave and after him the tenant farmer. I immerse into these collective expressions or voicing of self and selves in order to be made anew, baptized as it were, in the waters of my grandparents' culture. It seems that whatever route my pen takes it always leads back to the plantation shack where I was born.

At last, I visited the place known as South Africa in November and December of 1991. For the first time I confronted the continent out of which my ancestors were ripped in a genocidal fashion somewhere between the mid-sixteenth century and the end of slavery in 1889. The unusual synthesis of this encounter with my experiences of growing up in Mississippi and experiencing the Civil Rights Movement

and the Black Power and Black Consciousness in this land resulted in *Johannesburg and Other Poems* in 1993. Here my achievement is that I link my experiences with the expressions of the South African masses fighting to erect a new day for themselves. I see similarities between the various maids I see in Johannesburg, Kimberly, and other townships; I identify with the role music plays there and here; I sense the seminal role "blues" plays in empowering the spirit in both circumstances. I also adopt the experiences of those struggling in Kenya, Grenada, and Los Angeles as my own.

The demarcation line dividing *Johannesburg and Other Poems* in "Metamorphosis" and "Homeland" is not indelibly imprinted on stone. The former refers to the American South where I was born in Clinton, Mississippi. It also suggests the ethics of that region which I had to imbibe in order to survive. There is an allusion to the United States itself, this land of slavery and misery, where my ancestors and I have known its chains, its denial of humanity, and its deaf ears to justice and human equal-

Reading poetry at a restaurant in Jackson, Mississippi, 1986

ity. Within the boundaries of "Metamorphosis" I write poems that probe crises of grandparent, parent, uncles, aunts, a sense of place. Both "Blues from the Bloodseed" and "Sanders Bottom" retell sagas of family members. The former poem is my reinvention of my aunt and uncle's sojourn to Chicago where their memory of Mississippi still lashes their minds. "Sanders Bottom" is my retelling of my grandmother's telling of her life. Her narrative and my telling represent the lifeline to my past. Her one hundred and three years on this planet between 1890 and 1993 connect me back to slavery and slave ships.

Obviously "Homeland" is my sobriquet for Africa, my homeland, but it is also a metaphor for Mississippi and America where I was nourished as an African. In "Kimberly," "Orange Free State," "Townships," "Weaver," "Thaba Nchu," and "Johannesburg," I draw the connections between what I am witnessing in that changing apartheid state where the African majority has just "one more mile to go" be-

fore majority sets in—however dangerous that mile. I had requested to go to the Orange Free State since I was told that it was South Africa's Mississippi in terms of history and social mores. I initially set foot in this state at a place with the ironic name of Welkom (welcome) in the African township Thabong. "Township" recounts my day in Phomolong, an African township within South Africa's Mississippi where I spent a day viewing a children's celebration. "Orange Free State" is an account of my journey from Welkom to Kimberly (Northern Cape) where I visited a diamond mine and spent time in a cemetery in the African township of Galashewe.

I saw female hotel attendants with rags around their heads which brought to my mind that my mother had been a maid prior to her death in 1980. These hotel attendants wore a demeanor of subservience and possessed eyes which told me that they very rarely saw guests of my complexion. The journey to Kimberly reminded me of my travels through the Mississippi Delta where miles and miles of fertile soil have thousands of shotgun houses standing vigil over the acres. However, in Mississippi in South Africa, the houses were square and labelled "matchbox."

"Thaba Nchu" was part of the scatter-site—homeland—of Bophuthatswana located within the Orange Free State far from Bloemfontein. The soil is very dark and rich agriculturally. It has located within its borders a posh motel complex to house the whites who visit to gamble and engage in illicit sex. Thaba Nchu means Black Mountain. "Weaver" is my reaction to Zim Ngqawana, a brilliant young South African jazz saxophonist/flutist/drummer/composer-arranger I saw at the famous jazz spot Kippies, located in Market Square in Johannesburg. I saw Zim after I had been to Soweto and Alexandra at night and had also walked the streets of Johannesburg and found myself marvelling at how similar this place was to the Harlem of Langston Hughes and James Weldon Johnson.

The most poignant sight was during my visit to a park in the wealthy section of Johannesburg known as Hillbrow. I was amazed at the flickering lights so my guide stopped and we entered the park. Moving towards the varying lights we found numerous women lying on blankets and conversing intermittently in their various tongues. I was told that they were maids who lived too far away to commute back to their townships, who did not make enough money to rent a place to live, and whose employers did not provide a residence for them either. The sight of them brought me back to my mother in the house where my grandparents reared me.

However, "Weaver" and "Johannesburg" are about jazz, about blues, about music. I sensed that the music I heard and had heard arising from the spirits of South African singers and musicians and flowing from the pens of South African writers was my music. It was Mississippi and it was American and it was South African. I simply point to several strands that obviously are related.

In the year since the publication of *Johannesburg and Other Poems* (1993), I have continued to explore blues, my personal experiences, and ancestry as themes. *Home/Bass* is a book-length poem, in which a blues singer (Mississippi Delta traditional blues singer Willie Kent) comments on his art, his life, women, and history. I am also at work on a long epic poem, "Mfua's Song" which is based on the oral history of the maternal side of my family. Specifically, it relies on a story told me by Aunt Alberta, a sister of my maternal grandfather, about Tympe, a distant ancestor who was born in 1772 and died in 1908. Tympe narrates my family's chronicle by telling what Mfua told her. The epic is divided into three sections: Book One (Tympe) is told mostly in the language of the Negro spirituals; Book Two (Mattie) mostly in the language of blues; and Book Three (Poet) mostly in the languages of gospel and jazz. Each book extends to about two hundred pages. I am also writing a volume of poems tentatively entitled, "Breathing/In Winters," which pertains to sensuality and the necessity for humans to know other selves in order to fulfill and be fulfilled. I continue—very much in the fashion of my grandmother who collected various articles of rags, tossed them into a basket, washed them, and stitched them together in patterns— to bring order to the chaotic and ambivalent landscape of my mind with an artistic imagination. For it is, after all, the imagination which defines limits and possibilities.

My latest works are *Hornman, Home/Bass, The Ballad of Harriet Tubman*, and *The Ballad of Martin Luther King. Hornman* is my tribute to and attempt to personify bebop, the jazz of Parker, Gillepsie, Gordon, Blakely, Monk, Miles, and Coltrane—through the re-creation or retelling of tenor saxophonist Von Freeman of Chicago, who says she has played predominantly on the South Side (the traditional black area) since 1947. In *Hornman* I try to link my blues roots to jazz, the creative musical expression of improvisation and stylized individuality. The aforementioned *Home/Bass* tributes the blues by allowing a blues-singer-narrator to probe history, the metamorphosis initiated by migration from Mississippi to Chicago, the horrors of contemporary urban life for young black males, and the meaning of a place known as home, which crumbles under the weight of external forces. In his constant search on the road of existence, this blues-singer-narrator exclaims the meaning of life, of sexual and sensual engagements, and of the will to live. Both *The Ballad of Harriet Tubman* and *The Ballad of Martin Luther King* are ballads that have been illustrated as poetry in children's books. These two children's books represent my desire to reach a mass audience and to educate.

BIBLIOGRAPHY

Portable Soul, Third World Press, 1969, revised edition, 1974.

Half Black, Half Blacker, Third World Press, 1970.

(Contributor) Patricia L. Brown, Don L. Lee, and Francis Ward, editors, *To Gwen with Love,* Johnson, 1971.

Black Rituals, Third World Press, 1972.

Muslim Men, Broadside Press, 1972.

Steps to Break the Circle, Third World Press, 1974.

Clinton (poems), Broadside Press, 1976.

(Editor) *Somehow We Survive: An Anthology of South African Writing,* illustrations by Dumile Feni, Thunder's Mouth Press, 1981.

(Contributor) Joyce Jones, Mary McTaggart, and Maria Mootry, editors, *The Otherwise Room,* The Poetry Factory Press, 1981.

The Mojo Hands Call/I Must Go (poems), Thunder's Mouth Press, 1982.

(Contributor) *From South Africa: New Writing, Photographs and Art,* edited by David Bunn, University of Chicago Press, 1988.

Blues: The Story Always Untold (poems), Another Chicago Press, 1989.

Paul Robeson (for children), illustrated by Adjoa J. Burrowes, Third World Press, 1992.

Johannesburg and Other Poems, Another Chicago Press, 1993.

Hornman, Third World Press, 1995.

The Ballad of Harriet Tubman (for children), illustrated by Gregg Spears, Third World Press, 1993.

The Ballad of Martin Luther King (for children), illustrated by Gregg Spears, Third World Press, 1995.

Home/Bass (poem), Another Chicago Press, 1995.

Also contributor to all four volumes of *Mississippi Writers: Reflections of Childhood and Youth,* edited by Dorothy Abbott. Contributor to *Black World, Another Chicago Magazine, Black American Literature Forum, Black Scholar, AFRO-DIASPORA,* and *Journal of Black Poetry.* Editor for Third World Press, 1970—, and Institute for Positive Education; managing editor, *Black Books Bulletin,* 1971–73; poetry editor, *Black American Literature Forum,* 1982—. Historical advisor on "Promised Land," a five-hour documentary on the black migration from Mississippi, 1940–1971; premiered on the Discovery channel, February 12, 1995.

Kalamu ya Salaam

1947-

ART FOR LIFE: MY STORY, MY SONG

this is my story
my song, i will sing these blues,
tho they stole my tongue

Iwas born Vallery Ferdinand III on 24 March 1947 in New Orleans, Louisiana. My early publishing is done under the name of Val Ferdinand. In 1970, I changed my name to Kalamu ya Salaam (Pen of Peace).

Because I do a great deal of writing as a journalist, music producer (radio programs, album liner notes, and artist bios), dramatist, cultural critic, propagandist for various issues, fiction writer, and advertising executive, I usually shy away from identifying myself with any one genre of writing. Poetry is, however, my most developed, and my most comfortable, voice.

I consider poetry the song of literature and consider myself a griot, an African American praise-singer through whom sounds the voice and vision of my people.

one: in the beginning

I think the best thing I can do at this time is to try to get myself in shape and know myself. If I can do that, then I'll just play, you see, and leave it at that. I believe that will do it, if I really can get to myself and be just as I feel I should be and play it.

—*John William Coltrane*

Today, I am a poet, but I did not choose poetry; poetry found me. I was in eighth grade; Mrs. O. E. Nelson baptized me. I had been in the water before, but till that day I had never gotten religion.

I was familiar with poetry through church, as well as through segregated public schools where Black, mostly female, teachers imparted culture in both subtle and overtly obvious ways.

Kalamu ya Salaam

I will never forget the opening lines of the poem "Invictus": "Out of the night that covers me / black as the Pit from pole to pole / I thank whatever gods may be / for my unconquerable soul."

"Invictus" is not a "Black" poem, but the poem has special meaning when done "Blackly," as it was under the tutelage of Mrs. Wilson, my sixth grade teacher at Phillis Wheatley Elementary School.

Although our rowdy class had once sent a student teacher fleeing out of the classroom literally in tears, Mrs. Wilson had the power to render us dumb, to leave us literally holding our breaths and not daring to say a mumbling word when she confronted us. One day after lunch as we settled into our seats, she wrote "pussy" in big, shockingly bold letters across the blackboard. She asked us, any of us, to define "pussy."

I don't know why she chose that word, but it was a powerful lesson which culminated with one of the young ladies in the class reading out loud the dictionary definitions about pussy willows and pet names for cats, etc.

We all knew that the meaning of the word according to *Webster* was not the issue. Mrs. Wilson cared enough about us to force us to deal with defining ourselves. Even though after school we laughed and exchanged, in whispered conspiracy, other definitions, still from that moment we became, probably for the first time in most of our young lives, conscious of the need to define what we meant when we used a word. We had been challenged to take responsibility for every word we said.

Far more than solely academics, Mrs. Wilson taught pride to a classroom of Black youngsters who ranged in hue from the light-skinned "Creoles" (as mulattos are generally referred to among Blacks in New Orleans) to dark-skinned folk.

I had classmates who would pass for White on the buses after school. We'd get on together, however the darker skinned of us would sit in the back, behind the "colored" signs. We sometimes threw those "colored screens" out the window, but those were the rare sometimes. In general we just trooped to the back of the bus and followed the convention of the day, which convention also meant our fairer skinned schoolmates sat up in front passing for White. Somehow we knew there were no hard feelings. Some people could run faster than others. Some people were smarter at spelling or English or whatever, and some people were light enough to pass for White.

At the time we did not see "passing" as a particular pathology, because this was still public school and everybody was from the same or similar economic strata. Later, that would change, but for now we were all laughing, awkward adolescents who were made to stand in the front of the classroom and recite, with feeling, the concluding lines of "Invictus": "I am the master of my fate / I am the captain of my soul."

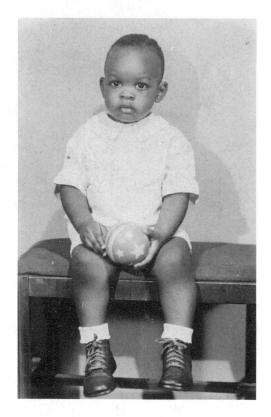

Vallery Ferdinand III, age fourteen and a half months

By eighth grade, while I had already been ushered into poetry as a social upliftment device, I did not yet have a conscious knowledge of "nommo" even though I had felt "the force of the orated word" as manifested by preachers in the church and by the brothers talking shit on the block, and also by the recitations which were an integral part of our education at that time.

We were taught Black poetry such as "If We Must Die" by Claude McKay, "God's Trombones" by James Weldon Johnson, and "When Malindy Sings" by Paul Laurence Dunbar. Additionally, there were school and church oratory contests and spring festivals.

I did not define all those oratorical touchstones, which I knew by heart, as poetry. They weren't poetry like the poetry we studied from books, the Shakespeare and stuff. Our textbooks concentrated on White worlds, and I associated poetry with that world.

The stuff I learned by heart and loved didn't come to me via a book. Most often those works came by word of mouth and by listening. Occasionally, a poem was run off on a sheet of paper and passed around for us to learn and recite.

Moreover, I never thought of reciting Shakespeare in the same way that we recited James Weldon Johnson. This is probably the beginnings of my belief that Black poetry must be heard to be fully appreciated. I know there are people who feel that way about Shakespeare, but Shakespeare's rhythms did not quicken my blood.

At the gut level—the blood pounding, getting excited, aroused, your heart literally racing, and you be grinning—for me there's no poetry like spoken Black poetry. When you experience a good Black poetry performance, the audience actually becomes a "congregation" joining in a quasi-religious cultural experience. I identified with that *collective* emotional experience, and I didn't know poetry attained that. I thought poetry was read alone, very intellectual, very far removed from emotive emotional involvement, and totally devoid of a collective experience. I thought I did not like poetry.

Mrs. Nelson changed that.

She dipped me deep beneath the waters by simply laying Langston Hughes on me. I received the word not from a book, not from my reading Hughes, but rather from hearing him, and hearing him with music, jazz no less, and blues.

"Put your books away. I want you to listen to something." I was not prepared for the Langston Hughes recording, because if this was poetry then poetry was me.

Until that moment I had a disdain for "poetry." Given the total psychological schema of segregated America, my dilemma was but a minor example of the schizophrenia that marks the Negro's being.

As I became conscious—or, as we often say, as I "woke up"—and tried to figure a lot of this out, I was confounded. In my ignorance I came up with some awfully dumb theories. I didn't know that all people had poetry, just had different ways of expressing it. Most of all I didn't know that, given who I was, there were ways of poetic expression that I preferred to others.

Although I had been taught and had absorbed certain lessons, I didn't "consciously" understand my people and my culture. Yes I was Black. I could feel my culture and be moved by my culture, but "feeling" is not "knowing." It is not enough to experience, we must also understand if we are to become subjects, and not just objects, of culture and history.

Not only was I ignorant of myself but, even worse, I did not know that there was such a thing for Black people as "knowing thyself." In school when I read Shakespeare saying "to thine own self be true," I thought it profound. What was truly profound is that I didn't know that "know thyself" was a maxim found on the temples of ancient Egypt and in the folktales of West Africa, indeed, found around the world.

For me and most Black people, the very process of traditional mainstream education is alienating and engenders a psychological sense of both individual and racial inadequacy. That's why I had not ascribed philosophy nor poetry to Black people, even though it was all there. I was not only truly ignorant, I was the perfect product of America's educational system which confuses Black people by rewarding those Blacks who evidence that they can "think" like Whites and have an "understanding" of White culture, and failing those who do not evidence receptivity to and absorption of mainstream pedagogy regardless of what else that person knows and can do.

Fortunately for me and my junior high school peers, Mrs. Nelson knew something her students didn't know. Mrs. Nelson knew we young Blacks needed to be put in touch with ourselves. She knew we needed intellectual self-empowerment that wasn't referenced to Europeans and American Whites as the paragons of culture, beauty, excellence, and achievement. I recognize now that this self-pride, or "race consciousness," was not accidental in my development. Nevertheless, at the time I wasn't thinking about philosophical questions of self-esteem. I was thirteen.

I attended Rivers Frederick Junior High School, a public school named for a New Orleans physician of color. Because my mother was an elementary-school teacher, I had not gone to a neighborhood school, but rather went across town to the schools where she taught: first Fisk Elementary for kindergarten through fourth. For fifth and sixth grades I attended Phillis Wheatley (named for one of the first published African American poets whose work I think of as a perfect example of Negro schizophrenia). I was sent to Frederick because, at that time, my parents judged Frederick the best of the Black public junior high schools. Frederick more than lived up to its reputation.

My first year at Frederick I got into photography via Mr. Conrad, the industrial arts teacher who set up a small darkroom in the industrial arts shop and started an after-school photography club. There were only about a half dozen or so of us who regularly participated. The impact of that experience has lasted throughout my life. After buying my first Yashica twin lens reflex camera in seventh grade, there has never been a time when I did not own a camera.

Up until the time I got deep, deep into performance poetry and drama via the Free Southern Theatre, photography was a major and, more often than not, "the" major form of self-expression for me. At Frederick I became so identified with photography that many of my classmates referred to me as "the picture man."

Mr. Conrad taught photography as an avocation and as a social development mission. He probably received little, if any, school funding, and, for certain, he supplemented our shortfalls in the money to buy camera, film, paper, and chemicals with funds out of his own pocket. Likewise, I'm sure, Mrs. Nelson had purchased that Langston Hughes record with her own funds.

My three years at Frederick were a cultural breakthrough for me. I learned of myself in a conscious way that was a culmination of all that had come before via my parents and my years in my grandfather's church. This was also a fitting prelude (and perhaps a critical spur) to my involvement in the civil rights movement and my conscious break with Creole and European goals and orientations.

I became conscious of myself as a positive and culturally active human being—I formed friendships that lasted far longer than those created at any other period of my formal education; I got involved in artistic self-expression; I experienced puppy love and first kissed girls; became conscious of the blues and of jazz; realized that there were languages other than English and began to learn French; traveled for the first time by myself to and from school; went out for the school football team (I didn't make it but found out later that even the coach who told me I "didn't have to come back" to practice expected me to show up the next day); fractured my leg playing sandlot football; became conscious of the petite bourgeoisie and the mind-set of Catholics; met kids who didn't

simply pass for White but who, as the sons and daughters of doctors and lawyers, educators and business people, actually acted White; made decisions about how to spend my time after school; and, all in all, had a ball growing up through what is generally the most tempestuous period in the coming-of-age saga. In short, at Frederick I became myself. Conscious self-development spared me the maiming conceptualization of myself as an intellectually and psychologically inferior victim of racism in America.

I know the exact moment I was saved as a writer: it was when I heard Langston Hughes reading his poetry with a jazz piano player in the background—all praises due Mrs. Nelson.

I have searched for but never found that record. Today I realize the record itself is of small consequence because, as is usually the case with such events, the memory is more potent than the reality.

I remember now and was absolutely astonished then by the concluding line of a poem about the death of a poor man in Harlem— too impoverished to afford a funeral, his widow went around begging for money to pay for the man's burial: "a poor man ain't got no business to die."

After school I went straight to the main public library on Tulane Avenue. Over the following weeks I checked out everything I could find by Langston Hughes. I was as excited and as self-absorbed with Langston Hughes as a crib-bound baby playing with its newly discovered hands and feet.

two: what Langston did

> . . . *I think that music, being an expression of the human heart, or of the human being itself, does express just what is happening. I feel it expresses the whole thing—the whole of human experience at the particular time that it is being expressed . . . I think music is an instrument. It can create the initial thought patterns that can change the thinking of the people.*
>
> —*John William Coltrane*

I had absolutely no idea about anything related to "formal" poetry, except that I was captivated by what Langston Hughes had done on that record. Being both ignorant and smitten, Hughes became my measuring rod.

For years, I thought to be a writer meant to be like Langston Hughes: meant to work, and work hard at it; meant to write in every genre and to produce anthologies as well as individual books; meant to travel and communicate with people around the world; meant to do both journalism and creative writing; meant to celebrate the humanity of the planet through a focus on one's own folk. This is what I thought being a writer meant.

I never thought of being just a poet or just a journalist, just a dramatist or just an essayist. I never thought that writing one's own books was more important than editing the works of others. Tutored by Hughes, I quickly learned that people of color were writers and had a valuable literature.

Because I was inspired by the recording, I of course examined Hughes's poetry first—I remember reading an early, if not a first, edition of *The Weary Blues* and some of Hughes's other early books which had those beautiful etchings by E. McKnight Kauffer used as illustrations. To this day I think poetry books ought to have pictures in them, at least artwork on the cover, and not commercial graphics but pieces by artists who think of their visual work as art and not as advertisement.

Oddly enough, while Langston's poetry deeply affected me, I moved quickly past what I initially thought was its stylistic simplicity. Of course, as I started trying to write, I found out that Langston's simplicity was far from simple to duplicate.

Here are two of my early attempts, written, as near as I can remember, sometime between 1963 and 1965. Both reflect the Langston Hughes influence and a definite use of blues. The second piece also evidences my interest in fantasy, or exaggeration, as a poetic technique.

2 SISTERS
STREET CORNER CONVERSA(OBSERVA)TIONS
OTHER TALK THAN WHAT YOU HEAR

What
I got
Ain't for SALE

what ails a woman
worst than any pain
is to fall in love
with another woman man

my boss he white
I swear he do not know
where his hands belong

whiteman tell me
the rent is due
like the 15th
don't come every month

Ain't no hope
He be home soon
He got paid today

that child lord,
that baby got her daddy's eyes
& my husband's ways

O hum let me go

EXPECTED YOU YESTERDAY

expected you yesterday & here you come
   today
a head full of pretty face & no excuses
about not coming till you came &
smiling from here to me
you know I gotta like the way you look
& the talk you puttin down
you're just taking advantage of me
you know I was going to wait
here have a star
what about a moon
do you like sky
the clouds are especially delicious
i ah . . . i ah
expected you yesterday & here you come
   today
a head full of pretty face & no excuses

Even though I was writing poetry heavily influenced by Hughes's style, rather than the poetry per se, Langston's autobiographies were his most important books for me, followed by the poetry anthologies he edited (particularly the collection of African poets). Another very influential Hughes book was *The Sweet Flypaper of Life,* a photo/text collaboration with Roy DeCavara. *Flypaper* set a photo-essay standard, approached only by Amiri Baraka's book with Fundi (Billy Abernathy), *In Our Terribleness.* My high opinion of *Flypaper* undoubtedly was fueled by my love of and training in photography.

The autobiographies were important because they served as a road map. For every writer Hughes mentioned—Black, White, African, Russian or Chinese—I went to the library and checked out a book. Some of the writers I liked, some I didn't.

By the end of ninth grade I had read my way through the Harlem Renaissance. I knew there were poets in Africa and the Caribbean. In high school I had started reading Turgenev and a little Pushkin, moved on to Chinese and Japanese writers, and generally found an alternative to Euro-centric classics as the touchstones of great literature. Thanks to Langston Hughes, once I started reading literature on my own, I never had an inferiority complex about literature. I never thought that anyone White was necessarily the greatest writer I ever read or that I would not succeed until I could write like White writers or be like them.

At the same time, early on I got into some of the socially relevant and experimental non-Black writers: John Dos Passos and e. e. cummings come immediately to mind, but also the beats and a lot of left-oriented literature from the thirties and forties. In these writers I saw alternatives to almost everything that was in our textbooks. I did try to read the classic English poets but they didn't hold me, as did few of the mainstream American poets, the collected works of Carl Sandburg being an immediate exception.

This was the early sixties, an explosion and proliferation of independence movements were happening on "the" continent, and, indeed, throughout the Third World with an accompanying movement in literature. Langston Hughes had introduced me to much of this literature. There was also our domestic liberation movement, the civil rights movement, with its church base and freedom songs.

Hughes was one side in the triangle of my conscious self-development. My civil rights involvement, picketing and sitting-in, was the second side. My interest in blues and jazz, which I pursued with a passionate intensity, completed the triangle.

I can remember all kinds of random specifics, such as joining the RCA record club and gradually getting to jazz through both White and Black artists. Before appreciating Duke Ellington and Ray Charles, I had a Chet Atkins record which had one Black-oriented cut on it, "Boo Boo Stick Beat." Chet Atkins was not a jazz artist but at that time what did I know.

I remember sitting in Mrs. Chavis's English class in ninth grade. We called her "say it and

don't spray it" Mrs. Chavis, because in her effort to enunciate clearly and to speak proper English there was an exaggeration that often led to spittle flying out of her mouth. Here was the major deformity of petit-bourgeois aping of White ways to the point of absurd caricature.

I dug Mrs. Nelson who moved us deeper into ourselves, and I abhorred Mrs. Chavis who had us chasing a white chalice, a chase which invariably included all kinds of soul-killing perversions and behavior entirely inappropriate for Black mental health.

By the time I went to St. Augustine High School, psychologically I was in total conflict with their mainstream-America cultural orientation.

St. Aug's major reputation was as our city's premier college-prep school for Black males. In my case, they brought me to the attention of Carleton College in Northfield, Minnesota. Carleton offered me a partial scholarship. I went, but lasted only two trimesters from September 1964 through March 1965. During both high school and college, I continued to read and write.

Although I moved stylistically past Hughes as a poet, I never moved past Hughes's sensibility and his approach.

Hughes kept working-class Black folk as the central focus and foundation ground for all of his musings and philosophizing. Since Hughes was ground zero for me, nobody could influence me to abandon a Black focus.

I believe that for any writer to create a literature of value, our work must necessarily be culturally specific, whether that culture be native or adopted. Hughes's folksy, blues orientation was more than culturally specific. What was most important to me was Hughes's resistance to assimilation voiced through a celebration of and insistence on the nobility of our race. Of the African American writers I knew at that time, only Zora Neale Hurston approached Hughes in that wonderful and essential celebration and insistence.

"I'm like that old mule— / Black—and don't give a damn! / You got to take me / Like I am," sang Hughes in one of his most popular poems. I liked that he saw nobility in the stubbornness of a mule, a stubborn insistence that is often ostracized as stupidity. Hughes knew who he was and presented himself without thoroughbred pretense, and for me, a young Black male racing into adulthood via involvement in the civil rights movement, Hughes's mule was a touchstone I continued to rub all the rest of my life.

This appreciation of one's people is not simply an intellectual activity. In America, one does not love Black people simply because one is Black. In fact, in America one cannot love Black people simply on the basis of being. We must be taught both by instruction and by example to both bond with as well as identify with those who are the most despised, the most exploited, the most misused people in America. The trick, if one is Black, is to do this without developing a victim mentality of either self-hatred or self-pity, and, at the same time, avoid the temptation of overcompensation in the form of reversing the polarity of raw racism and declaring everything Black good and everything White evil. This is a very difficult task to master, even more so in a public arena. It has never been easy for Black people to love themselves.

I was extremely blessed to experience the civil rights movement because this helped me to learn to love Black folk. When I was sixteen I spent many Saturdays going door-to-door doing voter registration and voter education work. At that time, in order to register you had to fill out an arcane form which, among other bizarre hurdles, required an applicant to figure out her age exactly to the day. My job was both to convince people to register and to teach them how to fill out the application correctly.

While we often worked in the poorest neighborhoods of the city, I was culturally enriched because all of the houses I entered viscerally taught me aspects about my people and myself that I had not previously known, particularly the blues. While I taught mathematics, grammar, and spelling, they taught me a music which literally wailed its defiance of status quo propriety.

There is nothing as defiant as the blues at 10 A.M. on Saturday morning, cranked up loud and reverberating from the wood of those row on row of sparely painted, if painted at all, shotgun houses.

Blues as tough as that woman who answered her door in bra and brown skirt, cigarette at an angle in her mouth, an angle which complemented the comb in her hair. She continued combing her hair as I tried to convince her to register to vote, neither smiling nor scowling at my naive attempts to bring what I thought would be an improvement in her life.

Twenty years later, reality supports this woman's stoicism in the face of my misplaced enthusiasm: the granddaughter of that woman is locked in an even deeper funk after generations of Black elected officials have presided over a worsening of social conditions for her and all the people like her. This woman standing before me knows that I'm a fool to think that registering to vote will change her life for the better. Yet, like Black women have for centuries in America, she balances the bubble of my foolish vision on a resigned and sophisticated agreement to take another stab at life by buoying the dreams of a Black man regardless of the certainty that his dream will never come true.

Realizable or not, Black women somehow "know" that a man cannot live without dreams, so they identify not with our perennially deferred dreams but rather they identify with us, the dreamers. This agreement is not with abstract ideals but rather with the flesh, blood, and soul vision of our manhood.

That is why there is a man moving to the back of the house as I enter the door; a man who does not even want to discuss voting; a man who does not belong to this house and who probably does little to support this house; a man that this woman lets into her life without any great expectations just like she allows me to enter her living room, her house, her life, without any great expectations.

I am looking at her breasts. She watches me, does not blush, and why should she? She probably assumes that if I have not seen breasts before, then now is as good a time as any to begin looking. I slowly explain the procedures as we sit on an old sofa, or on beat-up old kitchen chairs, or, I don't remember what we sat on. I don't remember anything except that inside that house was a whole world, a different world from the church-bred houses I usually inhabited. The difference was not the people but rather the way the people lived: the smells, the liquor, the absence of White gods on the wall (there were no pictures of Jesus or Kennedy in those houses), and, above all, the mule sound of the blues bleating in all its immutable Blackness.

In that house lived a blues so stark that when she raises her arm there is hair in her armpit and she still has not bothered to put on a blouse. By the time we are going through the questions, I find her smiling as I explain that there are some simple tricks she can use to get through this thing. Observing or ignoring our New Orleans custom of sharing sustenance with those who enter our spaces, she may or may not offer me something to drink. Soon we are both comfortable with each other, and a half hour later I exit back onto the streets with a notation of her name and address so that we can follow-up on whether she registers.

Her arm reaches out to close the door which sometimes has a shutter that opens out, and, even as the shutter closes, the blues continues to blow. Now she is smiling and maybe calls me "baby" with the conspiratorial smile that Black women fleetingly flash after pumping up a Black male ego, the smile which plants seeds designed to strengthen the recipient who must face a world designed to grind Black people down. The incubation period sometimes takes years, but eventually I realize who was really helping whom. Blues like that.

Nothing stops the blues because the blues were created precisely as a way to overcome. This is how I came to realize the power of the blues. The power is like that woman being herself and facing life just as it is and just as she is, and still believing in a naive high schooler knocking on her door.

This woman, with the blues as her song, survives an unconditional confrontation with life. She taught me exactly what Langston meant by "just like I am." We didn't need to clean up. We didn't need to talk differently. We didn't even need to wear socially acceptable clothes. And we didn't need to stop shouting the blues. If they wanted us: take us like we were. If we wanted to change, that was our choice rather than some alien requirement of life. Blues like that is what I learned going door to door throughout the community.

The blues remains self-referential, always grounded in the here and now. Some people think the blues is about submission because the blues is reality based and embraces the world as it is while at the same time wishing for, indeed, longing for the world to be different. The Christian worldview, on the other hand, is viewed as "uplifting" even though it is other-referential, about life in the hereafter, reality based on faith in things unseen, and a gen-

eral exclusion of anyone who was not also Christian despite its philosophical claims to being good Samaritans and doing unto others.

When I did my civil rights canvassing, I experienced the deep blues and found myself drawn to and responding to a side of my birthright that heretofore I had only read about in Langston Hughes's and Zora Hurston's work, and had only recently begun to listen to on records. Until then I had never really *heard* the blues, even though the blues was in my blood.

As I canvassed and listened to the music, and listened to the people talk, and as I tried to make them comfortable while giving my spiel about registering; as we walked the picket lines outside the department stores and talked to people trying to persuade them not to shop; all of that not only put me in contact with the working-class Black, more importantly, those experiences put me in contact with myself.

Regardless of whether these people thought what I was about was important, it was my job to convince them of the importance of what I was trying to get them to do, and in the process I began to understand that I was "them" and it was "we" who were important.

Once I accepted that what my people did or didn't do was important, then I could never look down on them, nor could I think that what happened to me personally was the only important part of life. I never felt that because I could read, write, and figure, I was somehow better off. Although I went to school with the sons of doctors, lawyers, and civil servants at St. Aug, because of the civil rights movement I identified more with the laborers than with the professionals, and I firmly believed that I could be of service to them.

This identification, furthermore, was consciously constructed because I not only learned from watching and working with people in the civil rights movement, I also started studying the blues: reading books about the blues, buying blues records, and the same with jazz. I had the world of gospel in my intimate upbringing, but I came to the blues as someone who did not share the blues world on a day-to-day basis and, aware of my distance, I closed the gap by study and by civil rights work.

I got the best of both worlds. My upbringing grounded me in a Christian community of caring folk, and my civil rights work and junior high school education grounded me in in-

Kalamu ya Salaam (second from left) leading an anti-police brutality demonstration/boycott

timate contact with blues folk. Again, I point to Hughes as a guide.

I loved Hughes's poem "Motto," which ended with: "My motto, / As I live and learn, / is: / Dig And Be Dug / In Return." Dig. Hughes said nothing specific about what to dig, so implicitly, at least to my way of thinking, that "dig" meant "dig" the world. In fact, in the opening stanza Hughes says: I play it cool / And dig all jive. / That's the reason / I stay alive." This is Hughes's great attraction for me: he told me to be myself and he told me to dig the world. Yes, and that's deep.

After Hughes, only Baldwin and Baraka significantly and permanently influenced my writing style. All three of them engaged the world with both an outsider's critical eye and a grounded Black person's love of Black folk.

I found Baldwin technically awesome. I can remember reading some essay he wrote with the word "proffer" in it. That became a word I used in my writings.

Critics often credit Baldwin's use of language to the Bible, but really it's not the Bible per se, it's the Bible mediated through the Black church, and it's also jazz, the complex outpourings of bebop. Look at the sentence structures, the very volubility of his sentences; everything and the kitchen sink pushed against each other in breathless rushes of prose. Baldwin's denseness was balanced by an unerring rhythmic logic that made his fanciful prose flights a joy to read.

When Baldwin took America to task, as he did so eloquently in his play *Blues for Mr. Charlie* and in his famous essay "The Fire Next Time," he did it with the same stylistic brilliance as evidenced by the creators of bebop. Baldwin's best prose had not only the Old Testament fire and brimstone, raunchy forthrightness and righteous indignation, but that prose also advanced the art of the essay as a genre. Baldwin's prose achievement was much like Charlie Parker and Dizzy Gillespie who ushered in a whole new musical style, a style which, at its core, had the grandiose, stubbornly elegant simplicity of Thelonious Monk articulating stark truths in a uniquely offbeat manner, a manner which both demanded an audience and made demands on its audience with the same explosive pronouncements as the drumming of Max Roach and Klook Clarke elevating rhythm to new heights.

I know that Baldwin loved gospel and blues, but he also loved jazz—so many of his major characters were musicians and lovers of music/musicians. Mary Ellison in her book *Extensions of the Blues* references a Baldwin quote from Baldwin biographer Fern M. Eckman's book *The Furious Passage of James Baldwin.* "When Baldwin was a keynote speaker at a conference on 'The Negro Writer's Vision of America' in the early sixties, he declared 'My models—my private models—are not Hemingway, nor Faulkner, nor Dos Passos, or indeed any American writer. I model myself on jazz musicians, dancers, a couple of whores and a few junkies . . .'" If you don't understand the music, then you will be blind to the music's influence on Baldwin.

In 1964 as a high school senior, praising Baldwin got me kicked off the student newspaper. Back in eighth grade at Frederick, after being introduced to Hughes, I joined the school newspaper. Mrs. Nelson was the advisor. I was writing and doing photography. Eventually I became the editor. We entered the paper in a contest sponsored by Columbia University in New York and won second place. Us. A little, Negro, junior high school paper. Winning made me know I was a match for the world, for the best of America. At St. Aug I wanted to continue with my journalism. I wrote a glowing review of Baldwin's incendiary "Blues for Mr. Charlie" which, while not rejecting religion, ended by espousing self-defense, picking up the gun.

The priests said not in this paper, not at this school, not in this life. I realized we were in direct conflict with each other. They wanted me to study and make straight *A*'s. They wanted me to give up or tone down my civil rights work. One teacher, Father McManus, who was a "liberal" on the Urban League board and all that, went completely out of his tree when he walked into the homeroom and I was sitting their reading *Muhammad Speaks.* I had no idea it would provoke him to turn redder than a redneck sheriff watching Sidney Poitier in *Guess Who's Coming to Dinner?*

Father Mac, who was known for his prowess at corporal punishment with the paddle, stomped the floor, bellowed at me, and over the next month took every opportunity to re

mind me that I would be better off studying than reading that crap. I laughed and wondered what was so threatening. They knew I was dangerous before I knew.

And there was the time an English teacher told me that I was going to write a term paper on fancy, fantasy, and some other "f" word in one of Shakespeare's sonnets. I immediately said I wasn't going to do it. "Well, if you don't do it, Ferdinand, you're just going to get an *F* for the semester." "You can just give me my *F* now, because I'm not going to do it."

I went home that evening and told my mother that I was going to get an *F*. Neither she nor my father forced me to return to school and apologize, or even to write the assignment. They let me happily hold onto both my *F* and my budding sense of rebellion and dignity.

Years and years later when my children were going through school, I never ever sided with the school administrators and instructors when any of the children rebelled. I made sure that the children understood that there were repercussions they would have to bear as a result of their actions, but the larger picture for me was that I refused to repress rebellion in the youth. Indeed, not only did I want to encourage that rebellion because I knew, ultimately, it was healthy, but also I recognized that the whole system was set up to smother our rebellious spirits. Why should I help the system to maintain the status quo? As a parent I made a conscious decision, as a high school student I intuitively concluded that St. Aug's discipline was a conscious attempt to season a slave.

Sometimes we exaggerate the severity of a situation because memory is selective and everyone wants to tell a good tale about themselves, but there were too many incidents at St. Aug to ignore. For example, when I went out for the drama club at St. Aug, I quit after attending one rehearsal where they were doing some English drawing room comedy with fake British accents, butlers, and dry jokes. In eighth grade at Frederick I had played Crispus Attucks in my civic teacher's drama. Under Mrs. Green's direction, my big scene was to leap out of the closet with a sword made of a clothes hanger and cardboard and confront the British soldiers with the declaratory line, "I am a desperate Black man who is willing to fight for my freedom." So you know I thought St. Aug's British bullshit was just that, i.e., British bullshit.

At Frederick they armed me. At St. Aug they tried to castrate me.

Most of my teachers at Frederick had been significant Black women with an important handful of bold Black men such as Mr. Conrad, Mr. Howard who taught me French, and Mr. Blanchard who gave me a love for mathematics. At St. Aug the instructors were mainly priests (who were mostly White) of the Josephite Order. The Josephite's were an order who focused on educating Black people. The lay instructors at St. Aug, except for the coaches and music instructors, were pious, intellectually oriented Black men who struck me as effeminate. The dichotomy between the instructors at the two schools was too ludicrous for words. I owed St. Aug nothing except my muleish contempt.

All of this time I was still reading and still struggling to write. By twelfth grade I finished an experimental novel that ended with the hero committing suicide. No matter how much I thought I was uninfluenced by St. Aug, no matter how much I fought against their example and instructions, still, I obviously was ingesting some of their messages, especially the message to become respectable by killing the Black blues self.

Baldwin's writings spoke directly to me because here I was confronting a sensibility, a system whose total intent was to turn the blues-based Black into a Christian American. In the St. Aug schema, integration meant effacing one's self. They taught young Black males that the highest achievement for Blacks was to speak, dress, conduct oneself and be around Whites as though we were not who we were. Ultimately, they wanted to put into our hearts the desire to be like Whites and into our heads the belief that being like Whites equated with being intelligent, civilized, and Christian.

My acceptance of such a mainstream scenario inevitably would have meant submerging every conflict, sucking contradictions up and in, and contorting my psyche just to be acceptable. I resisted and stayed in constant rebellion.

In that context, Baldwin's penetrating intelligence appealed to me because his example allowed me to confront the status quo norms in its own arena. Baldwin's use of language and mastery of the essay signified not only his ability to handle White words but also his ability to bend those words for his own use. Initially, that appealed to me.

Had I stopped there I would have been forever trapped, because ultimately striving to express one's self solely by mastering the master's language presupposes that language is value free, that language is neutral, and somehow, even though I did not "know" in a theoretical sense that language was the articulation of culture, emotionally moved by Black music, I did feel that I needed my own language. The Catholic rejection of gospel and blues was a confirmation of Black music's importance. Reading Baldwin, beneath his mastery of the "king's English," I heard, and felt, a love of Black music.

In later years Baldwin addressed the issue of language in his own eloquent way, noting that "Black English" was essentially a language and ought to be respected as such. While Baldwin was not the only person to address this issue, what distinguished Baldwin's contribution was his emphasis on the necessity of language. Baldwin's defense was an affirmation for me of a position that some of us had intuited. In fact, Baldwin's ability to penetrate to the *sine qua non* of this issue reinforced in me the necessity for developing an articulation of what we had been doing with language. But here I am jumping ahead of myself. Back then all I knew was that it felt right to speak, write, and listen to the language(s) I loved and understood.

Needless to say, the blues with its confrontation of pain appealed to me. Although I was unable to avoid both the positive and the negative influences: the Latin and English, the religion classes and the skewed history, the emphasis on getting high marks on SAT's and IQ tests, the uniform of wearing a tie every school day, and the insistence on proper English spoken at all times, even as all of that was influencing me, fortunately, there was the counterweight of the literature I was reading, the music I was listening to and studying, and, above all, the civil rights movement within which I was deeply and actively immersed. In Baldwin I found a companion who championed all that I found valuable.

After Baldwin came LeRoi Jones/Amiri Baraka. Baraka I dug because of his iconoclastic and boldly innovative stylings. He is always at his best breaking ground, making you go "damn" at the way he has hooked something up with the sarcastic aloofness of a hard bop hipster. Clearly, as the quantity and quality of his earliest work demonstrates, Baraka worked hard at being off the cuff. Like a great jazz musician, he had shedded (i.e., "woodshed," jazz parlance for practice and serious study) heavy so that whenever the time came to blow, he was able to blow with confidence and make his work sound effortless. Baraka also projected a cocky air of being ahead of the curve, always in the know, always the first one to arrive on the set wondering what took the rest of us so long to arrive. That appealed to the machismo in my adolescent male psyche.

But what most appealed to me was that Jones, too, was struggling in the White world, struggling to define and claim his persona as a Black man. Additionally, Jones was deep into the music, especially jazz and blues. Through Jones I also started to experience poetry as self-revelation.

Jones's own personal life experiences, conundrums, confusions, dreams, and aspirations were at the center of his poetry. On the stylistic surface, Jones's poetry was nothing like Hughes's, but yet, underneath it, there was a deep blues, a blues for the lost Black man, the man unsure of what being himself meant, the "dead lecturer." That title of Jones's second book of poetry said it all.

A lot of Jones I didn't understand, couldn't understand, and even if I had understood would never have really related to, but what attracted me, I think, to Jones before he became Baraka, as well as attracted me to Baldwin, was the way they confronted the White world and also confronted their complicity and love of that world; the way they articulated and embraced with critical consciousness their love of White literature which directly correlated with my own less ambivalent, but not totally uncontradictory feelings about what I was learning in school. Much of what they spoke about resonated in my experience.

Anyone who has not experienced it will find it nearly impossible to understand the schizophrenia that mainstream education engenders in working-class Black people, right down to the root of rejecting one's mother, which is the embodiment of rejecting one's culture. This is why Black studies was so immediately latched onto by students and so instantly rejected by the petit bourgeois oriented colored professors, and why Afro-centricism is often strongest in predominately White institutions of higher education. At no other time in one's life will the

intellectual challenge to and intellectual oppression of Black people be as clear as when you are a Black student in a predominately White school precisely because in higher education there are few, if any, status quo revered Black intellectual authority figures—and almost all of them are either conservative or seemingly apolitical.

On the other hand, there was no way for a sane person to reject learning, to reject intelligence. I wanted to embrace my people, embrace myself and the world I grew up in, but there was a conflict between the two. The wannabes stumbling and fleeing toward the status quo invariably would put down the blues folk, put down their ignorance, their uncouthness, their illiteracy, their blues essence. In what is easily perceived as a rejection of intellectual values, rather than a rejection of self-abnegating intellectualism, blues people seemed to be so short-sighted, so self-destructive and so incorrigible.

Hughes did not speak to this conflict as cogently nor as consistently as Baldwin and Jones/Baraka did. There is a detachment in Hughes's writing that maintains the privacy of the witness even as Hughes focuses almost exclusively on his people. Baldwin and Baraka, on the other hand, even with Whites intimately involved in their lives, focus much more on the contradictions of being a Black man in White America as a personal rather than an observed experience.

Hughes's reticence about his personal life was an alienating factor for me. Hughes had written two autobiographies, and, by the early sixties, neither Baldwin nor Baraka had written autobiographies, yet readers knew more about each of their personal lives than about Hughes's personal life. This is a line of demarcation. In later years I would develop my theory about the use of the "personal," but at that time I simply did the most expedient thing: I loved both approaches, the detachment of Hughes and the personal involvement of Baldwin/Baraka.

Baldwin and Baraka wrote in a modern intellectual style and that appealed to me. Yet, neither Baldwin nor Baraka had that element of blues based, holisticness that was the most marvelous quality of Langston Hughes, a writer so huge that his collected works define literature. Prose, fiction, poetry, drama, journalism, criticism, editing, it's all there, plus Hughes presented his work to the whole world, work which focused almost exclusively on Black people. Hughes was a "simple" Black writer who went around the world.

To an adolescent eighth grader in 1959/60 just waking up to literature, Hughes was both a blessing and a foundation. After Hughes, nothing was too deep to tackle. Hughes gave me a sense of self-confidence as a budding Black writer. Before I realized that there was such a thing as a literary ghetto, I was already literally looking at the whole world.

three. I choose to be a writer

Well, I tell you for myself, I make a conscious attempt, I think I can truthfully say that in music I make or I have tried to make a conscious attempt to change what I've found, in music. In other words, I've tried to say, "Well, this I feel, could be better, in my opinion, so I will try to do this to make it better." This is what I feel that we feel in any situation that we find in our lives, when there's something we think could be better, we must make an effort to try and make it better. So it's the same socially, musically, politically and in any department of our lives.

—*John William Coltrane*

I was slow to commit to writing. When I graduated from high school in 1964, photography was my first love and music my deepest passion.

After graduation I went on an eleven-year odyssey in and out of higher education, which culminated in a business administration Associate Arts degree from Delgado Junior College in 1975.

I have never liked college. I perceived college as an extension of high school from the pedagogical standpoint. Nevertheless, there is no denying the importance of many of the experiences I had in colleges.

First, I was one of eleven "American Negroes" (eight of whom were first-year students and two of whom were sophomores) at Carleton College in Northfield, Minnesota—the mythic site of one of Jesse James's last and most di-

sastrous attempts at bank robbery. Carleton was a great and expensive learning experience that I quickly rejected.

Even though I left at the end of the second trimester, while there I had written a lot of poetry and a second novel which revolved around the experiences of a desperate group of young Blacks at a predominantly White college.

During this period I also developed a relationship with Esim Bozoklar, a young student from Turkey. She inspired me to write a series of numbered poems called, as best I can recall, "mavi gok" which was Turkish for "blue sky."

Overall, at that time, my poetic influences were: Hughes for content and e. e. cummings in visual presentation (the breaking of words into letters and the explosion of one word erupting from another word or interrupting the word flow). Although I've lost most of my work from this era, here are two poems which exemplify both my state of mind and some of the cummings influence.

NO ENTRANCE

the vo
ice might
y voice
of Go
d visit
ed me la
st ni
te it sa
id "fuc
k you" &
so I tu
rned ov
er on m
y stomac
h that i
t might be
easier/not
that He ne
eded it—
He was real
ly doing su
ch a go
od job al
ready!

[untitled]

those good things there be that are
are more surely killers more deadly lethal
than any evil be
for sometimes even dreams become
poisonous & aspirations abortions of life
sometimes the very hope amputates
sometimes the better worsens
it is not the envisioning of dreams nor
the rise toward aspirations
only the survival midst this all
that can keep us
it sometimes matters not that you fail only
that you've survived it
somehow is the resurrection more
    cherished than the climb

to be the phoenix more surely is harder
    than ever the god to be
more straight more true
than any glory ever

In addition to musicians such as drummer Art Blakey and Ravi Shankar, at Carleton I was able to see and meet a variety of influential people such as socialist Norman Thomas and members of the budding White left organization Students for a Democratic Society. Also important for me was the opportunity to meet and talk with students from Africa and other foreign places. I became a radio programmer with my own jazz show on the college station. Carleton also exposed me to an enormous amount of foreign cinema. Although I never had any major desire to work in film, since Carleton I have been an avid cinema buff.

Through an improbable twist of circumstances, I even got to meet writer John Oliver Killens, whose World War II novel *And Then We Heard the Thunder* was my favorite piece of fiction. Carleton started an exchange program with the historically important Black school: Fisk University in Nashville, Tennessee. As the administrators reminded me in their attempts to keep me from going, the program was designed to send "White" students to Fisk in exchange for accepting Black students at Carleton. I reminded the administrators that the program guidelines said nothing about the race of students, besides who could better benefit from comparing the two. During the two weeks I was at Fisk, I went to a writing workshop conducted by John Killens. Years later, Killens chose to include my work in an anthology of Black southern writers which was posthumously completed by my friend Dr. Jerry Ward of Tougaloo College in Mississippi after Mr. Killens died.

The major benefit of going to Carleton, however, was that the experience forced me to self-examine myself in a challenging setting. At that point I was predictably confused.

When I quit Carleton, I returned to New Orleans and literally surrendered to the army. It was 1965, the height of the Vietnam draft. I had turned eighteen but had not registered. Finally, as a result of my mother's insistence, I went down to the draft board. I can still hear this elderly White woman shrieking about how I had broken the law, could go to jail, and had better report there the next day at noon. I don't volunteer for executions, so I went to the recruiting offices downtown and volunteered to go anywhere but Vietnam. The recruiter said he couldn't promise to send me to a particular place, but if I did well on a battery of tests, he would get me into a "mos" (military occupational service area) that they didn't use in Vietnam.

I never returned to the draft board and, in fact, didn't receive my draft card until after I was in boot camp at Fort Polk, Louisiana. I ended up in electronic repair of the "nike hercules nuclear missile," which meant a nine-month training period at Fort Bliss in El Paso, Texas. I served a year in Korea and finished out my army stint back at Fort Bliss. Throughout this period, I was into photography and music as well as writing. Most of my writing was fiction and poetry.

When I returned to Bliss I was a sergeant and had lots of free time. I lived in the darkroom, the music practice room, and the library, in that order. Because of my rank I didn't have to make roll calls and also had my own room. I would be the first at the USO, check out a set of drums, go into a practice room, and practice playing drums for an hour before any of the other musicians/soldiers arrived. After three or four months of intensive practice, I became good enough to jam with the other musicians, and later I developed into an in-demand drummer. I played in a soul band, as well as in a rock trio as a sub when their regular drummer couldn't make it, and eventually in a small band which played both jazz and rhythm and blues.

By then the photography was mainly on the weekends, and I would go back to my room and write at night. I didn't read as much as I had in college, partly because the army library was predictably conservative. The three journals I read and subscribed to were the *Liberator* magazine, *Negro Digest,* and the *Village Voice.*

By 1968, my fiction had developed to the point that I was good enough to get a publisher strongly interested in my work. I had sent a set of short stories, "Easy Rider, Dark Rider," to William Morrow (because that's where LeRoi Jones was published) and to Dial (because of James Baldwin). Phil Petrie wrote me back encouraging me to send him more. He noted, perhaps if I added two or three stories, then I would have a collection they would be interested in discussing. I was so ignorant of the publishing process that I took this to mean that he wanted me to do something else other than what I had written.

"Easy Rider" contains six stories comprising about seventy double-spaced, typewritten pages. The first five stories are written in the first person from the point of view of the protagonist. The last story is in the third person and makes a jump of about twenty years.

I know now that Mr. Petrie was simply asking for at least one more story to bridge the chasm of years. Had I done that and the book have been successfully published, I may have chosen to pursue fiction rather than poetry as my main voice. As it was, in 1971 I had a story published in *Young Black Storytellers,* edited by Orde Coombs, and in 1973 another story was published in *We Be Word Sorcerers,* edited by Sonia Sanchez. On a national level, I was more successful with fiction than with poetry.

I frequently tell people that fiction is the hardest form for me to write, but that's not entirely true. What is true is that in Black publishing circles there was an extremely limited number of publishing opportunities. After I got out of the army, except for anthologies, I had no desire to pursue publishing with mainstream publishing companies and looked exclusively for Black outlets. Looking back at my work, I recognize that fiction was actually the bulk of what I wrote before joining the Free Southern Theater (FST).

So, why didn't I continue fiction? The real answer is I don't really know. I suppose this is sort of like asking John Coltrane why didn't he continue to play alto rather than switch to tenor saxophone. Who knows?

Even though I wrote two novels early on, the novel has never appealed to me as a professional writer. Short stories, yes, but the novel, no. I have theorized about the novel being a bourgeois Euro-centric genre. I have made up off-the-wall arguments about fiction in general. I have even avoided writing fiction for a long time, but none of that addresses the central issue. For me, fiction lacks the oratorical element.

Both poetry and drama are recited, spoken aloud, or sung before an audience. I think those of us engaged in the Black aesthetic movement gravitate to the orated as opposed to the textual, partly out of personal taste and partly because, as currently demonstrated by rap music, our community responds more forcefully to the orated rather than the textual. Given our community's "church" and "street corner" orientation, each of which places a high value on oratorical abilities, the preference for spoken over written text is natural, i.e., grows organically out of our environment.

Additionally, for us, text is like lyrics separated from music. One cannot appreciate rap at all if one never hears rap and only reads the text of a rap. On the other hand, even if you don't or can't understand every word that a rapper says, you still can appreciate and be moved by the rap once you hear it.

Of course, in early 1968, looking forward to getting out of the army, playing music professionally, and writing at night, I had not come to any of these conclusions. I was writing fiction constantly, and I was not writing that much poetry. I was a closet writer. My writing was so deep in the closet, that I never hesitated to focus on my music at the expense of time spent writing. My writing was going nowhere but in a drawer, a box, a folder, a closet. But my music, that was another story.

By the time I mustered out of the army, our band had all kinds of gigs lined up, and we had become very popular. I promised my band mates I would return after I visited my family for a week or so. "Yeah, I'm coming back. I'm leaving my drums here and you know I'm not going to abandon my drums." I never saw those drums again.

I heard drummers in New Orleans who made my fingers and hands deny ever, ever holding a drumstick. Those cats beat me into a serious "inadequacy" crisis. No matter how hard I practiced, I would never be able to play as well as

Kalamu ya Salaam

they did. They nullified any aspirations I had to be a musician. I was too realistic to fool myself. On the one hand, I knew Zigaboo Modeliste of the Meters, Smokey Johnson of Fats Domino's Band, and David Lee, who eventually was snatched up by Dizzy Gillespie, plus "beaucoup" (a bunch, almost too many to count) other New Orleans drummers could drum circles around me. On the other hand, I didn't know or know of any New Orleanians who could write better than me.

Right then and there, I gave up music as a profession. I had not yet definitely decided to try writing as a profession, however my realistic choices had been narrowed considerably. I did recognize, however, that writing, like music, would always be a part of my life.

More so than hearing Langston Hughes while in eighth grade, more so than quitting college and going into the army, my decision not to pursue music as a profession, coupled with my strong desire to participate in the Black power struggle, defined the way ahead.

four. BLKARTSOUTH

. . . it seems to me that the audience, in listening, is in an act of participation, you know. And when you know that somebody is maybe moved the same way you are, to such a degree or approaching the degree, it's just like having another member in the group.

—*John William Coltrane*

Here it was, July 1968, and although I had rejected the profession of music and also was impelled toward participating in the Black power movement, in terms of specifics, other than a gradually cohering desire to write, I had absolutely no idea about what I wanted to do with my life.

Part of the problem was I really didn't know any writers personally, so I had no idea what the writing life was actually about or how to go about becoming a writer.

Unlike abandoning music, my decision to be a writer was not spurred by a specific incident or a specific realization. Over the next six months, I found myself writing more and more, and found the people around me responding to the poetry I was writing. So after getting positive feedback, I just kept on doing it.

In September of 1968 I tried college again. I enrolled as a freshman at SUNO (Southern University in New Orleans). I ran headfirst into academe and its ignorance of and disdain for the Black arts movement. I wrote a poem called "John Who," which focused on the overall ignorance of John Coltrane by various faculty members in the different departments. Then there was the incident that sealed any hope that I would reach some détente with SUNO's academe.

I was in Dr. Taylor's English lit class. We were studying ballads. In the textbook there were the Scottish ballads and some examples of American ballads. One of the ballads we studied was a blues ballad, I think it was "Frankie and Johnny," and there was the phrase "the window was throwed up high." Dr. Taylor, who had her Ph.D. in Chaucer or some other area of "olde English," asked did anyone know what the phrase meant. I smiled. That was easy. I told her it meant the window was wide open, "like in 'when you see me coming, throw yo' window high, when you see me leaving, hang yo' head and cry.'" She told me I was wrong. She said that what the phrase referred to was the architecture of the period and how the windows were built high off the ground. Well, I didn't know architecture but I did know bullshit.

On the other side of the coin, my writing was fueled in part by the impatience and arrogance of youth. Here is a short poem from that period. Imagine this piece read by a bushy-headed, sunglass-wearing (we was so cool we sometimes even wore sunglasses at night) militant.

MADPOET

the madpoet, mad, mad, mad
poet, the niggerpoet, the black
poet, mad, mad
how many black angels can dance on a
    watermelon seed
how many english teachers can fly
how many historians are white
how many records do J.B. sell for his
    white bosses
how many women wear wigs
how many women wear natural wigs
how many black folk vote for wallace
how many cadillacs parked in tenement
    lots

how many men do janitorial work in
  alligator shoes
how many men work
how many got alligator shoes
how many people think shelly pope is
  pretty
how many women with babies that look
  more like
       their man than their husbands
how many gods do christians believe, any
how many space ships the man gon build
how many rivers and lakes still fresh water
how many black students know how to
  read and write
how many black students go to school
how many schools do we have
how many colleges in the city are schools
how many so-called hip people is frontin
how many cigarettes you smoke
how many fifths can you drink
how many us think we together
how many us together

By the end of the first semester, I and a handful of other students, some of whom were veterans like myself, were in open rebellion against the administration. By the spring semester of 1969, we organized a takeover of the university, completely shutting it down. In New Orleans I became known as both a militant leader and the leader of a drama group, which meant that the two identities were fused in the public's mind.

I used my poems in various community programs where I was a volunteer and at community events. One of my first major pieces in that regard was "All in the Street," which spoke in poetic tones about the tidal wave of us dancing in the street with brass bands. The poem had the closing line which suggested, just like we took the streets, "the cities are next."

At this point I began experimenting with using New Orleans music in my work. It was conscious in that I knew I was doing it, but subconscious in that I had not figured out what I was doing other than emulating the music and/or being inspired by specific musical performances. As I developed, the music became more and more integral to both the structure and the performance of my poetry.

Here is where my basic style as a public poet got its start. I wanted to reflect and project the dreams and aspirations, the reality and history, the ethos and diverse ideologies of my community, a community on the move, in tran-

sition from oppression to liberation. Some view this simply as polemical poetry, but, for me, a particular party line was not the important thing. The important thing was the identification with the community-at-large and the desire to serve my community.

My desire determined a style. My work had to be mass-oriented. The images, the metaphors, the style, as well as the themes, the concerns and the emotional orientations, all had to draw on the social realities of our community or else it would be rejected or, worse yet, ignored.

Audience is a major force in the style of any and every poet. Some poets never think of or define their audience. Some say that they write from the heart, or write the truth, and that whoever appreciates that work is the audience. But, even in those cases, is it not true that the language of the poetry will determine who is in a position to relate to (both understand and appreciate) the poetry both stylistically and content-wise?

A critical part of my style was the utilization of the oral as a poetic *sine qua non*. For me and my community, it was not enough for the poetry to exist as text. Our poetry needed to be oral.

I remembered reading Langston Hughes explaining why he used rhyme and how rhyme could more easily be remembered by both the poet but especially also by the audience. I used rhyme but not at the ends of lines. Early on, I learned to use what I call internal rhymes and absolute rhymes. An internal rhyme was the use of the same and similar sounds in the middle of lines but rhythmically in the same place in different lines. An absolute rhyme was the repeating of the same word or phrase, usually at the beginning of the line, but sometimes at the end.

In addition to rhyme, irony and humor (particularly sarcasm and caricature) were important elements of my early style precisely because community people responded to these elements. Irony, deliberate understatement and/or the emphasizing of the split between the literal meaning and the contextual meaning of a word, phrase, idea or image, is a hallmark of African American humor. Irony is also a mask, a tool for resistance and rebellion presented in a seemingly innocuous or nonthreatening manner. Finally, irony is reinterpretation by causing the audience to reconsider a given reality from a different point of view. Next to the use of music, irony is probably the salient characteristic of our work from that period.

Here is a poem, "Leader," which is illustrative of the period. This is actually a choreopoem in that it was both a dance and a poem. Eventually, we had a whole set of dance poems which we did like a chorus line with different members taking the lead. Similarly, we had a set of "hair" poems.

"Leader" opens with me clapping and improvising a funky dance while encouraging the audience to clap along, which usually didn't take much encouragement. At some point in the dance I would stop, move directly to the audience, recite the poem with a cocky air, and at the conclusion go back to dancing.

LEADER

i saw a Negro at a dance
last nite who called himself
my leader & that nigger
couldn't dance to save his life
so how he gon lead me!

That summer and fall of 1968, just out of the army and full of fire, engaged in community activity, I found the perfect stage for my calling as a community-based writer at the Free Southern Theatre. I went to both the weekly writing workshops conducted by Tom Dent and to the weekly drama workshops conducted by Robert "Big Daddy" Costley. There were only a handful of us attending either workshop, with a core of three or four of us who attended both. Eventually the workshops combined and that led to the development of the writing/performing workshop which eventually developed its own identity as BLKARTSOUTH.

Excepting Tom Dent, none of the other workshop members thought of writing in terms of fiction or prose. Much of what would normally have been channeled in that direction was redirected into drama and performance poetry, partly because there was immediate feedback. Not only did we critique each other's work, we also would give the work dramatized readings. Inevitably, people began writing poetry and drama rather than prose.

Here are two of the first poems I published. Both of them are blues. "Love" is a traditional blues piece written under the influence of Langston Hughes, and "And Black Women!" is a more modern blues, self-referential and intentionally didactic.

LOVE

less you ever been in love
you can not understand
what I mean when I say
I love my baby so hard
it sometimes make me want to cry

[untitled]

And Black women!
the wet shining beauty
brown eyed and ebony hued
you mothers, sisters, wives, lovers all
we revere you, need you/build
stronger manhoods more worthy of you
than has been our fate to be in years
recent past, cowardly living like sheep
no longer, we rise with the noble
intentions of taking you into our
arms, into our homes, into
black families (. . . this propaganda of
words will sound strange to all who
do not know or realize the worth of
our beautiful black women) perhaps,
this poem can open the eyes of some
young Afro American to the beauty
of the black girl living in his
community; we have only to look with
our eyes & quit using a foreign
myopic blue eyed aesthetic and we will
see ourselves, and love ourselves

The late sixties and early seventies were a time when Black people literally were reading and reciting poetry on street corners, on buses, in churches and temples, at rallies and demonstrations, in playgrounds and in gymnasiums. This was a time when poetry mattered and was vital, had meaning for everyone whether young or old, male or female, college educated or a high school drop-out. In that context, to be a community respected poet was nothing short of being a messenger from the spirit world, a juju man/woman. To appreciate our theoretical approach to poetry, you must understand the context.

My first year in the workshop was the key to my decision to become a professional writer. I was developing a voice as a writer and I had found a writing community—actually, I had helped create a writing community. From the beginning I served as coeditor of *Nkombo* and later, when the workshop officially became BLKARTSOUTH, I became the director.

Scene from the London production of Blk Love Song #1 *with (from left) Patrick Miller, Heather Goodman, and Doyle Richmond*

While I do not separate developing a voice from the development of the writing community, the truth is that other than Tom Dent, I had done more writing than anyone else in the workshop and it was quickly apparent. At first I was recycling stories and poems I had written while in the army as well as writing new material, but then I hit on writing a play entirely in verse. *Blk Love Song #1* became one of my most successful plays on a national and international level, even though it never played as much as did some of the other more conventional pieces I wrote such as *The Picket* and *Mama,* which was our biggest hit.

While some of the other plays were more popular and had been performed throughout the South, they had not been published. In 1974, *Blk Love Song* was selected for inclusion in the monumental work *Black Theater USA: Forty-five Plays by Black Americans, 1847–1974,* edited by James V. Hatch with Black playwright Ted Shine serving as a consultant.

The immediacy of the workshop is what made it possible for me to write as much as I did and as quickly as I did. As soon as a script was drafted, we would get on the stage and walk through it, reading it aloud. All of our workshops were open, so oftentimes there were visitors and an audience checking out how we developed the work. Although I continue to write plays, I am not even one-third as productive as I was during the FST/BLKARTSOUTH years.

The success of the poetry performances and the drama inadvertently led to neglecting the publishing outside of *Nkombo.* For us, the written word was of secondary importance and we never really concentrated on developing it the way we did performance. After all, we were performing before hundreds of people monthly. We did not publish monthly, and when we did publish it seldom reached as many people as our performances did. Of course, we were making the mistake of focusing only on the present and not thinking about the future, not thinking about documenting what we were doing as a priority. Additionally, when we did publish we added a twist to our literary magazine which intentionally added to obscuring the individual personalities of the writers in favor of presenting the flavor of the group.

We viewed *Nkombo* as the textual voice of our collective. In my introduction "Food for Thought," I wrote:

> Blk writers' words are of only three forms
> 1. protest
> 2. revolutionary
> 3. blklife
> . . . . . .
>
> —protest writing is basically explaining to somebody how human you are, enough said
>
> —revolutionary writing is up against the wall
>
> —blklife writing is what we are
>
> most of what follows is directly out of our workshops where we write w/h only the preconceived notion of being honest to our senses, there is no pretension to it being high art

One of my poems in that first publication, "BLKARTS is the magic of ju-ju," delineated the direction our words would take:

> blkarts poets are crazy weird dudes
> whose vocabulary is in the streets&in the gutters& off the walls
> & round de corner & down the halls & whose ideas is like the same
> ones that hang on the edges of buildings where ever gathering throngs
> of blkfolk have spoken about their lives, churches, barstools & jail
> cells, jail cells, empty parking lots&the balconies of old tired cineramas

Except for the very first issue—an issue which was called "Echoes from the Gumbo"—we did not use authors' names on the poems included in *Nkombo* except in the table of contents. Flipping through the book, there were only the poems, the text itself to refer to rather than a name above or beneath the text.

In performance, we not only read our own poems, but we also developed a collective style and recited each other's poetry, sometimes solo but also as a choral group.

Before long we had moved to the idea of developing poetry shows with musical accompaniment, but only as much music as we could make ourselves. I of course played percussion, but also some recorder, penny whistle, and bamboo flute, plus thumb piano and occasionally balaphone.

Intuitively, we had moved to the jazz band as a metaphor and model of our poetry work. The poetry shows were flexible in that they could be altered at a moment's notice to accommodate a given reality we faced. Additionally, we could reduce or increase the number of poems and the number of poets without violating the overall structure. As far as we were concerned, just as most people didn't know the names of all the members in a big band, they didn't need to know our names individually. The band was more important than the soloist, in fact, it was the band that provided the platform for the soloists to blow and develop—even the most novice poet could be accommodated and given room to recite at least one poem.

Here is one of the most frequently performed pieces which was orchestrated for the whole group. Even though I wrote the poem, I was not "the featured voice." Different people had different parts in solo or duo, while all of us acted as chorus and musicians. I remember one particular performance we did at the Univer-

sity of New Orleans. There was a jazz band on before us and some of the musicians hung around for our set. The drummer and vibraphone player joined us once we got started on "Black Bones," which was how we referred to the poem whose formal title was "Names, Places, Us." This poem was published in the first issue of *Nkombo.*

Late in 1969 we published five small books of poetry: *The Reluctant Rebel* by Renaldo Fernandez, *Dark Waters* by Quo Vadis Gex, *Visions from the Ghetto* by Raymond Washington, *I Want Me a Home* by Nayo Watkins, and my debut book, *The Blues Merchant.*

I did not have any one particular style of writing. Some of the pieces were blues poems; some were wild, quasi-surrealistic screamers; some were long narratives; and some were straight out promo for whatever belief system I had at the time. In reviewing the work, I was immediately struck by a poem called "The Blues (in two parts)." Periodically, I would return to this same device, writing a poem specifically about the blues which used blues images and structure.

The two long narrative poems were written under the influence of LeRoi Jones of the *Dead Lecturer* period, but even so they are still very much me. They are also written as prophesy as they are poems about being married and caring for a baby, written at a time when neither were yet a reality for me. There are a few conceits built into the narrative, the main one of which is that I refer to my "wife" by the initial "V" which was actually my first initial at the time. The "wife" in this poem is a composite of various women I had been close to at that time. These long narratives are precursors of the "sun songs," except that the "sun songs" in general are purposefully much more didactic.

NAMES, PLACES, US

Who did they kill?
What were the names of those Blacks they killed then?
No One knows no one knows
no names no places just us to witness
they are dead, killed only because their skins were Black,
we are here only because their skins were black
Who did they kill? What, where, who? Who did they kill, murder?
What?
They killed you! Who? Who dead drift now who they killed
Are you hip to the middle passage? how many of our people rest now at sea
their bones & flesh chewed & eaten by fish, abandoned to die in a turbulent sea
whipped by the frenzied hands of white masters into their places
What were the names of those Blacks they killed then
Who did they kill? What are you?
WHAT ARE YOU BLACK PEOPLE!!!!???? WHERE ARE YOU!!!!????
I often go down to the sea & stand looking out across
wondering
How many of my people rest now out there their bones eaten by fish
thrown there, in those waters from slave ships years ago
abandoned to die in a turbulent sea whipped by the hands of white masters
who were they? What were the names of those Blacks they killed then
No One knows, no one knows, they are dead, killed only because their skins were Black
One day bones will wash from the sea and rest gleaming in the sun on eastern seaboard shores
let them then try to lie to you, let them try explaining where those bones come from
those bones, bones of our ancestors, dead, killed, murdered
nameless Black people, countless Black people we don't even know now
Black bones from the sea, Black bones
Bones Black bones washed upon the shore, washed upon the sand
Black bones resting in the sand from the sea, no home, no name, just bones
Legs & arms, large, small bones, Black bones Black bones thrown up from the sea
Black bones from the sea, Black bones
And when I die throw me too into that sea facing toward Black Africa
Let fish eat my hair, and my eyes, and my Black flesh
Let me go home again and if not home at least to the bottom
where I know others rest
Let me join others like me dead at the bottom
BLACK FOREVER MORE!!!!!!

THE BLUES

(in two parts)

I

Our best singers
can't really sing
you take like otis redding
that nigger never could sing
in fact I believe he only knew
maybe two notes at the most
& a couple of
phrases/no melody
strictly atonal stuff
i mean like what does
yes are am mean
or even na-na-na
what's da matter baby
mr. redding you is singing
like you is in a hurry or
something, maybe you
got to go to the bathroom
& now you take that
lil ugly no singing nigger
James brown
now he can dance his
ass off, ain't no
doubt bout that
but he can't sing
not a lick &
talkin bout a
lickin stick
somebody need to
beat him all upside
his haid w/h his own
damn lickin stick
& that band
he got, they don't know
nothin but one song
that's how come
they got to have
two drummers
them two dudes is suppose
to be among the best
we got/black
people we gon have to do better
or shut our mouth
cause I mean
what is mother popcorn and
for sho dum-dum de-de de-dum-dum
ain't no song

II

The blues is not song
it is singing
no voice
is needed
only the knowledge
the blues is not
not notes
it is feeling
it is not death
it is being
it is not submission
it is existing
you take the ing
it is the ing of th-ings
whether it be
laugh-ing or dy-ing
swing-ing or hang-ing
from a tree
sometimes it be
hurting so bad
when you is singing
or feeling the blues
till you just have to
drop the g trying
to e-eeee-eeee-asssssse
on in

FOR MY WIFE WHEN I DO THAT THING

1.

my blk girl
got out into the clearing somehow
looked out past the ocean's horizon into the sky
& it took her about
ten minutes to discover
it was blues/she returns
skipping/dancing
smiling in my stupid face
my face is ragged/toothy
sort of smile w/h big lips
through my beard
women are lovely & is
why they bear children in
stead of we men

2.

        is it still June
V. baby/pass me a color
you saw today & save
my tenderness w/h your lovely
brown fingers on my face
/she showed me a sea-shell
that was red/black inside & green
pretty—i would have passed
it by/in fact I wouldn't
even have been wading out into
the blue green water lapping
up over the seawall like she
was holding her dress folded above her knees
smiling back at me
& dodging small fishes

3.

she came home yesterday from work
tired & sleepy just before I did
like about fifteen minutes
& dinner was still on the table
". . . take me to the lake
tomorrow, huh, please . . ."
falling about my shoulders w/h her long arms
& a kiss on the ear
she fell into my lap & told me
about the devils she worked w/h
got up ironed, washed/i dried
the pieces of plastic that replace
china in our lives—the
apartment is so small on sunny days
you seem to always be running
into blocks of heat/at evening times
i believe they call it dusk
the sun sits on the funeral parlor's roof in
  back of us
on rainy days it can be nice to
lay around/she is quiet like
morns when we call each other in
sick for work & loll about in
each other's arms & discuss
plans for getting up to eat
orange juice & cheese

4.

we got up early sunday
& got into the volkswagen
which had sat cooling all night
& like the lake is only 5
miles from us

5.

on the highway going further out
leaving behind the seawall & concrete beaches
i stilled the wheel w/h my elbows
trying to light a cigar
which she eventually lit for me
nearly choking twice on her laughter
on the beach's empty stretch
we had no food & sat down in the sand
& planned for a family of three

6.

my baby's eyes are big & brown
big & brown & shiny
that look at me wide open
when I am sweet to her
like bringing home a bag of
big purple plums from on my way from work
or rub her back at night
before she sleeps or be
alone w/h her
or/
        i kiss her
lips once, twice & again & again
thanking her for keeping my life
soft in her heart

7.

we love each other
& that is good
i look at her sometimes I
tell her never let her bush
grow longer/i go to work
& come home
not yet brave enough to
risk a child
        weak, weak,
weak

8.

running the risk of injury
i sat up alnight
yesterday thinking of two suitable
names, one for a girl & the other
a boy/she made me laugh, she says
"what if we have twins"
let them be, let them be
my wife & I are both 23 year old
blk folk

FOR MY CHILD WHEN I DO THAT THING

1.
my little girl's name is winnie
we call her winnie la roo
who jump happy like a kangaroo
              i use to read the papers
              regularly/the price of peaches
              has gone up steadily
              what do you want me to do/
              be
              i scowl at my wife
              alnight sometimes combing her hair
              in the mirror small tufts
              coming out in the big wide tooth ivory
              of her african comb
              turn to the wall stroking my beard
the car ran out of gas
i sat there & hit the steering wheel a few licks
"that won't do any good . . ."
it's bad enough she makes sense
talking softly to me w/h winnie wrapped
in a blanket in her arms
              i rolled the window down &
              hollered out it & then turned around
              & looked at her & she had her hand
              on my arm
              i called my scream back
              the car seemed too small opening the
              door
              letting my sandal drag against the
              concrete
              right on the white line/i had to push
              it to the side
              out of the way of bus traffic

2.
V. must of been pregnant about twenty months
trying to play like her big belly wasn't hampering
   her
i'd catch her sometimes smiling to herself holding
   her stomach
              with her hands
once in bed I laid my head on her & heard
   winnie moving around
when it came time to go I had to call a cab
   cause she was too
big to get in the volkswagen
it was kind of dopey living w/h a pregnant
   woman
i use to could cook, winnie & V. came home to
   our first steak
dinner at home
V. breast-fed winnie & I stood around looking
   helpless

3.
i came home friday winnie was sitting on the
   floor
on a bunch of newspaper mushy spinach
all over her
V. sitting on the floor supposedly feeding winnie
   her dinner,
              mine was on the table
they had smothered liver & carrots I went down
   the street to a
              local bar & had a quart of beer
when I got back V. was giving winnie a bath
"if you want to eat now I'll fix your dinner"

4.
went to my mother's house
& sat w/h an orange pop resting on
my knee covered w/h a white, blue bordered
   paper napkin
my wife sits looking at stupid drug store pictures
on the chartreuse walls: "i like that one"
the technique is french impressionism
but it looks like it was done w/h a raggedy
   handkerchief
momma pulled me to the side to ask whose idea
   it was to
              cut winnie's hair short like it is
"Mine!"/
              i ain't got to come here to fight
              about the way my daughter's hair is
              on her head

5.
went out of
town last week
for a conference
forgot to bring even a postcard back
when I got back V. was at work
so I went round to momma's & picked up winnie
& came back & had to change her diaper
& tried to feed her but she wouldn't eat
i sat in the doorway w/h winnie in my arms
looking out across the open court filthy w/h trash
& made up poems about little blk children
   playing stick
              ball & tag in an apartment house courtyard
the mailman came w/h bills & advertisements
winnie'll be sixteen months next week
sixteen months shaking my head

In December of 1969, I wrote in the introduction to the volume 2, number 4 issue of *Nkombo:*

> September found us performing for some of the students of Southern University in Baton Rouge, Louisiana. There, as in most other places, we were performing before people who were experiencing a Black poetry show for the first time in their lives. Many times our frankness and willingness to discuss on stage many things that some Negroes dread to even think about seemingly shocked them. Often they reacted hesitantly as we performed; wanting to laugh at times but stifling it, wanting to scream but clamping their jaws shut. However, after the show, invariably they came forward to tell us that they enjoyed our work. And it was most often at the colleges where we found the more inhibited audiences. During our community performances the audiences never left any doubt as to how they felt about the shows.

Every performance led to a greater confidence and also greater insight. Soon we were doing what we called "sets," i.e., poetry shows which were thematically organized, choreographed, and highly musical. We even developed a few plays which consisted of both poetry and dialogue. Within a two-year period we were inspiring artistic developments all over the South, most notably in Houston, Texas, and Miami, Florida.

Another factor affecting our development as both writers and performers was that Tom Dent was introducing us to cultural workers everywhere we went. Some of these people, like Worth Long, were former "SNICK" (SNCC/Student National Coordinating Committee) workers. Others were just people who loved the Black arts. Most important of all, some of the people were cultural workers right at home in New Orleans whom most of us simply didn't know, didn't know about, and didn't initially understand how important they were. These included people like the poet Octave Lilly and above all the musician Danny Barker.

Danny Barker "above all" because he was a genuine African American griot. Not only was he a musician and composer, storyteller and entertainer, bandleader (he was almost singlehandedly responsible for the reemergence of the brass bands among young Blacks in New

Orleans), but Danny Barker was also a writer. He wrote short stories, character sketches, autobiography and history. Had not Tom understood the importance of hooking us up with people like Danny, I'm certain that our work would not have been as grounded in the community nor as lasting as much of it is.

Almost all of our attention was given to performing for our community and publishing our own work which we sold at our readings. We simply were not into sending our work around for others to publish. We knew who our audience was and how to reach them, and beyond our immediate audience we also knew how to publish ourselves. BLKARTSOUTH was a tremendous development vehicle but it also, paradoxically, led us away from interacting with the rest of the country outside of the South.

Occasionally, we would break through, but even then, we generally did so as a workshop rather than as individual poets. The best example of this is our inclusion in *New Black Voices,* an anthology edited by Abraham Chapman which is still used in college courses. We had a section in that anthology because the editor understood what we were trying to do as a collective. The poets were Issac J. Black, Renaldo Fernandez, Kush (Tom Dent), Nayo (Barbara Malcolm, who continues to write under the name Nayo Barbara Watkins), John O'Neal, Raymond Washington, and myself.

Here is one of the selections included in that anthology. It is one of my humorous poems which proved to be very popular.

[untitled]

whi/te boys gone
to the moon
plantin flags & stuff
why you boys goin
to the moon
dont yall think
yall done fucked up enuf
without messing
with somebody else's world

in the beginning
it was africa
you just wanted to see
you said
& once having seen
commenced to fucking up

open up them china gates

& let's hunt tigers in india

you whi/te boys sho nuff likes
what ever anybody else has
all ways got to be
digging in somebody's bag
always got to be plantin flags & stuff

whi/te boys done gone
to the moon
just like they come here
talking bout it's a
great adventure & we is
the first ones here
& plantin flags

whi/te boys gone to the moon
whi/te boys done gone to the moon
sho hope them lil brothers up there
dont show um how
to plant corn

In addition to the poetry, Chapman chose to include "BLKARTSOUTH/get on up!," an essay/manifesto I wrote, the opening half of which piece is a complete summary of our intentions (see pp. 206–207).

The other major exception to the trend of a low national profile was our inclusion in *Negro Digest/Black World,* edited by Hoyt Fuller. We were always included in the annual Black Theatre roundups, even though, as Tom pointed out to me, we often had to write about the theater scene in the South ourselves because no one came down from New York or Chicago to write about what was going on. Tom and I would take turns writing the annual roundup. But even so, this was more attention than we got from any other source outside the South.

As one of the most developed "writers" in the workshop, I published regularly, but not as a poet. In 1971 I won *Black World*'s first Richard Wright Award for excellence in criticism. Except for one of my plays, *The Destruction of the American Stage,* almost everything published was either directly related to our theater work or were political essays and cultural critiques. Of all the people in the workshop, only Lloyd Medley had a poem published in *Black World*. Moreover, I don't ever remember submitting any poetry to them.

During the time I was writing this essay, I ran into Lloyd Medley in the post office. We had not seen each other in literally over a year. I told him about what I was working on and the reference to his poem. He reminded me that the poem had won a first place award for a first poem published by a new writer. Before I could tell him the thrust of my reference, he went on to echo my sentiments: what we were doing was as strong as, if not stronger than, many of the other writers, but we weren't in New York or on the West Coast. Moreover, our emphasis was on reading to audiences, reaching people, and Lloyd felt that was better than publishing. Although we both recognized that had we published more, we would have received far more recognition, achieving "fame" was really not our aim.

This may seem unbelievable, but the fact is we were happy doing what we were doing. We were traveling throughout the South. We were performing. We were publishing our own work. We were influencing others. And we were young. What more was there? Also significant was our relationship to our community. Although we certainly wanted our work to be entertaining, we avoided like the plague simply being "entertainment." Always, for us, there needed to be relevance. Invariably, we challenged our audiences and critiqued "Negro" ways of thinking/acting. Our humor and sarcasm was withering. But there was also a great deal of warmth in what we did, and an overwhelming love for our people which was reflected in our love for each other. Again, because we came from New Orleans, we were a bit distrustful of a unity based on uniformity. We preferred the concept of a gumbo composed of diverse elements.

Our orientation was to include everybody in the pot and not to exclude someone just because they were of a different persuasion or had different thoughts than some of us did. This was not always easy, but it served us well. For example, I remember when some of us became Muslims. Even though most of us changed our names—(in 1970 at one of the first Kwanzaa celebrations in New Orleans, I had taken the Swahili name Kalamu ya Salaam, which means "pen of peace")—some of us never became converts to any particular religion or any particular political organization. What we wanted to be was relevant. Relevant to the people in our community: to the kids and to the elders, to the working class and to the daughters and sons of the working class attending college, many of them the first in their families to do so.

Philosophically, our workshop covered a wide range of opinions and beliefs and we tried our best to express the widest degree of tolerance. Can you imagine that within one poetry group we had practicing Catholics and practicing Black Muslims? Moreover, because we were from New Orleans, our skin hues, social/religious backgrounds, and individual expressions covered a very broad spectrum. One of our members had naturally blonde hair and blue eyes. Undoubtedly our collective's obvious broad spectrum of hues contributed to our concept of Blackness which stressed consciousness and culture much more than race.

My point here, and our point then, was to contextualize our artistic work. Whereas many, many artists are extremely uncomfortable with this sort of contextualization, the process was a spur to our development. I say "our" because not only I, but a number of other writers and theater people (including Tom Dent, Nayo Watkins who is in North Carolina now, Chakula cha Jua who is the head of one of the oldest continuing Black theater companies in New Orleans, Johnetta Barras who is a journalist in Washington, D.C., at the *Washington Times,* and Quo Vadis Gex Breaux who continues to write in our hometown of New Orleans) have testified to the value of what we achieved, attempted, and learned from our experiences in Free Southern Theater.

Two other important points. One, we never believed that everybody had to do the kind of theater we did. Ours was a voluntary commitment and, as poet Mari Evans pointed out in an important article first published in *Black World,* those who volunteer are not forced to parrot any particular line. They choose to believe and create out of their beliefs and experiences.

The second important point is that this view does not ipso facto lead to a lessening of artistic development in terms of techniques. Certainly no one would argue that Lorraine Hansberry wrote "propaganda" or parroted a particular political line, or that she did not write well. She wrote exceedingly well, nevertheless, she also believed in the social function of art. "I persist in the simple view that all art is ultimately social: that which agitates and that which prepares the mind for slumber. The writer is deceived who thinks that he has some other choice. The question is not whether one will make a social statement in one's work—but only *what* the statement will

say, for if it says anything at all, it will be social."

In the final analysis I saw myself as an artist, a writer, a dramatist, a performer, but also as an active participant in the liberation struggle. I saw no separation between the two, indeed, my whole professional life has been aimed at merging the two so that they are not only inseparable but also each developed to its most effective pitch.

While working at FST/BLKARTSOUTH, I had decided. I would be a writer, a professional writer. Later I expanded that vocation to include being a producer, mainly because a lot of the artwork I desired to create or assist in creating, the artwork I desired to experience and wanted to share with others, much of that work didn't exist and needed a midwife if it was to be born. Here again, the example of Langston Hughes impelled me forward without hesitation, whatever was missing I just had to figure out a way to create it. That was my task. My obligation as an artist was to create—and whatever necessary ingredients for creation that were missing, well, I would just have to marshal them by whatever means necessary.

five. a decade of development

My goal is to uplift people, as much as I can. To inspire them to realize more and more of their capacities for living meaningful lives.

—*John William Coltrane*

By the time *Hofu ni kwenu* ("my fear is for you"), my second poetry book, appeared in 1973, some of the BLKARTSOUTH crew had started Ahidiana, an activist oriented collective. Free Southern Theater closed down for a lack of funds. Due to an argument between John O'Neal, one of the FST founders, and some of us from the workshop, BLKARTSOUTH split off on its own.

Ahidiana ran an alternative school for preschool through third-grade aged children—and we always made sure that kids from working-class backgrounds were the majority of students. We were not interested in operating a little "private academy" populated mainly by the children of Black professionals.

BLKARTSOUTH/get on up!

BLKARTSOUTH started as a community writing and acting workshop under the direction of Tom Dent and Robert "Big Daddy" Costley. The Free Southern Theater had been disbanded for the year and they were the only two left in New O. (our name for New Orleans, Louisiana) to continue on the work of the theater. By that certain inventive process that Black people are famous for possessing, the community workshop grew into BLKARTSOUTH without the aid of funds, star attractions, immense programming, or anything else that is usually thought of as a prerequisite to developing a theater group. We started in the summer of '68 and by October of the same year we made a vow that we would publish and perform our original material exclusively. Within a year we were performing poetry shows and one-act plays throughout the South; plays and poetry we had written, arranged, directed, and produced. In December of '68 (note: this is a mistake, it was actually 1969), *Nkombo* celebrated its anniversary with a one-hundred page offset edition that included drawings, poetry, prose, fiction, and drama. From the very beginning we were attempting to actualize our purpose which was to develop and perform new/original literary and theatrical material for Black people.

We go deeper now with our purposes. We say that our art is aimed toward building the nation. A nation for Black people. We say that not only do we have to be new/original but that we have to be of some use/have some meaning to Black people in the struggle for liberation. And we mean it. Since we do not operate in a vacuum our motion has created friction and heat. In fact we've burned up some people. But we keep on keepin on just like Shine. BLKARTSOUTH is a whole lot of us striving toward the nation.

What we do, however, ain't mind lunges at paper targets. Our work is instead real spear movements we learned by putting our work out there. Just like the old/our folks used to wash clothes and then hang um out in the sun to dry. Hang um out where every/anybody could see how clean (or unclean) they were. The writing you *see* ain't academic (or un, or anti-academic either) but is some real stuff that's been hanging out in the sun. We are the results of doing/being our poems and stuff. The writing you *see* is not all the writing we are because you ain't seen nothing until you've *heard* us. That's important. That aura of hearing, feeling, seeing; experiencing this kind of writing. Our conclusions are drawn from our experiences and then maybe put down in books. Be aware of that. Be aware that the organization you are reading about is a living, performing group that produces its own material and that the production/performance of this material is an intentional fusing of technique, content, style, and ideology that necessarily gives a total shape to the whole of our work which cannot be realized or appreciated just by reading our writing in books. This does not mean that there is little attention paid to "literary" values per se, rather it means that as far as we are concerned just being "literary" is not and has never been sufficient.

We feel that what we're doing is a relatively new thing in our environment. Our molds aren't quite set yet. Like jazz, what we're doing is constantly moving; the changing same. Right now all we're trying to do is get our work out there and be honest about the things we put out. Maybe two or three years from now we'll be able to set down some standards to judge our work by (real standards and not personal considerations, likes and dislikes, theorizing from "one-eyed" critics). Like what standard was Louis Armstrong blowing by other than what he felt? We can tell now but who could have told then? Maybe not even Satchmo himself. The whole problem centers around the fact that critics invariably want to judge Black artists at their first note. They are afraid to allow the BLKARTS to grow. It took Black music less than seventy years to go from Buddy Bolden to Coltrane and beyond. So just as jazz grew, Black writing is going to grow, grow straight from the gutters, from the streets, the people. Grow from our people, which is where Louis Armstrong came from with his trumpet playing, his eye opening innovations. He got it all from a culture that accepted, emphasized and respected an African inspired, African-American heritage of music making. We as writers have a similar heritage we must tap, a spoken, verbal art that runs deep and long all the way back to the homeland. Slave narratives, field hollers, shouts, hard luck stories, animal tales, everything. A real heritage we have been taught to ignore and belittle, a heritage we must get next to or be like a tree without roots. We must grow to know this heritage and do as it advises us: Sing about what we are in a good strong voice and not get caught up in trying to imitate others or denying the worth of what we are. Sing our own songs.

We at *Nkombo* say that our goal is not to put out a magazine full of "little poetic masterpieces," but rather to publish a journal that will serve as an adequate medium of expression for Black artists of the South. We feel that Black writers are ignored (and as a result stunted in their growth) by the traditional publishers both Black, such as they be, and white. Many critics insist that there is very little "quality" Black writing available as an explanation for this exclusion. But the truth is that there is too little Black writing available period, "quality" or not. And furthermore there will never be a large body of so-called "quality" Black writing until there is an even larger grouping of Black writing published irregardless of "quality"; a larger grouping that is written to reach and take in Black people rather than to live up to some vague flat cultured concept of "quality." That sounds cold, defensive, and anti-good literature but it's true. It's an unbelievable trip to think that the absence of quality is the cause for the exclusion of Black writers when there is so much garbage being dumped on the heads of our people by white publishers. Check it out for yourself. Go to any local bookstand or drugstore and pick out what you consider to be quality writing. After you've done that, look at all the junk that's left. Quality??? Not hardly. And that's what we're out to change. Black writers are not published simply because the publishing industry is for the most part white and doesn't want to or doesn't know how to publish Black writing (that's not meant as a criticism but rather as a realistic assessment of fact and intentions; like we ain't out to publish white writers either). Our policy is that those Black writers who live in our area and participate in our workshops *will* be published, period! We are intent on making sure that any writer who is interested in writing will be able to get at least one of his pieces published in *Nkombo*. The future will decide what is of "quality." Let that be taken in, let it remain; throw the rest away.

We've been around for three years now darting in and out of the consciousness of Black people in the South and elsewhere. We feel like we ain't even off the ground yet, still just pecking away at this eggshell environment. But as soon as we break out of this straightjacket society/mind condition . . . we movin on up! We want to move, got to get away. Our art is functional art that's going to help all us Black people find ways to fly. We trying to get Black people together so that we can all consciously make that great migration east. To quote brother Kush (tom dent), "Anyway, our poetry, the beautiful thing about it has to do with making connections with, talking to, grooving with blk people, not with 'poetry' or 'great writing' or being a literary giant, or an ideological father, or any such shit as that. Just making connections giving blk people something they can value and use. This is what we mean by functional writing." If somebody can learn something from it, or it draws Black people closer together, then our writing has done its do.

We also had a food co-op to buy fresh fruit and vegetables. We had a small garden. We operated a bookstore and owned and operated a press. We brought speakers and activists (such as Amiri Baraka, John Henrik Clarke, Mari Evans, Yusef ben Jochannan, Maulana Ron Karenga, Haki Madhubuti, Sonia Sanchez, Owusu Saudaki, and Sweet Honey in the Rock) to the New Orleans community. And finally, we organized around community issues and around Kwanzaa activities.

Our organizing work included demonstrations against apartheid and police brutality, as well as challenges to the mainstream media based on Federal Communication Commission-mandated community access issues (which the Republicans dismantled as soon as they got in control at the federal level). Our organizing also included annual Black Women's Conferences, which attracted attendees from around the country.

Our experiences in FST/BLKARTSOUTH helped us understand how to organize and how to dramatize issues. Our experiences as artists raised the qualitative appearance of our political presentations to a very high level. Concomitantly, the political issues sharpened my artistic work. My work became both more explicit and more specific. Even though we had moved past simplistic sloganeering, I still had a lot to learn about writing poetry. Ahidiana was my graduate program.

Here are two poems which exemplify the merging of the artistic and the political. The first is a poem in support of the political prisoner Dessie Woods who was imprisoned for killing a White man who attempted to rape her. She never denied the shooting. This was one of the favorite performance pieces. It is an ironic commentary written in the feminine voice, a technique which I had developed not as a gimmick but rather as a way of making a statement not only about whatever particular issue the poem dealt with but also a statement about how I felt revolutionary male writers should be addressing issues and supporting the feminist anti-sexist struggle. Most often when we performed these type of poems, either my wife, Tayari kwa Salaam, or Shawishi St. Julien voiced the poem.

The second poem is a defense of Ntozake Shange which was published in an issue of Al Young and Ishmael Reed's *Quilt* magazine. This poem was written and published during the backlash against Ntozake Shange that many males were whipping up over "Colored Girls." This was the kind of piece that put me at odds with some of my fellow male writers. That was OK with me; in fact, I enjoyed the confrontation.

We in Ahidiana believed that confrontation of contradictions among our people was healthy as long as the contradictions were debated and hopefully resolved without resorting to violence among ourselves. I was aware, however, that in certain circles this piece amounted to "fighting words."

HIWAY BLUES

(for Dessie Woods)

Ain't it enough
he think he own
these hot blacktop hiways,
them east eight acres,
that red Chevy pick up
with the dumb bumper stickers
and big wide heavy rubber tires,
two sho nuff ugly brown bloodhounds
and a big tan&white german shepherd
who evil and got yellow teeth?

Ain't it enough
he got a couple a kids to beat on,
a wife who was a high school
    cheerleader,
a brother who is a doctor,
a cousin with a hardware store,
a divorced sister with dyed hair,
a collection of Hustler magazines
dating back to the beginning,
partial sight in his left eye,
gray hairs growing out his ear,
a sun scorched leathery neck that's
    cracking,
a rolling limp in his bow legged walk,
and a couple of cases of beer in the
    closet?

Ain't it enough
he got all that
without having to mess
with me?

Yeah, I shot the
motherfucker!

NTOZAKE SHANGE

(to those who wish she would shut up)

I.
if yr life had
happened to a man, the
whole world would know abt it,
but you a big legged woman
breaking the monopoly of male writers
talking bold about what has kept
you from walking off the ledge of life
and what drove you out the window
in the first place, about to
silently hit the sky falling
like a dropped drum stick
during the middle of the big number

II.
talk abt yrself
yr blkwomanself/neo-african
in the midst of a land caught up in
worshipping twentieth century minstrels
talk about womanness and exaltations
and never uttering the lie about being
sorry not to be born a boy, talk
like you think, like you feel,
like you move through decaying urban america
pass fashions, kitchen recipes, modern romances
and mythical holy vaginal orgasms

talk like our moses spake
in the middle of headin' north night
pressing a slack-jawed man who
couldn't keep his pants dry:
"once we get started, ain't no turning
back!"

talk like that lil sister, can't
remember her name, who shot hot
breath all up in a white boy's face
and double dared him to fuck with her
in the hallway, in class, after school, on
the bus or any other goddamn time, back in
1958, in one of *their* schools when,
at the time, you did good just
to stay proudly black and defiantly sane

talk like you an oracle
bearing witness to changing times
or the sphinx sitting on the secret
in the desert, not only was you blk
but, yes, possibly you were woman
when napoleon saw that he barked
the order for his battery
of cannons to commence
and left part of your nose,
and a piece of lip
pulverized and floating
a dusty cloud toward the nile

talk that talk
when the truth is revealed to the
light, the shysters will all scream
'taint fair, they'll cry
foul, say yo strikes smokin
clean down the middle are misses,
say you high, or low, or wide,
or you got spit on the ball,
you see you just ain't allowed
on the mound and there you
are talking like you ain't
never heard of being
quiet and pretty in the bleachers

talk Shange, talk
like a lioness putting
her jaw around a jackass' throat

III.
to some men
the sound of blkwomansong
is noise

but no matter,
many of us are dancing anyway
and in time most all of us will be waving
red bandannas and shouting: "amen,
amen, sister, amen"

well.
well.

Ahidiana was a product of its time. Today there is no similar Pan-African movement, no similar Black liberation struggle in the '90s. Yes, there is the Afro-centric movement, but that movement is far from community based. The majority of the Afro-centricity leadership is based on college campuses, and mainly predominately mainstream campuses at that. While I hear and understand a lot of the theory, the practice is not community rooted and community dependent. Nor is this movement linked to international struggles, which was another driving force supporting and encouraging our efforts in the early seventies.

Hofu was the first book produced by Ahidiana and it reflected our activist orientation. We described it as "A collection of essays and poetry written by Kalamu ya Salaam which explains and defines the natural functions of men and women and the relationship between men and women." From *Hofu* on, every poetry book I wrote during the Ahidiana years came out of specific social contexts and was meant to influence our community at large and to directly affect those of us engaged in the Black liberation struggle.

Those who have never volunteered to be a cultural guerrilla at war with the dominant and dominating culture probably cannot understand both the exhilaration and the freedom involved in creating socially committed literature.

The exhilaration is perhaps more obvious than the freedom. It is both humbling and uplifting to present your poetry and witness people react in honest and deep-felt ways: to see people laugh and, sometimes, even cry; to have people come up to you, their eyes shining about how your work helped them make it through the semester, through a marital dispute, while in jail, while in the army, etc.; to hear people chant your poems back to you, hear them clap and pat their feet as the audience participates; to hear them shout out to you, "teach," "right on"; to be there at the creation of a new consciousness, that is exhilarating, an exhilaration unknown to the literary poet whose work is appreciated in solitude. For here we have the circle completed, the feedback loop is immediate. Here we have the actualization of one of the cardinal tenets of the Black aesthetic: immediate "call and response."

The calabash of community is reconstructed, the circle is unbroken. At the deepest level one must ask what is art without an audience? Furthermore, if audience is necessary for art to exist, then should not the involvement of the audience be as timely as possible? Moreover, the audience responding not only exhilarated us, it pushed us to produce more and better art, art that was cleaner, leaner, and more pure in its connection with the audience.

No matter what "thought" we had, the test was to find a way to communicate it. How to convey the concept of dialectics in a poetry reading at a community center, on a playground, to preschoolers, at the college campus. Our audiences were wherever our people were, and our challenge was to reach all of them. Of course this required crafting and composing different poems for different segments of the community, and also required us to expand the general conception of poetry, but, as we became better and better at it, we perceived each challenge not as a problem but rather as an opportunity. This was an exhilarating time.

The freedom of it is less obvious but no less real. Essentially it boils down to the fact that we had no masters. We had broken off the plantation of literary poetry and had no maps, no set destination, no preordained models to which we had to adhere.

We had to be truly creative. We had to improvise. Our freedom was precisely that we could use any and everything we wanted to in whatever way we wanted to.

Some of us wrote in rhyme, others of us didn't. Some of us had a college education and had been exposed to all kinds of literature, others of us were people with a deficient public school education (when integration came, the quality of education which we had received at schools like Phillis Wheatley and Rivers Frederick suffered a serious decline). Some of us were writing in dialect, others of us weren't. But again, the principles of the Black aesthetic guided us: it's not what you do but the way that you do it.

Moreover, because our people are human beings who represent the broadest spectrum of emotions and intellectual proclivities of any community in the United States, there was always an audience for almost any style of poetry we wanted to write. Plus we had numerous poetic examples to draw on within our own culture: from the jazzy surrealism of Bob

Wife, Tayari kwa Salaam, teaching at Ahidiana Work/Study Center

Kaufman (who was from New Orleans), to the formalism of Robert Hayden, from the hip street talk of Don L. Lee/Haki Madhubuti and Sonia Sanchez to the literary arcaneness of Melvin Tolson and the classical rigor of Gwendolyn Brooks—it was all there for us.

Sonia would be killing with her signifying pieces one minute and kissing us with the awe-inspiring quiet of a haiku the next. Baraka could make us scream out loud or send us scurrying to a dictionary to figure out what he was talking about. And that was just on the creation side.

On the audience side, the people who came out to hear us were so hip. Some of them knew more poetry than we did. They would give us tips. Tell us about poets, some of them locals whom we had never heard of and whom we needed to know. Whatever idea we dropped, usually there was somebody in the audience who would pick up on it and afterwards want to rap about "that thing you said, well, you know I was thinking . . ."

In our audiences you might find a person who had ardently studied Shakespeare sitting next to a barroom bard for whom toasting, signifying, and reciting his own version of "Shine" was the highest form of poetry. Our task was to reach both of them, to feel free to draw on both of their experiences, and to use all of that and more of that in everything we did.

For us, being Black was a blessing. As Americans we could learn from, and if we chose (which few in our collective did), we could even emulate the mainstream literary world, and, at the same time, as African Americans we could draw on a rich culture of orature that the literary mainstream knew little, if anything, about. Moreover, we also had our music (the only indigenous American contribution to world culture) and our people's musical usage of English to draw on. We had so much, so much.

In addition to our abundance of influences and the dual traditions we had to draw on, we also had the seventies atmosphere of revolutionary freedom. In our poetry everything was permissible. There were no sacred cows. We could quote anyone we wanted to, or quote no one. We could use techniques from traditional poetry or invent techniques based on music. With so much happening daily around us, there was no excuse not to write.

In this context work just poured out of me. I would write about everything: hanging my foot out the window after making love, a demonstration against police brutality, hair styles, dance styles, Pan-Afrikanism, sexism. The window was throwed up high and, fortunately, by the seventies I had been writing for over a decade so I had a degree of facility that comes from practice, practice, and more practice—plus, I had an audience.

I was writing for the members of Ahidiana: I wrote wedding poems, praise poems, poems and songs for our kids who were now appearing with regularity. I was writing for the community: all kinds of demonstrations were happening and a rally wasn't a rally until at least one poet was called upon to give some "poetic inspiration." All kinds of Black journals were popping up and there was always a need for a cogent and timely or topical poem. I was also writing for myself.

As I worked out ideas, theories, and understandings of whatever I was experiencing or grappling with, I would know I had reached a degree of understanding when I could put it in a poem and communicate it to others. Eventually I called these poems "sun songs" because they were partly sermons delivered in the style of Baptist preachers, and partly because they invariably relied heavily on musical motifs, musical metaphors, and musical organizational methodologies and techniques. I would beat on podiums, stomp on floors. Sing. Shout. Jump up and down. Dance. After all I was a poet.

If I couldn't express myself in poetry, it just meant that whatever I was trying to express was unclear in my own mind, or else what I was thinking was out of phase with what I was feeling. In that sense my poetry was very, very private in its origins and orientation at the same time that it was public in its expression. That was the dialectic that made the most sense to me.

After *Hofu* came *Pamoja tutashinda* ("together we will win") in 1973, *Ibura* in 1976, *Revolutionary Love* in 1978, and *Iron Flowers* in 1979.

Those were the books of poetry written during the decade of my Ahidiana years. I also co-wrote two children's books with my wife, Tayari kwa Salaam, and *Our Women Keep Our Skies,* a collection of essays "In support of the struggle to smash sexism and develop women." *Skies* included three poems, two of which became among my most popular poems.

Hofu will always be fondly remembered. It was my first poetry book that was more than just poetry. The cover was a symbolic piece created specifically for the book. Inside we had symbols as well as text. We also mixed essays with poetry. And the poems included both tender and tough pieces. The book was printed in green ink on ivory stock. It set the tone for all the other Ahidiana publications which followed.

You could see growth happening in this book, but you could also see glaring blemishes, particularly a vehement strain of homophobia which Ahidiana would directly tackle within the next four or five years. I know that some people say that "homophobia" was part of the times, but there is no need to hide from the truth. On that account we were backward. Other poems and essays which tackle homophobia head-on would follow over the next few years, and thusly demonstrate through both criticism and self-criticism that regardless of where we started from, we kept on developing.

In 1973 we were what I would now call classic Black nationalists. Even though we thought we were being progressive, our position on the women's question was suspect. That too would change over the next couple of years. *Hofu* would have been stronger artistically, if I had been more progressive politically. The feeling was there, the ideas were lagging behind.

Hofu was then both experimental and limited, but it was an attempt to move past status quo examples of what a poetry book should be like.

Here are two selections which demonstrate where we were at in 1973. The first piece, "Lament," is written in the feminine voice and actually had been written somewhere between 1967 and 1968; it was published in the first issue of *Nkombo* and, because of its subject matter, I chose to include it in *Hofu.* Audiences used to get really, really quiet when we did this one.

The second, "Inspiration," is an example of some of the most progressive thoughts cohabiting with some of the most regressive. I used both the word and the image "faggot" in a negative sense. In later years, I would continue using the poem but substituted the word "freak." Also, in performance this poem was built on a chain gang chant, "Be My Woman," which Nina Simone also used a variation of in her song "Be My Husband." The chant metamorphosed into a Curtis Mayfield-like ballad, "Love a Good Woman" and ended on a Pharoah Sanders tip. Of course the music is not on the page, but this is an example of how I wrote poems which were designed to be sung, as well as spoken, lyrics.

LAMENT

/for black men everywhere/

when
   will our men be men
      not of fear and trembling
      feeding dark soil with their own
   dark blood or
      crying yes sirs and halting steps
   of broken airs about
   themselves
but men:
   simply able to love their lives
   as men are said to do?
God can you possibly
   replenish that lost seed
   who were once lovely African chieftains,
      princes and such, loving
      their queens
Can pride be restored
or must they suffer forever
attempting a shield of their
impotence from our knowing eyes.

In January of 1973 Ahidiana published my third book of poetry, *Pamoja tutashinda* ("together we will win"). In advertisements for *Pamoja* we described it as "A collection of political poems with an introductory essay by Kalamu ya Salaam which is a beginning projection of the ideology of Pan-Afrikan Nationalism." This was the most didactic of all the books. Strictly an organizing and conscious-raising tool. One of the poems, "give a speech/talkin abt 'da problem,'" is five typeset pages long in nine-point type. The five-part poem was read at many a rally.

INSPIRATION

The Flower in the House,
The Air We Black Men Breathe

love a good woman
love a good woman
for all the time there is
for all the life there is
for all the best we are
love a good woman
love a woman
love love a good woman
in sunshine, in rain, place
yr house in order, in
balanced on the tear drop of her happiness
on the hair back from her geled* head
on the soft steps she makes
moving toward you being the flower in the
   house
yr oxygen, yr gettin up fuel
yr no nonsense and strength to do what you
   got to do
the love of a good woman
loving you love a good woman
yr choice, companion and soul mate,
yr maker really, if you be man
then woman is yr maker, yr woman is yr
   maker
yr black woman is yr creator, woman
is what you should love yr good woman
is what you need yr good woman to love, to
   live
yr pleasant voice in the evening and smiles in
   yr morning
yr soft fingers touch on yr chest calling you
   king
calling you man, calling you god
you god the giver come on now love yr good
   woman
she creator the maker, love yr good woman
no man makes himself
woman makes man and love
love a good woman

sister i am incomplete
without you, i am vessel full
of holes, i am spirit begging
substance, i am shadow with
out form, i am baby wait
ing to be born, i am that faggot
walking down the street
not knowing what to do with myself
like singers without song
i need yr tender touch

*head wrapped respectfully Afrikan styled

Part one poetically asks the question:

> give a speech to reach
> the masses, to reach this, to reach us
> who are tired of words?
> give a speech

Part two responds to the question with cynicism which is itself responded to:

> somebodies, some bodies are sayin
> that's the problem nah
> niggers talk too much
> but is it? is that
> really the problem now
>   is talk why our life expectancy is so short
>   is talk why we eat so badly
>   is talk why we work a week for one day's
>   wages
>   is talk why everybody laughs at us on
>   television
>   is talk why we spend so much time in jail
>   is talk why we have no money, no power,
>   no land
>   is talk why all our schools are dumb, our
>   teachers dumber
>   is talk why nobody likes us
>   nobody likes the Negro
>   is talk the cause of that
>   are we here because of talk
>   think about that,
>   did talk rape your grandmomma, red?
>   did talk make you eat pork, abdul?
>   did talk cut off the gas&lights last night,
>   rhetta?
>   did talk do this or was it organized people
>   taking advantage of our ignorance

Part three rhetorically asks the question: "do we want out of this" and, assuming the answer is yes, goes on to suggest:

> then organize
> organize to control
> control the space we occupy,
> control all that space as best we can
> the first space being of course, the body, the
>   flesh and
> muscle, brain and mind body, control that from
>   hair tip
> to toenail, discipline it i.e., self-control it
> exercise power over it i.e., self-determine it,
>   self-defend it, self-respect it

Part four speaks directly to how to organize:

> start with the easy, give a dime a day
> start with the easy, run one block a day
> start with the easy, read for five minutes a day
> start with the easy, eat one fruit a day
> start with the easy, volunteer fifteen minutes a day
> start with the easy and organize to do the
>   undifficult
> don't worry about the heavy problems
> all the heavy problems ain't goin nowhere
> just develop self step by step and one by one
> we'll get to everything in due time

Of course, many, many people reject this as poetry, especially people who are not overwhelmed with social problems and actively seeking a solution. Similarly, people who are relatively comfortable with the status quo reject this as poetry. But what difference does the theme or content of a poem make in terms of whether we are dealing with poetry? It is not the content that makes a poem a poem, but rather the style and presentation.

Pamoja had a cover by Fred O'Neal who had done the cover for *Hofu* and was printed in black ink on a light tan paper.

In 1973 I made another major move. For two years I had worked as the first director of the Lower Ninth Ward Neighborhood Health Center. I had also been a founding member of the *Black Collegian* magazine in 1970. Both the health center and the magazine were growing. I was offered the assistant directorship of the whole neighborhood health care system with the promise of becoming the director within the next year. I was offered a salary of over $25,000 per annum with benefits. I enjoyed the work of directing an outpatient health care facility located in the neighborhood where I had grown up. But I quit.

By then, I knew: what I wanted to do more than anything was write. I never will forget, right after signing the contract papers to work at the *Collegian*, I went to the city welfare department, applied for food stamps and, based on the small salary I was drawing at the *Collegian*, I was eligible. I never regretted the move.

The *Collegian* offered me the opportunity to develop my writing and editing skills. Additionally, I had the opportunity to offer activists in the movement a platform to speak to Black college students across the country. I interviewed a wide variety of activists, artists, and politicians. Sometimes I had three or four interviews and/or articles in each issue. I was even able to help Hoyt Fuller when John Johnson closed down *Black World* and fired Hoyt. The first issue of Hoyt's new publication, *First World,* was published in the *Black Collegian* as a special insert. My stay as an employee of the *Black Collegian* paralleled my membership in Ahidiana, which had been officially founded in the summer of 1973.

The following year I was selected as a delegate to the Sixth Pan African Congress held over the summer in Dar Es Salaam, Tanzania, in East Africa. That trip marked the beginning of an ongoing pattern of traveling around the world as either an activist, a writer of socially committed literature, or a journalist. Before long, I went to the People's Republic of China, Cuba, Surinam, and numerous destinations in the Caribbean. At the same time that I was developing as a poet and performer, I was also traveling around the world meeting, being inspired by, and learning from activists and artists across the globe. My outlook was expanding quickly as a result of these developments and the interaction I was having nationally and internationally.

By late 1975 with two strong years of organizing and operating our programs under our belt, Ahidiana began to move seriously on dealing with radicalizing our position on the women's question. The next book came out early in 1976. *Ibura* (Swahili for "something special, miraculous or wonderful" and also our third child's middle name) was dedicated to my mother who had passed on 5 October 1975. The whole book was about women.

In addition to the poems, *Ibura* contained two short stories, one of which was later published in *We Be Word Sorcerers,* an anthology edited by Sonia Sanchez. This would be the last time for fiction for a good stretch.

There are two poems in this collection which have particular meaning for me: "Top 40" and "Ibura/Come Get to This."

"Top 40" was written for Maxine Maye, a good friend of mine who lives in Washington, D.C., and who was a stalwart in the independent Black school movement. "Top 40" demonstrates one of the techniques I frequently employed: I used the experiences of close friends as both a sign of how deeply I appreciated them as individuals and also to create poems

which addressed lessons to our community at large. Almost all of my work, regardless of theme or content, draws on real lives (myself, my friends, our community, the world) for details. Sometimes it's as minute as using a color as an image because a friend might wear that color often. In any case, "Top 40" was a very popular poem at readings. It opens with a cataloging of pain:

> babies, no babies
> children, single & multiple
> employment, exploitation
> scar tissue and wounds
> anger, hurt, disappointments
> . . . .
> weary, certainly, of the centuries
> of the necessary but nonetheless
>   crippling
> and often unacknowledged work of
>   forced soloing,
> sometimes seemingly single handedly
> having to handle the process
> of propagating and preserving
> our subjugated race, our
> wounded pride and indeed, our
> historically tested humanness
> you are, i'm sure, tired
> of being cursed and accused
> for the umpteenth million time
> of being damn aggressive
> when not aggressive but human,
> female and Black in a time
> callous & cruelly hard on such a
>   combination
> and too, terribly tired of taking shit
> and knowingly pretending it's sugar
> . . . .
> don't let her be misunderstood

This was a three-part poem based on a classic country blues form of AAB, i.e., make a statement, repeat the statement perhaps slightly paraphrased or altered, and then conclude with a statement that commented on the opening two statements. In part two we amplified the opening.

> babies, no babies
> house, apartment, bus
> stop, street corner, car
> man, husband, lover
> (scarcely ever three in one)
> and still seldom someone there
> who actually understands
> or even consciously tries to

the continuous struggle,
what to do,
supporting the dead weight
of unconscious brothers,
those bad black bodies pressing down
upon your breasts, but betrayals
notwithstanding, true to who you
actually are, you move on
giving sex, or giving money, or giving
  love,
or attention and indeed, giving your
  whole
aching life, giving that
taking that, not taking that
but moving on, liking life
hating it, wishing
you were dead, or joy
so in love, yet always
always moving on
Black woman, black woman
i hear you
i see you

Then the third part which sharply contrasted with, but did not contradict, the two-part litany of realities faced by women. What I was trying to empathize with was the real situation faced by women, and especially by single women such as my friend Maxine. Musically, this particular poem has an analog in Bill Whither's exquisite song "But She's Lonely," even though I actually refer to an Al Green song.

    III.
     . . . at a window, looking out
and looking in and just sitting
  sometimes,
stopped for a short moment
for a fast minute
just momentarily resting, catching breath
just, just basically reflecting
on the conditions of our collective
  existence,
cognizant and courageously critical of
the serious realities of our struggle,
unsurrendering, your voice is absolutely
bittersweet but strikingly strong as you
sing silently softly along
with the top 40 song drifting
pervasively around the solitary sunlit room,
from the radio . . .
  ". . . i'm so tired of being alone,
  i'm so tired . . ."

Where "Top 40" had been addressed to the sisters, "Ibura" was addressed to both sisters and brothers. It is a "sun song." There is no way that I can help you hear it except to ask you to read it aloud and think of a preacher in the pulpit. There are numerous musical references in the poem, some of them obvious ("Billie singing" referring to Billie Holiday), some of them obscure ("keep our eyes on the prize of life, hold on, hold on" referring to a freedom song from my civil rights days). The dedication is to Yvonne Mason whom I had first met during our civil rights days in the NAACP Youth Council when she and her younger sister Yvette joined our picket line. Later, in the mid-seventies, I would meet Yvonne when she was working as a typesetter for Edwards Printing Company, the company that first printed *Nkombo*.

Ibura was printed in black ink on an aqua blue paper stock. It had art work by Arthrello Beck, Jr., a Dallas, Texas-based artist whose work I came in contact with while I worked at the *Black Collegian* magazine as the editor.

After *Ibura* came *Revolutionary Love.* Even though *Iron Flowers,* a short book of poetry inspired by a trip to Haiti, is the tightest thematically, I still think *Revolutionary Love* is the strongest of all my poetry books from this era. At 114 pages plus fold-out illustrations, *Revolutionary Love* certainly was the largest book of poetry I had ever published—it contained more poems than all of the previous books added together. It is also the most overtly political, even as it had some of the most "personal" poems I wrote during those years. It contains the clearest articulation of what we came to mean by "art for life," a concept posed as an alternative to "art for art's sake," which we rejected.

While none of the sun poems in *Revolutionary Love* are as strong as "speech" in *Pamoja,* overall there is a greater diversity; and, technically, I achieved some alliterations and metaphorical reaches that still make me smile whenever I go back to review *Revolutionary Love.* Certainly here I have articulated the Ahidiana philosophy more cogently and with greater artistic skill than in any other collection of poetry. In *Revolutionary Love* the actualization most closely matches the intent, and the articulation is artistic to the max. Here are two of my favorite poems from *Revolutionary Love*— actually there are about fifteen or so of the poems in this collection that are my personal favorites of all of my work from this period,

IBURA/COME GET TO THIS

(for Yvonne A. Mason & many, many more)

Many of our brothers are actually afraid
somehow of you, feel weak in your
    presence,
sort of emasculated by your strength or so
    they say.
Can not stand your corrective gaze, find
    it near impossible
to move when you are in charge, so they
    question your femininity.
But is it you who should be questioned
    or we? Are we really
men, if we cannot deal righteously with
    our women,
our beautiful black women, who have
    remained toughly
together throughout this terrible
    tumultuous travel
cross water into new world named
    america? Our women who
have never stopped getting up, giving
    birth and supportive
succulent sweet satisfying love, never once
    stopped walking
home, alone, night after night, carrying
    big brown bags
full of clothes and used food to feed us,
    stolen from day work,
or sad hours spent silently suffering
    degrading labor
in offices and backrooms for chump
    change under the
lecherous eyes and hands of capitalist
    crackers.

Our women, our women, who, even on
    pain sometimes of death,
have never denied loving us. Remember
    Billie singing
"if it's one thing that I've got, it's my
    man and I
love him so"! Our black women who will
    wear their hair
anyway we want it, if only we knew what
    we really wanted,
our women, Tubman steady, Sojourner
    strong, Parks steadfast
Big Mama wise, young sister sensitive and
    song singing soulful.

Our women from town and country, life
    to death, something sure
to count on, consistent like sun rises, life
    bringing
life spring rain falling, our women, beauty
    catching in the throat
and the most nourishing love that a man
    can have and hold. Do we
understand that they, our women, are a
    guide given to us
to keep our eyes on the prize of life,
    hold on, hold on.

What we need now is a saner society, we
    need to create a place
where life can be lived to the max,
    enjoyed, improved and made
ultimately much, much better than when
    we arrived, we need to free
our women from all our own twisted anti-
    female chauvinistic
thoughts and actions, sad actions, many of
    which were foisted on
us by dog lovers, johns, and assorted
    other individuals who
come crawling forth from caves with weird
    ideas about women,
sometimes refer to themselves as "he-men"
    as opposed to their
women whom they sometimes call she-men
    which explains partly
how they really view life. What we need
    to do is encourage
our sisters' growth, encourage our women
    to get together and
speak out, to rush forward and take the
    lead on social and political
issues, to form associations that will
    organize around their concerns,
we need to be there supporting them in
    each and every way like we
like to envision them supporting us. What
    we expect of them is the same
as they need to have come from us. Like
    we need wives, they need
husbands, like we need love, rest and
    relaxation, they need the same,
need what we need, need us like we need
    them.

but we won't bore you with our personal preferences.

"Personal preferences" is an inside joke, making reference to a distinction we used to make in Ahidiana between what we called a "political point" as opposed to a point of "personal preference." The collective arrived at and agreed upon political points, but each individual had a right to hold points of personal preference. Most of us, of course, would frequently exercise our rights of personal preference to explain why we liked or disliked a certain thing, idea, action, person. This allowed us a way to express disagreement without getting disagreeable.

Of all the poetry books, I think *Revolutionary Love* best fulfills the promise of *The Blues Merchant*. There is a definite diversity of styles in the same way as that first book of poetry had except that I was by then a much better poet, as is exemplified by two of the poems.

The first poem is part of our ongoing struggle to move beyond race/racism as the sole definition of our condition. The second is an example of self-criticism.

At Ahidiana we actively studied political theory—Amilcar Cabral was our most respected theorist. We also were very much into criticism and self-criticism. We developed position papers which delineated a methodology for both giving and taking criticism.

While all of this probably seems strange and a bit far out to people who are used to functioning as individuals, in the context of a collective, there was always a need to monitor the motion of the group lest we end up in a state of cultish self-delusion. Part of that monitoring process was criticism and self-criticism. The balance for us was our ironclad rule that we made decisions by consensus, if and only if everyone agreed would we establish a rule, take a political position, or commit ourselves to an action. Other organizations and individuals repeatedly criticized us for our rule by consensus, but it served us well and kept the more articulate from browbeating the less articulate into accepting something that each in the group was not prepared to accept. Just the knowledge that each individual had veto power forced all of us to be sharper in presenting our ideas. We knew we had to convince each member.

Again, this probably seems to be a very restrictive situation for an artist to be in, but exactly the opposite was the case. The majority of my work from that period was sharpened by group criticism, and I was emboldened by the knowledge that these ideas were not simply an artistic idiosyncrasy, but valuable insights shared by a close community of committed individuals.

ALL THAT'S BLACK AIN'T BROTHER

1.
white people
come in all colors

their systems sink
past skin
anchoring into bone, mind
flesh, heart and soul

it is geno-suicide
to minstrel aliens
but some of us do die
strangled by our own
hands

2.
some of us
selfishly think that
self starts
and stops
with i

dream not of peace
but money, don't
dance, hate
our energy
and lust for
an equal opportunity
to turn the screws

see that
black boy over there,

he's white.

DIAPERS AND DISHES

i can thrust
my hand straight
into the toilet bowl, expertly
swirling a soiled diaper around
shaking loose all the stool
as I submerge the cotton cloth
agitating with a firm
back and forth action

i used to recoil
from the touch and texture
of warm masticated corn
kernel hulls and other leavings
smellingly ejaculated
from our babies' behinds
but now it is no bother

i used to be upset
coming home late at night
shake my head and suck
my teeth at the sight
of dirty dishes in the sink
now I willingly wash them

these tasks are so simple
since my thought
has been reformed

Tayari can read now at night
since we share house work
and mutually develop

now, after much self struggle, i
too can change
diapers and wash dishes

i laugh at my old self
sulking about bowel movement
and toilet water on my hands
or dishes that need only
a little time and hardly any
trouble to be made clean

i laugh at my old self
it feels good to improve

In a feature-length profile of me published in a local weekly, writer James Borders judged:

> More congenial now to dialectics, ya Salaam's work in *Revolutionary Love* reverberates with a new fullness that is more deeply personal and more deeply social than any of his past attempts. It is all statement and it has found its most effective distance. Published by Ahidiana and printed on the group's own press, the poems and essays that comprise the text are gorgeously embellished by the drawings of Douglas Redd and the photographs of Kwadwo Oluwale Akpan. If the words don't grab you, the visuals will.

Borders was impressed by the total package, which is exactly what we intended. Early on in FST/BLKARTSOUTH, we were using drawings and photographs in our publications as well as text. This was because a number of the members were visual artists as well as writers, and because, as we continued, both Tom and I believed it was important to include the visual artists in the presentation of our work. This was another example of our insistence on broad inclusion. We were always looking for ways to hook up with others. Eventually, we would also begin inviting blues and jazz musicians to perform with us.

This development was not accidental. We aspired to a holistic concept of the arts, even before we had the theories to articulate and rationalize why we did. We felt it and went with our feelings. Later, we would be able to define what our feelings were.

By the Ahidiana time period we went all the way. Ahidiana had a performing ensemble, composed of musicians and singers as well as poets, called the "Essence of Life." We produced a weekly radio program for six months or so which was also called the "Essence of Life." The name was taken from a song by Gary Bartz and Andy Bey whose chorus was "we must get closer to the essence of life." This was in addition to owning and operating our own press: not just a publishing company, but an actual printing machine which was run by Kuumba Kazi, a member of Ahidiana who had had experience operating a printing press. We were serious about actualizing the principle of self-determination and self-reliance.

All of this affected my writing. How could it not? What may sound like fantasies and exaggeration, reading it cold on the page, actually had a social basis in that we had an active organization whose total goal was to turn words and ideals into revolutionary deeds. Everything we did was designed to actively raise the liberation struggle to a higher level. We were much more than just talk, we were action—and that action inspired me to write like I had never written before.

The final book of poetry in the Ahidiana period was *Iron Flowers.* A trip to Haiti in August 1979 affected me so strongly that I started writing the book during the last couple of days in Haiti and finished everything within a matter of days upon returning. For this book the cover and borders were done by Douglas Redd, who by then was the main artist I worked with. But the book also included photographs which I had taken in Haiti. Next to *Revolutionary Love,*

I like this one the best from cover to cover.
In fact, in terms of consistency, unlike *Revolutionary Love,* I like all of the poems in *Iron
Flowers.* Again, there are two poems which stand
out. One is the last selection in the book titled
"Tomorrow's Toussaints." The other is "Beyond
the Boundaries," the poem I most often read
from the book. *Iron Flowers* was printed in black
and red ink on the cover with black only on
the inside, on a translucent, semi-parchment,
eggshell white paper.

TOMORROW'S TOUSSAINTS

this is Haiti, a state
slaves snatched from surprised masters,
its high lands, home of this
world's sole successful
slave revolt, Haiti, where
freedom has flowered and flown
fascinating like long necked
flamingoes gracefully feeding
on snails in small pinkish
sunset colored sequestered ponds

despite the meanness
and meagerness of life
eked out of eroding soil
and from exploited urban toil, there
is still so much beauty here in this
land where the sea sings roaring a shore
and fecund fertile hills lull and roll
quasi human in form

there is beauty here
in the unyielding way
our people,
colored charcoal, and
banana beige, and
shifting subtle shades
of ripe mango, or strongly
brown-black, sweet
as the suck from
sun scorched staffs
of sugar cane,
have decided
we shall survive
we will live on

a peasant pauses
clear black eyes
searching far out over the horizon
the hoe motionless, suspended
in the midst
of all this shit and suffering
forced to bend low
still we stop and stand
and dream and believe

we shall be released
we shall be released
for what slaves
have done
slaves can do
and that begets
the beauty

slaves can do

BEYOND THE BOUNDARIES

(meditating on the meaning of life)

I.
who am i
who visits
who stares at sights
who strains to catch the
drift of conversations
who bathes
who dresses
who eats
sometimes two or
more times a day?

what does my black skin
mean to similarly skinned people
when there is money
in my pockets
and no pockets
on their pants

or
when I glide pass
at a hundred kilometers
an hour as they
trudge step by step
cross rolling mountain side?

these are tense questions
testing my thought

II.
who asks for their lot
who chooses parents, or
selects birthing spot

i have I.D., U.S. certified,
but what is my identity
Haiti haunts me
there are eyes I saw
in those hills
in the silence of those
noisy nights, Haiti

i turn over
back to the wall
even in the dark
i keep seeing me
beyond myself
climbing to the side
of some overfull tap-tap*
singing out in comfortable tongue

"keep going,
keep going, don't stop
i'm alright!" Haiti,
are we,
are we alright?

congealed into too many urban areas
our people idly littering stolen
  streets, oh
these spaces are so bitter
Africa has had
to walk so many rough waters
we need rest
we need rest but must
press on, "keep going,
keep going,"
never mind that the
particulars of our nativity
are luck and circumstance
what we do
with our after birth
is the singular
importance

III.
who knows what Toussaint
lurks in the heart of Haiti
how can we new slaves
of an old world order
not be Haitian
not have fight
and freedom flowing
in our veins
flashing, flaming like
gold shooting through
sturdy human hills

never mind the language,
a barrier, breakthrough
the dress code
a barrier, breakthrough
the lay of the land
a barrier, breakthrough
breakthrough, yes
individualities do differ
but essences, our
essences rise and converge

IV.
go beyond the boundaries,
where we're coming from
matters
matters so much more
than where we've been
where we were born

if we fail to recognize
that there is no one
human who is totally foreign
then we ourselves will
fail to become anyone
oh Haiti, Haiti
Haiti, heart of hurt
Haiti, heart of hope
you hit so hard
at the meanings of life

the call of
conch shells
caper so softly
cross your verdant
land, cross valley
cross water, Haiti
everywhere
we hear your history

somewhere slightly west
of here, in Jamaica, we say
i and i

i and i
meaning I am
i and I am
you and you are i
and you are you and
it is getting late

and I fall asleep
awakened
by this important
Haitian hiatus

and become a
different person
more conscious
of all I am

---

*A colorfully and imaginatively painted, privately-owned Haitian taxicab.

At the time I had no idea how true a statement I had made regarding becoming "a different person." Ahidiana had survived the split in the Black nationalist movement, which might crudely be characterized as the cultural and/or revolutionary nationalists versus the neo-Marxists. By the early eighties we began to sense a development which we had not foreseen but which, in retrospect, had been accurately forecasted by Fanon in the *Wretched of the Earth*. Essentially, the Black Liberation struggle fractured and much of the energy that had previously gone into organizing oppositional activities and alternative institution building was now going into participation in electoral politics.

The first successes at getting Black politicians elected inevitably led to more and more, and more and more, and more people jumping on the electoral platform. The Congress of African People gave way to the National Black Political Assembly. It was as if the whole Black nation had been persuaded that the best course of action was working for reform from within rather than continuing to work at building alternative institutions outside of the system. Yes, we really were becoming different and most of our nationalist oriented organizations, Ahidiana included, did not survive past the mid-eighties.

In June 1980 we produced my last Ahidiana book, *Our Women Keep Our Skies from Falling*. It was my most radical and effective work. The title was a paraphrase of the Chinese line that "women hold up half the sky." The essays reflected our most thoroughgoing critique of sexism. By then we were presenting lesbians at our annual Black Women's Conferences.

This book was popular in women's groups across the country. Both complete essays and excerpts were reprinted in newsletters and anthologies. Some of the essays were published in major Black journals of the period, including *The Black Scholar* and *Black Books Bulletin*. But even more popular than the essays were two of the poems: "Pa Ferdinand" and ". . . And Raise Beauty to Another Level of Sweetness." Each poem has a story.

Skies was dedicated to my father. People would ask how did I come to such a point of view as expressed in my writings. I would invariably point to my father. From the civil rights days on, he actively supported me and my brothers. When I joined FST he told me with pride how he had been involved in drama at one time. When we went into revolutionary struggle at SUNO, including arming ourselves, he supported me. But more than all of that, he always evidenced a respect and love for Black women that never failed to inspire me. He would bust our behinds at a moment's notice, but he never struck my mother; in fact, seldom raised his voice even though he was

quite sarcastic in talking about some of her teacher friends whom he kindly described as "phony."

On the back of *Skies* there is a portrait of him and me, standing next to the pecan tree in our backyard which he planted when we first moved there in the mid-fifties. He was so proud of this book and I was proud of him. "Pa Ferdinand" was selected by Ruby Dee and included as part of the text of an article she wrote in *Ebony* magazine, whose readership is over a million.

"Raise Beauty" is altogether different. It was actually written as an advertisement for a special Black women's issue of the *Black Collegian* magazine. There was no particular person or incident inspiring this poem other than my publisher directing me to develop something "different." The brochure advertising that issue was sent out to recruiters in major corporations across the country. I didn't care whether they understood the poem or not, I wanted to make a statement of support for Black women. Over the years, church groups and community organizations would reprint the poem.

The community's acceptance and use of both "Pa Ferdinand" and "Raise Beauty" embody the most profound examples of what we considered to be the usefulness of revolutionary Black art, whether a personal statement such as "Pa Ferdinand" or a straight-out political statement such as "Raise Beauty." These, and other poems like them, achieved the broad community acceptance *and usage* which was the goal of my writing.

Ahidiana continued to publish pamphlets and journals. Much of my time was taken up with political organizing. The movement was reaching a point of transformation. When Black power zigged toward electoral politics, I zagged. Shortly after Ernest Morial was elected the first Black mayor of New Orleans, I was one of the leaders of a takeover of the mayor's office around the issue of police brutality. That was the culmination of one phase and the beginning of another.

By 1983 I left the *Black Collegian*. And that was just the beginning. Piece by piece, the foundation and inspiration for my artistic work crumbled, and I was forced to reexamine everything: everything I believed, everything I had achieved, and every dream I had ever conceived. Although I would write a great deal, it would be a long time before I would publish another

PA FERDINAND

(on this man's foundation i build
my political support of feminism)

my father
is a solid stepper
amid a generation
of soft shoers
& scuffling shufflers

was young with
WW II, did not die
nor get discouraged
but rather fought
on both fronts
and unflinchingly brought
the fight back
home, after
korea

a country boy
who walked miles
for school & job
he married the minister's
daughter (who was
a school teacher)
but never went
out to lunch for
class or church,
could sing but usually
kept his baritone
at home

i remember him home
making us work
rising with the sun
and planting food
in the city

i remember him home
waxing floors
on his knees
and requiring his sons
to follow his lead learning
to cook and clean

but mostly
i remember him man
teaching me
consistency: the
importance of principle,
the necessity of
struggle and the
immense beauty
of interrelating
with a good woman

what more could
a son receive
from a father
than the realness
of life lived
like a conscious
African (american)
man!
sho-nuff simply doing
his duty, in his own
context, in his own
space and time.

. . . AND RAISE BEAUTY TO ANOTHER
LEVEL OF SWEETNESS

You are a fresh flower
bursting boldly
into a hard world
with a softness
strong as steel

Reaching for sunlight
you raise yourself
up from down under
out of the degrading dirt
society has so routinely
dumped on women,
you have transformed
manure, muck and mire
into fertilizer

Springing self assertedly
past winter weather
you bring a sweet fragrant
incense and inspiration
into musty places
stale with the stuffiness
of misogynic sexist
status quos

You blossom, you bloom,
you expand and grow,
raising beauty
to a bedazzling higher
and healthier level of
light, life and love

Grow on Black rose
Black woman grow on!

book of poetry. In retrospect, I understand what happened, but at the time it was all touch and go, day-to-day struggling to survive.

six. the reconstruction of a poet

There is never any end. There are always new sounds to imagine, new feelings to get at. And always there is the need to keep purifying these feelings and sounds so that we can really see what we've discovered in its pure state. So that we can see more and more clearly what we are. In that way, we can give to those who listen the essence, the best of what we are. But to do that at each stage, we have to keep on cleaning the mirror.

—*John William Coltrane*

In 1985 I wrote a haiku which perfectly expresses the turbulence and searching that engulfed my life at that time. I had left Ahidiana, left the *Collegian* and was shortly to leave the Jazz & Heritage Foundation. Most emotionally wounding to me, I had also left my marriage.

haiku #7

summer rain showers
fall; in renegade silence
i strip search my soul

The breakup of my marriage deeply hurt me precisely because my "ideology" couldn't save it, nor could my deep "respect" for women and commitment to anti-sexist struggle. The breakup forced me to come to grips with understanding why women occupy such an important role in my life and why I often write in the feminine voice.

The answer begins back at the beginning. For example, the blues woman I met during the voter registration does not exist. She is not an individual. She is a composite, a composite not simply of the women I met doing voter registration work on the weekends, but also a composite of my perceptions of those women. But why is she so important?

She is important because Theresa Copelin, my grandmother on my mother's side, was important to me. Theresa Copelin reared me up until the time I went to school, and Theresa Copelin also released me from the tyranny of organized religion. She was the minister's wife, essentially the queen mother of the church.

The most socially revered female I personally knew. My grandmother whipped my butt when I did wrong. When I left the church, rather than whipping me with words or making me feel bad, she gave me a lesson in compassion.

I had been groomed to be a preacher in the tradition of my grandfathers. While still in grammar school I was reading verse and making statements from the pulpit. I quit going to church in high school. At the time it did not seem like a big deal to me, but for my mother and my grandparents it was the end of a dream.

In the customary metaphorical directness common to pre-sixties Southerners, my grandmother acknowledged my decision not to take up the call of preaching. One Sunday after church, we were all climbing into my grandfather's car and my grandmother told a joke. She said there had been this young man who had been coming to church regularly. The young man had declared he wanted to preach because God had called him to do so. Shortly afterwards he announced that he was going into the seminary to become a preacher. Well, the church didn't hear from him for awhile and then one day he came back. Everybody was glad to see him. They asked had he become ordained yet. He said no. They asked what happened, hadn't God called him? One of the deacons said, when God calls, it's best that you answer. I did answer, the young man replied. Well, then what happened? Well, said the young man, when I got there, God told me never mind.

All through my life there were strong women, caring for and teaching me, and every step of the way they supported me even when they didn't necessarily agree with me. That woman was also my mother who was the only teacher in her school to go out on strike, and then, after the strike was over, she returned without bitterness to work with and, yes, befriend her fellow teachers. My mother was that blues woman when she gave me this most remembered advice which sustained me in the awful decade of the eighties: "Do whatever you think is right, but always be prepared—no matter what anybody else may say or do—always be prepared to go it alone."

That woman was certainly also Mrs. Nelson, my English teacher who introduced Langston Hughes to me, and Mrs. Green, my civics teacher, who actually taught Black history.

So then, this is why women speak in my work. They not only created a major part of me, they also created the emotional space for me to be myself. How could their voices not be sounded by me?

Why then has my later work championed gay rights and spoken forcefully against homophobia and heterosexism? Did I have homosexual experiences which I've never revealed in print?

Of course. But these experiences were not sexual in nature. They were instead bonds of comradeship and friendship. Remember when I spoke of Hoyt Fuller? I remember writing a long essay on homosexuality in the Black Arts Movement of the seventies. I sent the essay to Hoyt Fuller at *Black World*. He commented that it was an interesting analysis from a heterosexual position. But he did not publish it. When Hoyt died I spoke at his funeral and wrote a praise poem for him. My biggest disappointment is that I had not created space enough for us to safely discuss Black gay realities and experiences. I vowed to work to create such a space for serious discussion and respect of the "other" in our community howsoever the "other" is defined.

Again, my life is also inseparable from my New Orleans acculturation where I would see "gay" men who affirmed their identify simply by refusing to hide or disguise themselves as straight men. They moved about, especially in the entertainment world, as though there was nothing in the least bit unusual about themselves and that was liberating for both them and, ultimately, even more so, for us who witnessed and came into contact with them. For example, there was Bobby Marchan, a singer who had worked with Huey Smith and the Clowns. Bobby was also a well-known emcee of rhythm-and-blues shows. He would do a stand-up routine which flaunted his homosexuality, and he especially enjoyed taking on macho hecklers.

Then the contact became more than a socially observed phenomenon, it also became an integral part of our liberation struggle. While at SUNO, one of the people who made sure that our newsletter, *The Black Liberation Express,* came out on time without fail was gay. I could never deny that brother's commitment nor his competence. Later, after some of the BLKART-SOUTH members joined the Black Muslims, there was a gossip campaign about one of our major

members. Did I know he was a faggot? Did they know that *that* didn't matter?

I realized through those and numerous other experiences that confronting homophobia required courage on the part of homosexuals who also wanted to participate in the liberation struggle, the Black Arts Movement, or wanted rather simply to be able to walk hand in hand down the street without being "stoned."

One day, coming out of the New Orleans Jazz & Heritage Foundation (NOJ&HF) office, there was a gay man at the bus stop and a woman who looked at him hard, seemingly with daggers in her eyes. He literally switched across the street. I turned to one of my coworkers and said, "People laugh at men like that but they have no idea of what his struggles were and how much courage it takes for him to openly be the way he is."

The verse play *Malcolm, My Son* was born that day, an expression not only of solidarity with the "other" but also an appeal to the rest of us. There are many other examples.

Some of what has made me what I am I will be able to remember only with great difficulty—the difficulty of keeping the mirror clean. If I am a true poet, eventually it will all be revealed, or, at least, as much of my history as I can (under)stand to uncover.

Social conventions are clothes on our psyche. The poet must be a worshiper of nudity, and, therefore, precisely in opposition to the merchandisers and social bureaucrats (e.g., government officials, business administrators, religious leaders) of the status quo whose essential tasks are to sell uniforms and to enforce dress codes.

To be a poet is to be at odds with the present if only because every dominant status quo has something to hide, something that needs to be revealed. I wrote a poem whose whole focus is on the question of what role for poetry.

The poem is structured into call and response. In introducing the poem I would reference "viva la revoluçion!" and ask the audience to respond with a strong "Viva" every time I said the word "poetry." I would tell them, however, only shout "Viva" if you agree with what I say.

The poem was actually inspired by an English/Spanish bilingual reading I did with Cuban poet Pedro Sarduy in New Orleans. He had written "The Poet," a poem about being a poet which he recited in Spanish. I recited the English translations after each stanza. I was impressed by what he had written and decided to do a similar kind of poem, hence, the "Viva" response which, by the way, does not appear in the text of the poem.

THE CALL OF THE WILD

Poetry is not an answer
Poetry is a calling
     a vision that does not vanish
     just because nothing
     concrete comes along, or
     because the kingdom of heaven
     is under some tyrant's foot

Poetry is not a right
Poetry is a demand
     to be left alone
     or joined together or whatever
     we need to live

Poetry is not an ideology
     poets choose life
     over ideas, love people
     more than theories, and really would
     prefer a kiss to a lecture

Poetry

Poetry is not a government
Poetry is a revolution
     guerrillas—si!
     politicians—no!

Poetry is always hungry
     for all that is
     forbidden
     poetry never stops drinking
     not even after the last drop, if we
     run out of wine poets will
     figure a way to ferment rain

Poetry wears taboos
     like perfume with a red shirt
     and a feather in the cap,
     sandals or bare feet, and
     sleeps nude with the door unlocked

Poetry cuts up propriety into campfire logs and sits
     around proclaiming life's glories far into
     each starry night, poetry burns prudence
     like it was a stick of aromatic incense or
     the even more fragrant odor of the heretic
     aflame at the stake, eternally unwilling
     to swear allegiance
     to foul breathed censors
     with torches in their hands

Poetry smells like a fart
     in every single court of law and smells
     like fresh mountain air
     in every dank jail cell

Poetry is unreliable
Poetry will always jump the fence
     just when you think poets are behind you
     they show up somewhere off the beaten path
     absent without leave, beckoning for you
     to take your boots off and listen to the birds

Poetry is myopic and refuses to wear glasses
     never sees no trespassing signs and always
     prefers to be up touching close to everything
     skin to skin, skin to sky, skin to light
     poetry loves skin, loathes coverings

Poetry is not mature
     it will act like a child
     to the point of social embarrassment
     if you try to pin poetry down
     it will throw a fit
     yet it can sit quietly for hours
     playing with a flower

Poetry has no manners
     it will undress in public everyday of the
          week
     go shamelessly naked at high noon on
          holidays
     and play with itself, smiling

Poetry is not just sexual
     not just monosexual
     nor just homosexual
     nor just heterosexual
     nor bisexual
     or asexual
     poetry is erotic and is willing
     any way you want to try it

Poetry

Poetry has no god
     there is no church of poetry
     no ministers and certainly no priests
     no catechisms nor sacred texts
     and no devils either
     or sin, for that matter, original
     synthetic, cloned or otherwise, no sin

Poetry

     In the beginning was the word
     and from then until the end
     let there always be

Poetry!

While I did not belong to the "church" and was not a Baptist preacher, as "The Call of the Wild" makes clear, I was a preacher. The Bible was not my text, my poems were.

I also believed in the "spirit" and in "possession," after all I had been reared Baptist. I remember once in the choir stand when the spirit hit a young sister who was our age. She was thin, and my brothers and I were hefty. I never will forget being unable to hold her still when she fell thrashing to the choir floor. I looked into her eyes—she was not there, something or someone else was, and she was making some sound, or should I say some sound was coming out of her, it was not screaming, it was something else. On other occasions I have felt myself almost crying (what do I mean almost—I cried) just listening to a singer.

Even though I left the church, I still believed. I still wanted to be a conduit for the spirit, for *that* spirit. Sometimes in poetry performances I reach it.

In *The Bluesman, the Musical Heritage of Black Men and Women in the Americas,* author and blues musician Julio Finn describes the role and function of the preacher in the prototypical Black church. Finn perfectly described the function I aspired to as a poet.

> . . . the black *preacher* performs his sermons. Standing straight and stiff would never rouse his congregation; he shouts, whispers, threatens, pleads, jumps, dances, quakes, sings—in a word, he seeks to *conjure* his flock, to bring them to the state where they can be possessed by the Holy Ghost. *"Can you feel it?"* he screams. Next instant, he is in a trance, rapt in the divine spirit, on the brink of revelation. At a flick of his hand the music mounts, the voices of the choir lift on high, and the tranquil glory of salvation descends. No black preacher will last for long if he is no good at transmitting his emotions to his assembly. It is no good feeling called to preach if you can't make your auditors *feel* your message. This transmission and the communal experience of God exists because they literally feel the power of the supernatural passing through their own minds and bodies. The "fits" black Baptists fall into are but the "possession" of the Vodun by the *loas.* Only the names of the gods have been changed, in order to protect the innocent.

When I recited my poems, I was a preacher not simply in style but also in my inclination to instruct, to delineate good from evil, to inspire to prescribed action, and in my elucidation of the finer points of my religion (my ideology).

I began "abandoning" the "politically oriented sun poem" in direct proportion to my own distancing from the *practice of* (as opposed to the belief in) socialism, revolutionary nationalism. This shift was moved from a push to a shove toward a fall by the general failure of the progressive movement to defeat capitalism and neocolonialism in the Third World. There was literally nowhere where we succeeded.

Of course, I still wanted to be free. But when I look at the structure of my poetry after 1983, I notice that I am less inclined toward the sermon form on political issues. Now when I take up the sun poem, I speak not as a preacher from the pulpit but rather as a blues singer on a stage articulating hurt, pain, suffering, and the withstanding of same. Now, I really have the blues.

No longer is the blues simply a form that I feel is relevant; now, in the face of all the changes, all the disappointments, victories denied, now, me, my life is the blues. I am not singing from racial memory. I am not singing for effect. I am singing my own song.

There is a confessional tone, a revealing of what life has been like for this traveler—truth told, weathered by the weight of failures albeit buoyed by compassion for the world and leavened by a sincere appreciation of the ultimate great goodness of life that only realizing oneness with the world can bring.

I still write sun songs, but now these are sagacious praise songs for my cultural traditions rather than optimistic revolutionary anthems. Whereas before I sang a song of my people and for my people as a witness, now, like the blues bards of old, I witness my own living for surely my living has become part of the history. Structurally, I am now more interested than ever in singing the blues—there is a melancholic edge in my voice—it's just that I don't have to go anywhere to find it because the blues has found me.

Question: what happens when a poet who has functioned in a collective for over fifteen years and has had all of his poetry books published by a collective, suddenly finds himself alone? Answer: nothing—literally nothing.

Although I knew and was known to numerous influential people in the Black Arts

Kalamu ya Salaam (fifth from left) with Amiri Baraka, Askia Muhammad Toure, Eugene Redmond,
Malkia M'Buzi, and Dingane Joe Goncalves at the first National Black Arts Festival
in Atlanta, Georgia, 1990

Movement, I had never published a book with anyone outside of New Orleans, and only rarely had published single poems. Moreover, I was completely outside of the college lecture circuit. When the movement slowed to a trickle and my own involvement also shifted, I was left literally on the outside. I had to reorient myself and, in the process, I examined not only my own history, but also the entire body of African American poetry.

From the very beginning, Black poetry has consisted of two trains running. One train accepted and emulated the Euro-centric literary traditions and the other train rejoiced in and propagated the folk-based, orated (semi- or quasi-musical) indigenously developed African American expressions. This is not simply a question of theme or content but also a question of technique.

A poet such as Michael Harper without question writes thematically from a Black perspective, and his work is particularly expressive and suggestive of the music, however, over the years his techniques have become more Euro-

centric in a literary sense. Is he, therefore, less "Black"? Of course not. He's just on the west-bound train, that's all. The same is true of Jean Toomer. His book *Cane* is considered a classic of African American literature. Part of the reason that it has achieved that stature is because the technically accomplished ("brilliant" and "gifted" is how it is often described) poetry of *Cane* is generally rhymed, iambic pentameter and is therefore accessible to literary critics. Although it's carrying coal, the poetry of *Cane* remains a westbound train.

In the preface to the 1970 edition of Bontemps and Hughes's *The Poetry of the Negro*, coeditor Arna Bontemps writes: "If the compilers had sought for a racial idiom in verse form among Negroes, they should have concerned themselves with the words of Negro spirituals, with folk rhymes, with blues, and other spontaneous lyrics. These song materials, no doubt, suggest a kind of poetry that is racially distinctive, that lies essentially outside the literary traditions of the language that it employs. But the present anthology consists of poems written within that tradition, by Negroes as well as others."

There we have it clearly stated: even Negroes have excluded the eastbound train when dealing with literary concerns.

Moreover, if both the poets and the poetry are perceived as threatening because they are on a train headed in the opposite direction, then is it not also understandable that there will be limited publication and support of this work? In February of 1994 I served on an NEA (National Endowment for the Arts) literature panel. It was expected that I would be familiar with the work of American poets and, in general, I was. One proposal we got was to reference Haki Madhubuti. I was the only African American on the panel of eight or nine. No one else was familiar with Madhubuti's work.

Haki Madhubuti has over a million books in print! He is America's best-selling African American poet. I would have been considered "unqualified" to sit on an NEA poetry panel if I were unfamiliar with the work of a contemporary White poet who had sold more than a million books of poetry and was also the head of a major publishing company, but the reverse is not true.

The majority of oral oriented, African American poets and poetry is unknown to America's general literary world. Most Americans have never attended a Black poetry reading nor heard any of the few recordings which are available. There is a wall of ignorance. Breaching that wall has not been my main concern, however.

One of my goals has been to develop and articulate a theory of poetics from an Afrocentric point of view. I wanted the theory to be more than a simple description of a few techniques or a reductionism to "dialect" combined with overtly "Black themes and content." For me a major part of developing theory happens through the conscious praxis of writing poems with very specific goals in mind. While I am no less interested in writing political poetry, I am much more interested in investing the politicalness of the poetry into the structure of the poems.

I think it is both fatal and facile to slip into the quagmire of using race to define aesthetics. At Ahidiana we defined Blackness as color, culture, and consciousness. I took the first for granted and set about the task of defining culture and consciousness.

I began "constructing" poems which detailed a particular facet of social existence and which painted an overt picture easily grasped, but which also had an underlying political thrust. The politics of this poetry is sometimes unconsciously intuited by the audience or, at other times, subconsciously ingested.

For example, "a moment in a mississippi juke joint" was written as a direct effort to deal with those who criticize social realism as unpoetic. Based on the old joke about Soviet movies of the sixties—*Q:* What do you call a Soviet romantic film? *A:* A Man and His Tractor. My effort was first to use the image of a tractor as genuine eroticism. Second, I wanted to deal with "peasants," which in my case was translated to Mississippi country folk. Third, I wanted to employ only those images that such people would know intimately. Fourth, I wanted to present these people with a positive sense of self-esteem and an aesthetic of personal beauty based on an appreciation of their own features.

a moment in a mississippi juke joint:
wilma mae looks at john l.

his slender eyes
and taut behind, bared arms
blackberry dark with grapefruit
sized biceps, but especially
the massive slope of his head
with broad textures like the Benin
bronze she didn't consciously know about
but subconsciously gravitated toward
and those teeth shiny like
lighthouses down on the gulf coast
flashing through the ink of stormy night

wilma mae looked at his feet
and the go slow grind of his hips
keeping time to the juke box
& sucked her breath in slowly, she
would have taken a seat
except she was already sitting with
her thighs pressed tightly closed

just then john l. threw his head
back and sprayed the ceiling
with the mirth of his laughter
and casually did a little dip
on the off beat of the break
in the undulating song

"god," she thought, "that man
look like a tractor, & i feels like
a field what ain't never been plowed . . ."

By now I had also figured a way to make an oral statement and simultaneously make a textual statement: don't combine them, separate them. "A Moment . . ." uses a song fragment, "oh, you poor, love sick child," as a call and response device but that device is not written as part of the text. Instead, whenever I recite the poem, I explain the call and response to the audience. Thus, I achieve the participation of the audience as part of the orality of the performance, and, at the same time, I can develop the text without worrying about how to include the oral. Of course, this means that the poem on the page ceases to be recognized as a lyric. Were it not for this explanation, the reader would have no way of knowing that there is even a performance aspect tied to the poem. While this approach does not work in every instance, I have found it the most effective in allowing me to fully develop the oral as well as the textual potential of a given poem.

Another example of this technique is the poem "Tasty Knees," which was written as a critique of male-centered sex which defines the success of the sexual act in terms of male orgasm. I chose to deflate the penile fixation by ironically elevating it and then revealing the alternative. When I recite the poem, the tempo increases, mimicking the act of making love. I get louder and louder, ending on the word "ejaculation," and then I deliver the deflating line "of course, I'm exaggerating." Invariably people laugh. But the critique is actually delivered by having the poet celebrate an aspect of the lovemaking which was not phallic oriented, namely the "tasting" of knees (thus, also, the title of the poem).

Many people do not realize that much of the structure of what we have been taught as good writing is based on a patriarchal perception of copulation. Is it not true that the high point of a story or plot development is called the climax and if a story goes on too long after reaching a climax it is said to have "petered out"? These are the philosophical questions with which I was consciously dealing.

In 1989 I produced and recorded "A Nation of Poets" featuring Amiri Baraka, Pearl Cleage, Haki Madhubuti, Wanda Coleman, Kalamu ya Salaam, Mari Evans, Askia Muhammad Toure, and Sonia Sanchez. A CD of that event was released by the National Black Arts Festival in 1990. I also self-published *A Nation of*

TASTY KNEES

in the dark of touch
my face pressed heavy
to your head i open
my eyes and see the
night hair of you dark
as the lightless black
of a warm womb's interior,
your wetness inviting touch
your earth quakes, shakes and opens
as my rod my staff
slides across your ground
though i want to scream i
resolve to remain mute
as a militant refusing to snitch
to the improper authorities, but
suddenly, a riot of joy breeches my resolve
and i disperse the moist quiet of our union
with an involuntary shout loud
as a bull elephant's triumphant ejaculation
of course i am exaggerating, but my, my, my
your knees did taste some good, yeah

Poets, a small book of poetry featuring all of the poems I presented.

I made no serious attempt to distribute or directly sell *A Nation of Poets*. I did not view the book as a written document but rather simply as a set of lyrics to accompany the recitation. At that time I was still struggling with figuring out how to compose my poetry so that it worked as both speech and text. But more than the technical questions, there was the fact that I absolutely abhor self-promotion.

All of my adult life as a professional writer had been spent in a context within which we pushed the collective rather than any one individual. After twenty-five years of functioning in one way, to suddenly begin self-promotion as an individual is not only very, very difficult, it is also distasteful.

Although the seemingly simple work of pushing my book was not my speed, serving as the producer (coordinating all of the activities and supervising the recording) for the NBAF poetry program was both acceptable and arduous but relatively uncomplicated for me to see through to successful conclusion.

Similar programs at the Schomburg Library in New York (in February of 1990) and for the Caribbean Cultural Center (in October of 1990) in New York followed. I also produced and recorded New World Poets for the Houston International Festival in April of 1991. The

Kalamu (third from left) performing with Anoa Nantambu, Maria "Gingerbread" Tanner, and Kenyatta Simon as the Word Band at the Snug Harbor nightclub in New Orleans, about 1992

New World Poets were multicultural: African Americans Jayne Cortez, Haki Madhubuti, Thomas Meloncon, and Kalamu ya Salaam; Asian American Genny Lim; Chicana Evangeline Pinon; Native American Jack Forbes, and Puerto Rican Tato Laviera. All of us worked out of a strong oral tradition. I coordinated and recorded a poetry night in New Orleans featuring Amiri Baraka from Newark, Jimmy Santiago Barca from New Mexico, John Sinclair from Detroit, and myself from New Orleans.

In November 1991 I produced Bright Black Words, a special two-nighter at the Contemporary Arts Center. The program featured New Orleans poets Labertha McCormick, Arthur Pfister, Mona Lisa Saloy along with myself and the Word Band and a workshop production of my verse play, *Malcolm, My Son*. In March of 1992, *Malcolm, My Son* won an award from Rites and Reason Theatre at Brown University. This two-person play deals with the definition of manhood in the context of a young, gay male coming out to his mother.

Writing it in verse was not a premeditated act. I was not trying to make a sentimental statement. I wanted an overtly political statement. But I realized this was an emotionally charged issue and, as I got started, I realized that poetry was easier to do than dialogue. For one thing, I was not trapped into using "realism" nor even "chronology." Once I got started, it took only four or five days to complete. Here is an excerpt in which the mother, Amina, responds to her son's questioning about the uniqueness of his condition.

MALCOLM: Were there ever any other gay men
  in our family?

AMINA: If you open the closet in the hall,
  If you root around in the corners of the attic,
  If you dig in the crevices of basements,
  Go to the old picture books
  And look into the eyes of our blood . . .
  The felt hat worn across that great aunt's eye
  With a man's tie dividing her breasts,

The big-eyed youth hiding on the edge of the
  picture
His hands clasped in his lap staring with terror
At something way beyond the camera . . .
In the tear-strewn trail
Of all those still-missing ones
Who left home and disappeared
Somewhere across the Rockies or into
The soft belly of Europe,
The cousin you never heard from again
After he reached fifteen and left the church
  choir
And had the beautiful voice
That broke your heart to hear him
Reluctantly sing good-bye,
Or the one you only heard from through
Occasional phone calls at odd times
During some randomly selected decade . . .
Like I said, this is nothing new.
We just keep pretending we've never
Dealt with all this before, pretending.
But we are now no more sick
Than we've ever been during this sojourn
In the wilderness of being forced to make do,
Striving, although often valiantly failing,
To create wholeness from the twisted scraps
Of what's left after labor rape
And racist assault on our human selves.
(Pauses.)
Do you understand?

The Word Band was a poetry performing ensemble which I directed. We had Kenyatta Simon, a percussionist, and two vocalists/reciters, Maria "Gingerbread" Tanner and Anoa Nantambu.

The Word Band, now in hiatus, was my most advanced articulation of poetry as music. Most of the poems were my own, although we also had "Answers in Progress" by Baraka and a Mari Evans poem in our repertoire. What was sweet about the Word Band is that I figured out a specific musical reference for each piece, and then did arrangements. The idea was to function as a band playing certain charts but also to maintain, indeed, to require improvisation. Each arrangement had cues so that the band members would know when to make the changes. While the poems were always in the foreground, they were recited as music. I consciously set out to cover the entire sweep of Great Black Music—everything from elemental blues and a cappella gospel moans to really "out" new music a la late period John Coltrane, Archie Shepp, and Pharoah Sanders.

Many people talk about jazz as a model for their poetry, most meaning simply that they reference the music. Some quote the musicians, some sing the music, some list song titles and album titles, some even describe musical scenes, or do comparatives between a quality and a known musician ("as blue as B.B. bringing black blues by stroking the strands of Lucille's singing hair"). While I share those techniques, I also believe there is a deeper region.

There are other possibilities such as using actual music forms: the AAB or AA'B of classic country blues; the AABA "standard song" form; and the more complex forms pioneered by Duke Ellington which are basically structured on theme variation (A, A', A'') within a three- or four-part development such as A, A'/BBC/D. This translates into an introductory statement with an embellishment, followed by a classic blues statement/statement/contrast or concluding statement, and finished off by a coda.

Although theme variation (A, A' with the A part established by a specific word or phrase which is repeated at the beginning or the end of a line) is a very common device in Black poetry, I'm not sure how many poets consciously work with this form as opposed to simply using it because it feels like the technique to use.

In addition to form there is also the use of words as sound and rhythm devices rather than for a specific meaning. This is particularly true of nonconventional slang and so-called "curse" words. In Black poetry the word "shit" is not used solely to literally refer to excrement. In fact, in the Black lexicon shit is a completely neutral word in and of itself. Its meaning (if there is a meaning) is purely contextual and sometimes, even then, used as a structural device to achieve rhythm, rhyme, or inflectional emphasis.

Another option is the employment of "dirty" tones which refers to playing notes off-pitch or sliding in and out of intonation. One can alter the spelling to use both the original meaning of the word as well as a comment on that meaning. One of the more common examples is spelling America in this way: "Amerikkka." Another way to use dirty tones would be to repeat the word with variations such as "America, Amerikkka, A Merry Caw, A-Murderer." These are just some examples of structural approaches to poetry based on music.

In this regard, some of today's rappers are really inventive in their word play and reflect a musical sensibility in how they rhyme. Unfortunately, rap is almost entirely a verbal art and therefore the printed words often don't even make it as lyrics because so much of the meaning is contained in how the words are "sounded," i.e., cadence, inflections, intonations, melody, etc.

My effort with the Word Band was to go to the next step of using vocal arrangements. Of course, this group has to be heard to be appreciated, and plans are underway to release two or three selections by the Word Band as part of a projected CD whose working title is "New Orleans Soiree: A Gathering of the Saints/ Kalamu ya Salaam & Friends." "Saints" is a collaborative recording of me working with New Orleans musicians in a wide variety of musical contexts ranging from a piece called "Congo Square" performed with Percussion Inc. (this selection is commercially available on a cassette called "America Fears the Drum," produced by Don Paul out of San Francisco), to totally improvised poetry performed with Kidd Jordan and Alvin Fielder's avant garde ensemble, the Improvisational Arts Quintet (with whom I performed at least once a year at the annual New Orleans Jazz & Heritage Festival). Other musicians are blues guitarist Walter Washington; legendary traditional jazz banjoist, guitarist, and vocalist Danny Barker; saxophonist Tim Green; a cameo by my brother, trumpeter Kenneth Ferdinand.

I had also developed a working relationship with Chinese American Fred Ho, a baritone saxophonist, composer, and political activist. We called our collaboration the Afro Asian Arts Dialogue. We did a tour through Detroit, Flint, and Lansing, Michigan. We performed at the Newyorican Theatre in New York City and at Brandeis University in the Boston area. We performed in Atlanta and at the University of Wisconsin-Madison. Recordings were made of our performances in New York and Madison.

With Fred Ho (right) presenting an Afro Asian Dialogue

My intention is to release this work in recorded form because I know that the fullest appreciation of poetry in the oral tradition will not happen unless and until it is heard. This necessarily requires getting into the "business" of recording poetry. Although there are a few publishing houses who regularly record poets, there are no companies currently specializing in producing, recording, and distributing African American poetry.

I have served an apprenticeship in the recording business by working as a producer with All For One Records (AFO), a small independent jazz label founded by Harold Battiste. I have the experience but lack an infrastructure and necessary capital. This is also a major part of my problem: I have the demonstrated ability to fulfill a variety of required functions.

I am not only a writer, I am also an entrepreneur, an administrator, an arts producer, a radio personality, and a father of five. Each of those areas has its own sphere of influence and expertise. I have developed myself in each and find myself very often pulled away from my writing and editing work to function in another area. How else could it be?

Creating and producing our poetry is really not the hardest part of our struggle, however. The most difficult step is to develop a theory and critique of what we were trying to accomplish.

Earlier on I mentioned Amilcar Cabral. In my office there is a poster-sized portrait of Cabral which I obtained in Cuba. It was Cabral's seminal essay "National Liberation and Culture" which opened the theoretical way ahead for me. I quote Cabral's "aims of cultural resistance" as they are the basic framework which I use to define my own cultural work.

Development of a *people's culture* and of all aboriginal positive cultural values;

Development of a *national culture* on the basis of history and the conquests of the struggle itself;

Constant raising of the *political and moral awareness* of the people (of all social categories) and of *patriotism,* spirit of sacrifice and devotion to the cause of independence, justice, and progress;

Development of the technical and technological *scientific culture,* compatible with the demands of progress;

Development, on the basis of a critical assimilation of mankind's conquests in the domains of art, science, literature, etc., of a *universal culture,* aiming at perfect integration in the contemporary world and its prospects for evolution;

Constant and generalized raising of feelings of humanism, solidarity, respect, and disinterested devotion to the human being.

Based on my study of Cabral, I advocate the importance of cultural specificity, cultural integrity, and the legitimacy of cultural accretion.

Cultural specificity reflects itself in the need to be grounded. One must really know one's culture (whether native or adopted). That calls not only for objective study but also subjective immersion. Being grounded (i.e., "knowing your culture") is not an anthropological study but rather is a commitment to the study, propagation, and perpetuation of the culture "as a citizen of that culture." In this way, culture is not simply an object of observation but rather is also a mode of operation—culture is not something which one studies outside of and detached from the self, but rather is also a way of living which defines the self.

Part of my struggle as a writer was to both learn and project New Orleans culture. In my work there were three ways to use the specificity of New Orleans culture: (1) as content, (2) as style, and (3) as a structural model. Although content is an obvious approach, and although I have written a large body of prose which focuses on New Orleans, I have very few poems that "image" New Orleans as a geo-cultural space. Indeed, the majority of my poems which reference New Orleans are praise poems for specific cultural figures. Given my oral orientation, it is understandable that my use of New Orleans culture would lean more toward style and structure.

Cultural integrity requires an honest assessment of strengths and weaknesses *plus* a genuine acceptance of one's cultural identity. One cannot hope to preserve or project cultural integrity if one (*a*) objectively does not know and understand the culture and (*b*) has not accepted that one's culture is a legitimate and valuable expression of human culture. Especially for African Americans, who live in both physical and psychological proximity to a dominant and dominating culture, accepting the legitimacy of African American culture is not easy.

A word about "knowing" African American culture. None of us truly knows our culture because so much of our culture is *unknowable.* This is true precisely because our culture has been destroyed, dispersed, masked, and disrupted. Indeed, those of us who champion African American culture are actually championing the reclamation, reconstruction, and reevaluation of our culture. All the surface aspects we talk about are just that: surface.

For example, no matter how much we claim to love Black music, how can we be "champions" of our culture, when we have done so few studies of our music? To the truism "one could tell how 'Black' an intellectual was by looking at her or his library," I used to respond with my own saying: if you really want to know "how Black" (meaning how "cultured") an intellectual is, check out their record collection. Why? Because our music is universally recognized as the greatest, if not the only, American contribution to world cultural arts. Because our culture has been recorded but not written. Because books may be assigned in school, but records you generally buy on your own, based on your own tastes whatever they may be. Because your record collection is the truest gauge of the depth of a person's appreciation for our culture—and here I am not elevating one genre of Great Black Music over another. I mean quite simply that the embracing of our music is a *sine qua non* of the embracing of our culture.

At the same time, I must recognize that "our" music is essentially American music in the totality of its expression even though the core of it is the creation of African American culture. We are both African and American. As paradoxical as it may sound, Elvis Presley, country and western, hard rock, all of those examples of American music are entwined in and cannot be separated from the core elements which African Americans created. There is no one more American than African Americans, even as there is also no one in America as African as African Americans.

Third, we must move forward and recognize that *cultural accretions* are not only inevitable, they are also essential. Accretionizing is a seminal force in the life of all Afro-centric

cultures in general, and African American culture specifically is an "American" culture which by definition means that it is a "Creole" culture. Our strains are various, and even though we may be eastbound, the west is in us.

The concept of cultural accretions helped me to put my high school experiences at St. Aug in proper perspective. My initial memories are full of anger and rejection, but those initial memories are not factual, in fact, they are self-serving. I hated the goals of St. Aug, but emotionally I both loved and hated St. Aug and all it stood for. I was a Baptist so there was a conflict of religious beliefs but, more important than that, I was working-class oriented by social experience and by ideological commitment (via the civil rights movement). St. Aug's agenda was to create the talented tenth: doctors, lawyers, politicians, scientists. It is no accident that many of my former classmates have gone on to become Black professionals. Further, it is no accident that many of the managers of city government post-1973 are alumni of Catholic schools in general and St. Aug specifically.

I was influenced by my fellow students—most of whom did not share my civil rights activism. I played ball and went to parties with them. I could not fail to be impressed by their intelligence (actually their "education" rather than native intelligence). My first true love, Thelma Thomas, was a physician's daughter. One of my best friends at St. Aug, Emile LaBranche, was the son of a pharmacist.

They all lived in a very different part of New Orleans. The physical differences between the neighborhoods where we lived was analogous to the differences between Black and White neighborhoods in other cities. Many of them were Creoles. My rejection of St. Aug was partially a reaction to that world's rejection of my world and my own inability to understand the attraction and repulsion I felt for the lifestyle of Black professionals.

All of the psychological turmoil notwithstanding, St. Aug gave me intellectual tools that were denied most of the people who lived where I lived. Later, in FST, and, to a lesser but still noticeable degree, in Ahidiana, the educational differences were obvious obstacles which we had to struggle mightily to deal with. At Ahidiana we called it "uneven levels of development." As I read more and more of Fanon and Cabral—especially Cabral with his work on "class suicide" of the petite bourgeoisie in the context of revolutionary struggle, and also his conceptualizations of "returning to the source" to define the integration of the professionals into the ranks of the masses—it all became clearer to me. I was then more able to understand the conflicts and separate the wheat from the chaff in those experiences.

While I never did get a four-year college education, my ability to read and write was clearly superior to most of the people in my neighborhood as a child and superior to many of the people with whom I shared civil rights and Black power/Black liberation struggle. Although certainly neither created nor ideologically defined by St. Aug, my reading and writing skills were qualitatively enhanced by having a strong college preparatory curriculum in high school. There are all kinds of dimensions to this question. Suffice it to say, Cabral gave me the intellectual tools to appreciate my history.

To some, none of this has anything to do with creating poetry. To me it has everything to do with creating an authentic African American poetry. Paradoxically, my codification of a Black aesthetic made significant leaps while working in haiku, a foreign form.

Haiku is a Japanese poetry form which structurally consists of three lines and a total of seventeen syllables (five on the first and third lines, and seven on the second line). Once I began writing in haiku, I wanted to figure out how to incorporate an African American aesthetic into that form.

For me this was more than simply a technical question of how to write it on paper, it was also a question of how to perform haiku. I would not consider myself successful until I had figured out how to recite haiku with the same force as I did my blues and jazz based poetry.

I knew I had to deal with at least three different elements: rhythm, rhyme, and sound—plus, they needed to carry the weight of irony. Of course, I did not expect each poem to contain every element, but I was striving to have each poem manifest at least one of those properties. I did not study any traditional haiku nor read any books on writing haiku. I was not interested in learning the Japanese tradition. I wanted to use the form in my own way.

This was a left brain/right brain problem. I needed a creative approach for the performance and a technical approach for the writing. I stored it away and let my subconscious work on the performance part.

The writing part was easy once I focused on what I wanted to do. Eventually, I did rewrites as I perfected my techniques. I moved away from similes and went straight into personifications. I made the natural world an extension of the human self. I used imagery but also dealt with the Afro-centric tradition of proverbs, mother wit and "mama say." I used alliteration, rhyme, and rhythm. I wanted to reach for the Creolization of concepts, bringing together concepts that were not usually thought of as part of a whole. Beneath all of that I wanted to maintain a feminine/masculine referencing.

This poem is a good example.

haiku #79

i enter your church,
you receive my offerings,
our screaming choirs merge

It's written in three with the emphasis on ONE-TWO-three. The "three" is an open beat, meaning I could recite it ONE-TWO-three or ONE-TWO-three/three/three/three-ONE-TWO-three. Usually, I recite it rubato, without any particular rhythmic emphasis, but I keep the three feel in mind so that the words are emphasized like this:

I EN-TER your church
YOU RE-CEIVE my offering
OUR SCREAM-MING choirs mergeeeeee.

Unfortunately, there is nothing on the page that can tell you how I am using rhythm except that I have set the poem up with the emphatic words at the beginning of each line. Additionally, each line opens with two words. The first word is one syllable and the second word is two syllables, which is also a reinforcement of the three feel, but it's a three *within* the first two counts of the larger three.

Here is a haiku which leans heavily on the use of the "ssss" sound contrasted against the abruptness of the terminal "t" sound.

haiku #37

savoring the flesh
of your kiss, i chew sun &
spit out midnight stars

The rhythm break is like this:

Sa-vo-RINGGG/the-flesh
of-your KISSSS, i-chew SUNNN
and-spit (pause) / out
mid-Night STARSSSS

Once again, I'm using three.

Here is a more ambitious piece. I wanted to write about sadness, the breaking up of one into two separate pieces. I wanted to capture the feel of separation. I use rhyme ("gone/ flown/song/sung" are all half-rhymes), and rhythm (the middle line sets up an interesting swing with the use of the "s" sound repeated five times within seven syllables), as well as image. The image alone would have been sufficient, but the rhyme and rhythm emphasis add the Afro-centric. In this selection the last word, "harmony," which is three syllables long, contrasts quite unharmoniously with all the preceding words which are either one or two syllables long; in other words, it breaks the unity that had been set up. The irony was that it is the word harmony which breaks the rhythmic unity of the poem.

haiku #123

love gone is bird flown
sad sunset song tartly sung
without harmony

Haiku #48 is what I call a "perfect" haiku, meaning it has exactly seventeen words. Here is an example of using blues imagery. This haiku is a direct variation on the blues line "fattening frogs for snakes." I personify the night, the quality of hurt, and then use a simile to make complete the reference to the blues line.

haiku #48

night moans grip my waist
the arms of hurt snake round me,
i feel like a frog

Here is a piece which has a rather involved origin. The basic line is taken from Ho Chi Minh, who wrote "when the prison doors fly open / the dragons fly out" referring to political prisoners. I had learned that Ho Chi Minh lived for a brief time in Harlem and had been influenced by Marcus Garvey. When Nelson Mandela was released from prison I wanted to capture the feel of that. Upon seeing Mr.

Mandela step into the sunlight, what immediately struck me was the beauty of his smile. Also, Malcolm X and George Jackson approached prison as a school. I had read about imprisoned African National Congress (ANC) militants also approaching captivity as a school. The implied cocoon is the school. Finally, it occurred to me that the whole process was one of transformation. So, I wrote this haiku.

haiku #112
(for Mandela)

emerging from jail
their dragon/our butterfly
his smile is so huge

I was well on the road to using haiku as text, but I still had to figure out how to make haiku work as speech. I don't remember when the answer came to me. It was probably when I heard a musical selection that reminded me of an Art Ensemble of Chicago (AEC) concert which I experienced in Atlanta. The AEC performed one number entirely on large bamboo flutes with shimmering gongs in the background. There was an incredible quality of peace and tranquillity achieved by using long, low, extended notes. I had already mastered the ability to mimic musical instruments and the key was to figure out how to achieve that feeling/sound. I tried and tried and eventually was able to achieve a sound similar to a bass flute but not quite as mellow as the big bamboo flute.

Once I had the sound, I figured then I could improvise the words in the sense of repeating them, extend them, repeat phrases, inbetween blowing the flute notes. The key was to get inside the sound completely. There is no set melody. No set rhythms. I use however I am feeling at the moment, close my eyes, and listen to my breathing. As I begin reciting, sometimes it takes a minute to begin, sometimes longer. Generally, I cannot do more than two or three haiku at a time because it takes so much energy. But I had figured it out. The test, of course, was to perform it. It works!

There is another component. I use microphone techniques which I have learned not only from performing but also from radio work. I know how to blow across, next to, and into a microphone so that the noise of the air mixes with the sounds/words emanating from my larynx to form the total sound of the haiku presentation. At one point, I wondered could

I do it without a microphone. The answer was yes, as long as I was in a small room and was very close to the audience.

What I had previously done in the long form, in the blues and jazz forms, I could now achieve in the haiku form—I was close to figuring out a theory of Black poetics.

I knew that I had to have an audience and that it had to be orated. Working with the haiku gave me a missing part: how to put the aesthetics into the text so that the piece could stand on its own as text *and, at the same time,* serve as lyric for the ultimate oration of the selection. I have been working on this for the last five years. Experimenting. Studying. Talking with other poets. Actually, I have been working on this for many, many years; it's just that over the last five years I have been focused. Why?

On the one hand, reciting poetry was easy. But explaining what I was doing and how I did it was not so easy. I wanted to be able to articulate the theory as well as articulate the poem. Moreover, I understood that there was a need to compete in the arena of text.

It was clear that if my poetry was going to be published by people other than myself, then it had to achieve viability on the page and be able to stand up as text in comparison to most English poetry. I wanted to create a body of poetry that would make a contribution to the African American literary tradition. I was not in search of popularity—what I wanted, and have always wanted, was relevance. The difference is that now I view relevance not in the present tense but rather in the continuum.

Tom Dent articulates a belief that I share. Rather than in the present, our most important audience may be in the future; those who find antecedent and inspiration in the work that we do. I want to posit poetry worthy of that audience's perusal and study. This is a major shift in my thinking. I have moved from immediate feedback from our contemporary community as validation. I now believe the validation of our work comes not solely from the community as it currently exists, but also from the community as it existed in the past and as I think/hope it will exist in the future.

How does one receive validation from the past? By consciously incorporating the tradition and keeping alive the spirit of the ancestors. How does one receive validation from the fu-

ture? By consciously creating cradles that will support future efforts.

I go back to Langston Hughes. It is not enough just to write poetry. I must also gather and uphold the dispersed work of early poets (many of whom were overlooked in their time much like many of us are overlooked now). I must close the circle, reconstruct the calabash. I must dare to care about my ancestors and make a fitting home for them within whatever contemporary space I call home because "my home" is not truly home unless and until my ancestors are there with me. At some point we must understand that "caring" for our history is also a creative act.

The western notion of "self" (in general, and of the artist in particular) as an autonomous individual is what we are struggling against. When I collect and cause to be printed (or recorded) the works of ancestor poets, I have, in the collective sense, written poetry.

This is why in 1990 I edited, and, in conjunction with Felton Eaddy, produced *WORD UP, Black Poetry of the '80s from the Deep South.* That anthology featured sixty-seven poems by forty (evenly divided female/male) poets, representing each of the nine deep South states excluding Alabama and Arkansas.

In my introduction I addressed both the question of "poetry" per se and the rationale behind the title. Listen:

> Poetry is a revealer. And a connector. By revealing the essence of us, our differences as well as our commonalities, poetry makes it possible for us to know our individual selves, our collective selves, and also know others on a visceral level through the power and impact of art.
>
> At the gut level, the only substitute for firsthand experience is art. Quality poetry emotionally connects us to the world—it both helps the world "know" and, hopefully, understand us while simultaneously and dialectically helping us to know and understand the world. When the poet is really poeting, the poet becomes the voice of our heart as well as the window on the souls of others.
>
> While it is important to look out on the world, we also desperately need to understand ourselves, our condition, and, yes, our slavery nurtured psychosis—it is painful to realize how well we aren't. Our art helps us recognize and cope with both our negatives and our positives.

Though this recognition of the reality of our condition might be unpleasant at times, rather than papering over these differences, art delves deeply into them. Great art is always specific, always telling in how well it details the interior lives of those who create the art and those who are the subject matter of the art.

Although African Americans are one people, there are contradictions and differences among us, especially now that the great leveler of segregation has been lifted slightly. The gender gap, or the age gap, or the class gap is sometimes so wide that often only the mediation of art enables us to make the connection between where we are and where our sister or brother is.

Only after we actually feel the difference, only then can the majority of us even begin to feel what the other feels, and only after making the emotional connection can we earnestly commit ourselves to building community and closing the gap between us. Art enables us to care about others, others whom we might otherwise ignore.

But beyond that, we are dealing with another need. This anthology is for those of us who not only love and recognize the connective potency of poetry, but indeed who actually need poetry to survive. Although music is generally considered the *sine qua non* of African American life, there is no contradiction in elevating poetry to the level of music because, from our perspective, poetry, which is the music of spoken language, is just another way to sing.

Listen some more:

We decided on the name WORD UP because it implied not only an (re)ascension of the Afro-centric aesthetic, the very name WORD UP also reverberates on the term "Word."

"Word" is both a popular expression of the '80s and a concept of historic resonance for African Americans. Most of our people are familiar with the concept of "word" from the Bible (as in: "in the beginning was the Word and the Word was with God, and the Word was God,"). But there is also the racial memory of traditional African concepts such as "nommo" which find their new world corollary in the concept of "word."

Additionally, by saying "Up" we not only implied that we were coming "up out of the South," we also implied that we were attempting to raise the WORD to a higher level.

So thus we created WORD UP as an effort to provide exposure for and to display the works of African American poets who were working in the deep South, and who also, consciously or unconsciously, espoused an Afro-centric aesthetic sense which bases their work in the day-to-day lives, loves, and aspirations of working-class African Americans. Although we did not impose any aesthetical or political guidelines, most of the poets who responded clearly adhere to this perspective.

Compare the "sound" of the introduction to *WORD UP* with the sound of the pieces quoted from *Nkombo*—I do not disavow nor repudiate those earlier works, for they accurately represent their place and time. I am simply speaking now from a different place, sounding what I see, and suggesting that while the objectives are approximately the same as we had in the past, and while the subject remains the same, the song/sound itself has been deepened by carrying the weight of experience.

From the specific standpoint of writing poetry as text, once I understood what I was trying to do, I then went back to theoretical text I had read, back to interviews, back to discussions I had had with others. I reviewed and updated.

There were several pieces that served as my major springboard in focusing on Afro-centric language as text. One was an interview I did with Toni Cade Bambara which was published in Vol. 2, No. 4 (1980) issue of *First World:*

FIRST WORLD: Are you consciously trying to do anything in particular with your style of writing?

TONI CADE BAMBARA: I'm trying to learn how to write! I think there have been a lot of things going on in the Black experience for which there are no terms, certainly not in English at this moment. There are a lot of aspects of consciousness for which there is no vocabulary, no structure in the English language which would allow people to validate that experience through the language. I'm trying to find a way to do that.

FW: Do you see yourself, then, essentially in search of a language?

TCB: That's one of the things I'm trying to do.

FW: Why hasn't this happened before? Do you think other writers have tried to do this and been unsuccessful?

TCB: I don't know. I do know that the English language that grew from European languages has been systematically stripped of the kinds of structures and the kinds of vocabularies that allow people to plug into other kinds of intelligences. That's no secret. That's part of their whole history, wherein people cannot be a higher sovereign than the state. The time when wise folk were put to the rack was also a time when books were burned, temples razed to the ground, and certain types of language "mysteries"—for lack of a better word—were suppressed. That's the legacy of the West. I'm just trying to tell the truth and I think in order to do that we will have to invent, in addition to new forms, new modes and new idioms. I think we will have to connect language in that kind of way. I don't know yet what that is.

The second part of the article on Toni, the commentary, is a cogent summation of the quest for language:

Achieving a written language is not simply about duplication, or even "replication," of the language we *hear* in our communities and neighborhoods. Because, like our music, as of this moment there is no adequate form of written notation which can fully render our sound to paper. The struggle of the committed African-American writer is to create the written forms which can adequately translate the reality and visions, the past, present, and hoped for future, into black-and-white on a page.

In an effort to give "currency" to our mother tongue and its "folksy" essence, some of our writers have taken to attempting to write in a way that mimics or mirrors African-American speech. This process, at one time called "dialect," is characteristic not only of African-American literature, but also characteristic of most of the literature of African peoples who have been colonialized in the Western hemisphere whenever diasporan-African writers attempted to *give voice to* or *be the voice of* the particular people from which they originate.

In the U.S.A. the most frequently cited paradigm of this process and style of writing was the "Negro" verse of Paul L. Dunbar. During the sixties, trying to get down to it,

we would "be" dropping g's and adopting a ditty-bopping style which was better understood and appreciated when *heard* than simply *read*. The elliptical spelling and speech-like patterns of Ntozake Shange are probably the best-known examples of seventies dialect writing. But words change, sounds change, tempo, rhythm, and the gestures associated with talk, all of that changes and, thus, I suggest that "dialect" alone has only a surface relationship to the actual quest for the mother tongue, for an African-American language.

In the Caribbean and in Central and South America, this process, the use of "dialect," generally is referred to as using the local *"patois."* The *patois* is generally the African-ization of the colonial language. What is sometimes referred to as "Black English" is actually African-American *patois*.

In a context within which the use of African languages was strictly forbidden (either *de jure* or *de facto*) and actively discouraged by force, our people's use of *patois* reflects not, as has been mistaken by some, the attempt of the ignorant and illiterate to speak the English (or French or Spanish or Portuguese) language; rather, the significance of *patois* is that it reflects the will of our people to inject our African root and essence into everything we do and say, and especially into the way we communicate *with each other*. Patois, in our case "Black English," is not the bastard tongue of aliens and slaves imitating the master. *Patois* is the affirmation of the African presence in the Western hemisphere.

Furthermore, language is not just style, it is not only "how" we say or write something. What makes one language fundamentally different from another is not how it sounds, but, indeed, its actual "structure," which is derived from the users' worldview, i.e., how the users of the language view themselves, other people, and the world. The creation of any language which is *fundamentally different in worldview* from the colonial language is the most subversive act, short of actual revolution, that any colonized people can conceive and carry out.

Unfortunately, most of us who are literate in the colonial tongue, especially those of us who are nonpolitical or apolitical oriented writers, have generally failed to understand the importance of establishing the mother tongue. Too many of us as writers have spent unretrievable time attempting to demonstrate that we had mastered the colonial language. Thus, much of our "writing" has an "outside" quality *vis-à-vis* our own people. We write from the outside looking in, we write as an observer/*voyeur* who is explaining to others (those who are equally "literate" in the colonial language) what these "people," our own people, are all about. It is essentially a pimp/peephole act/art.

In fact, the very act of writing and publishing in the post-chattel slavery period is often considered a sign that some writer has "made it," i.e., collaborated with and been accepted by the colonial master.

A major part of my search was not for content but for structure, and this is no simple search. For example, Jean Toomer eschewed the Euro-centric forms and embraced the *patois* when he wrote the prose of *Cane*. I believe this is the case precisely because prose is the everyday written usage of language susceptible to "common," as well as specialized, influences. Prose is also less literary in the sense that prose as a totality is not claimed as the province of a select group (i.e., the intelligentsia).

This was not always the case, particularly in those historic eras when writing in toto was the province of a special class. Yet, what was democratic in the history of writing in America was prose precisely because industry cannot do without prose. They need manuals and minutes of meetings, records of transactions and logs detailing merchandise, discoveries, exploits, and military operations. Why else was the slave narrative possible? Why not slave poems? Why not slave songs?

If you are interested, look at how many critical texts have been written about African American prose as compared to the number of critical texts written about African American poetry. Critical consideration evidences acceptance by the intelligentsia.

Prose is also more open to experimentation, hence we have the magic realism of Latin America or the *Memories of Fire* Americas history trilogy by Eduardo Galiano. But poetry, on the other hand, because it is a distillation of language, is the most codified. The poetic text is the last bastion of Euro-centric linguistic domination.

After Toni Cade Bambara, the second influence was Barbadian poet/historian Edward Kamau Brathwaite, the person whom I consider the greatest living poet in the western hemisphere. Period. In the early eighties I did an interview with Brathwaite which remains unpublished.

> **SALAAM:** What are you trying to do with your poetry now?
>
> **BRATHWAITE:** My poetry has been concerned, for a long time now, with the attempt to reconstruct, in verse, in metric, and in rhythms, the nature of the culture of the people of the Caribbean. This involves not only discovering what I would call "new poetic forms"—a breakaway from the English pentameter—but also, and more importantly, discovering the nature of our folk culture, the myths, the legends, the speech rhythms, the way we express ourselves in words, the way we express ourselves in song. That has been my concern for about ten years and is increasingly so. One has to develop technical resources of a very complex nature and at the same time one has to get an increasing knowledge of who our people are, where they come from, and the nature of their soul.
>
> **SALAAM:** What's so important about that?
>
> **BRATHWAITE:** Well, what's important is that until we can do that we remain "ex-selves," we remain nobodies, we remain just imitations of those who had colonized us. Considering that the man in the street, our own people, the common man has always been himself, it is ridiculous that the artists have remained a shadow of that self. What we have to do now is to increasingly bring the artist and the people together.
>
> **SALAAM:** Do you prefer working on the page or would you like to do more recordings?
>
> **BRATHWAITE:** Both. I wouldn't separate them. My poems start off as rhythms in my head, as patterns of songs which also have an objective. The patterns of songs have to say something, address themselves to some problems, or go through some dialectical process. From my head they have to be transferred onto the page, because that's how I started, but then from the page I instinctively transfer it on to song. In other words, every time I write a poem I have to either have it read or read it myself to some kind of audience before I'm satisfied that it's a real poem. The recordings are a necessary part of the whole process.
>
> **SALAAM:** What's the importance of the audience in that process?

BRATHWAITE: The audience gives me feedback. The audience completes the circle. The audience are the people I'm writing about and for, and therefore if they can't understand what I'm saying, it means that it might be that I've failed. There are some cases where I think I'm ahead of the audience, but then I would know that and they would know it too, but you've got to start from a base that the audience and yourself agree on and move from there.

SALAAM: Who is this audience that you speak of? Obviously you don't just mean people in general?

BRATHWAITE: I start off with a Caribbean audience which is representative of the people who have been down-pressed. The audience is usually a mixed audience, moving in terms of class from college educated to middle class right *up* to the laboring class, because that is how our society is composed.

SALAAM: What immediate reactions do you find valuable as verification and what long-range reactions do you find valuable as verification?

BRATHWAITE: The immediate reactions are one of assent or dissent. You can tell from face and feeling, body movement, if you are saying the right thing. That is clear. But the long-range reaction is very interesting. I'll give you an example: I'm starting to use a lot of possession (religious) sequences in my work. Because the work is culturally accurate, instinctively when people come to it they want to perform it, they don't just want to read it. Nearly all my work in the Caribbean is done as a performance with groups. Now, a young group of actors recently came into contact with my latest poem which was essentially involved with religion, native religion, Afro-Caribbean religion. They were not themselves fully aware of what I was talking about, but they could tell from the descriptions, the external aspects of the descriptions, the kinds of churches I was talking about. They went to those churches in order to experience for themselves what was happening, and many of them have now become members of those churches. As artists they find themselves now being fulfilled as members of those people's churches. I think that's a very significant long-term effect, because it is really motivating people not just to talk about their culture but to become participants in its

root basis. The Haitians have done it too. The Haitians are increasingly returning to vodun as a central experience. With the African person the religion is the center of the culture, therefore every artist, at some stage, must become rootedly involved in a religious complexity.

SALAAM: How do you deal with the mystification inherent in much of the religion?

BRATHWAITE: It is not mystification at all, that's the thing about it. The religion is so natural, it is so vital, it is so socially oriented, so people oriented that there is no mysticism—mental mystification—in it at all. That is really the difference between an African-oriented religion and a European one. Theirs is very mystified because they are not dealing with a living god, they're not dealing with man in relation to god in relation to community.

SALAAM: They're not people-centered.

BRATHWAITE: Right. In the African sense the religion is medicine, it is philosophy, it is martial arts, it is everything, holistic.

SALAAM: In that sense, the work you are doing is people-centered work as opposed to idea-centered?

BRATHWAITE: Right. As opposed to art-centered work, art for art's sake.

From a vision outside the U.S.A. but inside the African diaspora, Brathwaite grapples with the same issues I have grappled with throughout my life. While I agree with the overall tenor of what he said, I think he avoids dealing with the "blues," which is simply our response to the denial of our humanity by humans more powerful than both we and our traditional god(s). Brathwaite is not a "practicing" member of any particular organized religious group. He locates the center of religion in the people orientation. This is an avoidance of the most troubling question: why did our old gods fail us, what did we do to deserve our lot, to be(come) so Black and blue.

We reenter the question raised much earlier in this writing. There is a schism between the blues folk and the religious (particularly the Christians). I agree with Brathwaite that there must be a religious center, spiritual beliefs—but I do not believe that presupposes organized religions, whether Christian or Islamic. A central (and, some would say, existential) question ultimately must be addressed by every serious writer who confronts African American culture: the failure of "God" (religion) to provide earthly deliverance.

In search of the answer I went back to the beginning, to the core, to the people and placed my faith in them and in nature, in what I can witness and in what created me, thus:

haiku #58

> black people believe
> in god, and i believe in
> black people, amen

Ultimately, every African American poet worth her or his salt must address in one way or another, directly or indirectly, bluntly or subtly, this most basic of all questions: how come we must suffer so. Regardless of the specific answer posed or the specific solution suggested, I believe such wrestling is an essential characteristic of the Black aesthetic and is also the source of our characteristic melancholic tinge which colors, to one degree or another, every African American gesture.

My understanding of the phenomenology of Black poetry was further uplifted by Kamau Brathwaite through an instructive lecture published in text form as *History of the Voice*. In terms of explicating the structure of his poetic language and relating that language to the liberation struggle, Brathwaite had gone further than any poet I knew. Brathwaite's work has parallels in the work of some linguists, but the difference is: Brathwaite was dealing with the inherent revolutionary nature of Black expressive voice in the face of colonial domination, a paradigm which remains profoundly applicable today.

Brathwaite defines "nation language" thusly:

> National language is the language which is influenced very strongly by the African model, the African aspect of our New World/ Caribbean heritage. English it may be in terms of some of its lexical features. But in its contours, its rhythm and timbre, its sound explosions, it is not English, even though the words, as you hear them, might be English to a greater or lesser degree. . .
>
> Now I'd like to describe for you some of the characteristics of our nation language. First of all, it is from, as I've said, an oral tradition. The poetry, the culture itself, exists not in a dictionary but in the tradition of the spoken word. It is based as much on sound as it is on song. That is to say,

the noise that it makes is part of the meaning, and if you ignore the noise (or what you would *think* of as noise, shall I say) then you lose part of the meaning. When it is written, you lose the sound or the noise, and therefore you lose part of the meaning. Which is, again, why I have to have a tape recorder for this presentation. I want you to get the sound of it, rather than the sight of it.

> In order to break down the pentameter, we discovered an ancient form which was always there, the calypso. This is a form that I think nearly everyone knows about. It does not employ the iambic pentameter. It employs dactyls. It therefore mandates the use of the tongue in a certain way, the use of sound in a certain way. It is a model that we are moving naturally towards now. Compare:

> *To be or not to be, that is the question*

> to

> *The stone had skidded arc'd and bloomed into islands*
> *Cuba San Domingo*
> *Jamaica Puerto Rico*

> But not only is there a difference in syllabic or stress pattern, there is an important difference in shape of intonation. In the Shakespeare, the voice travels in a single forward plane towards the horizon of its end. In the kaiso, after the skimming movement of the first line, we have a distinct variation. The voice dips and deepens to describe an intervallic pattern. And then there are more ritual forms like *kumina*, like *shango*, the religious forms, which I won't have time to go into here, but which begin to disclose the complexity that is possible with nation language.
>
> The other thing about nation language is that it is part of what may be called *total expression*, a notion which is not unfamiliar to you because you are coming back to that kind of thing now. Reading is an isolated, individualistic expression. The oral tradition, on the other hand, demands not only the griot but the audience to complete the community: the noise and sounds that the maker makes are responded to by the audience and are returned to him. Hence we have the creation of a continuum where meaning truly resides. And this *total expression* comes about because people are in the open air, because people live in conditions of

poverty ("unhoused"), because they come from a historical experience where they had to rely on their very *breath* rather than on paraphernalia like books and museums and machines. They had to depend on *immanence,* the power within themselves, rather than the technology outside themselves.

What was important for me was that Brathwaite had clearly articulated not only structural differences but also the social basis for those differences. When I put Brathwaite's insights with Zora Neal Hurston's remarks about "Negro Expression," the shape of the poetry I wanted and needed to create became clear.

Zora Hurston's article, currently available in the volume *Sanctified Church,* is at once a timeless meditation on the nature of *why* and *how* we express ourselves, as well as a period piece obviously grounded in (but not limited by) the "slang" of her era.

> Very few Negroes, educated or not, use a clear clipped "I." It verges more or less upon "Ah." I think the lip form is responsible for this to a great extent. By experiment the reader will find that a sharp "i" is very much easier with a thin taut lip than with a full soft lip. Like tightening violin strings.

Zora's ruminations opened a number of doors of inner insight for me, especially when set in the framework constructed by Brathwaite. In essence, Zora Hurston advised me to study our people, totally and without shame.

Well before I could intellectually articulate my theory of a Black aesthetic, I had already accepted the basic tenets because I loved the music of John Coltrane. My love of Coltrane was not instantaneous. In fact, early on I would walk out of the room when Coltrane came on the Saturday evening jazz radio program which I listened to religiously. But there was something that pulled me into Trane's sound. Eventually, I realized "that woman" was in his horn, i.e., Trane was a profound blues musician. In him, once again I heard the cry of the blues, a cry that was both brutally raw in its sound and sophisticated in its articulation.

My ultimately successful efforts to feel, embrace, and understand Coltrane intellectually stimulated and spiritually focused my development of Afro-centric literary theories.

Throughout my life, music has always preceded intellectual discovery. The sound of the music would grab me well before I could make sense out of the structure and sophisticated articulation of both the country blues singers and the modern jazz musicians.

Modern jazz moved me to think, particularly John Coltrane. In modern jazz, Coltrane reintroduced blues as the dominant emotional vector as well as conceptual structure of his music. Afterwards, he began incorporating both spirituals/gospel and world musics in his work. Finally, he added a spiritual dimension to his work by proposing that we are all one, and all part of a much larger life force. Coltrane articulated key aspects of his philosophy in conversation with Nat Hentoff who wrote the liner notes for Coltrane's path-breaking release *Meditations*.

> Once you become aware of this force for unity in life, you can't ever forget it. It becomes part of everything you do. In that respect, this is an extension of A Love Supreme since my conception of that force keeps changing shape. My goal in meditating on this through music, however, remains the same. And that is to uplift people, as much as I can. To inspire them to realize more and more of their capacities for living meaningful lives. Because there certainly is meaning to life.

The awesome inclusiveness of Trane's music—a sound at once informed by the world yet unmistakably and unalterably Black—suggested to me the possibility of a nonracist approach to Afro-centrism. His music was like the sun, radiating ideas (shooting them out to investigate the depths of the universe) and at the same time gravitationally so strong that it pulled an entire galaxy into orbit around itself. Any question I could pose, the music had already addressed. Every answer I would achieve, the music would prepare me to accept. By 1992 I had begun formalizing my approach, or, as the musicians would say: I had found my sound.

What is interesting here is that although much of my work, particularly the oral, was immediately identifiable, the sound I had was not the sound I was reaching to attain. Again, the music is instructive. Jazz is generally created in a collective but simultaneously always celebrates the individual. In the best jazz combos, one can tell who each musician is just by hearing their own unique sound, yet it is paradoxical that an individual sound is developed by playing with others, never in isolation, even though the isolation of shedding is necessary to develop craft, develop technique. But technique is not sound. That is why Thelonious Monk, for instance, is immediately identifiable as a pianist even though he did not have the technical abilities of many pianists of lesser importance to the music.

All of these kinds of considerations are reflected in my poetry. While I spent years experimenting and performing, writing and rewriting, refashioning and/or jettisoning old ideas and techniques, discovering new ones and adopting others, through all of that I knew that ultimately it was about being myself. I had to find out who I was and had to articulate the truths that I found.

Eventually, I also understood that, if I were successful, not only would I create my own sound, I would also create my own sense. Like Black musicians have for hundreds of years, I would learn by reflection and projection, reflecting on myself and the world, projecting what I had discovered. I would have my own sound and I would conceive my own sense of what my life was about. This revelation is best expressed in a short poem contained in *What Is Life?*, a collection of poetry and essays published by Third World Press in 1994.

THE MEANING OF LIFE

sometimes I sit
　　and I wonder
　　　what is the meaning
　　　of life
I sit
sometimes
and I wonder
　　and then I realize
　　I am the meaning
　　of my own life
the meaning is me

In June of 1994 I finished a collection of love poetry titled *I Enter Your Church*. Containing a poem written in 1965 and including many others written over a two-decade period, this collection has a range that none of my previous poetry collections were able to reach precisely because I am now consciously working from a structure.

To create what I call revolutionary Black art within a dominant and dominating White supremacist culture requires me as an African American artist to develop a consciousness that strives for the purity of artistic expression rather than simply an uncritical and unartistic reversion to raw expression. All artists must study if their work is to move beyond naive expressionism into modernity. What is the difference between modernity and naiveté? Modernity is reflective while naiveté is reflexive. Modernity thinks before it acts. Naiveté acts simply as it feels. Regardless of what I or any of my contemporaries may feel, or think, the fact is we not only live in a modern age, more importantly we have been psychologically shaped by our modern context.

Regardless of the objective, whether the study of history or the creation of a revolution, whether collaboration with the dominant forces or construction of iconoclastic alternatives, whatever we do will inevitably be *done in the present* (or, as Charlie Parker said on his horn, "Now Is the Time"), a "time" defined by modernity. Inspired by the examples of Coltrane, Cabral, Bambara, Brathwaite, Baraka, Jones, Baldwin and literally hundreds of others, I have fashioned my own individual response to the problems posed by living in these modern times: how to move Black(ly) into the future.

I had chosen to be a writer, a task which by definition included mastering text and/or creating textual alternatives and which by my own personal orientation also required extending the oral tradition. As I grew more mature, I recognized that my task was a "both/and" rather than an "either/or." This was a complex undertaking.

There were numerous examples of great naive art in the fields of music and dance, but that could never be the case with language precisely because textual language is a product of consciousness. One cannot just "feel up" a language, a language must be "thought up." The very act of writing requires thought.

To "consciously" create a literature expressive of a Black aesthetic, we necessarily must first think up what we mean by a Black aesthetic. Dr. Cheikh Anta Diop's *The Cultural Unity of Black Africa* was as important to me in my "thinking up" process (i.e., codifying a Black aesthetic) as was the political theory of Amilcar Cabral in helping me recognize and define the revolutionary character of people-based cultural work.

Particularly applicable was Diop's critique of tragedy and his advocacy of African optimism. Diop located the seeds of the tragic view of life in acceptance of the concept of "original sin."

The themes [of tragedy] always deal, through the action of destiny, with a blind fatality which tends systematically to destroy a whole race or line of descent. They all betray a feeling of guilt, original with and at the same time typical of the Northern cradle. Whether it is a question of Oedipus or the Altrides and Agamemnon, there is always a flow, a crime committed by the ancestors, which has to be expiated irremediably by their descendants, who, from this fact and despite whatever they do, are utterly condemned by fate. Aeschylus tried to reduce the severity of this state of affairs by doing his utmost to introduce the idea of justice, which would allow an innocent posterity no longer to be punished, but to be absolved.

The Semitic conception is identical. The original sin was committed by the very ancestors of the human race and all humanity, condemned from this time to obtain its bread by the sweat of its brow, had to atone for it. This point of view has been adopted and taught by modern religions such as Christianity and Islam.

The importance to me of Diop was that without the mystification of Yacub (the mad scientist who supposedly created "White people") or any other resort to racialism to explain human activity, he offered both an interpretation of the Euro-centric worldview and a human-centered explanation of a sub-Saharan African worldview. Regardless of whatever dreams and aspirations I or any of my peers hold, without rigorously researched, intellectual conceptualizations we would always end up proposing a mystical conceptualization of a Black aesthetic— mystical in the sense that one is asked to simply accept "Blackness" based on a belief system rather than on an interpretation of reality.

Worldwide travel has disabused me of the notion of Black exceptionalism, e.g., "it's a Black thing, you wouldn't understand." Just as, to paraphrase Terrace, there is nothing human that is foreign to me, certainly I as a human being need neither be perceived nor projected as foreign to any other human being. My *chosen* task as a writer is to locate the Black experience within the continuum of human experience. If I could understand the world, then certainly the world could understand me.

Diop gave me insight not only into myself, but into the world at large, as well as insight into my relationship to others in the world. I am profoundly influenced by his conceptions of African culture. *I Enter Your Church* is Diopian in its concepts of relationships.

Hofu had been my first conscious attempt to do this. I intuitively stepped off into areas about which I had limited concrete understanding. From the beginning, I had *felt* the direction I wanted to go, and I had moved with that sensually perceived spirit in my heart. But now there is more than just a song in my heart. There is also something in my head.

For example, in ordering the poems in *Church,* I decided to utilize a structure of birth, maturity, death, and rebirth. After I had completed and assembled the manuscript, I read a reference to this same philosophical system in *Signs and Symbols, African Images in African-American Quilts* by Maude Southwell Wahlman. The author pointed out that the diagrams on some of the quilts were replications of African cosmographs. She went on to point specifically to a Kongo cosmograph built on the same four-part philosophy that I thought was my thought.

As soon as I read it, I was happy. I prefer to be *aboriginal* in my modernity rather than *novel* (or what some call "original"). In essence, the preexistence of African cosmology meant in part that I had intellectually aligned myself with my ancestral foundation. This was cause for great rejoicing.

For my part I had arrived at this place, as many artists do, via an intuitive leap. I had no specific concrete knowledge in hand, but I had cultural predispositions and subtextual teachings which were the result of years of study. Unavoidably, there was a buildup of theories and experiential reflections posited by a wide variety of writings and conversations. For me all of this reached a critical mass in the beginning years of the nineties. In one sense the structure for *I Enter Your Church* was an intuitive leap resulting in a coincidence of concordance with a Kongo cosmogram, but it can also be argued that the structure was simply a qualitative transformation of the quantitative mass of information I had consumed.

Regardless of whether coincidental or logical (albeit subconscious deduction), this structure illustrated the basic unity of African culture. The closer we get to our total selves (i.e., the selves we were, are, and will be/come), the more likely will be our convergence with both ancient and futuristic Afro-centered concepts.

Because I focus on culture, I believe that Africa is not simply land, Africa is people. In fact, not only are African Americans (all over the Diaspora) examples of Africa people, but the culture we produce is African culture even as it is also the product of accretions. In the final analysis, our people in general are always more important than any specific piece of land. I do not mean to imply that the continent of Africa is of negligible concern, but simply that it is not an abstract concern in and of itself, and it is a concern which can only be appreciated in concert with a concern for Africa people worldwide.

Some believe as the Bible says: there is nothing new under the sun. In philosophical essence that may be true, but, in fact, as Great Black Music demonstrates, out of Africa (the people), there is always something new. Africa is both the history and the future of my poetry.

Give thanx.

coda: in order for something to come out, you got to put something in

haiku #125

drum between my legs,
my horn blowing into the
dawn, dance with me please

A Black Aesthetic: Where I'm Coming From/ Going To

1. Affirm life.

No art is completed until it is connected to the people (at the very least another person). Everything of value I have ever experienced has been consummated in a social setting (even if the society was the elemental couple procreating/enjoying life), and this is particularly true of art.

Every expression requires a transmitter, a message, and a receiver—and, of course, whatever it takes to make all three work. In the West the artist is severed from the audience (or the "auditors" as Julio Finn says). My art is incomplete without an audience because our culture is a culture of affirmation.

The old folks used to say, when you enter a room, speak to the people who are already there. When we enter the room of Black culture we should speak to the ancestors and we should expect to get a reply—after all, *the ancients are culture(d)* and will surely respond when spoken to.

Affirmation leads us to appreciate the continuum of life. Louis Armstrong would never have been whole, not to mention noble and bold, without the ancestors (King Oliver and Buddy Bolden) in his horn even when he blew notes that had never been blown before. By creating something new from something old, Louis, and Langston Hughes too, became ancestors of the future. These are the people we go back to know who we are in the present. To be mature is to make yourself worthy of being an ancestor.

2. Make a joyful noise.

Step up and sing. Dance and music are the two most basic gestures of the soul. Yes, work is necessary for physical survival, but art is necessary for soul's survival. Dance because it is the movement of our bodies, our physical selves consonant with the grace and fluidity of life motions stylized in recognition of and emulation of the beauty and the power of the cosmos, the creator. Music because that is how we create imaginary worlds, how we enrich our imaginations, and it is our enriched imaginations which enable us to figure out how to withstand the mundanity of day-to-day slavery.

Dance, properly done, of course, is about being earthlike. Duke Ellington and Sun Ra were always playing for dancers because until you move like the earth circling the sun, like rings around Saturn, like the breezes shaking the leaves, like the motion of the ocean, until you move you do not understand that the basic throb of life is Eros. Stillness is death. At the core of every dance is the celebration of the physical which necessarily leads to arousal. All of our dances, to a greater or lesser extent, are erotic because they celebrate life. There

The Salaams: (seated from left) daughter Tiaji, Kalamu, daughter Kiini, son Mtume; (standing) daughter Asante, son Tutashinda, wife Tayari

is nothing more human, more basic than dance. Nothing.

I approach my poetry as song precisely because song is the synchronizing of the soul with the body. Black song is, or ought to be, the sound of the body moving through life, the sound of the body being beaten or being loved. Song is a cry—just what a baby does. Song expresses our feelings, anxieties, desires and longings, our aspirations and our despairs, both hope and resignation. What is strongest about our songs is the quality of our expressive emoting, declarations unmediated (and hence, uncensored) by the workings of the mind. The mind unavoidably is circumscribed by the rules and regulations, taboos and qualifiers, of whatever society or civilization one finds oneself in.

If you only (or even, *mainly*) think about what you are singing, think about the music you are making, then you are not sharing your truest feelings, emotions. You are not sharing your total self. You are legislating your life,

being a politician. There will necessarily be a discontinuity between what you *say* you are about and what you *feel* and *desire*. This discontinuity inevitably leads to guilt, anxiety, and/or rage (especially when we realize that the expression of some (many?) of our deepest emotions is restricted, if not prohibited, by this society.

The purpose of the noise, the joyful noise, in my art is to disrupt the status quo and free the captive emotions.

The reason our music and dance is about freedom is because it is uncivilized. Uncivilized in the sense of unregulated by the social and moral authorities of America. The profoundness of our song and dance is that expressive participation in the making of music reinforces our resolve to be free. After the music we are emboldened and are ready to take on the police—whether actually dancing in the street or simply rejecting bourgeois propriety. I believe that if I can write a poem which helps people feel what freedom feels like, then, experiencing it momentarily within the ritual of art, they will desire it in their daily lives, and hence, will, of their own accord, think of ways to free themselves from the restrictions of this society.

3. *Pro(Re)claim the blues.*

The blues is a musical response to the socially restrictive, psychologically suppressive, and physically oppressive life we endure in America. The essence of the blues is primal, elemental rather than elaborate (i.e., intellectually deep). The blues is the elegance of emotional survival stripped of any social pretensions or prohibitions—which is why the thematic range may appear limited to those looking for intellectual stimulation. But far from being a limitation, the blues' raw power is what has preserved us.

The blues did more than artistically describe or replicate the essence of life. Being the ritual music that it is, the blues actually inspired and activated two essential qualities: facing up to the brutalness of life and seeking the community of love.

The reason the blues makes us happy even as it moans about pain is because it is mentally healthy to face the facts of life, the painful, the "evils," the wrongs, the losts. Facing adversity rather than suppressing our rage, our anger, our shame, our inadequacies, whatever. Indeed, that is why there seems to be so much violence in the blues; people singing about killing a lover, murdering with a knife, poison, hands, hammer, or a gun. Those lyrics are expressions of real impulses and desires, the real rage that one feels when one is wronged. Rather than sublimate those seeming base emotions, the blues singer shouts them out in a cathartic voice which releases the individual from the need to express the desire through actual mayhem.

Do not misunderstand, the blues is not therapy, because therapy implies illness. The blues is the ounce of cathartic prevention which is better than the pound of psychiatric cure. The healthy personality/society prevents rather than treats mental illness.

Facing up is healthy. And it feels good to publicly acknowledge these facts of life. Polite society would have us suppress these feelings, but when we suppress our real feelings where does the pain go? If we push rage down deep into the personality and deny it an outlet, sooner or later it will manifest itself in one way or another. This is why *civilization* is neurotic,

particularly American life with its myriad denials of reality. After all is said *and done,* what is civilization but a seasoning process that makes a slave "polite and obliging"?

Those who consider the blues profane are reacting to what they consider an affront to their aspirations toward the norms of a society which has enslaved them. Resultantly, and not unsurprisingly in this context, the more Blacks become like the Whites they aspire to be, then the more those same Blacks oppress and/or exploit their own Black selves. We Blacks become collaborating agents and maintainers of our own oppression. This oppression also assumes an intellectual dimension manifested in our disdain for the earthy, the funky, the "primitive," all of which is precisely what the blues is.

In this context I have come to believe that my task as a poet is to confront the unmentioned, the avoided, the suppressed. My task is to emotionally confront rather than to intellectualize. In this connection, poetry is most persuasive in that it is built on a foundation of emotion rather than intellect, cathartic rather than therapeutic. Poetry is the linguistic expression of emotions. This is the structure that the blues gives to my work.

By extension, jazz is blues-based expression expanded by intellectual perceptions. In one of my poems I describe jazz thusly:

> you got to blues i believe, you Black, you
>   got to blues,
> or gospel, or rhythm & blues, or jazz, yes
>   jazz, jazz,
> now that's just another kind of blues with
>   a mind of its own,
> intelligent blues, thinking about things
>   blues, want to know
> blues, want to be blues, new day, sunrise,
>   yes, sunrise of
> that sun gonna shine when the morning
>   come day blues, but
> jazz is still blues, you can tell all them
>   great jazz players,
> they is blues, each and everyone of them,
>   blues masters,
> think of one, anyone, if they can't blues,
>   they can't jazz . . .

Blues and jazz, gospel (actually the whole of Baptist liturgy), and folk music forms, Black music as a whole is the basic underpinning of my poetry. Even when I use the haiku structure, I do so consistent with the aesthetic demands of Great Black Music.

4. Seek unity with all.

We are citizens of the world. We belong to the cosmos. We must stop viewing the world strictly in racial terms, i.e., as White, Black, and Foreign. We must understand that just as we socially belong to the world culture of humankind, in a very primordial *physical* sense we literally belong to and are inextricably part and parcel of the earth. In a *psychic* sense our souls belong to a larger cosmic scene: the great energy field of life. This is the necessary metaphysical component of our mundane expressions, the eternal analog to our temporal existence here on earth. Religion in general is simply (or complexly) an attempt to articulate this most profound connection.

I used the concept of energy field for specific reasons. All of life is relative, neither created nor destroyed, only transformed and, depending on where we are on the continuum at the moment, it is manifested in a physical form. But even when we are physical, within our physical bodies the life energy force cries out for reunion with the cosmos, thus our desire to become one with god (*the* life force).

As I worked out this ideology, I struggled to insert those discoveries into my work. The poem "Earth Day" is a good example.

EARTH DAY

daily, once we arrive
we should ask ourselves what are we
   doing
to make the earth glad
that we are here

walking its face
breathing and being

does our living
help or hurt other
life forms

every time we celebrate
a birthday we should use the
occasion to reaffirm our pledge

to make the earth
glad that we are here

So, at base (writing the word "so" at this point requires another aside). Here is Zora Neal Hurston's explanation for my linguistic use of "so."

In storytelling, "so" is universally the connective. It is used even as an introductory word, at the very beginning of a story. In religious expression, "and" is used. The trend in stories is to state conclusions; in religion, to enumerate.

So, at base, the blues (and by extension all the other forms of Great Black Music) signifies the structure onto which I affix my specific remembrance and life experiences, as well as my intellectual speculations and conclusions. That is how I write my poetry.

* * *

You've got to dream before you can analyze the meaning, and you've got to create a body of work before you can codify a poetic code. Thirty years is a long time. Only after you've gotten to the tail can you tell what the whole looks like.

I did not consciously start out trying to define an aesthetic. For that matter, I was not even guided by an aesthetic, i.e., a codification of beauty. I started moving strictly on a feeling, not a thought. I wanted to sing and I had to figure out how. Even though *I didn't know what I was doing,* I didn't hesitate to move forward with the verve and arrogance characteristic of youth.

To this day I don't know why I became a word singer. Carrying and concretizing the spirit was something I had to do, came crying into this world to do. Like breathing, I could not avoid creative expression. I was born to sing and knew it when I first heard the blues. My whole soul shook, something like when you come but with more passion and with more lasting effect.

But here I am. This is my story, this is my song. Reflecting on how I got over is how I developed my theory of climbing. I didn't learn this in school. It wasn't written in a book. I'm not sure my elevator will lift you up, but I've shared all the secrets I know.

A special shout out to my son, Mtume ya Salaam, who was the line editor for this manuscript. Once I decided to focus exclusively on myself as a poet, as I wrote the text, Mtume suggested cuts, questioned items to include, edited for both flow and comprehension, and served as an excellent sounding board for the overall development, as well as for some of the particular philosophical points. The effort to combine both autobiography and aesthetic theory would have been much less effective were it not for Mtume's valuable insight and editing skills.

Like we always used to sign off: If there is something of value here, take it and pass it on, the rest leave alone.

Everything's gonna be alright.

> *If somebody asks you*
> *Who sang this song.*
> *Tell them Kalamu ya Salaam,*
> *Been here and gone.*

—July 1994

BIBLIOGRAPHY

Poetry and prose:

(Under name Vallery Ferdinand III) *The Blues Merchant: Songs for Blkfolk* (poetry), BLKART-SOUTH (New Orleans), 1969.

Hofu ni kwenu: My Fear Is for You (poetry and essays), Ahidiana (New Orleans), 1973.

Pamoja tutashinda: Together We Will Win (poetry), Ahidiana, 1973.

Ibura (poetry and fiction), illustrations by Arthello Beck, Jr., Ahidiana, 1976.

Tearing the Roof off the Sucker: The Fall of South Afrika (treatise), Ahidiana, 1977.

South African Showdown: Divestment Now (treatise), Ahidiana, 1978.

Nuclear Power and the Black Liberation Struggle (pamphlet), Ahidiana, 1978.

Revolutionary Love (poetry and essays), drawings by Douglas Redd, photographs by Kwadwo Oluwale Akpan, Ahidiana-Habari, 1978.

(With wife, Tayari kwa Salaam) *Who Will Speak for Us? New Afrikan Folk Tales* (for children), Ahidiana, 1978.

Herufi: An Alphabet Reader (for children), Ahidiana, 1979.

Iron Flowers: A Poetic Report on a Visit to Haiti (poetry), Ahidiana, 1979.

Our Women Keep Our Skies from Falling: Six Essays in Support of the Struggle to Smash Sexism and Develop Women (essays and poetry), Nkombo (New Orleans), 1980.

A Nation of Poets (poetry), self-published, 1990.

What Is Life? (essays and poetry), Third World Press, 1994.

Tarzan Can Not Return to Africa/But I Can, Visions 3000, 1995.

I Enter Your Church, forthcoming.

Plays:

The Picket (one-act), first produced in New Orleans at Free Southern Theater, 1968.

Mama (one-act), first produced in New Orleans at Free Southern Theater, 1969.

Happy Birthday, Jesus (one-act), first produced in New Orleans at Free Southern Theater, 1969.

Black Liberation Army (one-act), first produced in New Orleans at Free Southern Theater, 1969.

(With Tom Dent) *Song of Survival* (one-act), first produced in 1969, published in *Nkombo*.

Homecoming (one-act), first produced in New Orleans at Free Southern Theater, 1970, published in *Nkombo*, August 1972.

Blk Love Song #1 (one-act), first produced in New Orleans at Free Southern Theater, 1971, published in *Black Theater, USA: Forty-five Plays by Black Americans, 1847–1974*, edited by James V. Hatch and Ted Shine, Free Press, 1974.

The Quest (one-act), first produced in New Orleans at BLKARTSOUTH, 1972, published in *New Plays for the Black Theatre*, 1989.

Somewhere in the World (Long Live Asatta), first produced in New Orleans at Art for Life Theater Company, 1982, published in *Black Southern Voices*, Meridian, 1992.

Erotique Noire/Black Erotica (poetry), Anchor Books, 1992.

Malcolm, My Son (verse play), first produced at Contemporary Arts Center, New Orleans, 1991, published in African American Review, Vol. 27, No. 1, 1993.

Work represented in anthologies, including *What We Must See: Young Black Storytellers,* edited by Orde Coombs, Dodd & Mead, 1971, *We Be Word Sorcerers: Twenty-five Short Stories by Black Ameri-cans,* edited by Sonia Sanchez, Bantam Books, 1973, and *In Search of Color Everywhere: A Collection of African-American Poetry,* Stewart Tabori & Chang, 1994. Contributor to periodicals, including *Black Scholar, Black World, Catalyst, Encore, Journal of Black Poetry, Negro Digest,* and *Shooting Star.*

Editor and publisher of *Expressions;* coeditor and publisher of *Nkombo;* contributing editor of *Culture;* advisory editor of *First World;* editor (with Felton Eaddy) and compiler of *WORD UP, Black Poetry of the '80s from the Deep South* (an anthology).

Edward Sanders

1939-

Iwas born on August 17, 1939, in Kansas City, Missouri. My mother was Mollie Cravens Sanders and my father was Lyle Sanders; she was thirty-six and he was forty. I was raised in Blue Springs, Missouri, not far from Kansas City, in a red brick house designed by my mother that sat near the bottom of Cemetery Hill, from whose summit the polished stones of the dead flashed at dawn in beaklike beams, an experience later depicted in my poem sequence "Cemetery Hill."

My family heritage came from restless wanderers escaping Europe who spread across America in the early nineteenth century from England and Ireland. It was of course a continuum, but recalled as a fragmentary experience, and family history was passed along through the casual anecdotes of elders and genealogies listed in family Bibles, augmented beginning early this century with the mnemonic influence of photographs. The elders when they were young heard from their elders the fragments of moiling centuries. From the many fragments I heard, I decided when I was a child that life for centuries had been made unnecessarily grim because of what seemed to me an unfair economic system that unduly awards the relentlessly hostile and the aggressive and which exposes humans to unnecessary catastrophe.

My great-grandfather on my father's side, Peter Sanders, had deserted the Confederate army and switched to the Union side during the Civil War. Family legend is obscure on the reasons. He had been born in Tennessee and moved after the war to homestead in southern Missouri. He built a farm north of Mountain Grove, Missouri, deep in the Ozarks and not far from what is now the Mark Twain National Forest. He and his wife, Emily Hardin Sanders, had a bunch of children, one of whom was my grandfather, Sam, who married a woman named Alice Raigain in 1893.

My father was born in 1899 in Mountain Grove. My mother was born in 1903 in Arkansas, but her family moved to southern Missouri

Ed Sanders with the Talking Tie, 1985

where they built a house near Cabool, not far from my father's town. My maternal grandfather, Graham Cravens, was a restless man and an inventor. He worked building railroads and invented a railroad ballast and rail straightening machine. For my older brother he once made a wooden life-size replica of a machine gun with moving parts.

My mother inherited this inventiveness. She could restore old paintings and prints through micropatching and gluing, and I once watched her take apart a grand piano, spread the hammers and levers all over the living-room rug, glue and repair the broken parts, then put it back together again so that it worked perfectly for our music lessons.

Most of my aunts and uncles on both sides left the Ozarks and agricultural life after several centuries of their ancestors working the rural soil for sustenance. When my mother and father met around 1922 they quickly moved north to Kansas City. Mollie had wanted to go to engineering school, but in the 1920s that route was virtually impossible for a woman, especially of modest means.

My mother's mother was Eugenia Cravens, a small but very tough woman whose life seemed greatly spent in the service of food. One of my aunts once described how hard my grandmother Eugenia had to slave: "Just think about Mama: canning all that stuff; she'd can meat, she'd can beets, she'd can fruit. She did everything. They cured meat, they cured ham, she made sausage—wrapped them in corn shucks and hung them in a smokehouse; and did the hams—soaked the hams in the salt and the brine and then hung them up to cure; and cured beef, for chipped beef."

My mother was both strong willed, with powerful opinions, and passive. I remember she asked us to keep our mouths open when we listened to a radio broadcast of a nuclear explosion, fearing the vibrations would shatter our teeth.

My parents lived in Kansas City for a few years, but when my older brother developed asthma they moved to a town twenty miles away for fresher air. They were fairly liberal, considering the conservative area in which we lived, a town which had boosteristic elements right out of a Sinclair Lewis novel. Mollie told anyone that would listen that Senator Joseph McCarthy's Red Scare was a scam.

My mother loved books. When I was around eight she began reading the novels of Charles Dickens to me at bedtime. She told me that a gentleman knew Greek and Latin, an influence that later pointed me toward a college degree in the classics. She had a fine collection of detective novels, and she subscribed to the English humor magazine *Punch*. She was very religious and taught a Sunday school class that was popular with teenagers. My parents' generation believed very strongly that the path out of poverty lay in education. I remember going with my mother to a small stilt-legged cabin near the foundation of the old Civilian Conservation Corps camp in Blue Springs and waiting in the car while she ferreted out a family who were not enrolling their children in school.

Around the age of five

My father traveled through Missouri and Kansas as a sales representative. Before I was born he traveled for a tobacco company and during my childhood he worked a few years for the O'Cedar Corporation, which manufactured furniture polish, oil mops, and newfangled sponge mops with squeegees. Sometimes I accompanied him. It was fun, staying at hotels in places like Hutchinson and Salina, Kansas, and Springfield, St. Joseph, and Joplin, Missouri. It was my first taste of my generation's thrill of "on the road."

My father divided his life into anecdotes—it was through listening to his countless tales that I realized how all of life's time-tracks are material for poems, tunes, and short stories. When I was very young, I would sit on his knee and he would sing spontaneous, rhymed story-songs, an influence that encouraged my interest in chant, verse, and tune.

When I was about six I asked my grandmother Eugenia, who was living with us, about death. She told me, "You will never die." In her Christian context she no doubt believed it was true, but I took it quite literally. I mentioned what she had told me to my mother, who instantly shattered the rosy picture my grandmother had drawn. Not only that, my mother asserted, the body begins to wither at age fifteen.

I remember walking out onto the terrace in front of our brick house, staring up to the top of Cemetery Hill at the sun flashing off the stones, and feeling a total loneliness and forlornerlonerhood shiver, my first sense of the metaphysical anguish described so well by Sartre, a moment described in my poem "Cemetery Hill."

Right around that time Franklin Roosevelt died. My parents were weeping and upset and we all went out on the terrace in front of the house and I was told I should cry, that a great man had passed away. It was my first experience of the overpowering agony of political death, which I would relive on John Kennedy's day, November 22, 1963; Martin Luther King Jr.'s on April 4, 1968; and Robert Kennedy's the following June.

My parents were always volunteering. They worked very hard to help create a consolidated central school district to replace a network of one-room schools. My mother volunteered to sew the drapes in the auditorium in the new elementary school (even though my brother and I were beyond elementary school). She made the drum majorette costumes for the high school marching band. My father was involved in what they called midget football, for boys in the fourth through seventh grades, and paid out of his own pocket for a number of my teams' uniforms.

It had a big impact on me, and to this day I usually say yes to most requests to serve on boards, commissions, committees, environmental newsletters, affordable housing fund-raisers, et alia multa. In my teens I discovered George Bernard Shaw as a model for living a life of art while regularly doing public service for a better world.

My early years were tinctured with the evil, dread, and compassion of World War II. We had huge Victory gardens during the war, which

The house on Cemetery Hill, 1940s

The author's parents, Mollie and Lyle, 1940s

were worked communally by our family and neighbors. We saved grease in containers and turned them in for the war effort; there were ration coupons, retreaded tires, and suspicion of German-speaking neighbors. My brother and sister both enlisted in the navy—Jacqueline was a flight instructor and David was stationed on a ship known as a submarine tender. I watched my father get up at 6 A.M. and lean his head very close to one of those old-fashioned round-topped radios with the cloth-covered speakers to listen anxiously to reports of the war. My mother would bake fruitcakes in small metal containers to send to my brother and sister and their friends.

I began to hate this thing called war. In the Midwest during and after World War II it was the Japanese who were depicted as the universal evil. My parents were aware of the German atrocities and kept my brother and me informed, but there was no mention of the Holocaust in the newspapers or the cultural milieu in which I was raised. However my parents strove to open their minds, I was exposed to considerable racist and anti-Semitic talk from

my extended family (but never from my cousins, brothers, and sisters), not to mention on the streets of the Midwest milieu. Some of my relatives on occasion were almost caricatures of raving crackers. Before I was a teenager I vowed to escape those prejudices.

The American economy was a rattling experience. When I grew up in the Midwest it seemed biased in favor of a hucksteristic, boosteristic in-crowd of bankers and land developers. My own politics were forged in my youthful observations of the Midwest economic moil. On the way to a family dinner once I heard my older brother mention the great socialist Norman Thomas. Many of my relatives seemed shackled to the rat race. I witnessed some of my uncles trapped for decades in jobs they seemed to detest. I vowed not to let that happen.

For a while I attended a classic American all-white one-room school, where the teacher rang a handheld bell to call us in from recess to a room crowded with eight grades. The fall of 1948 gave me my first real exposure to politics.

It occurred out in the play yard of the school when the partisans of Thomas Dewey lined up on one side and those of Harry Truman on the other. "Phooey on Dewey, phooey on Dewey!" my side chanted, and then the fistfights and mudball tossing began.

A relentless suburbanization and subdivision of farmland for commuters to Kansas City began in Blue Springs during my childhood, so that much of the rurality was seized away through thoughtless development. Ponds where we used to ice-skate were transformed to malls, and a fancy house now occupies the play yard for the one-room school I attended.

There were families when I grew up that still pumped their water by hand from iron spigots in their kitchens. Outhouses, which we would haul into town on Halloween and build barricades with in the middle of Main Street, were still in use in the countryside. The town once had a band shell in the middle of Main Street, but as cars became bigger and faster, and pavement arrived, it had to go. Some of the flavor of my hometown can be found in my story "Lophophora Roller Rink," in volume I of *Tales of Beatnik Glory.*

There was trouble at home and economic cycles of largesse followed by poverty the children only understood through parental bickering or a paucity of presents beneath the Christmas tree. My father became a heavy drinker, and there was shouting and turbulence. It looked as if my parents would break up. My dad hid his drinking and stashed hundreds of empty little whiskey bottles in a crevice in the basement. Sometimes I'd shine a flashlight into the fissure, across the field of shiny bottles that looked like huge water bugs. After a few years, my father stopped drinking, recovering his gentleness, and our childhood assumed a more normal American throb.

I discovered the out-of-doors—especially the woods along the creeks that meandered toward the Missouri River a few miles away. Ahh, I loved them. My grandmother had taught me the names of plants and herbs. The happiest times of my early years were all-day walks in the woods and overnight camp outs. This love of the forests and the natural world found its way into the nature poetry I would write forty years later in my book *Hymn to the Rebel Cafe.*

There was an inconsistency in my "march orders" in the late 1940s and early 1950s. My parents encouraged me to stand up and not "take any anything from anybody," yet I was at the same time encouraged to take as an absolute given the culture and particularly the economic system in which I felt even then my family was mired. I was told I was different—I was supposed to excel, and yet at the same time I was to melt into the big Midwest waffle. In a culture that resembled Brecht's *Rise and Fall of the City of Mahagonny* and worth was measured in money, it was difficult to feel fully that specialness, given the economic ups and downs my family experienced.

Yet, in many ways my life was very much in the Midwestern vein. I was in the Boy Scouts and the Order of DeMolay, and I took part in school theatrical productions. I was president of the junior class and president of the student body my senior year. I was on the football and basketball teams. I played bass drum in the high school marching band and took snare drum lessons from a woman with the Kansas City Philharmonic. I took the obligatory four years of piano lessons before miffing my mom by quitting, especially after all the work she'd done restoring the piano.

What Kenneth Rexroth called "the light from Plymouth Rock" shone brightly in our home where, for instance, my mother set the rule that we were not allowed to use the word "belly." "Stomach" was the acceptable word. Yet when my father was drunk he broke all rules of proper speech, and there was extremely erotic language of all kinds in the school yard beginning in the first grade.

Like a secret drum beat, the culture resounded with affection for the American Outlaw. I absorbed this ironic Midwestern phenomenon so that while I thirsted for affection and even got baptized to please my grandmother, at the same time I enjoyed getting into trouble with local authorities. Once a bunch of us broke into the local jail and liberated some friends who had been arrested for what was called in the Midwest "Halloweening." One of the stories told by my mother's family was how as a child my grandfather Graham Cravens used to ride on his uncle's ferry boat across the Missouri River from Missouri City to Kansas City. The outlaw Jesse James used the ferry and allowed my grandfather to sit on his horse during the river run. In the woods where I used to hike, not far from my house, were initials cut into trees (purportedly by the outlaw gang the Younger Brothers), which we visited like a shrine.

The road toward writing was casual and somewhat accidental. There was my father's love of anecdotes, his singing of made-up poems, and my mother's love of books. After an infraction in grade school, I had to write an essay, "Why I Should Not Talk in Study Hall," and I turned out spontaneous page after page. At just that moment, perhaps inspired by the humor pieces in *Punch,* I discovered satire.

I was increasingly unhappy within the milieu in which I was being raised. I knew I could get out of there in just a few years and I began plotting my escape. My family was very religious—I had been raised to look for "salvation" for "inspiration," and to have "optimism" to have "hope." It was part of my agrarian heritage: grumble, look at the sky, and plow. Then I discovered poetry, and I could see the doors of my earthly salvation swing open.

My first poetic discovery was the works of Edgar Allan Poe, whose poems brought grace to my crusty sense of loneliness and boy-anguish. I had no idea Poe had inspired, say, Allen Ginsberg or Charles Baudelaire and a million others. It was my first experience of being "stunned" by writing. After just a few hours' reading, I was sure he had given me the keys with which to find some threnodic solace in the Poe-like quality of my own life with unsettled, unhappy parents in a moiling, often mean little American town with the farmers selling their fields all around us to make subdivisions.

In the spring of 1955, when I was fifteen, I wrote some poems for an English class taught by Lecie Hall. Life was never the same after that. Lecie Hall liked my verse and encouraged me to write. She did not censor my Poe-like, young boy morbidity, and, although she was very moral and proper, did not discourage my voyage into forbidden imagery. Some of my early poetry was religious and years later Mrs. Hall would read them to her Sunday school class. I began to carry my poems with me wherever I went, though I showed them to no one, except once in a while to Mrs. Hall.

It was in ice-skating that I first discovered the thrill of the beauty of motion. Olympic champion Dick Button was my hero, and during Missouri's brief ice-skating season I would go at midnight down to nearby Lake Tapawingo and borrow someone's lawn chair and ice-skate

with it in waltzes of bliss for hours beneath a wintery moon.

I was interested in the theater and acted in a number of high school productions. When I was sixteen, I discovered jazz in Kansas City. On Sunday nights a bunch of us protorebels would drive to a place called Jazznocracy where we'd dance to ultrahot music. One Sunday there'd be Jay McShann and his band, and the next there'd be a wild sax player named Big Bob Dougherty and his band. We didn't call it jazz. To my crowd, it was music to which we could dance as wildly as we wanted without censorship. It was a chance to dance interracially. It was my first taste of the freedom of performance. It was wonderful. Sometimes they'd circle up around a dancing couple and shout the Beat era's favorite exhortation, "Go! Go! Go!" I loved rolling my girlfriend across my back and pulling her between my legs to early rock and roll.

All of a sudden, rock and roll became important. Once my friends and I went to see

A senior in high school on the edge of the prairie,
1957

Bill Haley, Chuck Berry, Frankie Lymon, and Bo Diddley at the Kansas City Municipal Auditorium, where I witnessed my first teen gang knife fights; I glanced nearby during Chuck Berry's duckwalk and saw a wounded kid on the floor. And then I was exposed to my first sense of the adoration of fans when my high school girlfriend tried to get into Frankie Lymon's dressing room after the gig.

My mother died in early 1957 from diabetes. It was the most horrible thing imaginable, and it happened during a time I was quarreling with her almost daily. A boy seeing his mother in the coffin—few things are more painful in the whole universe. I've seldom had what could be called spiritual experiences. One was when Mollie died in the hospital and yet miles away I heard her voice cry out—a moment described in my poem "Cemetery Hill."

Nothing could be more horrible, yet I realized that it set me completely free from my upbringing. I felt at once rootless and I realized I could define my life from now on exactly as I chose and could completely sever any contact with anyone whom I felt was trying to block or to hinder what I wanted to do.

It was spring and I had to return to school to finish my senior year in high school. My secret clipboard of poetry that I carried with me was almost my only source of hope. It helped me overcome the feelings of anger, worthlessness, and guilt over her possibly preventable death.

The fall after Mollie's death, I began a year at the University of Missouri in Columbia, where an accidental encounter in the university bookstore with the books of the Beat Generation changed the course of my life. I purchased Allen Ginsberg's *Howl and Other Poems,* with the introduction by William Carlos Williams, some issues of *Evergreen Review* (especially the one about the San Francisco writing scene), Lawrence Ferlinghetti's *A Coney Island of the Mind,* and Gregory Corso's *Gasoline.* My experience at the bookstore made me obsessed with bookstores (the churches of my generation), and I began to spend as much time as I could in their poetry sections.

For my own life, reading "Howl" was an epochal event. It was to me at eighteen what Poe had been at fifteen, except that Ginsberg was an energizer whereas Poe tended to calm one down. The Beats urged on us an intoxicating mix of spontaneity and scholarship, and they urged us not to be afraid to experiment both in our lives and in our art. When I returned to my hometown, I would chant whole sections of "Howl" to my drinking buddies as we drove aimlessly around at midnight drinking beer, an experience described in "A Book of Verse" in the first volume of *Tales of Beatnik Glory.*

After a year at the University of Missouri, I knew I wanted to go where the writers were, either to San Francisco or to New York City, so I applied to New York University and to the University of California at Berkeley. NYU accepted me right away, so I borrowed my father's suitcase, and he drove me about eight miles east on Route 40 toward New York City and sadly left me by the roadside with about $50 in my pocket so I could hitchhike in the direction of poetry.

I'd been to New York City during summer vacation when I was sixteen, and I was so hungry for it I might have crawled all the way along Route 40 and the Pennsylvania Turnpike just for the chance to get to the Gotham Bookmart, which I had read about in a number of articles. As soon as I arrived in New York City I checked my bag at the bus station and immediately went to Forty-seventh Street to the Gotham and spent almost all my remaining money.

The fall of 1958 I enrolled in New York University while living with my sister, Jacqueline, in Briarcliff Manor in Westchester County. In honor of my mother's dictum that a gentleman knows Greek and Latin, I took a beginning course in Greek, where I met Miriam Kittell. Miriam and I began to date and fell in love, the beauty of which can be traced in my poem "Ramamir," in *Thirsting for Peace in a Raging Century: Selected Poems 1961–1985.*

The first two years at NYU I studied mathematics and science. Both of my brothers were engineers, and I thought I HAD to be an engineer. I had read that NYU had a good graduate program, so I had a vague concept of becoming involved in the Mercury space program and actually going up into orbit above the Earth.

Poetry and the spectacles of the New York avant-garde were a powerful lure. Miriam and I attended the first New York City beatnik poetry readings, our first taste of the wild thrill of great readings. We saw Ginsberg, Kerouac, and Edward Dahlberg at the Gaslight Cafe. We saw Ginsberg, Corso, and Frank O'Hara at the Living Theater.

I discovered the twenty or thirty bookstores that then lined Fourth Avenue! I probably spent thousands of hours in those stores that were to me like sacred Zen rock gardens in Kyoto or Quaker zones of holy silence. Slowly I scrounged together a few milk-crate bookshelves of philosophies, scholarship, and books of verse that directed my destiny. A book on Sanskrit meter! Books on ancient Egyptian writing! The letters of Swinburne! An anthology of Middle English poetry! Building a boat of books for the big river.

It was at a book table in the Eighth Street Bookshop than I first viewed the pictures from Dachau. I'd been given virtually no information on the Holocaust, and now I stood for hours studying the book called *We Have Not Forgotten* and its photos more horrible than horrible.

I discovered small magazines such as the *Evergreen Review, Yugen, Beatitude, Semina.* My generation read these magazines till the pages were bent with use. My brain literally pulsed twenty-four hours a day with gnarls of lines from poems. Ginsberg's line from "America," for instance, "When can I go into the supermarket and buy what I need with my good looks?" was burned into my consciousness. I believed in that line of poetry with all my heart and I vowed to work for a revolution in America that stayed true to that line.

We were urged to "live in the Now," so I studied Zen and spent many hours pondering various Upanishads and the Bhagavad Gita. The phrase "best minds," from Ginsberg's epochal line, "I saw the best minds of my generation. . . ." had a profound influence. It taught me to search for the best minds of my own generation. I deliberately tried to place myself in the galleries, the bars, the performances, the protest marches where I thought it would be most likely to encounter the best minds of my generation.

I knew I had many many books and languages to study, so I deliberately became an apprentice without teachers. I would have endured a jail term rather than take a poetry workshop or writing class. I was determined to find my voice through reading, watching, and listening. I felt shy and did not have great confidence yet in my writing, and so at the

Beat poetry readings, for instance, I did not dare approach some of my heroes, who a few years later would become my friends. I intensely studied the classic poets: Homer, Catullus, Ovid, Pindar, and especially Sappho and Hesiod. I memorized Hesiod's elaborate genealogies of the gods and carefully studied all the books I could find on things like the Eleusinian Mysteries, which sowed the seeds for my first published book a few years later, *Poem from Jail.*

There were many, many elements of chance involved in my education in New York. For example, the ferment around the time of the Cuban revolution caused me to study economic conditions and slowly evolve into a social democrat. I found an article about a writer named I. F. Stone in the street near New York University. His brilliant publication, "I. F. Stone's Weekly," changed my life. His exact, pithy, brave radical investigations into the secrets of the Kennedy era helped shape my poetry. I waited with great expectation each week for the delivery truck to bring "I. F. Stone's Weekly" to the newsstand.

Meanwhile, there was considerable parental pressure against Miriam and me, in part because I wasn't Jewish. We persevered however, and ultimately overcame the opposition. A fictional account of our early relationship can be found in *Tales of Beatnik Glory,* in the story "The Mother-in-Law."

The summer of 1959 was the time of glory for me. It was one of the happiest of my life. I moved to a hotel just off Washington Square where Miriam and I could spend all the time we wanted together. I lived Edna St. V. Millay's poem on beatnik multiracial bongo parties at midnight on the Staten Island ferry.

It was that summer I began to feel power as a bard, beginning my first book, "The Vision of the Fist," which I never published, but which occupied me for two years. The final section of it was the first version of *Poem from Jail.* The stories "Johnny the Foot" and "Vulture Egg Matzoh Brei" catch the mood of the summer o' 1959.

I had begun to study the poetry of Ezra Pound and researched his activities in World War II for which he was charged with treason. Pound's great nature imagery had a big impact on me, and I admired his investigative techniques and somehow his stubbornness. It took years to fully research his ghastly politics and racism, which I ultimately understood all

Ed and Miriam Sanders shortly after they were married, fall 1961

too well after I had located the transcripts of his wartime radio broadcasts in the Library of Congress.

From the Beats I received reinforcement of a hunger for spirit and visionary experience. I had read of Ginsberg's auditory experience hearing the voice of William Blake intoning "Ah Sunflower, weary of time," in Harlem in 1948. So, eleven years later on a warm, spring morning, 1959, in Washington Square after class, I composed a melody to "Ah Sunflower," which later I recorded with The Fugs.

Early that fall, I read Ginsberg's great poem "Kaddish" in a magazine and memorized it. During the next several months, I wrote my own Kaddish for my mother which I shyly showed to Miriam who said, "You have to be a poet."

I discovered a strange zone "over there" by talking with hipsters in Washington Square park. "Over there" was the Lower East Side, as distinguished from Greenwich Village. The hipsters called it "The East Side," where rents were very, very low due to World War II rent controls still in place sixteen years after the war had ended. The East Side had a long history as a rebel, multicultural zone of great personal freedom, and soon I was spending more and more of my time there. Finally I moved from Westchester County, from where I com-

muted to school, to a $49-a-month apartment at 266 East Fourth Street in early 1960. It was my first beatnik pad, and it was paradise.

My studies had ventured into an area that would have a lasting impact on my poetry. I had become fascinated with glyphs and pictorial writing. I always had a strong visual imagination and had considered becoming a painter. The Egyptian believed that the hieroglyphs on their walls and crypts were actually alive. That's what I craved—words as life.

I was interested in the possibility of a modern hieroglyphic language, which is now only being realized through self-designed computer fonts and images. I experimented with placing glyphs, hand-drawn images, and sketches in my poetry, a practice I have followed now for over thirty years. The glyphs I used in such poems as "Sappho on East Seventh," "Farbrente Rose," "Hymn to Maple Syrup," "An East Village Hippie in King Arthur's Court," and in my nature poems, grew out of my glyphic researches in the late 1950s and early 1960s.

At NYU I took a course in Linear B, the archaic Greek dialect that was written in phonetic glyphs. The Classics Department gave me access to its Papyrus Laboratory where I could work at leisure, and I took a course in Egyptian hieroglyphics at the New School in 1961.

To augment the financial support of my older brother, David, who to my lasting gratitude paid for my college tuition, I worked off and on from the fall of 1960 through early 1965 on the late-night shift at a cigar and candy store on Forty-second Street and Broadway, which also had a lasting impact on my poetry.

Times Square was a genuine underworld where I met strange, loner, street people with interesting stories and obsessions. I would hang out in the great cafeterias of the era—at Horn and Hardart, at Bickfords, at Hector's on Forty-second Street, places that I knew some of my Beat generation heroes had frequented a decade earlier. My poem sequence "The Toe Queen Poems" and the story-poem "The Gobble Gang Poems," published in *Peace Eye,* capture some of the underground qualities of my Times Square years.

As 1960 went into 1961, I became a pacifist. I was burned by a young man named Miles in Rienzi's coffeehouse on MacDougal Street in the Village for a nickel bag of grass which turned out to be oregano. On New Year's Eve

I went to a party on Bleecker Street looking for Miles, whose face looked remarkably similar to that of the basketball star of twenty years later, Isiah Thomas. I confronted Miles, demanding my money back. Out of a back bedroom ran a naked beatnik named Ronnie who was holding a long-bladed kitchen knife. I rather stupidly challenged Ronnie also, and he dropped the knife, thank goodness, and punched me out.

I fell down and utterly lost my breath, whereupon a kind of numb bliss came upon me, and it was then I became a personal pacifist. I vowed to sever myself from the numberless generations in my genealogy of violence, spanking, and hitting. Shortly after my conversion, I began to take part in peace marches and antiwar protests. On a peace walk in New Jersey I heard Pete Seeger for the first time sing his great anthem "We Shall Overcome," which was an overwhelming experience similar to the moment when I first stood in the university bookstore and read the opening lines of "Howl" in 1957.

I dropped out of college for a year beginning in the spring of 1961, and I walked through Ohio, Pennsylvania, and Maryland for about 700 miles with the San Francisco to Moscow Walk for Peace. That summer I took part in Polaris Action, a protest against the launching and commissioning of Polaris submarines in Groton, Connecticut. The Polaris subs were "city sackers," each outfitted with sixteen missiles with multiple warheads, each capable of destroying a city in Russia.

It seemed evil to me, and with a small group of friends I attempted to swim across New London harbor and board the submarine called the *Ethan Allen* during its commissioning, around the moment that First Lady Jacqueline Kennedy was breaking a bottle of champagne across its bow. The appendix to my collected poems *Thirsting for Peace in a Raging Century* contains more information on Polaris Action. I was arrested and tossed into a local jail for a few weeks, during which time I wrote *Poem from Jail,* the first work that I felt fit in with the best of my generation. *Poem from Jail* grew from close reading of Hesiod's *Theogony* and my researches into Egyptology and the Demeter-Persephone myths of the Eleusinian mysteries. I had read Herman Kahn's book *On Thermonuclear War,* which was my first exposure to the concept of the "doomsday machine," a

At the Berkeley Poetry Conference, 1965

nuclear device which would blow up the world if triggered, and putatively the ultimate deterrent against the Russians. And so I created a story-poem that combined these mythic elements with the American tradition of protest poetry. Jail authorities would not allow my Egyptian grammar book in my cell so I refused food for two days, after which a guard brought it to me, muttering that it might be a "Russian code book."

Writing was not allowed in jail. I began writing a long poem on a length of toilet paper. I copied the poem then onto the insides of cigarette packs, then hid the poem up near the ceiling on the top side of a horizontal metal bar. The original manuscript on toilet paper I kept carefully rolled and hidden under my mattress. Once during a search of prisoners in the day room, I passed the poem under a table to a friend, and thus *Poem from Jail* was saved.

I wrote much of the work in the Greek meters I was studying. I would summon the throb of a particular meter, say an *Ionic a minore,* short short long long, and then I would form a line in that meter. The lines in *Poem from Jail* were perforce kept short because of the narrow width of my writing material.

I smuggled out the poem wadded into my tennis shoe, typed it on the typewriter at Polaris Action's headquarters, and soon sent it to Lawrence Ferlinghetti of City Lights Books, whom I viewed as the most important publisher in America. Ferlinghetti accepted it! I was overjoyed, and at last I considered myself worthy of joining the "best minds" club of American bards.

After I was out of jail I was living in a commune on East Thirty-sixth Street in New York City, where I was studying John Cage's book *Silence* and where, under Cage's influence, I wrote the opening sections of "Cemetery Hill" and other poems published in my 1966 collection, *Peace Eye*. In October of 1961, after many tribulations, Miriam Kittell and I were married at the Ethical Culture Society.

My generation was interested in what were then called "underground films." They were shot in either 8 or 16 millimeter format, and I was particularly inspired by a weekly column on films written by Jonas Mekas in the *Village Voice*. With friends from the Catholic Worker one night in February of 1962 I saw Mekas' film *Guns of the Trees* at the Charles Theater on Avenue B, after which we went to Stanley's Bar at Twelfth Street and Avenue B to carouse. I announced to my pals that I was going to publish a magazine called *Fuck You/A Magazine of the Arts,* and right on the spot I began to collect submissions.

There was a certain skepticism at the table but the next afternoon I bought a $36 mimeograph machine, borrowed some mimeograph stencils at the Catholic Worker office, and used their typewriter to cut some poems. Within hours, I had an issue of *Fuck You/A Magazine of the Arts* printed and out on the streets. I decided to give it away, and during its three years and thirteen issues, I handed out thousands of issues in the streets, galleries, and rebel cafes of the Lower East Side. There was no electricity in my apartment on Eleventh Street near Avenue A, so I learned over the months to draw fairly elaborate cover images with a stylus, holding a flashlight on my lap shining upward from underneath the mimeo stencils in the dark apartment.

I instantly became what was known at the time as the Mimeograph Revolution. My magazine made a big stir in the poetry world, and I began to publish many of my heroes—Charles Olson, Allen Ginsberg, Diane di Prima, Robert Duncan, Gary Snyder, and Paul Blackburn. It was instant fame—and my first taste of minor literary corruption, when at the open poetry readings, where before I always seemed to be slotted to read at 1 A.M. Now, with the fame of my magazine, I was invited by the MCs to read whenever my whim should decree. The mood of these months is caught in the story "An Editorial Conference" in *Tales of Beatnik Glory,* volume I.

With the impending publication of my first book, and the attention given my magazine, I decided that my apprenticeship was over and that I was at last prepared to approach the "best minds of my generation." I wrote a number of my heroes and even a few world leaders, enclosing copies of *Fuck You/A Magazine of the Arts.* I contacted Allen Ginsberg, who was traveling in India, Charles Olson, Fidel Castro, Samuel Beckett, Jean-Paul Sartre, Robert Duncan, Gary Snyder, Marianne Moore, Diane di Prima, and others. The great American bard Charles Olson became a big influence in the early 1960s.

When the United States resumed atmospheric testing of nuclear weapons in the spring of 1962, I joined with peace groups such as the Catholic Worker and the Committee for Nonviolent Action to sit-in at the New York City Atomic Energy Commission office, and I was given a short jail term at Hart Island jail. There I wrote some of my Times Square poems, including the poems about Consuela. These events are captured in "The AEC Sit-In" in volume I of *Tales of Beatnik Glory.*

That spring I took part in the Nashville to Washington Walk For Peace, which passed through vicious Ku Klux Klan territory in rural Tennessee. One night the church where we were staying was under siege by racists, and the local sheriff took us to the National Guard Armory to sleep. My story "Peace Walk" provides a fictionalized account of the spring of 1962.

The summer of 1963 was for me one of those blessed seasons when time still seemed to stretch luxuriously and benevolently, giving the summer's span an extra few months. There was the Great March on Washington in which Martin Luther King Jr. gave his "I Have a Dream" speech, and my little book from City Lights, *Poem from Jail,* was at last published!

I continued my studies in visuality by making some underground films. I was helped by filmmakers Harry Smith, Stan Brakhage, and Jonas Mekas. Jonas told me of a place to get very inexpensive 16 mm film and Harry what camera equipment to purchase, and Stan gave me instructions on filming techniques. I began filming my friends and found that it was not that difficult to get them to disrobe. One of the better sequences I shot was when I followed the actress Jane Mansfield around at an uptown art opening; another was a film called *Amphetamine Head,* about the abuse of power, the making of which I have described in fictionalized form in *Tales of Beatnik Glory.* Later the police pulled a nighttime raid without a warrant on the "secret location" on Avenue A, where I edited my films and published *Fuck You/A Magazine of the Arts,* and seized virtually every inch of my film, none of which I was able to get back.

In 1964 I graduated from New York University with a degree in Greek and Latin. Our daughter Deirdre was born in September. The brilliant bard of Cleveland, d.a. levy, had asked for a manuscript to be published by his Renegade Press, and I put together some current work which he hand set and published under the title *King Lord/Queen Freak.*

When I could, I hung out on what was termed "the coffeehouse scene." I'd met Ted Berrigan, the editor of *C Magazine,* influenced by his sonnets. We were experts at printing on mimeograph machines. Sometimes we shared the same mimeo machines at Izzie Young's Folklore Center or at Bob Wilson's Phoenix Bookshop. At the same time, I was inspired by the life and poetry of Paul Blackburn. Both Ted and Paul are commemorated, and those days, in the elegies "For Paul" in *Thirsting for Peace in a Raging Century,* and "Elegy for Ted Berrigan" in *Hymn to the Rebel Cafe.*

I was publishing a variety of tracts, manifestos, and small anthologies. I published *Roosevelt after Inauguration* by William Burroughs, *The Platonic Blow* by W. H. Auden, and my own anthologies, including *Despair: poems to come down by, Bugger: An Anthology of Buttockry, Poems for Marilyn,* and a small collection of my research of the milieu of Times Square, *The Toe Queen Poems.*

When I was in college I began to put out "rare book catalogs," which were a combination of satire and seriousness. I see my own catalogs now in rare book lists at outlandishly high prices. I sold an odd assortment of books "published in heaven," and literary relics such as Allen Ginsberg's autographed cold cream jar. Later, when I graduated from college, I wanted to find some other way of earning a living other than working on Times Square on the 5 P.M. to 2 A.M. shift, which I had been doing, in between peace work, publishing, college, and arrests at demonstrations, for over four years.

Since I had been so influenced by bookstores, the words "open a bookstore" appeared in my mind. And so in late 1964 I rented a former Kosher meat store on East Tenth Street, with groovy tile walls and chicken-singeing equipment, which I transformed into a vegetarian literary zone called the Peace Eye Bookstore. I left the words "Strictly Kosher" on the front door.

Next door above the Lifschutz wholesale egg market lived Tuli Kupferberg, one of my Beat heroes whose poems I had published in *Fuck You/A Magazine of the Arts.* I approached Tuli about forming a singing group of poets. I said, "Let's form a band. We'll chant poetry and we'll do a lot of partying."

Tuli eagerly agreed. We were somewhat aware of what was going on in popular music. The Beatles were happening, and in the saloons where we drank the jukeboxes of 1964 emitted tunes like "I Want to Hold Your Hand" and "A Hard Day's Night," Roy Orbison's "Pretty Woman," and the Shangri-Las' "Leader of the Pack."

We wanted to present ourselves as a cross between a calm happening and an outlandish beatnik spectacle. We drew inspiration for The Fugs from a wide assortment of sources—first of all from *Theory of Spectacle* outlined in Aristotle's *Poetics* and from the prancing dances of Dionysus I had read about in my classical researches, from Alfred Jarry's *Ubu Roi* in 1896, from the *poemes simultanés* of the Dadaists at the Cabaret Voltaire in Zurich in 1915, from Charlie Parker's wild noodles of saxophone freedom, from the silence of John Cage, from the placid pushiness of the Happening movement, and from our belief that there was oodles of freedom guaranteed by the United States Constitution that was not being used.

The first Fugs' performance was at the grand opening of the Peace Eye Bookstore in February of 1965, for which Andy Warhol made wall banners of his silk-screened flowers. After that, we began to appear at galleries and small theaters in the East and West Village. We were utterly amazed as what we were doing for fun and in order to party became successful.

During the next four years, The Fugs created six albums on which around fifty of my compositions appeared. At the same time I was determined to keep writing poetry and publishing books and magazines. At Peace Eye I operated a free community print center and published countless broadsides, posters, announcements of events, and booklets for the community.

Life from 1965 through 1967 was a nonstop chaos of partying, traveling, publishing, recording, and receiving great gobs of adulation and hostility. I was swept up into the vortex of Bacchic fame. I felt that to be an American bard, you had to be OUT THERE IN PUBLIC. You had to be controversial, you had to try OTHER FORMS. And so I was out there—part Bacchus, part Bard, part Hubris, part Husband, part Rake. It was a formula that was

guaranteed to disturb domestic tranquility. There were threats. Someone called and threatened to bomb first me then Frank Zappa of the Mothers of Invention. More seriously, someone sent me a fake but very real-looking "bomb" to my post office box, an array of batteries, wires, and fake explosives in a hollowed-out Modern Library edition of Dostoevsky's *The Idiot*.

In early 1966 the police raided the Peace Eye Bookstore and seized boxes of publications. I was arrested for possession of obscene material, including a poem by W. H. Auden and issues of *Fuck You/A Magazine of the Arts*. To my lasting gratitude, the American Civil Liberties Union agreed to represent me, and therefore I did not have to raise tens of thousands of dollars to defend my rights. Nevertheless, what followed was eighteen months of nightmare court appearances and numberless nights of anxiety before I would win the case and invite the arresting officer to a victory party at the Peace Eye Bookstore.

In 1966 my book *Peace Eye* was published by Harvey Brown's Frontier Press, with an in-

The Fugs at the Peace Eye Bookstore, 1967: (from left) Ed Sanders, Tuli Kupferberg, and Ken Weaver

troduction by my mentor Charles Olson. Nineteen sixty-seven was an interesting year—with the word "beatnik" being almost totally abandoned for a few years, and "hippie" coming into parlance as a substitution. Early that year I was on the cover of *Life* magazine. The Fugs were thrown off a major recording label, but were quickly signed by Warner/Reprise Records, whose president told me he played our album for Frank Sinatra to get his approval, and, to our gratitude, the great singer had said, "I guess you know what you're doing."

All through the history of The Fugs in the 1960s, the war in Vietnam throbbed like an ever painful sore. However much we partied, shouted our poetry, and strutted around like images of Bacchus, we could never quite get it out of our mind. It was like that Dada poetry reading that Tristan Tzara gave in 1922 in Paris, with an alarm clock constantly ringing during the reading. The war was THE alarm clock of the late 1960s.

It seemed as if the war might become permanent, so there were big demonstrations planned for October of 1967 to surround the nerve center of the war—the Pentagon in Washington, D.C. Somebody came up with the idea of holding an exorcism of this mystic pentagonal citadel of napalm and defoliation.

I agreed to help organize it. Tuli Kupferberg and I rented a flatbed truck and a sound system. The Fugs and a group of San Francisco Diggers climbed aboard and joined the protest march across a bridge from Washington, D.C., to the Pentagon. We positioned ourselves on the edge of a parking lot a few hundred feet from our target, while tens of thousands of marchers walked past, and I intoned a sing-song litany of exorcism after which we all began to chant "Out, Demons, Out!" over and over for about fifteen minutes.

When we had finished the exorcism, we walked onto the lawn in front of the Pentagon where lines of armed soldiers with rifles thrust forward stood guarding the entranceway. We were carrying dozens of white and yellow daisies. We paused in front of the young and obviously nervous soldiers and gently shoved some stems into some rifle barrels, then glanced back over our shoulders as we walked away, marveling at the vision of white and yellow petal jutting from dark metal.

It was a famous thing we did, and people praised us for our audacity, yet the Vietnam War went on for another seven years. So much for "Out, Demons, Out!"

A few months later, in early 1968, The Fugs, with Allen Ginsberg, conducted a controversial exorcism ceremony at the grave of Senator Joseph McCarthy in Wisconsin, wherein an attempt through chant and mantra was made to cleanse the red-baiting right-winger's "ghost" of its homophobia. This event was captured on tape and can be savored on the compact disc entitled "Fugs Live from the '60s."

In ways such as these, 1968 began in a mode of defiance, yet, for me, and I think for much of my generation, 1968 was an American Nightmare. The My Lai massacre occurred in February; President Johnson abdicated under strange circumstances in late March; Martin Luther King Jr. was assassinated a few days later; and the next likely president, Robert Kennedy, was killed next to an ice machine in a hotel in early June. August saw the Chicago riots at the Democratic Convention and November ushered in the years of Richard Nixon. Behind it all, the war wailed onward.

I became involved with what I felt to be the social democratic wing of the Youth International Party, otherwise known as the Yippies. I was feeling great despair about my country, about American culture in general and what an energetic minority perceived to be the unseemly power of the military and what was known as the "intelligence community." The uprisings in England, Columbia University, and Paris in the spring of 1968 gave a tincture of slight hope to the general despair.

In my partying and fragmented life, I'd composed many melodies, but actually wrote very little poetry between the time that the expanded *Peace Eye* appeared in 1967 through 1971, a four-year gap that seemed like four decades at the time. I'd been touring constantly and drinking too much—Bacchus was celebrating around the clock in my liver, whose contours I was beginning to feel as if it were limned in neon.

In the fall of 1968 I was on the William Buckley television show with Jack Kerouac, one of those events about which you are interviewed over and over for the next thirty years. It was just a few months before he died. I tried to tell him what a hero he was, but he swigged on a bottle and disported himself so drunkenly that William Buckley wanted to substitute Allen Ginsberg, who was in the audience. But we protested vigorously, and the program continued, with Kerouac attired in the same checked jacket in which he was buried in the cold December a little over a year later.

After a concert with the Grateful Dead in Pittsburgh in the spring of 1969, The Fugs broke up. I felt used up and depleted. Four years had seemed like forty and life was having a corroded quality as if I'd awakened inside a Samuel Beckett novel. Being the leader of a touring and controversial musical group is a job requiring at least twelve hours a day of nonstop work. I wanted to return to poetry and to write some fiction. I was very tired of the rock-and-roll rat race, and I thirsted to become a mere jittery unself-confident post-Beat researcher and bard.

So, I retired and rested during the summer of 1969, operating the Peace Eye Bookstore which I had moved to a better location on Avenue A across from Tompkins Square Park. I completed *Sanders' Truckstop,* a solo album for Reprise Records, and I began a satirical novel, *Shards of God: A Novel of the Yippies,* set against the background of the Chicago Democratic Convention riots of 1968, which Grove Press eventually published.

The murders by the Manson family occurred in early August of 1969. I paid very little attention to them until the group was arrested at the end of the year. I felt refreshed after nine months away from the rock and roll treadmill. The case intrigued me. There were more loose ends in the early stages of the Manson case than on a tie-dyed, fringed, hippie shawl. My agent Carl Brandt negotiated a book contract for me from E. P. Dutton, and with my wife, Miriam, and five-year-old daughter, Deirdre, I headed for Los Angeles to begin my investigation.

I worked nonstop day and night for a year and a half. It was my "Saturation Job," to borrow a concept from my mentor Charles Olson, who had died just as I was beginning work on the book to be called *The Family: The Story of Charles Manson's Dune Buggy Attack Battalion.*

In his *Bibliography on America for Ed Dorn* Olson describes it: "Best thing to do is to dig one place or man (or woman) until you yourself know more about that than is possible to any other man. It doesn't matter whether it's Bard Wire or Pemmican or Paterson or Iowa. But *exhaust it.* Saturate it. Beat it.

Sanders (in bed of truck) going up Goler Wash to investigate the Manson family, 1970

"And then U KNOW everything else very fast: one saturation job (it might take 14 years). And you're in, forever."

Even though I wrote very little verse during my "Saturation Job" researching the Manson group, the techniques I was learning would serve me well in the research-based poetry I was to write in the next twenty-four years. And when finally I was able to return to poetry in the fall of 1971 after the publication of *The Family: The Story of Charles Manson's Dune Buggy Attack Battalion,* I wrote a long political poem that the *Los Angeles Free Press* published tracing the entrapment by police of poet John Sinclair. The poem helped set up the movement that freed him a few months later. At the same time I wrote the short story-poem "The VFW Crawling Contest," which would be featured in my verse collection *20,000 A.D.*

Then 1972 arrived, another troubling presidential election year, and I recorded my second album for Reprise Records, *Beer Cans on the Moon.* There was turbulence in my private life, though I was active in demonstrations at the Republican Convention in Miami, Florida, against Nixon and the war that wouldn't stop. I coauthored a mass market paperback called *Vote!* which was published in the fall of 1972 and urged rebellious youth to vote for George McGovern, an urging that went very, very unheeded as Nixon won by a big margin.

While I was occupied with political agitation, I began research on a book on satanic cults called "Among the Damned" which I worked on during 1972 and 1973. After I had filled up a couple of file drawers with data, I decided to set the manuscript aside, because I felt that the graphic descriptions of despicable acts might excite some readers in such a way as to fuel the fires of transgression.

As an independent writer not connected to a college, I had as one of my main tasks setting aside enough time and money so as to write about anything I wanted. I vowed to get involved with extensive writing projects that would never make money or even find a publisher. I called it the Blake Route. I would have my own private world of research and projects—and follow the threads of certain researches no matter if there were no readers and no one was interested. In this way, over the years, I have created a number of book-length manuscripts, "published in heaven," a phrase Ginsberg used in the dedication to *Howl and Other Poems.*

My doctor had told me to stop drinking in the late 1960s because my liver was becoming enlarged. I laughed and continued to pour the vodka into my stomach by day and by night. In the spring of 1973 Miriam and I drove to visit Allen Ginsberg at his farm in Cherry Valley, New York. Passing through the town's main street, I glanced at the bar where I might bend elbows that night. It was then that I stopped drinking—I just didn't want to get stuck in that small-town bar with smoke-scented pretzels and beery chuckles. Stopping drinking gives a writer great vistas of free time that normally would have been spent gossiping in bars and incapacitated by excess, not to mention the thrill of waking up without a hangover for the first time in years.

In the spring of 1973, I began a verse study of Egyptian culture, which was published as a small book, *Egyptian Hieroglyphics.* It refreshed my interest in the power of the glyph in poetry. It was thrilling again to insert hand-drawn glyphs into the poems I was then writing, a thrill I hadn't experienced since composing the

At an antiwar demonstration in Miami, Florida, 1972

poems in *Peace Eye* seven years before. During those years I had a number of invitations to join faculties as a professor, but turned them town in deference to the Blake Route. I loved the thrill of the Blake Route—of being deliciously alone, without support, on the edge, combining shapes with words, and living by my wits.

To survive economically on the Blake Route also required considerable discipline. Once again Allen Ginsberg pointed out something important. He told me that Michael McClure was writing a couple of hours regularly every single day "like a German novelist." For someone like me who had been partying and living too quickly for a few years, it was a lifesaver. I called it "The Tom Mann two." Zola's dictum, *Nulla dies sine linea,* no day without some lines, became my motto, even though *Nulla dies sine linea* tends to make one's biography a tedious moil of then-I-wrotes.

I wanted to write about something for which I felt great love. I had collected rather extensive archives about the recent past. I went through my many boxes of files and spent time reading and studying what I had fairly recently lived, in a Saturation Job mode. I began a series of short stories set in the late 1950s and early 1960s with interlocking characters and themes, which I titled *Tales of Beatnik Glory.* It took me two years to finish.

While I was writing *Tales of Beatnik Glory,* I reorganized the extensive files I had developed in Los Angeles and began a secret investigation, which would occupy me for the rest of the 1970s, into the assassination of Senator Robert Kennedy. Meanwhile, I had had considerable trouble from a pseudo-leftist splinter group which had threatened me and had on several occasions vandalized my automobile. In addition, I was disliked by several satanic cults because of my book on the Manson group; I had received threats, and New York City no longer seemed suitable.

My wife, Miriam, was mugged in the West Village on New Year's Day, 1974, by a young junkie holding a butcher knife, so that summer we moved with our nine-year-old daughter Deirdre to Woodstock, New York. I was completing *Tales of Beatnik Glory,* and had begun my novel *Fame and Love in New York.* I wanted to write a humorous left-wing novel while I was still young enough to enjoy it. It took me five years to complete *Fame and Love.*

We lived in Woodstock on the edge of a twenty-acre meadow of such magnificence that I would walk through it over and over singing Blake's "How Sweet I Roamed from Field to Field." The summer of 1974 was one of those glory times for me, such as the summer of 1956 when I visited New York at age sixteen, the summer of 1959 when I at last chose to become a bard, the summer of love in 1967, and the summer of 1970, oddly enough, when I was beginning research in Los Angeles on the Manson group.

In 1976, after publication of the first volume of *Tales of Beatnik Glory,* which I projected as a three-volume work, I decided to codify my thoughts on poetics in a small book, *Investigative Poetry,* which to my gratitude Lawrence Ferlinghetti published and kept in print for over ten years.

With a certain nervousness, I gathered my poetry for my first collection since *Egyptian Hieroglyphics.* The life of a poet can revolve around the invitations of publishers, and in this case it was a letter from Richard Grossinger for a text for his North Atlantic Books. My friend George Butterick, who was overseeing the Charles Olson Archives at the University of Connecticut, had acquired for the archives my literary files from the 1960s, including many of the letters that Olson had written me. Butterick liked the title of one of my poems

in *Egyptian Hieroglyphics,* "20,000 A.D.," and so in his honor I titled my new book *20,000 A.D.,* which was published in 1976.

When I had first discovered poetry as a teenager, I was surprised at the number of elegies that bards wrote. Twenty years later I was at that time of life when friends were passing away, and learned well the lesson of the elegy. Included in *20,000 A.D.* are my elegies for Charles Olson and Paul Blackburn. I wanted to break new ground with a story-poem, "Holy Was Demeter Walking the Corn Furrow," in which I brought together aspects of the Demeter-Persephone myth, as I had done in *Poem from Jail,* but in a more direct and mythoerotic manner.

In 1975 and 1976, I created several filing cabinets full of information about what was called "domestic intelligence" activities by the government, military intelligence, and the secret police against the activities of the so-called counterculture and the antiwar movement. The investigation into domestic intelligence was a way to further my researches into the assassination of Robert Kennedy. Out of this research I wrote a sequence of seventeen short stories, gathered together under the acronym *Dom-Int,* for Domestic Intelligence, a project lurking in my archives for the books of tomorrow.

In the summer of 1975 someone sent me a large cow's tongue in the mail from Sacramento, California. The package had stamps of Christmas angels in red robes. A few weeks later Manson-follower Squeaky Fromme, attired in a red robe, pointed a loaded pistol at President Gerald Ford in Sacramento. I was very disturbed at receiving the tongue, and I noticed in a number of articles that in the West and Midwest some group using helicopters was mutilating cattle and removing body parts, including eyes and tongues. It intrigued me, so I began a three-year investigation, wrote articles and newsletters on the phenomenon, and put together another lengthy manuscript.

After a hiatus of five years, in 1977 I returned to music and began to create what I called an Electronic Bard System. After years in the rock and roll world, I had vowed never to sing again. I remember Jimi Hendrix telling me how much he disliked his voice, and I felt the same way. I had almost a puritanical revulsion hearing it. In the summer of 1977 I was teaching a course in investigative poetry at the Naropa

Institute in Boulder, Colorado, and I was preparing some remarks on metrics. Allen Ginsberg was visiting my apartment, and I sang for him the opening lines of *The Odyssey* in Greek and some of the complicated metrics of Sappho. He suggested I perform them at my poetry reading that night, with music provided by a small hand-held synthesizer. That evening I chanted Sappho's "Hymn to Aphrodite" in her Mixolydian meter, and in that way I was thrust back into music.

I wanted to be able to recite poetry with music so that the music could in no way overwhelm the words. Anyone who has tried to articulate complicated word patterns in the context of banks of rock and roll amplifiers will understand what I was trying to avoid. So I decided to invent an Electronic Bard System and build some instruments for my poetry.

The first musical instrument I created was the Pulse Lyre, which features twin keyboards, each mounted on small sheaths that fit on the fingers of my left and right hands. These keyboards are connected by computer cables to very small synthesizers I placed in wooden boxes. After a few years of upgrading the Pulse Lyre, I finally arrived at a pleasing sounding instrument with which I have performed Sappho, Blake, Catullus, and my own poems all around the United States and Europe for over fifteen years. In the movie *Poetry in Motion,* I performed my "Homage to Henri Matisse" on the Pulse Lyre, augmented by what may be the world's first use of scissors to provide Samba rhythms during the recitation of a poem.

In the early 1980s I built the Talking Tie, a polyphonic musical device with its keyboard attached to a clip-on tie, which also can be seen in *Poetry in Motion.* I also built inside a wooden Sumi painting box a tiny theremin, whose pitch and volume control are set by moving the hands closer or farther from the theremin. In subsequent years I experimented with devices using infrared beams as "strings" which could be intercepted by the fingers and thus trigger notes on a synthesizer. The results were the Light Lyre and the Singing Quilting Frame, the latter having arrays of infrared beam-emitting and beam-receiving circuits built along the upper and lower edges of a small, round, quilting frame. My 1994 instrument, the Lisa Lyre, consists of a print of the Mona Lisa on canvas, the back of which is outfitted with electronic sen-

sors so that the beam of a laser pen upon the surface of the Lisa will make music.

In 1978 I turned down an opportunity, if you can call it that, to write a book on the ghastly Jonestown suicide cult. Instead I took an assignment to write a history of the rock band The Eagles, which took me two years, and resulted in an 800-page manuscript. I had met one of the leaders of the Eagles when I was researching the Manson family in Los Angeles in 1970 when he was a struggling young musician. I was paid very well, and thus had the largesse to indulge in my passion for building instruments for the Electronic Bard System.

During the years I was working on the Eagles project, I wrote and produced *The Karen Silkwood Cantata,* a two-act dramatization in song, narrative, and chant tracing the life of the union activist who was killed while investigating plutonium contamination and possible theft of plutonium at a processing plant in Oklahoma. My novel *Fame and Love in New York* was published in 1980, and shortly thereafter my manifesto on political activism, *The Z-D Generation,* an homage to the techniques of the great activists, Denis Diderot and Émile Zola.

Beginning in 1981, I began writing story-poems that combined verse with sections in prose plus hand-drawn symbols and glyphs. Works that combine prose and poetry derive from a tradition that includes William Carlos Williams' *Spring and All* and the third century B.C. Greek satirist Menippus.

Few things are as thrilling to write as a long story-poem that requires research. The first work I completed in the poem/prose form was "Farbrente Rose," an extended history of a fictional early twentieth-century union activist. Out of my researches into the political history of New York City for "Farbrente Rose," I created the Pulse Lyre chant "Yiddish Speaking Socialists of the Lower East Side," which was later published in my collected poems *Thirsting for Peace in a Raging Century.* "Farbrente Rose" was published in volume II of *Tales of Beatnik Glory.*

I decided to write a lengthy story-poem for volume II of *Tales of Beatnik Glory,* which would at the same time be part of my next book of poetry. I vowed to go line by line, syllable by syllable, consonant by consonant, as long as it took, to create the modern ghost tale "Sappho on East Seventh." It was the poem I submitted when I won a Guggenheim Fellowship in 1983. I would return over and over to the sho-sto-

*Ed Sanders with his daughter, Deirdre,
and wife, Miriam, 1989*

po, or short story–poem, in the following years, in such works as "Cassandra," "Melville's Father," and "An East Village Hippie in King Arthur's Court."

Throughout the 1980s I worked regularly on the second volume *Tales of Beatnik Glory,* mixing that work with the bundles of poems, tales, manifestoes, articles, environmental work, musical inventions, lectures, bardic travels, family life, and the other frenzies of late-century bardic existence. I'd long found out that moving to the country from a big city does not make life simpler. It merely gives a rural gestalt and cleaner air and water to a writer's normal complication.

In 1986 I was invited by Allan Kornblum of Coffee House Press to put together a book representing the best of my career in poetry. The result, after much agonizing and search, was *Thirsting for Peace in a Raging Century: Selected Poems 1961–1985,* which was published in 1987. I wrote in 1985 and 1986 a three-act musical drama, *Star Peace,* which was set inside

the military-industrial apparatus that was working on the so-called star wars defense system. *Star Peace* had several productions, including one at the Oslo International Poetry Festival, and was released as a compact disc and double album in 1987.

Beginning with that highly symbolic year, 1984, and continuing every year or so thereafter, I organized reunion concerts of The Fugs, who had not performed since a concert with the Grateful Dead in the spring of 1969. Our reunions were well received, and during the 1980s we released four albums and compact discs of our new music.

In 1988 I recorded *Songs in Ancient Greek,* in which I paid homage to the poetry and prose of that great language, setting texts of Homer, Simonides, Sappho, Aristophanes, Plato, Archilochus, and the section of the Greek Ecclesiastes that begins "To everything there is a season," to a variety of musical forms. For the setting from Plato's *Republic,* "The Allegory of the Cave," I invented a microtonal instrument, the Microlyre, which plays a thirty-one notes-to-the-octave scale. The keyboard of the Microlyre consisted of rectangular panels of switching membranes mounted on a curved, wooden surface so that an octave of thirty-one notes could be played with one hand.

That same year I finished the second volume of *Tales of Beatnik Glory* while I was helping write a number of laws for the town of Woodstock, including a long and complicated zoning law and later a law to control the spraying of insecticides and herbicides from airplanes. I had decided in the 1980s to become minutely involved in protecting the environment in my hometown, Woodstock, New York, which necessitated becoming very, very politically active.

In 1989, on the occasion of the twentieth anniversary of the murders committed by the Manson group, I created an updated edition of *The Family,* which New American Library published. I went back to Los Angeles to interview police and prosecutors and, although he would not allow me to visit him in prison, I began a less than pleasing exchange of letters with Mr. Manson. It's very unpleasant to get a hostile card from a murderer at Christmas time, especially one festooned with a hand-drawn swastika.

In 1990 the thirty-two stories comprising volumes I and II of *Tales of Beatnik Glory* were published as a single volume.

I completed work on *Hymn to the Rebel Cafe: Poems 1986–1991* for Black Sparrow Press. It was a chance again to work on some more sho-sto-pos, including the research poem "Melville's Father" and the sixty-one page epic tale "An East Village Hippie in King Arthur's Court."

Meanwhile, I was considering translating a Greek play in which I would set some of the choruses to music and have them performed in Greek in order to bring to a modern audience the beauty of ancient metrical patterns. I considered translating Euripides' *Bacchae* or Aeschylus' *Prometheus Bound.* While I was reading various plays, I encountered several sections on the Trojan priestess Cassandra, whose story I discovered had never fully been told in any extant drama. The Cassandra myth seemed relevant to our modern yet ancient practice of ethnic cleansing.

So, I decided to stitch together from ancient sources a play called *Cassandra: A Musical Drama.* While the drama and music is mostly performed in translation, I included sections from Euripides' *Trojan Women* and *Iphigeneia in Aulis,* Homer's *Odyssey,* and Aeschylus' *Agamemnon* in the original Greek.

In order to create the drama, I first wrote a poem which served as the basis for the larger work. The poem version of *Cassandra* was included in *Hymn to the Rebel Cafe. Cassandra* was produced twice in Woodstock in 1992 and 1993 and again in New York City in 1995.

After finishing *Cassandra,* I was planning to write a drama in verse on the life of Sappho. Driving home from the theater after a performance of *Cassandra,* the word "Chekhov" came into my consciousness. Right away, I began work on *Chekhov: A Biography in Verse.* I visited libraries and electronic databases, acquired numerous books and articles on life in Russia in the late nineteenth century, and spent a wonderful set of months completing what may be the only book-length biography in verse of the great Chekhov. *Chekhov: A Biography in Verse* was published by Black Sparrow Press in the spring of 1995.

I became active in local cable-access television. Beginning in 1993 I produced a weekly one-hour show, "The Sanders Report," featuring environmental researches, politics, songs, and video poetry. With my wife, Miriam, we began to produce "The Woodstock Evening News," a weekly show of local issues. And I started the final volume of *Tales of Beatnik Glory,* taking this series of interconnected stories to its conclusion.

I am living in a late-century electronic dream and time drain. E-mail, faxes, the proliferation of specialized newsletters, the fragmentation of issues, the gross assault on benign government by forces of the right—all combine to make life at century's end a final test of the apothegm, "There are no weekends for poets."

In my fifties, I've tried to become more proactive and to pay careful attention to the planning of projects and less attuned to the happenstance of random inputs in determining the books and projects of my final decades. A mistake can cost a bard precious years. I hope to complete work transforming *Chekhov: A Biography in Verse* into a musical drama. I'd like to complete a book on *Creativity and Investigative Poetry,* growing out of my lectures and researches in that field, and if there's time, I have some ideas for some medical inventions to assist the feeding and oxygenation of the brain during trauma.

Also, I'd like to work on a musical instrument utilizing Self-directed Evoked Potentials, or self-induced brain waves, as a keyboard for music, as well as some experiments in hieroglyphic fonts for a type of glyph-based poetic language on color computers.

There's no certain way to end an account of my life except to say that I will continue my modest labors in service of the dream of a social democracy for my country, and that I hope to go out in a blaze of leaflets and a flow of pleasing poems.

Woodstock, New York
August 1994

BIBLIOGRAPHY

Poetry:

(Editor) *Poems for Marilyn,* Fuck You Press, 1962.

Poem from Jail, City Lights, 1963.

(Compiler and contributor) *Bugger: An Anthology of Buttockry,* Fuck You Press, 1964.

(Compiler and contributor) *Despair: poems to come down by,* Fuck You Press, 1964.

King Lord/Queen Freak, Renegade Press, 1964, 2nd edition, 1965.

The Toe Queen Poems, Fug Press, 1964.

A Valorium Edition of the Entire Extant Works of Thales!, Fuck You Press, 1964.

(With Ken Weaver and Betsy Klein) *The Fugs' Song Book,* Peace Eye Bookstore, 1965.

Peace Eye, Frontier Press, 1966, 2nd edition, 1967.

Egyptian Hieroglyphics, Institute of Further Studies, 1973.

20,000 A.D., North Atlantic Books, 1976.

The Cutting Prow, Am/Here Books, 1981.

Hymn to Maple Syrup and Other Poems, Poetry, Crime, & Culture Press (PCC Press), 1985.

Poems for Robin, PCC Press, 1987.

Thirsting for Peace in a Raging Century: Selected Poems 1961–1985, Coffee House Press, 1987.

Hymn to the Rebel Cafe: Poems 1986–1991, Black Sparrow Press, 1993.

Chekov: A Biography in Verse, Black Sparrow Press, 1995.

Fiction:

Shards of God: A Novel of the Yippies, Grove, 1970.

Tales of Beatnik Glory (short stories; also see below), Stonehill, 1975.

Fame and Love in New York, Turtle Island Foundation, 1980.

Tales of Beatnik Glory: Volumes I and II (short stories), Citadel Underground, 1990.

Nonfiction:

The Family: The Story of Charles Manson's Dune Buggy Attack Battalion, Dutton, 1971, revised edition, New American Library, 1989.

(With Abbie Hoffman and Jerry Rubin) *Vote!,* Warner Books, 1972.

Investigative Poetry, City Lights, 1976.

(Editor and contributor; with the Investigation Poetry Group of the Naropa Institute) *The Party: A Chronological Perspective on a Confrontation at a Buddhist Seminary,* PCC Press, 1980.

The Z-D Generation, Station Hill Press, 1981.

Solo recordings:

Sanders' Truckstop, Reprise, 1970.

Beer Cans on the Moon, Reprise, 1972.

Songs in Ancient Greek, Olufsen Records, 1989.

Recordings, with The Fugs:

Ballads of Contemporary Protest, Points of View, and General Dissatisfaction, Broadside, 1966, reissued as *The Fugs' First Album,* ESP, 1966.

The Fugs, ESP, 1966.

It Crawled into My Hand, Honest, Reprise, 1968.

Tenderness Junction, Reprise, 1968.

The Virgin Fugs, ESP, 1968.

The Belle of Avenue A, Reprise, 1969.

Golden Filth, Reprise, 1970.

Refuse to Be Burnt-Out (live reunion album), New Rose/Olufsen Records, 1985.

No More Slavery (reunion album), New Rose/Olufsen Records, 1986.

Star Peace (two-record set; also see below), Olufsen Records, 1987.

Songs from a Portable Forest, Gazelle Records, 1991.

Musicals:

(With Eli Waldron, Ilene Marder, and Martin Fleer) *The Municipal Power Cantata* (performed at Woodstock Town Hall, 1978), PCC Press, 1978.

The Karen Silkwood Cantata, first performed at Creative Music Studio, Woodstock, New York, 1979.

Star Peace (three-act drama), performed at Oslo International Poetry Festival, 1986, and at Syracuse Stage, Syracuse, New York, 1986.

Cassandra: A Musical Drama, performed by River Arts Repertory Company in Woodstock, New York, 1992 and 1993, and in New York, New York, 1995.

Also author of *Love and the Falling Iron,* Yanagi, 1977, and a history of the rock band The Eagles.

Editor and publisher of *Fuck You/A Magazine of the Arts,* 1962–65; contributor of poems, articles, reviews, and investigative reports to anthologies, including *New Writing in the USA,* Penguin, 1967; *Anthology of New York Poets,* Random House, 1968; and *The Postmoderns: The New American Poetry Revisited,* Grove, 1982; contributor to many periodicals, including *Crawdaddy, Esquire, Los Angeles Free Press, New York Times, Oui, Paris Review,* and *Village Voice.*

James Simmons

1933-

LIFE AND WORK

James Simmons with daughter Anna and son Ben on holiday
in Donegal, Ireland, 1991

Today is the second of April 1994. I am sixty-one years old, looking out the window of the study in Portmuck at the sun on the Irish Sea. At the moment I can't see Scotland. It comes and goes on the horizon—Jura, the Mull of Kintyre, Ailsa Craig. Every few hours one or other of the Larne Stranraer ferries comes out of the mist, shining white . . . very romantic.

I live in a coastguard "cottage" called The Poets' House with my young American wife, two children, and a dog called Charlie. My wife, Janice Fitzpatrick Simmons, is from Boston. She is a poet too, and we run a school of poetry —six weeks of courses in the summer and M.A. students all year round, mostly Irish and American. Ben is our son, and Anna is the daughter of a previous marriage, so we only have

her at weekends and on holidays. She is eleven and writes really good poems. Ben is five and won a cup last year for reciting verse at a local festival. Apart from their talents they are good-looking nice-natured children, although Ben is a little foul-mouthed when he loses his temper. They are both walking down the lane to Crawford's farm to borrow some cake tins. Janice is going to bake a cake.

I took early retirement from university teaching at The University of Ulster in Coleraine in 1984. Since then I have worked at home, apart from three years as Writer-in-Residence at Queen's University, Belfast. Last autumn I was invited to Japan to read my poems and lecture and sing. This January it was Germany for a week. The year before, I did a tour of the United States. It is a busy writing life . . . and I have

Sherod Santos and Derek Mahon,
"new friend meets old friend," 1992

to say I enjoy performing my songs and poems. I also enjoy helping younger writers to get on with their work and to study the work of other poets. We hire poets to help us with the teaching: from America Jean Valentine, Sherod Santos, David Keller, Bill Matthews among many; from Ireland Derek Mahon, Paul Durcan, Seamus Heaney, John Montague, Medbh McGuckian, etc. Bernard O'Donoghue, an Irish poet teaching at Magdalen College, Oxford, is our external examiner. It is a very rich and privileged life, working and carousing with such creative minds.

So how did I get to be so lucky?

I was born in Londonderry in 1933, the son of a stockbroker. A few generations back they came up from Athlone. My grandfather, Sir Frederick, started work in the office of a Mr. Bible at fourteen and did so well that he became a partner in Bible and Simmons, and mayor of the city during the Second World War. He wore a black homburg hat and his white curls poked out underneath, like Lloyd George. My father went to the local grammar

school, Foyle College, where he was a good athlete and scholar. He served in the Royal Navy during the last few years of the First World War and came home to sell insurance and eventually become a stockbroker. He was a clever, energetic person and did well at business. He was also very convivial, which separated us a little from his parents who were strictly teetotal. I remember having to hide the fact that my father had lost his license for drunken driving from the grandparents. It seemed like a family joke then.

My mother's people were Montgomeries who came into Derry from farming in Donegal. Pacha Montgomery ran a carting company in Foyle Street. They were still using horse-drawn carts when I was a boy. The Montgomeries lived in a fine Georgian farmhouse, Elagh Hall, on a hill north of Derry. We went there every Sunday for a big Sunday lunch, and it was a child's paradise, with trees and endless roofs of barns to climb and little streams to dam. It was near enough to Derry for me to ride out on bikes with my friend Derek Kelso.

I had three elder sisters, all beautiful girls. We came at three yearly intervals so I wasn't very close to the two older sisters. Closest to me was Norah Anne. We fought quite a lot . . . in fact there is a family photograph of us standing on the back verandah with our arms round each other's shoulders, smiling. We had called out to my mother, "Quick, take a photo-graph of us. We're not fighting."

The first twelve years of my life were pretty tranquil, with long holidays in Donegal by the sea, reading books, listening to records, playing board games like Monopoly or Buccaneer, swimming, playing golf, exploring the beautiful, barren countryside. Those houses by the sea or in the country surely enriched my imagination. At that time adults and children listened to the same records, and my mind is still filled with the songs of Frank Crumit and George Formby and John McCormack, well-crafted whether funny or emotional.

At Elagh there were huge volumes of the *Children's Encyclopedia* which had folktales and fairy stories and myths. I certainly read children's adventure books, those about Biggles and the Saint and Bulldog Drummond and, later, maybe, Robert Louis Stevenson and P. C. Wrenn. These inculcated love of adventure and all sorts of heroic values, just like the adventure movies; but most authors and movies have other qualities that have nothing to do with the plot. For instance, John Buchan's *The 39 Steps* has the hero running away from villains all over the Scottish moors, just like Stevenson's hero in *Kidnapped,* and those places and that weather was the weather and landscape I grew up in . . . so that the ambition of your life can become subconsciously the need to live where waves roll in on beaches, where you have access to mountain country, where boats knock against stone harbours, and you smell turf smoke in the air. The heroes tended to be laconic and brave and capable of rowing boats and sailing yachts, swimming and running, maybe even drinking whiskey and smoking pipes and winning the love of beautiful women.

The first poems that attracted me were melancholy:

> Under the wide and starry sky
> Dig the grave and let me lie:
> Glad did I live and gladly die,
> And I laid me down with a will.
>
> This be the verse you grave for me:
> Here he lies where he long'd to be;
> Home is the sailor, home from sea,
> And the hunter home from the hill.

It seems a curious thing that very young people should be so satisfied contemplating death.

Of all our M.A. students at the moment, only one wants to deal in rhyming verse; but when I started to write, it never occurred to me that poetry should not be salted down in rhyme and rhythm, euphonious and easy to remember. That was the beauty of it, that it was clinched into a musical shape that allowed it to blossom in your mind.

In 1945 I was sent to a boarding school at the age of eleven with my friend Derek Kelso. It was frightening but we were able to cope with it. Campbell College was an Irish public school, a local version of Eton, a reduced world where we worshipped prefects and rugby players a few years older than ourselves. Fairly strict masters taught us Latin and science and geography, etc. Standing out from that pantheon of stuffy old-fashioned teachers was a French teacher called Storcy who played jazz piano at the end-of-year party. Instead of the black academic cloak, he wore a heavy leather jacket and was the first local human being who had

some flavour of the international world of the cinema. He sang "Frankie and Johnny."

Such schools represented the tail end of the tradition of empire. Most of it fitted in with the films like *They Died with Their Boots On,* which had Errol Flynn playing General Custer, a bad student but a great soldier . . . that was the message. So we had our fights with authority, but we still wanted to succeed, especially at sports. I wanted to be head prefect and play for the First XV. The growth of my mind estranged me from my teachers and the ethos of the school. There were also some catastrophes. My friend Derek was knocked down during a sparring session in the gym. He was taken to the infirmary and died.

The housemaster took me to his office the next morning and broke the news. Before he opened his mouth, I knew what he was going to say. They let me wander in the school grounds for an early morning hour while the headmaster spoke of death to the school at assembly. I wandered down paths in the beautiful overgrown grounds at the back of the school, past a little lake with an island at the centre totally covered with rhododendrons, trying to take in the notion of death.

They said Derek had some sort of brain tumour and that his death had nothing to do with Clive Bew's blow; but his mother queried the school's behaviour. She wanted to punish someone for the death of her son. The clash produced an inward quarrel in me. It seemed the school was hiding something. They stopped boxing in the school, which implied that something dangerous was going on. It didn't answer Mrs. Kelso's questions. She was an equally difficult novelty, an adult behaving in an hysterical and bitter way, spilt emotion, hatred. Then my grandfather Pacha Montgomery died, he who owned Elagh Hall, and it turned out that his wife had never liked the country, so they sold the farm. Elagh, that was somehow the centre of all that was most lovely and secure in life, was gone.

Derek and I had been inseparable. For all those years we had gone to so many pictures together, and he had a wonderful ability to relive the stories and mimic the actors. He was my one companion at Elagh. He could swim and box just that bit better than me that made him particularly interesting. After this, confusion fell thick and fast, common things like the first stirrings of sexual feeling. After some clumsy and confusing adventures I met my first real love, Margaret Kirk.

Margaret and I met at a dance at The Palladium Ballroom in Portrush when I was about sixteen. We walked out to the sandhills and kissed in that exploratory and passionate way of young people who do not know the intricacies of sexual intercourse. I invested huge passionate interest in this. It was all I wanted to know about. Everything I had heard of love began to make sense, and nothing else in my life had this sort of importance; but I was sixteen and she was a working girl a good few years older. This caused a natural turmoil that school had no place for. It caused me to break all the rules in efforts to be with her. In school terms it turned me into a delinquent.

At the same time my academic success had narrowed in towards arts subjects in a pretty confused way. Intellectually I was beginning to take religion and politics seriously in conversation with my new cleverer friends. Poetry was beginning to matter, those poets who spoke of the real world like Rupert Brooke and Louis MacNeice, novelists like D. H. Lawrence . . . and of course Shakespeare. I played hookey from school to see *The Lady from Shanghai* in which Orson Welles puzzled my mind with all sorts of strange emotions, and the beauty of Rita Hayworth was overwhelming. I made confused stands against the ethos of the school, refusing to do military training, refusing to go to church . . . not in a confident revolutionary spirit, but out of desperation, wanting a girl, wanting to think about pacifism, hating the bullying of schoolmasters, and suddenly being surrounded by fellow pupils who had conceived a hatred of me because I was handsome and charming and thought they were grotesque.

I came from a family of handsome charming people. I pause before saying this because it sounds so glib, but it was so. Whatever the shortcomings of our family, it had a sort of free-wheeling liberal quality. It was good fun. Nobody was blamed unless they were pompous. At school I met all sorts of poor distorted souls, clumsy, ugly, vain, wicked. There was one companion called Malseed I christened Cleo because he had huge lips like the cartoon goldfish. I didn't seem to realise how this might hurt him. He was also vain and bad-tempered, couldn't bear to be beaten at table tennis. Bad losers were beyond the pale.

Anyway, my treatment of these people gave them offence, and when they became prefects they wanted revenge. I was confronted by this big ugly boy telling me he could ruin my reputation at the school by spreading word that my father had lost his license for drunken driving. The family joke could be seen as a public shame. It wasn't that I shared his view of my father's crime, but the shock that a stranger could know of our family affairs, and that he was blackmailing me. He wanted me to be his friend, or I would suffer. He tried to bribe prefects to beat me.

I went immediately to my housemaster, thinking he would strike at once against this evil; but to him the issue was much more blurred. I had made myself unpleasing to the school, and my desire to see girls and not serve in the military training must have seemed similar in his mind to the blackmail I was being subjected to.

Such moral ambiguity confused me. I have always been terrified of anger and hate. Not that my terror stopped me from doing what I needed to do, but I could never respond adequately to the anger. I could neither be a tough guy and tell them to fuck off, nor even summon a cool rhetoric to state my position. I could and did resist in a blurred, uncertain, and frightened way.

The Higher Certificate was the top exam you did before leaving school unless you stayed on to work for university scholarships. My results in the H.C. were not such as to suggest I could get a university scholarship. Still, it was a shock when I got a letter from the headmaster at the beginning of my school holidays, saying there was no point in me coming back. Instead of playing for the first fifteen, being a prefect, going to university, I was suddenly out in the world with no rites of passage, a failure. I didn't understand that the struggles I had gone through were real and important, that I had begun to think. I had made some friends who would be more important than schoolteachers. I had begun to read and even write with some sense of purpose. I had taken some singing lessons. All sorts of things were beginning, but I didn't know enough to be confident in them.

My poetry tends to be dramatic or narrative. I have published eight books of verse. If

The "handsome" Simmons family: (from left) sisters Norah Anne and Joan, Sub Lieutenant John Miller (whose ship was in Derry during the 1939–45 war), sister Mary, my father and mother "with her hands on my shoulders"

you want to sample it there is a reasonable selection in Anthony Bradley's *Contemporary Irish Poetry,* University of California Press, or in *The Penguin Book of Contemporary Irish Poetry,* edited by Derek Mahon. Very little of it deals with those early years; but there is one poem in the Penguin book that shows how haunted I was by that affair with Margaret Kirk. I wrote it years later before any of my poems got published, and I was working at menial jobs, very much in the dark and insecure. It seemed I might never have love affairs so intense and satisfying as I had known with Margaret Kirk, hence the title "The Archeologist":

> Portrush. Walking dead streets in the dark.
> Winter. A cold wind off the Atlantic
> rattling metal in the amusement park . . .

I looked back at the early innocent days before sexual intercourse:

> Nothing is tawdry, all our jokes are funny,
> the pin-table is brighter than Shakespeare's
>   works,
> my handful of warm coins is sufficient
>   money . . .

I always wanted to write songs that were as rich as poems, and poems that were as easy and memorable as songs, without denying complexity or subtlety. One reason I am so happy at the moment is because I feel I brought it off, not always, but often.

Meanwhile in 1950 at home a worse disintegration was taking place. My father had conceived a love for a married woman, and left home for her. My sister, who had been at drama school, came home pregnant (this was still disgraceful in our society, though not altogether in our home). My mother badgered her into marrying the boy, Robert Stephens, who became a fine actor. The following year I worked as a clerk in my father's office. I hated the work and in fact did very little. I was shadowed by a sense of failure; but in a way it was great to be free of school. I was reading and writing poems, playing a little rugby, dancing, acting, singing, going to the pictures, and falling marvellously and painfully in love with a girl called Eileen Mitchell.

There was nobody I met in Derry who took art seriously. When a year had passed, it was evident that the sort of artistic activity I was after was not available. I resolved to leave home and try my luck in London, to be a singer and/or a writer. It was still very vague and unresolved, I was only eighteen; but the worries of the world were on me. Just before I left home my father's mistress killed herself! This was horrible; but my father wanted to come back to my mother, so it took the responsibility of her welfare and happiness out of my hands.

Max and I left one night in September. I had saved £20. Another friend, Terence McCaughey, came down to wave to us on the boat to Liverpool. We remembered that Rupert Brooke had paid a little boy sixpence to wave good-bye to him when he left for the South Seas. Max was a far more sophisticated boy than I. He had read autobiographies of Stephen Spender, etc., and knew a little of contemporary literary life, although he was probably twenty years behind the times. We arrived in London and spent one night in a B & B near Euston Station. It had all the grotesquerie one might wish for if you were Sam Beckett. A lap dog was sick on the dirty sofa. We were locked into our room. When we got up next morning we were offered jelly for breakfast. The next night we tried to save money by sleeping out, first in one of the London parks; but when police flashlights scared us off the park bench we ended up in one of the old red telephone booths, trying to sleep on the four London directories.

Thereafter we went to Blackheath and found more regular accommodation. Max had an urge to go on to France, and I wish we had. I might have a second language now. I also had one tentative connection there. One Easter vacation, when I was still at school, I had gone with some friends to Paris, sung at a night club, and met an older woman who took me to a small hotel where I experienced sexual intercourse for the first time. It was confusing and unsatisfying, but felt like an heroic achievement . . . and there was real tenderness. Such a woman might have helped us to escape from the society we had been brought up in to something more exciting and expansive.

I thought London was the place for me to try out as a singer. So we stayed in London. Max got a job selling tickets for shows. I worked as a waiter and dishwasher in a Lyons Corner House. Then he went home to tend his crippled mother who had fallen downstairs.

We had three small literary adventures: the first was to attend the Blackheath Writers' Circle where we felt very superior because the members seemed only interested in getting published in middlebrow magazines like *Argosy* and *Men Only*. I can remember bursting out from that modest gathering in suffocated joy to be out on the heath, breathing fresh air, our youthful ambitions still bursting out of us. The second was a visit to Stephen Spender's house. Max had the address. Spender was away on holiday. The last was a visit to T. S. Eliot, a popular poet of the day. We went up in a lift to his apartment, and an angry man in a wheelchair, Hayward, told us we were trespassing and should get out quick. I wouldn't have had anything to say to Eliot anyway. I hated "The Hollow Men," his poem in our school anthology. Max thought better of him. Max was a wonderful friend, and we met and corresponded for many years after. He was also a good poet and could have made his way in that discipline; but at a certain point he stopped trying and became a philosopher.

I was left alone in London. This time of my life gets into my poetry in some detail in the sequence "No Land Is Waste, Dr. Eliot," which came out by itself from the Keepsake Press in the '70s, and later in a volume called *Judy Garland and the Cold War*. I often feed off other people's poems, old and new, just as poems often feed off myths and historical characters and paintings. A classic plot helps to shape your own experience. The "Marital Sonnets" grew out of reading Daniel's "Sonnets to Laura." My London sequence contests Eliot's miserable vision:

> Stearns' Londoners are just as phoney as
>   Yeats'
> Irish peasants. Ignore the fella who hates
> too much, who spurns women with false
>   teeth . . .

Visions of horror conjured out of air,
the spiritual DTs. The pompous swine . . .
that man's not hollow, he's a mate of
   mine.

In fact I was often lonely and sad and frustrated, never "one of the boys"; but in writing poems about the life I saw and imagined I often gave the impression to careless readers that all my poems were autobiographical. Because Eliot and I might be shy and neurotic, it shouldn't stop us from seeing the dance of life as it is often enjoyed. He found the pleasure of ballroom dancing when he married his secretary in later life; but I enjoyed it from the beginning. For about three years on and off I lived there, visiting theatrical agents and attending auditions with almost no success. I moved from Blackheath to Kensington Gardens Square near Bayswater and got a job as an usher in the Odeon Cinema, Leicester Square.

The greater part of my sequence on London is filled with portraits of the deprived but resilient characters I lived among. Max and I once or twice paid £1.50 to have sex in a taxi with a prostitute called Betty. There were no real sexual thrills, but we were very frustrated and determined to have the experience, and it was rewarding in its own way:

Apart from sex she is humane and funny:
talks of her son at Eton, her love of
   plants,
what England owes to Churchill . . . just
   like my Aunts . . .
worth thirty bob of anybody's money.

I still get great pleasure from this sequence as from most of my poetry. I worked hard at my poems and wrote from the heart. I am intelligent and open to life. I never could understand why Larkin and Betjeman became so popular, including so much less of life, with no more art. Can it be that my poems have an in-built demand that people should go out and live better, while these two popular English poets relished frustration and failure. Eliot was the same. There is nothing profound about cowardice.

Some lines of Donald Davie stick in my mind (and that is a good sign with poetry):

For courage is the vegetable king,
the sprig of all ontologies, the weed
that beards the slagheap with its
   hectoring,
whose green adventure is to go to seed.

It is an elegant assertion of a heartening truth.

One of his critical truths sticks in my mind too. "After the first stanza the smell of blood is a question of style." This seems to go to the heart of certain questions that readers raise naively. All poems have some sort of truth to life, but it isn't literal. We don't want to know if Larkin actually lived at Mr. Bleaney's address or who Mr. W.H. is in Shakespeare's sonnets. All we need to know is if the poems question our souls and satisfy our ears. My most famous poem, "The Ballad of Claudy," was written in 1973, commissioned by the BBC for a radio programme on the troubles. A television crew came last week to ask me again about the wonder of getting so much feeling into a simple format.

The truth is that the poem was written out of professional skill and imagination. My withers were not wrung. By that time I was a lecturer, a well-known poet and singer-songwriter. The BBC asked me to write some songs for a programme, so I went through the papers looking for key events that might lend themselves to song. One was the recent series of car bomb explosions by the IRA that had killed twelve people in a pretty village in the Sperrin mountains. It was, as they say, a mixed population, Protestants and Catholics living well enough together as they often do. Someone put me in touch with a teacher who worked there and he showed me round the village and pointed out where people had been killed. I took notes and versified what he told me. I expected to draw some sort of moral at the end; but that turned out not to be appropriate.

This is where Davie's line about the smell of blood comes in. There have been songs about war since poems began. I knew I was adding to the tradition, I knew where I was expanding the tradition, I knew where I was avoiding the partisan nature of Irish political songs. The real decisions were aesthetic. And maybe courage and coolness come into it. I didn't let the horrific subject bully me. I could imagine a true picture of carnage and put it into poetic form:

How peaceful and pretty if the moment
    could stop,
McIlhenny is straightening things in his
    shop,
and his wife is outside serving petrol, and
    then
a child takes a cloth to a big window pane.

In truth the poem is also a lyric in praise of
the ordinary. The first half describes people
going about their business on a sunny day. The
second half tells about their sudden deaths:

An explosion too loud for your eardrums
    to bear,
and young children squealing like pigs in
    the square,
and all faces chalk-white and streaked with
    bright red,
and the glass and the dust and the
    terrible dead.

The last stanza hints at the cause of the carnage. By and large the IRA had not intended
to blow up innocent civilians (just innocent
soldiers and police); but quite often they made
catastrophic mistakes, and somehow their carelessness and incompetence angered someone who
was prepared to believe the "armed struggle"
could be inspired by serious ideas and true
feelings, however misguided. In this case they
had blown up the telephone exchange so that
their warning could not be phoned in. Hence
the last line:

Meanwhile to Dungiven the killers have
    gone,
and they're finding it hard to get through
    on the phone.

I think that is a nice piece of understatement.

In fact I resent the popularity of this song.
Anyone who knows anything about life or
poems should love other poems of mine much
better, where more skill does more important
work. Yeats was irritated in a similar way by
the popularity of "The Lake Isle of Innisfree."
You couldn't write that charming poem unless
you had talent, but even before, and certainly
after, Yeats wrote many poems that make
Innisfree seem trivial.

But I have leapt on from timid anonymity
to complaining about a popular and much
anthologised piece. I even compare myself to

Yeats! What a world goes in between, and yet
the shifts are fairly imperceptible. "One writes
well before one is recognised."

During the early years I was reading books
and listening to songs, often in an haphazard
way. During the years in London I hit on a
lot of classics . . . Joyce and Lawrence led to
Tolstoy and Turgenev and Flaubert. I was also
bowled over by Saroyan and O'Connor. In the
poetry line, Auden became important, his "Sonnets in Time of War" and his ballads . . . and
Hopkins: "Felix Randal" and "Thou art indeed
just, Lord. . . ." At that time Auden was bringing
out a five-volume anthology of poetry in English. From my weekly salary of £7.50, I bought
one volume each week. His introductions were
very stimulating. At school we learnt bits of
Keats and Wordsworth and Browning by heart,
and I stumbled on Blake's "Marriage of Heaven
and Hell." I should say that Shakespeare was
at the heart of my inspiration to write. Nobody else ever had his weight and variety and
humanity. No innovations superseded him, and
I still measure excellence against his work, although lesser figures can release ideas and subjects in you, tones and forms. In Derry a girl
had given me a copy of "The Rubaiyat of Omar
Khayyam." Lawrence's poems inspired me, and
still do, and lesser talents like Andrew Young
and Edward Thomas. It is wrong for me to
talk about major and minor talents. It is
particular poems that inspired me and sing
in the memory. I don't want to make a case
for Lawrence being a major poet; but I will
say over in my head the poem about his
mother:

My love is like a girl tonight
but she is old,
and the plaits that lie along her pillow
are not gold,
but threaded with filigree silver
and uncanny cold.

So it is with painting. I seem to prefer sketches
to large finished oils, though I love lots of
Van Gogh and Rembrandt and pre-Renaissance
painters whose names I forget. I think I also
prefer chamber music, Bach violin partitas,
Schubert quintets and Mozart trios. . . . Some
yes. Some no. Laughter and tears and conundrums. I like to be moved. I like to laugh and
cry . . . and to be intrigued:

The cut worm forgives the plough!

Is that poetry?

Those sort of questions were turning in my brain in those early years when I was going to The Hammersmith Palais, looking for a girl. Then back to Ireland to work behind the bar at The York Hotel and sing with Ernie Mann's dance band. In London I met the characters that turn up in "No Land Is Waste." In Portrush, behind the bar, I came across my father's drinking cronies who feature in some of the songs. I also observed my parents and relations, and boys and girls of my own age, and wrote about them sooner or later.

Then, one year, at the end of another frustrating summer I saw an article in the *Belfast Telegraph,* that *The Yacht Squall* had sailed from Belfast to go round the world and was now stuck in St. Ives because the crew had opted out. One could join the expedition by buying in for £50. I don't remember having to argue too hard with my father. He gave me the money and I set off. I remember my uncle Alec was driving, and we missed the train at Coleraine but caught it at Ballymoney. Some driving! Through the dark night, in my new duffle coat, I headed for Cornwall.

The captain of the yacht was Billy Stokes, a former shipyard worker with a peaked cap and a blazer. The yacht was leaning against a wall of the harbour in St. Ives, a racing yacht, too low in the cabin to stand up. Stokes was full of stories of his years at the Belfast shipyards, sleeping on mattresses they smuggled in when he ought to have been working on the construction of great ships. He had inherited the boat from some rich amateur, and here he was, heading off for a world tour with little money. We put our heads together to find sponsorship, but it didn't amount to more than some tinned food and some cheap lights. I certainly felt my middle-class upbringing and natural shyness.

The only other crew member was a bearded artist who smoked a pipe. In September we set off, and before Lands End, the artist had been careless at the tiller, the mainsail gibed and six feet came off the mainmast. This was clearly not a boat for a world cruise; but what did I know? Nothing. I watched with admiration as Billy Stokes climbed the mast and cut away the debris, and we limped round to Mousehole. There Billy fixed her up with a gaff rig and I bent myself to the common task of sewing the sail to fit the new rig. It was not work I was accustomed to. Then we sailed on to Falmouth and eventually headed south into Biscay. It was too late in the year. We sailed into foul weather and *The Squall,* with its elegant protruding prow, went bang bang bang into every choppy wave. The cheap lights went out. We were all wet and cold. Out of the mist huge liners loomed, likely to cut us in two. It was very frightening. Paralysed, we stood to our watches (the only competent sailor being Billy Stokes) and almost wept with relief when Billy declared the boat would break up if we endured the same punishment for much longer. We turned and sailed back to Falmouth, still through foul weather.

The press had kept some note of us, and a headline appeared in a Belfast paper, YACHT "SQUALL" MISSING, BELIEVED LOST. Apparently my father had some sort of seizure. He never expressed intimate emotion to me; but that didn't stop him from loving me and being shattered by my supposed watery death. I now have one or two of his old diaries. His whole war experiences are registered by games of badminton. I think he slept through the battle of Jutland. And when the love of his life married someone else, he notes "M.L. married C.B. Left for Belfast."

When we reached Falmouth, those who attend to damaged sailors were at the quayside and friendly locals put us up for the night. I will never forget the ease and comfort and relief of Mrs. Brewer's spare bedroom, the large brass bed with fresh linen in a room where apples must have been stored. I was suddenly back at Elagh Hall, safe, exhausted, comforted. What a sleep that was. In the weeks after, I enjoyed a few months of playing the piano at the Sailors Rest, eating Cornish cream pastries, helping Billy to work on a more spacious wreck he had acquired in exchange for *The Squall.* It was moored up a creek in the river and we had a long row into town, when I would visit Mrs. Brewer, who had become a tender but demanding lover.

A lot of this material turned up last summer in a sestina.

I was lying out on the grass with my daughter under a flagpole belonging to the local coastguards. The halyard was slapping against the metal mast, and it reminded me of all the halyards I had heard slapping against masts. My daughter, who is getting interested in poetry, took down the images that came into my head and told me the form of a sestina. Janice had just written one:

The nylon rope slapping the metal mast,
a forest clapping coldly in the dark,
and I alone unsleeping, close to the roof.
No other vessel had a man on board.
The small yacht strained against the
     mooring rope.
"Rangoon by morning!" Captain Billy
     cried.

This will be in my forthcoming collection, *Mainstream*.

I went home for Christmas. In Portrush, that strange little seaside holiday resort, my father said if I would forsake the sea he would pay for me to go to university. I accepted this offer; but over the holidays I met Laura Stinson at The Arcadia Ballroom, and, after an inauspicious start, we became very close. I had been singing "Blue Moon" with the local dance band. When I descended from the glamorous heights of the stage, she was standing in a waterproof, looking like a fascinating leader of the French resistance. I offered her whiskey from the half-bottle I had in my hip pocket. I hope the drinks I stole from my father's bar weren't too much of a factor in his losses.

All this material turns up in poems, most of them written long after the events, especially in the book *Constantly Singing*. Laura stayed over at the hotel several nights when she missed her bus to Coleraine and we slept together. My father came to the door one night and knocked. "I know she's in there," he said. It was a crucial moment in our relationship. His authority had winnowed away. I had found him out in the backyard trying to make it with one of our waitresses. He and my mother quarrelled continually over old letters he had from his former mistress (the one who killed herself). Although I was still unproved and incompetent in almost every way, I had energy and talent, and could see that he mixed all the time with clowns (Henry V in reverse) who were easy drinking companions. He seemed to have lost his way. The moral authority of this immensely talented man had eroded. So I found myself saying through the door, "Daddy. Go away," in a patient, unscared voice. And eventually he went. Nevertheless he was sometimes rude to

With first wife, Laura, on their honeymoon, 1955

Laura when we ate together, and so was my sister. This pushed us into a corner, and one night we left the hotel and begged a bed of a young man called Ronnie Brackenridge who was working in another hotel. We stayed with Laura's people in Coleraine for a while, and then we got married, about a month after we met.

This became a quarrel in my mind for many years. Were we in love or was it just desperation? Whatever it was, we weathered twenty years together. When we got married, my father felt it broke the bargain of his sending me to university, so Laura and I went off to Leeds where I had been accepted by Professor Bonamy Dobree in an earlier time when I lived in Bradford with my sister. A kind Egyptian had introduced us, and he thought well of my poems.

I was underqualified to get a grant, so Laura worked in factories and various other jobs to see us through that first year. Then, having passed the first year exams, I was eligible for government support. I couldn't overestimate the gratitude I owe to Laura for doing that work, or the excitement we both felt, renting our first flats and easing ourselves into university life. (It turns up in a recent poem "Hens' Feet.")

I worked in a brewery during the summer of 1955; but we couldn't have survived without Laura's work. However, the spectrum of life in

Leeds was much wider than anything I had encountered before, surrounded by people from all walks of life who had a fanatic interest in the arts. It became a haunting irritant that I had made my choice of wife before meeting all these more sophisticated and educated women. Laura quickly became pregnant and we had five children in not much more than five years. None of them planned. In one of Frank Loesser's marvellous lyrics in *Guys and Dolls* the perplexed wife says, "Have a pot roast, have a headache, have a baby . . ." And Laura told me afterwards she engineered her pregnancies to cope with marital crises. We were both radically ignorant of issues that are now carefully explored.

Leeds University was teeming with people of real talent: Wole Soyinka and Tony Harrison were fellow students, Geoffrey Hill was on the staff as were Wilson Knight and Arnold Kettle. People who never fulfilled their promise were immensely talented: George Campbell, Keith Waddams, John Chappell, Bill Ireland. There were several guitarists, a good jazz trumpeter, Pete King, and a comedian, Barry Cryer, who later made his living out of that art. Bonamy Dobree had set up a marvellous department, although he retired the year I arrived.

After a first year in which I bent myself to pass exams, I exploded into wildness and, I suppose, arrogance, believing more and more in my talent, editing the poetry magazine, acting in plays, singing, writing and reading, tempted continually by the beautiful talented girls who sowed a seed of discontent in my marriage to Laura without providing a serious competitor. Laura wasn't stupid. She made her own impact on this community. Sexual liberation and sexual confusion characterised this period, and many of my poems explore the results. Coming from Northern Ireland it was particularly important to fight the good fight against puritanism and obscurantism; but, like most pioneers, we found ourselves in painful situations beyond the simple optimism of our ambitions.

There are three key poems that come out of my time at Leeds: "Ode to Blenheim Square," "Me and the World," and "Soliloquy for a Ghost." They are in my first collection for the Bodley Head, *Late But in Earnest.* In the former I use the form of the ode to praise the down-at-heel area we lived in. The poem, originally called "Leeds 2," was much praised at the time. They both explore a theme that comes up again and again in my work . . . that the highest emo-

tions can be set off in the humblest surroundings. I keep discovering it in work I enjoy, from Chekhov and Hardy through Edgar Lee Masters to Raymond Carver. It is the poetic endorsement of democracy:

> . . . Even the trees are dirty to touch,
> the undug clay, hard:
> a bit of Nature, but not much
> better than a concrete yard.
> You can't lie down for dog-shit.
> But every morning, lovely, lonely,
> through white mist, lit
> by the hidden sun, only
> greenness and brightness show,
> and, sharp against the sky, aloof,
> as your eyes reach from below,
> the everywhere elegant lines of branch
>   and roof. . . .

Perhaps this is a good place to say that my first published poem came about by my aunt Norah sending me an entry form for a competition in *Varsity,* judged by Day Lewis. I sent in a poem about one of my schoolteachers, C. W. Bion. It won second or third prize, and to tell you the truth I have no memory of my emotions at the news. Great joy, no doubt; but life was so confused and my knowledge of the literary world so sketchy. Maybe I thought fame was within my grasp, that I had arrived! Almost certainly it went out of my mind as I approached the dance hall looking for love. When I eventually got to Leeds University, I might even have had another poem in the *New Statesman* or the *Listener.* I had certainly stepped out of private endeavour into some sort of modest public recognition. That sort of thing is so important and so irrelevant at the same time. There is no guarantee that you are going to write another poem; but when you have spent a long time in the wilderness, writing, you are likely to have a lot of poems in your folder, finished or half-finished. They aren't there because you want to win prizes, but because of the "inspiration" that made you think you had something to say. At the same time, in a writing career there can be a fairly business-like connection between writing and publishing. I am reading a biography of Wagner at the moment, and it is obvious with him that the need to write and the need to be heard were very close.

Romana Huk, the American scholar, visited me some years ago doing research on "The

Leeds School of Poetry." This satisfied me, because it was certainly the nursery of some brilliant talents; but there was no particular ethos that united us. I lay it all at the door of Bonamy Dobree for hiring and admitting talented people, and laying down a law that there should be money available for a poetry magazine. That is how good things happen; but the people who came out of that good seed bed cannot be characterised by any stylistic similarity or any purpose other than to write well. Bonamy didn't have a regional programme or a stylistic programme. People like Tony Harrison must have been entirely unforeseen, because he came in through classics. The teaching department had no special sympathies. I don't know what you would find in common between Gregory Fellows like Tom Blackburn, Martin Bell, John Heath-Stubbs, Jon Silkin, Pearse Hutchinson. Yet Leeds must have been the first university to have resident poets in England.

When I got my sorry 2/2 degree, I found it very easy to get a good teaching job in Ulster. I couldn't stay in England because I would have had to join their army for two years; but I was offered a post at the Royal Belfast Academical Institution (RBAI), one of the best schools in Ulster. It frightened me, because I had never intended to be a teacher. School teaching was to be a better bet than washing dishes and bar-tending, not a vocation. I took the second offer from Ivan Gray, a job at a Quaker grammar school in Lisburn. I wanted ease and tranquility.

In fact my first years at Friends School had nightmarish episodes, in that I couldn't keep order in the lower forms, partly because of total ignorance of teaching techniques and a sort of cavalier feeling that I was above all this nonsense. . . . I suppose it is characteristic that the bad was balanced by much good. I was asked to direct the school plays because I had acted Captain Boyle in *Juno* at Leeds. Teaching myself to be a director taught me about theatre and gave several waves of students insights into life and drama.

Friends School was a very modest version of Campbell College. It had none of the empire ethos, but it had the lyric qualities of avenues and trees and tennis courts and playing fields. That was a joy, and the atmosphere turns up in songs like "The Sun." Flirtations with colleagues turn up in other poems. Really it

was where I grew up. It was there I felt the shift from personal ambition to a notion of service. There were boys and girls in the sixth form who grew up to be novelists and professional musicians and actors. From being a boy myself I began to get the notion that I was an adult who had to help other people. This came, very happily, in enjoying their intelligence and creativity, their desire to act and write pieces for magazines, and to give me their reactions to literature that challenged my own. There was also a very intelligent man, George Craig, my friend and companion, who taught French and Russian and knew about Marx. We fostered our pupils together and enjoyed their company. He was also a good tennis player.

In those years in Lisburn so many other things happened. I had a bicycle to ride into Belfast. I began to write songs and had them broadcast on local radio, and met Sam Hanna Bell, a good novelist who worked for the BBC and was revolutionising the local radio by making it more truly regional. He was part of a national revolution that allowed provincial accent to become glamorous in the throats of Albert Finney and Tom Bell and Robert Stephens. Local drama had found new life in the radio series Joseph Tomelty wrote, "The McCooeys."

Stewart Love wrote a play for the Edinburgh Festival in which one of my pupils had a part. He asked me to write songs for it. Stephen Wray, then a student, was the leading actor in it. Michael Emerson who produced the play later started The Belfast Festival (and is now agent for James Galway). Kevin Boyle did lights. He has been Professor of Law at Galway and now writes Penguin books with Tom Hadden about Ulster politics. That is a measure of the times. Ulster has always produced talented people from the Duke of Wellington to C. S. Lewis and Helen Waddell; but in my time the province they sprang from became part of the fame of its illustrious sons and daughters.

In poetry I began to become conscious of younger talents, like Mahon, Heaney, and Longley, brought together for workshops by Philip Hobsbaum. These famous workshops had no effect on my work because I had been at Leeds with equal or superior talents. Hobsbaum was an enthusiastic facilitator, but I did not much like him or his poems. The local poets were getting to know each other independent of his workshops. I remember with more enthusiasm the burgeoning folk scene. For years singing in pubs had been frowned on as likely to cause trouble if people sang rebel or Orange songs; but by a curious twist of fate some Irish Americans, the Clancy Brothers, put Irish folk songs into the Top Twenty, and by so doing released the people at home into their heritage. Rebel songs were no longer rebel songs, they were internationally popular. To do the Clancys justice, they had taste and sang a whole spectrum of good songs in their Aran sweaters. Of course they were part of a larger movement led by Ewan MacColl and A. L. Lloyd in England, the revival of a sort of left-wing movement reintroducing the people to their own rich heritage of words and music.

I had been part of this folk revival in my university days. Arnold Kettle played us recordings of Irish songs by Patrick Galvin. In fact in my last year at school Terence McCaughey had played me 78's of MacColl singing medieval ballads like Sir Patrick Spens . . . but now it was coming to life in Belfast. Folk clubs were springing up everywhere, and I found an audience in them. Michael Emerson was a far more important figure than Hobsbaum. It was he who brought Sean O'Riada and The Chieftains north and set up new standards for traditional music, started the Belfast Festival, encouraged drama, and generally gave new energy to the people of Belfast. Hobsbaum's success was to pick out Seamus Heaney and set him off on the career we all know about. But when the folk scene was at its height, there was a feeling that the old sectarian grudges were fading away in the light of this new socially conscious movement. The Irish rebel songs were sung in the same spirit as "Van Dieman's Land," which emphasises class persecution rather than Nationalist fervour. We were all against oppression everywhere, as well as boosting our egos in performance.

For myself I was being forced to grow up in many ways, to cope with wife and children and job, at the same time as I was becoming almost a celebrity, writing topical songs for a radio programme and appearing on TV. At this time also my father had begun to die of cancer, and I used to cycle down back roads to his hospital to play desultory games of chess and not quite communicate with a man in pyjamas who was suffering various unsuccessful treatments, being inspired myself to all sorts of vague romantic poetic impulses as I rode my weary way through beautiful twilight looking up at the Belfast hills. These never became poems.

I have always been badly organised. I still come across the beginnings of poems, jotted down in notebooks, that were never completed. I was inconsistent about sending my work off to magazines; but so much was going on, perhaps most importantly a real sense of being alive and active in my own country. Apart from mixed public successes there was contact with other literary people, especially those of an older generation like Sam Bell, and more intimately, James Boyce, actor and intellectual bohemian who lived in a housing estate between Belfast and Lisburn. Sometimes I would get off the bus on my way home late at night and visit his house to savour his encouragement, the liveliness of his mind, the assurance that poetry mattered. It was a very ordinary small house. He was not a rich mandarin. Perhaps he was not a great actor or critic, but he was devoted to the literary life. His son, Patrick, was a pupil at Friends School, and he introduced me to a vital widow woman who kept a similar sort of poor but lively house in Lisburn. These were the people that mattered more to me than the local poets. They wove into my life. They were the sort of people who might have been friends of my father and mother.

Tony Harrison was still writing to me copiously from England and came over several times with his wife Rosemary to visit us and spend holidays in Donegal. He spent a year in Czechoslovakia and eventually went to Nigeria to teach at Ahmadu Bello University. When I had spent five years teaching he summoned me out there and we all went. It was a crucial move.

With my mediocre degree I was not eligible for university teaching at home; but at that time standards in African universities were lower, and with Tony's help I was appointed. It cut across the success I had achieved in Belfast and might have been a bad career move. It would have suited my temperament to move into professional performance; but the mystery of Africa and the glamour of university teaching lured me and became my life.

If you wake up in Philadelphia on a wet day it might as well be Belfast; but Africa was a total change. The seasons that dominate our lives where I grew up didn't apply. There was a long dry hot winter and a very wet hot summer. Getting off the plane in Kano was like stepping into an oven. All this is evoked in my one-man show *Doilly McCartney's Africa,* which I performed in Coleraine and at the Edinburgh Festival but has yet to be published. The African experience was also a step back in history. The university was built in the bush outside the small town of Zaria; but in the old town lived an emir in a mud palace with harem and devoted subjects. When we went down to watch his birthday celebrations, his tribal chiefs rode up to his throne and reared their horses in salutations. In the crowd was a jester with an inflated bladder, knocking people playfully about as they did in England a thousand years ago.

Our housing was quite European and familiar. The novelty was that we were expected to hire a houseboy to do the cooking, who went off to his own primitive accommodation at night. You also hired a "garden boy" for a few shillings. You could hardly do without them, and thus were lured into a dubious colonial style of living. Like my colleagues, I went along with it. The heat was frightening and exciting, like the thunderstorms and the new landscape of dead flat glistening plain as far as the inselberg where we sometimes went for celebratory breakfasts. Not far from our house you could see Stone Age farmers living in straw huts and hacking the earth with ancient tools.

University teaching meant we dealt with sophisticated texts like the novels of D. H. Lawrence, which did not always make sense to the students. If you brought up the notion of a boy being in love with his mother, you got responses like, "Not in Africa, sir." Teaching poetry you had to explain the symbolism of our seasons: winter/death, spring/revival, autumn/harvest, etc. Such novelties made you think again about familiar things and see them in a new light.

Before the family left Lisburn (we now had five children, four girls and a boy), I went out at Easter to take up my job at Ahmadu Bello. Tony had painted the scene in dark Conradian colours, but on the whole it was very pleasant and comfortable. The only dark side was the discrepancy between our lifestyle and the people who worked for us. You could be faced with a houseboy trying to sell you his wife or child or some other young person for your sexual pleasure. The bars in the town were also brothels. I must say I was fascinated and tried it out three times; but I have a low sexual drive.

Without love and affection I get frightened and frustrated. I almost never come to climax more than once in a night, so that if I am saddled with an unsympathetic partner there is no joy. I totally regret a night with an unattractive woman I shared with Tony Harrison (shared in the sense that he was there to mock my endeavours); but the other two had a sort of humanity about them, totally divorced from the sort of sensual satisfaction one's fantasies might associate with the notion of hiring a prostitute. One was very beautiful.

After that term I went back to Ireland for the summer, and brought the whole family out by boat in September. The voyage had some beauty (I remember leaning over the bow in fearful fascination to watch the prow far below, cutting through blue water); but the arrival at Lagos was totally scary. A new world of black people, and us, skinned (i.e. poor) as usual, unable to make ourselves understood, worried about losing our luggage, having to hire men to carry it to the train. However, we made it and suffered the long, miserable but fascinating train journey through jungle and scrub to Zaria.

We were given a large modern house at the edge of the campus and the freedom of the nursery to choose trees and plants for our garden. The speed of growth was awe inspiring. Saplings that we put in along the drive, perhaps forty of them, were almost full-grown trees in a year's time. The heat was amazing to us, to be always walking around in shorts and singlets, to sit in our large living room at night with the French windows open while regiments of insects, some huge and black like medieval knights, sailed into the light out of the bush. They were all dead in the morning and had to be swept up like rubbish.

With servants my wife's life changed radically, and instead of giving us more leisure for joy it opened up all sorts of cracks in our relationship so that we fought continually, had more time to resent our sexual hang-ups, perhaps felt no social eye controlling us in this strange environment. I suppose anyone looking back has to pick out the significant moments, and that can distort the picture. As far as our children were concerned we all had a wonderful time. They were young and in bed when we were quarrelling. By day we both functioned well enough as parents, the children attended school, we went to the swimming pool

En route home from Africa with four daughters: (from left) Rachel, Penelope, Helen, and Sarah, on holiday in Spain, 1964

every afternoon and relished the water and the warmth. They had good fun with other children . . . the American Tabachnicks I suddenly remember who had a horse . . . and lots of others, picnics and cookouts, afternoons at the club where the staff sat out in the verandah drinking huge cold bottles of lager, and the children ran about on the scorched grass among swings and slides. In most ways it was a very happy and privileged life. There' was a cinema club and a dramatic society, both very good. Some of us started a jazz band, very shaky for quality since I was the incompetent pianist, but exciting if you were keen to make music.

It certainly wasn't as interesting as the local music; on rough stages the Nigerians made good music. As I remember, the groups in the Sabon Gari hotels had plenty of drummers and a few solo instrumentalists, a guitar, a saxophone playing through an ancient public address system; but there was a totally relaxed

confidence and competence in the singing and the drumming. They weren't trying to imitate something else. They were at home in what they knew, their songs, their rhythms for dancing, what they wanted to get out of the Western instruments. It was different from the folk clubs I had enjoyed at home in which a minority were trying to resurrect a broken tradition. That was exciting and very rich because so many different artistic impulses were at work. My feeling is that a lot of self-conscious people left their unmusical homes and came out to a special arena to create the music of their dreams. It was some sort of escape rather than our daily bread. Perhaps that is true of all Western art.

The Nigerians dancing to this music were of all ages, dressed in their heavy beautiful robes, moving with unself-conscious pleasure. We joined in, eager to be part of this happy, satisfying ritual. No one discouraged us, but we were visitors. The same easy music-making characterised student parties.

The most dynamic educational experiences occurred in drama when I put on a play written by one of the students alongside one of Wole Soyinka's. It made me realise how European Wole was. Tony and I did a version of *Lysistrata* set in Nigeria. Tony is a natural scholar, and not only was he familiar with the Greek original, but he picked up enough knowledge of Nigerian gods and myths to find parallels. The cast was made up of students (Tony and I were two halves of a pantomime donkey). The strong Christian element on the campus tried to get the production banned on the grounds that it was obscene and would offend Muslims. Northern Nigeria is a chiefly Muslim community. There were enough good souls in power to fend them off, and during the event no one was offended. We played to packed interested audiences in the main hall.

Local dignitaries lacked the inhibitions of audiences we were used to, and strode the aisles discussing the action with each other. We had unusual problems in rehearsal with girls who were sometimes reluctant to show their faces too publicly, and brought in little shawls to hide themselves behind. The men had no such inhibitions and were inclined to demand that their roles be enlarged if they were not worthy of the importance they attached to themselves. The enterprise has slipped into a mythology of my mind. I don't really remember any details, just a general feeling of excitement and success, of having pulled off something worthwhile and confounded our critics.

A sentence keeps recurring in my mind: "One does not expect much of a Christian." It is true to my experience (my heart sinks when someone announces him or herself as a believer), and yet the society I live in (and obviously America and England) still seem to be haunted by lip-service to the worst excesses of Christian superstition, unleavened by the tender and exciting innovations that can be culled from certain speeches attributed to Jesus Christ. For a century or so these seemed to have inspired the positive side of society, the left wing, socialism; but at this moment the English socialist party, having jettisoned all its egalitarian principles, is now coming on as Christian! By which they can only mean prayer and family values, puritanism, conservatism, not the duty of man to love and care for his neighbour.

I find myself in relative old age back where I started, rebelling against the crude puritanical ethos of my local church, which was a cover for the simple-minded lust for power and money that characterised the elders of the city in which I grew up. They were humourless, unhappy, authoritarian, anti-art, and very suspicious of strangers. So it is now here. So it is in England and America, not to mention Russia and Yugoslavia.

Proclaiming love, sexual and social, brotherhood and equality and the courage people need to claim their own freedom are therefore still central to my work. In the '60s before I went to Africa and after I came back, it seemed that some sort of revolution in the human spirit was taking place. That was at the heart of the folk revival where the music of the people was set up against the music the people were offered by Denmark Street and Tin Pan Alley. I relish the frothy wit and fantasy and pathos and tunefulness of commercial popular music; but I am aware it is thin diet for souls. I was part of the folk revival, and, in the smaller world of poetry, my running battle with T. S. Eliot (Royalist, Anglican, etc., and mandarin) was a symptom, an effort to show that we were more in need of "The Ballad of Jo Hill" than "The Wasteland," on all counts, politically and aesthetically.

Towards the end of our stay in Nigeria, their civil war was breaking out. There were riots on campus. Frustrated Hausas, unprepared

for modern life in the Islamic schools, were hunting down their Ibo fellow-countrymen who were more attuned to progress, having had a Christian education in the southeast, and were getting better jobs. It was no place for a family to be brought up, so we went home to Ireland in 1967 where I was unemployed for a year, living in a beautiful gazebo on Castlerock— a year before the Irish showed themselves to be as violent as the Nigerians.

In writing this account I see that there are no simple patterns in my life. Success, happiness, and good work done vary wildly and seem to have no connection with each other. The writing has gone on constantly in fits and starts. Projects that I spent years on have come to nothing, poems written on the back of a cigarette packet have found prompt publication. My marriage to Laura which petered out after ten bitter years of quarreling and infidelity on both our parts coincided with many happy times with friends and children, picnics, sing-songs, dinner parties, play productions, teaching, with

*With son Adam in the backyard
of Westport, 1970*

productive and barren periods. Life happens day by day, hour by hour. How do you balance a fascinated hour or so listening to music or practising an instrument against a family quarrel? How do you balance a happy love-making against a frustrating night at the writing table? Looking back, the lost richness of detail is astonishing. I suddenly remember the huge room I had to write in, in Castlerock, how I set out my papers on shelves and in boxes day after day and couldn't write a line. I remember the grand piano we had in Lisburn. I remember watching Helen being born in Bachelor's Walk. What about our first car, the big Daimler, bought for £200 when I won the Gregory Award in the late '50s, the smell of the leather. The long happy journeys to Portrush. My father's death in 1963.

At the end of the '60s I began to publish books and pamphlets. The collection (always changing slightly) I had sent round the publishers for years was suddenly accepted by James Michie of the Bodley Head (some of the poems I had written before going to university) . . . just like that, out of the blue. Grahame Greene was looking over his shoulder in the office and got interested in the manuscript. He wrote the blurb . . . "the best collection of ironic poetry since Norman Cameron died." So *Late But in Earnest* came out in 1967. Was that more exciting than the *Ballad of a Marriage* coming out the year before? All such occasions are joyous in their way, but then you get upset if there are no reviews, and next you are caught up by other things.

In 1968 the New University of Ulster opened in Coleraine. Walter Allen, the novelist and critic, was head of English, and he appointed me to his staff. I could see that as wonderful luck which led to many productive years teaching. I can also see it as a distraction from the serious business of being a singer and poet. I'll never resolve these things in retrospect, for whatever decision I took, I kept other irons in the fire. Just before I joined the department I spent the last few hundred pounds of my father's legacy starting a literary magazine, *The Honest Ulsterman*. You could write a book on that enterprise. On the positive side, it was a local outlet for all the new talents in Ireland from Brendan Kennelly to Derek Mahon. It published Stevie Smith and helped to resurrect the career of Gavin Ewart. Frank Ormsby and Michael Foley and Paul Muldoon had their earliest

poems published there. It is still going today under younger editors. The early editorials spell out the huge ambitions I had for it, to bring poetry to the people, etc. That didn't work out on a large scale, and yet, because I brought it to small local news agents each month, it reached people in small towns and helped to change their lives. They have told me. I thought it might provide a living for my talented but delinquent nephew, Michael Stephens, but it never made a profit. It just survived. So it goes.

My mother moved to a bungalow in Portstewart and gave me her mansion in Kerr Street, Portrush. It had seven bedrooms and was generally very beautiful, but I never had enough money to keep it up to scratch, so it was a slightly poisoned gift, and yet so many of us had such joy in it, how could you balance the good and bad? You just had to cross the road to be on the West Strand, so that we got in the habit of early morning dips in the ocean, right up to Christmas. I was able to buy a small fibreglass sailing dinghy, which gave us endless hours of horror and delight. Once you sailed out of the great harbour in Portrush, you were in the Atlantic. One of my daughters, now thirty, rang up a moment ago, and we had a long talk about her present condition and her hopes, etc., and she was suddenly saying that her early life had been so happy and stimulating in that big house and our excursions from it, that she and all of our kids had found it hard to settle to life thereafter. Although Laura and I could betray each other, we did not for most of our life together and apart betray our children or our notions of the good life.

Artistically I just kept making poems and songs out of the life around me, the ups and downs of family life and affairs, but also slants on that life from outside and from the past. For example, the poem "Stephano Remembers" came out of playing Stephano in a production of *The Tempest* directed by Tony Bareham. This colleague of mine was a sort of friend; we meant well towards each other, but matters of temperament and taste drove us apart. In this instance, he was producing the play with no recognition of its political implications. He was a "man of the theatre," and we had a student who had been a star of the English Youth Theatre, so Tony was spending all his energies getting this euphonious young man to suggest the magic power of Prospero, concentrating on this tall student drawing rings with his stave and choreographing the movement of people around him, while I was feeling more and more the injustice to the minor characters:

> We were no good as murderers, we were
> clowns.

So too, sailing on the sea gave insights into Homer and produced poems with that weight and emphasis. On one of our trips to Donegal I carried the selected poems of Emily Dickinson that got soaked by waves, and the act of separating the soaking pages became an act of criticism . . . what poems were worth preserving? It produced a sharp feeling of distinction between poems that failed by blurring their effects, and those that shone on the page as worth learning. It suggests the physical feeling I get about poems. Is the poet disappearing up his/her ass or is she/he part of the struggle for liberation? It isn't a matter of ideology, but just of doing some human thing well. One of the poems I kept and set to music is a sustained joke; but a great joke:

> I drink a liquor never brewed
> from tankards scooped in pearl.
> Not all the vats along the Rhine
> yield such an alcohol.

To turn a good verse is an unusual virtue. Rare in all poets. Rare in the folk poets. Just as I detest the distinction made between men and women poets . . . either they write well or not. So I detest distinctions of class. John Clare is good when he is good because he is good. His working class origins give him certain advantages and certain disadvantages. I don't know any poet who finds difficulty with Emily Dickinson or Elizabeth Bishop or Stevie Smith. They just write better than most of us at their best. So it is with Tony Harrison and Geoffrey Hill, working class poets . . . you like them or dislike them on their merits. Other criteria just distract us from the human enterprise.

In the '70s my cup of ambition overflowed. New books came out every few years. I gave readings and appeared on television. I began to lecture at The Yeats Summer School. In my job there were plenty of stimulating students who found my teaching worthwhile. My beautiful and talented children were blossoming. Some of my colleagues were very interesting. John McVeagh and Bridget O'Toole were true and amusing friends. I got bad reviews and wonderful reviews. Laura and I reached the nadir of our marriage without disgracing ourselves. The sunny and the disastrous mixed. One great year at the Sligo Summer School I met this wonderfully intelligent and beautiful Canadian woman after my family had gone home. We made love happily, and during the winter her letters were a constant source of encouragement because she understood exactly what my poetry and songs were about and wrote to me about them.

It seemed that this was going to be the relationship that would finally wean me from my wife. Laura and I obviously had no future together, and the children were on the point of becoming independent. The youngest was sixteen. We had never healed since the quarrels in Africa; but we had never been able to discuss separation. There was just a sequence of affairs on my part, often with wonderful women (I can't speak for Laura), that never had the force to break up the marriage, partly because the family was a very strong unit. Partly because of money, I suppose. But in the end it happened quite gracefully and disgracefully. The sympathetic Canadian was coming back next summer when I met Imelda Foley, young enough to have been at school when I brought out *The Honest Ulsterman*. Perhaps there is no need to go into all this. She was the Arts Council organiser of a reading in Strabane that I gave with John Morrow, the short story writer, an old friend from folk days. Almost nobody turned up. We all drank a great deal, and Imelda and I ended up in bed and never looked back. She was my dream of female sexuality come true, and also practical, friendly, and intelligent.

I moved out of Kerr Street to a humble house in Coleraine, and my marriage was over. You could hardly overestimate the importance of this. Some people hang onto their first marriages forever. Not so many nowadays, but Laura and I had been together for twenty years, even if the last ten had been waiting for a way out.

In the early '70s the Bodley Head stopped publishing poetry, and at the same time Jim Gracey and his wife started The Blackstaff Press in Belfast. It was a natural progression for me to join him to support new local creativity, and my next five books came out from that imprint although he eventually sold out to Michael Burns and Anne Tannahill. Two of my happiest collections came out from Jim's successors. The first three were *The Long Summer Still to Come* and *Judy Garland and the Cold War.* These volumes were a mixture of new and early poems, some included song lyrics.

During my ten years with Imelda I made a new start, humanly and artistically. We lived together happily in Derry and then Belfast for five years while I worked on the poems that were to come out in the volume *Constantly Singing,* still with the Blackstaff Press in Belfast.

Imelda Foley (second wife), 1979

Living at a distance from the university cut down my contact with students and made teaching less rewarding. However, I managed to write a critical biography of Sean O'Casey for Macmillan. It may be the best book on O'Casey for he has not attracted the more intelligent critics, presumably because there is not much subtlety in his portrayal of politics or human psychology.

My teaching at Coleraine had narrowed down to drama and Anglo-Irish literature. I enjoyed seminars, especially at M.A. level, but was never quite at ease with lectures where, in my mind, you had to pretend to an omniscience I never felt I had. I enjoyed doing a high-powered lecture once a year at The Yeats Summer School; but

I couldn't turn it out three times a week. What I really enjoyed was directing and acting in plays, so I contrived to emphasise the practical side of drama and was involved in stimulating productions of *The Three Sisters, The Beaux' Stratagem, The Chalk Circle, The Good Person of Setzuan, Juno and the Paycock, The Measures Taken, Little Eyolf.* I also wrote some plays myself, one of which—*Black Eye*—was well received at the student drama festival in Galway. It is based on *The Bacchae* of Euripides, radically rewritten and set in Northern Ireland, with songs instead of choruses. It has never been performed professionally or published. The quality of work done at the university in Coleraine has never been properly recognised. It was established under a shadow. Many people felt (quite rightly) that Londonderry was a more appropriate site for a second university in Northern Ireland, which already had Magee College. In practical terms it made sense to establish a university at Coleraine among holiday resorts that had accommodation for the students in winter. In Derry there was no such accommodation; but it was hard not to suspect that the powers that be were nervous of raising the profile and economy of a rebellious city with a Catholic majority that had long been kept out of power by gerrymandering.

However, once it started in that site, The University of Ulster certainly achieved marvellous things in drama and other areas. To my mind it had much more vitality during the '70s than the older university in Belfast, yet, because of the shadow, many good people were unwilling to acknowledge these achievements.

There was an exciting folk-music life in the local pubs like the Harbour Bar, where you could hear Brian Mullen and Len Grahame and Eithne Murphy and many other fine musicians and singers. The student creativity was integrated into the life of these small towns. Similarly we produced plays in all sorts of local venues, held bonfires on the sandhills, and dances in the hotels. The university was alive and kicking.

I also put a lot of energy into song-writing and singing with my talented students. We called ourselves Resistance Cabaret and sang mostly in local pubs, but also at festivals in Belfast. I made two LPs of my songs with student musicians, *City and Eastern* and *Love in the Post.* These were busy productive years that included tours of America and visits to the continent. However the university was a less happy place to work when Walter Allen left for America. He was relaxed and humorous and had no trouble controlling the English department and keeping its needs before university committees. There was also more government money about in the early '70s. His successors were good men, but not great leaders or politicians. There was a lot of dissension in the department, student numbers declined, and bureaucracy increased. By 1984 the policies of the Conservative government helped to run down the universities, so I was glad to take early retirement in 1984. By this time I had married Imelda, and we had moved to a farm-house near Ballymoney. Soon a daughter, Anna, was born to us, and I became a house husband. Anna and I had great times traipsing the country lanes, talking to cows, and watching the train go by; but Imelda, failing to find interesting work locally, continued her job as Arts Officer in Belfast. The pressures of travel began to undermine the marriage when it had hardly begun. In fact, it sometimes seems we very foolishly got married to give a new start to an ailing relationship.

In 1984 I visited America for a month as part of an exchange programme between the Tyrone Guthrie Centre in Monaghan and The Frost Place in New Hampshire. I had a very productive month, living in Robert Frost's old house up in the Franconian mountains. I wrote the guts of *From the Irish* there, adapting and modernising classic Irish texts, turning "The Lament for Art O'Leary" into "Elegy for a Dead Policeman." I don't speak Irish, but I had been reading Irish literature in translation for many years and was keen to learn something from Irish forms, keen also to be part of an important tradition in modern Irish poetry (in English) since Yeats and the revival, i.e., translating and adapting Gaelic poems and using Gaelic mythology.

Yeats wrote, "Gaelic is my national language but it is not my mother tongue." We Irish poets live with that anomaly. We are cut off from a copious national literature because the Irish language was beaten out of us by the English oppressor over centuries. It is even more anomalous for those of us with Scottish and English background. We are surely Irish now, but we are the great-grandchildren of the oppressors. Anyway, nearly all modern poets here do their bit of translating and adapting. I made a play out of old saga material called *The Cattle*

Rustling. Just last week I was persuaded to try my hand at storytelling and had great excitement at a festival in Omagh telling of Deirdre and Neisha and the goddess Macha. It is a mixture of writing and acting skills that I enjoyed.

The assistant director of The Frost Place was a sweetly beautiful young woman who met me at the bus station in Boston and drove me up to Franconia in her little Volkswagen. Her plump husband was with her. She gave us a fine dinner in her wooden house where we were joined by a woman friend. Then we walked down to a little river. I was suddenly aware that Janice's husband was kissing the other lady, and it seemed only proper to kiss my hostess gallantly, in case she was feeling humiliated. She kissed me back warmly.

I always think of that night as comedy. I could not be deeply engaged, but I felt I had dropped into one of those sexually liberated societies that I had read about, but never experienced. Although my marriage was troubled I had great hopes of it surviving . . . our child was scarcely a year old. I had come out here to work. Janice's beauty was so wholesome as to be unsexy to my taste. Tired, a little drunk, in a dream I could not resist following this strange scenario wherever it led. And it was not too long before I was drawing the boots off the firm legs of my hostess. Like Oscar Wilde I could resist anything but temptation.

In fact I worked long and well at Franconia, loved the solitude and wrestling with the ghost of Robert Frost. As well as all the new poems, I wrote an essay on Joyce Cary for a new book edited by Edna Longley, and reviewed Heaney's "Sweeney Astray" for one of the Boston papers. Janice looked after me. I did not see much of my nominal host, the director. We dined once and he lent me a bicycle. He was on some sort of pseudoreligious vegetarian kick with which I had no patience, and it became apparent that he was letting his assistant director do all the work, without giving her proper payment.

Janice crept up on me. She was always there to show me around, buy me food, take me to readings. And, having broken the ice sexually, we did not go back on it. She did not push herself forward, but she was obviously fond of me. During that month I became aware that far from being part of a happy wife-swapping syndrome, she was married to a sick man who was incapable of work. He would hang around and take photographs and record my songs. At first I was half-embarrassed by his apparent complacency; but that first night had shown that he had sexual interests elsewhere.

It was only in the last few days that the reality was almost apparent. Janice and I had gone down to Boston to give some readings and meet Seamus Heaney who took us to his final workshop of the term, introduced us to his students, and put us up in his Spartan flat. It was a lovely outing. He took us out for a fish meal which appealed tremendously to Janice; but I hate squid and am suspicious of clams. However, his friendliness and generosity were apparent, and there was a nice homeliness about us grinding away at old differences happily enough, while Janice was nervous we were fighting bitterly. My pleasure in and reservations about Seamus's poetry are spelt out in essays and reviews; but his company is always rewarding and there is a special delight in homeboys meeting each other abroad where they have achieved some sort of celebrity. It reminds them of their boyhood ambitions, and how little they might have been expected to be dining out in America when they started on their careers. I was, of course, dissatisfied with Seamus's introduction to my reading, in which he emphasised my energy rather than my genius. In his workshops I thought I could have done a better job; but that is the natural combativeness of fellow practitioners. There was no bad feeling.

At the party we danced and sang. Walking home I felt he was making a pass at Janice, and perhaps it was then I began to realise that there was serious feeling between us. I felt closer to her than I did to him. Things escalated in the last few days. One morning I was awakened by Janice's husband (Do I only dream he was carrying a gun?). He told me she had had an accident and that he was to drive me to the day's reading. Then it turned out she was seriously hurt, and we drove down to some distant hospital and picked her up with a metal cover over her nose. I still didn't know he was a wife-beater; but as he drove us back, she in the backseat, my hand crept back to hold hers. Then they drove me up to Montreal to catch the train for Toronto where I was to reunite with Imelda.

Janice Fitzpatrick Simmons (present wife), in the kitchen of their Belfast house, 1988

I knew I was involved with something serious. Pain always escalates the emotions; but I couldn't read their situation, and even if I had, I was still going back to my wife and child. It was very puzzling and painful to be leaving this good woman to her nominal husband with her broken nose after the sweet intimacy we had shared.

Having been lucky all my life in the love of good women, perhaps I thought this was one more poignant farewell that would have no sequel. In fact Imelda and I had an heroic reunion in Toronto, including confessions, which is celebrated in two poems. It was genuine and deeply moving and exciting, as far as I am concerned, but I think there was something in Imelda that made her subject to other people's feelings. She found it hard not to cooperate. After the great reunion, we had all sorts of quarrels and miscalculations staying with my sister, Joan, in northern Ontario. One night, in measured drunkenness, I called her "a mediocre administrator." We had a great deal going for us and had tremendous times, fun and companionship and good sex, perhaps more than many people experience. I think we might have lasted forever; but she grew tired of me.

When we moved back to Belfast we were more impatient with each other. I thought her

With Ben and Janice, 1989

work in the Arts Council was corrupt and humiliating for her. She was determined to succeed in that milieu, and it became apparent that she was more at ease with her colleagues than she was with me. We had a bad Christmas holiday with her mother in which Imelda kept wandering off with old friends, flirting and taunting me, and I eventually hit her painfully on the nose, and that was the end.

We lived in the same house for a few months until I found my own place. At first it was one of the most civilised divorces. She took the car and the house because I could not afford them, but she gave me three thousand pounds to help me get started on my own. I had bought the car with my golden handshake, and we had put down deposits on the house together. It was a very equitable parting, and we have since been at our best dealing with our daughter, Anna, who is a brilliant and happy child, spending the week with her mother and the weekends with me.

About this time I became Writer-in-Residence at Queen's University and lived in a lovely little house in the Protestant ghetto of East Belfast. Being retired I could meet my daughter off the school bus and have her at weekends. I was desolate and lonely, not quite understanding why Imelda had fallen out of love with me.

Then the unimagined love story completed itself. Janice, the American poet, turned up in Dublin to do a Ph.D. at University College Dublin (UCD), having completed her M.A. at the University of New Hampshire. In Dublin she watched a television programme, "Hanly's People," where I was being interviewed about my poetry and my broken marriage, etc. It was a good programme. I wish I still had a copy. Janice drank a few bottles of wine and rang me up. Being a born husband I summoned her up north, and we have never looked back. She transferred from UCD to Queen's, and shortly became pregnant, despite being "on the pill."

We had a sickly baby, Ben, who survived fearful complications. Janice had a series of illnesses. This had the effect of cementing our relationship quickly. There was no time to indulge in petty quarrels or dwell on our differences, having to visit Ben in the intensive care unit of The Royal Hospital every day for five months. Janice had a temporary teaching post in the university at Coleraine seventy miles away. It was very hard on her, but we needed the money. I wrote her a Valentine poem some years later:

> Here is my old man's love, serene and
> mild,
> for your asthma-haunted body, your
> bladder burning,
> your collapsed lung, sick father, stillborn
> child.
> You watch the mirror for your shape
> returning . . .
>
> . . . .
>
> New England self-improvers, we're in
> league.
> The signs of love flash like a steady glow
> at meals, at work, in sickness and fatigue,
> in bed when Ben cries.
>
> "O.K. Let *me* go,"
> either might say, and both would calculate
> who is too drunk or if it's you or me
> most needs a rest. . . .

From our neat house opposite the noisy but friendly country-and-western bar in the heart of the city, we moved out to Portmuck, a little harbour twenty-five miles north of Belfast. I would have been content to try and get by on my pension and whatever teaching Janice could find; but in fact temporary posts are very unsatisfactory. She seldom got to teach subjects she was interested in and was often badly treated. There always seemed to be a hassle, so we resolved to follow her dream of running a school of poetry from our own house. At first the Arts Council seemed interested in helping us get started; but for some reason they turned away.

I had the promise of a substantial amount of money from the sale of my archive, so we went ahead. Neil Shawcross, a local painter, painted us a marvelous poster and wouldn't take a fee. We printed brochures and fliers and posted them off to all the American universities with M.F.A. programmes and to workshops and art centres in Ireland and England. Then the sale of the archive fell through and we went into debt; but there was no turning back. Janice approached various foundations and scraped up some money, and we have kept going ever since. It is a wonderful project. All summer the house is filled with interesting students and fine poets from Ireland and America coming in for the day to run workshops and read their work. More people come each year, and now we also run an M.A. in creative writing (poetry), the first in Ireland, endorsed by Lancaster University.

All this took a lot of courage and boldness. I feel very proud of Janice's vision and equanimity in the face of difficulty and disappointment. She just sweeps me along and things work out. Because we are doing work we love, there is no difficulty in lecturing now. We offer experience and a love of poetry, which we have in abundance.

We have suffered from the enmity of people we thought were friends for reasons we can't yet understand. That has been sad; but we have survived and managed to keep enemies at a distance. We just hear of their gossip and bad-mouthing secondhand, and shrug our shoulders. As for our poetry, it is very stimulating living with another writer; you get instant serious reaction to new work. We have helped each other to develop and try new forms, and by happy accident we have books coming out from the same publisher, Salmon/Poolbeg.

Ben is now in perfect health, clever, active, good fun, cheeky as hell, handsome, with a freckled nose. He will soon be six and enjoys school. Janice loves Anna like a daughter and Anna loves Janice like a mother. So here I am. Here we are.

> . . . My love, my freckled gardener
> busy with balm and briony,
> Americanly kind and conscious
> of the limitations of irony . . .
>
> supportive to a fault, hurt
> by local abrasiveness, our wit,
> the winding up and putting down,
> brilliance that has no heart in it.
>
> I grow less Irish every year
> with ardent love to lean upon.
> Our home and garden is my nation,
> my freckled gardener, my swan.

BIBLIOGRAPHY

Poetry:

Ballad of a Marriage, Festival, 1966.

Late But in Earnest, Bodley Head, 1967.

Ten Poems, Festival, 1968.

In the Wilderness and Other Poems, Bodley Head, 1969.

Songs for Derry, Ulsterman, 1969.

No Ties, Ulsterman, 1970.

Energy to Burn, Bodley Head, 1971.

No Land Is Waste, Dr. Eliot, Keepsake, 1972.

The Long Summer Still to Come, Blackstaff, 1973.

West Strand Visions, Blackstaff, 1974.

Memorials of a Tour in Yorkshire, Ulsterman, 1975.

Judy Garland and the Cold War, Blackstaff, 1976.

The Selected James Simmons, edited by Edna Longley, Blackstaff, 1978.

Constantly Singing, Blackstaff, 1980.

From the Irish, Blackstaff, 1985.

Poems 1956-1986, Bloodaxe Gallery, 1986.

Elegies, Sotto Voce, 1994.

Mainstream, Salmon/Poolbeg, 1995.

Plays:

(With Tony Harrison) *Aikin Mata,* adaptation of *Lysistrata* by Aristophanes (produced Zaria, Nigeria, 1965), Ibadan, Oxford University Press, 1966.

The Cattle Rustling, Fortnight Educational, 1991.

Editor:

(With A. R. Mortimer) *Out on the Edge,* Leeds University, 1958.

Ten Irish Poets: An Anthology, Carcanet, 1974.

Soundings 3: Annual Anthology of New Irish Writing, Blackstaff, 1975.

Other:

Sean O'Casey, London, Macmillan, 1983, New York, Grove, 1984.

Editor of *Poetry and Audience,* 1957–58; founder of the literary magazine *Honest Ulsterman,* 1968. Sound recordings: *City and Eastern,* Outlets; *Pubs,* BBC; *Love in the Post,* Poor Genius; *The Ballad of Claudy,* Poor Genius; *The Rostrevor Sessions,* Spring Records, 1987.

Work also represented in anthologies, including Anthony Bradley's *Contemporary Irish Poetry,* University of California Press, and *The Penguin Book of Contemporary Irish Poetry,* edited by Derek Mahon. Contributor to periodicals, including *Atlantis, Encounter, Missouri Review, Paris Review,* and *Spectator.* Simmons' manuscripts are archived at Emory University, Atlanta, Georgia.

Cumulative Index

CUMULATIVE INDEX

The names of essayists who appear in the series are in boldface type. Subject references are followed by volume and page number(s). When a subject reference appears in more than one essay, names of the essayists are also provided.

INDEX